MASTERPLOTS II

SHORT STORY SERIES
REVISED EDITION

MASTERPLOTS II

SHORT STORY SERIES
REVISED EDITION

Volume 4
Hor–Loo

Editor, Revised Edition
CHARLES MAY
California State University, Long Beach

Editor, First Edition
FRANK N. MAGILL

SALEM PRESS
Pasadena, California   Hackensack, New Jersey

Editor in Chief: Dawn P. Dawson

Editorial Director: Christina J. Moose
Project Editor: R. Kent Rasmussen
Production Editor: Cynthia Beres
Copy Editor: Rowena Wildin

Assistant Editor: Andrea E. Miller
Research Supervisor: Jeffry Jensen
Acquisitions Editor: Mark Rehn
Layout: Eddie Murillo

Library of Congress Cataloging-in-Publication Data

Masterplots II : Short story series / editor Charles May. — Rev. ed.

    p.   cm.

Includes bibliographical references and index.

ISBN 1-58765-140-8 (set : alk. paper) — ISBN 1-58765-144-0 (vol. 4 : alk. paper) —

1. Fiction—19th century—Stories, plots, etc. 2. Fiction—19th century—History and criticism. 3. Fiction—20th century—Stories, plots, etc. 4. Fiction—20th century—History and criticism. 5. Short story. I. Title: Masterplots 2. II. Title: Masterplots two. III. May, Charles E. (Charles Edward), 1941-

PN3326 .M27 2004

809.3′1—dc22

2003018256

First Printing

PRINTED IN THE UNITED STATES OF AMERICA

TABLE OF CONTENTS

TABLE OF CONTENTS

TABLE OF CONTENTS

MASTERPLOTS II

SHORT STORY SERIES
REVISED EDITION

A HORSE AND TWO GOATS

Author: R. K. Narayan (1906-2001)
Type of plot: Realism
Time of plot: The twentieth century
Locale: In and around Kritam, a South Indian village
First published: 1965

Principal characters:
MUNI, an old, poor Indian villager
HIS WIFE, who is equally ancient but sharp-tongued
THE SHOPMAN, the owner of the village store
THE FOREIGNER, an American tourist from suburban Connecticut

The Story

After setting the scene in Kritam, a tiny South Indian village, the story introduces old Muni and his wife, a poor, childless couple: "She was old, but he was older and needed all the attention she could give him in order to be kept alive." The two have been married since he was ten and she eight: "He had thrashed her only a few times in their career, and later she had the upper hand." At one time Muni was a relatively prosperous herdsman, with "a flock of forty sheep and goats." He sold the sheep's wool and sold the animals for slaughter to a town butcher, who brought him "betel leaves, tobacco, and often enough some bhang." However, those high old times are past. Now Muni's flock, struck by "some pestilence" (though Muni suspects a neighbor's curse), has dwindled to two goats. Still, Muni follows his daily routine of taking the animals to graze near the highway two miles away, where he sits on the base of an old clay statue and watches the world go by.

Normally Muni's wife starts the day by boiling him some millet for breakfast, then sending him on his way with a ball of leftover millet and a raw onion for lunch. This morning, however, there is no food, so Muni goes out of the hut, shakes the drumstick tree, and gets six drumsticks. His wife offers to boil them with salt, but Muni hankers for something richer—a drum-stick curry. His wife agrees to satisfy his "unholy craving" for "big things," provided that Muni can gather the ingredients: "a measure of rice or millet. . . . Dhall, chili, curry leaves, mustard, coriander, gingelley oil, and one large potato." When Muni goes to the village store, however, the shopman refuses him further credit (he already owes the store "five rupees and a quarter") and belittles the old man in front of other villagers. Muni returns home defeated, and his wife sends him off to graze the goats and to fast for the day. His hope is that she will earn enough money somewhere for an evening meal.

As he passes through the village each day with his two goats, people talk about his diminished status, and Muni quietly hangs his head. Only when he reaches the statue near the highway can he relax and enjoy a little peace. Here Muni sits all day in the shade of the statue—a horse rearing next to a fierce warrior—and watches his goats and an occasional passing vehicle. The vehicles are something to tell his wife about when he goes home at night.

Today Muni will have much to tell, for as he sits enjoying his somnolence, the big world abruptly intrudes. A strange vehicle—a van or station wagon—suddenly runs out of gas and coasts to a stop in front of Muni. Out steps "a red-faced foreigner" dressed in khaki. He asks Muni about gas stations, then sees the statue. He is transfixed by the clay horse, which he immediately desires to own. Muni, meanwhile, is terrified by the official-looking foreigner, who he thinks has come to arrest him. Thus begins one of the most hilarious negotiations in literature, the foreigner speaking only English; Muni, only Tamil.

Muni asserts his ownership of the two goats, despite what his slanderous neighbors might say. In turn, the foreigner smiles, takes out his silver cigarette case, and offers Muni a smoke. Surprised, Muni happily accepts: "Muni drew a deep puff and started coughing; it was racking, no doubt, but extremely pleasant. . . . No need to run away from a man who gave him such a potent smoke." Still cautious, however, Muni shuns the foreigner's business card, thinking that it is a warrant. He disavows any connection with a recent murder, blames it on Kritam's neighboring village, and promises to apprehend any suspicious character and "bury him up to his neck in a coconut pit if he tries to escape."

Observing that the deal must be conducted at a leisurely pace, the foreigner sits beside Muni and relates how he was working last summer "on the fortieth floor of the Empire State Building" when a power failure precipitated a personal decision: "All the way in the train I kept thinking, and the minute I reached home in Connecticut, I told my wife, Ruth, 'We will visit India this winter, it's time to look at other civilizations.'" Muni tells how his village turns thieves from the neighboring village into mincemeat, and the suburban New Yorker says that he also enjoys chopping wood. Noting the stranger's gestures toward the horse, Muni launches into its history and meaning: "This is our guardian, it means death to our adversaries." An embodiment of "the Redeemer" (apparently Vishnu), the horse will come alive at "the end of the world," save the good people, and trample the evil ones. The American promises to install the statue in the middle of the living room: At cocktail parties, "We'll stand around him and have our drinks." Muni then runs over a list of other avatars, tells how he used to enact their stories in village dramas, and concludes by asking the American if he knows the *Rāmāyaṇa* (c. 500 B.C.E.; English translation, 1870-1889) and the *Mahābhārata* (c. 400 C.E.; *The Mahabharata of Krishna-Dwaipayana Vyasa*, 1887-1896).

Seeing a chance to clinch the deal, the American pulls out a hundred rupees and offers them for the horse. Muni, thinking that the American is buying the two goats, is ecstatic: "His dream of a lifetime was about to be realized . . . opening a small shop on this very spot." Leaving the two goats with the American, Muni rushes home to show the money to his wife. Meanwhile, the American flags down another car, buys some siphoned gas, gets help in loading the clay horse, and drives off with it. At home,

Muni's wife suspects Muni of stealing the money, which seems to be confirmed when the two goats come trailing in. "If you have thieved," she declares hysterically, "the police will come tonight and break your bones. Don't involve me. I will go away to my parents."

Themes and Meanings

This comic masterpiece, which first appeared in *The New Yorker,* has the dimensions of an updated fairy tale: A childless old couple find their cupboard empty, but the old man goes out and meets a stranger who buys his last two goats for a small fortune. The tale is updated in that the poverty shown, with each day a new search for food, is only too real. Also real are the related conditions of village life in South India—the close-knit community with its malicious gossip and concern for status, the credit system exemplified by the village store, the bickering of husband and wife, the occasional violence and rough justice, the pervasive influence of religion.

However, the story's main updating is the clash of this village culture with American culture, represented by the American tourist. The stereotyped American tourist with his monoglot outlook and moneybags is perhaps less real than the story's other characters, but he is individualized somewhat by his New York background: Here the typical suburbanite of *The New Yorker* goes east. As usual, he is an object of gentle satire. He moves about on the floating world with ease thanks to his financial means, but otherwise he is a total nincompoop. He reduces existence to getting and spending, buying an avatar of the just god to install in his living room. His cocktail guests had better stay on their best behavior.

However, even the American tourist is not entirely oblivious to the existential void: His experience of a New York City power failure—a technological version of the Caves of Malabar—moves him to visit other civilizations. Although dimly understood, his basic instinct to bring the god back home is correct. The clash of cultures is symbolized by the different languages that the tourist and Muni speak, but, amazingly, in the long run they do communicate. Their misunderstandings are hilarious, but they share an understanding beyond language—that is, the human condition. In their little drama of the absurd, they serve as each other's sympathetic listener, and their cooperation enables each man to cope with his particular need. The two men, like their two cultures, complement each other, but they are more alike than different: Muni is simply a village counterpart of the New York commuter. As they face the universe, society, and their wives, each man no doubt wants to resemble the fierce warrior standing beside the horse, but in actuality they are more like the two goats.

Style and Technique

Part of the fairy-tale element in this story is the result of the author's use of coincidence. From a Western point of view, the story's big coincidence—Muni's opportune meeting with a rich American—may seem a fault: It undercuts the Western sense of probability, of order. However, that is apparently R. K. Narayan's purpose. From a Hindu point of view, which sees the universe in flux, the coincidence is quite logical.

In the Hindu view, anything can happen, though contingencies (or actions of the gods) usually balance out over time: Muni is wiped out by the pestilence but reinstated by the American. Just as Muni sells the American an avatar of a Hindu god, so Narayan slyly introduces the Hindu context into this story, complete with a lesson in theology, a reference to the great Hindu epics, and a wild conversation that mirrors the Hindu universe.

Narayan's ability to present Hindu culture to the West is aided by one of the smoothest English styles in the world. Narayan has developed his style over a long career, and "A Horse and Two Goats" shows the style at its best—simple, supple, subtle, able to encompass the Hindu worldview and the demands of *The New Yorker* at the same time. The style entertains without calling attention to itself.

Harold Branam

THE HORSE DEALER'S DAUGHTER

Author: D. H. Lawrence (1885-1930)
Type of plot: Domestic realism
Time of plot: The 1920's
Locale: A small town in rural England
First published: 1922

Principal characters:
JACK FERGUSSON, a doctor
MABEL PERVIN, the horse dealer's daughter, twenty-seven years old
JOE PERVIN, her oldest brother, thirty-three years old
FRED HENRY PERVIN, her middle brother
MALCOLM PERVIN, her youngest brother, twenty-two years old

The Story

The three Pervin brothers, left destitute by their late father, sit smoking and talking around the breakfast table in the family ranch house. They badger their sister, Mabel, whom they call "bull-dog," asking what she intends to do with her life now that they all must leave the ranch; she answers them as always, with stony silence. Dr. Jack Fergusson, a physician and friend of the brothers, calls. As he sits talking with them, he becomes intrigued by the gloomy, proud, and strangely detached sister.

Later, while walking about making his rounds, Fergusson sees Mabel in the cemetery, where, clad in black, she is tending her mother's grave. He follows her to a pond and, with continuing fascination, watches her walk into and finally disappear under the murky water. He runs after her, drags her out of the pond, and takes her home. There, he undresses her, rubs her skin dry, and warms her next to the hearth fire.

Mabel awakens in a daze, recognizes the doctor, and asks him what she has done. Realizing her nakedness beneath the swaddling blankets, she asks him, "Do you love me, then?" and becomes certain of the answer herself: "You love me. . . . I know you love me, I know." The doctor, who "had, really, no intention of loving her," is horrified at her words and her kisses, yet he feels overwhelmed and must embrace her and admit that her words are really true. Mabel's joyful assurance of his love soon passes, however, and she sobs, "I feel I'm horrible to you." "'No, I want you, I want you,' was all he answered, blindly, with that terrible intonation which frightened her almost more than her horror lest he should not want her."

The title, "The Horse Dealer's Daughter," suggests that the protagonist is Mabel, but actually she shares the center with Fergusson. At the crucial moment, however, this strange love story, recounting the emergence into passion of both these characters, gives the lead to Mabel. She and Fergusson come to their union from opposite directions, Mabel from the "animal pride" of the Pervins, Fergusson from the logic-dominated repression of science and the conformity of his educated class. The story itself chronicles how they make the journey, and for what conscious and unconscious motives.

The story's opening scene in the dining room emphasizes the family dynamics of the four children still present in the dead horse dealer's home; there is a Cinderella-like quality to Mabel's life—true poverty now, and the solitude of a decade of scrub-work, of holding things together, of living with a stepmother's indifference and without a mother's love. Her brothers, too, have ignored her, except to tease or criticize. That crude life has written its message as an "impassive fixity" on Mabel's face. However, her "steady, dangerous eyes" have an unsettling effect on Fergusson, and there are abundant hints of strong emotion under her facade. She manages by means of a dumb endurance: "She thought of nobody, not even of herself." Emotionally, she is already dead, and thus feels herself coming closer to her mother.

Fergusson, with his active mental role, dominates the crucial, central part of the story. In the strictest sense, however, his intellect is largely misleading: He tells himself that he hates the "hellish hole" he lives in, but the people there, "rough, inarticulate, powerfully emotional," excite him. The intense emotion of his witnessing Mabel's suicide attempt, and of his saving her from the pond, forces him out of the comfort of allowing thinking to dominate.

His entering the pond, in fact, is a kind of baptism: In his desperate grab to reach her, "he lost his balance and went under. . . . After what seemed an eternity" he reenters the world, and faces, though reluctantly, the passion that a revived Mabel intuits in him and reveals in herself. She reads events symbolically, from the primitive, unconscious wisdom to which fairy tales speak: On a logical level, her seeing love in the fact that he undressed her is preposterous, but Fergusson's "soul seemed to melt" when she speaks the thought. He fights the realization of his love, his intellect throwing obstacles before it: "his whole will was against his yielding"; to love her would be "a violation of his professional honour" as a doctor. This voice of a conformist society cannot withstand the force of passion; his decision to love seems to be the first nonrational choice of his life.

Finally, Mabel's and Fergusson's awareness of what they have promised each other inspires the confusion and shyness of the last pages, and the adjustment of roles: Fergusson takes the lead by ridiculing Mabel's self-reproaches and by reassuring her of his desire ("We're going to be married, quickly"), and she takes on a subtle and manipulative manner ("'Kiss me,' she said wistfully," and "I don't like you in those [her brothers'] clothes"). Passion might be blind, and is so described even in the final paragraph, but they must live with a knowledge of love, and that will not be simple.

Themes and Meanings

The story occupies itself with D. H. Lawrence's major theme, the difference between what he called "mental consciousness" and "blood consciousness." The characters are first introduced with this theme in mind. The brothers, "callous" but cowed by failure, are revealed as lacking that crucial tension: Joe is in a "stupor of downfall," "a subject animal now"; Fred Henry is "not master of the situations of life" despite his mastery of horses; Malcolm is "the baby of the family," "looking aimlessly." All have a "sullen, animal pride," and after years of living a brutal and coarse life, fathering illegitimate children with women of "bad reputations," they lack Mabel's "blood consciousness," her ability to see the situation and respond deeply to it. Fergusson, whose "slight Scotch accent" foreshadows the severe repression he later reveals, represents "mental consciousness," which has all the power of logic and science, but which cannot by itself do more than deny the instinctive forces of life. Their confrontation combines the wisdom of instinct and the wisdom of logic but does not suggest that the forces will coexist quietly.

Another important theme is the repressive role of society. It shows itself in Mabel's life after poverty strikes down her pride and forces her to buy cheap food and avert her gaze on the town streets. For Fergusson, on the other hand, success increases the social repression he feels; his sense of class, of professional status, makes him claim to hate the town and feel ashamed of his attraction to its people. Even after his confession of love to Mabel, the shame haunts him: "That he should love her? That this was love. . . . Him, a doctor! How they would all jeer if they knew!" Though Lawrence keeps society in the distance, its power is clearly in evidence, and the actions of his characters show his eagerness to strike against the still dominant Victorian sense of propriety he believed to be very destructive.

Style and Technique

"The Horse Dealer's Daughter," as is typical of Lawrence's short fiction, has a strong sense of plot, and because the two characters are of almost equal importance to his antibourgeois theme, he adopts the technique of convergence, alternating his focus from Mabel to Fergusson and causing them to meet three times: at the Pervins', at the graveyard, and finally at the pond, where the narrative brings them together and forces them for the first time to communicate. Lawrence accentuates the tension and feeling of inevitability by increasing the pace of the story: The first scene is leisurely, with a large cast, and the scenes following center on Mabel or Fergusson, sometimes both, and are briefer and given more to internal than to external description. They give way to the longest but most dramatically intense scene, that taking place at the pond and continuing beside the Pervin hearth.

Lawrence also illustrates here his pioneering attempts to use language, especially by means of metaphor, to communicate passionate inner states. In the beginning, the story is dominated by dimness and numbness: All the Pervins are "sullen"; the brothers' glances are "glazed" and "callous"; they refer to Mabel as "bull-dog"; her emotions only "darken" her face, and she passes "darkly" through the town and goes "darkly" through the "saddened" fields and the "falling" afternoon to the shadow of the churchyard to her mother's grave. It continues to fall while Fergusson watches Mabel move "in the hollow of the day" to the pond; as the water closes over her, the afternoon is "dead."

Lawrence then makes metaphors of hope (with a suggestion of religious passion) dominate the rescue scene. Fergusson finds, after his own full descent into the pond water that "clasped dead cold round his legs," that Mabel's body has "risen" from the pond, and he himself "rose higher" carrying her out of it. Once by the fire, he drinks "spirits" and revives her instantly by pouring some into her mouth. His watch has stopped; his old spiritless life, dominated by schedule and exactitude, is over.

From numbness to this revival of awareness, Lawrence moves in the final scene to metaphors of heat as the true physical passion of his characters comes to life, from the warmth of the fire and the friction of Fergusson's rubbing Mabel dry to the agony of his "burning" and "melting" heart. Throughout, the narrative conveys by means of its imagery the violent and contradictory nature of passionate love. Among all of Lawrence's quests in his fiction, this was the most significant.

Kerry Ahearn

THE HOUSE BEHIND

Author: Lydia Davis (1947-   )
Type of plot: Allegory
Time of plot: The 1990's
Locale: Saint-Étienne, France
First published: 1997

Principal characters:
THE NARRATOR, who lives in a house at the rear of a courtyard
M. MARTIN, the murderer

The Story

The narrator lives in a house at the rear of a courtyard and can look across to the bathroom and kitchen windows of the house in front. The dwellers in the front house—many of them high civil servants—enjoy greater economic and social advantages than their neighbors to the rear, who tend to be store owners, salespeople, retired postal workers, and single schoolteachers. The people in front occupy comfortable, spacious apartments; those in the rear endure small, awkward quarters. These differences create resentment in the house behind and condescension in the one in front.

One of the rituals of daily life for residents of both houses is the emptying of their plastic garbage pails in the big metal trash cans in the courtyard. The narrator recalls the shocking murder that occurred at the trash cans a year earlier. A woman from the house in front appeared in the courtyard just as M. Martin, a married man from the house behind, dumped his garbage. The woman, one of the "few kind people" in the front house, spoke to the man. He perhaps interpreted her apparently friendly words as patronizing, for he immediately stabbed her in the throat with the hunting knife with which he had been scraping his pail.

The sudden murder astonished the residents of both houses, who stood in their doorways staring at the tableau before them—a woman on the ground with blood gushing from her throat, a man standing over her, and garbage spilling from the pail she still clutched by its handle. It was the location in a kind of no-man's-land that paralyzed everyone, or so the narrator speculates. Finally, the concierge stepped out to take charge, the coroner carried away the body, and the police took M. Martin to jail.

The shock of the event intensified the ill will that already prevailed between the two houses. The tenants of the two houses began to avoid each other and fell into frequent violent engagements. People from the front house would not approach the courtyard alone, and old ladies from the front house ventured to the trash cans only in pairs. The night nurse living in the house behind quit dusting the banisters every afternoon and kept to her room and her radio; another woman, the older Lamartine sister, forbore her usual vigil at the crack in her door and stayed hidden except for early-morning Mass on Sundays; and the narrator's neighbor ignored for days the laundry on her line. Foul

odors drifted in the hallways, making tradespeople uncomfortable; people wore rain-
coats outside to conceal their poorly kept clothes; and surliness overtook everyone. A
year after the murder, the narrator confides that the situation has become intolerable
and realizes that before he becomes incapable of making the effort, he must go and
find an apartment in another part of the city.

Themes and Meanings

"The House Behind" is a bitter parable, less than four pages long, of the frustrations, resentments, and social upheavals engendered by class differences. The living
conditions emphasize the gap between the social classes. The tenants in the front
house have maids who live in rooms on the top floor with a view of the spires of the
city, but the tiny cubicles of the house behind open only onto a dusty corridor that
leads to a bathroom near the back stairwell shared by the indigent students and bache-
lors. No spires grace their horizons as they peer out from under the eaves of the house
behind.

However, the narrator insists that these discrepant living conditions do not explain
all the hostility between the two houses. To be always at the rear is humiliating to the
spirit. The students in the house behind may consider their situation to be only temporary, a mere rough patch on their road to success in the whole wide front house of the
world, but for the narrator's neighbors, working women without husbands or solace
from family, the sense of worldly defeat must be intense. The narrator speculates on
the motive of the murderer, a seemingly respectable married man. He wonders if he
was frustrated because he had come to understand that his dreams of living in the front
house would never be realized.

The murder poisons the already unpleasant air. Class conflict breeds fear in the
front house and sullenness in the house behind. People from the house behind never
speak first to those from the front house. The murder by the trash cans increases the
tensions that prevail in all the gradations up and down the social ladder. The narrator
observes that when M. Martin killed the woman from the front house, he destroyed
the last traces of self-respect among the people from the house behind, as they assumed the collective guilt for the murder. Such a remark betrays the narrator's intuition that M. Martin in a sense acted on the feelings of all the tenants of the house behind. The murdered woman was a kind woman, but the narrator imagines her saying
something to M. Martin that was just condescending enough to make him see that he
would never be her equal, provoking his brutal response, an outburst of hatred that had
been swelling in his soul for decades. The narrator's vision of society is essentially
Darwinian. The resentment of the underdog generates festering sores around the
globe, explaining much of the morning news everywhere.

Style and Technique

Lydia Davis writes direct prose with no dialogue and only a minimum of proper
names: M. Martin, the Lamartine sister, and the narrator's neighbor, Mme Bac. Davis
is rather fonder of the colon than most writers, using it effectively ten times in a story

of less than four pages, and she also works the dash well. Her plain diction suits her bleak tale, and her paragraphs develop in satisfying mixes of sentence lengths and patterns. Adjectives are permitted with restraint, but adverbs are largely banished. The first paragraph constructs a neat series of antitheses, and clauses march in parallel formations throughout the story. Doublets abound, and coordinate constructions depending on "and" or "but" advance the narrative two steps at a time. These features create a vigorous prose that is easy and pleasant to read.

As is usual with allegories, symbols play a considerable role in "The House Behind," most obviously in the role of the houses themselves. When the cold war between the classes erupts in violence, the narrator calls the murder strangely gratuitous, but it is not really. That is, although the victim is guilty of nothing more than being well off (the narrator admits she cannot be blamed for her status in life), her death becomes quickly understood as an event in the ongoing unfairness of life's distribution of goods. Surely, many of the globe's dispossessed agree with the nineteenth century socialist philosopher Pierre-Joseph Proudhon that property is theft, and for them, the woman's murder spells rough justice. Supporters of the Reign of Terror did not consider their brutality gratuitous, and modern terrorists who seek revenge on countries that are rich and powerful do not see their violence as gratuitous.

The narrator is transfixed by the suddenness of the bloodletting and the contrast between the strong, well-built man and the slight and graceful woman. The man and his hunting knife represent the latent power of the working class, and the slight and graceful woman symbolizes an elitist culture in which hunting knives are as foreign as arrowheads. The courtyard is the public space in which all classes meet and mingle— the supermarket, the motion picture theater, the athletic arena—and convention dictates civility in these settings. However, riots can be touched off quickly, and when they ignite, people in the big houses all over the world have to safeguard their heirlooms. Karl Marx and Charles Darwin preside over this fable.

Frank Day

THE HOUSE IN TURK STREET

Author: Dashiell Hammett (1894-1961)
Type of plot: Mystery and detective
Time of plot: The 1920's
Locale: San Francisco
First published: 1924

> *Principal characters:*
> THE CONTINENTAL OP, the narrator, a private detective
> MR. AND MRS. QUARRE, an affectionate elderly couple
> HOOK, a rough-mannered hood
> ELVIRA, a greedy, seductive hood
> TAI CHOON TAU, a clever, well-mannered hood

The Story

The Continental Op, a private detective who works for the Continental Detective Agency, has learned that a man whom he is hunting is living in a certain block of Turk Street in San Francisco. After canvassing all the houses on one side of the block and four on the other, he knocks on the door of the fifth house. At first no one answers. As the Op is about to leave, the door is opened by a friendly, fragile-looking old woman who insists that he enter. The Op, after a mild protest, enters the house and is taken into a sitting room, where an equally friendly old man, the woman's husband, is seated comfortably, smoking a cigar. With a twinge of conscience, the Op gives a phony name and tells a phony story in order to obtain information about the man whom he is seeking. As the old couple, Mr. and Mrs. Quarre by name, do their best to provide something helpful, the Op is served a cup of tea and given a cigar. He sits back, entranced by the relaxed atmosphere, and lets his mind wander from the sordid world of private investigation. He longs for the fast-approaching evening so that he can be finished with his work for the day and go home.

Suddenly the Op feels an object against the back of his neck and hears a gruff voice behind him demanding that he stand up. At first he thinks that he must be dreaming, but he feels the object and hears the voice again. He is frisked by the old man, then made to turn around. He faces an unpleasant-looking man holding a gun. Before he can interrogate the Op thoroughly, "Hook" is called into another room by a young woman, named Elvira. The old man covers the Op with a gun, and the old woman cordially invites the Op to be seated again. The Op hears Hook, the young woman, and a third gang member discussing his fate. Hook is in favor of killing the Op, but he is overruled by the calm, British voice of the third gang member, Tai Choon Tau. The Op is thankful.

The Op is tied up and gagged by the old couple, who then leave the house for a pre-arranged rendezvous. Elvira comes into the sitting room with Hook, goading and seducing him into getting rid of Tai. Carrying a traveling bag, Tai enters the room. After subtle encouragement from Elvira, Hook strikes the much smaller Tai. Tai, however, draws his gun even as he is falling and gets the drop on Hook. He takes Hook's gun, lectures the other two on unity, and matter-of-factly announces that the three of them will double-cross the old couple. Magnanimously, Tai gives Hook back his gun. As the dispute settles down, the Op notes a change in the room. Thinking back quickly, he discovers that Elvira has used the fight as a diversion, replacing the contents of the traveling bag with some of the room's books and magazines. He figures that the original contents of the bag are now hidden in the couch.

The three gang members depart. Tai, the last one to leave, places a gun within the Op's reach and loosens his bonds. The Op manages to get loose and reach the gun just as Hook returns to the house, entering the sitting room with his gun drawn; the Op fires first, and Hook falls dead. The Op quickly examines the couch, finding a cache of bonds. He examines his gun as well as Hook's: Both are without ammunition. Tai was taking no chances when he returned Hook's gun and set up the confrontation between Hook and the Op. The Op takes the bonds upstairs, hides them, and waits for Tai and Elvira to return. Tai and Elvira do, indeed, return, and the Op tries to turn the two against each other. Tai offers to trade the girl for the bonds. Just then, the Quarres return, convinced that they are being double-crossed by Tai, Elvira, and the Op. The old woman covers Tai as the old man takes away his gun, but Tai has two more guns hidden. He shoots the old couple dead. The Op is able to subdue Tai in the resulting confusion. Elvira escapes, reappearing in a later Hammett story.

It turns out that the gang worked a scam in which Elvira would seduce bank employees and get them to embezzle funds. Hook would then play the jealous husband, scaring the victim off minus Elvira and the loot. Tai was the mastermind. The old couple provided a hideout. On the gang's last job, the victim refused to be scared off and was killed in a fight with Hook. Thus the gang thought that the heat was on and that the Op had tracked them down.

The story's twist lies in the Op's ignorance of all this. The Op was unaware of the gang or their crimes. In fact, he was not working on a criminal case at all. Tai refuses to believe the Op. He goes to the gas chamber convinced that the Op is lying to him.

Themes and Meanings

Dashiell Hammett's Continental Op stories were derived from "pulp" fiction, a popular form of reading material in the United States during the first half of the twentieth century. The pulp magazines, so called for the cheap paper on which they were printed, fed the country's growing literacy by providing easy-to-read, sensational stories of adventure, the Western frontier, the supernatural, science fiction, sex (steamy, though not very explicit by modern standards), and crime. The pulps provided what seemed to many to be low-grade entertainment for the masses. On the other hand, some authors who began by writing for the pulps managed to transform the genre into a vehicle for serious commentary on the human condition and on contemporary society. Hammett's work, for example, treats a number of profound themes.

"The House in Turk Street" well illustrates this point. It is, first and foremost, a story about the deceptiveness of appearances. Almost nothing in the story is as it seems. The kindly old couple turn out to be accomplices to murder. Their house, which at first appears to be a haven in a heartless world, is a den of thieves. Hook appears to be tough, but the more gentle and cultivated Tai is tougher. The gang is in the business of deception, using Elvira's appeal to lure young men in search of romance to their ruin instead. Even the Op is not what he seems. He deceives people intentionally in order to gain information, and the entire story is based on the misleading appearance that he is hot on the gang's trail when nothing could be further from the truth.

In Hammett's stories, most of the characters are driven by greed or lust of some sort, social institutions are corrupt, and attempts at social reform are costly and possibly futile. Even Hammett's heroes are anything but saintly. On the other hand, the Op and other Hammett heroes also have a firm sense of duty. Thus, Hammett's skepticism (regarding appearances) and realism (regarding human motives and institutions) do not translate into nihilism, the absence of moral values. Instead, the Op does his duty in Turk Street, helping to uncover truth and bring a criminal to justice.

Style and Technique

Hammett's writing style also elevates his work beyond its start in the pulp magazines. A model of leanness and economy, Hammett's prose has served as a guide for many later writers. These include Raymond Chandler and Ross Macdonald, who went on to continue successfully the tradition of "hardboiled" detective stories. Hammett's style remains a fine model for young writers, particularly those who strive for clarity and who wish to produce a compelling narrative.

Indeed, Hammett's prose lent itself well to the conventions of the detective story, always keeping the reader interested and in suspense, yet moving along quickly enough so that readers would not become impatient. One of Hammett's techniques for accomplishing this was his masterful use of dialogue. Hammett's story lines are often advanced efficiently by conversation between characters, and Hammett's detectives most often seek truth by asking people questions. "The House in Turk Street" is no exception in this regard, though for much of this particular story, the Op is reduced to being a spectator.

Ira Smolensky

THE HOUSE OF COBWEBS

Author: George Gissing (1857-1903)
Type of plot: Social realism
Time of plot: The nineteenth century
Locale: London, Surrey, and Derbyshire, England
First published: 1900

Principal characters:
GOLDTHORPE, a young would-be novelist
SPICER, his landlord

The Story

"The House of Cobwebs" is told in the third person through the consciousness of Goldthorpe as he progresses from struggling writer to successful novelist. George Gissing provides detailed descriptions of the primary setting and other places his hero visits.

The twenty-two-year-old Goldthorpe estimates that he needs three months to complete his first novel, but he does not have enough money to continue living in his lodging house. He hopes to find a place where he can live on fifteen shillings a week. Walking rather aimlessly in the suburbs of Surrey, Goldthorpe comes upon three deserted houses in a row in a middle-class neighborhood. Their once well-tended gardens are overrun with weeds, and the houses are in severe disrepair. From one of the houses, he hears someone playing "Home Sweet Home" on a concertina. Moving closer, he sees the musician, a middle-aged man dressed like a clerk or shopkeeper. Learning that the man is the owner of the three houses, Goldthorpe asks immediately to rent a room. At first suspicious, the man changes when he discovers Goldthorpe is a literary man because he is a great admirer of such writers as Oliver Goldsmith and Samuel Johnson. Goldthorpe engages the man, who identifies himself as Mr. Spicer, further by complimenting him on the flowers and vegetables growing in the garden, which the owner hopes to improve.

Spicer explains the complicated legal means by which he has come to inherit the lease on the properties from an uncle. The lease has a little more than a year to run, and Spicer explains that he plans to occupy a room in one of the houses until then. Spicer asks only that his tenant pay half the water bill, but Goldthorpe cannot accept such generosity and offers to pay two shillings a week. Goldthorpe copies his landlord by acquiring the bare essentials for his room: a camp bed, table, chair, and oil stove. After these expenditures, he must exist on fifteen pence a day.

As Goldthorpe's tenancy continues, he and Spicer become friends. Little by little, Spicer reveals his life story, beginning as an errand boy for a chemist (the British term for pharmacist) and eventually becoming a chemist's assistant before leaving his job on receiving his inheritance, which also includes a small amount of money that will enable him to live once the lease expires. Goldthorpe promises to remain with Spicer until then and to pay a higher rent once his book is sold. The success of Goldthorpe's novel becomes the center of the lives of both men. The sight of the growing manuscript fills Spicer with reverence.

When the book is rejected by the publisher on whom Goldthorpe has most been counting, he becomes ill and leaves for his mother's house in Derbyshire. Spicer sends letters describing the progress of the garden while the writer convalesces. When the novel is accepted by another publisher the following January, Goldthorpe returns to the house of cobwebs to find its roof collapsed just above his old room after a storm has toppled the chimney. He learns that Spicer has sustained minor injuries in the accident. When Goldthorpe visits the hospital, Spicer's first concern is with the novel. On hearing the happy news, he pronounces himself cured and announces that although the house is no longer habitable he will continue cultivating the garden.

Themes and Meanings

"The House of Cobwebs" is in part a portrait of the optimism of youth. Goldthorpe has the courage to succeed not because of naïveté but because of his firm belief in his goals, a belief that a more experienced person could not have maintained. Such optimism is also present in the older, but even less worldly Spicer, who combats his loneliness with thoughts of everything turning out for the best. A potentially maudlin story is presented, however, with little sentimentality and subtle irony.

Goldthorpe and Spicer are parallel personalities. Spicer is what the younger man might have become had he not aspired to the literary life. The two are also similar in being solitary figures relatively comfortable with spartan existences. Spicer shares Goldthorpe's passion for literature, though on a more limited scale, and his evolving skills as a gardener are meant to mirror Goldthorpe's writing talent.

Spicer combats loneliness with literature, having inherited from his father thirty volumes, none published in his lifetime, which he reads over and over. He speaks of Lord Byron as if they are contemporaries and has little understanding of the modern ideas Goldthorpe, who hopes to be the leader of a new school of fiction, expresses in his novel. Nevertheless, the importance of literature to Spicer helps emphasize the significance of Goldthorpe's achievement. Creating art is far from a selfish act meant merely to assuage the artist's ego.

As with much of his fiction, Gissing explores the inequities of life in Victorian England and the unfairness of the way most people live. Spicer's sole ambition is to have a house of his own, a place of any size in which to live and die, and after working hard for twenty-five years, suddenly he is presented with three houses. However, they are in declining condition and his only for a brief period. Spicer says he was bitterly disappointed on seeing them.

Property remains a powerful weapon not only in the distinctions between the working class, the middle class, and the aristocracy but within each class level as well. Ownership is the stuff both of dreams and nightmares. Goldthorpe declares that fate has played a nasty trick on his friend, yet Spicer remains optimistic and accepting of the law even though it has dealt him an injustice. Goldthorpe truly admires Spicer's response to his fate. As does Charles Dickens, Gissing attacks the inequities of the British legal system.

"The House of Cobwebs" reflects Gissing's concern with the hardships, especially economic ones, of the literary life. As such, it is a companion piece to his best-known novel *New Grub Street* (1891). It resembles his other short fiction in presenting, with a lightly ironic tone, the ordinary events in the lives of undistinguished people.

Style and Technique

Although essentially a realistic story about an unusual friendship, "The House of Cobwebs" also offers some gothic elements that would ordinarily appear in much more melodramatic works. The abandoned houses with their overrun gardens establish a mood of foreboding. Gissing creates a sense of mystery by having Goldthorpe, on first seeing them, spot something he cannot identify at a window of the top story of one of the houses. Gissing's atmospheric touches add another layer of texture to what could have been merely a story of an odd friendship.

As the title suggests, the story is replete with cobweb imagery. Wherever Goldthorpe goes in Spicer's house, the windows and walls are covered in cobwebs. Every angle and projection is draped in cobwebs, and the stuffy, musty air smells of them. Although other writers might use cobwebs similarly to establish a milieu in which melodramatic events are likely to unfold, Gissing uses them to emphasize the stale aimlessness of Spicer's life before Goldthorpe's arrival.

In a more positive sense, the energy of the spiders corresponds to Goldthorpe's work on his manuscript. The spiders and their webs also point out the persistence of nature. Spicer observes that even if the houses are pulled down after he leaves, the spiders and their creations will remain and continue. Only the insects are really at home there. Nature outlasts humankind's laws and possessions.

Spicer's is a disused life; except for playing the only three songs he knows on his concertina, he does nothing until the young novelist spurs him into activity in the garden. The pride he takes in his Jerusalem artichokes makes these vegetables symbolic of the transformation of both men's lives. They will not be ready to eat until the first frost of autumn, about the same time Goldthorpe's book is judged by the publishers. Both the artichokes and the novel are their great hopes for the future.

Social criticism and examination of unfulfilled lives are not Gissing's only goals in "The House of Cobwebs." He also distances himself from didacticism by observing that Spicer judges literature solely from a moral perspective and is incapable of understanding any other. (It is interesting that Spicer is suspicious of Dickens.) Gissing intertwines strong characterization, theme, and a vividly descriptive style to achieve his desired effects. Without the painstaking attention to detail in depicting the milieu of the two protagonists, "The House of Cobwebs" would not have the same impact. Aesthetics is as significant as social criticism.

Michael Adams

HOUSE OPPOSITE

Author: R. K. Narayan (1906-2001)
Type of plot: Philosophical realism
Time of plot: The 1980's
Locale: The fictional town of Malgudi in South India
First published: 1985

> *Principal characters:*
> THE HERMIT
> THE PROSTITUTE

The Story

R. K. Narayan's "House Opposite" appears in his collection of short stories, *Under the Banyan Tree, and Other Stories* (1985). As suggested by the word "opposite" in the title, the story deals with two fundamentally opposite ways of life, represented by the hermit and the prostitute. The story is told in the third person, in a delightful ironic mode, with its spotlight on the hermit's consciousness.

The story opens with the hermit's shock when he discovers one day that the house across the street is occupied by a prostitute, who is being visited frequently by her male customers. With his preconceived notions of good and evil, the hermit immediately censures the prostitute and her clients for indulging in a sinful life.

The omniscient narrator fills in the details that the hermit has renounced his family, possessions, and all comforts and pleasures to attain his goal of liberation from worldly bondage. He leads a regulated life of austerity, asceticism, and stern discipline, mortifying his body and eschewing any food that could stimulate his carnal desire. He retires early at dusk, sleeps on the bare floor using a block of wood as his pillow, wakes up at four in the morning, and after a ritual bath sits down to meditate. Sometimes, during the day, he teaches little children simple lessons of morality derived from the scriptures.

A turning point in the plot comes one afternoon when the hermit happens to see the woman standing on her doorstep. His eyes explore the woman's sharp features, her soft, voluptuous flesh, and the seductive curves of her body. Driven by blind desire, he can hardly take his eyes off her body. Then, suddenly imagining her to be the devil incarnate out to lead him astray from his quest for purity, he angrily commands her to get in her own house and not ruin his spiritual merit.

From this moment onward, the story deals with the hermit's inner turmoil. As the woman abruptly goes in, the hermit shuts the door of his house tight and goes to the farthest corner of the room to meditate. No matter how hard he tries to concentrate, his thoughts keep wandering to the woman and her male customers, young and old, coming from all walks of life, ensnared by her.

To concentrate, the hermit chants different kinds of potent mantras. He prays to Lord Siva, the god of destruction in Hindu mythology, to destroy the prostitute. He composes a speech in his mind and resolves to confront the shameless woman and tell her that she is the contaminator of humankind and that she should either drown herself in the river or perform a most austere penance and pray for a cleaner life in her next birth. Despite all these efforts, the thought of the woman keeps tormenting him, and he cannot sleep at night.

Finally, he decides to leave his house immediately and move to the other side of the river where he could spend his life in quiet meditation in a temple or under a tree. He recalls a story told by his spiritual teacher long ago that a harlot went to heaven and her self-righteous reformer was condemned to hell because the woman sinned only with her body, but her detractor was corrupt mentally.

In the last climactic scene, as the hermit quietly steps out of his house the next morning, he hears a mournful voice from the house opposite. He sees the prostitute approaching him with a tray full of fruits and flowers. She bows before him with reverence and asks for his blessings on her mother's day of remembrance. As the woman bends to touch his feet, he looks at her closely and notices her sagging body, a bald patch in her discolored hair, and dark circles under her eyes. The hermit forgets the angry speech he had rehearsed in his mind. His heart is filled with pity for the woman. He touches her tray with the tip of his finger as a token of accepting the offering and walks away in silence.

Themes and Meanings

Thematically, "House Opposite" poses a universal question: What is sin? The nature of sin is explored through the characters of the hermit and the prostitute. Because both these characters are nameless, they represent types, not individuals, personifying two opposing ways of life and value systems. It is important to note that because the hermit is the focus of attention in the story, the prostitute is seen primarily through his eyes.

Because the hermit believes in asceticism and total renunciation of worldly pleasures, he looks down on the prostitute as a temptress, a contaminator of humankind, and an adversary to his moral view of life. He thinks that both the prostitute and her male customers are wallowing in sin and illicit pleasures. He therefore decides to admonish her to leave her present profession and atone for her sins to ensure a life of virtue in her next birth.

The irony is that the self-righteous hermit, for all his asceticism, meditation, and rigorous self-discipline, has not been able to conquer his erotic desires. Even a chance vision of the woman arouses in him desires that he had successfully suppressed for so long. He is so tormented by lustful thoughts of the woman that he cannot concentrate in his meditation or sleep at night.

The theme is clearly suggested in the hermit's recollection of the ancient Indian tale in which a prostitute is sent to heaven after her death, but her self-righteous reformer is condemned to hell because of his mental obsession with the prostitute.

This tale becomes a catalyst for change in the hermit's attitude. At the end of the story, as he is about to leave his house for good in order to save his soul from corruption, he encounters the woman. When he looks at her closely, he sees her in a new light as if a film had been suddenly removed from his eyes. She no longer appears to him as a seductive temptress, but a victim of social circumstances and male exploitation. In this moment of illumination, he suddenly becomes aware of his own secret sin, as he recognizes the prostitute essentially as a human being and a loving daughter.

The moral implications of the story are that sin and virtue are relative, depending on an individual's circumstances or way of life. No one therefore has the right to judge others who lead a different lifestyle. Though the story is embedded in a distinctively Hindu world, it conveys a universal theme: the need for tolerance, understanding, compassion, and acceptance of human foibles.

Style and Technique

"House Opposite" is written in a delightfully ironic mode, which is generally considered to be Narayan's strength. The language of the story is lucid, concise, and unlabored. However, because the story is imbued with Indian culture, it contains a number of references and allusions to Hindu religion and mythology. They do not, however, hamper the story's readability, nor do they obscure its meaning.

The plot of the story is simple, compact, and well structured. It involves one connected episode in the life of the hermit. There is very little external action; the main drama is played in the hermit's psyche. The author's choice of a third-person point of view allows him to intensify the conflict by showing a dramatic interplay between external events (the activities of the prostitute and her clients) and internal consciousness (the hermit's mental turmoil and struggle to control his senses). He uses the technique of ironic reversal to give the story a surprise ending.

In fact, the entire plot hinges on Narayan's ironic use of setting. Traditionally, a hermit lives in a secluded place or a forest retreat, but Narayan locates the hermit's house in a narrow, crowded street straight across from the prostitute's house, thus making the conflict inevitable.

Irony is the most important aspect of Narayan's narrative technique. It helps him reveal the disparity between the ideal and the actual. As the story unfolds, it becomes clear to a perceptive reader that things are not what they seem to be. The hermit, who has supposedly given up all pleasures of life, is seen caught in the web of lascivious desires. It is ironic that the prostitute regards the hermit as a saint when she seeks his blessings; she does not know that he has been tainted by mental prostitution.

The last scene underscores the contrast between appearance and reality. The hermit's romantic image of the prostitute, earlier projected by his repressed libidinal yearnings, suddenly changes on close scrutiny. In reality, she looks tired, wasted, and melancholy—a victim of social circumstances. The irony becomes double-edged when, in a moment of self-recognition, the hermit is silenced by the shame of his own hidden sin.

Chaman L. Sahni

THE HOUSE WITH THE GRAPE-VINE

Author: H. E. Bates (1905-1974)
Type of plot: Domestic realism
Time of plot: The 1950's
Locale: England
First published: 1959

Principal characters:
THE SMALL BOY, a lover of the natural splendor of England's past
THE FATHER, the parent who instills this love in the boy
THE OLD WOMAN, the resident of the house with the grapevine

The Story

A small boy growing up in a factory town in England enjoys hearing his father describe what the place was like before it became industrialized. The boy is fascinated to learn that most of the older houses were once covered by grapevines, on which small, dark grapes grew. That his father, when he was eight, worked in a grapevine-covered farmhouse half the day while going to school only part-time is especially appealing. The boy imagines such a life as ideal, but his father reveals that he hated working there, although he will not explain why. The romantic aspects of such a life, however, obscure any possible deficiencies for the boy: "How marvellous it must have been . . . to have stables and a pigeon-cote in the yard instead of only a water-barrel and a slat fence where people beat their mats. What days they must have been—he simply couldn't believe his father hadn't liked them."

The boy waits eagerly for three months before he can go to the farmhouse to see and taste the ripened grapes. When he arrives, an old woman with "a long face like a parsnip that had a few suspended hairy roots hanging from the chin" grabs him and accuses him of coming to steal apples. When he says he is after grapes, she denies ever having any and threatens to have him arrested. The boy breaks away and runs home. He never tells his father about going to the farmhouse or asks him again why he had been unhappy working there. He continues, however, to believe in the story of the grapevine.

Themes and Meanings

In the approximately six hundred short stories by H. E. Bates, one of the most frequent subjects is the glories of rural England. Bates dealt with this subject not only in his stories and novels but also in several nonfiction works and a column in *The Spectator* entitled "Country Life." He recognized throughout his career that what he considered an idyllic way of life was undergoing drastic changes, and his writing celebrates what had been and what remained of this peaceful splendor. Bates describes what has been lost in *The Vanished World* (1969), the first volume of his autobiography: "The world of television, jets and space craft dazzles our generation with new if sometimes near useless wonders, but for myself I would cheerfully exchange it for . . . the smell of wood-smoke, the scent of bluebells, cowslips, primroses and the Maiden's Blush, the Turk's Cap lily and the voice of nightingales."

A nostalgic longing for the natural magnificence of the English past dominates "The House with the Grape-vine." Both father and son would prefer their town to be "a place of green fields, with oats and barley and meadows where there were now factory yards, and little spinneys of violets and a farmhouse with apple-trees and a brook at the foot of the hill where sticklebacks swam among the cresses." The boy wants "to make a link with the past" and wants to discover "what it was like before the brick boxes and the factories with the gallows-cranes came to smother and obliterate it all." The impossibility of recapturing the past is emphasized when the old woman drags the boy to the wall his father has so lovingly described: "That was the wall all right, but there were no grapes on it. It was empty; there was nothing there."

However, something positive comes out of the boy's frightening experience. Loneliness and the need for companionship and compassion are other frequent Bates concerns. The boy's father associates the grapevines with the grandmother with whom he lived when he worked at the farmhouse. His mother had died, the grandmother did not live long after that, and there is no mention of his wife. He and the boy seem to have no one but each other. In refusing to explain what happened to him at the farmhouse, the father says, "Perhaps some day there will be something that will make you unhappy and you won't know why it is. I hope not. But you can't always explain things." Finding out about such unhappy things in much the same way that his father did and deciding not to say anything about it help the boy to understand his father better: "When he passed the gates of that house, he remembered the grape-vine. . . . [H]e too hated that house, and, because of it, loved his father so much more."

Style and Technique

Bates uses the grapevine to unify the elements of the story. It is no longer on the farmhouse wall because the old woman has either neglected or destroyed it because she is incapable of appreciating its beauty. She does not remember it because she cannot understand its possible significance. For Bates, the boy, and the father, the grapevine represents the past, the English countryside, childhood, innocence, and optimism. The grapevine can survive only as people and ways of life do: through care and love.

"The House with the Grape-vine" also gives evidence of Bates's descriptive powers. The boy will always remember the day he went to the farmhouse: "It might have been chosen specially from all the days of the autumn because the air was so yellow with sunshine that the stone of the house seemed almost the colour of a piece of plain Madeira cake, and because even the small white clouds seemed warm." Such affectionate evocations of time, place, and nature seem Bates's most lasting achievement in his short stories.

Michael Adams

THE HOUSEBREAKER OF SHADY HILL

Author: John Cheever (1912-1982)
Type of plot: Domestic realism
Time of plot: The 1950's
Locale: Shady Hill, a fictional suburb of New York City
First published: 1954

> *Principal characters:*
> JOHNNY HAKE, the narrator and protagonist, a thirty-six-year-old
> businessperson
> CHRISTINA, his wife

The Story

"The Housebreaker of Shady Hill" recounts the process by which Johnny Hake, a stable citizen of a quiet New York suburb, briefly becomes a thief, suffers remorse, and reforms. In the process, it comments satirically on the mores of modern suburban-ites. Johnny's career in theft begins shortly after he resigns his job with a company that makes parablendeum—a kind of plastic wrap. Fed up with office politics, Johnny strikes out on his own, only to discover that he cannot earn a living comparable to his old salary. Unwilling to burden his wife with his financial worries, reluctant to borrow from friends or relatives, Johnny one night enters a neighbor's house and steals a wallet containing nine hundred dollars.

Immediately appalled by what he has done, Johnny finds that his crime preys on his mind all the next day. Everywhere he looks he seems to encounter crime, from the stranger in the restaurant who pockets a tip left by a previous customer, to his old friend who tries to cut him in on a business deal that is "just like stealing." The very word "steal" seems to have a powerful effect on him; he suddenly feels he is a part of the force destroying the peace and order of the world. At church the next Sunday he imagines that he hears a rat gnawing away at the floorboards, and he is so distracted that he misses the opportunity to take Communion. He comes to a further crisis when his children surprise him for his birthday with the gift of an aluminum extension lad-der. In his new paranoia, Johnny imagines the gift to be an indirect comment on his ca-reer as a thief. He becomes sharp with the children, fights with his wife, and has packed a suitcase and left the house before the two reconcile.

A few nights later, Johnny attempts another theft. He enters the house of Tom and Grace Maitland, a wealthy but melancholy couple. Creeping into the Maitlands' bed-room in quest of Tom's wallet, Johnny discovers that Grace is in bed with the boy who cuts the Maitlands' grass. Shocked, he hurries home and reflects on the altered picture Shady Hill presents by night.

The next night, on his way to attempt another theft, Johnny has a revelation that turns him away from his life of crime. As he heads for the home of yet another neighbor, the wind begins to stir and suddenly rain is falling, reconnecting Johnny with his sense of the pleasures afforded by mere existence, and reminding him of his love for Christina and the children. His obsession with money seems to fall away, and he is able to go home and sleep peacefully. He even has a restorative dream of sailing a boat on the Mediterranean. The next day, he is offered his old job in parablendeum, and he accepts. Taking an advance on his salary, he returns nine hundred dollars to his neighbors, the Warburtons, and is finally at ease with himself.

Themes and Meanings

"The Housebreaker of Shady Hill" offers two themes that, although seemingly contradictory, in fact are complementary. On the one hand, the story satirizes the values and manners of a certain class of well-to-do suburbanites, suggesting the shallowness of their morality and the limits of their dreams. On the other hand, the story's resolution affirms the worthiness of life's simple pleasures and asserts man's freedom to direct his own life. In some measure, the story's strength comes from the tension between these themes. The overall tone is ironic, and yet there is ultimately an endorsement of certain facets of suburban existence—a nice house and garden, cooking on an outdoor grill, playing softball with the neighbors.

Throughout the story, John Cheever introduces characters whose affluence is emphasized, as is their unhappiness. The protagonist is established on the story's first page as a product of an upper-class New York upbringing: He was reared on Sutton Place, an exclusive address, and attended St. Bartholomew's, a fashionable Episcopal church. However, his parents, long divorced, are depicted as lost souls. His mother lives alone in a Cleveland hotel, refusing to forgive him for getting married. His father, whom he rarely saw, once took him to the theater and offered to buy him the services of any chorus girl whose looks he liked. Johnny fled after plucking fifty dollars from his father's wallet. In his current crisis, he broods on what he perceives as the unlucky origins that have led to his present "sordid destiny."

The wealthy residents of Shady Hill are also satirized. The Warburtons, husband and wife, are described respectively as "the kind of man that you wouldn't have liked at school" and "an aging mouse." Of the very rich Tom Maitland the narrator remarks, "His wife is the fattest woman in Shady Hill, and nobody much likes his children." Other potential robbery targets are the Pewters, "who were not only rich but booze fighters, and who drank so much that I didn't see how they could hear thunder after the lights were turned out." Amid this sea of moneyed unhappiness, Johnny Hake's yearning for affluence seems a misguided quest.

During his brief career as a thief, Johnny is haunted by images of his parents and his neighbors. Their depressing lives, as well as the dark events of the world at large, come to dominate his thoughts. However, suddenly, in one clear moment, his sense of balance is restored. He stops lamenting his life and returns to a celebration of possibilities. A brisk rain shower awakens his senses, and he realizes that neither his parents nor his recent misdeeds will trap him forever. He thinks with pleasure of his wife and children. The next day, New York City again seems sweet and exciting rather than dark and criminal. Overall, the story affirms the individual's right to choose his way of life and underscores his responsibility to do so honestly. Johnny may have been the accidental offspring of unpleasant parents, he may live in a world riddled with crime, but he has many blessings to contemplate as well.

Style and Technique

Despite its serious topic—the quest for an honest existence in a fallen world—"The Housebreaker of Shady Hill" is often humorous in tone. By interjecting humor, Cheever escapes the risk that his story might seem sermonlike, a cautionary tale warning modern-day sinners not to fall into the trap of worshiping money. This humor emerges principally in the melodramatic imagination of the narrator. Although Johnny can see the humor in the concerns of others, his own problems assume the status of major trauma. Having a cigarette late one night, he feels a twinge in his lungs and becomes suddenly convinced that he is dying of bronchial cancer, fated to leave his wife and children penniless. After his act of theft, he imagines himself as a "child of darkness" and "a miserable creature whose footsteps had been mistaken for the noise of the wind." Raking leaves while his neighbors play softball, Johnny complains, "Why should I be left alone with my dead leaves in the twilight—as I was— feeling so forsaken, lonely and forlorn that I was chilled?" Conscious of his slide into self-pity, Johnny nevertheless commits the ultimate in silly self-absorption when he sees a dogwood tree that has lost its leaves and reflects, "How sad everything is!"

Other poignant humor emerges from the degree to which Johnny's theft has changed his perception of things. The stained glass at church "seemed to be made from the butts of vermouth and Burgundy bottles." His fight with Christina is a lesson in domestic banality. When he discovers his suitcase is torn, he exclaims, "Even the cat has a nice traveling bag." It is a particular indignity to him that he cannot find enough clean shirts to last a week. At the height of his self-dramatization, he hammers a "For Sale" sign onto a tree in the front yard. He marches off to the train station only to discover, anticlimactically, that he cannot get a train until four o'clock in the morning. So, he goes back to Christina, and all thought of divorce is forgotten.

By persistently introducing a humorous tone into the scenes of Johnny's despair, Cheever indirectly reassures the reader that Johnny's fall into sin will not be permanent. A story with this kind of tone will surely end happily, as this one does.

Diane M. Ross

HOW BEAUTIFUL WITH SHOES

Author: Wilbur Daniel Steele (1886-1970)
Type of plot: Psychological
Time of plot: The early twentieth century
Locale: Rural Virginia
First published: 1932

> *Principal characters:*
> AMARANTHA DOGGETT, a teenage farm girl
> MRS. DOGGETT, her deaf mother
> RUBY HERTER, her betrothed, a farmer
> HUMBLE JEWETT, an escaped killer

The Story

On a remote farm in rural Virginia in the early part of the 1900's, an almost totally deaf Mrs. Doggett calls to her daughter, Amarantha, who prefers being called Mary or Mare. It is spring, and Amarantha has finished some of the more laborious farm chores, milking the cows and feeding the pigs, when her fiancé, Ruby Herter, stops by with his horse and carriage to remind the young girl that she belongs to him. Just as Ruby Herter kisses his betrothed, they hear a car driving up to the farm with the news that someone who is believed to be a killer has escaped from Dayville Asylum.

Ruby Herter immediately joins the other young men in their search for the crazed murderer, as Mare secures the team of horses and runs down the road to tell Ruby's father. Shortly after she returns to the farm, her mother calls her to come and meet a young man who has stopped to see her, and Mare is puzzled by his presence. On meeting her, the young man says, "That's poetry . . . Amarantha in Carolina! That makes me happy!" Mare immediately realizes that this seemingly harmless looking young man is the escaped killer but does not want to alarm her deaf mother. She lures the young man away from her mother and then bolts into the forest. The young man easily catches up to her and begins wooing her in the words of the seventeenth century English Cavalier poet Richard Lovelace, quoting from one of Lovelace's famous love lyrics, "To Amarantha, That She Would Dishevel Her Haire." He not only identifies Mare as the Amarantha from Lovelace's poem but also literalizes the words of the poem: "Do you know how beautiful you are, Amarantha, 'Amarantha sweet and fair?'" He suddenly reaches behind her and begins to unravel the meshes of her hairbraid, saying, "Braid no more that shining hair!" At that instant, Ruby and the other searchers capture him, tie him up, and take him to be locked up at the local courthouse. A neighbor tells Mare that the murderer's name is Humble Jewett, and that he was a teacher in an academy school. Five years earlier, he attacked the headmaster with an axe and tried to strangle a girl.

A few hours later, Ruby returns to tell Mare that Humble Jewett has escaped from jail, killed a man, and set the courthouse on fire. As soon as Ruby leaves, Humble Jewett quickly and calmly abducts a terrified Mare into the woods near her home. As they move deeper into the forest, he continues to quote both the Lovelace poem and erotic lines from the Old Testament's "Song of Solomon," while running his fingers through her hair. They come on the empty cabin of old Mr. Wyker, and Humble breaks down the door and takes her inside. Humble notices Mare's new shoes and recalls the lines from the seventh chapter of the "Song of Solomon": "How beautiful are thy feet with shoes, O prince's daughter!" Humble articulates quite clearly, during his meandering monologue, the exact nature of the tragedies of his life: "I've never lived . . . I knew I'd never loved, Beloved." As he catches his foot in a crack in the wooden floor and falls to his knees, he also admits that he never knew he had never lived. After Mare fails in a second attempt to escape from Humble's embraces, he calls her Blossom, and Mare angrily reminds him that her name is Mary. Hearing that name transforms the mad Humble into the persona of Jesus Christ on the cross addressing his mother Mary.

Finally Humble falls asleep. Old Wyker eventually returns to his cabin, sizes up the situation, and shoots Humble as Mare nimbly escapes from the madman's arms. Although Mare returns home shaken and exhausted, she cannot get the resonating lines from the "Song of Solomon" and Lovelace's poems out of her head; they obsess her to such an extent that she tells everyone, even her mother and her fiancé, to go away and leave her alone. She begins to perceive dimly the connection between words and experience, and the more poetically compelling the verbal images, the more vivid the experience: "Last night Mare had lain stupid with fear on groundpine beneath a bush, loud foot-falls and light whispers confused in her ear. Only now, in her room, did she smell the groundpine. Only now did the conscious part of her brain begin to make words of the whispering." As Mare stares at the wallpaper in her room, she has a romantic vision of herself running through moonlit fields with a young man: "And the world spread down around in waves of black and silver, more immense than she had known the world could be, and more beautiful." She wonders if only crazy people say such things. When Ruby Herter tries to get her to show her gratitude, she violently pushes him out of the door, crying, "Go 'way. . . . Lea' me be!"

Themes and Meanings

The major theme throughout "How Beautiful with Shoes" is the fall of Mare Doggett from ignorance into knowledge. Wilbur Daniel Steele presents both Mare and her fiancé, Ruby Herter, as a couple naïvely treating each other with animal affection: "They were used to handling animals, both of them; and it was spring. A slow warmth pervaded the girl, formless, nameless, almost impersonal." Although Humble Jewett forcefully carries her off into the woods, his habit of quoting from some of English literature's most compelling love poems eventually registers in Mare's consciousness because of the sheer force of their poetic beauty. Humble's first words to Mare, "Amarantha. . . . that's poetry," become the agents of her fall. Those lines and others propel Mare into a world of romance, beauty, and ecstatic declaration that she never knew existed. She begins to understand that there may be more to life than the obvious animalistic level that her names suggest: Mare, a female work horse, and her surname, Doggett. She slowly perceives, through the agency of poetic beauty, that there may be more to life than the brutal drudgery of being a farmer's wife.

Although Humble Jewett is quite mad, he has found the resonating power of these immortal lines of poetry sufficient to sustain him in creating a world of his own, a world resplendent with grace, romance, and loveliness. When Mare returns from her traumatic journey with a madman, she is unable to shake off the transforming effects of hearing those lines, lines that reveal to her both the empty banality of her life and, simultaneously, the richness of the life of the imagination, of which she never had been aware before. The story concludes with an image of the young girl suspended, quite miserably, between the animal consciousness of life on a farm and an unattainable yearning for the romantic ecstasy that these magnificent lines of poetry seem to promise. A recurrent question that she cannot stop asking in the concluding pages of the story—"Is it only crazy folks ever say such things?"—accurately summarizes her agonizing confusion.

Style and Technique

One of the techniques that Steele uses throughout this well-constructed narrative is making the proper names of the major characters contribute to a deeper understanding of both their characters and their plights. The Doggett family leads a life that shares characteristics with the animals they care for as they pursue, doggedly, their rather brutal lives on a rural farm. Although Ruby Herter does not directly hurt Mare, his behavior toward her is little better than his treatment of other farm animals. After Humble Jewett connects Mare to the highly romanticized Amarantha in the Lovelace poem, she identifies with her actual name, Amarantha. Once Jewett mythologizes such common names and highly romantic lines of poetry from Lovelace and the Old Testament, Mare begins to understand her life in larger perspectives: She sees what she is not, as well as what she has missed and can never have. Steele's technique of constantly repeating these lines and interweaving them in the text enables them to resonate with greater significance each time they appear. The reader experiences with Mare the painful process of transformation that she undergoes.

The line that Mare repeats as the story concludes, "Is it only crazy folks ever say such things?" cannot be answered, and that knowledge is what causes Mare to reject everyone, even her fiancé, with the concluding, recurring line: "Go 'way! Go 'way! Lea' me be!" Although Humble Jewett is quite mad, he has taught Mare a terrible lesson—that she will never be able to enter the world of grace and loveliness that these glorious lines express and embody.

Patrick Meanor

HOW CLAEYS DIED

Author: William Sansom (1912-1976)
Type of plot: Philosophical realism
Time of plot: Shortly after the end of World War II
Locale: German countryside
First published: 1947

> *Principal characters:*
> CLAEYS, the protagonist, a teacher from Belgium
> TWO ENGLISH OFFICERS AND A DRIVER, his companions in a car
> EXPATRIATES FROM EASTERN EUROPE, former prisoners of a Nazi
> labor camp

The Story

A Belgian named Claeys, temporarily attached to the British army on a civilian mission, is riding in Germany with two officers and a driver two months after the end of World War II. He is a teacher who has volunteered to assist in the rehabilitation of the enemy. He is traveling to one of the camps of displaced persons, mostly Slavs, from a German forced-labor camp.

The car drives through a verdant landscape, where vegetation is already camouflaging the evidence of war, burying the carcasses of abandoned war machines in grass and vines. However, there is also a bombed-out town that is quite dead, grim evidence of humanity's power to bring a total disorder that at least temporarily defeats every effort of nature to restore life.

As the car approaches the area of the labor camp, the riders hear a chorus of men singing Slavic songs and a large group preparing, apparently, to march home. The driver advances cautiously with a hand on his gun; there has been trouble recently between the former inmates and a former German soldier returning to his farm. However, expatriates generally respect the English military. Claeys says that he wants to speak to these men and asks the driver to leave him there alone, drive out of sight around the bend, and wait.

The expatriates approach Claeys, uncertain about who he is and what he wants. Claeys smiles and speaks to them in English, but they obviously do not understand. Then he tries French—again no response. He breaks into Dutch, which comes more naturally—this time there is some interest and arguing among the men, even some menacing gestures. Then he thinks that perhaps some of them might have learned German and reiterates his friendly overtures in that language. Now, the ranks close around him, the looks grow darker. Though they evidently recognize the language, they still do not seem to understand his now desperate "Bitte ein Moment . . . ich bin Freund, Freund." Slowly he raises his hand in a plea for order and understanding. A man steps forward and swings a scythe, cutting him down. The others close in, shouting and kicking.

Shots from the two officers bring a halt to the mob action, bringing down two of the attackers. Claeys, now dying, tries to speak to the officer who kneels by him but can only gasp out "mistake!" Claeys lifts his right arm to shake hands with the officer, then gestures to his attackers. The officer, believing that he understands the dying man, walks toward the group of watchers extending his hand. Because it is now bloody, however, he first wipes it, then shakes hands with the Slavs as a sign of peace. The displaced persons do not know if he is vicariously offering the hand of the dying man in friendship or, by wiping his hand first, expressing a repudiation of the man they killed.

Themes and Meanings

The expatriates in this story are obviously confused about the identity and intentions of this stranger in civilian clothes, and when he speaks German, they attack him with the hatred built up for their longtime oppressors. Strangely enough, the reader may also be somewhat puzzled by him. He is apparently willing to forgive his killers in a magnanimous gesture of friendship even as he dies. However, there is something ambiguous about his character, what little the reader knows of it.

Perhaps the most puzzling statement about him comes early in the story: "Claeys was a teacher, engaged then on relief measures, a volunteer for this work of rehabilitation of the enemy, perhaps a sort of half-brother-of-mercy as during the occupation he had been a sort of half-killer." Does this mean he was a "half-brother" to Germans? A collaborator, perhaps, or simply one who did nothing while others were killed and who thus feels half-guilty? Was he one whose resistance to the Germans was only theoretical, not actual? "Now he wanted to construct quickly the world of which he had dreamed during the shadow years; now he was often as impatient of inaction as he had learned to be patient before."

The only clues that the reader is given to comprehend his nature come from the burden of his thoughts as he rides through the countryside. He seems to be philosophically inclined, more a man of thought than a man of action. He meditates much of the time on the evidence of both chaos and order in nature, and he wonders about the impact of man on that larger framework of nature. Much of what he sees suggests that even the devastation of war does not seriously unbalance the natural order. Some of the wreckage even seems to suggest organic forms; an abandoned tank nosing up from a cornfield, for example, looks like a large gray toad. Claeys is disturbed, however, by the barren, bombed-out town, which seems beyond reclamation. Its sheer vacuity contrasts forebodingly with the unconcerned fecundity of the fields outside of town.

Perhaps Claeys's tragic flaw is his unrelieved propensity to theorize with little actual experience of what wartime has meant to those in the midst of action. He overestimates his own ability to communicate and help his fellowmen, or perhaps he underestimates the psychological effect of accumulated resentment in the former prisoners.

Some of his philosophical phrases, such as "the time for compensation," make an ironic background to the brutality of his death.

At the point of death, he is still racked by confused questions, though he cannot express them: "Broadly, if they could have been straightened out, these questions would have been: 'Order or Disorder? Those fellows were the victims of an attempt to rule men into an impeccable order, my killing was the result of the worst, that is, the most stupid disorder.'" Absolute control over men's lives apparently brings on such outbreaks of irrational chaos.

Style and Technique

William Sansom's sure command of visual images is vital to this story—the sense impressions both of vigorous vegetation and of the residue of war. The unique method of the story is the apparent demonstration in concrete terms of its philosophical burden. The protagonist (if not the author himself) is extending what he calls at one point "the intricate anarchy" of nature, which at the human level seems successful and orderly but which involves the continual, indifferent destruction of individual plants and animals, to include the effects of war on individuals and groups. The victims of warfare are like seeds that fall on stony ground.

The author illustrates this intricate, but random principle of nature in a vivid image of the wind-borne seed, such as that of a dandelion:

> Look at the parachute seed—this amazing seed actually flies off the insensate plant-mother! It sails on to the wind! The seed itself hangs beneath such an intricate parasol, it is carried from the roots of its mother to land on fertile ground far away and set up there an emissary generation! And more—when it lands, this engine is so constructed that draughts inch-close to the soil drag, drag at the little parachute, so that the seed beneath actually erodes the earth, digs for itself a little trench of shelter, buries itself! Amazing! And what if the clever little seed is borne on the wrong wind to a basin of basalt?

In the completely bombed-out town, the protagonist apparently senses, but does not verbalize even in his thoughts, the obvious analogy to "stony ground." He does, however, meditate at length on the frustrated displaced persons, men from Bulgaria, Poland, and Russia, as analogous to seeds that have no chance to develop. The men, even when released from servitude, are far from home and have no means of support in an alien land: "ten thousand displaced souls, newly freed but imprisoned still by their strange environment and by their great expectations born and then as instantly barred."

Perhaps this somewhat fatalistic perception allows the protagonist to accept even his own death as a natural accident, a "mistake," for which blame need not be assigned. The protagonist has been accustomed to thinking in somewhat impersonal, general terms, what a philosopher might call the "view from eternity," wherein local disasters may be, if not rationalized, at least unemotionally accepted.

The error, or perhaps merely the impracticality, of living thus removed from the gritty, concrete experience of human misery is also suggested through natural imagery. The car has been driving on a straight, endless road lined by great beech trees at regular intervals—a seemingly endless order. Ironically, when the beech rows stop and the protective arch of leaves is broken, the effect is a greater confinement, wherein the sky, traditionally called "infinite," is likened instead to a lid over a plate. This image also suggests the freed, yet imprisoned situation of the displaced persons.

> Those who deny the flatlands forget the sky—over flat country the sky approaches closer than anywhere else, it takes shape, it becomes the blue-domed lid on a flat plate of earth. Here is a greater intimacy between the elements; and for once, for a little, the world appears finite.

This revelation of the accordionlike qualities of human perception of time and space is one of the most striking characteristics of Sansom's writing. The open sky as finite reflects the existential reality of each person's individual life, which cannot experience the broad sweep of history in which short-term disaster is comfortably lost in long-term survival of the species. At least one interpretation of this story, therefore, may be as the journey of an abstract thinker into the concrete, existential reality of the "stony ground" created by modern warfare.

Katherine Snipes

HOW I CONTEMPLATED THE WORLD
FROM THE DETROIT HOUSE OF CORRECTION
AND BEGAN MY LIFE OVER AGAIN

Author: Joyce Carol Oates (1938-   )
Type of plot: Psychological
Time of plot: 1968
Locale: Detroit suburbs
First published: 1969

Principal characters:
"THE GIRL", the sixteen-year-old narrator and protagonist
HER FATHER, a physician
HER MOTHER
CLARITA, her female companion
SIMON, her thirty-five-year-old boyfriend and pimp

The Story

"How I Contemplated the World from the Detroit House of Correction and Began My Life over Again" probes the case of a young girl from a "good" family who turns to crime. The opening lines of the story perfectly identify its content: "Notes for an essay for an English class at Baldwin County Day School; poking around in debris; disgust and curiosity; a revelation of the meaning of life; a happy ending." The narrator uses the occasion of a school essay to examine the psychological "debris" of her recent life—the emotional turbulence and confusion that led to a stay in the Detroit House of Correction.

The narrator's search for the meaning of her delinquency begins as she mentally revisits Branden's, the large and luxurious department store where she was arrested for shoplifting. The store's plushness and material glitter serve as an immediate symbol of the comfortable, insulated, middle-class existence of her parents against which the narrator rebels. With no logical transition, the girl's notes move readers from the store's interior to the parents' sumptuous home (with "a small library"), where the astounded parents confront her for stealing a pair of gloves. The narrator knows that "there is a connection" between her bridge-playing mother and her physician father (doctor of the slightly ill), and between them and the manager of the store, his doctor, her brother, and the family's maid. She knows that her "salvation" is bound up in these relationships, but their meaning is a painful blur.

The narrator's next notes highlight the tragic alienation between daughter and family. The mother wonders why her daughter is "so strange"; perpetually in motion, she has no clue to the girl's inner life, her secret obsession: "I wanted to steal but not to buy." A status seeker like the mother, the father is equally oblivious to the girl's needs.

He is off reading a paper at a medical convention in Los Angeles at the moment the daughter is arrested for shoplifting. The father would agree with the ironic, impersonal note sent home from school, that though the girl made off with a copy of *Pageant Magazine* for no reason and swiped a roll of Lifesavers, she was "in no need of saving her life." The parents' evasion of responsibility leads them to conclude that their daughter's problems are attributable solely to "a slight physiological modification known only to a gynecologist." The girl hardly remembers her brother, who has been sent to a preparatory school in Maine.

Further notes establish that the atmosphere of affluence that intoxicates her parents nauseates and suffocates the girl. The neighborhood is heavy with conspicuous symbols of upper-middle-class success, yet its rigidly conformist social patterns leave no room for individuality or spontaneous emotional expression. Things appear to matter more than people; the people are mere adornments, attachments like pools, garages, or automatic sprinklers. It is her unarticulated desire to escape this "airproof, breathproof," environment that leads the girl to become a truant from school and to become involved in a social milieu diametrically opposed to her own: a Detroit ghetto where, in a sense, she is befriended by a street-hardened girl named Clarita. There, she meets Simon, a desperate, exploitative man who becomes her lover and pimp. Simon prefers a needle in the arm to the girl's embrace, and he turns her into a prostitute. If Sioux Drive was heavy with material possessions, this environment is heavy with fear and pain, climaxing in the girl's prostitution and then a brutal beating by female inmates of the house of correction. The girl perceives her attackers to be avenging themselves for the cumulative social injustices in their lives.

Out of the hospital, the girl, in her final notes, tells of her return to her safe and comfortable home. Her vow never to leave home again, her declaration that "I love everything here," has a desperately false ring to it. Despite the temporary capitulation to a world that is unreal and plastic as ever to her, she weeps in her living room over the falseness and emptiness of lives that seek salvation through material acquisitions, that look "for God in gold and beige carpeting" or in "the beauty of chandeliers and the miracle of a clean polished gleaming toaster and faucets that run both hot and cold water."

Themes and Meanings

On the one hand, the girl's notes are an indictment of the soulless materialism of her parents, which stifles the girl's emotional and artistic growth. On the other hand, the notes are, like the art of fiction itself, a gesture of liberation, of purgation and self-discovery. Clearly, this is a portrait of the artist as a young woman, albeit a girl who must take to the streets to search for life-affirming experience to fill the void she feels. So uncertain is the girl's sense of personal identity that she is "a secret" to herself—one more stranger in the sea of bewildering events and faces whose connections and meanings she records and hopes to understand.

In the sterile, suburban utopia of the parents, people are viewed as possessions, adornments, or attachments, valued not for their human qualities but for their ability to function harmoniously in the community's regulated social machinery. The door to the girl's home has a brass knocker "never knocked," and even the weather is described as "planted and performing." In this plasticized environment, people experience "ecstasy" not in relation to one another but in response to a smooth bathtub of bubbly pink water, a man's trouser pockets filled with coins, keys, dust, and peanuts, or income tax returns.

It is her quest for a more honest and spontaneous way of being that takes the narrator into the violent world of Simon and Clarita. The narrator must make herself vulnerable to life, exposing herself to its ravages, to test her own nature in a world not protected from suffering or true ecstasy. If the emotional weather here is erratic and stormy, its turbulence is preferable to the superficial well-being of her previous life— to no weather at all. Desperate love is better than no love, and despite the filth, injustice, and brutality, the day-to-day struggle for street survival is life-affirming. In short, this is an atmosphere in which the girl can breathe (Simon, she says, "breathes gravity into me"), in which people are ready for laughter or tears, and in which, however accompanied by pain, compassion and creativity have a chance to grow.

Still, salvation for this incipient artist is no more likely to come in Simon's anguished, self-destructive world than in the uniform anonymity of her parents' life. Although her emotional confusion drives her once more back into the protected world of wealth and privilege, her reference to the "movieland sun" that breaks over her doll's house of a home and to the unfamiliar face that peers back at her from the shiny toaster shows that her crisis is far from resolved, that the role she is trying to assume is incompatible with her future artistic destiny. Suggestive of the final image and words of Dorothy in the film *The Wizard of Oz* (1939), the girl figuratively draws up her legs into a fetal position and vows never to leave home again. However, a healthier, more positive ending is in store. These notes are her promise to herself that, like James Joyce's Stephen Dedalus, she has an artist's awareness, honesty, creativity, and active social conscience that will allow her entrance into a world of her own artistic creation.

Style and Technique

Rather than presenting her story by means of a smoothly unfolding plot in which actions mount spirally to a climax and then unwind to a denouement, Joyce Carol Oates here juxtaposes a series of emotionally charged vignettes, impressions reminiscent of picture slides.

These vignettes are filtered through the narrator's confused, half-formed artistic consciousness; she does not yet comprehend the logical connections, the cause-and-effect relationships, of the events she relates. That she writes "Nothing" under the heading "People and Circumstances Contributing to this Delinquency" suggests her present inability to digest and interpret the painful flux of experience. The key to the story's style, then, is the fact that the girl's fragmentary notes are a rough draft. The finished product should give coherence to her jumbled experiences and lead to understanding of her predicament. Ultimately, with emotional distance and greater artistic awareness, she will see what the careful reader sees—that these impressions are an indictment of the obsessive materialism of her parents. She will gain greater control over her art, but her artistic perception of experience is already evident here, in such unconscious devices as the repeated association of the color pink with her plush but corrupt surroundings, in the metaphorical use of weather to suggest emotional states, and in references to sexual abuse and incest that symbolically link her father to Simon.

For now, it is enough to get these hostile impressions on paper as a purging of fears and uncertainties. The glut of uninterpreted physical detail, the detached, impersonal, third-person point of view (she refers to herself always as "the girl"), the choppy sentences and objective observations, all combine to convey the narrator's numbness of spirit, the aftermath of trauma. Conveyed, too, is the isolation of the girl's inner self— separated for a while from the outside world and from that battered external self who appears to her as a stranger. To heal this split between the perceiving self and the self perceived is an essential quest of the story.

Lawrence Broer

HOW I FINALLY LOST MY HEART

Author: Doris Lessing (1919-   )
Type of plot: Psychological
Time of plot: The mid-twentieth century
Locale: London
First published: 1963

Principal character:

THE PROTAGONIST, an anonymous English woman in her forties

The Story

In this first-person narrative, an anonymous woman in mid-life reflects on her life and loves and recounts an experience that she has recently had, the experience of losing her heart. She loses her heart neither in the romantic metaphorical sense of being powerless before desire for another nor in the literal sense of cutting her heart out of her body and throwing it away, not that she has not wished to do both in her life. She loses her heart in a transfiguring, dreamlike encounter with her own inner being.

In the narrator's ruminations on her past loves, she distinguishes between the affairs and entanglements and even marriages, however numerous, that "don't really count" and "serious loves." She points out that not only she, but also most people today, fly from lover to lover, ever seeking "serious" love. Acerbically, she observes, "We are all entirely in agreement that we are in the right to taste, test, sip and sample a thousand people on our way to the 'real' one." Although she carries the scars of many loves, she has never lost her heart.

The occasion that precipitates her finally losing her heart takes place on a day on which she lunches with her first "real" love, a man she terms "serious love A." By chance that same afternoon she has tea with another past love, serious love B. Meeting these two loves "that count" and anticipating a meeting with a new man that evening engender in her a startling insight into the nature of her affairs of heart. Standing at a window looking out on Great Portland Street, ready for an evening with the man who might be serious love C, she has a vision of the dynamics of her romantic life. She imagines C, too, standing in his window, anticipating their meeting, hoping like her to be able to give his wounded heart to another. She imagines calling C and asking him to agree that they should keep their wounded hearts to themselves, not hurl them at one another. Her fancied appeal to C is interrupted by an awareness that a large, unknown object has appeared in her left hand. She recognizes this unknown object as her own heart.

She is in turn irritated, appalled, and a bit disgusted by the heart in her hand, but soon enough the problem it presents is clear. How will she get rid of it? Unable to pull the heart off and throw it away, she cancels her date with the man who might be serious love C and sits for four days examining the layers of memory in her forty-year-old heart. She is struck by the realization that examining her heart and its memories will affix her heart to her hand permanently. Freeing herself of her heart will require more than introspection.

Concealing her heart on her hand first in tinfoil, then in a scarf, she moves out on the street and into the London subway system. Sitting unnoticed in a crowded train, she observes a young, rather shabby woman. The woman sits in a twisted posture, stares at nothing, talks to herself in a "private drama of misery" over some betrayal of love. The narrator describes her as absorbed in a "frozen misery," a "passionless passion."

As she stares at this stricken shell of a woman, the narrator suddenly feels the heart in her hand roll loose. She stands and places the heart wrapped in its tinfoil on the seat next to the woman, like a poignant valentine. The grieving woman clutches it to herself as if it were a precious gift, a gift that compensated for all of her pain. The narrator rises and leaves the underground, laughing. Heartless, she is free.

Themes and Meanings

This story portrays a contemporary woman's consciousness surveying the ruins of the myth of romantic love. It is an ironic rumination on the emptiness of the cliché of losing one's heart in love. At the center of the story is the drama of a psychic crisis and its resolution, staged in the chamber of a middle-aged woman's mind. She metaphorically moves into the room of her own being and then into the underground world of her own unconscious. The tale is both the story of a woman's crackup, her intense experience of her divided self, and the story of her development and new wholeness. The narrator's cool detachment has long covered her submerged torment of disappointment and failure to connect in love. Captive to the myth of losing her heart in love, desiring another to claim responsibility for her and absolve her of her pain, Doris Lessing's contemporary woman explores her own disillusionment and moves toward becoming a "free woman."

The pale, thin, self-absorbed woman on the train is a projection of the narrator's dissociated and long-denied mourning, her inner being gripped by pain. To her tormented doppelganger, her own living ghost, she gives her heart, at once symbolically freeing herself of the myth of romantic love and confronting and uniting with her own despair. No lover can redeem one from pain. Freedom is found in acknowledging and claiming the pain of love as one's own, thus becoming whole.

Style and Technique

The unifying force of this story is the narrator's voice. Her personal voice, however, is not the language of the heart but of the head. Her style, sophisticated, coolly analytical, even cynical, is the manifestation of her conscious denial of the pain of disappointed love. Lessing uses the device of this voice as a controlling metaphor for her character's detachment from her own grief. The intensely preoccupied tone of the narrator's self-scrutiny reveals her lack of connection, the emptiness of a quest unfulfilled and unfulfillable, the pain of repeated loss and the undiminished hope that "He might turn out to be the one." She long has been victim of such women's magazine phrases, and, like Anna Wulf in *The Golden Notebook* (1962), the narrator has been a woman "who cannot feel deeply about anything." After encountering her two serious loves on the same day, her conventional behavior patterns, including her habitual return to the search for serious love represented by the date with C, crumble under a torrent of new self-awareness.

The appearance of her heart in her hand is a symbol with many valences. It is an ironic literalization of the cliché of losing one's heart or approaching another with one's heart in one's hand. The exteriorization of her heart is also a surreal representation of her moment of psychic upheaval, her revolution in attitude toward love, which leads to a new state of freedom. Her conscious self, embodied in her narrative voice, confronts her unconscious, suppressed pain in the depths of the London underground. Her live, clinging heart wrapped in silver becomes a stylized gift of love to herself. Offered and accepted, it represents an integration of her conscious and unconscious selves and her entry into a new personal realm of freedom.

Like so many of Lessing's characters, this narrator is absorbed in reflection on her aloneness in a journey where loves are not ends but rather way stations. She recounts an experience in which she makes herself, her actions, and her feelings visible to herself. In giving her heart away, she does not die but is reborn in acceptance of and freedom from her own disappointments in romantic love.

Virginia M. Crane

HOW I MET MY HUSBAND

Author: Alice Munro (1931-   )
Type of plot: Domestic realism
Time of plot: The early twentieth century
Locale: Ontario, Canada
First published: 1974

> *Principal characters:*
> EDIE, the narrator, a fifteen-year-old maid
> CHRIS WATTERS, a pilot with whom she falls in love
> ALICE KELLING, the pilot's fiancé
> LORETTA BIRD, the nosy neighbor and town gossip

The Story

A red-and-silver plane lands at the old fairgrounds across the road from the home of the Peebles, for whom Edie works. Edie's first close-up view of an airplane leads to her first encounter with romance.

Edie is both eager for and rather innocent about romance. She is quite proudly aware of her blossoming womanhood, and the day after the plane lands, Edie gets the impulse to dress herself up in Mrs. Peebles's finery, put on makeup, and play the part of a sophisticated beauty while Mrs. Peebles is out for the afternoon. This is how she is discovered by Chris Watters, who is looking for a drink of cool water from the pump. Edie is embarrassed but also irresistibly attracted to the pilot when he tells her she looks beautiful.

That attraction leads Edie to cross the road that same night. Chris Watters has finished giving airplane rides for the day and shares a smoke with his young visitor. Edie, concerned that Mrs. Peebles will discover her improprieties of the afternoon, convinces Watters to promise not to say anything about the dress-up episode. Her short visit reinforces her impression that she is somehow special to the friendly pilot.

Their casual relationship continues as the pilot regularly stops by for drinks of water. One day Alice Kelling shows up, guided to the Peebles's place by the ever-present Loretta Bird. Edie critically notes that Alice is neither young nor pretty, that her bust looks low and bumpy, that she has a worried face, and that her engagement ring features but a single, tiny stone. That night Alice and Chris go off somewhere in her car. Much later, through the slats of her blind, Edie watches them come home. She is not unhappy to observe them get out of opposite sides of the car and walk away from each other.

When Alice accompanies the Peebles on a picnic to the lake the next day, Edie bakes Chris a cake and learns that he has decided to pull up stakes and make his getaway. The visit turns into a rousing but tender farewell party. It becomes Edie's initiation in physical intimacy with a man. The pilot sensibly does not allow his urges full rein; when they say goodbye, he promises Edie that he will write to her.

Later that evening, Alice discovers that her fiancé has left. To her own surprise, Edie lies for him, but also for herself, saying that Chris has flown to another nearby field. Alice becomes suspicious of this sexy young girl; in response to Mrs. Peebles's questions, Edie readily admits to intimacy with Watters. Alice explodes in rage and sobs; Loretta, cliché-loaded and always functioning as a kind of parodic Greek chorus, comments that all men are the same; and Mrs. Peebles finally discovers that, to Edie, being intimate meant kissing.

Throughout the summer and well into the fall, six days a week, Edie waits at the mailbox for the promised letter, but the letter never comes. Finally, Edie's absolute faith in the promised letter crumbles and her heart turns to lead. She stops meeting the mail, for she refuses to become like so many other women who wait all their lives for something that never comes.

Then, however, the mailman calls and says he has missed her. They begin to go out, and after two years become engaged. They marry, have children, and find happiness.

Themes and Meanings

In this uncomplicated, traditionally plotted story, Alice Munro uses the same motif that informs most of her stories—the quest for fulfillment by girls and women. The focus is on the younger Edie, an untutored country girl who, in her first job away from home, discovers the human inclination to pursue wished-for truths that often turn out to be forms of self-deception.

Loretta Bird is one character who exhibits this proclivity. Loretta, who has trained her eyes and ears to miss nothing of inconsequence and whose tongue never utters anything of consequence, preens with a sense of self-inflated importance. To Loretta, life is drama, full of intrigue and corruption, and she is an essential player whose information and commentary are vital to the outcome. What Edie observes, but Loretta is ignorantly or willfully blind to, is that others regard her more as a pesky blackbird that screeches, squawks, and squats regardless of anyone's welcome—a general nuisance whom others tolerate out of a reluctant sense of propriety.

Alice Keller suffers from an even more serious case of self-deception. Alice is in pursuit of a life with Chris Watters, but Chris proves to be an elusive prey. Ever since Alice nursed him back to health in a military hospital, he has been on the move. After they became engaged, he left for overseas duty. Perhaps Chris did have noble intentions someday to honor his commitment, but when he returned, Alice observed that he had become terribly restless. Several years later now, Chris is still on the run, flitting from place to place offering airplane rides and trying to stay ahead of his pursuing fiancée. Alice ignores the clues of his rejection. Although he never leaves a forwarding address, she tracks him down relentlessly with the blind faith that she will yet prevail: Chris will park his plane permanently, marry her, and become her loving husband. All the characters in the story sense the futility of that dream, except Alice. Munro shows that people tend to believe what they wish to believe, regardless of the facts.

Observing such frailty in others, however, does not guarantee anyone's exemption from succumbing to the same weakness. That is Edie's most significant discovery in the story and occasions its title. From the moment Edie lays eyes on Alice, she feels the surge of her own superior physical charms, which certainly must be sufficient to attract Chris away from the well-worn Alice. When Chris, after their steamy tumble in the tent, promises that he will write, she knows she has won him. All of this leads her to an unshakable faith that his letter will come. It does not, of course. Like Alice, she, too, has fallen to self-deception. In the moment of that realization, she stops meeting the mail.

Although she does not realize it, Edie has already met her husband. Munro's surprise ending leaves the reader with a smile. The smile deepens when the husband, too, is exposed as one who lives by self-deception, although of an innocent kind. For Edie, the married woman who long ago realized what she had been saved from, has just confided something that she has never told her husband: the real reason for her daily appearance at the mailbox. Her husband believes it was for him, and because that makes him happy, she allows him to believe that vital falsehood.

Style and Technique

Like many of Munro's stories, this one has a tone of charming intimacy and confidentiality about it, mediated in this case through the double perspective of its first-person narrator. Edie tells her story as a memoir: She is no longer the fifteen-year-old romantic, but the middle-aged Mrs. Carmichael who understands what her younger self did not and could not.

Perhaps more than anything else, it is Munro's remarkable gift of rendering her central characters as persons one can know, understand, and feel close to that attracts one to her work. Even the less sophisticated characters such as young Edie often yield meanings that surprise by their depth and spirituality, meanings that flow from the author's deft touches of detail through her character's perception: Loretta hooking her legs around the chair rung; Alice's freckled and wrinkled fingers; and especially Edie remembering Chris after all these years, not bitterly for the unkept promise, but almost wistfully for the kisses, the kindness in his face, and the words, "I wouldn't do you any harm for the world." Such authentic detail animates both style and character and rewards the reader with moral significance and aesthetic delight.

Henry J. Baron

HOW IT WAS DONE IN ODESSA

Author: Isaac Babel (1894-1940)
Type of plot: Realism
Time of plot: The early twentieth century
Locale: Odessa
First published: "Kak eto delalos v Odesse," 1923 (English translation, 1955)

> *Principal characters:*
> THE NARRATOR, who listens to the story
> REB ARYE-LEIB, the storyteller
> BENYA KRIK, a Jewish gangster
> SAVKA BUTSIS, a member of the gang
> RUVIM TARTAKOVSKY, "Jew-and-a-Half," a wealthy Jewish
>   merchant
> JOSEPH MUGINSTEIN, a clerk
> AUNT PESYA, Joseph's mother

The Story

"How It Was Done in Odessa" belongs to a cycle of four stories known as the *Odessa Tales*, which were written by Isaac Babel between 1921 and 1923 and published as *Odesskie rasskazy* (1931; *Tales of Odessa*, 1955). All these tales concern the adventures of a Jewish gangster, Benya Krik. "How It Was Done in Odessa" is begun by a first-person narrator, who asks Reb Arye-Leib how Benya came to be known as "the King." The story that follows is told by Reb Arye-Leib in response to that question.

Reb Arye-Leib's story begins when Benya is twenty-five years old. Benya appeals to the then leading gangster for permission to join the gang, and the gangsters decide to test him by asking him to rob Ruvim Tartakovsky, one of the wealthiest and most influential Jews in Odessa, who has already been robbed nine times before.

Benya accepts the gangsters' challenge and sends an extremely polite letter to Tartakovsky requesting his cooperation. Tartakovsky actually replies to Benya's letter, but the reply is never received, and Benya and his companions proceed to Tartakovsky's office as threatened. When they arrive, the office is occupied only by the frightened clerk, Joseph Muginstein. The robbery proceeds without incident, but as they are emptying the safe, another member of the gang, Savka Butsis, arrives late and drunk. The drunken Savka accidentally shoots Muginstein in the stomach, and the gang runs away.

The shooting of Joseph Muginstein is an accident. It is the way in which Benya behaves after the shooting that earns for him the title "King." As the gang leaves, Benya threatens that if Muginstein dies, he will bury Savka alongside of him. Later, Benya visits the hospital and tells the doctors to spare no expense. If Joseph dies, Benya threatens, each doctor, "even if he's a doctor of philosophy," will receive six feet of earth for his pains. Joseph does die, however, and Benya next drives his red automobile, the horn of which plays the first march from the opera *Pagliacci*, to visit Aunt Pesya, Joseph's mother. There he meets Tartakovsky, who accuses him of "killing live people," but Benya in turn reproaches Tartakovsky for having sent Aunt Pesya a mere hundred rubles in compensation for her son's life. The two men argue and finally agree on five thousand rubles in cash and a pension of fifty rubles a month for the remainder of Aunt Pesya's life.

In the final scenes of the story, Reb Arye-Leib describes the magnificent funeral that Benya arranged for Joseph. Benya himself delivered a funeral oration, at the end of which he invited the crowd to pay their respects to the late Savka Butsis as well. It was at this funeral that the epithet "King" was first applied to Benya.

Themes and Meanings

All the Odessa tales have as their background the Jewish way of life in Odessa at the beginning of the twentieth century. Conventional images of the Jews do not generally include gangsters who tear around in opera-playing red automobiles, however, and "How It Was Done in Odessa" should not be read as a documentary account of the life of the Jews but rather as a burlesque of that life.

This burlesque, although comic, refers to a serious reality. In "How It Was Done in Odessa," casual references to a pogrom remind the reader of the precarious position of the Jews within Russian society. Benya himself addresses this theme when he asks Aunt Pesya, "But wasn't it a mistake on the part of God to settle Jews in Russia, for them to be tormented worse than in Hell?" It is significant, however, that the only violence that occurs within the story itself is perpetrated by the Jews, and great stress is placed on the fact that both Benya and Tartakovsky, who is generally referred to by his nickname "Jew-and-a-Half," belong to the same people.

The narrator, who plays no role in the action of the story, plays a crucial role in developing its theme of appropriate attitudes toward violence in modern society. He has obviously asked Reb Arye-Leib to tell the story because of his admiration for Benya, but Reb Arye-Leib compares the narrator unfavorably with Benya throughout the story and describes him both at the beginning and the end of the story as having "spectacles on [his] nose and autumn in [his] heart." In other words, Reb Arye-Leib represents him as a stereotypical ineffectual intellectual, who is incapable of action although he finds it attractive. The narrator's ambivalence, although not central to the action of the story, nevertheless occupies a central place in any understanding of it.

Style and Technique

Babel was a noted practitioner of what is known in Russian as *skaz*, a dramatic first-person narrative technique that duplicates as closely as possible the natural idiom of the speaker. In "How It Was Done in Odessa," the primary speaker is Reb Arye-Leib, and his language is rich in the rhythms and idioms of his milieu. However, "How It Was Done in Odessa" is not written in a single uniform style. At the beginning of the story the narrator's manner is reminiscent of medieval Russian epics. Later, Reb Arye-Leib embeds long speeches by the other characters (which he could not possibly have known from his own experience) into his narrative. Benya's excessively genteel letter to Tartakovsky and his address to the doctors fall into this category, and their humor derives from his misuse of the language and ignorance of the conventions generally associated with such occasions.

The effectiveness of "How It Was Done in Odessa" depends on a discrepancy between the manner of speaking and what is actually said. Despite the very funny way in which the story is told, it is actually concerned with robbery and murder, and it is the narrator's ambivalent attitude toward these acts of violence that creates much of the story's interest. The narrator's excessively literary style stands in sharp contrast to Benya's colorful abuse of the language and heightens the reader's awareness of the differences between the two men. Reb Arye-Leib's constant hectoring of the narrator and his frequent suggestions that the narrator emulate Benya and become a man of action himself keep this conflict present in the reader's mind, but such acts of violence are clearly alien to the intellectual narrator. The tension that exists between the light manner of narration and the brutal events depicted reinforces the atmosphere of ambivalence by producing a similar reaction in the reader, who finds the story appealing while at the same time being unable to accept the values of its attractive hero.

Sandra Rosengrant

HOW MUCH LAND DOES A MAN NEED?

Author: Leo Tolstoy (1828-1910)
Type of plot: Parable
Time of plot: The late 1800's
Locale: Russia
First published: "Mnogo li cheloveku zemli nuzhno?," 1886 (English translation, 1887)

> *Principal characters:*
> PAHOM, a landowner who strives for security in owning more and more land
> THE CHIEF OF THE BASHKIRS, who offers Pahom as much land as he can walk around in a day
> THE DEVIL, the tempter who arranges Pahom's land deals

The Story

An elder sister from the city visits her younger sister, the wife of a peasant farmer in the village. In the midst of their visit, the two of them get into an argument about whether the city or the peasant lifestyle is preferable. The elder sister suggests that city life boasts better clothes, good things to eat and drink, and various entertainments, such as the theater. The younger sister replies that though peasant life may be rough, she and her husband are free, will always have enough to eat, and are not tempted by the devil to indulge in such worldly pursuits.

Pahom, the husband of the younger sister, enters the debate and suggests that the charm of the peasant life is that the peasant has no time to let nonsense settle in his head. The one drawback of peasant life, he declares, is that the peasant does not have enough land: "If I had plenty of land, I shouldn't fear the Devil himself!" The devil, overhearing this boast, decides to give Pahom his wish, seducing him with the extra land that Pahom thinks will give him security.

Pahom's first opportunity to gain extra land comes when a lady in the village decides to sell her three hundred acres. His fellow peasants try to arrange the purchase for themselves as part of a commune, but the devil sows discord among them and individual peasants begin to buy land. Pahom obtains forty acres of his own. This pleases him initially, but soon neighboring peasants allow their cows to stray into his meadows and their horses among his corn, and he must seek justice from the district court. Not only does he fail to receive recompense for the damages but also he ruins his reputation among his former friends and neighbors; his extra land does not bring him security.

Hearing a rumor about more and better farmland elsewhere, he decides to sell his land and move his family to a new location. There he obtains 125 acres and is ten times better off than he was before, and he is very pleased. However, he soon realizes that he could make a better profit with more land on which to sow wheat. He makes a deal to obtain thirteen hundred acres from a peasant in financial difficulty for one thousand rubles and has all but clinched it when he hears a rumor about the land of the Bashkirs. There, a tradesman tells him, a man can obtain land for less than a penny an acre, simply by making friends with the chiefs.

Fueled by the desire for more, cheaper, and better land, Pahom seeks directions for the land of the Bashkirs and leaves on a journey to obtain the land that he thinks he needs. On arrival, he distributes gifts to the Bashkir leaders and finds them courteous and friendly. He explains his reasons for being there and, after some deliberation, they offer him whatever land he wants for one thousand rubles. Pahom is pleased but concerned; he wants boundaries, deeds, and "official sanction" to give him the assurance he needs that they or their children will never reverse their decision.

The Bashkirs agree to this arrangement, and a deal is struck. Pahom can have all the land that he can walk around in a day for one thousand rubles. The one condition is that if he does not return on the same day to the spot at which he began, the money will be lost. The night before his fateful walk, Pahom plans his strategy; he will try to encircle thirty-five miles of land and then sell the poorer land to peasants at a profit. When he awakes the next day, he is met by the man whom he thought was the chief of the Bashkirs, but whom he recognizes as the peasant who had come to his old home to tell him of lucrative land deals available elsewhere. He looks again, and realizes that he is speaking with the devil himself. He dismisses this meeting as merely a dream and goes about his walk.

Pahom starts well, but he tries to encircle too much land, and by midday he realizes that he has tried to create too big a circuit. Though afraid of death, he knows that his only chance is to complete the circuit. "There is plenty of land," he says to himself, "but will God let me live on it?" As the sun comes down, Pahom runs with all his remaining strength to the spot where he began. Reaching it, he sees the chief laughing and holding his sides; he remembers his dream and breathes his last breath. Pahom's servant picks up the spade with which Pahom had been marking his land and digs a grave in which to bury him: "Six feet from his head to his heels was all he needed."

Themes and Meanings

"How Much Land Does a Man Need?" is a classic Leo Tolstoy tale of a man's grasp exceeding his reach. Seeking security in the acquisition of wealth or land instead of seeking it in the humble family life of the peasant, Pahom mocks God and falls into the clutches of the devil. Tolstoy's story greatly resembles the parable of the rich fool told by Jesus in Luke 12:16-20, in which a wealthy farmer tears down his barns and builds bigger ones to store his wheat, thinking to himself that he has achieved security for the rest of his life. Instead, at the very moment when he surveys his domain with complacent satisfaction, God rebukes him: "Thou fool, this night thy soul shall be required of thee."

Tolstoy's Pahom is thus a man discontented with his lot in life who fails to seek his contentment from the proper source. His boast that with enough land he would not fear the devil himself is actually a rejection of God as his protector and benefactor. However, unlike Faust, who openly bargains with an agent of the devil, Pahom is a victim of his own greed, which obscures his judgment; so obsessed is he with more land, he is unable to recognize the hand of the devil behind his opportunities. This, clearly, is the moral fault that Tolstoy seeks to underscore in the tale: The sacrificing of a basic trust in God and the surrender of basic human kindness and responsibility for the acquisition of possessions brings a man earthly ruin and eternal damnation.

Style and Technique

Tolstoy regarded the telling force of a moral and the power to reach a wide audience as the key elements in a story. These two elements are bountifully present in "How Much Land Does a Man Need?" In referring to the tale as a parable, critics draw attention to its didactic function. In a parable, the focus is entirely on one or, at most, two characters and a specific circumstance that provides the conflict or challenge that the protagonists must face.

The only fully developed character in Tolstoy's tale is Pahom; neither his wife nor her elder sister nor any of his fellow peasants is given a distinct identity. Tolstoy intends his readers to focus entirely on the plight of Pahom as he seeks his fortune. This, like his other parables, is meant to transmit feelings of God's love and the importance of love of one's neighbor.

The parable form is meant to convey a deliberate sense of "artlessness"—that is, a simplicity of narrative style and content in which a story seems inevitable, or self-telling. In fact, the parable form requires careful attention to achieve this "artless" effect, and Tolstoy has no equal among such storytellers.

Bruce L. Edwards, Jr.

HOW THE DEVIL CAME DOWN DIVISION STREET

Author: Nelson Algren (Nelson Ahlgren Abraham, 1909-1981)
Type of plot: Ghost story
Time of plot: The 1930's
Locale: Chicago
First published: 1945

> *Principal characters:*
> ROMAN ORLOV, the protagonist, who recounts how he became the
> "biggest drunk on Division Street"
> PAPA ORLOV, an accordionist and janitor
> MAMA ORLOV, who has second thoughts about the "miracle"
> TERESA, Roman's sister

The Story

The "story" in "How the Devil Came Down Division Street" is narrated by a person who heard the tale from Roman Orlov, the "biggest drunk on Division Street." As the story begins, several drunks in the Polonia Bar argue about who the biggest drunk is, but the discussion is decided by the appearance of Roman, who is unanimously accorded that title. Pressed for an explanation about his life and the reason for his drinking, Roman tells the narrator his story in exchange for a series of double shots of whiskey. Roman claims that he has a "great worm inside" that "gnaws and gnaws"; the whiskey helps him "drown the worm." Roman also "obscurely" (as the narrator puts it) states that "the devil lives in a double-shot," but not until the end of the story does the reader learn what Roman may mean. In effect, then, the story is filtered through the personality of the narrator, who treats his subject and subjects with light irony.

Roman's story, as told to the narrator, takes him years back to his early adolescence. It seems that the Orlov family lives in a small tenement apartment that is too small for the six Orlovs and their dog. There are only two beds: Mama and eleven-year-old Teresa sleep in one of them; thirteen-year-old Roman sleeps between the squabbling younger twins to prevent them from fighting. As a result, there is no bed for Papa, who spends his nights playing his accordion for pennies and drinks in bars. When he comes in late, he sleeps under Roman's bed, unless the dog is already sleeping there, in which case Papa sleeps under Mama's bed. Papa never crawls, "even with daylight, to Mama O.'s bed," because he does not feel "worthy" to sleep there. The narrator adds that Papa apparently wants to remain "true" to his accordion, which replaces Mama. At this point in the story "strange things go on in Papa O.'s head," and Teresa is a slow learner at school, but Roman is fine.

Things change with a mysterious knocking at the Orlov apartment. Soon afterward, Mama dreams of "a young man, drunken . . . with blood down the front of his shirt and drying on his hands." Knowing this for a sign that the "unhappy dead return to warn or comfort . . . to gain peace or to avenge," she consults Mrs. Zolewitz, who confirms her fears by telling her about the previous tenants of the Orlov apartment. It seems that the young man who lived there was "sick in the head from drink"; more important to the conservative Mrs. Zolewitz, he lived there "with his lady without being wed." On New Year's Eve, he came home drunk and beat his woman until her whimperings stopped completely, and there was no sound at all until noon the next day, when the police arrived: The woman was dead and the man had hanged himself in the closet. According to Mrs. Zolewitz, the couple was buried together in "unsanctified ground." Mrs. Zolewitz reassures the frightened Mama by telling her that the young man does not intend them any harm but searches, instead, for peace. The Orlovs' prayers, she suggests, will bring that peace.

Meanwhile, Papa has lost, sold, or loaned his accordion, and the lost accordion and Mama's dream coincide, leading her to believe that a change is coming. The change occurs when the prayers begin and when Papa stays home because he lacks the accordion. After Papa prays, he goes to bed with Mama "like a good husband," and she informs the priest that she knows now the knocking was a good omen. He declares that it is the will of God that "the Orlovs should redeem the young man by prayer and that Papa O. should have a wife instead of an accordion."

The results of the changes are immediate and salutary: "For lack of music," Papa becomes the best janitor on Noble Street; the priest blesses Mrs. Zolewitz for her part in the miracle; the landlord, who now has an unhaunted house, frees the Orlovs from their rental payments; the "slow" Teresa "goes to the head of the class"; even the squabbling twins make their peace. In effect, the entire Orlov family, with the notable exception of Roman, benefits from the knocking, the prayers, and the new sleeping arrangements. Because Papa is sleeping with Mama, Teresa replaces Roman between the twins. For four years Roman replaces his father under one of the two beds, and his parents' bed has springs that squeak "half the night as likely as not." Finally, Roman begins sleeping during the day so that he will not have to sleep at night, "and at night, as everyone knows, there is no place to go but the taverns." The narrator notes that Roman consequently took his father's place not only as a person without a bed but as a drinker.

At the conclusion of his tale, the narrator pauses to reflect about Roman's story. Is it, he asks, "a drunkard's tale or sober truth?" Complicating that answer is the passage of years since the changes: Mama now believes that the knocking young man was the devil because she believes she gave the devil a good son, Roman, "in return for a worthless husband." This development causes the narrator to ask if the devil lives in a double shot, if he gnaws "like the worm," or if he knocks, "with blood drying on his knuckles, in the gaslight passages of our dreams?"

Themes and Meanings

Although the story begins in a bar and contains a humorous turn of events, it explores the nature of guilt, the need to justify one's behavior and one's weaknesses, and the nature of evil. On the superficial and superstitious level, the bloody young man seeks atonement and peace, both of which he apparently receives through the Orlovs' prayers, but the narrator mocks the "miracle" through Mrs. Zolewitz's morality (un-wed sex leads to death) and the priest's liberally bestowed "blessings." Mama also suffers guilt for her neglect of Roman, but her guilt is "after the fact" of her renewed sex life with her husband and his eventual death. Hers is the comic guilt of one who repents only after the opportunity for sin no longer exists. Roman's guilt, however, is real, for that "worm" that "gnaws" within him is his own awareness of his wasted life. It is that awareness that prompts his explanation and justification of becoming the "biggest drunk on Division Street." His "lack of a bed" is his "excuse" for his behavior, but the narrator notes that his father's "excuse" at least involved an accordion. Because he still does not have a "home," Roman expects sympathy and understanding, but clearly his psychological wounds have been self-inflicted. Although it may help Roman to believe in the devil as an active presence in the world, the devil is "within." On the other hand, Nelson Algren also suggests that Roman's environment contributes to his fate. Brought up in a community that confuses superstition with religion, that restricts morality to sexual matters, and that regards drinking as a means of achieving status, Roman does not have much chance to escape the confines of the Polish ghetto in Chicago. Like other Algren characters, Roman is trapped, paralyzed, and incapable of action.

Style and Technique

The narration in "How the Devil Came Down Division Street" is atypical of Algren, whose style tends to be figurative and naturalistic in its use of animal imagery, rather than literal and matter-of-fact. In addition, Algren generally relies on omniscient, third-person, rather than first-person, narration. The narrator in this story recounts Roman's story, but he embellishes it, filters it through his own values and attitudes, and then poses questions about the story itself. There are two narrative "voices" or styles in the story. The first is the narrator's retelling of Roman's story "as closely to what he told as I can," without the "sobs" and the "cursing," but with a touch of mocking irony. For the most part, the narrator offers a straightforward account with almost mathematical exactitude. Given the number of people and the number of sleepers, there is domestic trouble; when Papa is added to the equation, someone else will be in trouble. In fact, the narrator begins the paragraphs at the end of Roman's story with the phrases "Thus it came about," "So it was," and "This is why," thereby lending the story an air of logical precision. The other narrative voice occurs at the end of Roman's story, from which it is separated by a break in the text. The second voice is more abstract, philosophical, and questioning, and the language is much more figurative: The narrator asks if the devil is "the one who knocks, on winter nights, with blood drying on his knuckles, in the gaslit passages of our dreams?" Because the short story concludes with this pessimistic speculation about evil, despair, and the unconscious, Algren apparently intends Roman's story, amusing and touching as it is, as the springboard for some searching questions about the nature of evil.

Thomas L. Erskine

HOW TO TALK TO A HUNTER

Author: Pam Houston (1962-   )
Type of plot: Psychological
Time of plot: The 1980's
Locale: Alaska
First published: 1990

> *Principal characters:*
> THE NARRATOR, a single woman
> A HUNTER, her lover
> HER BEST MALE FRIEND
> HER BEST FEMALE FRIEND
> PATTY COYOTE, another of the hunter's lovers

The Story

"How to Talk to a Hunter" is told in the second person through what appear to be notes or journal entries. In Alaska's bleak midwinter, as Christmas approaches and the days grow colder and shorter, an independent young woman has a relationship with a hunter. When the story begins, the hunter has given the narrator a key to his cabin. The two are not so close, though, that she has given up her own cabin—nor has the hunter given up his other girlfriends.

The narrator spends so much time at the hunter's house that he cannot play back the messages piling up on his answering machine. Clearly, though, a woman has been calling, perhaps more than one woman. While making love to the hunter, the narrator hears a female voice leaving yet another message.

Perhaps this voice belongs to Patty Coyote, who calls one day while the hunter is out. A few days before Christmas, the hunter tells the narrator that he has a friend in town and so cannot see her. Though the hunter does not mention the friend's gender, the narrator knows that Patty has come from Montana to be with him. The narrator spends the night with an understanding male friend. When she returns home the next morning, she finds a tin of chocolates and a loving note on her pillow.

The hunter finds the narrator sufficiently attractive to visit her under the pretext of going to work, even though Patty is still in town. The narrator makes clear that she knows that the hunter is cheating on her. He replies with excuses: The visit was all the friend's idea (still no mention of the friend's gender), some good will come from this experience, and after holding the narrator, he cannot be comfortable holding anyone else. At night, though, he goes back to his cabin and to Patty. Once Patty leaves, the hunter returns to the narrator. Together they will finish decorating the Christmas tree and then make love beneath it as the stereo plays Willie Nelson's "Pretty Paper."

Themes and Meanings

Pam Houston here demonstrates how different men and women are. Some of these differences are peculiar to the couple in the story. He likes top-forty country music; she does not. He is a Republican; she is not. Other differences are stereotypical. Thus, the (male) hunter fills the (female) narrator's freezer. He kills animals, whereas she could never shoot anything. His cabin is warmer than hers, presumably because he is better at chopping wood. He can find the faulty bulb that eludes her on the string of Christmas lights.

As a male, the hunter also avoids commitment and fidelity. When the narrator speaks about monogamy, the hunter launches into a long speech about being hurt by his previous lover. He says he wants to spend every night with the narrator, but he still has some unanswered questions. He is still afraid of getting hurt again and still confused. He sleeps around because he seeks to satisfy his desires. When Patty Coyote visits the hunter, the narrator spends a night with an understanding male friend because she seeks reassurance that she is still desirable.

As the title suggests, the biggest difference between the genders lies in language, whether verbal or nonverbal. When the hunter gives the narrator a key to his cabin, she thinks that he is making a commitment to her. She similarly misinterprets making love. When he talks about opening a guest ranch or spending summer in Alaska and spring in Hawaii, he is making chin-music; these are not serious plans for the future. When she tells the hunter she loves him, he replies, "I feel exactly the same way." The word "love" does not cross his lips. Leaving a tin of chocolates on the narrator's pillow is as close as he will come to saying the "L" word, and the narrator informs him that she does not speak chocolate.

Houston shows that this failure to communicate does not result from a male's inability to express his thoughts. The hunter seeks refuge in that stereotype, claiming that he is not good with words. However, he shows remarkable skill at talking about his visiting friend without revealing her gender. When he talks about his future, he conceals whether the narrator is included in those plans. Leaving the narrator so that he can have sex with Patty Coyote, he says that he has to go home to sleep, emphasizing that last word to mask his cheating.

Writing from a feminist perspective, Houston highlights male perfidy. At the same time, she recognizes that women need men. The last sound in the story is that of the narrator's dog howling, lonely and cold in the quiet, frozen night. The narrator has accepted the hunter as the only alternative to the dog's fate. When spring comes, the narrator will reclaim her independence. However, in the physical or metaphysical cold and darkness, she cannot live alone.

Style and Technique

To highlight differences between men and women, Houston introduces the narrator's best female and best male friend. In the course of the story, the narrator discusses her affair with each of them, and their differing reactions reflect the way that men and women understand themselves and each other. The best female friend distrusts men.

When the narrator talks about hearing a woman leave a message on the hunter's answering machine, the female friend says that anyone who sleeps under a dead moose skin (as the hunter does) is incapable of commitment. This friend is not surprised when the hunter cheats on the narrator. "So what did you think?" she asks. "That he was capable of living outside his gender?" The best female friend warns the narrator not to say "I love you" to the hunter. This friend is also critical of the narrator for her choice of lovers and of women in general for raising men to behave as they do. Houston seems to imply that in matters of love a woman is not likely to get sympathy from another woman.

The male friend reacts differently. Whereas the female friend is appalled by the tin of chocolates, the male friend says that the gift shows how much the hunter cares for her. This friend tells her that she has nothing to fear from a rival named Patty Coyote and that the hunter's sleeping with Patty means nothing. Perhaps the male friend is merely being supportive. More likely, he thinks and behaves like the hunter. He speaks the language of chocolate rather than the language of love. He, too, would cheat on his lover and then think that a box of candy is adequate apology. For him, as for the hunter, sex does not imply a world-without-end bargain. Indeed, he warns the narrator not to talk about commitment. When she says she used the word "monogamy," not commitment, he replies that it means the same thing—an attempt to deprive a man of his freedom.

Houston uses the unusual second-person point of view, with the narrator referring to herself as "you." This device highlights the distance between the female "you" and the male "he" and invites the reader to identify with the former. Houston's point of view also emphasizes the universality of her tale, a point she makes again by refusing to name any of her characters except Patty Coyote, whom the narrator never sees, or to specify a time other than the eternal present. Like the cycle of the seasons, Houston indicates, the relationship between the sexes will continue its never-ending ebb and flow. She also indicates that men and women, however close they may get physically, will always live in different emotional and linguistic worlds.

Joseph Rosenblum

A HUNGER ARTIST

Author: Franz Kafka (1883-1924)
Type of plot: Parable
Time of plot: Unspecified
Locale: Unspecified
First published: "Ein Hungerkünstler," 1922 (English translation, 1938)

> *Principal characters:*
> THE HUNGER ARTIST, the protagonist, a tormented performer of
>   the macabre art of fasting
> THE IMPRESARIO, the hunger artist's manager during the years
>   when spectacles of fasting are popular
> THE SPECTATORS, insensitive, skeptical amusement seekers
> THE OVERSEER, the circus attendant who hears without
>   understanding the artist's dying confession

The Story

Franz Kafka's dark parable describes the hunger artist's ritual of self-annihilation and shows the ironic use of dissatisfaction as a stimulus for art. The narrator describes two periods of the artist's life—that of the past, when people took a "lively interest" in spectacles of fasting, and that of recent times, when fasting has lost its popularity. Even in the early days of his career, the hunger artist feels the ingratitude of his audience, which continually questions his honesty. To demonstrate that no trickery is used, the artist sings during his fast. The watchers only consider him more clever for being able to sing while eating. No matter how much he craves respect for his achievement, the artist cannot gain his audience's trust. More important, the hunger artist cannot even please himself, for he knows that he is indeed dishonest, not because he breaks the fast—he never does this—but because he alone knows how easy it is to fast. The fast, then, is not an act of self-fortitude and spiritual purification but rather an expression of the artist's disdain for life.

The impresario reveals himself to be as uncaring as the public toward the hunger artist. The impresario sets a forty-day limit to the fast, not out of concern for the weakened artist but because public interest cannot be sustained beyond forty days. The impresario is concerned only with promoting the performance just as the watchers are interested only in their own amusement.

Epitomizing the isolation of the hunger artist is the description of the artist's defeated reaction to the impresario's display of photographs. When the hunger artist reacts violently to a comforter's advice that the artist's melancholy springs from fasting, the impresario apologizes for the hunger artist, explaining that his moodiness and irritability indeed result from fasting. Photographs are then shown of the artist, who on the fortieth day appears almost dead from malnutrition. The hunger artist watches the audience accept the lie that his depression is caused by fasting. He alone knows that the opposite is true, that his depression comes from knowing that he will soon be forced to eat. As the photographs support the impresario's lie and reinforce the public's misconceptions, the hunger artist feels more frustrated in his desire for understanding: "as soon as the photographs appeared he always let go and sank with a groan back on to his straw, and the reassured public could once more come close and gaze at him." The words "come close" point to the physical nearness and the psychological distance of the audience, while the word "gaze" emphasizes the superficiality of the public's way of seeing.

The second part of the story describes the hunger artist's life after the spectacle of fasting has lost its appeal. The hunger artist is now forced to dismiss the impresario and join a circus. Because he has no manager now to limit his fast, the artist hopes to achieve a record that will astonish the world. The other professionals smile at this boast, for they know that no one really cares about fasting anymore. The emaciated artist's cage is ironically placed near the menagerie, where the artist must suffer the odors of the animals and of the raw meat that is served them. Although, in former days, the skeptical public at least displayed curiosity, the public now pays little attention to the hunger artist. The occasional visitors who wish to stand and watch him are jeered by those who believe that their journey to the animal exhibit is being impeded. The circus attendants also neglect the hunger artist. They forget to replace his straw and to change the placard indicating the length of his fast. Finally the hunger artist is forgotten altogether.

The discovery, the confession, and the death of the hunger artist provide the climax of the story. Curious about the seemingly empty cage, an overseer pokes the straw with a stick and finds the hunger artist. When asked if he is still fasting, the hunger artist whispers, "Forgive me, everybody" and explains that no one should admire his fasting because he could not help but fast. When asked why he cannot help it, the artist says, "because I couldn't find the food I liked. If I had found it, believe me, I should have made no fuss and stuffed myself like you or anyone else." With this confession that there is nothing nourishing in life, the hunger artist dies. The nourishment that the hunger artist has craved has been the food of human compassion.

The story ends with the image of the wild panther that now occupies the hunger artist's cage. The contrast between the defeated, malnourished, and spiritually imprisoned artist and the young, vital animal that seems "to carry freedom around with it" is striking. The animal that cares nothing for audience support ironically achieves the understanding and admiration never attained by the starving artist.

Themes and Meanings

The lack of specific names for the hunger artist, the impresario, and the members of the audience suggests the symbolic nature of the story. The hunger artist may represent any artist or any person whose art or existence is grounded on a conviction of life's meaninglessness. The hunger artist, as his name implies, craves nourishment.

As the story progresses, it becomes clear that the food desired is spiritual and that physical starvation is merely a metaphor for the soul's malnourishment. The artist's devotion to the art of starvation ironically demands that while consciously attempting to win understanding, he unconsciously must discourage human sympathy. He thus encages himself, turns himself into a grotesque, appeals to the sympathy of people who relish freak shows, refuses to verbalize his feelings, and in the end buries himself under straw.

Reflecting a tasteless, monotonous world, the performance proceeds by an absence of action. This passive art ensures the slow deterioration of an already fragile bond between the performer and his viewers. The many allusions to Christ emphasize the parodic nature of the hunger artist's martyrdom. When the hunger artist at the end of a forty-day fast is helped from his cage by two frightened women, his outstretched arms form a cross. The hunger artist, however, unlike Christ, suffers not to affirm spiritual life but to reveal the absence of hope. The hunger artist's consummate performance, the perfection of the art of negation, is death.

The alternatives offered by the story are bleak. The hunger artist with his heightened sensitivity and unhealthy narcissism stands for one way of experiencing life, and the impresario, the public, and the overseer, complacent and uncaring, reveal an alternative way of seeing and feeling. The panther that captivates the interest of the public is placed against these human extremes. Unlike the hunger artist, the panther will devour anything. The animal possesses the joy of life and the sense of freedom that is beyond human reach: "Somewhere freedom seemed to lurk; and the joy of life streamed with such ardent passion from his throat that for the onlookers it was not easy to stand the shock of it." The cat displays a vibrant, wild beauty, for its predatory nature is fitting to its species. However, although the crowd and the impresario possess a similar voracious appetite and hardness, they are despicable caricatures of human beings. However, their lack of insight makes them, like the panther, survivors.

Style and Technique

The narrator poses as an objective, unemotional chronicler of a dying social phenomenon. He records the early years of the profession of fasting with cold detachment and with more than a modicum of irony. For example, he exaggerates and then undercuts the moral claim of the hunger artist, describing him as "this suffering martyr, which indeed he was, although in quite another sense." When the public loses interest in fasting, the narrator seems to smile, "at any rate the pampered hunger artist suddenly found himself deserted one fine day by the amusement seekers." The amused tone of this cosmic chronicler adds to the reader's sense of the artist's growing isolation. As the historian describes the hunger artist's experience in the circus, the tension of the narrative increases.

In this section, the narrator often expresses the yearnings and frustrations of the hunger artist: "Just try to explain to anyone the art of fasting! Anyone who has no feeling for it cannot be made to understand it." The narrator's voice again merges with the feelings of the artist when the viewers question the accuracy of the numbers posted on the placard: "that was in its way the stupidest lie ever invented, by indifference and inborn malice." By shifting from an objective to a subjective perspective, the narrator emphasizes the unbridgeable gulf between the longing artist and the world. The final shift in perspective and tone comes in the description of the hunger artist's death. The narrator now returns to the earlier, uninflected style. The rapid pace of the prose and the cold, impersonal tone emphasize the total insignificance of the artist: "'Well, clear this out now!' said the overseer, and they buried the hunger artist, straw and all. Into the cage they put a young panther." The closing image of the public's admiration of the panther is a disturbing reminder that even a person's death by slow starvation is not sufficient to disturb the placidity of the self-indulgent world.

Catherine Cox

THE HUNGRY STONES

Author: Rabindranath Tagore (1861-1941)
Type of plot: Ghost story, frame story
Time of plot: The late nineteenth or early twentieth century
Locale: India
First published: "Kshudita Pashan," 1895 (English translation, 1916)

> *Principal characters:*
> THE NARRATOR, who is returning to Calcutta with his kinsman
> SRIJUT, a man whom the narrator meets while waiting for a train
> MEHER ALI, a madman whose shouting wakens Srijut
> KARIM KHAN, an old man who works in Srijut's office

The Story

"The Hungry Stones" uses two first-person narratives. It begins and ends with the voice of an unnamed narrator, who describes himself as a traveler returning to Calcutta on a train with his kinsman from a *puja*, or Hindu religious pilgrimage. While waiting at a junction for the train, the narrator and his kinsman meet a man who impresses them with his learning and knowledge of current events. The man, Srijut, launches into his own story, which becomes the main part of the tale.

When he was young, Srijut recalls, he was appointed collector of cotton duties at Barich. Nearby stood a marble palace that had been built 250 years earlier by the emperor Mahmud Shah II. Karim Khan, an old clerk in Srijut's office, warned the young man not to stay in the palace. Srijut ignored him. After staying in the palace for less than a week, the young man began to hear footsteps and the sounds of maidens running to bathe in the nearby river.

Although during the day, Srijut's nighttime experience seemed like a fantasy, before dark he was drawn back to the palace, leaving his work unfinished. Entering a spacious hall at the top of a staircase, he heard the sounds of fountains, strange music, and tinkling anklets. His normal identity began to seem an illusion until his servant entered and left a lamp. After going to sleep, however, he was awakened and led through the palace by an Arabian or Persian girl, who seemed to him like someone out of a tale from *Alf layla wa-layla* (fifteenth century; *The Arabian Nights' Entertainments*, 1706-1708). She took him past a black eunuch. As Srijut attempted to step over the eunuch's legs, the guard woke up and dropped his sword. Suddenly, Srijut was back on his camp bed and could hear the shouting of Meher Ali, a local madman.

Srijut says that he began to feel a separation between his nights and his days. During the day, he was tired and his nightly fantasies seemed empty. During the night, however, his English-style clothes and his job seemed petty and unimportant. He would wander through the palace, hearing the music and other sounds and sometimes seeing a reflection of the Persian girl in a mirror. One night, he heard a voice crying out from the foundation of the palace, begging him to rescue her. As he was wondering about the voice of the young woman and asking how he could rescue her, the scream of the madman Meher Ali, shouting "Stand back" and "All is false," broke his fantasy again. Srijut decided he could no longer stay in the palace and moved back to his office.

By evening, Srijut began to long to go back to the palace. When he returned to it, though, it seemed dark and desolate, as if he had deserted it. He had the impression of a woman with blood on her face lying under a bed. He wandered through the dark palace, hearing Meher Ali's shouts from outside. In the morning, he ran back to Karim Khan at the office. The old man explained to him that unsatisfied desires and passions in the old times had made the stones of the palace thirsty. They swallowed anyone who stayed more than three nights. The only exception was Meher Ali, who had been driven mad. Karim Khan began to explain that there was only one way to escape the curse and began to tell the tragic story of a Persian girl who had lived in the palace.

At this point in the story, the voice of the original narrator returns. The train arrives and an Englishman in a first-class compartment sees Srijut, recognizes him, and invites him into his compartment. Because the narrator and his kinsman are traveling second class, they cannot hear the end of the story, and the narrator complains that the stranger was making fools of them with his story. Mysteriously, the narrator remarks that the conversation that followed began a lifelong break between himself and his kinsman, a theosophist.

Themes and Meanings

"The Hungry Stones" has the form of a simple ghost story, but its main underlying themes are the contrasts between imagination and skepticism and between reality and fantasy and the difficulty of clearly distinguishing which is which. During Srijut's days, the impressions he had in the palace seem like pointless flights of imagination. During his nights, however, his English clothes and his undramatic job make up a life that seems pointless and illusory. Srijut responds to the shouts of the madman Meher Ali by asking, "What is false?" He never receives an answer.

The historical fantasy of the night and the routine of the day call each other into question and draw attention to the shortcomings of each. The night world, seen from the perspective of the day, is a dangerous dream that threatens to destroy the dreamer. The day world, considered from the night, is tedious and colorless.

Both Srijut's narration and that of the unnamed narrator end without satisfactory conclusions. This may be disturbing to many readers, but Rabindranath Tagore undoubtedly intended it to have that effect. Just as Srijut never learns what is false, neither the reader of the story nor the narrator ever learns how Srijut escaped the fate of those destroyed by the palace and the fate of Meher Ali. In addition, the author leaves it to the reader to decide whether Srijut's story was a true account of his own experiences or a fanciful lie told to two strangers to pass the time while waiting for a train.

The story ends with a reference to a disagreement between the narrator and his kinsman that causes a lifelong break between them. The key to the cause of this break is the identification of the kinsman as a theosophist. Theosophy was a religious and philosophical movement of the late nineteenth and early twentieth century that blended elements of Western mysticism with esoteric Hindu and Buddhist traditions. The narrator's rejection of the story as a lie marks him as a skeptic and a believer in day-to-day reality, and his disagreement with his kinsman represents a clash between the doubting materialist and the believer in otherworldly things, a clash that mirrors the conflict between Srijut's days and nights.

Style and Technique

Tagore said that he developed the idea for "The Hungry Stones" when he was seventeen years old and stayed in an old Muslim palace. The time of the Mughal emperors, the Muslim rulers of India, seemed to him to be a mysterious and romantic period. The story, therefore, employs the style of a romance from *The Arabian Nights' Entertainments*, and Srijut refers repeatedly to these classic stories. Lush descriptions and exotic details contribute to the sense of wonder and fantasy that characterizes Srijut's account of his nights.

Having a character meet a stranger who tells a tale is a fairly old device in storytelling, but Tagore uses this device effectively, and the technique fits the story's theme of the difficulty of distinguishing between reality and fantasy. The setting at the opening is important. The narrator and his kinsman are at a junction on a return journey from their pilgrimage. They have temporarily stepped outside their ordinary lives and are on their way back when they meet this unknown and impressive man. Although the bulk of the story concerns events in Srijut's life, even his name is mentioned only in passing and his listeners never know anything about him aside from the weird events that he claims happened to him during a short time in his youth. He disappears as suddenly as he appeared, without having explained what the unsatisfied passions that cursed the palace were or how he escaped being destroyed by them.

Carl L. Bankston III

THE HUNTER GRACCHUS

Author: Franz Kafka (1883-1924)
Type of plot: Parable
Time of plot: Unspecified
Locale: Riva, Austria
First published: "Der Jäger Gracchus," 1931 (English translation, 1946)

Principal characters:
SALVATORE, the burgomaster of Riva
GRACCHUS, a hunter from the Black Forest who has long been
dead

The Story

As various inhabitants of the town of Riva, situated on Lake Garda, go about their apparently customary activities—shopkeeping, reading the paper, drawing water at the well, or simply idling away the time—a boat enters the harbor and ties up at the quay. Two men in dark coats with silver buttons debark, carrying what seems to be a person's body on a cloth-draped bier. The townspeople pay them no particular attention. The boatman, who seems to be their guide, directs the two men to a nearby house. All three enter it with the bier, noticed as they go in by a boy at an upstairs window. A flock of doves arrives and alights in front of the house.

A man in mourning dress, looking somewhat troubled by the appearance of the neighborhood, approaches the house from one of the streets, knocks at the door, and is admitted at once. Some fifty little boys standing in two rows the length of the entry hall bow to him, and the boatman descends the stair and leads the visitor upstairs to a large room at the back of the house, in which the two bearers are busy placing and lighting candles at the head of the bier. The cloth has been drawn back, and on the bier lies a man with tangled hair and beard and tanned skin, looking rather like a hunter. Although his eyes are closed, and he is motionless and seems not to breathe, it is really only his surroundings that suggest that he may be dead.

The man in mourning approaches, touches the forehead of the one lying there, and kneels to pray beside him. The two bearers withdraw, and at a sign from the visitor so does the boatman. At once the man on the bier opens his eyes, turns his face to the mourner, and asks: "Who are you?" "The Burgomaster of Riva," the other replies, getting to his feet. In fact, both know already who the other is, since a dove came to the burgomaster's window during the night and announced to him, "Tomorrow the dead Hunter Gracchus is coming; receive him in the name of the city." Gracchus explains that the doves precede him wherever he goes. He asks the burgomaster if he believes that Gracchus is to remain in Riva. The answer seems to depend on whether Gracchus is truly dead.

He tells the burgomaster that a great many years ago, while hunting a chamois in the Black Forest in Germany, he fell from a precipice and died. The burgomaster observes that he is nevertheless still alive. "In a certain sense," Gracchus answers. His death ship lost its way, he explains, so that ever since that time he who yearns only for the mountains of his homeland has been ceaselessly traveling the waters of the earth, a hunter transformed into a butterfly, as he says. He spends his days on a wooden pallet in the boat's cabin, dirty and unkempt, with a candle at his head, and on the wall of the cabin a small picture, evidently of a bushman, who is aiming his spear at Gracchus and taking cover behind a lavishly painted shield.

Gracchus's great misfortune, as he tells it, was not his death, but the wrong turn, the brief inattention of the pilot, the distraction of his native land—whatever it was that caused the ship to stray from its course. Gracchus had lived and hunted happily, and he welcomed his death as the most natural thing in the world. He believes that he was faithful to his calling and to his fate; the mishap was the boatman's fault, not his. Gracchus says that there is no help for him. None will come to his aid; even if they were asked, people would hide in their houses, under their bedcovers. No one knows of him, and if someone did, that person would not know his whereabouts; even if someone did know it, that person could not halt the boat's voyage and could do nothing for the voyager. "The thought of helping me," Gracchus says, "is an illness that has to be cured by taking to one's bed." So, wish as he might, he resigns himself to his fate and does not call out for help. He needs only to look around him and remember where he is, and any thought of calling out vanishes. The burgomaster asks him if he intends to stay in Riva. Gracchus replies that he intends nothing, that he can know only where he is at present; his ship rides with the wind that blows in the undermost regions of death.

Themes and Meanings

The parable of the hunter Gracchus, with its overtones of both classical mythology and Germanic legend, is perhaps most reminiscent of the folk saga of the Flying Dutchman, the man whose blasphemous boasting condemned him to sail the seas on his ghostly ship forever unless released from his punishment by the faithfulness of a woman. He too, like Gracchus, sought death as a liberation from his endless wanderings, but he found himself powerless to end his own life. Like Gracchus, the voyager of the legend was accorded the chance to come ashore from his ship periodically to seek that which might free him from the curse.

However, Gracchus is condemned to sail wherever the winds may drive his boat without the benefit of knowing the offense of which he is guilty, and this is where his story differs so significantly from the legend of the Flying Dutchman and what makes his plight so characteristic of the human condition as Franz Kafka confronts it. Indeed, as he says, Gracchus lived his life as he had been meant to live it: joyously, proudly, and with distinction. His labors were blessed. He was known as the Great Hunter of the Black Forest. The death that he thought was his, and for which he still wishes, is not a desperate wish but rather the natural consequence and fitting reward for the life that went before it. He met death gladly and expectantly, donning his shroud as a bride would her wedding gown. "Then came the mishap."

It was the fault of the boatman, Gracchus claims, and if anyone could explain what went wrong in his crossing from life into death, it would be this enigmatic figure. A number of Kafka's novels and stories include such persons. It is sometimes unclear whether they are the guides who show the way or the guards who bar it. Often they appear to be both, seemingly helpful but then again frustratingly ineffectual or even perversely obstructive. The boatman in this story does not speak a word and is no longer present when Gracchus tells his story to the burgomaster, yet he seems to control the course of events. His actions, even if arbitrary and inexplicable, are not subject to question, and the passenger, whatever his station and distinctions otherwise in life, is at his mercy. The boatman calls to mind the mythical ferryman Charon, but he is a Charon in reverse: not the guide who makes entry into the realm of the dead possible, but the one who presumably committed the fatal error and now keeps Gracchus a wanderer while maintaining silence about the reason for it and about the eventual fate of his passenger.

Gracchus (still a hunter, even though he once believed his hunting days were happily over) hovers between two worlds. He tells the burgomaster that he is dead but also still alive. One might also say that he is neither and that the "no man's land" he now inhabits may help to explain the open end of the story. It has been said of Kafka himself that, occupying a kind of border territory between sociability and solitude, he could not live; but that condition enabled him to observe how life was lived. So it is with Gracchus. He cannot intend to stay in Riva or to leave again because intending is not within his power now. He can say only, "I am here, more than that I do not know, further than that I cannot go."

Style and Technique

Although parables in the traditional sense are thought of as didactic stories with a moral truth or insight, Kafka's tales do not purport to have arrived at such truths. Instead they record observations on the human experience. Because the human condition, at least to Kafka's eye, is experienced as a fragmented, incoherent, sometimes mystifying, and frightening existence, stories such as "The Hunter Gracchus" do not proceed from a clear beginning through a logical series of developments to a conclusive ending. They are marked by apparent disjunctions of thought and seemingly arbitrary, extraneous elements. Told—like parables—in analogous, not literal terms, they nevertheless embody a realism of their own. However, it is not Gracchus's fantastic story that is realistic; it is rather the sense of unending limbo, a twilight existence between life and death, and the helplessness that he feels that constitute Kafka's realism.

Certain elements of "The Hunter Gracchus" are palpably symbolic—the doves that announce the hunter's arrival, the fifty or so little boys who form the receiving line for the burgomaster, and the picture of the spear-wielding bushman in Gracchus's cabin. Exactly what the symbolism means is difficult to say; this is the sort of device that gives rise to interpretive disputes over Kafka's writings.

There is also a familiar, superficial realism about the story. The waterfront setting in which it begins, with boys playing at dice, a man reading his newspaper, the denizens of the café, a monument to some military hero, the fruit peels littering the street, the exterior and interior details of the house where the bier is taken; these lend the story a "realistic" overlay. However, in fact they parody traditional realism because they distract from, rather than explicate or complement, the main idea of the parable. This level of realism, especially as it focuses on the ordinary and unswept corners of life, may establish an initial credibility for the narrative, but there is humor in its dull ordinariness, and because of that, it contrasts all the more starkly with the grave existential "illness" that Gracchus's fate engenders in the rest of humanity.

Michael Ritterson

HUNTERS IN THE SNOW

Author: Tobias Wolff (1945-   )
Type of plot: Existential
Time of plot: The 1980's
Locale: Countryside around Spokane, Washington
First published: 1981

Principal characters:

TUB, an overweight hunter
FRANK, a former hippie who sometimes inserts clichés from New
    Age philosophy into his conversation
KENNY, a bully

The Story

A third-person narrative, "Hunters in the Snow" is the story of three men from Spokane, Washington, who go on a hunting trip. Kenny drives up on the sidewalk where Tub has been waiting for him and Frank for an hour; he would have driven his pickup over Tub if he had not run. They drive out to hunt the same patch of ground they unsuccessfully covered for the past two hunting seasons. The driver's window of the truck has been broken out, and the wind and snow rush in.

Arriving at the site, Tub scouts one side of the river and the two other men take the other. Quickly winded by the effort of moving through the sometimes deep snow, Tub can only struggle to keep up and soon forgets about everything else. When Frank and Kenny cross over to Tub's side, they see that he has walked over deer tracks and signs without alerting them. They heap more scorn on him, then follow the tracks until they come to a fence with a No Hunting sign. They hike back to the truck in order to drive to the farmer's house to obtain permission to keep tracking the deer over the posted land.

Tub tends to wallow in the deep snow, sometimes breaking through the hard crust that supports the lighter weight of the two other men, but Kenny and Frank make no allowances for his relative weakness. Kenny rather transparently teases Frank about a baby-sitter, but Frank does not appreciate the humor and refuses to explain the situation to Tub. After they gain permission to hunt, a dog rushes from the house, but Kenny drops down to snarl, and the dog, intimidated, runs back to the barn.

Their hunt is unsuccessful, but as they walk past the farmhouse, Kenny suddenly declares his hatred for a fencepost and shoots it. He does the same to a tree, and when the farmer's dog again rushes out toward the hunters, Kenny declares that he hates it and shoots the animal between the eyes. Tub and Frank are stunned. Next Kenny announces that he hates Tub, and Tub beats him to the draw by shooting him in the stomach.

When Frank and Tub return to the farmhouse to call for an ambulance, the farmer informs Tub that he had asked Kenny to kill the dog. The farmer was too fond of the animal to shoot it himself but had not wanted it to suffer. Tub realizes that Kenny had only been playing another practical joke on him.

No ambulance is available, so the other men find a board on which to carry Kenny to their pickup. When Tub accidentally drops his end, Frank castigates him for his clumsy obesity. Tub attacks the smaller man, shaking him until he apologizes. They get Kenny into the back of the truck, cover him with blankets, and Frank drives off to the hospital.

Finding the cold unbearable, the two uninjured men stop to warm themselves but leave Kenny in the back of the truck. In the congenial atmosphere of the tavern, Frank reveals his love for Roxanne Brewer, a fifteen-year-old baby-sitter for whom he is thinking of deserting his wife and children.

Despite Tub's wanting to develop his friendship with Frank, his initial reaction to Frank's offer is more telling than his eventual acceptance of the relationship. First, he confuses Roxanne with Juliet Miller, an even younger and less sexually mature child, and he then asks what Frank's wife thinks. Frank provides the conventional response that Roxanne is more special than other children and, indeed, other people. He also admits that he has not yet told his wife and wonders if Tub thinks him a complete bastard. Tub promises to remain Frank's friend regardless of his actions.

Returning to Kenny, they again cover him with the blankets that had somehow slipped off him. Frank urges Kenny to keep repeating that he is going to the hospital. After they return to the highway, Tub realizes that he had left the directions to the hospital on a table in the bar, but Frank says he can remember them.

Again suffering from the cold, Frank stops at the next roadhouse. This time it is Tub's turn to entrust Frank with a secret. Although he attributes his obesity to his glands and pretends to always be dieting, in fact he stuffs himself with food. Frank rewards his openness with four orders of pancakes with butter and syrup and watches while Tub rather sloppily enjoys them.

Returning to the pickup, they find the blankets have again slipped off Kenny. Because Kenny cannot keep them on, Frank suggests they take the blankets to the cab of the truck so at least someone can get some good out of them. He also insists that Kenny repeat that he is going to the hospital. It is unclear if this is to keep up his optimism, to distract him from the pain, or just for cruelty. Kenny is obviously getting weaker as Frank drives on in the wrong direction.

Themes and Meanings

In keeping with the hunting theme, the men act according to a natural pecking order. The more physically fit Kenny plays a series of harsh practical jokes on Tub, who is seemingly the weakest member of their trio because of his excessive weight.

As an existential work, "Hunters in the Snow" immerses its characters in an indifferent universe in which the moral signposts have been obliterated, just like the signs on country roads during a winter storm. Such bonds as individuals are able to form under these conditions are necessarily tentative, and they sometimes try to fill this void by consciously adopting the tacit rules of the groups to which they want to belong. At the outset, the hunters have bought into the myth of a rugged individual independence in which rigid personal boundaries are enforced by bullying. Even seemingly close friends are kept at a distance by constant ribbing and a willingness to ridicule their predicaments or shortcomings. Any sign of affection between the men or even basic courtesy is perceived as weakness. The futility of this approach to life is demonstrated by Kenny's plight at the end of the story; his companions are as out of touch with his suffering as the distant stars over his head.

As an example of reductio ad absurdum, the story takes the typical banter and hard-edged joking that is sometimes part of the bonding experience among a certain class of men to its ridiculous conclusion. The special bonds of friendship developing between the two uninjured men are so unique and highly valued that they do not care that Kenny could die from their neglect. Apparently feeling that the bonding experience is more important than a human life, they do not want the moment to end.

Style and Technique

The narrative is told realistically, with an emphasis on concrete sensory details. As a sign of the unconditional friendship growing between them, Frank is not disgusted by the syrup that drips from the gluttonous Tub's face like a goatee, nor does Tub criticize Frank for the domestic mess that he will create. Such unattractive details suggest that the author does not endorse the choices the characters are making.

The major plot elements of the story develop in accordance with a basic principle of Zen Buddhism as that religion is understood by the popular culture of America's Northwest. Boiled down to its essence, the tenet is embodied in the saying that whatever goes around comes around. Hence, because the three men go hunting only as a diversion, it can seem like cosmic justice when one of them is shot. Similarly, Kenny is the most adept at maintaining the emotional distance among his companions. When his life is endangered, however, they are so distant that they have neither empathy nor sympathy with his suffering. They react with less pity than they would have had Kenny been a legitimate game animal.

From a psychological standpoint, the story is realistic in showing how Frank is more receptive to male bonding as a consequence of the strain he is placing on his marriage. Because his affair has lessened his intimacy with his wife, he emotionally clings to Tub to fill the void. Although he argues that Roxanne is more alive than other people, he has essentially been reduced to functioning at an irresponsible early teen level. Both Frank and Tub are selfishly focused on their own gratification, and by the end of the story, Kenny is almost reduced to being only a symbol.

Randall Huff

HUNTING SEASON

Author: Joanne Greenberg (1932-   )
Type of plot: Pastoral
Time of plot: The early 1970's
Locale: The western American mountains
First published: 1972

Principal characters:
JOSEPH, a young boy who suffers from epilepsy
HIS MOTHER, who is extremely concerned about her son's well-being

The Story

On a winter day, Joseph, a youngster of four, nonchalantly mentions to his mother that he wants to go down to the creek near the house. The family lives in a mountainous area, where, during the winter, hunters abound, making it somewhat dangerous for young children to play in the woods. The mother, busy at household tasks, puts off her son briefly before acknowledging his request. She gives in, but only grudgingly, making sure that he is dressed warmly in a jacket that marks him out for hunters so that he will not be mistaken for a target. Additionally, she recites a litany of "dos" and "don'ts" for the boy, which he bears patiently.

When her son is gone, the mother reflects on her behavior toward him. Sorry that her son does not realize that she, too, was once young, the mother begins to realize how little time she has given to communicating with Joseph. In her fussing over details, she has "missed the important things." However, suddenly, she realizes that this day marks a week since the boy had been put on new medicine for his epilepsy. Though the doctor had assured her that there would be no ill effects, the mother nevertheless has spent the past seven days waiting for the moment when a seizure would strike. Now, her son gone off to wander in a dangerous environment, she fantasizes how he might fall into the creek and suffer a sudden seizure and drown. The mental anguish becomes too much, and she rushes out of the house to find him.

Outside, she searches for the trail that her son has taken. Carefully she picks her way over the mountain, trying to go quietly so as not to let her son know that she is after him. Finally, she spots his turquoise jacket. Trying to remain unobserved, she stalks after him, noting with indignation that he is wandering from the route that he told her he would take. In the distance, the sounds of the hunters are discernible. For a moment, the boy disappears from view, and the mother is again seized with a vision of horror. Then she spies him beside the creek. Suddenly, she realizes that she is intruding on his privacy, spying on him. For his part, the boy remains oblivious to his mother's presence. He begins to talk to the rocks across the creek, challenging them as if they were animate creatures. "You're not so tough," he shouts; he tells them that he will learn all about them, and therefore be master of them when he is old enough for school, but that they will never know about him. The outburst, delivered in a tone that the mother recognizes as one she herself uses, makes her retreat quietly to let her son engage this "world of rape and murder" alone, as he must in order to grow up.

Themes and Meanings

It is not surprising that Joanne Greenberg included "Hunting Season" in her 1972 collection entitled *Rites of Passage*. This is a story about a passage from innocence to experience. One might expect the story to focus on the young boy's experiences in the forest. Ironically, however, the central interest in "Hunting Season" is the effect that a boy's growing up has on his mother, who must make the hard decision to let her offspring make his way, in whatever small way he can, into the world of adulthood.

Though adults have all been through the process themselves, it nevertheless appears to be a terrifying trial when their children are the ones who are trying to break away from parental control. The mother in "Hunting Season" is not unaware of what is happening. She is disappointed that her son cannot see that she was once a carefree girl who enjoyed many of the same things that he does now. Nevertheless, she is caught up in her role as homemaker, wife, and mother to such an extent that she has little time to share her life with her son. To her, he is simply a child, something to be cared for but not given serious attention.

The mother's world is clearly defined by the limits of her house. She is no longer a part of the outside world; her domain is inside the home, where she brings order and provides for all of her family's needs. As a consequence, she has lost something of herself; the days when she would "stamp windowpanes out of frozen puddles" are gone, and though she is "a little ashamed," she cannot find the time to treat her young son's emotional problems with the same degree of seriousness that she gives to his physical disability: The boy does not know the suffering that epilepsy brings, but he has felt the pain of losing his best friend, who has moved away.

The world outside appears to be a harsh one, and the contrast between "inside" and "outside" is magnified by the presence of the hunters and the physical dangers of the landscape. Psychologically, Greenberg suggests that the comforts of the womb stand in sharp contrast to the world outside. However, the child must leave that womb, both physically and psychologically, if he is to grow in the world. At the same time, the mother must be willing to set the child free from her body and from her influence if his growth is to be successful. The "passage" in "Hunting Season" occurs primarily on this psychological level.

Style and Technique

The most noticeable feature of "Hunting Season" is its imagery. Virtually every detail in the story focuses the reader's attention on the hunt, which Greenberg uses as an ironic symbol of the mother's pursuit of the child whom she must release. The literal presence of hunters in the woods near the home provides the most significant sign of the dangerous environment outside the warmth and security of the home, which is clearly the domain in which the mother is supreme. The "world of rape and murder" that the mother sees when she ventures out after her son is really there: The land has been ravaged by miners, and the hunters seek to destroy the living creatures that inhabit the mountainous region.

When she dashes out to follow her son, the mother herself becomes a hunter, her son the prey. Searching for him, she "nosed the wind like an animal." A noise prompts her to ask herself "Was that his cry?" When she spots his jacket, she begins "tracking" him "warily," until she finally realizes that she is simply "a middle-aged huntress." Her action—backtracking to avoid his seeing her, treading carefully so as not to make noise, reinforce this portrait. Greenberg also suggests the nature of this pursuit in her description of the boy, who appears with the characteristics of the wary animal: "He put his head up," when stopping on his trek toward the creek, "reading the air for something."

More subtle is Greenberg's handling of point of view. The opening paragraphs give the reader a glimpse into the minds of both characters: the mother realizing that she is being a bit overprotective, the son patiently enduring the preparations that his mother makes him undergo before venturing into the forest. When the boy leaves the house, however, the reader is forced to follow the story only from within the consciousness of the mother. This technique heightens the sense of suspense that characterizes the mother's pursuit of her son: Will he be safe? Will he be killed by hunters? Will he fall into the creek and drown? The realization that the mother is actually intruding on the boy's privacy and may actually hinder his maturation is made particularly poignant by Greenberg's decision to have the story seen through the eyes of the woman who must make a crucial decision not to interfere if her son is to grow to manhood.

Laurence W. Mazzeno

I-80 NEBRASKA M.490-M.205

Author: John Sayles (1950-   )
Type of plot: Fantasy, tall tale
Time of plot: The 1960's
Locale: Interstate 80 in eastern Nebraska
First published: 1975

>   *Principal characters:*
>   RYDER P. MOSES, a long-distance trucker whose voice dominates
>   the citizens band (CB) radio communications
>   "SWEETPEA," a woman trucker who tries to lure Moses to a truck
>   stop
>   "COYOTE," a long-distance trucker who follows Moses

The Story

"I-80 Nebraska M.490-M.205" covers one night in the life of a big rig driver who calls himself Ryder P. Moses. No one has ever seen this larger-than-life trucker, but his voice rules the night citizens band (CB) radio on which the long-distance haulers depend. These eighteen-wheelers travel the highways, carrying their huge loads from coast to coast, and their drivers use their CB radios to warn one another of police cars ("Smokey Bear") or errant passenger cars ("four-wheelers") and to entertain fellow truckers with stories and information. All the truckers have colorful names such as "Gutslinger" or "Oklahoma Crude," except for Ryder P. Moses, who in the last few weeks has come to dominate the thoughts and conversations of the other truckers. No one has ever seen him, which makes them suspicious when they see one another in the cabs of their trucks or at truck stops until they can identify one another, but he appears on the radio each night with powerful messages conveyed in apocalyptic language.

On the night the story describes, Moses first taunts other drivers with thoughts of where their wives or girlfriends may be and with what other men, and then he lets loose a rant on drugs such as amphetamines that truckers use to stay awake. "Sweetpea," called the "Grande Dame of the Open Road," tries to lure Moses into the open by suggesting over the CB radio that they meet at Bosselman's, a truck stop on Interstate 80 somewhere between Lincoln and Grand Island, Nebraska, and when Moses agrees, all the truckers on that section of the road pile into the truck stop to see him, but it is soon clear that Ryder P. Moses is not there.

A boy at the Husky gas station three miles away later reports that he saw a cattle truck filled with dead cows getting gas, and back on the road again, the drivers hear Moses claim that he stopped at the Husky because the gas was a few cents cheaper. He continues his rant, westbound on Interstate 80, this time on the problems of the economy and corporate America as they affect independent truckers such as his listeners. He tells them that he is educating them and continues on about life, eternity, history, and other essentially philosophical, even mystical, questions, urging them to break through life's cycle by never stopping.

Another trucker, "Coyote," is following a cattle truck he believes to be Moses through Kearney and then Lexington, headed west on Interstate 80. He sees that the truck is fishtailing, so he breaks into the CB chatter to try to warn Moses. Moses signs off without ever acknowledging Coyote, and then apparently collides with a concrete overpass support somewhere before reaching North Platte, for the story's last line describes Coyote swerving to miss the wreck "as the sky begins a rain of beef." Moses has been killed, readers assume, his load of dead cattle scattered along the roadside, but John Sayles leaves the ending ambiguous. Was that trucker really Moses?

Themes and Meanings

"I-80 Nebraska M.490-M.205" has a number of themes, and its central meaning may be found in a combination of several of them. On the simplest level, the story is a celebration of workers seldom noticed before in literature: blue-collar truck drivers, doing their difficult and dangerous jobs with a casual style and with pungent, colorful language. This story was first anthologized in *On the Job: Fiction About Work by Contemporary American Writers* (1977), edited by William O'Rourke. Like John Steinbeck, Nelson Algren, Charles Bukowski, and other important twentieth century American writers, Sayles celebrates the world of real work and real workers.

The character of Ryder P. Moses, however, elevates the story into something beyond a simple celebration of working men and women. Moses can be called a mythic figure—a larger-than-life character who takes on the aura of myth and legend. None of the truckers has ever seen him, and yet they talk about him incessantly, discussing his exploits and speculating about him. In this sense, Moses partakes of the tall-tale tradition in American literature (he himself mentions Paul Bunyan), and he even resembles a Christ figure in the truckers' rumors of his earlier death. He is superhuman, if not supernatural, for he has no physical presence in the story except as a voice over the radio.

What is the purpose of this comparison? Toward what end does the mythic buildup drive? On one level, the presence of Ryder P. Moses elevates the occupation of trucker itself. His mystery and legend lend seriousness to this often ignored but vital profession. More important, his CB diatribes provide a critique of the very profession to which he belongs and of the economy that depends on truckers like those listening to him. There is a driven and poetic quality to Ryder's rants on American culture and American capitalism that makes them both truthful and poignant.

In the end, Moses dies—or at least readers think that he has. There is something mysterious even about his death. On this level, Ryder P. Moses must be seen as fulfilling his Christ role as dying to save the world. His final monologue has a kind of apocalyptic quality to it that can end only with his self-immolation. In the prophetic tradition of Walt Whitman, Jack Kerouac, Ken Kesey, and other American writers, Sayles has created a mythic figure who warns his listeners about their world. The dead cattle that he apparently hauls, however, like his own fiery end, suggest that he is a figure of death as well, a modern version of the Grim Reaper driving the roads to warn other truckers of the dangers of their jobs.

Style and Technique

Meaning and technique are closely interrelated in "I-80 Nebraska M.490-M.205." The pace and momentum of the story mimic the life it describes: the jobs of long-distance haulers driving large loads of goods through the night across the United States. The rhythm of the road is faithfully rendered in the story, and the pace of life on the road is reflected in the language of the CB radio: the staccato, colloquial outbursts of truckers as they call to one another through the night. It is similar to the language, as Sayles acknowledges in the story, used by American astronauts, talking with ground control in dozens of televised space missions, especially during the 1960's and 1970's.

Sayles's language itself—in the exposition as opposed to the dialogue of the story—is as metaphorical as the conversation of the truckers, with numerous figurative expressions. In his first expository paragraph, for example, Sayles compares the line of big rigs to a river, a flood, lava, and then a stream. The language of Ryder P. Moses is the most colorful of all, a voice out of the darkness that is at once both philosophical and earthy. Moses's language accelerates during the course of the story until he reaches his flaming end. Near that conclusion, he talks about metaphors, about how drugs are metaphors for sleep and about how the lesson he is trying to instill in his listeners is to keep driving: "Rest not, rust not." The story's language is as vivid and pulsing as the scenes it describes.

The story defies classification because, while realistic in its setting and subject, its central character is fantastic and mythic. In some ways, "I-80 Nebraska M.490-M.205" is a throwback to older forms of short fiction that combine realism with fantasy and myth, such as Harriet Prescott Spofford's short story "Circumstance" (1860) or the tales of Charles Brockden Brown or Edgar Allan Poe. However, the language and drug references place the story firmly in the psychedelic strain of much of the music and literature of the 1960's.

David Peck

I LOOK OUT FOR ED WOLFE

Author: Stanley Elkin (1930-1995)
Type of plot: Realism
Time of plot: The early 1960's
Locale: Urban America
First published: 1962

Principal characters:
ED WOLFE, the protagonist, a ruthless bill collector
LA MECK, his boss at the loan company
OLIVER, a black stranger who agreed to take Wolfe to a party
MARY ROBERTA, a young black woman who keeps Wolfe
 company at the party

The Story
Ed Wolfe is a loan officer whose aggressiveness in collecting bills for Cornucopia Finance Company ("Can you cope?" is Wolfe's sardonic rechristening) verges on the maniacal. On the day the story opens, he is fired for doing his job too well: His zeal has transformed into a practice of vicious harassment of delinquent clients, and he is accused by his boss, La Meck, of having degenerated into a gangster. As the story's title suggests, Ed Wolfe is exclusively self-absorbed, a champion of detachment and a heartlessly efficient operator.

Receiving his severance pay initiates a bizarre ritual of dispossession, as though Ed Wolfe, a man obsessed by his orphanhood, has chosen to quit the world rather than accept its dismissal of him. So begins a wildly comic personal liquidation sale: He sells his car and his furniture, he closes his savings account, cancels his insurance policy, pawns his clothes, and disconnects his telephone. He sells himself off with single-minded fervor, melting himself down into dollars, orphaning himself as completely as possible. When he has nothing left to sell—he imagines that his senses, his very skin, have been exchanged—he inventories his worth: $2,479.03. This is the sum total of his accumulated past and his ransomed future, as translated into cash flow.

It is also the measure of his distance from death. The exhilaration of freedom sours quickly as Ed Wolfe realizes that he cannot stave off the inexorable leakage of his assets into the few necessities he has managed to pare his life down to. Ironically, this Thoreau-run-amok, who carries the famous dictum to "simplify, simplify, simplify" to absurd extremes, has not reached his essential being so much as abraded himself into anonymity. Freedom is irresponsibility.

The lone Wolfe becomes an urban nomad, a contemporary Wandering Jew. He aimlessly makes his way into a hotel bar, where he gets drunk and accosts a black man. Apparently, even Ed Wolfe craves human contact after all; beyond inhibition, he awkwardly forces himself on the stranger, all the while stressing their camaraderie as social pariahs. Oliver, the black man, invites him to a party. Although Wolfe momentarily hesitates—the reflex anxiety of being at the mercy of murderous blacks—a few more drinks and an ever-deepening sense of fatality finally combine to rid him of all restraint. He is introduced to and dances with Mary Roberta, a young black woman (a prostitute?), to whom he confesses his despair. He then makes some vaguely racist remarks that culminate in a boozy effort to sell her to the increasingly angry onlookers. The story concludes with Ed Wolfe casting his remaining money to the crowd at the party, until the black woman he has witlessly abused silently squeezes his pallid hand.

Themes and Meanings

Stanley Elkin's stories are populated by chronic complainers, whose energies are devoted to lamentation over failures of health, business, love, or aspiration, and by glib finaglers, who ooze oily confidence and dispense inside dope. These are the residents of Elkin's short-story collection *Criers and Kibitzers, Kibitzers and Criers: Nine Stories* (1965); each has a code, myth, or obsession to sum up society and his place in it. Testifying to the precept that the limits of one's language are the limits of one's world, they share a faith in verbal extravagance as a means of staking out claims for the self. Whether he is after influence, sympathy, or simply an audience, every character is an ear-bender, a salesperson, a cajoler, a philosopher. Talk is the common currency of the anxious and the fanatical alike.

Ed Wolfe is a particularly proficient negotiator in an environment that highlights the intimate relationship between identity and expression. The exploitative way he handles people over the telephone, however, dehumanizes the bill collector as well as those he duns. It intensifies the orphan's divorce from the human community. Wolfe's subsequent selling off of everything he owns looks like the programmatic suicide of a man at loose ends; moreover, it may be interpreted either as the bullying method of the bill collector turned inward or as an upgrading of what for him has been a prolonged search for authenticity. At the end of the story, Ed Wolfe, shaved to the bone, has reached bottom; yet even though he is dislocated and desperate among strangers, the closing image of Mary Roberta's brief act of compassion may be a foundation on which to begin rebuilding his life.

In other words, Ed Wolfe's humiliation may be prefatory to a return to life. The vitality of a strange black woman may serve as an energy transfusion for a man who has been riven by guilt and spiritual isolation. However indifferently he observes the climactic event of the story (and even if he is still not ready to be groomed for virtue), there exists the possibility of a reversal of his depletion. Perhaps he has been purged, in which case he may now be prepared to discover the self for which he has been searching.

Style and Technique

Unlike his novels, which are generally categorized with those by such linguistically venturesome, self-referential writers as Robert Coover, William Gass, and John Hawkes, Elkin's short stories resemble the more conventionally realistic style of so-called Jewish Renaissance fiction of the 1950's and 1960's—the literary territory carved out by Saul Bellow, Philip Roth, and Bernard Malamud. Nevertheless, what has become the Elkin trademark does occasionally appear in "I Look Out for Ed Wolfe": the establishment of outrageously comic circumstances that spur what might best be called lyrical exhibitionism. Elkin is responsible for some of the most richly imaged verbal flourishes in American fiction.

Ed Wolfe is a vocation vocalized, for Elkin has mastered the jargon, pace, and patter of the salesperson and granted it poetic status. Verbal rhythm and drive: They lend even Ed Wolfe's willful deterioration an optimistic charge—and a plenitude. Rejoicing in voice, the beleaguered ego perseveres.

Arthur M. Saltzman

I SEE YOU NEVER

Author: Ray Bradbury (1920-   )
Type of plot: Psychological, social realism
Time of plot: The mid-1940's
Locale: Los Angeles, California
First published: 1947

Principal characters:
MRS. O'BRIAN, a fastidious and kindly landlady
MR. RAMIREZ, a Mexican airplane-factory worker

The Story

Mr. Ramirez, the landlady's best tenant, is in the custody of two police officers, but he is initially unable to speak and therefore explain the reason for his arrest. Mrs. O'Brian knows his past: that he traveled by bus from Mexico City through San Diego to Los Angeles, where he found work in an airplane factory during the final years of World War II. Throughout this time and into the postwar period, he had roomed with Mrs. O'Brian. With his good salary, he was able to buy a radio, a wristwatch, and even a car, which was repossessed when he forgot to keep up the payments. He enjoyed going to restaurants, films, the theater, and the opera, occasionally with one of his few girlfriends.

Mrs. O'Brian eventually learns from Ramirez and the officers that her tenant had only a temporary visa and he had been an illegal resident for the last six months. Ramirez's reappearance at the boarding house is to let her know that he has to give up his room. He is there to collect and pack his belongings for his return to Lagos, his small hometown north of Mexico City.

Ramirez smells the pies that his landlady is baking and sees the kitchen table that she has set with shining silverware and carefully prepared food for her three sons and two younger daughters. After packing, Ramirez returns his house key to Mrs. O'Brian, who tells him what a good tenant he has been and how sorry she is that he has to leave. She once visited some border towns in Mexico and therefore has some sense of the impoverished world to which he is returning.

With deep feeling, Ramirez tells Mrs. O'Brian that he likes his job and life in the United States and that he does not want to go back to Mexico, but she can do nothing to change his situation or mitigate his pain. With tears streaming down his face, Ramirez clasps her hand desperately, shaking and wringing it, while saying in broken English, again and again, "Mrs. O'Brian, I see you never, I see you never!"

Ramirez picks up his suitcase and walks away with the police officers. Mrs. O'Brian closes the door and sits at the kitchen table. Despite the pleas of one of her sons, she lacks the appetite to enjoy her steak. When her sons asks what is wrong, she replies that she has just realized that she will never see Ramirez again.

Themes and Meanings

"I See You Never," with its third-person narration, pivots between the minds of the two chief characters. The thrust of the story concerns the epiphanies of a Mexican expatriate and his American landlady that their thirty-month relationship of admiration and respect has been irredeemably ended by the California police. Ray Bradbury, who had recently traveled to Mexico before writing the story, expressed sympathy for Mexicans and Mexican Americans, and "I See You Never" contains a sensitive portrayal of a successful, albeit now illegal laborer, who reluctantly has to confront his alien status.

In whatever type of short story he writes—fantasy, horror, science fiction, or realism—Ray Bradbury is often concerned with the theme of metamorphosis, the transformation of human experience under the pressure of past or present events. He therefore uses his stories to bring to the surface hidden emotions or forgotten selves, and these revealed feelings or personalities may frighten, amuse, or enlighten the reader. In "I See You Never," Mr. Ramirez discovers his deep feelings of attachment to the United States when he realizes that he has to leave it. Mrs. O'Brian finds that she has become emotionally attached to her tenant of two and a half years when she realizes that she is never going to see him again.

Unlike Bradbury's science-fiction stories, "I See You Never" has ordinary settings (Southern California and Mexico) and conventional characters (a plump landlady and a Mexican laborer). In response to a criticism about his use of stock characters, Bradbury replied that he created characters to personify his ideas. Furthermore, he said, all his characters were, in some way, variations on himself. In this story, Mrs. O'Brian represents the orderly, comfortable, prosperous world of the United States, and Ramirez is the alien who is cast out of an edenic California.

This story was written not long after Bradbury made a two-month trip to Mexico, during which he felt like a stranger in a strange land. Bradbury, like many Californians of the time, was Protestant, individualistic, and ambitious, and he consequently felt alienated in a culture that was largely Roman Catholic, communalistic, and preoccupied with survival in the midst of poverty, suffering, and death. This theme of alienation became important in many of his stories, for he came to see that many modern human beings were alienated from their culture, their technologies, and even their own thoughts and feelings. In some of his other stories about Mexicans, Bradbury showed his admiration for their lack of materialism and their pastoral virtues and his anxiety over the dehumanization brought about in such a materialistic, technological society as the United States. This story is also an early manifestation of Bradbury's social conscience because it exhibits his concern for the plight of foreign workers in the United States.

Separations have been called little deaths, and "To See You Never" is also about the permanent loss of persons to one another. Several critics have observed that below the surface of many of Bradbury's stories lies an ominous vision of the human condition. Bradburian characters occupy a fallen world, where periods of sunny happiness may sometimes occur, but they are destined to be overwhelmed by darkness. Ramirez was beginning to think of himself as an American because he worked hard, saved his money, and became an appreciative consumer of American products and entertainment, but his dreams of a prosperous future were doomed to be dashed, not because of any fault of his or Mrs. O'Brian's, but because they were both inhabitants of a sinful world.

Style and Technique

A knock at the kitchen door of Mrs. O'Brian's rooming house is the story's incipient event. Bradbury has spoken of moments when doors open and the future floods in, and this story certainly illustrates the power of pending events, but the story's subject is also the pastness of the present.

Bradbury's style has been traced to the Bible, William Shakespeare, Ernest Hemingway, and motion pictures, and it has been variously described as romantic, poetic, gothic, and realistic. The reason for this motley of characterizations is his penchant for choosing a style to match his subject.

The style of "I See You Never" is clearly realistic throughout, from the soft knock on a door that begins the story to Mrs. O'Brian's face in her hand that ends it. However, Bradbury's realism is symbolic, not naturalistic, because he chooses realistic details to point to other meanings. For example, he describes Mrs. O'Brian's kitchen table as covered with clean white linen, and on this table all is meticulously displayed (even her oranges are precisely cubed and sugared). This is the orderly, affluent setting within which Ramirez has found a new home. On the other hand, when Mexico is described through the consciousness of Mrs. O'Brian, Ramirez's native country consists of streets covered with dead or dying insects, and the food and drink—spicy sauces and warm beer—stand in stark contrast to her crisp, brown pies, whose color is like Ramirez's complexion and whose slits are like his eyes.

Many classic writers advised followers to show rather than state the meaning of their stories, and Bradbury's technique is in line with this advice because he reveals his themes through his characters, their words, thoughts, and feelings, and also through the places they inhabit. Both the landlady and the Mexican reveal through their thoughts, words, and actions that they are basically good and decent people, but their situation is tragic. This tragic situation is suggested at the very start of the story when Ramirez is described as "walled in" between the two police officers. The secondary characters also reinforce this feeling of mutual respect within a dehumanizing context. The officers understand that Ramirez poses no threat of violence or escape. Though he decries his fate, he is reconciled to it. Mrs. O'Brian is genuinely sorry about her tenant's predicament, but she, too, accepts its inevitable unhappy outcome. Implied in the way Bradbury writes about this quandary for his characters is a critique of the injustice involved in Ramirez's expulsion from the United States, but it is a gentle protest because the story ends with an acceptance of what cannot be changed. Mrs. O'Brian returns to her children, and Mr. Ramirez returns to his Mexican hometown.

Robert J. Paradowski

I STAND HERE IRONING

Author: Tillie Olsen (1913-   )
Type of plot: Psychological
Time of plot: About 1950
Locale: A city in the United States
First published: 1956

Principal characters:
THE MOTHER, the narrator of the story
EMILY, her daughter

The Story

The title of the story reveals that the narrator is engaged in a simple, routine household task. While she is ironing, she meditates about a note she has received from a teacher or adviser at the school her daughter, Emily, attends. She feels tormented by the request to come in and talk about Emily, who the writer of the note believes needs help. However, the mother has no intention of going to see the person who wrote the note. "Even if I came, what good would it do?" she asks.

The rest of the story is an interior monologue, reviewing the lives and relationships of the mother and daughter, followed by a brief exchange of dialogue between the mother and Emily, and a final paragraph of summary of the circumstances in which Emily grew up. At the end, the mother is still standing there ironing.

There is no action and no apparent plot in this story. The interior monologue rehearses the things that the mother might say to the teacher or adviser who wrote the note. Her memories of the daughter's infancy and childhood serve to explain much about the personality and the difficulties of the girl. Her love and tenderness for the girl, and the barriers that separated them physically at first and then emotionally later, are revealed.

Emily was the first child of the mother, who was only nineteen at the time she was born. The mother adored her beautiful baby but was forced to leave her with an indifferent sitter when the child was only eight months old because the mother had to earn money to support them. The father had abandoned his wife and child, and in those days of the Depression and no welfare help, the mother had no choice but to leave the child and find a job. Emily greeted her with a cry each time she rushed anxiously home to gather up her precious infant, and the pain she felt is clear when she notes that the crying was "a weeping I can hear yet."

The child was still an infant when the young mother had to take her to the father's family to keep her for a while. When she finally raised the money to pay for Emily's return, the infant got chicken pox and could not return for yet another period of time. When she came back, the child was thin and so changed that the mother scarcely knew her. The mother was advised to put the two-year-old in nursery school, and it was indeed the only way that they were able to be together at all, because the mother had to spend long hours at work. She recalls that she did not know at the time how fatiguing and cruel the nursery school was. It was only a parking place for children, and she came to realize how Emily and the other children hated it, but there was no other recourse. Emily did not clutch her and beg her not to go as some of the children did, but she would have reasons for staying home. The mother wistfully remembers the child's goodness in never protesting or rebelling.

The young mother married again and was able to be with the child more for a brief time, but even then she and her new husband would go out in the evenings and leave the child alone. Emily was frightened and had to face her terrors alone. Then another daughter was born, and the mother was away at the hospital for a week. When she returned, Emily was ill with measles and so could not come near her mother or the new baby. Even after the disease was over, Emily remained thin and subject to nightmares, so finally the mother was advised to send her to a convalescent home for poor children. The place turned out to be little more than a prison, where the children were denied almost all contact with their parents, not allowed to have any personal possessions, and discouraged from forming any friendships with other inmates.

After eight months of effort, the mother was finally able to get her child released, but when she tried to hold or comfort her after that, the child would stiffen and finally push away. The new baby, her half sister Susan, was a beautiful, plump blond, which aroused fierce jealousy and a painful sense of inadequacy and plainness in Emily. Although the worst of the poverty and deprivation were over, Emily was needed to take the part of an adult during her growing years; her stepfather was away at war, and her mother needed Emily's help in caring for the four younger children. Emily's schoolwork suffered, and she had little chance to be a carefree child during these school years. She did, however, occasionally try to cheer up her mother by imitating happenings or types of people at school.

The mother once casually suggested that she might do some comic routine in the school amateur show, and Emily entered and won first place. After that she began receiving invitations to perform and displayed a genuine gift for comedy. However, the mother says that they were not able to help her to develop her talent and the gift has not grown as fully as it might have.

At this point the girl comes in, and the mother senses by her light step and bantering comments about the perpetual ironing that Emily is feeling happy. The daughter chatters as she fixes herself some food, and her mother dismisses the idea that her daughter has any unmanageable problems. She feels confident that the girl will find her way. Then the girl asks her mother not to rouse her in the morning even though it is the day that her midterm exams are scheduled, explaining that the exams do not matter because everyone will be dead from an atom bomb in a few years anyway. The mother knows that Emily believes it, but she has just been reliving the tenderness and the agony of the making of this human being, and she cannot bear to dismiss the life of this girl so lightly.

At this point she makes her statement. She will not try to explain to anyone the events and the anguish that shaped the girl's life. She tells the note writer (in her mind) to let Emily be. She is not worried that the girl will not achieve her full potential: Not many people do. Emily will still have enough to make a life for herself. However, she does want Emily to know and believe that she is not a helpless, passive victim of circumstances, or fate, or an atom bomb.

Themes and Meanings

The mother-child relationship is the focus of "I Stand Here Ironing." The close bond created in the days of infancy is threatened as soon as the mother must consign the child to a sitter. Both the mother and the child regret and resist the absences that weaken the bond and make it difficult for the mother to express her love for the little girl, but poverty and the demands of other family members prevail, so that by the time the story takes place, the mother believes that she can be of no help to the girl's further development.

The daughter's view of the relationship is expressed only as it is perceived by the mother. However, the mother's memories of the infant crying, the small child finding reasons not to be separated from the mother, but never rebelling or begging, the stiffness and silence of the bigger child when her mother tried to hold or comfort her, the help in mothering and in cheering up her mother when the stepfather was away all suggest that the complexity of the relationship has been developing for a long time. Hurt and deprivation and anger have not severed the bond of love, but they have created barriers so that the mother and daughter are very separate people now.

The mother's confidence that the daughter's common sense will prevail if only she can be persuaded that life is not futile is an acknowledgment of the daughter's maturity. The mother was persuaded against her own common sense to feed the child only at set intervals, to send the child to nursery school, and finally to place her in the convalescent home. In acquiescing to the advice of others instead of following her own instincts, she realizes now, she hurt the child emotionally; she will not make the same mistake again.

Style and Technique

The first-person narrative technique permits the development of a very personal interior monologue and the examination of an entire lifetime of events. These reveal the development of the child Emily and her relationship to her mother in a way that exposes the mother's anguish and sadness. The language of the mother in describing the daughter is always loving and tender. She speaks of her as a miracle, beautiful and happy. The simple, direct sentences are appropriate to the interior monologue and reinforce the sincerity and seriousness of the thoughts expressed.

The calm, reflective tone serves to emphasize the resignation of the mother to her ineffectiveness in influencing the course of her daughter's future. It also provides a fitting contrast to the intensity of the final lines of the story, in which the mother admonishes the note writer to let the girl be but still urges this unnamed figure of authority to convince the girl that life is not futile.

Betty G. Gawthrop

I WANT TO KNOW WHY

Author: Sherwood Anderson (1876-1941)
Type of plot: Psychological
Time of plot: Probably the early twentieth century
Locale: Beckersville, Kentucky, and Saratoga, New York
First published: 1921

> *Principal characters:*
> THE UNNAMED NARRATOR, a fifteen-year-old boy who loves
> horses
> HIS FATHER, a small-town lawyer
> JERRY TILLFORD, a horse trainer
> BILDAD JOHNSON, a black cook at the racetracks
> SUNSTREAK, a thoroughbred racehorse

The Story

The protagonist of "I Want to Know Why" is an unnamed boy nearing his sixteenth birthday. The events that he relates have occurred almost a year previously, just as he turned fifteen. The boy recalls these events in a mixture of confusion and desperation: He needs to understand exactly what happened and how it has affected him so that he can get on with his life.

The boy lives in Beckersville, a small Kentucky town, and he is fascinated with horses and horse racing. His father is the town lawyer, but the boy wants more than anything else to be a part of the racetrack environment. He remembers that when he was ten, he tried to stunt his growth by eating a cigar stolen from his father so that he might remain small enough to be a rider. "It made me awful sick and the doctor had to be sent for, and then it did no good," he recalls. "It was a joke. When I told what I had done and why, most fathers would have whipped me, but mine didn't." Thus, even in this early action, the boy expresses the sense of disappointment that marks the whole story.

With the realization that he can never be a jockey, the boy turns to other aspects of the racing scene. He hangs around the stables, listening to the touts and stable hands and trainers talk. He learns the lore of horses, absorbs the knowledge and hones the instinct that goes with a true appreciation of the animals. His foremost teacher at this time is Bildad Johnson, a black man who works as cook around the track each spring. The boy appreciates Bildad's honesty and trust. He also gathers from the old man an awareness of the beauty of horses that goes beyond simple admiration—that, in fact, approaches the spiritual: "It brings a lump up into my throat when a horse runs. . . . It's in my blood like in the blood of . . . trainers," he says.

The central event in the story occurs when the boy and three of his friends sneak away and hitch a freight train to Saratoga, New York, to watch a first-class horse race.

When they arrive, they look up Bildad and some of the other Beckersville racetrack men who have arrived earlier. The race is the Mullford Handicap, in which Sunstreak, a stallion, will run against the gelding Middlestride. Both horses are from near Beckersville, but the boy pulls for Sunstreak because the horse is special:

> Sunstreak is like a girl you think about sometimes but never see. He is hard all over and lovely too. When you look at his head you want to kiss him. . . . He stands at the post quiet and not letting on, but he is just burning up inside. Then when the barrier goes up he is off like his name, Sunstreak. It makes you ache to see him. It hurts you.

Before the race, the boy visits Sunstreak's stall, where the horse is being groomed. Jerry Tillford, Sunstreak's trainer, notices the boy, and when they share a glance, the boy knows that Jerry is as moved by the horse—by its courage, strength, grace, and vitality—as he is. "Something happened to me," the boy remembers. "I guess I loved the man as much as I did the horse because he knew what I knew. Seemed to me there wasn't anything in the world but that man and the horse and me."

The race between the two horses is barely described by the boy: Sunstreak's victory is a foregone conclusion. Nevertheless, the boy is moved by what he has seen, and that night he parts company with the other boys so that he can be alone to consider the events that he has witnessed. He also wants to be near Jerry Tillford, the one person who most shares his feelings. He has watched Jerry leave in a car with a group of men after the race. With little hope of finding them, he strikes out on the road they took and soon sees the car turning into the driveway of an old farmhouse. The boy creeps up to a window to find out what is going on inside:

> It's what give me the fantods. I can't make it out. The women in the house were all ugly mean-looking women, not nice to look at or be near. . . . I saw everything plain. . . . The women had on loose dresses and sat around in chairs. The men came in and some sat on the women's laps. The place smelled rotten and there was rotten talk, the kind a kid hears around a livery stable in a town like Beckersville in the winter but don't ever expect to hear talked when there are women around. It was rotten.

As the boy watches and listens, Jerry Tillford begins to brag about the race. He takes credit for Sunstreak's win, which the boy knows is foolish. Then the trainer begins to look at one of the women, and the shine in his eyes is the same as the shine that the boy noticed when Jerry looked at Sunstreak before the race. It is this realization that so angers and confuses the boy. When Jerry then kisses the prostitute, the boy is racked by disgust: "I wanted to scream and rush in the room and kill him. I never had such a feeling before," he says. Instead, he retreats into the darkness and, after a sleepless night, heads for home the next day.

In the time that has passed between this event and the present time of the story, the boy has continued to mull over the adventure. His life has changed: "At the tracks the air don't taste as good or smell as good," he says. "It's because a man like Jerry

Tillford, who knows what he does, could see a horse like Sunstreak run, and kiss a woman like that the same day. I can't make it out." Thus the story ends, with the narrator still puzzled, trying to understand the adult world into which he has been so abruptly initiated.

Themes and Meanings

The boy-narrator is a young man growing into the adult world, although he would rather, in a sense, remain a child. This idea is suggested by his wish to stunt his growth by eating a cigar. Although he is thinking in terms of staying small enough to be a jockey, in the larger context of the story it is clear that he is unwilling to face the realities of adulthood. The racetrack, with its magical allure, is a perfect fantasy world for the boy.

The boy's father, the town lawyer, is something of a disappointment to his son. "He's all right, but don't make much money and can't buy me things, and anyway I'm getting so old now I don't expect it," the boy says. In comparison to his friends' fathers—one is a professional gambler—the narrator's father seems rather bland, although the boy appreciates his understanding nature. The reader can recognize that the father is, indeed, a good and wise man, but the narrator, at this age, prefers Jerry Tillford. In fact, he substitutes Jerry for his father on the day of the race. Thus, his shock and his disappointment at Jerry's transgressions are profound: They are a betrayal of the highest order.

The boy's horror takes on an even greater significance when the reader reconsiders the boy's attitude toward horses. As an adolescent, unable to sort out his powerfully confused feelings, the boy has sublimated his sexual urges into the beauty and excitement of racing. Sunstreak is described as a girl whom the boy wants to kiss. The ache, the pain he feels at the horse's running is also vaguely sexual but made acceptable and understandable to the boy because it is pictured in the terms of his childhood world. When Jerry bridges the gap between the spiritual appreciation of the horse and the sexual lust for the woman, he is unknowingly forcing the boy to face the truth about his own feelings and needs. Because the boy has vested Jerry with the role of father, Jerry's act precipitates a distinctly Oedipal crisis. The boy at first wants to kill his "father," whose overt sexual needs reflect the boy's hidden, confused ones. Thereafter, the world is no longer simple; there are no easy, clean answers.

Style and Technique

The most obvious stylistic device in this story is Sherwood Anderson's use of the first-person narrative voice. The naïve speaker finds it difficult to tell his story; he fumbles for the right word, the accurate description. He hesitates to get to the central event. In fact, he circles the event for several pages, nearing it only to withdraw until he can better face it. When he does describe the scene, he can do so only in vague, almost childish language. The house is "rummy-looking"; the women are "ugly" and "mean-looking"; and the place "smelled rotten." How much does the boy actually see? "I saw everything plain," he says. The loose dresses reveal the women's bodies.

The men, some of whom "sat on the women's laps," apparently participate in sexual activities before the boy's eyes. He is obviously fascinated and appalled by what occurs and by the reactions he feels within his own body.

"I Want to Know Why" can be compared to "Death in the Woods" (and numerous other Anderson stories) in its rendering of sexual awakening and confusion. In "Death in the Woods," the narrator is a grown man looking back on his childhood. The boy in "I Want to Know Why" does not have that sort of perspective; less than a year has passed since his experience. Still, he does understand that his childhood is over and he no longer has the luxury of innocence. "That's what I'm writing this story about," he says. "I'm puzzled. I'm getting to be a man and want to think straight and be O.K." At the end of the story he still cannot understand—or cannot make himself admit that he understands—but his desire to "be a man" and "think straight and be O.K." indicates that he is beginning to face the obligations and realities of growing up.

Edwin T. Arnold

THE ICE HOUSE

Author: Caroline Gordon (1895-1981)
Type of plot: Social realism
Time of plot: 1866
Locale: The South
First published: 1931

> *Principal characters:*
> DOUG, a fifteen-year-old southern youth
> RAEBURN, his friend, also fifteen
> A YANKEE CONTRACTOR, unnamed, who hires the boys

The Story

Doug, an enterprising southern lad, has found a few days' employment with a Yankee contractor. He has been hired to remove from a pit in an ice house the skeletons of Union soldiers who were killed in a battle about four years earlier, in 1862. At that time, the frozen December ground precluded digging graves, and the bodies were placed in the ice house to await a future burial.

After enlisting the aid of his close friend Raeburn, Doug waits for him early on an April morning. When Raeburn is late, he becomes irritated, fearing that the contractor might not pay the agreed-on sum. Arriving at about six, Raeburn explains his tardiness, saying, "I ain't going to work for nobody on an empty stomach," but Doug argues that they should earn their pay and provide a full day's labor.

The two youths meet the Yankee contractor at the ice house and begin the task of separating the tangle of bones. Working inside, Doug passes armfuls of bones to Raeburn, who places them in a wheelbarrow. The contractor then deposits the bones in the waiting pine boxes. Because the skeletons are not intact and are often without skulls, however, the boys question whether the contractor knows when he has a complete body in any one of the coffins.

At noon the three rest and have their dinner. Raeburn, more sensitive to handling the skeletons than the other two, drinks some coffee but is unable to eat the biscuit and cold meat that he has brought. Doug and the contractor have no such trouble, for to Doug, "handlin' a dead Yankee ain't no more to me than handlin' a dead hawg." Even so, Raeburn offers to exchange places with him because Doug's job of untangling the bones is the more difficult of the two. On their return to the ice house, however, Doug resumes the same position because, as he points out, "I'm used to it now. You have to kind of get the hang of it. It'd just be wasting time now if we changed places." Because the bodies are lower in the pit, he requests a ladder. In search of one, the contractor inquires at the nearest house, but Mrs. Porter, having lost three sons in the war, is unwilling to help a Yankee, and she directs the contractor to a distant house that he discovers to be abandoned. Unable to obtain a ladder, he returns, but because it is dusk, the boys are finishing up for the day.

As the contractor pays the lads for the day's work, he mentions that he no longer needs them. Doug is surprised; originally he was hired for three or perhaps four days. Furthermore, skeletons of Union soldiers still remain in the ice house. As the boys leave, Doug turns into the woods, and Raeburn soon follows, discovering Doug peering through the undergrowth at the contractor in the distance. The contractor is rearranging the bones, taking some out of the full coffins and placing them into the empty ones, thus making it appear that all the bodies have been removed from the ice house. Doug quickly figures it out: "He's dividing up them skeletons so he can git paid double." The thought amuses him, and he laughs, "There ain't a whole man in ary one of them boxes."

Themes and Meanings

Caroline Gordon is often associated with the Agrarian movement of the 1920's and 1930's, which advocated a return to an economy tied to the land and opposed an industrialized society. Indeed, "The Ice House" can be read as a criticism of the North and its commercialism. The contractor is a Yankee who has come south for the opportunity it provides, a character type often found in Agrarian literature. He is preoccupied with attaining success. He advises Doug, "Farm work's all right if you can't get nothing else to do, but a smart young feller like you wants to be looking out fer oppertunity." At the conclusion of the story, the contractor is more eager to make a profit than to fulfill an obligation. In addition to swindling the government, he deceives the families of the men who died in battle. They will assume that their sons have been buried while, in fact, some of them remain in the pit in the ice house. The contractor does not consider the implications of his action, however, only his profit. In Gordon's fictional world, a character who is concerned solely with money is morally bankrupt.

Gordon, a southerner, is not limiting her criticism to the North. Rather, "The Ice House" is a comment about commercialism everywhere. The contractor is materialistic, but so is Doug. He is prepared to go to work before six in the morning; he worries about not getting paid the full amount; he is preoccupied with getting ahead. Engaging the contractor in conversation, Doug inquires, "Had he ever worked for the government before? And how was he paid? By the day or so much for the job?" Doug's concern with the skeletons is all business. He even appreciates and almost seems to admire the contractor's solution to the remaining empty pine coffins. Doug's attitude suggests that materialism is not specifically a northern trait but one that seems to have replaced or is replacing the old order.

Although initially the tension appears to be between the North and the South or between the contractor and the two friends as representative figures, actually the contractor and Doug, both of whom are materialistic, occupy one side of the spectrum while Raeburn occupies the other. Raeburn insists on eating breakfast before working. He notices the dogwoods and the sprouting new growth on the pokeberry and the sassafras. He understands the channel catfish and has devised a successful method for catching it. Raeburn's appreciation of nature provides him with a sense of the meaning of life that the other two lack. In Gordon's fiction, nature is important because it represents order in a world threatened by chaos. The characters who are close to nature are laudable figures with a strong moral sense. Furthermore, Raeburn's interest in fishing is a positive action that is seen in some of Gordon's other fiction, including *Aleck Maury, Sportsman* (1934), her most acclaimed novel, in which the protagonist resorts to hunting and fishing as a means of withstanding the pressures of contemporary life.

In addition to his awareness of nature, Raeburn is sensitive to the emotions of others. He realizes that Mrs. Porter would not lend a ladder to a Yankee. In contrast, Doug, who sees only the practical side, comments, "Tain't nothin' to lend anybody a ladder." Doug, as a southerner, should anticipate Mrs. Porter's hatred, but he does not. Raeburn is more in tune with the natural rhythms of life, with the budding trees, the catfish, and with the emotions of others. Unfortunately, the contractor and Doug represent the future.

"The Ice House" is a lament for the traditional ways of an agrarian society that bespoke an ordered existence and a criticism of the new values of a technological one that seem to encourage chaos. Although opposed to romanticizing the past, Gordon longed for the stability and order found in the pre-Civil War South, a stability that was based on a hierarchial arrangement of classes and a close relationship to the land. She was convinced that twentieth century life bordered on anarchy. Later, after converting to Catholicism, she found, in her religion, the order that she was seeking, but at the time she wrote "The Ice House," she saw nature as the only counterbalance to the confusion and disorder that accompanied the industrial society.

Style and Technique

The spare, economical style and the objective point of view that distinguish "The Ice House" are also found in many of Ernest Hemingway's stories. Like Hemingway, Gordon presents her tale in a straightforward fashion: The author is unobtrusive, and the story appears to evolve and develop by itself. In *How to Read a Novel* (1957), Gordon labels this approach dramatic; she suggests that characters should be revealed by their actions as they respond to others and to the environment.

Therefore, because it exposes or displays characters, the environment assumes an enhanced position. Although the details and events in Gordon's fiction are realistic, she invests objects with more than a literal significance because of their role in determining character. For example, in "The Ice House" the manner in which the characters view the bones of the dead soldiers is indicative of their moral stance.

In "The Ice House," the details of the landscape and the use of dialect serve to recreate the atmosphere of the southern countryside, closely based on the Kentucky tobacco region of Gordon's childhood. Because she evokes the South in her fiction, Gordon has been labeled a regional writer, implying a limited appeal, but although her setting is often the South, her themes are universal.

Barbara Wiedemann

THE ICE WAGON GOING DOWN THE STREET

Author: Mavis Gallant (1922-   )
Type of plot: Psychological
Time of plot: 1950-1960
Locale: Toronto, with extensive flashbacks to Paris and Geneva
First published: 1963

> *Principal characters:*
> PETER FRAZIER, a middle-aged Canadian, home after ten
>   unsuccessful years abroad
> SHEILAH, his wife
> AGNES BRUSEN, a former colleague in Geneva

The Story

Peter and Sheilah Frazier console themselves on Sunday mornings by remembering the people they met during the decade they spent trying to live a charmed life abroad. Now they are "back where they started," in Toronto, living with Lucille, Peter's down-to-earth sister. They do not have plans for the future, and they have become soured by "the international thing"; unlike other expatriates, Peter was neither "crooked" nor "smart" enough to find shady business opportunities in postwar Europe. Now as in the past, they try to believe that "hazy and marvellous" experiences lie ahead of them. In order to believe in this wonderful future, they must avoid the dreary present, so they spend their Sunday morning recalling the years that they spent in Europe, carrying the reader back with them to the Paris and Geneva of their past.

In their decade of genteel drifting, only four months in Paris are charmed. Peter does not need to work, for his comfortably endowed childhood has been extended by an inheritance, and Sheilah loves him. They live "in the future" until the money runs out, and then they are "never as happy again." When Lucille finds Peter a lowly job as a filing clerk in Geneva, Peter keeps his self-esteem by convincing himself that a position befitting his social status and family connections will come his way. He rationalizes his situation by deciding that there is a conspiracy among Canadian diplomats and businesspeople to punish him, and he becomes secretive about his job. He tries to cultivate connections so that he and Sheilah can move in the proper social circles. Peter behaves as if he "had been sent by a universal inspector to see how things in Geneva were being run," and as if "his real life [were] a secret so splendid he could share it with no one but himself."

His image and his secretiveness are put to the test when a young Canadian woman, Agnes Brusen, becomes his boss. His first assumption, that she is there to spy on him, soon evaporates when he sees her transparent character and is able to recognize her origins. He categorizes her as a provincial person, the product of simple immigrant ambitions; she is devout, purposeful, hardworking, unsophisticated, and direct. She does not seem to have anything that she wants to conceal or of which she is ashamed, and this makes Peter even more defensive and secretive. At a fancy dress party, where Sheilah is in her element and seems to find a lover, Peter recognizes that this social scene has unnerved Agnes and left her "gasping for life." When he helps her home, she tells him of her childhood in Saskatchewan: "I'm not from any other place." Now and two days later, she emphasizes a memory of early morning in her childhood home when she got up alone before her large family crowded the house. Unlike the freezing winter scene in Geneva, this is a picture of summertime, when she looked through the window and saw the ice wagon going down the street: "It's you, you, once in your life alone in the universe. You think you know everything that can happen. . . . Nothing is ever like that again." Agnes's disillusionment with the world of educated people strikes a chord in Peter; he feels that if it were not for Sheilah, he would be like Agnes.

The story ends rather suddenly when Peter shifts back from his memory of Agnes to the present in Toronto. It is implied that not much has changed in the years after Geneva. Nothing has been as important for Peter as that moment of self-disclosure with Agnes, the one secret he has kept from Sheilah. However, whatever the private importance, it is clear that nothing has changed in Peter's attitude toward himself, toward Sheilah, or toward other people.

Themes and Meanings

This is a story of evasiveness, the portrait of a man who wants to avoid the judgment of his own character and of his accomplishments in life. It is a story without a real climax because the Fraziers have settled into a flat, self-protective lifestyle, without significant action, purpose, or emotion. As the narrative moves forward, their present is replaced by recollected incidents, but these incidents are remarkable for their insignificance and inconclusiveness, and the Fraziers' memory game is designed to free them from the emptiness of the present so that they can daydream of a glorious future.

In a sense, Peter breaks the rules of the memory game on this particular Sunday morning. He remembers Agnes Brusen, with whom he almost had an intimate relationship: "It is almost as if they had run away together, silly as children, irresponsible as lovers." It is appropriate that they do not become lovers and do not "run away"; Peter does not even fantasize about what might have been. The emotional flatness of his temperament leads him to conclude with relief, "Anyway, nothing happened."

However, the image of Agnes Brusen has become embedded in his memory. His half-conscious recognition of her significance to him is, perhaps, the climax of the story, although that recognition has such low voltage that Peter finds it easy to remind himself, "Sheilah is here, it is a true Sunday morning, with its dimness and headache and remorse and regrets, and this is life." It is evident that Peter does not want to face the fact that his life might have been more true or more real, and that Agnes Brusen is an image of the narrow but authentic life that he has missed.

The contrast between Peter and Agnes is more striking than the similarity that Peter wishes to recognize. It is true that they are both "lost" in "the international thing," but he only partly realizes that she has a strength of character that he lacks. The image that she recaptures from memory reflects, as he knows, Agnes's integrity as a person and the self-confidence to lead a more purposeful life. Although the content of Agnes's childhood vision is so ordinary that it hardly excites interest, what is important is the depth of feeling and wonder with which she invests the scene. Peter's own children are cheered by the return to Toronto, which they want to call home; Agnes has a sense of continuity and rootedness in her identity, whereas Peter realizes that he does not and that the best for which he can hope is that "everything works out, somehow or other."

Style and Technique

This is a psychological sketch of a man who fails to develop and who has replaced action in the world with a compensatory world of recollection and wishes. The form of the story mirrors his state of being. It is a narrative in which nothing happens; there is no climax, and what almost happened has become the object of circular recollection. Apart from the framing scenes in the present, the story is made up of scenes arranged chronologically, but the movement forward that occupies the reader leads to new images and situations that only confirm the initial psychological insights. Peter does not change, nor is he really revealed to the reader more fully. Temporal and spatial displacement are emphasized to heighten the sense of a lost character without any sense of direction.

The story is not an intensive dramatization of this state of being, however, for the narrative voice is a prominent part of the texture of the story. This sardonic voice is counterpointed with the material of Peter's experience, and the satiric and ironic commentary becomes more engaging than the lives and situations presented to the reader. This commentary joins with key images, such as the ice wagon going down the street, to entertain and challenge the reader intellectually while the realistic detail of Peter's experience loses dramatic impact. As the character becomes less coherent, the authority of the omniscient narrator becomes more reliable. In this way, the strong voice that might have seemed intrusive establishes itself as the only stable center in a story that lacks the order that has been traditionally guaranteed by plot and character.

Denis Sampson

THE ICICLE

Author: Abram Tertz (Andrei Sinyavsky, 1925-1997)
Type of plot: Fantasy
Time of plot: The 1950's
Locale: Soviet Union
First published: "Gololeditsa," 1961 (English translation, 1963)

Principal characters:
VASILY, the narrator of the story and its intended reader
NATASHA, his girlfriend
BORIS, her estranged husband, who is still in love with her
COLONEL TARASOV, the officer in charge of Vasily's case

The Story

"The Icicle" is a structurally complex story. It is told by a first-person narrator to "Vasily," who, the reader later learns, is a future incarnation of the narrator himself. In the story's preface, the narrator urges Vasily to find and marry Natasha "before it is too late." The narration that follows will explain this advice.

Shortly before New Year's Eve, the narrator, who has yet to be identified, and Natasha are sitting outside discussing the unseasonably icy weather. During their conversation, the narrator attempts to push his memory as far as it will go and suddenly finds himself projected into what is apparently an Ice Age landscape. The unnerving experience lasts only a moment, but as the couple begin to walk home, they are approached by a large woman walking on the ice. The narrator fancies that he knows her life's story and that in the near future she will slip and fall on the ice. His prediction comes true, and in the conversation that follows, his surmises about her past are confirmed as well.

Against his better judgment, the narrator is persuaded by Natasha to attend a New Year's party at which her former husband, Boris, is also expected to be present. As the New Year approaches, the narrator compares the candles burning on the tree to a man's life. He identifies with one particular candle, and as he whimsically attempts to guess how long he will live, he has a compelling vision of himself approaching death at age eighty-nine. In an effort to dispel the mood of his vision, he offers to read the minds of the party guests. His performance is entirely convincing, but in the course of it he begins to perceive more than one individual in each of the people present. In particular, he realizes that one young man has in previous existences been primarily either prostitutes or priests. He tries to avoid subjecting Natasha to this kind of scrutiny, but as they leave, he realizes that she is missing part of her head.

During the days that follow, the narrator becomes acquainted with his own various pasts and futures. At one point in the twenty-fourth century, he is addressed as Vasily by his wife, who asks him about Russian literature. On another occasion, he realizes that the incarnation that he is watching is aware of him as well. The threat to Natasha that was suggested by his vision of her at the New Year's party is finally articulated: She will be killed by a falling icicle on the nineteenth of January. In a vain attempt to avoid fate, the narrator extorts fifteen hundred rubles from Boris in order to take her out of town. Boris, however, denounces him to the police, and they are arrested before they reach their destination. The narrator attempts to warn Natasha, but as he does so, he realizes that by articulating the threat he has made it inevitable. The narrator's considerable gifts are put to the service of the state, and Natasha, at his request, is put under surveillance, but at the appointed hour on the appointed day she does walk under the icicle and loses her life at the same moment that the narrator loses his gift. In one of his last visions, the narrator sees himself as Vasily standing outside a lighted window trying to attract the attention of Natasha, who sits inside reading. His story is addressed to that Vasily of the future whose happiness with Natasha is still possible.

Themes and Meanings

In one sense, "The Icicle" is about writers and writing. The narrator's reasons for undertaking the story are certainly compelling, but readers can assume that all writers have equally compelling reasons for their work. Practical aspects of the trade are addressed: The narrator hopes that his story will come out in a large edition not for money or glory but because he hopes to increase his chances of reaching Vasily, his future reader. The question of who this future reader will be is central to the story. In an epilogue, the narrator observes that because, like any other writer, he must reread his work, he already has at least one reader. The idea of writing only for himself does not present a difficulty for him, because he realizes that he is writing for a future self. Writing to this future self is his way of combating the inevitability and senselessness of death. Indeed, he observes that "most books are letters to the future with a reminder of what happened."

Another central theme of "The Icicle" is the continuity of life. As the narrator watches the parade of past existences at the New Year's party, he realizes that anyone who examines himself closely will find simultaneously existing within himself thieves, liars, and cheats as well as perhaps great creative artists. Following Natasha's senseless death, it is also important to him to realize that none of these multiple existences is lost, although they may be forgotten. "The Icicle" is his letter to the future, his attempt to remind a future incarnation of his present existence during the Soviet 1950's.

Style and Technique

"The Icicle" is unified by the image of ice that runs through the entire story. The Russian title of the story, "Gololeditsa," refers not to the icicle that killed Natasha but to the icy conditions that produced it. The narrator's first vision of the past takes him to the Ice Age, and he first feels alarm for Natasha after helping the woman who has fallen on the ice. Following that experience, the narrator feels that he must treat Natasha as he would a bag of eggs, and he decides to take her home by trolley because "it really was very slippery." Later, after he knows precisely what will happen to Natasha, he is depressed by the sight of icicles that grow "like mushrooms" on the neighboring roofs.

There is, however, another "icicle" in the story that contributes as much to Natasha's death as does the one that strikes her. Following the narrator's arrest, he is asked to predict the future of Colonel Tarasov, who is handling his case. As he absently answers the question, he has a vision of the entire world covered with ice, and the colonel, who in every incarnation has achieved one rank higher than he did in the previous one, has become a gigantic gleaming icicle in control of everything around him. Specific references to the political climate of the Soviet Union in the early 1950's are infrequent in "The Icicle," but in the epilogue, where the fates of the various characters are summarized, the narrator states very clearly that people such as Colonel Tarasov were not needed following 1953 (the year of Joseph Stalin's death). When one recalls that the period of general relaxation that followed Stalin's death is referred to as the "Thaw," it becomes possible to see Natasha's arbitrary death as produced by the political climate of the period rather than by specific meteorological conditions. "The Icicle," however, is more than mere allegory. Its fantastic hypothesis (the possibility that each of us contains multiple past and future existences) raises it above the concrete reality of the Soviet 1950's and gives it universal significance.

Sandra Rosengrant

IDIOTS FIRST

Author: Bernard Malamud (1914-1986)
Type of plot: Fable
Time of plot: The mid-twentieth century
Locale: New York
First published: 1961

> *Principal characters:*
> MENDEL, the protagonist, a poor man
> ISAAC, his retarded son
> A PAWNBROKER
> MR. FISHBEIN, a wealthy man
> YASCHA, an old rabbi
> GINZBURG, a mysterious figure

The Story

"Idiots First" begins with the stopping of Mendel's clock as the old man awakens in fright. The importance of time in the story is foreshadowed in the opening paragraph when the reader is told that Mendel "wasted minutes sitting at the edge of the bed." Once moving, he dresses, summons his son Isaac, and, pocketing a paper bag containing his modest savings, leads his son into the night. The old man seems very fearful, and he warns Isaac to avoid Ginzburg, who came to see Mendel the day before. "Don't talk to him or go with him if he asks you," Mendel cautions. Then as an afterthought he adds, "Young people he don't bother so much."

Though Mendel always refers to him as a boy, Isaac, who has "thick hair greying the sides of his head," is not the child his father perceives him to be. Rather, he is the "idiot" of the title, a thirty-nine-year-old man with the mind of a child. Facing his own death, Mendel attempts in the course of the story to provide for Isaac in the only way he can, sending him by train to California, where he will live with his Uncle Leo. The story traces Mendel's efforts to raise train fare to secure Isaac's safety before his own time runs out.

Their first stop is the pawnbroker's shop, where Mendel tries to get the thirty-five dollars he needs to make up the difference between his savings and Isaac's ticket to California by pawning his watch. Despite Mendel's protestations that it cost him sixty dollars, the pawnbroker will allow him only eight dollars for the old watch. Though Mendel's desperation is obvious as he despairs of finding the money he needs, the moneylender ignores his pleas.

Next Mendel and Isaac visit Mr. Fishbein, a wealthy philanthropist. He proves no less hard-hearted than the pawnbroker as he, too, turns down Mendel's entreaties. Insisting that his "fixed policy" is to give money only to organized charities, Fishbein shows scorn for Mendel's plight and contempt for Isaac's condition. Though he does offer to feed them in his kitchen, the philanthropist throws the pair out of his house with the advice that Mendel should put Isaac in an institution.

As they approach a park bench to rest, a shadowy, bearded figure arises before them. Mendel pales and waves his arms, Isaac yowls, and the stranger disappears into the bushes. The clock strikes ten. From earlier hints, the reader suspects this figure to be the mysterious Ginzburg. He is encountered again when Mendel takes Isaac to a cafeteria for food and they flee from a "heavyset" man eating soup.

His other options exhausted, Mendel now goes to see an old rabbi, to whom he appeals for charity. Although his wife insists that they cannot help, the old rabbi, though he has no money, gives Mendel his new fur-lined coat. The wife tries to snatch it back, but Mendel tears it from her. As Mendel and Isaac run into the street, the wife chasing them, the old rabbi diverts her attention by falling to the floor in an apparent heart attack. As they "ran through the streets with the rabbi's new fur-lined caftan," after them "noiselessly ran Ginzburg."

It is very late when Mendel buys a ticket for Isaac and they hurry to the train. The train is still standing in the station, but the gate to the platform is shut; a heavy, bearded man in uniform guards the entrance and refuses to allow them to pass. "Too late," he tells Mendel, "Already past twelve." Mendel begs for a favor, but the guard callously refuses. "Favors you had enough already. For you the train is gone. You shoulda been dead already at midnight. I told you that yesterday. This is the best I can do."

Recognizing his antagonist for the first time as the mysterious Ginzburg, Mendel begs again: "For myself . . . I don't ask a thing. But what will happen to my boy?" Isaac is not his responsibility, Ginzburg tells Mendel, and when the old man asks him what his responsibility is, he says, "To create conditions. To make happen what happens." Later he claims that he serves the "law," and when Mendel asks which law, he says, "the cosmic universal law."

His pleas unsuccessful, Mendel attacks Ginzburg, who responds by threatening to freeze him to death. As Mendel's life fades, he thinks only of dying without helping Isaac. Mendel sees his own terror reflected in Ginzburg's eyes, while Ginzburg sees his terrible wrath mirrored in Mendel's eyes. Suddenly, Ginzburg "beheld a shimmering, starry, blinding light that produced darkness." In the grip of some greater power, Ginzburg allows Mendel to put Isaac on the train. After he is settled and the train is moving, Mendel returns to the platform to see what has become of Ginzburg.

Themes and Meanings

In this simple story, Bernard Malamud explores the power of love to change the universe. Throughout the story, the world appears bleak, cold, and dark, and the mood of the tale is one of despair. In a world characterized by the mercenary pawnbroker, the heartless philanthropist, and the greedy wife of the old rabbi, Mendel seems foolish even to hope he might save Isaac, but it is finally his hope in the face of desperate odds that turns the events at the end of the story. Though Mendel's time has run out, some power greater than death stays Ginzburg's cold stare for the final minutes Mendel needs to complete the task for which he lives.

When, in the final scene of the story, Ginzburg identifies himself with a mechanical cosmic law that binds him as well as everyone else, the reader recognizes in him more than a symbol of death, though he is that as well. He is the representative of a meaningless universe in which human beings can only play out their destinies against a background of impersonal forces or "laws." Cold and heartless, Ginzburg, as Mendel tells him, does not "understand what it means" to be human. His world, like that of the other selfish, unfeeling, and greedy characters in the story, is a world without love.

Ginzburg's opposite is the old rabbi; he says to Mendel, "God will give you," and offers his own new coat to help Isaac. The rabbi has faith in God, but he also acts himself with charity and love, proving that these qualities are not so dead as other characters make them seem. It is through men such as the old rabbi that God works and by their faith that He lives.

Mendel, a long-suffering old man, might be expected to welcome death as an end to a painful life. His love for Isaac has been the meaning of his life, however, and his determination to see his son safe gives him strength to go on even in the face of the inevitable. He sacrifices his last strength in a final attempt to get Isaac to the train, and in that moment the power of love in the universe is revealed. As Ginzburg's power over Mendel fails before a "starry, blinding light that produced darkness," love, faith, and hope triumph over the meaningless universe.

Style and Technique

Superficially, this story is typical of the dark mood of literary naturalism. Its realistic setting and effective Yiddish dialect heighten these effects. Beginning with his first hints that the mysterious Ginzburg might be more than simply another character, though, Malamud gradually builds toward the mystical vision at the end, which totally changes the meaning of the piece. With the exception of the role of Ginzburg, symbols are used sparingly and seem an uncontrived aspect of the narrative. This is true of the various characters who represent the failure of human values, and even more true of the several references to the sky and stars. Only at the end of the story, when Ginzburg beholds the "shimmering, starry, blinding light that produced darkness," does the reader connect the heavens and the stars, points of light in a dark universe, with God. Malamud's ability to combine realism and mysticism in a style that does justice to both in large measure accounts for the powerful impact of "Idiots First."

William E. Grant

IDLE DAYS ON THE YANN

Author: Lord Dunsany (Edward John Moreton Drax Plunkett, 1878-1957)
Type of plot: Fantasy
Time of plot: The early twentieth century
Locale: The River Yann, in Dunsany's imaginary Lands of Dream
First published: 1910

> *Principal characters:*
> THE UNNAMED NARRATOR, a traveler
> THE CAPTAIN, whose ship is the *Bird of the River*

The Story

The narrator arrives at the Yann, where, as prophesied, he finds the *Bird of the River.* Singing sailors swing the ship out into the central stream, while the narrator is interviewed by the captain about his homeland and destination. The ship sails from Fair Belzoond, whose gods are "least and humblest," not very threatening, and easily appeased. The narrator discloses that he hails from Ireland, in Europe, but is mocked, for captain and crew deny the existence of any such places. When he reveals the lands where his fancy dwells, they compliment him, for these places are at least imaginable, if unknown. He bargains for passage to the Gates of Yann.

As the sun sets and the darkness of the adjoining jungle deepens, the sailors hoist lanterns and then kneel to propitiate their gods, five or six at a time, so that no god will be addressed by more than one man at any moment. Meanwhile, the helmsman, holding the ship in midstream, sings the helmsman's prayer, common to all helmsmen of whatever faith. Not to be alone, the narrator also prays, but to a god long ago deserted by humankind. Night descends as the prayers die out, yet the sailors feel comforted in the face of the Great Night to come.

During the night, under the guidance of the ever-singing helmsman, they pass a number of cities and tributaries with exotic names. Finally, shortly after daybreak, they harbor at Mandaroon. While the sailors gather fruit, the narrator visits the city, silent, moss-covered, and apparently deserted. A sentinel at the gate informs him that questions are forbidden, because when the people awake the gods will die. When the narrator inquires further about these gods, he is driven off.

The ship sets forth again under the full sun, accompanied now by choirs of insects, including the butterflies, whose hymns are beyond human ears, rising to pay homage in flight and song to the vivifying sun. The sun works otherwise with people and beasts: It puts them to sleep. The narrator himself is lulled into dreams of a triumphant but mysterious return.

He awakes to find the captain buckling on his scimitar; they have arrived at Astahahn, where an open court surrounded by colonnades fronts the river and where the people follow ancient rites of dignity and solemnity; antiquity is the rule. The people ignore the passing ship, intent on their ancient rituals, but one bystander states that the occupation of the city is to preserve Time, in order to preserve the gods. These gods, moreover, are "all those . . . whom Time has not yet slain."

Beyond Astahahn the river widens, and a second evening descends. The sailors pray, as before, and the helmsman's prayer guides the ship onward into the dark. In the morning they have arrived at Perdondaris, a fine and celebrated place, welcome after the jungle. The captain is haggling with a fat merchant. The contest proceeds as if by script, with extravagant rhetorical gestures, the captain at one point threatening suicide because the price offered would disgrace him. Finally he entreats his lesser gods of Belzoond—whom he had previously threatened to loose on the city—and the merchant yields. The watching sailors applaud. The captain breaks out a cask of wine, and their thoughts are soon back home.

In the evening, the narrator visits the city, a formidable place with a massive, tower-surmounted wall bearing plaques advertising the fate of an army that once besieged it. However, the people are dancing in honor of "the god they know not," because a thunderstorm has terrified them with images of the fires of death. The narrator admires the wealth and prosperity of the city until he comes to the outer wall, where he finds a gate of ivory, carved out of one solid piece. He flees to the ship, fearing the wrath of the animal from which the tusk was taken but revealing his secret to no one.

Finally he tells the captain, who agrees that the gate is recent and that such a gigantic beast could not have been killed by a human. The captain decides to escape immediately. Later the narrator learns that some force has indeed wrecked the once mighty city in a single day.

Again they pass a night on the river. As before, the helmsman prays the helmsman's prayer, to whatever god is listening, beseeching safe return to all sailors. His voice rises above the silent river in the songs of Durl and Duz, and fair Belzoond. The narrator awakes to lifting mists and a broadened river tumbling as it mingles with the brawling Irillion from the crags of Glorm. Freshened, the river shrugs off the torpor of the jungle and sweeps through cliffs. It broadens again to wind through marshes, then reaches further mountains with a number of villages, passed by night to the helmsman's songs.

They pass more cities before arriving at Nen, the last great city, where they anchor. The Wanderers, a weird, dark tribe, are also in the town for their once-in-every-seven-years visit. These savages have taken over the city, dancing like dervishes, playing strange music, and performing feats of desert magic, to the consternation of the people of Nen.

The narrator must leave before he can hear the Wanderers' night-hymn, echoed by wolves on the heights surrounding the city. They sail on in silence under the setting sun, until they reach the Gate of Yann, formed by two barrier-cliffs at the mouth of the river, before the sea. Anchoring at the foot of the cliffs, they take a lingering farewell, for they sense that they will not meet again. The captain commends the soul of the narrator to his humble gods of Belzoond.

Themes and Meanings

The story offers little overt material for analysis, for the plot is slight and lacks the conventional conflict and resolution of narrative. In fact, Lord Dunsany stated repeatedly that his material was the stuff of dreams and spontaneous storytelling, that he was not aware of promoting any themes, even by symbol or allegory, and that the only meanings in his stories were those that emerged subconsciously. That does not seem to leave much with which to work.

However, a little examination reveals subtle patterns. The gods are repeatedly alluded to, and the helmsman's prayer stitches the story together. Peoples are distinguished and identified by their god or gods; yet these tribal, or at best, regional, gods are not in conflict with one another. Furthermore, there seems to be no rivalry among them: The helmsmen along the river pray indiscriminately to "whatever god may hear." This is a continent of mutual toleration.

However, if the function of the gods is protection and there is no antagonism among them, from what, then, do the gods protect? The story itself gives some clues. Although there is little conventional plot, the structure reflects the action depicted: It is a journey interrupted with stops, and each stop provides a climax of a certain intensity. On the first day, the ship passes the preserved city of Mandaroon, where life is spent in sleep that the gods may not die; that afternoon brings the wordless choral dance of insects and butterflies in praise of the sun, in whom they find life for the moment, regardless of the future. That afternoon they come to Astahahn, where stately rites charm Time into immobility, for otherwise he will destroy the gods. The second day records the bargain at Perdondaris, mediated by the gods, and the discovery of an impending doom that cannot be deflected by prayers to the god they know not; it ends with the helmsman's prayer to all gods. On the next day, the ship reaches Nen, where the strange gods of the Wanderers have intimidated the people, and finally there is journey's end, which closes with celebrating the little gods of Belzoond who have guided the expedition. Threaded throughout is the chant of the helmsman to all gods.

This sequence does not add up to a definitive statement, and it is not intended to. However, the story consistently suggests that although the gods may be powerless, people need to defer to and respect them in order to survive their voyages—as, on the first night, the narrator finds himself impelled to pray by the example of the sailors.

Style and Technique

The term most often associated with Dunsany, also appearing frequently in his writing, is "dream," with its relatives "dreamy" and "dreamlike." Some of this derives from his subject matter, for in much of his writing he gives substance to the beasts, men, and gods of his Lands of Dream, a fantasy world distinct from the waking here and now, one endowed with the power of myth. However, much of it can be attributed to the peculiarities of his style. This story is a good example.

"Idle Days on the Yann" resembles dreams first in its narrative inconsequence. Instead of following an action with a clearly defined beginning, middle, and end, it merely floats along the surface of the river; what happens does not seem to connect with what preceded or follows, except as marking stages of passage. There is no apparent reason why Astahahn should appear on the first day or Nen on the last. There is danger, as there is danger in dreams, but it all seems to come from beyond. Danger is something that happens, not something caused.

The themes are also as evanescent as the meanings of dreams. The reader senses connections in the way that a dreamer gropes for significance; yet the links fragment and the strands part. Meaning drifts off, dangling somewhere just beyond reach, to be replaced by wonder and vague foreboding.

Beyond all else, however, Dunsany accomplishes this creation of a dreamworld by his use of language. This is most apparent in the place-names and the regions that he creates—Belzoond, Darl, Duz, Yann, Irillion. However, more subtle and more telling are three other qualities. First is the flat, deliberate narrative style, in which events are sketched as if they were taking place on a screen in front of the narrator; he records them, rather than taking part in them. This trance-narration has elements of both children's literature and biblical apocalyptic literature. Second is a use of adjectives and adverbs as modifiers at the expense of more graphic metaphors and images; this lack of definition blurs the events and forces the reader to complete the outline. The third is a habit of compound construction: Long series of clauses are butt-joined by "ands," as in stories told by children. These combine to create a unique representation of pseudodreams in words.

James L. Livingston

IF THE RIVER WAS WHISKEY

Author: T. Coraghessan Boyle (Thomas John Boyle, 1948-   )
Type of plot: Domestic realism
Time of plot: Probably the 1970's or 1980's
Locale: A lake in the mountains
First published: 1988

> *Principal characters:*
> DAD, an alcoholic who has recently lost his job
> CAROLINE, his wife
> TILDEN ("TILLER"), their son

The Story

Tilden, a sixth-grader who is also called "Tiller," is the son of an unemployed alcoholic father. In a vain effort to turn his life around, the father, his wife, Caroline, and Tiller have gone to spend a month at Caroline's father's cabin on a lake. Caroline sits in her deck chair watching as Tiller rises to the surface of the lake where he has been snorkeling, jumps out of the water, and immediately casts a fishing line into the water. Back at the cabin, Tiller's depressed father pours himself a tall vodka and soda from a plastic half-gallon jug, although it is not even noon. He needs a couple of drinks just to begin to feel good. Later, Tiller is sitting in a local bar where his parents are drinking heavily with another couple. The men talk at cross-purposes, the stranger about building supplies, his father about his failed career as a blues musician. The women gossip about people his mother has never met. Both parents ignore their son, who sits quietly watching a neon beer sign flash on and off.

Tiller spends much time alone on this family vacation. In the early mornings, while his parents still lie sleeping, he rows across the lake to fish a certain cove where large pike are said to lurk, according to an old man who lives in the cabin next to Tilden's. Tiller dresses warmly for these outings and always wears the lifejacket his mother insists on. The lifejacket obstructs his casting, however, so he removes it as soon as he begins to fish. As the day warms up, he removes one article of clothing after another, sometimes remaining nude in the privacy of the cove.

The narrative shifts from this tranquil scene back to the cabin later in the day, where Tiller's father and mother are having an ugly row. The father rouses from a semiconscious, alcohol-induced state to overhear his wife tell their son that his father is a drunk. Furious, the father leaps from the bed and grabs his wife by the shoulders. Tiller escapes from the cabin, leaving his parents barking mutual accusations. The father accuses his wife of being just as drunk as he; she retaliates by pointing out that at least she has a job. He says he will get another job; she accuses him of spending no time whatsoever with their son and calls him a lousy father. He grabs a bottle of cheap whiskey, her drink, and pours a large serving. They declare their hatred for each other and she leaves.

Tilden tries not to think about his parents, but when he does think of his father, he remembers the day he came home from school to find his father home, playing the guitar in a darkened, smoky room with empty beer bottles and a liquor bottle within easy reach. His father ignored his greeting; he just kept playing "If the River Was Whiskey" repeatedly on a guitar that he rarely uses. His father could not explain the meaning of the song, but he offered Tiller his first sip of beer.

Tiller's dad decides to prove his wife wrong: He is not a drunk and not a lousy father. He will spend the day fishing with his son and not drink a drop. Tiller excitedly packs a lunch, little realizing that his father is already feeling queasy from lack of alcohol. He takes his father to the cove in search of the special pike, and they fish until dark. Although his father is tired and out of cigarettes, he suddenly comes to life when a fish takes his line and he fights to bring it in. He triumphantly hauls in a big pike, but Tiller knows better: It is no pike, but a bottom-feeding carp, a garbage fish that no one eats.

At 2:00 A.M. the next morning, Tiller's father reflects on what is to come: Caroline is leaving him and consequently he is losing his son. Almost suicidally depressed, he falls asleep and dreams he is out in the boat with Tiller, utterly incapable of any action, when suddenly they are sucked deep under water. He sees his son going down, and he can do nothing to save him.

Themes and Meanings

Many stories in T. Coraghessan Boyle's collection *If the River Was Whiskey* (1989) deal with similar themes of illusion become disillusion. Tiller's father once had the illusion of becoming a professional musician, but the reader sees him as a disillusioned man who has failed in every aspect of life. Not only did he fail as a musician, but he also has failed as a breadwinner for his family, as a husband, and, most important, as a father to his son, Tiller. Caroline, Dad, and Tiller form a dysfunctional nuclear family in which each member seems to be in his or her own world. Caroline is a background character who comes forward to proclaim her hatred for her husband. Once sweet lovers, they are now worst enemies. She watches her son swim, but does not join him; in the bar, her attention is completely focused on a stranger she has just met. Tiller's father is incapable of sharing anything with him. On the contrary, when they are in the boat together, Tiller seems to take on the role of his father's caretaker, and Tiller's illusions of having a great time with his father and catching a great fish change to disillusionment with his father's condition and the carp his father catches.

This story is one of loss and alienation: the father's loss of hope, of family, of pride, of self-respect, and the son's alienation from both parents, but especially from his father. Although he avoids thinking about his parents in the same way he avoids thinking of "bald-headed stick people in Africa" and other equally disturbing and inexplicable topics, it is his relationship with his father that suffers a death blow in the futile effort to connect through a fishing trip.

Style and Technique

Cutting from one scene to another with no more transition than a series of asterisks between scenes, the narrative might be difficult to follow if it were not for the shift in point of view from father to son. The shifting point of view guides the reader through a vague chronology and minimally sketched settings; more important, it allows the reader to feel the isolation and increasing alienation of young Tilden while simultaneously registering the inner torture of the failing and ailing father.

Much of the story revolves around water imagery. The song from which the story takes its title figures prominently in the narrative: "If the river was whiskey/ And I was a divin' duck/ I'd swim to the bottom/ Drink myself back up." It is this song that the father plays repeatedly after losing his job, that Tiller tells his dad he likes a lot, that the father explains to his son by saying, "I guess he just liked whiskey, that's all." Caroline drinks Four Roses whiskey, but Dad's "whiskey" is vodka. Dad has been in a river of vodka and has drunk his way down. He has lost his job, his wife is leaving him, and as a result he also is losing his son.

The story closes with the father's drunken dream replaying the failed fishing trip, but with tragic consequences. Just as in the actual fishing trip, the father is a powerless figure, but in his dream he and Tilden are suddenly sucked under water. (Here the reader may recall that Tilden makes a habit of removing his lifejacket.) He watches his son being pulled farther and farther down and cannot save him. His son is dying, drowning in a river of whiskey of his father's making.

Linda Ledford-Miller

I'M A FOOL

Author: Sherwood Anderson (1876-1941)
Type of plot: Psychological
Time of plot: About 1919
Locale: Rural Ohio
First published: 1922

> *Principal characters:*
> THE NARRATOR, the protagonist, a nineteen-year-old boy
> LUCY WESSEN, his "girl"
> WILBUR WESSEN, her brother
> BURT, the black stableboy

The Story

The narrator is a nineteen-year-old boy whose life revolves around his job as a swipe at a local racetrack. Though it is a menial job with no future, the young man brags to the reader about it, describing it in a sort of homespun lyricism that purportedly shows his genuine feelings about his career among horses, jockeys, and trainers. Significantly, his best friend and fellow worker is a black man, Burt, and the young man boasts of the good life that they lead, traveling from track to track tending the horses. What the reader infers from all this is that the swipe's protestations are clearly part of a deep-seated dissatisfaction with his life. In narrating his "adventures" at the track, for example, the swipe remarks on the college men in the grandstand, who "put on airs" and think that they are superior because of their education. However, the narrator himself does precisely the same thing. One payday, he walks into a bar, orders a drink and expensive cigars, and spurns a well-dressed man with a Windsor tie and a cane who is standing near him and whom he accuses of "putting on airs."

It is the narrator's detestation of the false front and his own use of it that is at the heart of the story. Sitting in the grandstand, the narrator meets Wilbur Wessen and his sister, Lucy. The Wessens take a liking to the swipe, and he in turn becomes attracted to Lucy. He is impressed with her breeding, her charm, and her gentleness, and in an impetuous moment he introduces himself as Walter Mathers, the son of the owner of a noted racehorse.

Later that evening the narrator and Miss Lucy go off to a quiet spot by the lake, and the young man describes his feelings, revealing a sensitivity and gentleness that belie the demeaning crudity of his life as a swipe. He learns that she and her brother are leaving soon by train, and he realizes then that he has lost her. By lying to her, giving her a false identity, he has cut off any possibility of her writing to him and of his being honest with her. He is hurt all the more by his realization that she genuinely cares for him, not because of his name or supposed wealth, but for himself.

At the end, Miss Lucy leaves, and the swipe has tears in his eyes, hating himself, convinced that he will never see her again and that he has been a fool.

Themes and Meanings

"I'm a Fool" is a poignant treatment of an adolescent's inferiority complex and of his painful journey to maturity and self-knowledge. The narrator is not conscious of his feelings of inferiority, but his constant comparing of his honest, good life at the track with the false, hypocritical life of the rich and cultured clearly gives the reader insight into the young man's problem.

In many of Sherwood Anderson's stories, young people struggle with unconscious desires and with an inability to explain or understand their feelings. The swipe does not understand why he lies to Miss Lucy, for example; he senses only that he was foolish to do so. When he declares that he wishes he could die or at least break a bone so that he could hurt, the young man expresses his feelings but does not understand that their source is not in his "love" for Miss Lucy but in his unconscious dislike for himself, his position in life, and his lack of security about a future—a security symbolized by the man with the Windsor tie and cane, who reappears as an image of contempt in the narrator's thoughts at the close of the story.

On another level, the young man's companionship with Burt is an example of his naïveté about the implications of his social status. As a black man with no education, Burt occupies the lowest rung of the social ladder. As his friend, therefore, the swipe puts himself in the same position, though he invests it with the glories of romance and adventure, oblivious to his low-class family origins. He is, in effect, a fool, not because he lies but because he deludes himself about his background, his present, and his future.

Style and Technique

Anderson's use of the first-person narrator is crucial in creating the subtlety of "I'm a Fool" and illustrates the instinctive quality of Anderson's best work. A third-person narrator, for example, not only would have robbed the character of his emotional intensity but also would have revealed the fragility of a commonplace plot. Instead, the narrator's voice gives the almost banal situation an earnestness, an honesty, that is both powerful and moving.

Though the use of the first-person narrator was certainly not new, Anderson's adaptation of it for this kind of story is significant. Mark Twain had already created the character of Huck Finn in 1884 by allowing Huck himself to record his adventures in his Missouri vernacular. There is, in fact, even an echo of *Adventures of Huckleberry Finn* in "I'm a Fool" in the relationship between the narrator and the black man, Burt.

However, the relationship is suggestive more of the narrator's frustration than of his freedom and moral superiority, as is the case with Huck's relationship with Jim. Besides, Huck's narration is often of stirring action, satiric comedy, and shrewd character portrayal. By contrast, the narrator of "I'm a Fool" speaks more about his feelings;

he records in his ungrammatical English not the external action, but the internal, the private, the quiet experience of his emotions.

The indebtedness of "I'm a Fool" to Twain's *Adventures of Huckleberry Finn* is further evident in the skillful use of irony; like Huck, the swipe communicates deeper meanings than he intends. When, for example, the narrator describes the lakeside setting of his tryst with Miss Lucy, he uses the simplest analogies, comparing the evening to the sweetness of an orange. In so doing, the swipe reveals not only his simplicity but also his sensitivity, his almost poetic "soul."

Furthermore, when the narrator seems to stumble and digress from his "story," he is inadvertently giving clues to the reader about his feelings of inferiority, as when he discusses his family background and begins to mention his proud grandfather in Wales; "but never mind that," he concludes.

Thus, the use of the first-person narrator not only establishes a sensitive personality but also makes the story a collaboration between that personality and the reader, forcing the reader to draw inferences from the narrator's offhanded remarks. Collaboration such as this is a characteristic technique of twentieth century literature.

Finally, if "I'm a Fool" is indebted to *Adventures of Huckleberry Finn*, it is also in its own right a literary ancestor of such modern works as J. D. Salinger's *The Catcher in the Rye* (1951). Anderson's handling of the sensitive young narrator was emulated by Salinger in the characterization of Holden Caulfield, highlighting the conflict between the compromised world of the adult and the idealistic world of the adolescent. Though Holden is not uneducated in the same way as the swipe, he is as confused and frustrated as his predecessor.

"I'm a Fool" is a modern classic whose deceptively simple style is the chief method by which the emotions and personality of the central character are portrayed.

Edward Fiorelli

1936

I'M DREAMING OF ROCKET RICHARD

Author: Clark Blaise (1940-   )
Type of plot: Realism
Time of plot: Winter, 1952
Locale: Montreal and Florida
First published: 1974

> *Principal characters:*
> MANCE DESCHÊNES, JR., a ten-year-old boy
> MANCE DESCHÊNES, SR., his alcoholic father, a janitor
> MRS. MANCE DESCHÊNES, his mother, a thrifty homemaker
> LISE SCHMITZ, his mother's sister
> HOWIE SCHMITZ, Lise's husband, a successful dry cleaner

The Story

Mance Deschênes, Jr., is an industrious ten-year-old paper boy who lives on Montreal's Hutchinson Street with his alcoholic father and thrifty, caring, but tired mother. Mance works hard and does not think his life of poverty is a hardship. He enjoys going to hockey games and other simple pleasures in life. When his Aunt Lise Schmitz and Uncle Howie Schmitz, a successful dry cleaner with three stores, visit from New Hampshire, Mance begins to see his life in a different light. Howie and his wife always have a new car when they visit, and their children whine because they want things they do not have. Mance does not understand what his wealthy cousins could want when they have many wonderful possessions already.

Mance's father is hired as a janitor for a new, sixteen-room apartment building that winter. He is paid well, and the family receives a free three-room apartment in a safer and cleaner part of the city. They formerly had lived in the damp basement of the last building in which he worked. Now that they are on the ground floor, however, Mance's father is unhappy with the incessant ringing of the doorbell. His new income gives them a better standard of living, however, and the family even manages to save some money.

In the meantime, Uncle Howie and his family have packed up to leave their home and successful business in New Hampshire for North Hollywood, Florida. Soon afterward, the family buys a used Plymouth to make the long trip to Florida to visit the Schmitzes for Christmas at their request. Mance's father has his brother Réal and his family move into his apartment to look after the apartment building during their trip. The journey takes much longer than the Deschênes family had anticipated, and they arrive in Florida with little money left, despite Mrs. Deschênes's strict frugality. Before they arrive, Mance finds out that his father intends to sober up so that he can become the manager of one of the new Schmitz Dry Kleeneries that Howie plans to open in the North Hollywood area.

They arrive in time for Christmas week, but Mance has trouble enjoying the season as he normally does, because he is unable to fit into this foreign situation. He dreams of being back home with his ice rink and his hockey games, where he feels comfortable and complete. The Christmas carols here are in English and not his native French; there is no snow on the ground; it is too hot; and his father does not fit into the Florida scene with his blotchy red tan, his enormous hockey tattoo of Rocket Richard, and his ill-fitting clothes. Suddenly, Mance wishes that he were not a Deschênes, but sees himself becoming "Schmitz-like."

Later that week, he sees his mother and aunt on the beach talking about the wonderful plan they have arranged for his father and uncle to be business partners. Unfortunately, the women's planning turns out to be useless. Later, Mance watches his father and uncle walking on the beach and talking together, and he realizes that Howie is telling his father that such a partnership cannot work. Mance's father finally tells his family of his failure and resumes his drinking.

Out of money, the family drive back to Montreal. The trip takes almost a month because they have to stop in Georgia for a time to work and then sell the car to get bus fare back to Montreal. On their return, they find that Réal has taken such good care of the new building during their long absence that he has taken over his brother's job. Mance is surprised that his father takes the news so quietly, after trying the hardest he has ever tried in his life to do well, only to fail miserably.

Themes and Meanings

Clark Blaise's tragic story focuses on the ideas of familiarity, alienation, and, ultimately, rejection. These ideas are lived out by Mance, Jr., sometimes on his own, and often vicariously through his father. Mance does not realize how important his familiarity with daily life in Montreal is until feelings of alienation begin during his Christmas at Uncle Howie's. He hears foreign voices singing familiar carols on the radio, there is no snow as he is accustomed to at Christmas, and he cannot even console himself by listening to hockey scores on the radio. He feels alienated from the world of his relatives and wishes he could be in Montreal watching his hero, Rocket Richard.

When his father tries to fit in by removing his shirt like the others on the beach, his blotchy complexion and tattoo of Rocket Richard embarrass Mance. The image of his hockey hero now elicits shame instead of admiration. Mance's last foothold of familiarity has been removed; his hero has fallen, as has his estimation of his father. His father is oblivious to his own awkward appearance, and Mance sees himself wanting to become a Schmitz.

His father wants desperately to have a job in the dry-cleaning business but cannot fit Uncle Howie's ideal as a business partner or a man. He is turned down by Howie as he scampers along the seashore like a dog at Howie's heels. He understands that this is his last chance for greatness, but it is not until he returns to Montreal and finds that Réal has taken his job that he plummets from feelings of alienation to final rejection. In retrospect, the narrator sees that his father cannot even return to the familiarity of

Montreal for a respite and understands that he himself has rejected and alienated not only his father but also his hero, Rocket Richard, in an attempt to find a way out of his feelings of rejection toward himself.

Style and Technique

Blaise writes in a realistic, almost naturalistic, style with a minimum of symbols to convey his meaning to the reader clearly. The narrator speaks from the vantage point of age and experience. This perspective creates a credible character who is open and honest. Thinking back on his life, the narrator does not exhibit malice toward the difficulty he had in being poor. All of his memories of those days are nearly shining, as he describes with fervor the trips to the forum in his team shirt and how he cheered for Rocket Richard.

When the narrator was younger, he did not consider himself and his family as living in poverty. His life was filled with pleasure. It is only by comparison with the Schmitzes that he realizes his life is not as materially endowed as that of others. Blaise's use of a first-person narrator is skillfully done, as his narrator conceals the coming alienation and rejection until the last possible moment at the end of the story. There is little foreshadowing of this moment, and the reader is suddenly empathetic not with the determined and industrious Mance, Jr., but also with Mance, Sr., who is perhaps the most pathetic character presented.

In a sense, Blaise has created a tragedy of the common man. It is a tragedy that lacks a hero of noble birth, but Mance, Sr., has two fatal flaws—alcoholism and covetousness. He is unable to see when he has a good thing going and is never happy with where he is. When he tries to go beyond what he is capable of, he fails miserably and loses not only his best job but his very place in life as well.

James Kurtzleben and Mary Rohrberger

I'M YOUR HORSE IN THE NIGHT

Author: Luisa Valenzuela (1938-   )
Type of plot: Allegory
Time of plot: The 1970's
Locale: A city in Argentina
First published: "De noche soy tu caballo," 1982 (English translation, 1985)

> *Principal characters:*
> CHIQUITA, a woman in love with a revolutionary in Argentina
> BETO, her lover, the revolutionary

The Story

"I'm Your Horse in the Night" is narrated in the first-person voice through the consciousness of a woman who is in love with a persecuted revolutionary who calls himself Beto and is involved in secret activities. Beto visits the woman, whom he calls Chiquita, at night to avoid getting caught by the police. In the story, the narrator recreates in her mind his last visit as she is imprisoned and tortured because of her relationship with him and her refusal to betray him.

The story begins in the middle of the night, in an Argentine city. The narrator is annoyed because she has to get up when the doorbell rings several times. It sounds like the signal used by Beto, but Chiquita fears the possibility of a police trap. She opens the door to her lover. Extremely cautious about his own security, he locks the door of the house behind him.

Beto is a man of few words; he embraces and kisses Chiquita to communicate his emotions. Happy to see him, she tries to talk about his experiences during his long absence, but he silences her. He tells her that her safety depends on her ignorance of his activities. She concludes that he must have been in Brazil because he brings with him a drink and a record from that country. She realizes that he risked his life coming to see her and worries about their future.

The lovers drink and dance while they listen to the Brazilian song "I'm Your Horse in the Night." Chiquita explains that the song is about a saint in a trance who considers herself the mount of the spirit who is riding her. Beto criticizes her esoteric talk and tells her that the title refers to a sexual relationship in which the woman plays the role of a horse for the man who is riding her. They fall asleep after enjoying a night of passion.

Chiquita wakes the next morning to the sound of the telephone. She hopes that Beto is calling her because he left while she was asleep. At first she thinks that the voice on the phone belongs to someone called Andrés. When Chiquita is told that her lover has been found dead, after floating down the river for six days, she shouts that it cannot be Beto. Soon she realizes that the call is a trap, but it is too late. The police arrive in a few minutes and search the house. They take her to jail and interrogate her; she tells

her torturers that Beto abandoned her a long time ago and that she does not know anything about him. Chiquita tries to convince herself that her night of passion was just a
dream. The fate of her lover is never discovered. She hopes that Beto's spirit will visit
her.

Themes and Meanings

Like many of Luisa Valenzuela's works, "I'm Your Horse in the Night" deals with
politics, power, language, and gender issues. This story illustrates Argentina's history
during the military repression or dirty war in the 1970's and early 1980's, when torture was common and thousands of people disappeared. The principal characters in
the story have fictitious names, implying that they fear to reveal their true identities in
a terrorized society. When Chiquita hears the doorbell ringing at night, she fears a
visit by the ubiquitous and dreaded secret police.

The relationship of Chiquita and Beto serves as a metaphor for Argentina's society,
torn by violence and despotism. The expression of the couple's fears, passions, and
desires represents the private and the public story of this society. The pair also symbolizes the opposition between individual freedom and dictatorship and the struggle
between female dignity and the macho syndrome. The female protagonist longs for
love and togetherness with Beto, but she is dehumanized by his condescending language and acts of differentiation. He enforces his male superiority by calling her
Chiquita—the little one. He shows off his masculinity and power by stripping her of
human qualities and defining her as his obedient and passive horse.

All Beto's attention is focused on Chiquita's body, and his relationship with her is
based on male sexual domination. He does not like to speak with her, does not care
about her feelings and thoughts, and ignores her interpretation of the song that gives
the story its title. According to her, the song refers to the supernatural connections between a woman's body and spirit and her magic power to dream; he scorns her vision
of reality and associates it with witchcraft. He also fails to understand that her sexuality and eroticism are expressions of female desire and creativity.

Much as the military regime represses the Argentine society, Chiquita's guerrilla
boyfriend dominates her by silencing her creative thoughts and language. Like her society, the woman becomes a conquest and a possession as well as a victim of circumstances created by the male repressive power. Although Beto leaves unharmed,
Chiquita is arrested and taken to jail. As a prisoner, she is forced to speak on topics of
interest to the police and is tortured and interrogated about Beto's whereabouts.

Although Chiquita finds herself in a nightmarish situation, she resists submitting
totally to the system. She tries to create a language of her own to convince the police
that Beto visits her only in bad dreams. She reaches into her dream world and searches
for new ways of expressing herself. She re-creates the love scene with her absent lover
to escape the dark reality surrounding her. To save Beto, Chiquita must deny his existence in the real world. She realizes that she is empowered to will objects out of existence with her mind. In the end, Beto does not exist outside her imagination. Chiquita
may be physically imprisoned and abused, but she sublimates the real violence and

takes refuge in a dream of erotic and sensual love that is her only possession. In a dangerous world in which people suffer and lose their lives, Chiquita confronts death with a tale of love. She finds spiritual escape and survival by means of her imagination.

Style and Technique

Like other stories in Valenzuela's *Cambio de armas* (1982; *Other Weapons*, 1985), "I'm Your Horse in the Night" may be read as a political allegory, an erotic tale, or a detective story. It is a literary construction of a violent and abusive power that must be denounced. The author's revision of the historical reality of her country places her within the context of the Latin American literary boom. The subconscious aspect of the narration symbolizes the power of female language and storytelling to reach into social and historical issues while reflecting the female experience in contemporary society.

Valenzuela dramatizes a world of binary opposites such as history and fiction. The relationship between history and fiction is explored through Chiquita's recollection of events. The female-male dichotomy, which is centered on the meaning of the horse as a magical or sexual element, provides a structural and thematic framework for the narrative. The first section of the story deals with the lover's visit, and the second reveals Chiquita's arrest and torture as a result of his visit. Beto's actions prefigure the actions of the police when they force themselves on her. The voices of Beto and the police inhabit Chiquita's story. The story shifts from interior monologues to dialogues, which weave in and around each other, and offer opposing perspectives. The female narrator seeks to appropriate the text by using her language to confront the dominant male language and include it within the framework of her own story.

Valenzuela uncovers oppressive systems and, at the same time, re-creates a woman's literary thinking process. As Chiquita creates a dream-world version of Beto's visit, it is difficult to tell whether she is telling all that really did happen. She offers a version of reality that may be true and may be a fabrication. Her inclusion in the story is accepted as a fact, but the confusion of what is real and what is not creates a surrealistic atmosphere and a sense of ambiguity. In her mind, Chiquita speaks to the torturers and dares them to take away her dreams. She also addresses Beto and offers to be his mount and carry his spirit—like the horse in the song, according to her interpretation. Chiquita has the last word because her version of the truth ends the story.

Ludmila Kapschutschenko-Schmitt

IMAGINATION DEAD IMAGINE

Author: Samuel Beckett (1906-1989)
Type of plot: Fable
Time of plot: Possibly after a nuclear holocaust
Locale: Unspecified
First published: "Imagination morte imaginez," 1965 (English translation, 1965)

Principal characters:
AN UNNAMED NARRATOR, who discovers the rotunda
TWO UNNAMED HUMANS, one female, one male

The Story

The terse, ambiguous title of this story is consistent with the tale itself, in which a narrator describes flatly the real (or imaginary) discovery of a small rotunda in a white wasteland, the investigation of the same with some scientific care, and the final withdrawal from it after its dimensions, shape, and occupants have been systematically examined. The narrator leaves, convinced that there will be no chance of ever finding the building again.

The obvious thinness of such an overview may sufficiently convince a reader that something more is going on, and that a more detailed account must be given to make sense of the story. Detail is important in Samuel Beckett's world, and this tale is full of it.

The story begins in mid-conversation, in which the oral shorthand must be deciphered by the reader. The speaker seems to be rejecting with abrupt arrogance a comment that there is no sign of life. Unconcerned, the speaker suggests that it is irrelevant so long as imagination exists, but he immediately accepts the possibility that even imagination is dead. Good riddance to it and its inclination to describe the world in terms of the old nature as humankind knew it. The narrator posits a world of unrelieved whiteness, one in which a small building appears. He gets inside the building and measures the interior, a circle divided into two semicircles. Without evidencing any surprise, he records the presence of two human bodies, one in each semicircle. He checks the structure inside and out, testing its solidity, commenting on its bonelike quality. Inside, it is intensely bright and hot. The bodies are sweating.

The narrator goes out, moves away, and ascends. One must presume that there is some kind of vehicle, although it is not mentioned. As he ascends, the building disappears in the landscape and then reappears as he returns. This time, inside the building, the lights start to dim. Over a twenty-second period the room goes black, and the temperature drops to freezing. Then the light and heat come on again. These changes begin to happen irregularly, and the passage back and forth is sometimes interrupted, at which time everything, including the ground, shakes. There is some comfort in the stillness at the extremes of light and dark, and, significantly, a comment is made that such calmness is not to be found in the outside world.

At this point, then, some connection with a past world is established, and some modest feeling is expressed. The building is commented on as a miraculous discovery, and the further point is made that there is no other like it. After what seems to have been a long space voyage through perfect emptiness, a place of peace, albeit a limited peace, has been found.

The story starts to make some sense as a record of the discovery of the last remnant of the world, but at almost the same time, the light and heat patterns become erratic. Attention turns to a precise description of the humans, lying in their jackknife positions back to back. There is now little calm in the room, and the bodies are difficult to observe closely because of the increasing agitation of their surroundings. They are alive, sweating, breathing, and occasionally opening an eye.

There is a very muted suggestion that a sigh might barely raise some reaction in the form of a quickly repressed shudder from the figures, but the narrator does not pursue it. The narrator leaves, suggesting and immediately denying the possibility of a better example of this sort of thing somewhere else. There is no expectation that the rotunda could ever be found again.

Themes and Meanings

Beckett, as an absurdist, avoids meaning if he can, although the very avoidance is caused by a belief that the world and human life are meaningless. Beckett's stories are aesthetic structures proving that simple idea. It is, however, true that he often illustrates that idea in works that use the landscape and the characters that might be imagined as existing after a nuclear holocaust. This story may (with the stress on "may") be read as an example, a comment on humanity's disastrous possibilities. The narrator can be seen as a survivor, possessed of some technological capacity to travel, coming on this isolated haven. It is, significantly, a shelter in which the male and female, turned away from each other, simply survive in a fetal position.

That, however, is too easy. The title and the first fines suggest that it may be an exploration of the last vestige of mental life. The rotunda could be a skull, the interior a brain close to death, the two pallid figures representing the weakened capacity of the mind to create and the mind's inability to project creation further because, as the narrator suggests, the imagination is dead. Imagine what it would be like if the imagination were dead, and still try to imagine.

Both these readings lead to the idea that life in general is absurd, without meaning, without hope. Sometimes in Beckett that proposition can be relieved by saucy humor. Here it is relentlessly morbid.

Style and Technique

Beckett often uses solitary characters—nameless, wandering, talkative; they are often tramps. In this story, however, the man has a touch of the professional, the specialist, about him. He seems to be recording his comments, making a detailed report on this unusual discovery of isolated life. The determination to get the details right has a pseudo-scientific fastidiousness about it. If the story is read carefully, it will make sense physically; there is a clear picture of when and where everything happens. It is stylistically impersonal, often pedantically so. It is, in a way, simply a more artistically successful form of the overview of the story in this article. It is really a précis of a story—compressed, sticking doggedly to the facts.

It should be no surprise that it is a fragment of what was supposed to be, originally, a longer work. Beckett calls it, outrageously, a novel, and some critics see it as a plot for a novel. It does contain the structure of a short story. Framed by the elusive idea of the imagination fore and aft, it has a beginning, a middle, a slight touch of last-minute reversal, and a conclusion.

The remark about the imagination starts the whole sequence with the discovery of the rotunda (beginning). The narrator stays long enough to record the peculiar situation and the change from pattern to chaos (middle). At the last moment, he notices, possibly, a touch of feeling in the shudder caused by the human sigh, which is quickly suppressed (reversal). The narrator leaves, certain that in the great meaningless cosmos, it will be impossible to find that place ever again (end). It is all very cool, tonally indifferent.

Charles H. Pullen

IMAGINED SCENES

Author: Ann Beattie (1947-   )
Type of plot: Psychological
Time of plot: A winter during the 1970's
Locale: Evidently the northeast United States
First published: 1974

> *Principal characters:*
> AN UNNAMED YOUNG WOMAN, the protagonist
> DAVID, her husband
> AN OLD MAN, for whom she provides night care
> HIS SISTER
> KATHERINE AND LARRY DUANE, new neighbors, who never
> actually appear in the story

The Story
　　Like much of Ann Beattie's fiction, "Imagined Scenes" is more evocation of a situation than plotted tale. The seven sections of the story cover three days in the life of the female protagonist, who sits nights with an old man while his daughter and son-in-law take a midwinter vacation in Florida. The garrulous old man reminisces about the terrible winter he spent in Berlin and produces photograph albums and postcards, one of which, a silver-spangled picture of Rip Van Winkle walking through a moonlit forest, provides one of the story's many ambiguous echoes. The old man's chatter provides contrast with the scenes between the protagonist and her husband, David. Their marriage seems a wary one, dominated by silences, clichéd expressions of concern, and David's ambiguous disappearances and his relationship with the new neighbors, the Duanes.
　　The opening section establishes the protagonist's dependence on her husband, who seems to her energetic and supremely competent, able to anticipate her needs and alleviate her fears. However, their relationship seems very much like that which a brother and sister might have. There is no hint of passion or even deep caring on David's part. Instead, there is a smugness about him, communicated in the first section by mention of his "surprise" decision the previous summer to quit work and return to graduate school and by his guessing that she has dreamed of Greece and then insisting, without asking her opinion, that they will go there. Though the protagonist would rather go to Spain, she silences her objection with the significant line, "She should let him sleep."
　　The subjects of wandering and sleeping dominate the story. During the three nights she spends watching the old man (the third, fifth, and seventh sections of the narrative), she is increasingly cut off—by the ever-falling snow and by David's absences and ambiguity about the new neighbors—from the comfortable reality of her marriage. She is forced to imagine his whereabouts, and in the fourth, sixth, and seventh

sections, to question him without seeming to intrude into his privacy. Appearances suggest that he no longer studies for his Ph.D. orals, and his having given their house-plant to the Duanes puzzles her, as does his reluctance to take her to the Duane home. His failure to answer the telephone late the second night causes her to imagine once again the dream scene of ocean and mountains and to name it this time, as if in obedi-ence, Greece. His apparent absence the third night when she calls at four in the morn-ing visibly depresses her and reminds her of his previous excuses, that he was walking the dog through the forest at night and that he "could have been anywhere." His sur-prising appearance the next day to help the old man up from the snow and his excuse for the night before ("I was sleeping") reinforce the connections between him and the Rip Van Winkle figure and at the same time seem to reinforce his image as an eccen-tric but caring man, magically able, as in the opening section of the story, to anticipate her needs.

Most important, the scene leaves the protagonist in a true dilemma: The old man has told her that the aged, lacking power to "improve things," learn to make up stories, "to lie all the time," and this young woman, finding her reality to be an indeterminate mixture of speculation and apparent fact, does not know what to make of it. She dis-trusts David without wanting to, yet she sleeps through the ringing of their telephone even as her subconscious mind registers the sound—just as David claims to have done. "You don't know what it's like to be caught," the old man's sister tells her, but clearly that is not true.

Themes and Meanings

Collected in *Distortions* (1976), this story offers an angle of that theme, presenting a young woman about whom the reader actually knows very little except that she feels as trapped in her life as the old man for whom she cares. However, whereas he can name some of the distortions to which he has resorted in an effort to manipulate those around him, the protagonist cannot even define the conditions that cause her malaise. Like many of Beattie's characters, she seems to have no interests that define her; she comes to the reader as a collection of perceptions and impressions, so uncertain as to be incapable of anger or of confronting the possibility of getting angry. Her inability to admit her emotions even to herself also means an inability to communicate them to anyone else.

The progression of events in the story, however, implies change. The mystery of David's whereabouts preoccupies her more and more, and as the tension builds, the reader is encouraged by the story's recurrences to wonder if confrontation and/or res-olution will result. During the story, the protagonist has come to recognize what tenta-tive knowledge she possesses about her husband. From what she hears about loneli-ness and powerlessness from the old man, she is invited to see the possibilities of loneliness and powerlessness in her own life. The old man's postcards and photograph album provide him with a refuge of sorts, but the image of Rip Van Winkle takes on a cruelly ironic quality when the old man is knocked down by children in the street. The images of David's walking at night connect him with the postcard Rip Van Winkle and bring to mind that old sleeper's urge to escape his wife. In addition, the old man in Beattie's story has established a kind of truce with his sister, who serves him diligently but not without bitterness, and who, though claiming that she is trapped, insists on maintaining the unpleasant conditions, partly out of a kind of love for her brother and partly perhaps because she has nothing else. All of this hints to the young woman something about the possibilities of life, but the story does not lead to a sudden awakening or epiphany for her. She is at present too timid to look hard at her situation. The story communicates this theme of limited possibilities, as it were, over her head.

In this regard, the crucial set of imagined scenes comes near the end of the story, when the narrative implies that she does not wish to confront directly the essence of her relationship with David. On the way home, with David angry because she allowed the old man to go outside, she hints at her suspicions, but faced with his simple denial of what seems obvious to her, she takes refuge in a series of four dream images: She imagines him sleeping, as he claims to have done; then walking with the dog in snow "too deep to jump out of"; then "asleep, under the covers"; and then walking up the hill. Something ominous about this willed dreaming—perhaps in the sequence of deep snow and David asleep under covers, or perhaps the alternate acceptance and rejection of his excuse for not having answered the telephone—prompts her to stop. However, she remains suspicious.

To measure distortion, one must be able to fix an image to serve as a standard, and this is precisely what this young woman cannot do. Her suspicions cannot be escaped or glossed over by her dreams; she has neither illusions nor truths, and that is the worst condition of all.

Style and Technique

Beattie's manipulation of narrative techniques made her one of the most recognized and original writers of the 1970's, and "Imagined Scenes" gains much of its force from her preoccupation with narrative objectivity and the fragmentation of time's flow.

There is a reportorial quality about the narrative voice that gives the story a very cool ambience. Events are related, but the internal world of emotions remains outside the narrative's view except for what the old man and his sister tell about their feelings of anger, rejection, and powerlessness. With this as counterpoint, the narrator, with the objectivity of a camera's eye, examines the interactions of the younger couple, who do not speak of their inner feelings. This technique effectively creates great emotion by making emotion's absence so obvious. For example, when first describing the new neighbors, David tells her, "He's very nice. Katherine and Larry Duane," and never again does he refer to the woman. That the protagonist does not react to this omission makes her inner torment all the more clear. David touches his young wife only twice during the story: once "on his way out" to the Duanes' house, and once (his cold cheeks sting her) coming back from the same place. Without consulting her, he gives their plant to the Duanes. He takes to making his own coffee and abandons other of their private rituals. When upset, he refuses to speak to her. The narrative records these details with noncommittal economy; in fact, nothing in David's behavior assures a reader that he is anything more than mildly dislocated by having his spouse away every night for a week.

However, the technique only makes the emotions and judgments more forceful because they remain unstated: Finally, during the last telephone conversation with the old man's sister, the young woman seems overwhelmed by the images and emotions she has suppressed, and she mixes them together into a fearful vision of a deserted, snow-covered earth to match the table that David cleared of, perhaps, suspicious evidence.

The fragmentation of the story into seven vignettes nicely complements the apparent disintegration of the young protagonist's marriage or at least of her naïve confidence in her husband. The first vignette gives the impression of what for her was an ideal past, one of shared instincts: "she expects him to wake up when she does"; "by unspoken agreement, he has learned to like Roquefort dressing." That this situation evolved without apparent effort makes plausible her silence in the subsequent chronological sequence when he seems to drift away; her passivity before life makes it impossible for her to impose a coherence on its events. The last and longest of the narrative sections shows her feeble attempt at inquiry, the continued suspicion, and the vertigo that results. In this marriage of a passive-aggressive pair, the lack of unity that the story objectively sets out in fragmented sections seems inevitable.

Kerry Ahearn

THE IMITATION OF THE ROSE

Author: Clarice Lispector (1925-1977)
Type of plot: Psychological
Time of plot: The mid-twentieth century
Locale: Brazil
First published: "A imitação da rosa," 1955 (English translation, 1980)

> *Principal characters:*
> LAURA, a housewife
> ARMANDO, her husband
> MARIA, her maid

The Story

Laura, a Brazilian woman, is back in her home after spending time in an institution to recover from an undisclosed mental illness or breakdown. Happy to be home and well again, Laura returns to her old routine of tidying up the house and waiting for her husband, Armando, to return from work. Laura looks forward to doing the things she used to do with her husband. At the same time, she begins to reflect on her fading youth and the fact that she has never had children.

Sitting in her home, she is tempted to doze off, but she reminds herself that she and Armando will go to dinner at her friend Carlota's house that evening, and she still has much to do to prepare. In a reverie, Laura reviews the things she must do, noting that Carlota would surely despise her liking for routine. She paints a mental picture of how she and Armando will leave the house, with her low, thick hips transformed by a girdle into a more attractive shape. Continuing to daydream, Laura admits to herself that she is neat and ordinary, and a little boring, but seems happy she can let herself go with Armando. Although she realizes Armando seldom listens to her, she is content that she can tell him things without his getting annoyed, as do the maid and others.

Opening her eyes, she sees a vase of flowers, wild roses she bought that morning at the market at the florist's insistence. Their beauty and perfection strike her as she gazes at them, although she feels a moment of unease and a touch of perplexity, which she vaguely attributes to the roses' beauty. Hearing the footsteps of Maria, the maid, she decides to have Maria carry the roses to Carlota's house and leave them as a gift. Slightly disturbed by the roses yet attracted as well by them, Laura again slips into a reverie as she justifies to herself why sending the roses would be for the best. Feigning decisiveness, she orders Maria to call at Carlota's and leave the roses. While preparing the flowers, however, Laura begins to have doubts about giving the flowers away, doubts that become frighteningly strong a moment later. First she thinks of why she should keep the roses; moments later, she realizes that there would be no turning back. Sad but terrified at her own confusion, she resolves to give the roses to Maria.

As Maria takes hold of the roses, Laura briefly draws back her hand in a feeble attempt to keep them for herself, vowing, however, never again to be tempted by perfection. For several final seconds, Laura frantically considers how she might get the roses back, going so far as to consider stealing them from Maria, yet again does nothing. Soon Maria is gone and Laura is alone, missing the roses—whose absence has left her feeling an intense sense of loss. "In her heart, that one rose, which at least she could have taken for herself without prejudicing anyone in the world, was gone."

Deeply fatigued from her struggle, Laura tries to envision the roses within herself, which she finds is not difficult. Her tiredness lifts, and she begins again to plan what she will wear that evening when she and Armando go to Carlota's. She imagines how Armando will arrive, relieved as always that nothing had happened while he was gone—her husband, whose sense of well-being is somehow dependent on Laura's being ill. When Laura calmly and sweetly tells Armando that her illness, or at least some of its symptoms, came back while he was gone, he pretends not to understand, although he surely does. Laura's uncharacteristic serenity and lack of haste unnerve her husband, causing him to question her harshly. The story concludes with a dejected Armando staring at Laura as she sits serenely on the couch, distant from him in both mind and spirit.

Themes and Meanings

Like many of Clarice Lispector's works, "The Imitation of the Rose" focuses on an individual's subjective perception of the world in which she lives. Although it is clear that Laura has recently returned from an institution at which she was treated for a breakdown, Lispector is concerned with portraying the complex mental processes of her protagonist and how these processes structure her reality, rather than presenting a case study of the illness itself. The history of Laura's illness is obscure, yet certain suggestions are given as to the nature of her ailment, probably a form of manic-depression, coupled with obsessive behavior.

Lispector's story invites comparison to another fictive account of a woman suffering from mental illness, Charlotte Perkins Gilman's "The Yellow Wallpaper" (1892), because the real cause of her illness appears to lie not in a personal defect but in the suffocating social environment in which she lives. Laura's doctor and husband both take an uncompromisingly patronizing attitude toward Laura, treating her like a child who cannot do anything for herself or make important decisions. Her mental and emotional vacillations are symptoms of how she has been treated by others, mostly the men, in her life.

Laura's decision to send the wild roses that she has bought to her friend Carlota represents a small, yet significant, even if unconscious, attempt to make an independent decision and establish a more secure sense of her own identity. The perfection of the roses represents not the former obsession of tidying, cleaning, and counting but the possibility of a truer, probably happier, self, which unfortunately turns out to be still out of her grasp. Laura's confusion about whether to send the roses or keep them for herself seems to foreshadow a relapse of her illness, yet also reaffirms her desire to have something of her own. All of this frightens her, however, as she thinks to herself that she might still have them simply by telling Maria, who after all is merely her maid, that she has changed her mind. Seemingly forced to give up the roses, which are lovely but disturb her, she concludes that "something nice was either for giving or receiving, not only for possessing. And above all, never for one to be. Above all one should never be a lovely thing." These thought confirm her ambivalence toward and fear of truly doing or being.

After giving up the roses, Laura is disappointed, rebellious, sorrowful, obstinate, resentful, and enraged, a range of emotions that signals improvement over her former obsessive monomania. Laura now is able to "imitate the roses deep down inside herself," a particularly significant accomplishment and one that brings her an unexpected serenity. Lispector closes this story by reminding the reader that Laura lives in an oppressive social environment in which she has been trained to think only of the comfort and wants of others, a situation exemplified by her sympathetic but obtuse husband, who is oblivious to Laura's real needs as a woman.

The reader is further reminded that Laura has sacrificed much to make her husband happy and is allowed only submissive happiness, not the "imitation of Christ." (The title of this story is a reference to Thomas à Kempis's *The Imitation of Christ* [1441], which Laura had been given to read during her schooling at a convent.) As if to reinforce the dilemma of women such as Laura who attempt even small changes in the way they live or feel about themselves, the author presents a cautious, suspicious, disinterested, annoyed Armando, who is mortified by his wife's shamelessness. In the end, it seems to be she who triumphs, for an "aged, tired, and strange" Armando merely watches her, "luminous and remote," as she sits tranquil and alert on the couch.

Style and Technique

Lispector's style is characterized by a deliberate indeterminacy, meant to mirror the internal processes by which individuals perceive the world, themselves, and others. Laura's fragmented thoughts are reflected in the author's prose by sentences that are difficult to interpret or groups of sentences or phrases that seem not to go together. This creates an effect similar to what the protagonist must be experiencing, that is, a sense of the unfinished and inconclusive nature of reality and thought. The reader, however, is likely to be more aware of this than is Laura because the process of reading typically involves some level of introspection and analysis. In her use of fragmented interior monologue, Lispector has been compared to Virginia Woolf, although her narration is reminiscent in some ways of Gustave Flaubert's *Madame Bovary* (1857; English translation, 1886), whose narrator is neither first nor third person, but some combination of the two.

Howard Giskin

IMMIGRATION BLUES

Author: Bienvenido N. Santos (1911-1996)
Type of plot: Social realism
Time of plot: The early 1970's
Locale: San Francisco
First published: 1977

Principal characters:
ALIPIO PALMA, a retired Filipino American widower
MRS. ANTONIETA ZAFRA, the wife of an old friend of his
MONICA, her sister, a Filipina schoolteacher

The Story

Alipio Palma, the protagonist in this story, is a Pinoy, an old-timer, as the Filipinos in the United States have been called. One summer day, when Palma looks through the window curtain, he sees two women dressed in their summer dresses, the way the country girls back home in the Ilocos of the Philippines would dress when they went around peddling rice cakes. One woman seems twice as large as the other. The slim one could have passed for his late wife Seniang's sister as he remembers her from pictures that his wife kept. He is correct in a sense.

Hearing the gentle knock on his door, Alipio limps painfully toward the door—not long after Seniang's death, he was in a car accident that left him bedridden for a year. He opens the door to find himself facing the two women he has just seen through the window. Although he does not know them personally, he welcomes them into his house.

The fat woman introduces herself as Mrs. Antonieta Zafra, the wife of Carlito Zafra, who was Alipio's friend in the 1930's. Hearing that his old friend is still alive, Alipio recalls their happy time back then: Being young and romantic, they were like fools on fire, wowing the blondies with their gallantry and cooking. Alipio also re-members that Carlito liked cockfighting more than the girls, and he is surprised that his friend got married.

Mrs. Zafra tells Alipio that it is she who wanted to marry Carlito. She had been a nun at St. Mary's in California, but life in the convent turned sour on her, and she found the system tyrannical and inhuman. If she left the order, however, she would no longer have been entitled to stay in the United States and would face deportation. She had to marry an American citizen within a week to avoid a shameful deportation to her home country. After a week of private talks with God, she was guided to find an el-derly Filipino who was an American citizen to marry her, which was how she had found Carlito. Now Monica, Mrs. Zafra's older sister who has come to the States on a tourist visa, is facing the same fate: She will be deported in two days if she cannot marry an American citizen.

Alipio is already familiar with similar stories of heartaches and deportations, because his deceased wife went through the same predicament. Facing deportation, Seniang came to him to ask for marriage, willing to accept any arrangement that would suit him. Although not interested in the proposal at first—for he believed that marriage should mean children, a possibility denied him because of his advanced age—he agreed to marry her after he realized the problem she faced. It had been a happy marriage, and now he is presented with a similar case. Maybe his first impression, that Monica is Seniang's sister, is correct in a sense.

The two sisters mean to tell Alipio honestly the purpose of their unexpected visit—as Seniang had done before—but at first are unable to do so, because he welcomes them like long-lost friends and family members. Alipio, still recovering from both his loss of Seniang and his car accident, is eager and happy to see his fellow countrywomen. When the sisters manage to tell him their real intention, although not without regret and difficulty, Alipio is a little surprised at first. When he comprehends the situation, he begins pondering in his mind what a nice name Monica is. When the two sisters beg him for forgiveness, he asks what there is to forgive. Uttering "God dictates," he accepts Monica as he did Seniang years ago: Both are God's wish.

Themes and Meanings

Bienvenido N. Santos once commented on his increased interest in the comictragic predicaments of the exiled Filipino: He is not truly at peace with himself, but resigned somewhat to a fate he has to accept to spend the rest of his life with as much grace as he can summon. This is found in his portrayal of the protagonist in "Immigration Blues." In this sad but heartwarming story, Santos portrays a Filipino "blues singer," Alipio Palma, whose bittersweet songs are the praisesong of the indomitable human spirit.

Alipio's strong faith in God is the source of his strength day in and day out, especially in his old age. When Seniang is taken away by God, he accepts it as best he can by dwelling on the happy years they spent together. When a terrible car accident threatens to render him unable to walk, God makes it a miracle that he is able to walk again in a year's time. In spite of all of his sufferings, he welcomes Antonieta and Monica as friends and relatives, without a trace of doubt as to the real intention of their visit. Even after they have disclosed their objective to him, he receives them with a warm heart and open arms.

Santos's characterization of Alipio belies the argument that Filipinos and other Asian immigrants in the United States cling tenaciously to their own customs, traditions, and way of living because they cannot assimilate into the mainstream culture. He portrays Alipio's nostalgia for his home country and things Philippine as a positive factor, the one force that has enabled him to face his life in an alien land. After many years in the United States, he still prefers to eat rice, the major food in his home country. The two sisters in the story remind him of the country girls at home peddling rice cakes; the chilly summer nights in San Francisco awaken his memory of home, where the climate is warm and agreeable all year round; and the waves of the Pacific Ocean make him feel closer to home. In a sense, those nostalgic memories have helped him to overcome the loneliness that has been with him all of his life; at the same time, they have made his assimilation into American society less painful and difficult—however partial it may have been.

Alipio is not completely at peace with himself yet, but he is not resigned in desperation. Like a blues singer, sometimes he sings happy songs; other times, he sings sad songs. It is the singing that matters.

Style and Technique

A fine storyteller with a keen sensitivity, Santos is credited as the leading fictional spokesperson for his fellow expatriates in the United States. This comes out of his personal encounter with exiled Filipinos. "Immigration Blues" is a convincing example. His portrayal of Alipio Palma is vivid and powerful.

To let the readers sink into the tragic life experience of the protagonist, Santos uses a slow and controlled narrative tempo: It is as if Alipio, being old and recovering from a terrible car accident, cannot be rushed. He does things according to his own timetable. His slow movement provides a striking contrast to the urgent matter of the two sisters. This slow tempo allows several flashbacks to take place, such as his accounts of his early, carefree days in the United States, and his marrying of his first wife. These bits of information are necessary to help the reader understand what has happened to the protagonist and why he has become what he is today.

Santos also uses concrete details in the story to dramatize Alipio's desire to live—which offsets the tragic subject matter of the story. Alipio's drawers and refrigerator are stacked with food that may last longer than the rest of his life—the sight of the foodstuffs seems to enliven the old man and erase years from his eyes. This is an old man who knows that food means life and sustenance, and provides energy and health.

Weihua Zhang

IMPULSE

Author: Conrad Aiken (1889-1973)
Type of plot: Psychological
Time of plot: About 1920
Locale: Boston
First published: 1932

Principal characters:
MICHAEL LOWES, the protagonist, who yields to an "impulse" to steal
DORA LOWES, his wife
SMITH,
BRYANT, and
HURWITZ, Michael's card-playing acquaintances
A STORE DETECTIVE

The Story

Although Conrad Aiken's title might suggest that "Impulse" concerns a whimsical, unpremeditated action, the story actually examines an ostensibly "impulsive" action and finds, instead, that the "impulse" is really the logical culmination of a series of actions in the life of Michael Lowes, the protagonist. If fact, the story is a fictionalized psychological study of a paranoid "loser," whose attempts to escape from reality are self-destructive acts that lead to his arrest and conviction for theft and to an impending divorce from his wife.

Just as he is left alone in his cell at the end of the story, Michael is significantly alone when the story begins, and because he is shaving, he is also characteristically narcissistic. As he shaves, his thoughts reveal a gamut of psychological problems: Ready "to do a new jump," he projects his "restless" feelings on his wife, Dora; "fate is always against you"; his "friends" are inferior, "cheap fellows, really"; and he twice mentions his need for "escape." Michael uses his "friends" to enhance his own self-image, while he maintains a distance from them (he denies that he "likes" them), and he also seems threatened by Dora and the family relationships and responsibilities that the marriage represents. Those responsibilities are represented by the "bills," which he procrastinates paying and which are the result of the "bad luck" that hounds him.

To gain needed respite from his responsibilities, he schemes to meet Smith, Bryant, and Hurwitz for dinner, drinks, and an evening of bridge and conversation. During an intermission from bridge, the four men begin to discuss the nature of impulses and the civilizing social forces, particularly the fear of the law, that prevent people from yielding to those sudden, irrational, and subconscious desires. Michael feels "relief" when he learns that he has not been alone in having "both these impulses," theft and sex, and although his friends turn to other topics of conversation, he recalls the "thrills" he experienced earlier in his life when he stole a conch shell.

When the game ends, Michael leaves for the subway station but stops at the nearby drugstore to get some hot chocolate. Once in the store, he realizes that his real motive for stopping at the drugstore was "to steal something," "to put the impulse to the test." After viewing the "wares," he steals a safety-razor set, but despite his dexterity he is apprehended by the store detective and taken to a back room, where he unsuccessfully attempts to explain the theft as a "joke," the result of a "bet." He is equally unsuccessful at the police station, where a sergeant calls Hurwitz and Bryant to check on his story about the bet; both deny the existence of the bet, and Hurwitz adds that Michael is "hard up."

Dora adds to Michael's predicament because, although she is willing to get him a lawyer and to contact Hurwitz, Bryant, and Smith, her "cold, detached, deliberate behavior" indicates that she does not believe in his innocence. Moreover, she is unwilling to use her own savings in his defense. When his lawyer reports that his friends are unwilling to be involved, his fate is sealed, and he receives a three-month sentence. After his first week in prison, he receives his first post-trial communication from Dora: It is a note informing him that she is instituting divorce proceedings and requesting that he not contest the divorce. Realizing that opposing the divorce would be futile, he resolves that on his release he will "go west . . . get rich, clear his name somehow," but he does not know how to accomplish his immature, unrealistic goals and retreats into his memories of his childhood in Chicago. At the end of the story, he concludes that his "whole life . . . had all come foolishly to an end."

Themes and Meanings

In "Impulse" Aiken depicts the psychological problems of a repressed, insecure "loner" who attempts to escape from his problems and whose immature concern for self prevents him from seeing things as they are. His "impulsive" theft is clearly premeditated, the act of an adult who has never "grown up" and who has never had to accept the consequences of his actions. Though he is directly responsible for the theft, the paranoid Michael Lowes sees his predicament as the result of betrayal and "bad luck."

Michael's bridge game is twice associated with "escape" from what he sees as a dreary routine naturally repugnant to a man of his education and cultivation. He seeks a diversion, significantly a "game," which is how he persists in seeing shoplifting, a crime usually associated with youngsters. Alcohol is one method of escape, and although Aiken stresses its importance to Michael, it is not the alcohol that prompts the theft. If Michael is a "trifle tight," he is not unsteady on his feet, and his behavior is extremely methodical. He "examines" the "wares" with a "critical and appraising eye" and carefully considers what to steal. Because Aiken has associated "impulses" with sex and theft, it is significant that Michael's reaction to the safety-razor set is "love at first sight" and that the set is twice described as a "victim." The theft of the set becomes a hostile act for the repressed Michael, who bitterly resents the nagging of his wife, who reminds him of his "non-success." The safety-razor set suggests both hostility and caution, and although Michael is drawn to the "heavy gold," the box is made of "snakeskin," with its association with archetypal evil. (The detective who apprehends Michael has a voice that conveys "venom.") Thus, the literal theft is also quite symbolic.

Michael simply does not regard an "impulsive" theft as a crime, but instead sees it as an adventure, even a "discovery": "Why not be a Columbus of the moral world and really do it?" When he is apprehended, he sees himself as a "thief by accident" (perhaps a reference to the bad luck that "hounds" him). When Dora and his friends tell the truth and will not reshape their accounts to square with the "facts" that Michael has created and now believes to be true, Michael sees himself as persecuted martyr: What Michael sees as a "monstrous joke; a huge injustice" is really the impartial functioning of the legal system: The judge decides that it is "a perfectly clear case of theft, and a perfectly clear motive."

Michael cannot impose his vision of truth on others, but he nevertheless attempts to create a future with which he can live psychologically. That future is expressed in immature terms more appropriate to a child with a temper tantrum: "He would show them. He would go west, when he came out—get rich, clear his name somehow. . . . But how?" Horace Greeley's advice about "going west" is no longer appropriate, and riches and reputation necessitate hard work, behavior that is not consistent with Michael's past. Rather than vowing to change his life—such a vow would be an admission of his faults—Michael regresses to thoughts of his childhood.

Style and Technique

Aiken's "Impulse" relies heavily on psychological terms and concepts, and his language is a blend of literary symbolism and the psychological case study. To understand Michael, the reader must know what Michael thinks, but there must concurrently be some distance between Michael and the reader. Aiken's choice of point of view is particularly fitting, because it creates distance—as a first-person account would not—while it allows the reader to see events as they are screened through Michael's distorted perspective. At times, the third-person limited point of view becomes so intimate that it approaches the stream-of-consciousness technique, with its series of impressions that only seem to be unrelated.

As he sits on the bed in his cell, Michael thinks of the past, and Aiken offers a series of memories that account for the "impulsive" decision to steal. Michael's Chicago memories involve his mother (the missing father is important psychologically), who nags him, as Dora does, about being responsible; Michael's theft is perhaps a rebellious act against domineering women. (He is both attracted to Smith's "Squiggles," whose name suggests irresponsibility, and disgusted with her, for he blames her for the police's failure to contact Smith.) The other memories suggest, without being explicit (Michael cannot bring himself to admit weakness), failures and past crimes: The "crowded examination room at college" may well involve an "impulsive" decision to cheat; the lost stamp collection seems innocuous, but the reader knows that Michael had been tempted to steal Parker's stamp collection; and the broken conch shell refers to a stolen conch shell.

The references to the boat ride and the dead boy next door are enigmatic, but given the context of failure and guilt, they doubtless are allusions to other "impulsive" acts that Michael subconsciously remembers but cannot consciously admit as failures. In fact, the reminiscences constitute, for Michael, only a series of "trivial and infinitely charming little episodes." When he again assures himself that "he had really been a good man," Michael indicates that he cannot admit past errors and learn from them; instead, he deludes himself again and remains in a state of arrested emotional development. Michael's "end" does not come, as he believes, "foolishly," but logically, as the inevitable outcome of the rest of his life.

Thomas L. Erskine

IN A FATHER'S PLACE

Author: Christopher Tilghman (1946-   )
Type of plot: Domestic realism
Time of plot: The 1980's
Locale: Chesapeake Bay
First published: 1989

> *Principal characters:*
> DAN WILLIAMS, a lawyer and widower
> NICK, his son
> RACHEL, his daughter
> PATTY KEITH, Nick's girlfriend

The Story

Dan Williams is a middle-aged man seeking to come to terms with ghosts from his familial past and with the discordances of his familial present. The Williams family, of which Dan is now the patriarch of sorts, is a venerable Maryland clan, with roots that can be traced back to the American Revolution. Dan, a widower with two grown and relocated children, now lives alone in a house that is a physical emblem of familial tradition and history—antiques stand on the oaken floors, two-hundred-year-old oil portraits hang on the walls.

Into this house, Dan welcomes his children for a rare weekend reunion. His daughter, Rachel, a corporate lawyer working in Wilmington, Delaware, is a robust, physical woman; a lacrosse player during her college days, she shares a heartiness with her father that bonds them in an athletic way. She returns with the news that she is leaving the homegrounds of the Chesapeake and relocating to Seattle. Dan's son, Nick, is a writer currently living in New York City. Dan sees his relationship with his son as problematic—he laments to his daughter that he has "made a hash" of Nick. To complicate matters further, Nick has brought his girlfriend, Patty Keith, with him.

Tragedies, large and small, shadow Dan's life. His wife, Helen, died in a hit-and-run accident soon after their marriage, leaving a huge gap in his existence as a husband as well as his existence as a man. Dan subsequently sought to fill that gap through a relationship with Sheila Frederick, who years before had been merely a high school fantasy object. This romance left a slightly smaller, but equally jagged, hole in Dan's heart. Meanwhile, Dan handed over the raising of his two young children to a housekeeper—an act that he now perceives as an abdication of his fatherly responsibility and as a partial cause of his lack of connection with Nick. Dan thinks, too, of his own father and his relationship with that man; Dan worries about being one of a "generation that lost its children."

The facts of Dan's personal past impinge on his present. Part of his purpose in having his children temporarily back in the fold is to attempt a reconciliation between himself and his son, although the estrangement is not so dramatic that it is apparent to

Nick. What exacerbates Dan's problem, however, is the addition of the fourth party, Patty. A woman seemingly without humor, she enjoys reading literary deconstructionist Jacques Derrida. She is also without tact; she seems to appraise the house as well as the family within it, gathering some sense of the ultimate worth of both as if considering some financial settlement.

Dan and Rachel work to appreciate Patty, to allow her into their lives for this short space of time, but it proves difficult. Communication between Dan and Patty is tense, fraught with suspicion and mistrust. Patty figures as an interloper, as a woman looking to control Nick in ways that Dan would never wish him to be controlled. Worried as he is about his own failure to help Nick's passage from boyhood to manhood, Dan worries just as seriously about this woman's submerged desire to subordinate Nick's will to her own, to somehow possess him as she might possess a piecrust tea table or a letter from George Washington.

Nick feels the agonizing pull of both his father and his lover. He also has complicated matters by bringing his work home with him—that work being a novel loosely based on his familial history. As Patty tells Dan, Nick supposedly is trying to deconstruct his family, looking for those crucial and ultimately limiting points of contradiction in the familial weave. As much as Dan wants to understand the complex fabric of family, with its intricate and puzzling mesh of past and present influence, he fears the radical rending of that fabric.

To keep the family momentarily whole, Dan and Rachel join forces against Patty's intrusive presence and construct a strategy to liberate Nick from her witchlike hold. They first manage to separate Nick and Patty so that Dan can have his son to himself, beyond the baleful influence of Nick's lover. As Patty perceives the ploy, her resentment builds.

Later, Rachel hauls Nick off to go sailing, an act that recapitulates their childhood. A storm blows up on the bay, and the drama of the story builds partly around the fate of brother and sister. Their experience is a test of their abilities both as sailors and as independent human beings, with the storm reaffirming their intense and preeminent relationship as siblings. While Nick and Rachel maneuver on the bay, Dan weathers a more figurative storm at home, taking on Patty's rage when she realizes what Dan and Rachel have done. She first lashes out specifically at Dan, and then more expansively, and expensively, at the family. Accusing them of hypocrisy, of seeking to transform family into history and artifact, Patty carries out the deconstruction that Nick supposedly pursues in his novel: She exercises that of which Nick (and Derrida) only write. Dan reacts by evicting Patty from the house and from the family, thus reassuming some of the fatherly responsibility he has long left unclaimed. By asserting his paternal will, Dan experiences an epiphany, an authentic rush of joy that is part of a private celebration of his own identity as father.

Themes and Meanings

A central concern of Christopher Tilghman's story is the agonizing pressures placed on the individual as member of the family. Participation in the family carries with it a vast collection of historical baggage that shapes that participation. Tilghman looks to this historical weight as the essence of family: When one claims familial ties, one claims also the long line of familial action and memory that defines the character of that family.

Tilghman also explores what it means to act as father within the family. He examines the difficulties of acting individually as a father to a son, while at the same time carrying, almost genetically, the fact of being a son to one's own father. How does one exert a will of one's own, and how does one judge the rightness of that willful act? How does one resolve the in-betweenness of being both father and son without repudiating one or the other of these roles? Tilghman understands the inherent tragedy of parenthood, of fatherhood: that one inevitably missteps and misjudges, that so very much is left to guess and hope and instinct.

What redeems the familial circumstance is the fact that love generally operates through the mess one makes of things. Plagued as he is by his own failures as a private, desiring man, Dan Williams still arrives at a kind of resolution—an epiphany, even—by the story's end. The wind that brings the storm, and his own apprehensiveness over the condition of his children out on the bay, also brings a cleansing of Dan's vision. He perceives the confirmation of all that he has done, the work of his days. Tilghman asserts an almost spiritual presence in the family that works toward wholeness and that flows through the past and the present, keeping all connected and continuous.

Style and Technique

Tilghman is often seen as a traditional writer who builds his fiction on careful and extensive development of character and story. He is a patient storyteller, willing to spend time and words on detail that ultimately builds toward dramatic or spiritual climax. "In a Father's Place" demonstrates this patience in the sheer length of its telling—it is nearly a novella—and in its depth of character detail.

Tilghman also uses a traditional narrative method here, avoiding the postmodern trend toward the self-conscious storyteller. The third-person omniscient narrator is neither ironic nor self-reflexive; we have no sense that Tilghman is drawing attention to the fact that he is telling a story or that he is somehow poking fun at that story.

Tilghman is also a traditionalist in his willingness to invest his fiction with a certain spiritual element. His fiction finally and meaningfully affirms the humane character of one's endeavors, without lapsing into sentimentality or preachiness. He seems to practice what novelist John Gardner defined as "moral fiction"—fiction told to celebrate the ultimate humanity of the ambiguous, baffling, and often contradictory human heart.

Gregory L. Morris

IN A GREAT MAN'S HOUSE

Author: Ruth Prawer Jhabvala (1927-   )
Type of plot: Domestic realism
Time of plot: The 1970's
Locale: India
First published: 1976

Principal characters:
    KHAN SAHIB, a renowned Indian classical singer
    HAMIDA, his wife
    ROXANA, his sister-in-law, Hamida's sister
    THE GIRL, his wife's niece, Roxana's daughter
    SAJID, his son, who attends a boarding school

The Story

In the great man's house, the word of Khan Sahib is law. A renowned musician who attracts listeners, students, and researchers from far and wide, Khan Sahib is the undisputed lord of the house. His wife, Hamida, is torn between her pride in him and her bondage to him. The story opens as Hamida receives a letter from her brother, who resides in the town where she was raised, inviting her to attend his daughter's wedding. When Hamida tells Khan Sahib about this invitation, he rules that she cannot attend the wedding because it will take place at the same time as a music conference at which her services as a hostess are needed. Hamida is upset, both by Khan Sahib's high-handedness and by the thought of missing a joyous family gathering.

Later that morning Hamida's younger sister Roxana visits her to discuss travel plans. This visit further upsets Hamida's equilibrium. Although she wants to impress on her sister the importance of Khan Sahib's role at the music conference and the importance of her own role there (mainly to supervise the kitchen), she also envies Roxana's freedom to attend their niece's wedding—whose organization she herself would manage, were she to attend. Roxana sympathizes with her sister's disappointment, but it is clear that she has actually come to her wealthy sister looking for financial help. To help advance her cause, she has brought her daughter and son along.

Roxana wastes no time in throwing her children at Hamida and Khan Sahib. The latter, uncomfortable in family situations, immediately orders Hamida to take the young girl shopping to buy her fineries for the wedding. Hamida resents Roxana's greedy readiness to leave her daughter behind for the shopping expedition. After her sister leaves, Hamida again pleads with her husband to let her go to her niece's wedding. While reclining majestically on his bed, Khan Sahib dismisses her pleas and orders her to massage his legs. Hamida then collapses in tears and moans about her greatest sorrow—as she always does in such situations—the fact that her husband has sent her only son, Sajid, away to a boarding school in the hills. Tired of Hamida's tears, Khan Sahib wearily dismisses her.

In the other room, Hamida finds her niece waiting patiently for her. She tries to be kind to the girl, telling her stories about her cousin Sajid, who will be home for the holidays in two weeks, and she questions the girl about the food that she eats at home—suspicious that her sister's household does not feed the children properly. At this moment, a telegram from her brother arrives, asking her to come immediately as she is urgently needed for the wedding preparations. Khan Sahib remains unimpressed by this new call for Hamida's presence at the wedding. Although Hamida shrieks that she will go anyway, both she and her husband know that she will not go.

Hamida now amuses herself by feeding Roxana's daughter, whom she believes is too thin. She takes the girl to Khan Sahib and is touched by his gentleness with the girl. After she attends to his needs as he dresses for company and finishes preparing refreshments for his guests, she is exhausted. Her niece surprises her pleasantly by rubbing her forehead with cologne, dispelling her headache. In a rush of tenderness, Hamida dresses the girl in her own silks and jewels, and they enjoy each other's company until Roxana returns.

Roxana's undisguised glee at the turn of events spoils Hamida's good mood, and the girl is embarrassed by her mother's open display of greed. Hamida is further dismayed to hear that Roxana's entire family is preparing to leave for the wedding almost immediately. In a weak moment, she begs Roxana to leave her daughter behind to keep her company. Though excited at the thought of what gifts her daughter may get out of her aunt, Roxana cannot allow that, but she promises to bring her back immediately after the wedding. She insists that her daughter keep the clothes that Hamida has dressed her in, and Hamida, too weary to protest, agrees.

After her sister and niece depart, Hamida lies down and listens to the sounds coming from the room in which Khan Sahib is merrily entertaining his guests. Feeling abandoned and sorry for herself, she sheds a few tears as the soft strains of the romantic song that her husband is singing reach her. It is a song about a woman suffering from unrequited love. Hamida is once again struck with amazement at how movingly such a coarse man as Khan Sahib can express the depth of a woman's feelings. His beautiful voice fills her with complete joy, and she gives herself up ecstatically to the wonder of his music.

Themes and Meanings

"In a Great Man's House" explores the psychological complexities in the marital relationship between a talented, famous man and his adoring but heavily fettered wife. It concentrates on the turbulent feelings of Khan Sahib's wife, Hamida, as she conducts her life torn between joyous pride in her husband's "greatness" and talent, and sorrow in knowing that she has no rights or powers of her own. Hamida is not a terribly intelligent woman who suffers a great moral dilemma in this conflict, however. Her tale is basically a simple one, a snippet of domestic realism that has undertones of irony in its characterization of a "great man," talented but coarse and unfeeling in the ultimate analysis. It is, therefore, possibly the story of many a marriage in which a prominent man uses his "greatness" to secure the bondage of his less talented spouse, while she is confused as to whether she should allow her personality to be totally consumed by his or should assert herself periodically.

Hamida does occasionally attempt to demand her rights—usually by throwing tantrums—but they are of no avail in the face of her husband's mountainous power. Therefore, she has become increasingly acquiescent, now confining her expressions of sorrow to tears and sulks. On the other hand, she has not lost her ability to revel in her husband's talent. She can even drown her sorrows in it, finding in his song a kind of sublime happiness, even though he sings it for other people, not to her. Hamida can, apparently, exist in the great man's house only by accepting her inferior status. She can be happy only if willing to undermine her own needs and take pleasure in catering to his. Her ultimate happiness is derived from a true appreciation of that which makes him great, his musical ability, for it is only through his love songs that she can feel close to him.

Style and Technique

Although Ruth Prawer Jhabvala is not a native of India—where she spent twenty-five years while married to an Indian—she has shown a remarkable ability to capture the essences of everyday life in the country in her short stories and novels. The story of Hamida and Khan Sahib takes a brief look at a situation obviously not uncommon to middle-class Indian households in which the husband happens to be well known in his field. It is usual in such a case for him to be the noisy and demanding center of a small universe that revolves completely around his desires and whims, and Jhabvala clearly conveys this idea through what appears to be a rambling account of a day in Hamida's life. Her stylistic strength lies in her low-key storytelling that quietly captures meaningful moments and emotions.

The story's anticlimactic end makes it powerful. If the reader expects that Hamida will finally rebel or merely collapse in a heap of sorrow, her swift change of mood inspired by the strains of her husband's song gives the story an interesting psychological twist.

Brinda Bose

IN A GROVE

Author: Ryūnosuke Akutagawa (Ryūnosuke Niihara, 1892-1927)
Type of plot: Mystery and detective
Time of plot: The twelfth century
Locale: Heian-kyo, modern Kyoto, Japan
First published: "Yabu no naka," 1922 (English translation, 1952)

Principal characters:
THE WOODCUTTER, who discovers the body of a dead samurai
    soldier
THE ITINERANT PRIEST, who saw the victim a day earlier
THE ARRESTING OFFICER
AN OLD WOMAN, the victim's mother-in-law
TAJOMARU, a notorious thief
THE WIFE, who confesses to the murder
THE SPIRIT OF TAKEHIRO, the victim

The Story

Seven characters speak to a magistrate about their knowledge of a man found stabbed in the chest in the woods near Kyoto after a woodcutter discovers a dead samurai soldier in a secluded grove. The woodcutter reports to the magistrate the details of the scene of the crime and the condition of the body, recounting that the well-dressed victim was stabbed in the chest, but that there was no sword nearby. A priest saw the soldier with a woman and a horse the day before. The man had a bow and a lacquered quiver holding more than twenty arrows. An officer has arrested a notorious thief named Tajomaru and has no doubt that this criminal committed the murder. Tajomaru's weakness for women and his violent activities are well known, explains the officer; the fact that the lacquered bow and arrows found in Tajomaru's possession belonged to the dead man further convince the officer that he has arrested the right man. The quiver, however, contains only seventeen arrows. The thief also has a horse that matches the description given by the priest. An old woman approaches the magistrate and asks the court to find her missing daughter. She defensively acknowledges her daughter was spirited, but she insists that the young woman was devoted to her husband, twenty-six-year-old Takehiro.

Tajomaru confesses that he has murdered the samurai because he wanted the man's wife: When he saw the couple, he decided he must have the woman. He lured Takehiro into the dense grove by appealing to his greed, promising to sell him some valuable swords and mirrors at a bargain. He attacked the samurai from behind and tied him to a tree, then went back outside the grove where the woman waited on the horse. He led her into the grove by telling her Takehiro had been taken ill, and seeing her husband tied up, she pulled out a dagger and fought Tajomaru. She was a spirited fighter, Tajomaru agrees, but he overcame her without difficulty. Although murder is not difficult for him, he did not plan to kill the husband because it was not necessary. Although he has ravished women without compunction on other occasions, he insists that this time he fell in love with the woman. He claims that she then cried that she could not bear for two men to know of her shame, and she suggested that the two men fight to the death and vowed that she would go with the winner. After twenty-three runs with the sword, a number that demonstrates the samurai's incomparable strength, Tajomaru finally succeeded in killing the soldier. During the fight, the woman disappeared, leaving her horse behind. Tajomaru appropriated the horse and other items and rode off.

A young woman appears at a temple and identifies herself as the wife of the victim. She claims that she was ravished by Tajomaru while her bound husband watched her contemptuously. Tajomaru left immediately afterward. The wife insisted that she could not bear for her husband to know of her shame and suggested that they both die. Her husband agreed that she must kill him and then kill herself. She stabbed her husband, but to her greater shame, she did not have the courage to kill herself.

The spirit of the victim, speaking through a medium, maintains that he killed himself. Takehiro says that his wife chose to go with the thief but insisted that Tajomaru kill her husband before they left. Even the amoral Tajomaru grew pale at the woman's cruel suggestion, Takehiro asserts. Tajomaru asked Takehiro if he should kill the woman, but she ran off and Tajomaru chased after her. To preserve his honor, Takehiro thrust the dagger into his own chest. As he gasped his last breaths, he could feel someone pull the valuable, bejeweled dagger from him.

Themes and Meanings

Rather than focusing merely on discovering the identity of the murderer, as in most mysteries, Ryūnosuke Akutagawa forces the reader to examine issues involving motive and characterization. The story's initial question—who committed the murder?—soon yields to the more provocative question of why anyone would confess to a murder he or she did not commit. At least two, and possibly all three, characters are lying. Nor does the story simply address the issue of varying points of view of the same event. These characters are not honestly reporting their distorted perceptions of what transpired. Each presents the story in a way that makes him or her look better, given the values of their respective cultures. The wife professes to value her honor above her life; her greatest guilt comes from her ravishment by Tajomaru and her inability to carry through with her suicide plans, not from having killed her husband. That act, after all, was done in accordance with the Japanese code of honor. The thief speaks from another culture, that of outlaws. He blatantly flaunts his lawlessness; brags about his past crimes, which include other murders; and even proclaims that his life is more honest than that of the establishment, which hypocritically exploits people and ruins lives through the abuse of power and wealth. The husband, whose suicide would be more honorable than being murdered by a thief or a dishonored, disloyal wife, wants to defend his reputation, even after death.

All three characters cite courage as an honored virtue. Tajomaru boasts that he is courageous, both in his criminal exploits and in his fearless acceptance of his fate, which is to be hanged. This latter certainty, he argues, should give his account credibility, as he has no reason to lie. The wife is ashamed that she did not have the courage to kill herself, and Takehiro's suicide would be the ultimate act of courage.

Style and Technique

The story is divided into seven sections, each presenting a first-person point of view of one of the seven characters. The first four narrators are not directly involved in the crime, and the seven narrators are arranged in order of increasing involvement. The woodcutter, for example, is merely a witness and reports factual details and makes no judgments or inferences. The priest, who has seen the couple, does not know them personally but comments on the brevity of life and expresses pity for the victim. The arresting officer seems intent on proving that he has arrested the right man and jumps fallaciously to the conclusion that the thief's possession of the victim's bow and arrows is proof of his guilt. He has a vested interest in claiming the capture of this nefarious villain to boost his own professional reputation. The mother, the last of the indirectly involved characters, is concerned about the safety and whereabouts of her daughter and feels the need to defend her daughter's reputation.

The last three narrators, the principal characters involved, are presented similarly in order of increasing subjectivity. The thief is involved in the crime, yet he feels no remorse for the acts he has confessed to or for his other past criminal deeds; nor does he betray any fear or regret at having been arrested, although he will surely be hanged. The wife, emotionally as well as physically involved in the event, nevertheless is alive. She has not only the murder to answer for, but also the accusations regarding her relationship with Tajomaru to deny. The concluding narrative, that of the victim himself, presents the point of view of the character most dramatically affected by the events described. Akutagawa uses overlapping details in the seven accounts to give some credibility to each of the three confessions. For example, Takehiro's claim of suicide raises questions about the absence of the weapon, yet he recalls someone pulling the sword from his chest as he is dying. The priest's description of the horse implicates Tajomaru.

Critics have noted that this story reveals the influence of Victorian poet Robert Browning's dramatic monologues, particularly *The Ring and the Book* (1868-1869), which similarly presents twelve different accounts of a murder. "In a Grove," along with Akutagawa's story "Rashōmon," was the basis for the film *Rashomon* (1950) by Japanese director Akira Kurosawa.

Lou Thompson

IN ANOTHER COUNTRY

Author: Ernest Hemingway (1899-1961)
Type of plot: Psychological
Time of plot: The late 1920's
Locale: Milan during World War I
First published: 1927

> *Principal characters:*
> AN AMERICAN OFFICER, a young man being rehabilitated after having been wounded
> THREE ITALIAN OFFICERS, young men of the same age who have received medals for their bravery
> A FOURTH ITALIAN SOLDIER, whose nose was blown off within an hour after arriving at the front
> AN ITALIAN MAJOR, formerly a great fencer, who is now disabled with a withered hand

The Story

Ernest Hemingway's "In Another Country" describes the relationships that develop in Milan among an American and five Italian soldiers who have been wounded and are receiving physical therapy. The story is told from the perspective of the American. The townspeople, with the exception of the café girls, resent the young men because they are officers; this resentment, in addition to the young soldiers' war experiences, sets them apart from the street life in Milan.

Within their group, however, there are also differences. The American has received a medal for his accidental war injury. Three young Italians from near Milan, in contrast to the American, have received wounds and medals because of bravery in battle. Another young Italian from a good family was wounded after only one hour on the front line. The American feels close to this young man because his bravery could not be tested. After cocktails, the American thinks that he might have done all the things that the Italians did to receive their citations. However, he knows that he "would never have done such things" and acknowledges that he is "very much afraid to die."

All the wounded men go to the hospital every afternoon to use machines for physical therapy. The doctor assures the American that he will again play football even though his knee does not bend. An Italian major, who used to be the greatest fencer in Italy before he was wounded, befriends the American, assisting him in learning to speak Italian grammatically. Although the youth of the American and the Italians is emphasized, the major seems to be more mature. Unlike the three young "hunting-hawks," the major does not "believe in bravery."

Near the conclusion of the story, the major's young wife suddenly dies. He is distraught and lashes out at the American but then apologizes and tells him of his loss.

After three days of mourning, the major returns to the hospital wearing a black band on his sleeve.

Themes and Meanings

Still significant in the consciousness of the wounded men is the war, which represents both a challenge and a threat. Because of the war, the three young Italians with medals know that they are brave. In addition to representing a test, the war also heightens the soldiers' awareness of death. The story opens with the line: "In the fall the war was always there, but we did not go to it any more." The tall, pale Italian who has three medals is described as having "lived a very long time with death." As a result, their experiences in the war have left them all "detached."

The nature of courage is one of the central themes of "In Another Country." The American officer is afraid of dying and lies awake wondering how he will behave when he goes back to the front. His fear is contrasted with the bravery of the three young Italians who earned their medals: "The three with the medals were like hunting-hawks; and I was not a hawk." The bravery of the three "hunting-hawks," however, is also contrasted with the courage of the major, who is not a hunting-hawk. The American does not understand the major, but he does recognize that he "had been a great fencer" and that he does not "believe in bravery." The major's self-discipline and courage prompt him to befriend the young American. He insists that the American learn to speak Italian grammatically. The major's concern about speaking Italian grammatically illustrates the importance he gives to "form," to living in terms of a strict code of behavior.

The major's courage does not spring from the heedless self-confidence that often passes for bravery; he is willing to continue to try in spite of the likelihood of failure or defeat. Even though the major comes regularly to work with the therapy machines, he tells the doctor that he has no confidence in them.

The major's courage in the face of his wife's death equals his courage in accepting his disability. The death of his wife is particularly tragic as she was very young and as the major had postponed their marriage until after he had been permanently disabled from his war wounds. The major's courage in coping with his young wife's death is contrasted with the bravery of the three "hunting-hawks" in facing danger. In addition, the major's compassion (for the American) sets him apart from the others.

Although war offers the challenge of living with death, those who do battle are not the only ones vulnerable to it: The death of the major's young wife from pneumonia underlines the fact of human mortality. The major's courage thus becomes a model of the heroism required to live.

The source for the title "In Another Country" is Christopher Marlowe's *The Jew of Malta* (1589), in which Friar Barnardine says to Barabas: "Thou hast committed—"; the sentence is finished ironically by Barabas, who says, "Fornication—but that was in another country/ And besides, the wench is dead."

The title thus suggests the detachment that the young men feel after living with death during the war. The conclusion of Barabas's speech, "the wench is dead," brutally reinforces the tragedy of the death of the major's young wife. The irony of her death suggests the difficulty of living with courage.

Style and Technique

Hemingway tells the story from the point of view of the young American, but in the objective or pseudo-third person. By telling the story from the American's point of view yet not making him the narrator, Hemingway manages to objectify and distance the surface of the narrative without affecting the intimacy established between the reader and the American.

The restraint with which the characters experience and voice their emotions is reinforced by the stylistic restraints that Hemingway imposes on his narrative. The central issue of the story, that courage is necessary for life as well as death, is not revealed until the end, when the doctor explains the tragedy of the death of the major's young wife. The major's intense grief at his wife's death is conveyed by language that avoids labeling the emotion he feels: "The photographs did not make much difference to the major because he only looked out of the window." The American may or may not understand the major's bitter loss, but the reader inevitably perceives the major's emotional wound and his courage in not giving up.

Hemingway uses images to suggest the feelings of his characters; the emotions of the characters are conveyed indirectly by what they see. The mood or tone of the story is established in the first paragraph, in which the dead game outside the shops is described as "stiff," "heavy," and "empty." The American's awareness of death controls the way he experiences the streets of Milan. Death is a haunting refrain playing quietly under the surface of the narrative. Though the hospital is "very old and very beautiful," the American observes: "There were usually funerals starting from the courtyard."

Irony is used quietly, but with force. The American comments that the wounded men are all very polite when they go to sit in "the machines that were to make so much difference." Because these men are the first to use the machines, the photographs of restored limbs that the doctor first shows the men and then puts on the wall do not inspire great confidence. The machines are not likely to restore their limbs; in any case, nothing can ease the internal wounds epitomized by the suffering of the major.

In spite of his lack of confidence in the machines, the major continues to come to sit in them, even after his wife's death. His regular attendance is like his interest in having the young American learn grammar. The major's discipline and courage in the face of almost certain defeat are powerfully underscored because they are never overtly mentioned.

Jean R. Brink

IN DARKNESS AND CONFUSION

Author: Ann Petry (1908-1997)
Type of plot: Psychological
Time of plot: 1943
Locale: Harlem, New York
First published: 1947

Principal characters:
WILLIAM JONES, a drugstore porter
PINK JONES, his wife
ANNIE MAY, Pink's niece

The Story

William Jones, his wife, Pink, and her niece, Annie May, occupy an apartment on the top floor of a Harlem tenement. One Saturday morning, as William eats his breakfast and prepares for work, it is apparent that this will not be a good day. He usually enjoys this first meal of the day—the quiet before the house awakens and the coolness before the sun's heat penetrates the thin walls and makes the small apartment unbearable. This morning, however, the heat is already intolerable, the coffee tastes awful, the eggs are overcooked, and the warmed-over cornbread tastes like sand in his mouth.

William cannot seem to rid himself of the worries that have plagued him of late, especially the anxiety for his son, a soldier stationed in Georgia. He has not heard from Sam in a long time, and both he and Pink are concerned that the boy may be in trouble. To add to William's distress, Annie May is out of control and constantly indulged by her doting aunt, who excuses the girl's every indiscretion by saying, "I don't care what she's done, she ain't got no mother or father except us."

As William sits at the kitchen table, consumed by these thoughts, he is brought back to consciousness by the sound of movement in the bedroom. When Pink comes into the kitchen, he mumbles something about the heat, then quickly retires to the bedroom. He does not want to talk to his wife just yet. After a while, he comes out of the bedroom, dressed for work. Heading for the door, he stops to question Annie May about the late hours she has been keeping, and she gives him a flippant answer. Her answer seems to meet with approval from Pink, whose laughter mingles with Annie May's, as William goes out of the door and down the stairs to the mailbox.

There is no letter. Disappointed by another day with no word from Sam, William makes his way through the dismal streets, struck again with their meanness—many of the dilapidated buildings are inhabited by pimps, prostitutes, drunks, and drug addicts. Thoughts of the morning return, and he finds himself reliving incidents of his life. He recalls the many unsuccessful efforts he has made to extricate himself from this ghetto, to find decent housing for his wife, whose health is threatened by having to climb the steep stairs to their apartment. He thinks, also, of the many wonderful plans he has made for his son.

When William arrives at the drugstore, he puts on his work clothes and begins his routine of cleaning the floors and stocking the shelves. As the day wears on, three young girls come in, laughing and giggling as they seat themselves on the stools at the counter. They remind William of Annie May, who quit school at the age of sixteen, with Pink's sanction and over his objections.

At the end of a weary day of work and worry, William goes to the barbershop for a haircut. There, in a chance meeting with one of Sam's soldier friends, William learns that his son is in prison. Sam has been court-martialed and sentenced to twenty years at hard labor for shooting a military police officer who had shot him for not moving to the back of the bus. Devastated, but determined to keep this discovery from Pink, William goes home, gets into bed, and feigns sleep so as not to have to talk to his wife when she comes home from work.

When William arises on Sunday morning, Pink is already dressed for church, and William pretends to be deeply absorbed in the newspaper until she leaves. Later, finding it impossible to remain alone in the apartment, he dresses and heads for a bar in a neighborhood hotel. While he is drinking and brooding over his son, he glances casually toward the hotel lobby, where a white police officer is arguing with a black woman. When the police officer threatens the woman with his nightstick, a black soldier intervenes and is shot by the police officer. This act of violence against the soldier is a painful reminder of all that William has been trying to forget; suddenly, all the anger and frustration that he has been suppressing bursts forth. Without thinking, he rushes through the lobby, followed by the other barroom patrons. They hear the sound of an ambulance, which pulls off just as they reach the street. They are then joined by others who are also angered by the incident, and this anger explodes into a full-scale riot.

In a matter of minutes, a sea of humanity is surging through the streets—hundreds of black people, venting their rage against a system that has held them in bondage. They rush wildly through the streets, pillaging, pilfering, destroying. Suddenly, amid the chaos, William encounters Pink returning from church. In trying to tell her what has happened at the bar, he blurts out the news about Sam. Her first reaction is stunned silence, then uncontrollable rage—rage that sends her on a destructive rampage through the streets of Harlem. When, finally, her rage is spent, she collapses a few blocks from their apartment—dead.

Themes and Meanings

"In Darkness and Confusion" is clearly about the destructiveness of poverty and the terrible consequences of unfulfilled dreams. Ann Petry suggests that a dream too long deferred can, and often does, have catastrophic effects, not only for the individual but also for the community. This theme begins to unfold early in the narrative, as William descends the dark, steep stairwell of his apartment building. He wants desperately to find a way out of his situation. He dreams of finding a place, perhaps a first-floor apartment, that would be easier on his wife, but cost is always the deterrent. His thoughts continually return to that one all-consuming dream—release from this environment that is so damaging to his family—but always he comes up against the maddening reality that his meager finances hold him captive in this place.

William's dream intensifies as he thinks about the deleterious effects of the ghetto environment on his young son, for they could not walk down the streets without being propositioned by prostitutes and pimps. Although he had warned Sam about the dangers in these streets, he is discomfited by the thought that the boy had already explored what the block offered. At such times he would think, "We gotta move this time for sure. This ain't a fit place to live." Neither anguish, nor outrage, nor dogged determination will free him, however. Dire poverty has assigned him this place, and it is a place from which there is no escape.

Despite his destitute condition, William still dreams of a better life for his son than that which he and Pink share. Even while sweeping the drugstore floor, he vows that Sam will not have to earn his living this way. He will earn it "wearing a starched collar . . . shined shoes and a crease in his pants." Looking at his employer, William decides that being a pharmacist would be a good occupation for Sam because it is clean work and pays well. With Sam's imprisonment, however, it seems that the fulfillment of this dream also will be denied him.

Style and Technique

In showing the devastating effects of poverty on the lives of individuals, Petry employs a third-person point of view, setting William Jones at the center of the narrative and filtering all the incidents of the story through his consciousness. This gives the story a sense of immediacy by allowing the reader to experience events firsthand. The reader relives all of William's fears and frustrations: fear for his wife's physical health and for his son's emotional well-being, as well his frustrations at being trapped in the stultifying ghetto environment. The reader walks beside him as he makes his way to work in a dead-end job, and as he operates on the fringes of a world to which he can never really belong.

In following William throughout the weekend, sharing his past disappointments and disillusionments as well as his hopes and dreams, the reader is better able to understand how the tremendous buildup of tension can result in riot. In looking through the eyes of the protagonist, one can see how an entire community might be overwhelmed by circumstances and finally driven to commit unspeakable acts of violence.

Gladys J. Washington

IN DREAMS BEGIN RESPONSIBILITIES

Author: Delmore Schwartz (1913-1966)
Type of plot: Dream vision
Time of plot: 1909
Locale: Brooklyn
First published: 1937

> *Principal characters:*
> THE NARRATOR, the dreamer of the story
> HIS FATHER
> HIS MOTHER
> THE USHER, who works in the theater where the narrator "views" the silent film
> THE OLD LADY, who is one of the theater audience
> THE PHOTOGRAPHER, who poses the parents at Coney Island
> THE FORTUNE-TELLER, who provokes a quarrel between the parents

The Story

The first-person narrator sets a tentative tone at the beginning with his uncertainty: "I think it is the year 1909." The reader then learns that the narrator is dreaming that he is in a motion-picture theater, viewing a Sunday afternoon in 1909. He sees the man who is to become his father walking the streets of Brooklyn on the way to visit the woman whom he is courting. As the narrator dreams and casts the characters, he can know their thoughts and feelings: his father's awkward impressiveness, for example, his hesitancy about marriage.

The couple—the narrator's "prospective parents"—go to Coney Island, where they stroll the boardwalk, watch the bathers, and stare at the ocean. Throughout this section, the narrator reacts to their movements and is shocked by the seeming shallowness of his father and mother. He knows that the father is hesitant about marriage, exaggerates his earnings, and has always believed that "actualities somehow fall short." The narrator begins to weep but is consoled by an old lady in the theater of his dream. Unable to control his tears, he leaves the theater momentarily but returns to view his parents riding on a merry-go-round, after which they walk at dusk to a fashionable restaurant "so that they can look out on the boardwalk and the mobile ocean." As they eat, the father talks about his plans for the future, about his achievements, about his independence since he was thirteen, until, moved by the music of the waltz being played, he almost accidentally proposes to the mother.

The narrator stands up in the dream theater and shouts, "Don't do it," but when the audience, the old lady, and the usher urge him to be quiet, he resigns himself. The next scene shows his father and mother having their picture taken, although the photographer has difficulty posing the two and is certain that "somehow there is something wrong in their pose." The father impatiently goads the photographer, who takes the picture, and as the parents wait for it to be developed, "they become quite depressed."

The final dream sequence features a fortune-teller, whose booth the mother wants to enter, while the father does not. Although the father momentarily concedes, inside the booth he again becomes impatient and in anger strides out. The narrator at this point once more shouts to them to consider what they are doing. The usher drags him out of the theater, telling the young man that he cannot do whatever he wants, that he cannot behave so emotionally. The narrator wakes then, to the "bleak winter morning of his 21st birthday, the windowsill shining with its lip of snow, and the morning already begun."

Themes and Meanings

The young man, through his dreams, is able to expose his ambivalence toward himself and his parents, and toward the imminence of manhood and responsibility. As he re-creates his parents' lives before his birth, he judges and evaluates their personalities, their shortcomings, and their incompatibility. In that dreamworld, the youth can also become aware of his own consciously repressed sense of terror and anguish. Although he feels detached and anonymous as the film begins, the succeeding images force him to confront his own fate—his birth and his impending responsibilities as he enters manhood on his twenty-first birthday. The ambivalence of youth toward parents is clearly revealed as he deplores his father's materialism and smugness, his mother's stubbornness. The sensitivity of the narrator is paralleled by the seeming stolidity of his parents, who sense nothing of the menace in the power of the ocean or in their awesome responsibilities as prospective parents.

Throughout the dream, the narrator's place in society is also explored, when, for example, the old lady in the theater admonishes him or when the usher establishes the conventions of proper behavior. Fluctuating between his need to stay in the theater (society) and his ambivalence toward the incompatibility that he senses in his parents, he is yet caught with the desire to be born—to live. What could have been a banal story of the generation gap, of youthful sensitivity versus parental callousness, of coming of age and the acceptance of responsibilities, is transformed by means of Delmore Schwartz's technique.

Style and Technique

Schwartz combines two imagistic devices—the whole a dream structure within which the narrator is watching a film. The dream device permits quick switches of time and place, distorted focus, and shifting images. The narrator, though unable to control or choose his parents in real life, has control in the sense that he is able to know their thoughts in the past of the film and contrast them with his emotional reactions in his own present. The narrator, once the silent-film atmosphere is set, can then posit a surrounding audience, which serves also to reinforce the theme of the young man's growing awareness of the restraints and judgments in society. The film device combined with the dream permits abrupt shifts in scenes, time telescoping, and sharp, telling visual images. The narrator thus can both view and feel because of the interaction between the internal dream and the seemingly external film.

With the swings between the narrator's understanding and rejection, the paradox of denying his parents' fitness and yet desiring his own existence, Schwartz uses the dream device to suggest the youth's ambivalence and to compress the whole family life into a few pages. The focus is on the narrator's reactions, but without the overt self-pity that a direct first-person "realistic" narration might have engendered. The narrator's level of perception suggests his sensitivity without explicit statement. His perceptions provide insight into his capacity to feel. The narrator does not need to "tell" the reader. His growing awareness is set with sharp images, bleakness contrasted with shining, the reiteration of the paradox of rejection and acceptance, and the suggestion that he realizes through the dream that after all, for everyone, what one does matters very much.

Eileen Lothamer

IN GREENWICH THERE ARE MANY
GRAVELLED WALKS

Author: Hortense Calisher (1911-   )
Type of plot: Social realism
Time of plot: About 1950
Locale: New York City
First published: 1951

Principal characters:
PETER BIRGE, the protagonist, a twenty-three-year-old journalism
  student
.ANNE, his mother
ROBERT VIELUM, Peter's older friend, a "perennial taker of
  courses"
SUSAN, Robert's twenty-year-old daughter
VINCE, Robert's current young roomer
MARIO OSTI, Robert's new young friend, an Italian painter

The Story

As the story opens, Peter Birge has just returned from Greenwich, where he left his
mother, Anne, at a sanatorium. Peter's father, a Swedish engineer, died when Peter
was eight, but his patents have provided income for Peter and Anne ever since. When
not in sanatoriums, Anne has maintained an apartment for herself and her son in
Greenwich Village, to the consternation of their more conservative, suburbanite relatives. This unconventional upbringing taught Peter early the limitations of life's
promises for many and inevitably alienated him from the optimism common to his
age group. Not surprisingly, therefore, the friend he seeks out on his return to town is
an older man, Robert Vielum.

Robert, who in many ways is a mystery to Peter but in whose apartment Peter and
other young students have found "a heartening jangle of conversation and music,"
takes courses but avoids degrees and has no known source of income beyond the
money that he earns renting the extra bedroom in his apartment to a series of young
male students. Peter's arrival discovers Robert entertaining a new young man, an Italian painter named Mario Osti, much to the dismay of his current renter, Vince. Vince
is further upset, Peter learns, because Robert is expecting a visit from his daughter Susan and has offered her Vince's room for the remainder of the summer while Robert
and Mario vacation in Rome. Robert had been planning a trip to Morocco with Vince
before Mario and Susan entered the picture.

Vince's dismay threatens to become violence just as the doorbell rings. As Vince
retreats to his bedroom, Robert ushers in Susan, who is caught between camp and

home while her mother and stepfather are finishing divorce arrangements. Susan's mother apparently "marries" for a living; the current stepfather is Susan's third. "I wouldn't want to be an inconvenience," she assures her father, "with a polite terror which suggested she might often have been one."

With the cast now complete, the real action begins: Vince leaps from the bedroom window to his death. After the confusion of police and ambulances, Robert exits to the police station, and Peter escorts Susan to a restaurant before inviting her to use his mother's room if she has nowhere else to stay. After checking her stepfather's home and finding it bolted against her, she accepts his offer. "It was a nice room I had there. Nicest one I ever did have, really," she remembers. Then she admits that she really does not care about "my parents, or any of the people they tangle with," although she wishes that she could. As they drive to his apartment, Peter thinks about taking her for a drive the next day—to Greenwich.

Themes and Meanings

In her preface to *The Best American Short Stories, 1951*, Martha Foley describes the reaction to this story in a classroom of Columbia University: "The younger generation in the room considered it a heartbreakingly beautiful story of two young people, lost like themselves, in a world they never made." Susan and Peter, much like the eponymous characters Franny and Zooey in J. D. Salinger's novel, were more familiar to the youth of the 1950's than were, perhaps, the television role models promising the happy days of ideal American families such as the Nelsons. Ozzie did not divorce Harriet, nor did Harriet become an alcoholic. How could David and Ricky represent the generation growing up in the aftermath of World War II? Susan and Peter, on the other hand, respond to the sensitivity in each other and passively resign themselves to the insensitivity and sordidness of the world around them.

Hortense Calisher chose to open the 1975 edition of her collected stories with "In Greenwich There Are Many Gravelled Walks," so that the book would follow what she explains in its introduction as the "natural rhythms" in her work. One of these, she explains further, is going "from an untrustworthy reality to a joyously recognizable fantasy." Her later works include, in fact, two novels that can loosely be described as science fiction in that search for the fantasy. This story, as part of her first published collection, best represents the "untrustworthy reality" of which she speaks.

What is "untrustworthy" in the world of Peter and Susan is not the sordid surface of broken homes and children assuming responsibilities while parents pursue pleasure or escape. Rather, it is the greater society, which offers an American Dream and ignores individual nightmares. Peter cannot communicate with his cousins, whose "undamaged eyes were still starry with expectancy"; Susan admires even the neurotic Vince, who can care enough to commit suicide. In finding each other, each has finally discovered the company that misery loves. It took Calisher another twenty years to discover the "joyously recognizable fantasy" that perhaps first emerges in the two works that she published in the mid-1960's: *Journal from Ellipsis* (1965) and *The Railway Police and The Last Trolley Ride* (1966).

Style and Technique

Not surprisingly, the "untrustworthy reality" of this story is captured in a style rich in social realism. With almost classical restraint, Calisher limits the time to one afternoon and evening in early August, the primary action to the meeting of Peter and Susan, and the primary place to Robert's apartment. The action that would seem to demand center stage, the suicide, is presented only after the fact, as first Mario and then the young couple look out the window to see the body lying below.

The story is offered from Peter's perspective; the reader learns of the others only what Peter knows about them or what they reveal about themselves in the course of the story. The homosexuality implied by Robert's relationships with "young male students" is never stated; neither Peter's nor Susan's parents actually enter the story, although the reader learns much about Anne because the experience that drives her back to the sanatorium is fresh in Peter's mind.

Most notably, as the title intimates, the story is conveyed by setting. Peter and Susan are products of urban America; even the suburbs seem to be out of their reach. Peter's cousins at Rye can claim "the hot blue day, the sand, and the water, as if these were all extensions of themselves," while Peter's escapes from his mother's Village reality have only been brief respites in boarding school, an abortive attempt to move uptown to Central Park West, and a stint in the army. Her latest trip to the sanatorium will cost him his latest hope for a summer abroad.

Susan does have one setting that frees her from her mother's residences in Reno, her stepfather's brownstone, and the hotels at which she and her mother have stayed "in between." She counsels at a children's camp and can at least say that "I like helping children. They can use it." However, even this setting is prematurely denied her as a polio scare closes it down early and sends her to stay with Robert.

Robert, too, is defined by his "old-fashioned apartment, on Claremont Avenue," and by the places to which he has traveled, which he seems to share with his guests by assuming that they, too, are familiar with both the places and the languages. Even Mario and Vince can be seen in the temporary status of the room for rent and the vacation companion.

Finally, it is the mother's place that closes the circle of Peter's world and provides the symbolic title. The "gravelled walks" of the sanatorium in Greenwich, lined with nurses rather than trees, are the only "country" reality that Peter has to offer Susan, as she agrees to fill his mother's room at least temporarily. Theirs is the reality that Calisher, a New Yorker herself, knows most intimately and can best convey to the reader.

Thelma J. Shinn

IN SEARCH OF EPIFANO

Author: Rudolfo A. Anaya (1937-   )
Type of plot: Fantasy
Time of plot: Probably the late twentieth century
Locale: Sonora and Chihuahua, Mexico
First published: 1992

> *Principal characters:*
> THE OLD WOMAN, who is journeying alone into Mexico
> EPIFANO, her dead great-grandfather

The Story

An old woman, almost eighty years of age, is traveling alone in her jeep, heading deep into the Mexican desert, searching for a man named Epifano. At her advanced age she is ready for death and not afraid of it. In her childhood, she had heard whispered stories about her great-grandfather Epifano, about how he had built a great ranch in the desert. Her family album included a picture of him, which remained her only concrete link to this segment of her past.

Her vehicle experiences problems, and the mechanic who repairs it attempts to dissuade her from continuing on her journey, knowing that such a trek would be difficult for anyone, let alone for a woman of her age. She remains firm in her resolve despite the physical discomforts associated with her failing health: her liver or her spleen, she does not know which, has a dull, persistent pain, and in her heart there is a tightness. She is searching for the answers to many unresolved issues in her life. Her foremost concern is what purpose her life has served. The mental picture that she has formed of Epifano guides her through the doubts and the difficulties of the voyage. She can hear his voice, the voice of her Mexican heritage, the heritage her family forgot long ago.

As she progresses in her quest to reach the land of Epifano, somewhere in the desert of the state of Chihuahua, she becomes increasingly thirsty, but it is a thirst not only for water but also for life. She reflects on how many of her desires were never satisfied. She thinks her sketches and paintings are the only evidence she will leave of her existence, and considers them an attempt to give meaning to her empty life.

In the solitude of the Mexican desert, she is overwhelmed by the magnitude of nature. She thinks she is only a moving shadow that crosses a vast, dusty, hot land. She is dwarfed by the Cañon de Cobre, the ancestral land of the mystical Tarahumara Indians, as she drives along its northern rim. As vultures circle overhead, she is flooded with memories of her marriage. She had married a man of ambition while she was young and believed that she was in love, but after many years, she discovered that he lacked desire and passion and thus could not fulfill her needs. To fill the void, she painted, took classes, and traveled. Her most intense and meaningful recollection was of her wedding day, when an Indian entered the chapel and stood in the rear. She turned around and spotted him just before he vanished. She later wondered if his appearance was real or imagined, but she had never forgotten him. He had the features of a Tarahumara. In retrospect, she believes that he was a messenger from Epifano bringing her a warning about her impending marriage. She chose to ignore the warning, however, and her unhappy union with this unfeeling man produced a daughter and a son.

In the emptiness of her marriage, she had turned to her dreams for solace, for it was there that she heard the voice of Epifano. After leaving her husband, she decided to seek out the origins of these voices to better understand them, and every spring she makes a pilgrimage to the south. Each year, she travels a little bit farther into the desert, getting closer to the location of Epifano's ranch.

At last, she reaches her destination. She drinks from a pool of water and gives thanks to the gods for quenching her thirst. As she looks out over the land where Epifano's ranch once stood, she sees the outlines of the foundations of the buildings, which is all that remains. She thinks about how his family had spread from this point toward the north until they reached Southern California.

The old woman, dressed in white, "the color of desire not consummated," sits observing the desert, feeling sad over the completion of her quest, when a noise causes her to turn. Among the desert plants, an Indian appears. She tells him that she came in search of Epifano, and the Indian holds his hand to his chest indicating that she has found him. She recognizes his kind, deep blue eyes. The figures of many Indian women emerge from the desert and surround her, forming a circle. As her sadness disappears, a flash of light fills her being. It is a light full of desire, which makes her quiver. At last, she is engulfed in light, love, and life.

Themes and Meanings

The search for Epifano constitutes a quest for meaning. The protagonist seeks something that she has never experienced in her life: fulfillment. She embarks on this journey, a journey that may be her last, hopeful of establishing meaning for a life lived for others rather than for herself. The old woman passionately clings to her almost forgotten ancestry, because it provides her with a sense of self. She stands alone, independent from the rest of her family, who treat their Mexican heritage with aloofness.

The voices of her dreams have become more meaningful to her than the voices of her family. The former have a mystical, otherworldly power that promises to quench all of her thirsts and satisfy all of her desires. Every detail of her life in Southern California is rendered meaningless by virtue of the seductive voices of the past. Her search obligates her to abandon the rational nature of her American culture for the subjective and spiritual world of the Tarahumara Indians. It has come down to this for the old woman: Fulfillment and meaning can be found only in the remote world of her tenuous ancestry.

At the story's end, she is enveloped by light and encircled by ghostly figures, including that of her great-grandfather Epifano. Her despair is replaced by a joy and a satisfaction that she has never known before. The blinding flash of light pierces her, "like an arrow from the bow of an Indian," and reaches the innermost core of her desire. It represents the supreme moment, a moment when she is complete. There is no pain and no fear. The old woman has returned to wed her ancient past and, in so doing, she satisfies her quest. The last lines of the story reflect this: "The moan of love is the moan of life. She was dressed in white." It is the end of her search but the beginning of her fulfillment.

Style and Technique

The style of Rudolfo A. Anaya's "In Search of Epifano" is not explicit. The narrative contains many symbols, representations, and clues to its meaning. It is as though the reader also joins the central character on her quest for meaning. The story's conclusion is open-ended, which necessitates a careful rereading in order to fully understand the tale. The clues that Anaya supplies throughout the story are many, and he plants them strategically. "The Tarahumaras," "death," "the loneliness and harshness of the desert," "the search for one's ancestors," "unfulfilled desires and unquenchable thirsts," "voices and apparitions," and "wearing white" are leitmotifs that recur throughout the narrative. Reading the story requires care and skill, for the journey to the story's end is fraught with mysteries that need resolution if the reader is to find satisfaction in his or her endeavor.

At the end of the story one primary question arises: Does the woman die? Anaya refuses to be explicit in his conclusion. The answer lies in the metaphor of the blinding light, which represents the old woman's passage into another dimension, a transition to another world that is carefree and fulfilling.

Silvio Sirias

IN THE AMERICAN SOCIETY

Author: Gish Jen (1956-   )
Type of plot: Social realism
Time of plot: The 1980's
Locale: An unnamed American suburb
First published: 1986

> *Principal characters:*
> RALPH CHANG, the proprietor of a pancake restaurant
> MRS. CHANG, his wife
> CALLIE, the narrator, his elder daughter
> MONA, his younger daughter

The Story

The Changs are a Chinese American family on track in the pursuit of the American Dream, which is also, in Ralph Chang's case, the immigrant dream. They are newly prosperous because the pancake house in which Ralph and his wife have invested to secure their daughters' college educations in the future is doing handsomely. Ralph has never felt so secure and expansive. He revels in his new role as benevolent dictator over his staff, not quite grasping the fact that his style of management is too much to take for many of his workers.

Mrs. Chang and their two daughters, Callie and Mona, have plans of their own. To them, one measure of their success in their new American society would be membership in the local country club. Although Mrs. Chang is pragmatic enough to realize that joining the club is not totally practical, she cannot help but aspire to membership. The biggest drawback, she and the girls realize, would be that Ralph would be forced to wear a jacket to dinner there.

Ralph's overbearing management style soon leaves the restaurant drastically understaffed. When the only applicant for a job is an undocumented Taiwanese student named Booker, Ralph hires him. There are petty jealousies among the staff, and when a disenchanted former worker divulges to the immigration authorities that Ralph is hiring illegal aliens, Ralph has to answer to the immigration agency. Fortunately, it turns out that it was not illegal to have hired aliens, and Ralph, in his well-meaning meddlesomeness, posts bail for his illegal help, Booker and Cedric. Ralph glows with self-righteous satisfaction until a note is discovered from Booker and Cedric: They promise to repay Ralph, but they have decided to flee before their trial.

On the home front, Mona has inadvertently mentioned that her mother is keen to join the country club, which leads to an effusive offer from Mona's friend's mother, Mrs. Lardner, to sponsor the Changs for membership. Mrs. Chang has little chance either to accept or to decline. Now it has become a matter of waiting to hear from the club. As it turns out, the club informs her that it has filled its quota of new members for the year. To soften the blow, Mrs. Lardner invites the Changs over for a party she is throwing for a friend. It is the opportunity for Mrs. Chang to get Ralph to buy a proper suit. Ralph does not have a chance to get alterations for the suit before the party, so the salesgirl tacks the suit up temporarily for him. Ralph then insists on wearing the tacked-up suit with the price tag intact.

The party starts well for the Changs. Ralph mingles in his temporarily tacked-up suit, while Mrs. Chang is held in conversation by someone who has been to Asia. Short of help, Mrs. Lardner puts Callie to work as a server. Trouble starts when the drunken guest-of-honor, Jeremy, confronts Ralph. When he thinks that Ralph is making fun of him, he becomes belligerent and demands to know why Ralph has crashed his party. Mrs. Lardner whispers to him and manages to calm him down. In a turn-around, Jeremy immediately becomes cordial. To make it up to Ralph, he wants to pay Ralph in kind; he takes off his polo shirt and insists that Ralph accept it. He wants Ralph to try it on and takes Ralph's jacket off. Jeremy sees the price tag still on the jacket and starts taunting Ralph. He tells Ralph he will throw the jacket into the pool if Ralph will not try on the polo shirt.

Ralph throws the shirt into the pool, then throws the jacket in after it. He gathers the family together and stomps off. Only when they are outside walking to the car does Ralph divulge that the car keys and house keys were in his suit jacket. Mrs. Chang suggests they walk to the pancake house and wait there till the party is over to call Mrs. Lardner.

Themes and Meanings

"In the American Society" is about finding one's place in society and trying to fit in. It also hints strongly at racism. Ralph and his wife are immigrants who have found some measure of success in life. They own a thriving business, they live in the suburbs in their own house, they own a car—outwardly they have all the trappings of being comfortably ensconced in their adopted society. Being accepted for who they are in the society is another thing.

The story is cleverly separated by the subheadings, "His Own Society" and "In the American Society." The first half shows Ralph in his own restaurant, the milieu in which he is comfortable. In the setting of his thriving business, Ralph feels he has come into his own in the United States. His daughter Callie, the narrator, notes that now that he is a success, he is finally able to talk about his past in China. Because Ralph has taken care of the necessities, he is able to allow himself extravagance. In his restaurant and with his employees, he even likens himself to "that Godfather in the movie."

The test of whether the Changs are fully accepted in their adopted society, however, comes when they leave the milieus of home and family business for environments that are beyond their control, environments that seem to have different sets of rules. At Mrs. Lardner's, the Changs are strange, exotic specimens, present through the generosity of their patron-hostess. Callie is shanghaied into waitressing, and her mother alternates as the center of attention between a group of women and a male guest. The former titter over her complexion while the latter tries to impress her with his knowledge of "the Orient," from which he has picked up a few Chinese words. Both the women and the man are engaged in degrees of patronage of the "exotic Orientals," something that seems to be as natural as Callie walking around with a tray of food.

The most offensive gesture of the occasion comes from Jeremy. He feels comfortable patronizing Ralph with the "secret-code," supposedly Chinese-charactered handkerchief, but when Ralph tries in return to humor him, he turns ugly. To cap his performance, he tries to press his shirt on Ralph, in effect assuming that his disgraceful display can be erased with a gift—an unwanted gift at that—and worse, that Ralph can be bought off. The incidents at Mrs. Lardner's suggest that although the Changs may be able to hold their own economically, being naturalized as full members of American society is a different matter. They seem to be Mrs. Lardner's demi-guests, and by extension the perpetual demi-guests of American society.

What marks the Changs as different and, therefore, not fully acceptable seems to be the color of their skin. It is no accident that the club to which Mrs. Chang aspires to belong is the country club—the Changs may seem to be part of their country, the United States, but they have not gained access to certain clubs, certain communities. In her own way, Mrs. Lardner seems to be trying to include the Changs in the club of her friendship, but she does so from a misplaced sense of duty, of being the good patron, so that when she is overly effusive, her supposed benevolence is nothing more than benevolent racism.

Style and Technique

"In the American Society" is a lively and humorous story. The narrator seems to be chuckling to herself when she tells it. There are many comic turns and hilarious situations, and it is filled with an assortment of zany individuals. Although it is primarily about the Changs, the side attractions are just as integral. One such subplot is that concerning Ralph's experiences with Booker and Cedric. Booker and Cedric's joint farewell letter is sheer comedy, from its appearance after they have availed themselves of Ralph's largess to its many misspellings and overall naïveté. The cast of pancakehouse characters is similar to the cast of a situation comedy—one can easily picture Ralph being godfatherly and tyrannical in turn, as his staff members add color to the scene.

Although the party carries negative undercurrents, there is a parallel hilarity to it. The narrator's tone of voice seems to be matter-of-fact, but it is always edged with irony. The narrator does not need to name the negative, but she conveys her meaning through description and dialogue. The well-placed phrase then speaks volumes. For example, at the end of the story, when the Chang family decides to wait out Mrs. Lardner's party at the pancake house, Mona moans that they will have to "dive for them." She is probably rolling her eyes when she says this, but it captures the Changs's debut in the American society—as performing seals.

Pat M. Wong

IN THE BASEMENT

Author: Isaac Babel (1894-1940)
Type of plot: Autobiographical
Time of plot: 1906
Locale: Odessa, Ukraine
First published: "V podvale," 1931 (English translation, 1948)

Principal characters:
THE NARRATOR, a twelve-year-old Jewish boy
MARK BORGMAN, his classmate
LEIVE-ITZHOK, his grandfather
BOBKA, his aunt
SIMON, his uncle

The Story

The narrator and protagonist of the story is a lonely and fanciful boy from a poor and odd Jewish family living in a basement. The reader learns about the boy's imaginative and artistic powers and his artistic method at the beginning of the story. In the first scene, the narrator overhears his rich classmate, Mark Borgman, telling the other boys about the Spanish Inquisition. Having just read a book on Baruch Spinoza, and disappointed with the lack of poetry in Mark's narration, the protagonist gives a brilliant picture of old Amsterdam, the philosophers who cut diamonds, and the death of Spinoza. The bookish child, whose imagination is always working overtime, attracts his classmate with his fantastic tales, and they become friends. Mark is a top student, and the narrator, who is too engaged in reading fiction, gets a pass because the teachers cannot bring themselves to give him a grade of very poor.

Mark invites the boy to the family villa. Mark's father, the manager of the Russian Bank for Foreign Trade, has risen so high that he refuses to speak Russian, preferring the coarse, fragmentary English language. The narrator is flabbergasted by the riches of the Borgmans. Everything is excessive in the home of these Jewish parvenus, including their guests, especially the women: "Drops of the sunset sparkled in diamonds—diamonds disposed in every possible place: in the profundities of splayed bosoms, in painted ears, on puffy bluish she-animal fingers."

The narrator, on the other hand, lives in poor and queer surroundings. His grandfather Leive-Itzhok, a former rabbi, was expelled from his town for forging a Polish count's signature on bills of exchange. All his life he has been writing a book in Hebrew, entitled "The Headless Man," in which he describes all his neighbors. His uncle Simon, with his crazy fits of enthusiasm, shouting, and bullying, is a drunk. The narrator's family includes people who have seduced the daughters of generals and abandoned them afterwards. The only sensible person is his Aunt Bobka. What can the impressionable boy give in return for what he has seen in the Borgmans's luxurious villa?

The only thing he can do is make up stories about his relatives' adventures and their virtues.

He continues doing it when the young Borgman returns his visit. His fantasies sound convincing, because in his heart of hearts he believes in what he is saying. In describing his uncle's strength and magnanimity, he admits, "If you go by the heart, it was not all that untrue." It was just hard to tell the truth looking at and listening to his unfortunate uncle. Being ashamed of his grandfather's and uncle's looks and behavior, the boy gets rid of them before Borgman's visit.

He and his Aunt Bobka welcome the guest. The aunt, proud of the boy's friendship with Mark, has baked apple strudel and poppy-seed tarts. Now, with nothing in his way, the narrator is free to allow his imagination to run wild, and he does. He cannot stop. He even resorts to the help of William Shakespeare, declaiming Marc Antony's speech over Julius Caesar's corpse.

Suddenly his drunken uncle, accompanied by a friend, returns to the basement. Uncle Simon has bought an odd and useless piece of furniture—not for the first time, as it turns out. Aunt Bobka is in despair. The grandfather, Leive-Itzhok, joins the party. To drown the noise of quarreling, cursing, and fighting, the embarrassed child continues to recite poetry at the top of his voice. He is almost frantic. The guest retires in haste.

That evening, the humiliated boy, who does not know yet what to do with reality, tries to commit suicide by drowning himself in a water barrel. Saved by his crazy grandfather, the child breaks into tears. "And the world of tears was so huge, so beautiful, that everything save tears vanished from my eyes." Thus the boy's anxieties are resolved.

Themes and Meanings

"In the Basement" is the third of the four stories of the *Dovecote* cycle devoted to Isaac Babel's Odessa childhood. The first two are "The Story of My Dovecote" and "First Love"; the fourth is "Awakening." They are presented as autobiographic tales, and they are indeed quasi-autobiographical in the sense that Babel observed such families in the Odessa Jewish quarters. The narrator is the same boy at different ages.

The main theme is growing up Jewish in czarist Russia. The difficulties of growing up and the boy's identity problems stem from his feelings of social inferiority. His love for reading and the power of imagination help him to escape the mundane reality, the poverty, the vulgarity, and the hysteria of Jewish life. He is ashamed of that world, but he is still a part of it. The lifestyle of the Borgmans does not present an alternative either. The satirical description of Mr. Borgman and his guests, especially the women, proves it.

The boy's far-fetched tales, which help him to escape reality, are nourished by the emotional richness of his Jewish heritage, his grandfather's exercises in writing, and the uniqueness of his family. The boy's tales breathe poetry and truth and are indicative of his vocation to literature. Literature, an important theme in this story, is the subject of the last story of the cycle, "Awakening."

Style and Technique

Johann Wolfgang von Goethe's definition of a short story as "a story about an unusual occurrence" was Babel's favorite. Comparing his prose to Leo Tolstoy's, Babel said that whereas Tolstoy described what happened to him minute by minute, he, Babel, was trying to depict the most interesting five minutes in twenty-four hours and put it all on several pages to make it as compact as possible. Therefore he had to choose words that were significant, simple, and beautiful. All of his life, Babel fought against adjectives. He mentioned that if he ever wrote an autobiography, it would be called "The Story of an Adjective." According to Konstantin Paustovsky, his six-page story "Lyubka the Cossack" (1924) was rewritten twenty-two times, totaling about two hundred pages.

"In the Basement" is told in a more relaxed manner than Babel's other stories and sometimes reminds the reader of a comedy of manners. Still it is pithy and full of colorful epithets and remarkable metaphors, such as "I was an untruthful little boy," "My twelve-year-old heart swelled with the joy and lightness of other people's wealth," "Night towered in the poplars, stars lay heavy on the bowed leaves," "I had nothing to give in return for all this measureless magnificence." Babel also uses satire to enliven the story.

The element of contrast plays an important part in the story. The description of the poverty and strangeness of the narrator's family, living in the basement, and the depiction of the lifestyle of the wealthy Borgmans, illustrates that. The grotesque and the romantic, the tragic and the comic, are very close. The boy's fantastic tales about his relatives' adventures and about the death of Spinoza are romantically heightened. His attempt to commit suicide is both tragic and comic, and represents the resolution of the conflict.

Babel portrays his characters so vividly and his visual images are so powerful, it is hard not to mention his cinematic technique. It is also important to remember the relationship of his art with painting, both with the old masters and with the new, especially Marc Chagall. It is as if the characters from the story jump right from Chagall's paintings. Babel's art is indeed expressionist. Therefore he is using the "untruthful little boy" (instead of, for example, Mark Borgman) to portray the world and to express his ideas on the art of writing.

Grigory Roytman

IN THE CAGE

Author: Henry James (1843-1916)
Type of plot: Psychological
Time of plot: The late 1890's
Locale: The Mayfair section of West London
First published: 1898

Principal characters:
THE PROTAGONIST, an unidentified female telegraph operator
MR. MUDGE, her fiancé, a grocer
CAPTAIN COUNT PHILIP EVERARD, a roué and the primary object
of the protagonist's attention
LADY BRADEEN, who is destined to be Everard's wife
MRS. JORDAN, a florist and occasional confidante of the
protagonist
COCKER, the man who owns the store that houses the post-and-
telegraph cage

The Story

The protagonist of "In the Cage" is a young woman whose identity is never revealed by Henry James, thus reinforcing the very anonymity of her status in life: She works in the post-and-telegraph cage of Cocker's store in the Mayfair section of West London. From the outset, James makes clear two facts about her personal life. First, she has grown up and still lives in relative poverty. As a consequence, she does not look kindly on the many idle rich who come to Cocker's day after day to send telegrams.

Second, she is engaged to a grocer named Mr. Mudge. He is a most caring, decent man; he is, however, also dull and pedestrian. She does not encourage him as he sets forth tentative wedding plans. The principal reason for her reluctance to marry has to do with her fascination with the upper-class patrons of Cocker's. For some time she has carried on a love/hate affair with them—in her mind. She knows that these privileged people are boring and profligate, and often engage in illicit liaisons. Although she has confided to a friend that she sees them as "selfish brutes," she is driven by a genuine fascination with them. Like many of James's characters, she is an inquisitive person: She has to know what is going on in their lives. When she waits on them, she sharply scrutinizes them; she carefully listens to their conversations; and she quickly memorizes their telegrams. From these gleanings, her hyperactive imagination is quite capable of rendering for her in most dramatic fashion their current anxieties, intrigues, and crises.

When she encounters at Cocker's a Captain Count Philip Everard, a smiling, handsome aristocrat, she makes a quantum leap from simply immersing her acute imagination in the affairs of her wealthy clientele to becoming a part of their lives. From the beginning, she understands that he is what she has been waiting for. (In an ancillary way she is also caught up in the life of a patron named Lady Bradeen, who has some kind of shadowy connection with Everard, although her eventual single focus will be on him.) Not only can she re-create Everard's romantic life with all of its selfishness and immoral behavior, but now—from her modest position as telegraphist—she also will be able to do him eager service in whatever humble way she can. Her imagination wills her to believe that Everard needs her, depends on her advice, and is singularly attracted to her.

"In the Cage" moves toward its climax when the protagonist wants to expand her connection with the captain beyond the confines of Cocker's. To that end, she begins to haunt his residence, the exclusive Park Chambers, during her off-hours. They meet early one evening, and he invites her to sit on a nearby park bench. In vintage Jamesian dialogue, her speeches to him assume all that she has assumed these many months: to inform him that theirs is a passionate and reciprocal relationship. Everard, in his turn, apparently has only one purpose in asking her to sit with him in the August twilight: to tell her that as a public servant she is greatly appreciated for all of her favors to him as a patron of Cocker's.

He is perplexed when she announces that she may be induced to move on (this is a reference to Mudge and the wedding plans). Startled by the news, Everard selfishly cries out that he will be upset if she goes: "I shall miss you too horribly." Taking his hyperbolic rhetoric at face value, she leaves Everard with a stern warning that she will not give him up. Later that summer, while on vacation at Bournemouth with Mudge and her mother, she advises Mudge that her duty now is to stay at Cocker's, to go on assisting her captain in his dalliances.

Weeks later, a troubled Everard comes to Mudge's betrothed and asks about a particular telegram that Lady Bradeen had sent earlier in the year. James does not explain why Everard is upset, but when the telegraphist is able to recite the contents from memory, Everard is relieved inasmuch as Lady Bradeen has sent the wrong message. The crisis is over. Everard departs without a gesture or word of thanks or good-bye. She never sees him again.

Once more, weeks go by and the telegraphist is chatting with a friend of hers, a Mrs. Jordan, who is a widow but is soon to be married to a Mr. Drake. He is a servant of Lady Bradeen, and Drake tells Mrs. Jordan that Everard and Lady Bradeen will also be marrying soon. Mrs. Jordan is unable to supply pertinent details, but several facts emerge from her conversation with the telegraphist: Everard is not wealthy; he is a philanderer and a fortune hunter; Lady Bradeen once went so far as to steal something in order to protect him; and, finally, Mrs. Jordan concludes that Everard is wedding Lady Bradeen because she has the power to coerce him into marriage.

"In the Cage" ends with the disillusioned telegraphist ready to take Mudge up on his offer of marriage—as soon as possible. Further, she is perturbed at having to hear all this scandalous news from Drake through Mrs. Jordan. The protagonist has long seen herself as being a principal source of reliable information on the doings of the

Everard-Bradeen set. Mudge's betrothed thinks of the disturbing description of Everard by the future Mrs. Drake. It reinforces in a most succinct way what the telegraphist has known all along. No longer can she idealize him; she can see him now with merciless clarity for what he is: unscrupulous, selfish, and materialistic. There is no shatteringly powerful scene as the protagonist comes to terms with Everard and her association with him—both the imagined and the real. After she bids good-bye to Mrs. Jordan, she walks alone along the Paddington canal. James writes that her mind is jumbled with thoughts. Knowing, however, that her obsession with Everard is over and that marriage to Mudge is inevitable, the telegraphist curiously muses on one aspect of all that has happened: "It was strange that such a matter should be settled for her by Mr. Drake."

Themes and Meanings

James's life, both private and professional, was rather limited in its own way. He had little to do with the lower strata of society. On occasion, however, he could do dramatic justice to a woman such as the telegraphist, whose position in London life is both lowly and uneventful. To that end, two of James's standard themes surface in this tale: the need to take advantage of life, or, to use different words, to live all that one can; and the reductive power of leading a life of renunciation. At first these themes might seem to be antithetical, at odds with each other. They are—but they are both present within the life of the protagonist. She is the embodiment of both themes as she embraces Everard figuratively and pursues him literally. Indeed, the telegraphist is one of those well-known James characters who is eager to live pleasurably in an imagined world, while at the same time, and without regret, she is happy to set aside her life in the real world.

More specifically, these themes coalesce in the life of the protagonist as she lives all she can in her fantasized relationship with Everard; unfortunately, she is at the same time forfeiting the potential in her own young life by giving Everard many months of selfless servitude at Cocker's. In time, her imagination becomes the controlling factor in the calculus of her life: For her, nothing is more genuine and central in her day-to-day existence than the Everard interlude. In fact, there is every reason to assume that she would have gone on for months—perhaps years—in her persistent attraction to Everard had he not so abruptly ceased to do his business at Cocker's. Oddly enough, she knows from the beginning the sordid nature of his dalliances. She is not blind to his vices. When they have their one meeting away from Cocker's, she bluntly reveals to him that she is aware of his adulterous activities. However, she continues to live her life through his until the Lady Bradeen-Everard marriage is arranged.

So far as renunciation is concerned, the telegraphist is fully conscious of the double life that she is leading as she preoccupies herself with Everard's activities. James unambiguously describes that consciousness: "She was perfectly aware that her imaginative life was the life in which she spent most of her time." However, the lady telegraphist considers it time very well spent.

Style and Technique

"In the Cage" provides James with the requisite length (about forty-five thousand words) for him to explore as fully as he wants the whole range of emotions that his telegraphist experiences as her life becomes entangled with that of Everard. In the hands of another writer, "In the Cage" might have been a much shorter tale: relatively taut, compact, and efficient. James, however, had a passion for telling it all, and his principal narrative technique was to explore the mind of the protagonist until all—or almost all—had been said.

James's saturation technique is seen most directly in his presentation of the telegraphist vis-à-vis Everard. That is, she is always the protagonist, but different moments with Everard call for a different persona. Like a chameleon, she manages to become a variety of women while still remaining a telegraphist. In a sense, then, she is an actress who writes her own script—and chooses her own parts.

When Everard first comes to her attention, she is the dazzled, awestruck clerk. Shortly thereafter, once she has recognized his value to her and to her imagination, she becomes the enamored young woman, one of her favored roles. From time to time, while waiting on him, she sees herself as the dreamy, soulful paramour. On occasion, when she fears that her admiration for Everard may be showing on her face, she assumes the role of the poker-faced minion who singles out no patron for special attention. When she strolls by his residence of an evening, she is the lover hungry for even a fleeting glimpse of her beloved. Everard, so taken with himself and his ongoing intrigues, is conscious only of her presence as a helpful clerk at Cocker's.

Most of her various roles are enacted briefly and then only in response to a given situation. Even after their evening meeting at the park near his home proves conclusively that he has no romantic interest in her, she persists in the old myths. Strangely enough, in their last meeting, as he anxiously asks her to recall a telegram sent by Lady Bradeen some months earlier, the protagonist presents a new face to Everard, a smug, knowledgeable face. She knows that she is easily able to quote the telegram from memory, but as playful teaser she holds off doing so until she deems it to be the right moment. Again, Everard does not recognize that his telegraphist is a competent and self-assured actress in the little theater of her own mind. Everard is a constant in the tale: He is always merely the adulterous roué.

Gerald R. Griffin

IN THE CEMETERY WHERE AL JOLSON IS BURIED

Author: Amy Hempel (1951-   )
Type of plot: Psychological
Time of plot: The 1970's
Locale: Los Angeles, California
First published: 1985

Principal characters:
THE NARRATOR, an unnamed woman
HER DYING FRIEND, a former college roommate

The Story

The unnamed narrator, a young woman in her twenties, has come to visit her former college roommate, who is dying in a Los Angeles hospital. The friend asks the narrator to tell her useless stuff that she will not mind forgetting. Much of the story thus consists of meaningless bits of trivia told by the narrator; for example, that insects can fly through rain without getting wet and that no one owned a tape recorder in the United States before Bing Crosby did. The narrator also tells her friend that when scientists taught the first chimp to talk, it lied, and about a "hearing-ear dog" who wakes up a deaf mother and drags her into her daughter's room because the child has a flashlight and is reading under the covers.

When the doctor enters the hospital room, the narrator goes to the beach, a few miles west of the hospital, where she recalls being afraid of earthquakes and flying— neither of which her friend feared—when they were college roommates. However, she knows that her friend is now afraid and that she will not try to talk her out of her fears, for she feels her friend has a right to be afraid. When she returns to the hospital, she finds a second bed in the room and knows that her friend expects her to stay; she thinks that the friend wants every minute: "She wants my life." The narrator continues to joke with her dying friend, reading her a story from the newspaper about a man who robbed a bank in Mexico City by pointing a brown paper bag containing a barbecued chicken at a bank teller, only to be tracked down by the chicken's smell. Because the story makes her friend hungry she goes out and buys ice cream bars, which they eat in the hospital room while watching a movie on television.

When the dying woman is given an injection to make her sleep, the narrator also goes to sleep and dreams that her friend is a decorator who adorns her house in black crepe and bunting. When she awakens, she says that she must leave; she thinks of getting in her convertible in the parking lot and driving to Malibu, stopping for wine and dinner and picking up beach boys. "I would shimmer with life, buzz with heat, vibrate with health, stay up all night with one and then the other." Her sick friend becomes angry, storms out of the hospital room, and hides in a supply closet from which she must be coaxed by nurses.

The story ends with the friend being buried in Los Angeles, in a well-known cemetery where a memorial to the film star and singer Al Jolson is visible from the freeway. The narrator enrolls in a fear-of-flying class, but she sleeps with a glass of water on her nightstand so that she can see whether it is the earth or herself that is shaking. She recalls the story of the chimp that was taught to talk with sign language. When its baby died, it stood over it, hands moving with animal grace, forming the words, "Baby, come hug, Baby, come hug . . ."

Themes and Meanings

Amy Hempel has said that the idea for "In the Cemetery Where Al Jolson Is Buried" was suggested to her by her teacher Gordon Lish, the fiction editor of *Esquire* in the 1970's, in a fiction-writing workshop that she took at Columbia University. Lish told his students to write on their "most terrible, despicable secret, the thing you will never live down." Hempel has said that she knew immediately what that secret was for her: "I failed my best friend at the moment when I absolutely couldn't fail her, when she was dying." "In the Cemetery Where Al Jolson Is Buried" (dedicated to her friend) is Hempel's fictionalized account of what she considers to be her own failure based on fear. Although Hempel has said that not a word of dialogue in the story was spoken by either her or her friend, she claims that it is a true story. In response to a critic's judgment that she "leaves out all the right things," Hempel said she left out some of her friend's anger, for it would have made the dying friend look less sympathetic. "I was convicting myself" in the story, Hempel said. "I wanted to be the one who did things wrong, not my dying friend."

Much of the story focuses on the narrator's efforts to distance herself from the fact of her friend's dying. Underlying the banter and jokes that dominate the dialogue is the narrator's own fear of death and her guilt at not having come to see her friend earlier. When she describes the hospital masks she and her friend wear, she says she kept "touching the warm spot where my breath, thank God, comes out." When a nurse tells them they could be sisters, the narrator thinks that the hospital staff must be wondering why it took her two months to come see her friend. She tries to explain her failure to herself by recalling a story (told to her by a friend who worked in a mortuary) of a man who wrecked his car on the highway: When he looked down at his arm from which the flesh had been torn to the bone, it literally scared him to death. The narrator says that she does not dare look any closer at her friend's dying, for she fears it will scare her to death also.

The narrator's fear of death is made more immediate by the fact that she and her friend are indeed almost like sisters—for example, when they were in college her friend's mother could not tell them apart on the phone. She thus has an irrational sense that she will somehow become infected with death. When she comes back from the beach and sees the other bed in the room, she fears that her friend, vampirelike, wants her life. Her dream that her friend is not content with dying alone but must also decorate her own house with death suggests that somehow she will be caught up in the dying of her friend. She imagines escaping, driving her convertible to a bar in Malibu where she will "shimmer with life."

At the end of the story, the narrator recalls the events of her visit to her friend, wondering why looking back should reveal more than looking at something. She tries to block out everything painful by remembering useless things, but when she recalls the talking chimp story and the part that her friend did not want to hear because it would "break your heart," the wall that she has built around her grief and guilt breaks down. She thinks of the chimp making sign language, indicating the loss of its child, for, like the narrator, it has become "fluent now in the language of grief." Hempel, like her most admired writer, Anton Chekhov, knows that grief, by its very nature, resists ordinary attempts to articulate it. Grief cannot be talked about; it can only be objectified in efforts to avoid it.

Style and Technique

Hempel's story is a textbook example of a central technique of the short story prominent among writers, from Chekhov to Ernest Hemingway and Raymond Carver. It expresses a complex inner state by presenting selected concrete details, rather than by creating a parable, or by the supplying of direct statements. Significant reality for Chekhov and those short-story writers who have followed him is inner rather than outer reality, but the problem that Chekhov solved is how to create an illusion of inner reality by focusing on external details only. The answer for Chekhov, and thus for modern short-story writers within his tradition of lyric realism, is to find an event that, if expressed "properly," that is, by the judicious choice of relevant details, will embody the complexity of the inner state.

The relevant details in Hempel's story are precisely those that seem irrelevant, even as their very triviality suggests the pain that they attempt to cover. It is this inability or unwillingness of modern short-story characters to confront pain directly that has made many readers mistakenly believe that such so-called "minimalist" writers as Chekhov, Hemingway, Carver, and Hempel are hard-boiled and unfeeling, failing to create caring characters about whom the reader can in turn care. The heart of Hempel's story focuses on just this impossibility to speak directly the language of grief. At its beginning, when she tells her friend that she could tell her more about the talking chimp but it would "break your heart," the friend says "no thanks." However, by "looking back," the narrator has, at the end of the story, come to terms with her guilt and has learned how to express the language of grief.

Charles E. May

IN THE GARDEN OF THE NORTH AMERICAN MARTYRS

Author: Tobias Wolff (1945-   )
Type of plot: Satire
Time of plot: Unspecified
Locale: Colleges in Oregon and upstate New York
First published: 1980

Principal characters:

> MARY, the protagonist, a history teacher at an Oregon college
> LOUISE, Mary's former colleague, a professor at an upstate New York college
> TED, Louise's husband
> JONATHAN, Louise's lover
> ROGER, a student campus guide at Louise's college
> DR. HOWELLS, the history department chairman at Louise's college

The Story

"In the Garden of the North American Martyrs" begins with a summary of Mary's career, a sort of curriculum vitae establishing her credentials as an uninvolved person: a college history teacher who "watched herself." Early in her career, she witnessed the firing of "a brilliant and original" professor whose ideas upset the college's trustees. To diminish the chances of similarly offending, Mary carefully wrote her lectures "out in full" beforehand, "using the arguments and often the words of other, approved writers." She just as carefully avoided entanglement in departmental politics, the cliques and ongoing quarrels of her colleagues. Instead, Mary adopted the role of a campus character, cultivating little eccentricities and making people groan with her corny jokes, culled from books and records. She was also such a good listener that eventually she had to get a hearing aid.

Thus, Mary's innocuous career of playing it safe coasted along for fifteen years at Brandon College. Then, suddenly, Brandon College went bankrupt (the result of the business manager's speculations) and closed. Shocked, Mary was forced into a tight job market. She did get another job, but in a miserable Oregon college housed in one building (apparently a former high school or junior high). Mary found the weather in Oregon equally miserable: The incessant rain troubled her lungs and hearing aid, flooded her basement, and encouraged "toadstools growing behind the refrigerator." Mary kept applying for jobs elsewhere but received no further offer.

When the story's main action begins, Mary is in her third year at the Oregon college. One day she receives a surprise letter from Louise, a former Brandon colleague who "had scored a great success with a book on Benedict Arnold and was now on the faculty of a famous college in upstate New York." Louise says there is an opening in her department and invites Mary to apply for it. Although Mary has never considered Louise to have much "enthusiasm for other people's causes," she sends in her application. In rather short order, Louise, chairwoman of the search committee, calls to schedule an on-campus interview for Mary. Mary thinks things are looking good, but as she flies east she cannot get over a strange feeling of déjà vu.

Mary's feeling intensifies in Syracuse, where Louise meets her at the airport. She even mentions the feeling to Louise, but Louise brushes it aside: "Don't get serious on me. . . . That's not your long suit. Just be your funny, wisecracking old self. Tell me now—honestly—how do I look?" Obviously Louise is still her egotistical old self, just as she expects Mary to assume her old roles, particularly the role of good listener. Seeking Mary's approval and occasional flattery, Louise talks almost nonstop about herself during the hour's drive to the college. The most interesting news is that Louise has a lover, Jonathan, and that Ted (her husband) and the children are not at all understanding about him. Finally, Louise turns the talk to Mary, telling her not to worry about the interview and lecture. Mary is shocked to learn that she has to deliver a lecture, unprepared as she is, but Louise offers her unpublished article on the Marshall Plan for Mary to read. Mary hesitantly accepts, concerned that "reading Louise's work as her own . . . would be her first complete act of plagiarism."

After dropping Mary off at a college guest cabin, Louise returns later in the night, distraught and in need of further sympathy. That scoundrel Jonathan, whom she has been with, had the nerve to tell her that she was not "womanly" and had "no sense of humor." Eventually Louise calms down and stretches out on the couch, but for the rest of the night before the big interview, neither woman gets any sleep. The next day during Mary's private campus tour, Roger the student guide informs her that, even though the school is a replica of an old English college, it is up-to-date: "They let girls come here now, and some of the teachers are women. In fact, there's a statute that says they have to interview at least one woman for each opening."

Mary's interview is one of the most perfunctory on record. The interviewing committee is twenty minutes late, giving Mary an opportunity to discover that no one has read her two books lying on the table. When the committee members arrive, they are all men except for Louise. After a preliminary remark or two, Mary and Dr. Howells, the department chairman, briefly discuss the Oregon rain. Dr. Howells, a native of Utah, likes a dry climate: "Of course it snows here, and you have your rain now and then, but it's a dry rain." Then the interview is over, and Mary realizes that she has been the token woman candidate. Questioned afterward, Louise confirms that Mary has been interviewed only to satisfy the statute. Louise thought Mary would not mind the free trip, and, anyway, Louise needed to see her old friend: "I've been unhappy and I thought you might cheer me up."

Mary decides not to give the lecture, but Louise tells her that she must, after all of their expense. Mary goes into the lecture room, looks over the crowd of students and professors, and dispenses with her prepared text on the Marshall Plan. Instead, she speaks extemporaneously: "I wonder how many of you know . . . that we are in the Long House, the ancient domain of the Five Nations of the Iroquois." Her new subject is the cruelty of the Iroquois, who slaughtered people mercilessly and tortured prisoners fiendishly. She presents the example of the two martyrs Jean de Brebeuf and Gabriel Lalement, Jesuit priests who went on preaching even as the Iroquois tortured them. Mary describes, in detail, the tortures inflicted on the priests. She pretends to report Brebeufs sermon, telling her audience, "Mend your lives. . . . " The professors are aghast. Dr. Howells and Louise leap up and wave, shouting at Mary to stop, but Mary turns off her hearing aid and goes on speaking: "Mary had more to say, much more. . . . "

Themes and Meanings

This story is a wicked satire of American academia, shown here in three of its guises: a college going bankrupt, "a new experimental college in Oregon," and a pretentious Eastern college that is "an exact copy of a college in England, right down to the gargoyles and stained-glass windows." None of these colleges inspires confidence in American higher education, nor do the faculty members shown: mousy Mary, tediously copying out her lectures; egotistical Louise, expert on Benedict Arnold; Dr. Howells, native son of Utah, with his "porous blue nose and terrible teeth"; the young professor who talks around the pipe in his mouth; and assorted other members of the faculty menagerie. They are shallow, conventional, and phony, like bad actors in an academic *commedia dell'arte*, with Louise as stage manager. The only exception is the "brilliant and original" professor who is fired.

If the trustees make an example of the outspoken professor, the author makes an example of Mary, but of the opposite sort: She illustrates what can happen to people who sell themselves out for security. From the professor's firing, Mary takes warning: "She shared his views, but did not sign the protest petition. She was, after all, on trial herself—as a teacher, as a woman, as an interpreter of history." The irony of these words reverberates through the story because Mary is a failure in all three respects because of her career of self-censorship. She stifles her own ideas until "without quite disappearing they shrank to remote, nervous points, like birds flying away." She deliberately molds herself into a faintly ridiculous role until her eccentricities, jokes, and hearing aid qualify her for the ranks of the collegiate grotesques. However, ultimately, Mary's self-betrayal does not prevent her from being betrayed by her college and by her colleagues, who tend to accept her at face value.

Mary's betrayal by the system, however, might also be what saves her from it. As a college history teacher, she has denied not only her own authenticity but, ironically, her involvement in history. Her hard knocks, along with the Oregon rain, begin to cleanse her soul, to make her see that even a college campus is not a safe refuge from life. In the story's remarkable ending, Mary at last finds her own voice via a "brilliant and original" interpretation of history that encompasses herself and the system.

Style and Technique

There are several lines of symbolic imagery in the story—references to birds and "winging it" (in lectures), to rain and dryness—but the most important imagery expands on the story's title by developing parallels between Mary and the two martyrs. The closer Mary gets to Iroquois country, the more she feels a sense of déjà vu. The strained appearance of Louise the hatchet woman reminds Mary of "a description in the book she'd been reading, of how Iroquois warriors gave themselves visions by fasting." In the lecture room that Mary calls "the Long House" sunlight streams through windows of "stained glass onto the people around her, painting their faces." Mary is, in effect, being roasted at the stake: "Thick streams of smoke from the young professor's pipe drifted through a circle of red light at Mary's feet, turning crimson and twisting like flames." Like the priest who kept preaching through torture, Mary delivers her lecture; in the words that Mary imagines the priest speaking, time past and time present come together.

Mary herself is perhaps intended as a representative figure of higher education in the United States. In her days of clownish conformity, she became Brandon College's presiding spirit, "something institutional, like a custom, or a mascot—part of the college's idea of itself." Her "martyrdom" is also typical of horror stories about cruel hiring practices in academia. "In the Garden of the North American Martyrs" should be on the required reading list of everyone contemplating a career in higher education.

Harold Branam

IN THE GLOAMING

Author: Alice Elliott Dark (1953-   )
Type of plot: Domestic realism
Time of plot: The 1990's
Locale: Wynnemoor, Pennsylvania
First published: 1993

> *Principal characters:*
>> JANET, a middle-aged suburban housewife and mother
>> MARTIN, her husband
>> LAIRD, her thirty-three-year-old son

The Story

"In the Gloaming" focuses on a mother's efforts to come to terms with her son's dying of acquired immunodeficiency syndrome (AIDS). The story begins when Laird, the thirty-three-year-old son, comes home to die and says he wants to get to know his mother, Janet. Martin, the father, is obsessed with his work and has never had much time for his wife or children. On a summer evening, after they have eaten on the terrace and the father goes to his study to work, Laird looks at the sky and says he remembers that when he was a child his mother told him that this time of day—the late afternoon just before dark—was called the "gloaming" in Scotland. He says he has been remembering a lot recently, mostly about when he was small, probably, he says, because his mother is taking care of him now as she once did.

Laird is well aware of his father's work obsession and feels that his dying is just one more in a long line of disappointments that he has caused his father. When Janet tells him that Martin's failure to spend time with Laird is his loss, Laird says it is his father's loss in her case also. Janet has always known that Martin is an ambitious, self-absorbed man who probably should never have gotten married in the first place. In one of their conversations, Janet says she does not like reading about sex, not because she is a prude but because she believes that sex can never really be portrayed, for the sensations and emotions of sex are beyond language. She asks Laird if he has loved and been loved in return, and when Laird says "yes," she says she is glad.

Laird also tells his mother what he wants for his funeral; he says that he does not want it to be too gloomy, that he wants some decent music, and that he wants her to buy a smashing dress, something mournful, yet elegant. It is during the time of day known as the "gloaming" that Laird dies. As his fingers make knitting motions over his chest, Janet presses her face against his and puts her hands down his busy arms, helping him along until he "finished this last piece of work."

After the funeral, when Janet goes up to Laird's old room and lies down, Martin comes in, and they weep together. Janet says that Laird could not decide about the music, and Martin says he was moved at the bagpipes played at her grandfather's funeral.

When she says she thinks that Laird would have liked that idea very much, Martin says, "Please tell me—what else did my boy like?"

Themes and Meanings

Called a brilliant Jamesian classic by some reviewers and a predictable piece of popular slick fiction by others, "In the Gloaming" received considerable attention in the three years after it was first published; not only was it the subject of two film treatments, including a highly praised 1997 HBO television drama, but also John Updike chose it for inclusion in the *The Best American Short Stories of the Century* (1999).

Although the word "AIDS" is never used in the story and the son's homosexuality is not a thematic issue, except for an oblique reference that it may have been one of the ways in which Laird disappointed his father, it is probably true that if he had come home to die of any other ailment, the story would not have been filmed or so highly honored. Although it seems to avoid social issues to focus on the universal dilemma of facing death, the underlying AIDS/homosexual theme certainly supplies much of the story's timely power.

Even though the story depends on the AIDS issue, Alice Elliott Dark avoids exploiting it by focusing throughout on the mother's emotions about her son's inevitable death. She also avoids lapsing into sentimentality by making both the mother and the son witty and sophisticated enough to banter about the process of dying. The most risky, and therefore perhaps the most successful, thematic tension in the story is the fact that the mother engages in a flirtatious relationship with her dying son, realizing that he has been the love of her life. At one point, Janet scolds herself for behaving like a girl with a crush, behaving absurdly, having a feeling she thought she would never have again. What makes this theme even more risky is the danger of the story's falling into a stereotype about the cause of homosexuality—the doting mother and the distant father.

The bittersweetness of the story derives from the fact that whereas most mothers seldom get an opportunity to spend much time with their children once they are grown, now, because of Laird's dependence on her, Janet gets a rare chance to rediscover the joys of parenting—the intimate conversations, the child's need of the parent, and the genuine sense of closeness and mutual dependence. As when Laird was a child, he and his mother are once again "captive audiences" to each other. The poignant identification between mother and son reaches its inevitable climax when, as Janet is knitting, Laird begins to make knitting motions over his chest, "the way people did as they were dying." Laird dies as Janet puts her hands over his hands and they both make the fretful imaginary stitches together.

A parallel theme throughout the story is Janet's sense of loneliness because of her husband's neglect. Although she tells her son that she has had the usual fantasies of being a heroic figure like Amelia Earhart or Margaret Mead, she says she was never even close to being brave enough. Janet's sense of never having achieved any of her fantasies, of being only average, is balanced by her sense that the one extraordinary thing about herself is her children. Indeed this is a story about the bittersweet realization of a mother's dream—to be the complete mother, the needed one. Janet says she often finds it hard work to keep up with the conversations with Laird, but she knows "it was the work she had pined for all her life."

Style and Technique

The central metaphor that holds the story together is the idea of the "gloaming," that bittersweet transition period of twilight when "purple colored curtains mark the end of day." When he was a child, Laird thought his mother said "gloomy" when she told him about the "gloaming." He thought it hurt her that the day was over, but she always said that it was a beautiful time because for a few moments the purple light made the whole world look like the Scottish Highlands on a summer night. This metaphor of a transition, both sad and beautiful, colors the tone of the entire story.

The dominant technique of the story is the creation of the unsentimental dialogue between the mother and the son, a dialogue so stripped of the usual cross-purposes of conversations between parents and children that it often sounds as if the two are lovers. At one point when Laird says he wants to get to know his mother, she says there's nothing to know, for she is average. When he says, "let's talk about how you feel about me," she laughs, "Do you flirt with your nurses like this when I'm not around?" However, the story is not all dialogue. The conversations between the two are interspersed by third-person self-conscious musings by Janet as she tries to find ways to cope with Laird's approaching death. She feels quite alone but often turns around expecting someone to be there. Then she realizes that she is inviting a villain, an enemy that could be driven out by a mother's love. However, she knows that the enemy is actually part of Laird, and neither she nor the doctors can separate the two.

The story ends after Laird's death with Janet and her husband, Martin, together. Martin uses the same shy, deferential tone that he used when the children were young, the tone that made her feel "as though all the frustrations and boredom and mistakes and rushes of feeling in her days as a mother did indeed add up to something of importance."

Charles E. May

IN THE HEART OF THE HEART OF THE COUNTRY

Author: William H. Gass (1924-   )
Type of plot: Antistory
Time of plot: The 1960's
Locale: A small town in Indiana
First published: 1967

> Principal characters:
> THE NARRATOR, a self-proclaimed poet and a college teacher who
>   has lost his lover
> MRS. DESMOND, an elderly lady who often visits him
> BILLY HOLSCLAW, an elderly man who lives near him
> UNCLE HALLEY, an elderly man who shares his collection with
>   the narrator
> MR. TICK, the narrator's cat, which the narrator envies

The Story

Following the modernist tradition of elimination of traditional narrative line, this story could be loosely described as a series of thirty-six prose poems, repetitious in subject and title, connected only by two devices—the setting (a small midwestern town) and the first-person narrator. The shorter titles within the story at first glance seem quite straightforward: abstract, factual, almost guidebook dull. The longer titles tend to emphasize possessions of the narrator: "My House, This Place and Body."

Closer inspection, however, reveals that the content of a given section may have only a tenuous connection with the title. In the "Politics" section, only five lines refer to the Cuban Revolution; the rest of the section attempts an extended and overstrained comparison of love and politics, which veers entirely out of control. At one time, the narrator may have only a sentence or two to say about his ostensible subject of the moment; at another, several paragraphs or pages. Nor do the topics recur in any definite pattern, but in an almost obsessively arbitrary one. In addition, the narrator's implied objectivity often slips away, giving the reader several different versions of a place or a character. In short, if the reader does not fairly quickly grasp that the real story is the self-revelation of the narrator, he or she will soon be floundering amid seemingly unconnected, repetitious, or even contradictory data. Nothing much actually happens in the present tense of the story.

From the multiple sections, however, a relatively old-fashioned plot line emerges, introduced in the last line of the first paragraph: "And I am in retirement from love." Rearranged in a linear fashion, the action preceding the beginning of this story is fairly simple. The first-person narrator, a forty-one-year-old college teacher and self-proclaimed poet, came to B——, Indiana, full of the hope of establishing a new beginning for himself: a new job, new companions, a new home, and new roots—perhaps, he suggests, even a new youth. He also found a new lover, a young, tomboyish girl with whom he believed that he had escaped from his old routines. Soon, however, it is she who escapes, leaving both him and the Midwest far behind.

As the story begins, he is reminiscing about the failure of all of his hopes, especially his lost love, and occasionally trying to pull himself together, to get back to his poetry, to understand his sense of being trapped in coldness, isolation, and fragmentation. He tries to give an objective examination of the town—its businesses, clubs, politics, churches, schools, some of its inhabitants, the land, and the seasonal cycles of the weather. However, he reveals much more about himself than he ever understands or intends.

Living totally within himself, looking at nature through windows or from platforms, and running from actual encounters with real people and real problems, this narrator egotistically and sentimentally wallows in self-pity, coloring every piece of data with the despairing, cold grayness of his own mind and heart. Lacking in self-discipline and willpower, he asserts that he "cannot pull himself together." He acknowledges that in B—— he has not been able to find a new youth; he has merely confirmed his advancing age. His poetry, which he considers only a "physical caress," will die as his senses diminish until death.

Themes and Meanings

William Faulkner once said that the basis of all great literature is the human heart in conflict with itself. William H. Gass's intellectual first-person narrator (a college professor and poet) is a perfect example of carrying this conflict to an undesirable end. The title and opening lines of the story identify the most crucial conflict: the heart of the country (a clichéd metaphor for the Midwest) is presented as withered, too long deprived of love and true union with others, with nature, or with any real order beyond the individual's own mind. In turn, the heart of the Midwest is presented through the words and mind of one individual, who both typifies and identifies the conflicts that have crippled his own heart and, by extension, the heart of his vast country.

Although the reader can and must see beyond the narrator's acknowledged narrow point of view, the reader cannot deny the strength of the conflicts that the narrator exposes. The heart cries out with longing for love of and love from others but seldom finds lasting union and harmony, and even then, it knows deeply that they will pass. Humankind, like the narrator, desires an always blooming spring of youth and a fruitful harvest of fame, always full of new hopes and promises, only to find that, because the pruning and spraying of the fruit trees has been neglected, there is only rotten fruit to harvest. The heart, then, becomes fearful, depressed, isolated, and cold, retreating before the forces of the other half of the natural cycle—decay and death—leaving only the intellect to cope with these facts.

This isolated mind of humanity becomes chaotic and disorganized; not united with the heart or the body, it recognizes only partial truths, as reflected in the narrator himself and in the structure of the story. In a world of entropic chaos, he cannot will himself into order. He sees harmony in body, will, and nature existing only in animals—a cat, some birds, flies that are unaware of the implications of time and death. His heart longs for an affirmation of some sort, perhaps any sort, of harmony. However, neither humanity's senses nor its intellect, grasping at received data, finds evidence of any order or eternity. Baffled, like this narrator, the intellect may simply give up in despair.

Gass, however, suggests that another avenue to experience and recognition is open to human beings. Because he has an intellect, the narrator may be more isolated from nature than the cat, but he also can have revelations received from literature, most important, from poetry. Poetry may be a sensual caress, as the narrator claims, but it also can enlarge and enrich the intellect. Art, nature, spirit, and cycles of time can be affirmative alternatives to despair. Rules, responsibility, and, most important, the imposition of self-will and the rejection of self-pride are necessary if human beings are to find patterns of harmony in the universe. It is this type of harmony that the narrator knowingly rejects in his remarks about Rainer Maria Rilke's concerns with poetry helping the spirit of man, and it is to his eternal isolation and death that the narrator does so.

Style and Technique

Gass has used multiple techniques to emphasize the complexity of theme and subject of this story. The story's title and structure, its patterns of imagery, allusions, and brilliant stylistic transformations all add to the reader's ability to understand and respond, both intellectually and emotionally. The fragmented, nonlinear structure suggests the manner in which the mind actually works, as opposed to the rules of logic. The narrator is both lacking in will and obsessed with thoughts of his lost love, with fears of death and age, and with his isolation from his environment and his community. These topics appear again and again; even when he tries to concentrate, his mind moves in circles, and he sees similar patterns wherever he looks. The Ferris wheel, seasons, old records—all these cycles the narrator identifies as deadening ruts. He is unwilling to consider the cycle as an image of natural completion and harmony.

Stylistically, Gass uses sentences that move, almost unnoticeably, from flat, blunt, factual realism to highly evocative, poetically imaginative flights of fancy. He will even alternate the two types of sentences in one section, suggesting the internal conflicts of the narrator. Finally, his use of allusions to other poets illuminates the story and offers the reader standards for judging the narrator's conclusions. The use of Whitmanesque lists, the narrator's rejection of Rilke's spiritual poetry, and, most significant, the opening quotation from William Butler Yeats's "Sailing to Byzantium" hand the reader keys to a poet's ideal belief in something beyond this physical world and beyond his isolated intelligence. The line from Yeats, for example, is a triumphal affirmation of an eternal world of pattern and artistic design achieved by acts of will, a world of the soul and imagination, to replace this natural world, in which time, age, and death make humans seem paltry, only a heart fastened to a dying animal. In contrast, the poet-narrator of this story, eloquently but with pity and hate, can only describe the dying animal's longings, for he lacks both the will and the imagination of a Yeats. His heart and that of "his country" remain thin and gray.

Ann E. Reynolds

IN THE LAND OF THE FREE

Author: Sui Sin Far (Edith Maude Eaton, 1865-1914)
Type of plot: Sketch
Time of plot: The early twentieth century
Locale: San Francisco, California
First published: 1909

> *Principal characters:*
> HOM HING, a Chinese merchant in San Francisco
> LAE CHOO, his wife
> JAMES CLANCEY, a young lawyer

The Story

After discovering that she is pregnant, Lae Choo, the dutiful, obedient wife of Hom Hing, returns from California to China so that her child will be born in her homeland. While she awaits the birth of their first son, her husband's aged parents fall ill. A good Confucian wife, Lae Choo remains to care for them. After the death of both parents, she returns to San Francisco with her young son. At the immigration desk, Lae Choo and Hom Hing have a problem. They filed their immigration papers before the birth of their child, so their baby does not have proper certification. The first customs officer says that he cannot allow the boy to go ashore. "There is nothing in the papers that you have shown us—your wife's papers and your own—having any bearing on the child." Because of bureaucratic red tape, the immigration authorities keep the infant, telling Lae Choo and Hom Hing to return the next day to learn the disposition of his case.

The parents are confident that the authorities will return their child, but after five months the child is still in the care of the missionaries with whom the immigration authorities have placed him. In desperation, Hom Hing hires a lawyer, James Clancey, to petition the immigration service for the release of their son. Unsuccessful in this attempt, the lawyer asks for five hundred dollars to go to Washington, D.C., to petition the government personally. Hom Hing does not have the money, but Lae Choo offers her jewelry instead. "See my jade earrings—my gold buttons—my hair pins—my comb of pearl and my rings—one, two, three, four, five rings; very good—all same much money. . . . You take and bring me paper for my Little One."

Another five months pass before Clancey succeeds. At last able to regain her son, the joyful mother goes directly to the mission to bring him home. After so much time away from her, however, the child runs back to the white missionaries. "Go 'way, go 'way!" he says to his mother.

Themes and Meanings

Edith Maude Eaton (Sui Sin Far), an early feminist, freelance journalist, and short-story writer, was the first person of Chinese ancestry in the United States to write stories and articles containing positive portrayals of the Chinese. She was a Eurasian, born of a Chinese mother and an English father, whose appearance did not show her Chinese heritage. Despite her European appearance, she chose to live and write as a Chinese American during a period of powerful anti-Chinese sentiment. The deletion of her English name and her choice of the pseudonym, Sui Sin Far, "Water Lily," or narcissus, indicates her identification with Chinese immigrants. She produced a small but important body of work that provides rare insights into the lives of Chinese and Chinese Americans in the early twentieth century. Her writings, including a collection of her short stories, *Mrs. Spring Fragrance* (1912), deal sympathetically with their problems.

Lured by the California gold rush, many Chinese came to the "Gold Mountain" or the United States. Later, thousands more Chinese laborers were imported to finish the western stretch of the transcontinental railroad. After the completion of the railroad line in 1869, many Chinese men went to West Coast urban areas, where the only work permitted to them was cooking, gardening, and laundry. Because of their numbers, their appearance, their preference for their traditional Asian ways and customs, and the perception that they jeopardized white labor opportunities, anti-Chinese sentiment grew. They faced prejudice from white demagogues, whose slogan, "the Chinese must go," further increased prejudice against the Chinese.

This bias manifested itself in violence and anti-Chinese legislation. The Chinese were robbed, stoned, lynched, and murdered. Besides the brutality they suffered, the popular media stereotyped them as loathsome, vile, opium-addicted gamblers whose very presence endangered the American way of life. Many laws were enacted against them, culminating in the federal Chinese Exclusion Act of 1882. After 1882 only Chinese government officials, merchants, students, teachers, visitors, and those claiming United States citizenship were admitted to the United States. Immigration officials detained others until their claims could be verified. "In the Land of the Free" explores the effects of such detention on one couple.

The title of "In the Land of the Free" is ironic. In the early twentieth century, professed American ideals and patriotic rhetoric did not apply to the Chinese. The title, and thus the story, is a gentle protest against American injustices. The story presents Chinese characters sympathetically—as deserving the full rights of American citizenship, not as one-dimensional heathens whose goal is to overwhelm the United States with their numbers. Lae Choo and Hom Hing are at the mercy of a biased immigration system whose unequal laws penalize them. Sui Sin Far, in this brief story, tries to give a balanced view of the situations that many Chinese faced, portraying their condition realistically.

Style and Technique

Using the form of the sketch that lacks the depth of a short story, Sui Sin Far stresses the psychological atmosphere surrounding the mother's deepening depression. As is appropriate in a sketch, an economy of incidents combines with an ironic ending. The author's journalism background gives a documentary mood to this short work. This format, with its air of topicality, suggests that the story is drawn directly from actual events. Sui Sin Far's characters are an ordinary family, law abiding, unassuming, gentle, and passive. "In the Land of the Free" contains a basic human theme: parents' love for their child. By careful manipulation of this theme, she elicits the reader's sympathy. Unlike Bret Harte and others who depict Chinese characters from a European American perspective, Sui Sin Far gave American readers the Chinese perspective.

Sui Sin Far avoids a didactic, confrontational tone to protest the legal outrages committed against the Chinese. However, the horror of a child taken from its parents is forceful and convincing. She lays out the situation in which she has placed her characters, and the reader comes to the conclusion that the immigration laws were unfair to the Chinese. Though at times the portraits of Lae Choo and Hom Hing may seem humorous and picturesque, they are not mere caricatures from local-color stories, such as those written by Bret Harte. Sui Sin Far's intention is unmistakable: to portray the humanity of the Chinese. In this she follows the lead of Mark Twain, whose "Goldsmith's Friend Abroad Again" (1870) treats a similar theme.

Though Sui Sin Far writes well, the sketch form limits her ability to deal with her subject and her characters in depth or in length. Trapped in the stylistic conventions of the time, her language seems stiff and stilted to contemporary ears. For example, in describing his wife's announcement of her pregnancy, Hom Hing says, "When my wife told to me one morning that she dreamed of a green tree with spreading branches and one beautiful red flower growing thereon, I answered her that I wanted my son to be born in China." Though Sui Sin Far tries to reproduce the speech patterns of Chinese immigrants, her dialogue is forced and her dialect is artificial. For example, Lae Choo tells James Clancey "you are a hundred man good!"

The immorality and corruption in the story come not from the Chinese, but from European American society. To protect American citizens, prejudice becomes illogical, values become distorted, and laws unjustly persecute the innocent Chinese. While Sui Sin Far avoids a preachy, aggressive tone in this story, the inhumanity of a repressive, biased bureaucracy that takes a child from its parents is credible and powerful.

Mary Young

IN THE PENAL COLONY

Author: Franz Kafka (1883-1924)
Type of plot: Allegory
Time of plot: The early twentieth century
Locale: A penal colony on an island in an unspecified, remote region of the world
First published: "In der Strafkolonie," 1919 (English translation, 1941)

> *Principal characters:*
> AN EXPLORER, who arrives in the penal colony to investigate its
> conditions
> AN OFFICER, who believes in the organization of the colony as
> devised by the dead commandant

The Story

An explorer arrives in a penal colony, at the invitation of its new commandant, to investigate its organization and report his findings to a commission created by the commandant. Franz Kafka calls the explorer *Forschungsreisende*, a "research traveler," and in the story's context he is clearly more than an amateur: He is an enlightened modern naturalist and relativist, trained to observe and analyze dispassionately the customs of diverse cultures—such comparative anthropologists as Bronislaw Malinowski (1884-1942) come to mind.

The explorer is introduced to the machine that is the central edifice of the colony's structure by an officer zealously loyal to the former commandant's administration of the colony. The machine is an instrument of torture and execution, the complex operation of which is described in devoted detail by the officer. "It's a remarkable piece of apparatus," he exclaims in the story's opening words, and he proceeds to explain, with the rapture of a totally committed believer, the coldly glamorous intricacy of the coordination of its three main parts: the "Bed," on which the condemned prisoner is strapped; the "Designer," whose cogwheels control the machine; and the "Harrow," which adjusts its needles to the dimensions of the condemned man's body and then engraves his sentence on it. The prisoner is thus literally forced to feel the pain of his punishment, in a ritual that lasts twelve hours.

The criminal whose execution the explorer is invited to witness is a servant/sentry assigned to a captain. His duties are bizarrely twofold: to serve his master by day and to protect him by night. The previous night the captain had found him derelict in his obligation to rise every hour and salute his master's door. Has he had a trial? No. Does he know his sentence? No: It is "HONOR THY SUPERIORS!" and "He'll learn it on his body." After all, says the officer, he is acting in the spirit of his former commandant's plans for the colony, and his "guiding principle is this: Guilt is never to be doubted."

Such monolithic simplicity in applying an ethic of unrelenting vindictiveness and cruelty appalls the explorer, whose temperament has been shaped by Western concepts of due process, tolerance, and humaneness. He therefore refuses the officer-judge's plea that he intercede on behalf of the Old Order's judicial system when appearing before the liberal new commandant. Because he is "fundamentally honorable and unafraid," he tells the officer, "I do not approve of your procedure." However, he adds, "your sincere conviction has touched me, even though it cannot influence my judgment."

The officer's response is cryptic: "Then the time has come." He frees the condemned prisoner, adjusts the Harrow's legend to read "BE JUST!" and submits his own body to the machine. However, instead of redeeming him, as the officer insisted that it would, the machine kills him and in the process disintegrates, ending the Old Order's execution of "justice."

Shaken by this strange martyrdom, the explorer decides to issue no report to the new commandant. Instead he seeks out the grave of the old commandant, reads the inscription on the tombstone, which prophesies his return, and then leaves the penal colony by boat, refusing to take with him the liberated former prisoner and a fellow soldier.

Themes and Meanings

The story is a fantasy-allegory portraying the critical condition of religion in the modern world. The explorer, representing the humanitarian outlook of a secularist culture, visits an earth that is in a state of sin. The old commandant created and organized the penal colony and invented its dreadful machinery of justice/injustice—call him the god of an authoritarian faith. Somehow he lost his hold over the colony, but one day he may return and reclaim it. Meanwhile his fanatic disciple, the officer, serves the colony as its police officer, judge, and executioner.

What the explorer must choose on this island is either morality or spirituality, for Kafka regards the two as having suffered schism. The Old Order is revoltingly sadistic, but, according to the officer's testimony, it does offer humankind redemption through an agonizing ritual of pain. "How we all absorbed the look of transfiguration on the face of the sufferer," exults the officer. "What times these were, my comrade!" Nevertheless, the explorer has no difficulty condemning the Old Order's inquisitorial severity: "The injustice of the procedure and the inhumanity of the execution were undeniable."

The New Order is humane, sentimental, and concerned with the colony's economic and political recovery. It allows the machine to fall into disrepair while improving the island's harbor installations. The New Order, however, lacks the strength of conviction to confront the practices of the Old Order directly and abolish them outright. It is slack, shallow, and worldly, unable to offer humanity more than palliatives and fleshly indulgences. The new commandant immerses himself in a sea of admiring women, who weaken the law's rigor through erotic enticements.

The victory that the New Order achieves over the Old Order is therefore unredemptive and pyrrhic. The explorer, while convinced of the Old Order's injustice, is also careful to keep his distance from the new dispensation's slovenly ways. He admires the officer's dedication to his faith and willingness to martyr himself to the machine. "If the judicial procedure which the officer cherished were really so near its end . . . then the officer was doing the right thing; in his place the explorer would not have acted otherwise." Unlike the officer, the explorer is adrift in a sea of aimless, situational ethics, anchored to no absolute standard, trained only in rational positivism.

Why does the machine execute the officer and in the process commit suicide? Possibly because the injunction it is asked to write—"BE JUST!"—contradicts the despotic nature of the Old Order and therefore violates the nature of the machine's tyranny. In the hour of its self-destruction, the machine becomes animated as a horrifying monster that shows its teeth as it jabs the officer's body and drives its iron spike into his forehead, murdering him without granting him absolution or transcendence. Like the hunter Gracchus in Kafka's later sketch by that title, the dead man remains earthbound and unredeemed.

The story's conclusion has puzzled many readers. Because the explorer has denounced the Old Order as inhumane for its cruel treatment of the soldier-prisoner, he might be expected to exhibit his own humaneness by taking the freed man aboard his boat as he leaves the island. Instead, he threatens him with a heavy rope to prevent him "from attempting the leap." Perhaps Kafka means to have the explorer show his contempt for the condemned man's previously demonstrated refusal to extricate the officer from the machine's harrowing needles. In effect, the explorer enacts the adage, "A plague on both your houses!" In allowing the explorer to escape the colony, Kafka also allows him to evade a meaningful choice between a purposeful but blood-drenched religion and a purposeless but humane secularism.

Style and Technique

Kafka's allegory does not establish a strict, point-for-point parallelism between its literal and abstract levels of meaning, as do Edmund Spenser's *The Faerie Queene* (1590, 1599) and John Bunyan's *The Pilgrim's Progress* (1678, 1684). The Old Order does not pointedly correspond to the Hebrews' Old Testament era or the strictures of John Calvin's Christianity. The deadly purpose of the old regime's machine violates the Sixth Commandment: "Thou shalt not kill." Nor does the Old Order's ethic confirm a reciprocal covenant between God and humankind, as the Judeo-Christian Scriptures do.

Still, the Old Order does symbolize all religions that base their authority on transcendent rites and absolute decrees. The machine's Bed is an altar on which humans are sacrificed to appease the wrathful majesty of a Moloch-like Law. Its creator clearly corresponds to a Lord of Hosts, and the labyrinthine script that guides the machine's operation stands, not necessarily for the Hebrew Torah recording Judaism's laws and learning, but for Scripture in general. When the explorer, unable to read the script, describes it as *sehr kunstroll*—that is, "highly artistic"—he defines himself as a representative modern man who can admire the Bible as literature but refuses to accept it as dogma.

Kafka's style is realistic in its Swiftian accumulation of plausible detail, stressing a sober sense of documentary verisimilitude. After all, the explorer is an empirically trained social scientist, conditioned to observe cultural patterns dispassionately and maintain an attitude of suspended judgment. As the onlooker through whose perspective Kafka chooses to filter the action, he validates what might otherwise be an incredible fantasy by convincing the reader that a fable that violates ordinary notions of probability is nevertheless credible: "I, an accredited anthropologist, saw and heard all this."

Kafka was never wholly satisfied with the ending of this story. He wrote an acquaintance that "two or three pages shortly before the end of the story are contrived." In these pages, the explorer kneels before the tombstone over the old commandant's grave so that he can read the "very small letters" on it, which promise that the commandant "will rise again and lead his adherents . . . to recover the colony. Have faith and wait!" Does the explorer's physical gesture of obeisance signify his subconscious respect for the Old Order? Does Kafka want the reader to accept the Old Order's relentless religion of victimization and painful punishment as morally superior to a sentimental, mild materialism? His conclusion is inconclusive.

Gerhard Brand

IN THE REGION OF ICE

Author: Joyce Carol Oates (1938-   )
Type of plot: Psychological
Time of plot: The 1960's
Locale: The Midwest
First published: 1970

> *Principal characters:*
> SISTER IRENE, a nun in her early thirties beginning a teaching
>   position in a Jesuit university
> ALLEN WEINSTEIN, a bright young Jewish student with emotional
>   problems

The Story

Sister Irene is praying for the energy and resolve to get through her first semester of teaching at the Jesuit university at which she has arrived. Although she is fully confident of her teaching ability and her vocation as a nun, she is somewhat anxious and timid about the world outside her classroom, which frequently startles and confuses her. Two weeks after the semester begins, a new and impetuous young man turns up in her class. In a breach of classroom etiquette, he interrupts her as she attempts to answer his not altogether relevant question, so she asks to see him after class. He argues vigorously and somewhat chaotically for permission to attend her lectures. Against her better judgment, Sister Irene allows him to join her class. Passionate and needy, the new student, Allen Weinstein, causes a sympathetic resonance in the usually restrained and self-sufficient professor.

Sister Irene notices that her excitement about her William Shakespeare class is heightened because of the presence of Allen's inquiring and disquieting mind. Her emotional and intellectual sympathy with Allen leads her to have expectations of him, and consequently to be capable of being disappointed by him. When he fails to meet his first paper deadline, she finds herself making an unusual concession for him, only to be given a paper that is twice as long as she has assigned, entitled "Erotic Melodies in *Romeo and Juliet.*" Allen becomes increasingly emotionally demanding and yearns inarticulately for some kind of human intimacy. He presses her urgently to walk with him, to talk with him, to read a long and rambling poem he could show only to her. In his great need, he is immune to subtlety; he does not respect the conventional glass wall between teacher and student. His obsessive manner, his instability, and his desperate rudeness become more and more terrifying to Sister Irene, whose cloistered life has left her unprepared to deal with such raw and undigested emotion. Because she is a contemplative person, she is forced by Allen's very existence to consider the limits of Christian charity and her obligation as a teacher. Can one reach out to such a person and still save oneself?

For a while the question is a moot one, as Allen does not return to class to pick up his "A" paper, or to enliven the classroom discussion with his energetic defenses of humanism. Just as Sister Irene is beginning to relax into her familiar and comfortable academic routine, she receives a letter from Allen, who is in a sanatorium; it contains a veiled suicide threat, couched in references to Claudio's speech to his sister in William Shakespeare's *Measure for Measure* (1604). It is clear that just as the play's Claudio wants his sister to part with her purity to save him from Angelo's malice, Allen wants Sister Irene to risk some small part of herself to answer his overwhelming need. This she partially does, by going to Allen's parents and trying to persuade them of their son's despair in Birchcrest Manor, where he is being given shock treatments. The parents' frustration and unwillingness to yield to this stranger, so new on the scene of their chronic troubles, give some idea of the turmoil that their son Allen has been causing them over the years. Sister Irene returns defeated after her charitable exploit, far from the mystery of Christianity with which she had begun, but curiously resigned to her own human frailty.

A month later, Allen comes back into Sister Irene's life one last time—to tempt her into some real gesture of affection—and finally to alienate her entirely by a request for money to escape to Canada. His exaggerated anger at her emotional frigidity and her lack of generosity is unwarranted and explosive, and it paradoxically purges her of any ambiguity, guilt, or responsibility she might have felt for him. Months later, when she hears of his suicide by drowning in Quebec, her mind drifts vaguely for a moment; then she pulls herself together and accepts the fact that she can only be one person in her lifetime, and that person could not even truly regret Weinstein's anguish and death. She feels no guilt, precisely because she cannot really feel anything at all.

Themes and Meanings

Joyce Carol Oates has returned repeatedly in her prodigious fictional output to the theme of the complexity of human relationships. *The Wheel of Love* (1970), the collection in which "In the Region of Ice" appears, contains many stories of men and women struggling with issues of physical and emotional intimacy. For the characters in most of these stories, the risks of human connection appear to far outweigh the benefits, and violence is always about to happen.

Sister Irene is a particularly touching character, because of the huge disparity between the depth of her feelings and the narrow range in which she is able to act. When she sets out to talk with Allen's parents about his desperate cry for help, she feels an intense affinity with the mysteries of Christianity and the sufferings of Christ; this would be remarkable hubris if it were not for her obvious personal insecurity. When Allen asks Sister Irene in her office for permission to touch her hand, that simple human act of human affection takes on such dramatic proportions for her that it becomes an impossible favor to grant.

In the classroom, where Sister Irene is in complete control, she can let her brilliance range freely, and she can be what the student Allen requires of her. Outside the classroom, in the chaotic, messy world outside the "region of ice," she is passive and sterile in ways that infuriate him. Sister Irene is not physically and emotionally alienated because she is a nun; she is a nun because she has made a conscious choice to remain isolated, alone, and, most of all, safe. Although some readers might see Allen Weinstein as a possible avenue of redemption in her life, Sister Irene clearly experiences him as a possible agent of annihilation. She consciously chooses the ordinary over the heroic, and she is patiently resigned to the consequences.

Style and Technique

Oates has shown herself to be one of the most versatile stylists of twentieth century fiction. From Joycean short stories with powerful epiphanies, to academic satires, to mock translations, to epistolary experiments, to southern gothics, Oates has succeeded brilliantly in almost every style devised for the short story. For "In the Region of Ice," she has chosen a straightforward third-person central-consciousness narration. This is a modern story told in the traditional style of psychological realism.

It is a story, however, that is greatly enriched by Shakespearean allusions. All three Shakespearean plays mentioned in the text have the same basic theme as "In the Region of Ice": the terrible risks involved in human relationships. The allusion to *Romeo and Juliet* (c. 1596-1597) illuminates an erotic subtext to the interaction between Sister Irene and Allen Weinstein. It also suggests that such connections between men and women may have precisely the tragic outcomes that Sister Irene so vividly fears. *Measure for Measure*, only nominally a comedy, is also fraught with the dangers of human interaction: Claudio is condemned to die for his intimacy with his fiancé Juliet. Angelo's lust for Isabella makes her life a misery and a hopeless conundrum, and even the duke himself fails everyone by not being capable of judging and ruling his subjects. It is Claudio's pathetic consideration of suicide that Allen calls to Sister Irene's attention in his allusive letter from the hospital. *Hamlet, Prince of Denmark* (1600-1601), whose human relationships are nothing if not problematic, is also mentioned briefly. Hamlet's famous indecisiveness is a good reflection of Sister Irene's inability to act, in spite of tremendous emotional and perhaps moral provocation.

Cynthia Lee Katona

IN THE SHADOW OF WAR

Author: Ben Okri (1959-   )
Type of plot: Magical Realism, postcolonial, fantasy
Time of plot: Between 1967 and 1970
Locale: A Nigerian village
First published: 1988

> *Principal characters:*
> Omovo, a young village boy growing up in war-torn Nigeria
> His father
> A woman, who covers her face with a black veil
> Three Soldiers, who follow the woman

The Story

"In the Shadow of War" is told from the perspective of a young boy, Omovo, who takes a short trip from the sleepy innocent boredom of his sunny village into the dark shadowy forest, where he experiences the terrors of war. In this story, as in much of Ben Okri's fiction, the world of reality and fantasy merge seamlessly.

The story begins one hot afternoon in an unnamed Nigerian village. Omovo, a boy of about eleven, waits for his father to go to work. Only the radio, with its announcements of war and an impending eclipse of the Moon, intrudes on their peace. Before the father leaves, he warns Omovo to be careful because during an eclipse, the world turns dark and evil things can happen. He gives the boy his ten kobo allowance and tells him to turn off the radio. Children, he insists, should not listen to tales of war. After his father gets on the bus, Omovo turns the radio back on. He has been watching a mysterious woman veiled in black who passes his house every afternoon. He decides to wait for the woman, whom the village children believe to be a ghost, to appear.

Through the window, he watches three soldiers drinking outside at a nearby bar. When he sees that they are playing with, and giving money to, neighborhood children, he goes out to see them. The soldiers pay attention to him as well and offer him money to report on the whereabouts of the mysterious black-veiled woman. However, unlike the other children, Omovo refuses the money, the same amount as his allowance, and returns home to his window.

Soon, Omovo is lulled to sleep in the afternoon heat. The whole village becomes drowsy, and even the announcer on the radio yawns. When the boy wakes up, the woman has just passed by, and he surreptitiously follows her into the forest. Brandishing rifles, the three soldiers also follow her for a while and then circle around to catch her unawares.

Hidden in the forest, Omovo watches in wonder as the woman, who carries a red basket filled with food, enters a cave, where she encounters shadowlike people hiding from the horrors of war. The people, decrepit and dressed in rags, approach her with gratitude and deep respect, as if they might never see her again.

The soldiers appear and threaten this mysterious woman at gunpoint. They rip the black veil off and expose her face and head; she is bald and severely disfigured, and a slash extends the length of her face. In a matter of moments, the woman picks herself up, screams in defiance, and spits in a soldier's face. He shoots her dead. Omovo screams, and when he attempts to flee, he trips and falls down, passing into unconsciousness. When he wakes up, the world is entirely black. He has forgotten the coming eclipse of the Moon and believes himself to be blind.

Shortly, he wakes up at home where he sees his father drinking in comradeship with the three soldiers. Omovo is delirious; everything remains blurry. Was what happened in the forest real? His concerned father tells the boy to be grateful to the soldiers, who were kind enough to bring him home from the forest, as he carries Omovo off to bed.

Themes and Meanings

Human survival lies at the heart of this hypnotic story. Okri has been the recipient of many awards, including the Booker Prize for his 1991 novel, *The Famished Road*, about the exploits of Azaro, a spirit-child, who in the Yoruba tradition of Nigeria exists between life and death in the throes of war.

Similarly, "In the Shadow of War," from his second collection of short stories, *Stars of the New Curfew* (1988), Okri presents war through the eyes of Omovo, a young Nigerian boy, who while not a spirit-child, enters a sort of spirit world where the people might, or might not, be alive. This much-anthologized short story deals with the devastating impact of war on everyday people. The Nigerian Civil War, first as insubstantial as the radio waves transmitted by a sleepy radio announcer, becomes deadly real to the young boy, as the author details the abuses, the hunger, violence, and disease that result from the political disaster and are witnessed by the innocent youngster.

The mysterious veiled woman is important to Omovo. Early in the story, there is no sign of a mother in the boy's home, and it seems natural that the child would wait willingly every day for the veiled woman to appear. Could it be his mother is dead? Is this why he follows the woman so easily into the forest? Two of the soldiers are intimidated by her and cry out "witch," and her ravaged appearance suggests she hovers between life and death. Possibly, this woman represents Nigeria, already deeply wounded but, nevertheless, attempting to feed its starving people.

Style and Technique

"In the Shadow of War," like much of Okri's work, contains a good deal of surrealist imagery and phantasmagoric happenings, which has led some critics to compare his works to those of Latin American writers Jorge Luis Borges, Isabel Allende, and Gabriel García Márquez, all known for their use of Magical Realism, which mingles realistic and fantastic details. This melding of worlds also defines Okri's work. However, Okri argues that his stories realistically represent people's consciousness of life in Nigeria, a country that is inhabited by three hundred different tribal groups and therefore at least this many belief systems. What seems surreal or fantastic to one group, Okri insists, will not seem so to another group.

The art of storytelling comes naturally to Nigerian people, Okri explains. As a child growing up in postcolonial Nigeria, stories were an intricate part of daily life and every aspect of culture. Parents and other authority figures, he remembers, would tell their children stories as parables to teach a moral or to manipulate them to do what they wanted. Likewise, children were encouraged to let their imaginations run wild and to invent stories.

Okri shifts between the material world and the world of spirits with seamless grace. Although the protagonist, Omovo, is grounded in reality in his solid village world—the radio plays; people shave, leave for work, carry briefcases, and catch buses—the boundaries between the real world and the ever-present spirit world remain blurred. In the otherworldly forest, Omovo fades in and out of wakefulness, sleep, delirium, and unconsciousness and, for a while, blindness. The faceless mysterious woman hidden behind a black veil, whom the village children believe to be a ghost, appears every afternoon and reputedly has no shadow, and her feet seem to glide, never touching the ground. This character and the wraithlike starving women in rags and their malnourished children in the forest contrast vividly with the real-world, fleshy soldiers, bursting out of their clothes and concerned with drinking palm wine.

Okri uses the setting to dissolve the solid world. Waves of heat permeate the village, and heat mists, the canopy of leaves, the half-light of the cave, the muddied river, and the darkening of the Moon constantly blur Omovo's surroundings, so that nothing remains clear. The boy cannot tell the real world from the spirit realm. Flaking signboards, collapsing fences, and the skeletal remains of animals decry a worn, war-ravished world coming apart at the seams.

Okri also uses foreshadowing as a literary device to enable the reader to enter this shadowy otherworld without question or hesitation. At the beginning, the radio, covered with a cloth so it looks like a household fetish, takes on the role of mythic oracle when it presages an impending eclipse of the Moon. Because his father warns Omovo that the dead will walk and that the world will turn black, it is hardly surprising when the child happens across the ghostlike mysterious walking woman, who brings food to the starving refugees, and after he mistakenly believes he is blinded, the world turns black during Omovo's sojourn into the forest.

Okri adds a touch of Christian symbolism to define Omovo's character. The rooster's crowing signals the betrayal of Christ by Peter in the Garden of Gethsemane, and Omovo's refusal of money from the soldiers to spy on the mysterious woman casts him in a positive light, unlike the biblical Judas who took the Roman's bribe of silver.

M. Casey Diana

IN THE WHITE NIGHT

Author: Ann Beattie (1947-   )
Type of plot: Domestic realism
Time of plot: A winter night, evidently in the 1980's
Locale: A suburb or town
First published: 1984

Principal characters:
CAROL and
VERNON, who have been married twenty-two years
MATT AND GAYE BRINKLEY, their longtime friends
SHARON, Carol and Vernon's daughter, who is dead
BECKY BRINKLEY, Matt and Gaye's daughter

The Story

Ann Beattie's story narrates the events of scarcely more than half an hour, the time that it takes Carol and Vernon to leave a party at the home of their friends Matt and Gaye Brinkley, drive home through the snow, and lie down to sleep. The story takes on greater spaciousness, however, because of its focus on the consciousness of Carol, whose thoughts range through time and among a number of persons and events. She thinks first of the party and of a childish game that Matt Brinkley had played (significantly, the game is called "Don't think about . . ."), and by association moves to thoughts about her daughter, Sharon, and Becky Brinkley when they were very young together, and from that to an account of Becky at present, and then to a reminiscence of Sharon's death from leukemia and that trauma's continued effect on Vernon despite his dedication to optimism. After all this, Carol returns to the present to ask Vernon if Matt had mentioned Becky; he answers that nothing was said of that "sore subject."

The narrative breaks and then takes up a comparison between the two married couples: Vernon claims with some seriousness that the Brinkleys are their alter egos, suffering crises in their stead. Clearly, he refers to the many difficulties Becky Brinkley has brought into their lives, and thus obliquely refers to the death of Sharon and the absence of children in his and Carol's lives. This thought makes Carol consider the randomness of events and the impossibility of finding sanctuary. At home, she disguises the fact that she is crying, hides for a few moments in a bathroom to compose herself, and emerges to find Vernon asleep on a sofa, her coat "spread like a tent over his head and shoulders." Carol lies down on the floor under his coat, and her last waking thought is of Sharon as an angelic witness who could understand the significance of this tableau of sleepers.

Themes and Meanings

Children and parents, a frequent theme in Beattie's earlier fiction, appear in this story as the dramatic center, but it is the parents' isolation and loneliness that preoccupies her here, not the children's. Similarly, the parents are not characterized as the irresponsible, never-to-grow-up breed Beattie presented so deftly in her fiction of the 1970's. This story is a subtle evocation of the pains of adulthood and points to the larger theme of sanctuary, summarized by Carol's thinking, "Who could really believe that there was some way to find protection in this world—or someone who could offer it?"

The theme develops from the paired situations of the two couples, analogous to Carol's memory of the range finder camera that superimposed two images of the subject to make it leap into clearest focus. Both have had a child, thus making themselves more vulnerable to fate, and both have suffered thereby: Becky Brinkley's teenage troubles—her having had an abortion at age fifteen and her lack of direction even at the present—alter her parents' lives in ways Vernon and Carol cannot truly know. However, Vernon's notion that he and Carol have been spared misfortune and "chaos" because of their Sharon's early death is to Carol's mind a piece of sophistry—his optimism seems to her a frightening thing, based as it is on the twisted assumption that the great misfortune of Sharon's death, having struck them early, has somehow insulated them against further shocks. Carol remembers the small traumas since: Vernon's mononucleosis (what an "unbearable irony," the hospital attendant had said, "if Vernon had also had leukemia"), the exploding Christmas tree, the pet put to sleep—all had hinted that life might again exact a great price from them.

The alternative is to play Brinkley's game of "Don't think about . . . ," and the early image in Carol's mind of Matt and Vernon's acting like children at the party invites the interpretation that only the women are serious. Gaye must, after all, pull Matt into the house at the end, and Carol suspects that it had been Matt's idea to have the party so soon after the death of Gaye's father. Toward the end of the story, however, Beattie reveals that the perceptions of husband and wife, as represented by Vernon and Carol, provide another double image, and when they are superimposed, another theme emerges clear. Their responses, his optimism and her supposedly clear-eyed realism, are belied by other gestures, such as her foggy-eyed crying and his habit of reacting physically to that; something about Vernon's unexpected bedding down on the couch under Carol's jacket causes her to revise her opinions and reminds the reader of Vernon's continued self-accusations over Sharon's death. His optimism is simply a cover, as was Matt's game. Whereas Carol had hidden in the bathroom, fearing that he would want to rid her of sadness by making love, she is now reminded that they "had learned to stop passing judgment on how they coped with the inevitable sadness that set in, always unexpectedly." Carol's last thought is nothing if not escapist and optimistic: "In the white night world outside, their daughter might be drifting past like an angel."

The inevitability of sadness and pain, this story suggests, can hardly be coped with by a single response. Nor can any single response be judged better than another. Among the adults described, all do their share of compensating, pretending, escaping, and standing firm one way or another. However, in the juxtaposition of two responses, Vernon and Carol seem able to find perspective and avoid pessimism and cynicism.

Style and Technique
    Irving Howe, introducing an anthology entitled *Short Shorts* (1982), claimed that in very brief stories ("In the White Night" is little more than two thousand words long) "situation tends to replace character, representative condition to replace individuality." Indeed, the reader knows very little about Carol and Vernon and much less about anyone else in the story. The reader knows, for example, how many bedrooms the house has, but not what Carol and Vernon do for a living or what color their eyes are or what political views they hold, if any. Beattie has presented Vernon and Carol as individuals who think of themselves as parents though they do not seem to have any children, and thus the spaciousness of their house, a seemingly insignificant detail, conveys a powerful emotion. Their relationship with the Brinkleys is to a large extent controlled by the contrasting fates of two daughters: What can or cannot be talked about, as well as what is talked about, inevitably finds a referent there. In the context of the evening portrayed, the same might be said of Vernon and Carol's relationship with each other. The vacuum left by Sharon's death is the center of these lives. In this way, the story deals with types rather than individuals (Vernon's mental gymnastics to promote optimism and Carol's emphasis on visual and emotional connections remind one of male and female stereotyping), but its use of ambiguous characterization instills a mystery about the characters that saves them from becoming clichés.
    The narrative moves, as is suggested by the progression of events summarized above, by association, which helps characterize Carol's mental processes. Superimposed on that is a habitual pairing whose real purpose is contrast: Matt's loud garrulousness against Vernon's quietness (he speaks directly only three words), the death of Gaye's father (in the normal progression of generations) against Sharon's death, Sharon's bed as a "battlefield of pastel animals" against Vernon's refusal this night to use a bed, Sharon's leukemia versus Vernon's mononucleosis, Sharon versus Becky, the implications of Carol's hiding in the bathroom to avoid sex (the situation of the stereotyped bride) versus Becky's abortion at fifteen, the idea of inevitable sadness versus the recognition that "very few days were like the ones before." Such definition by contrast means that much is implied about the complex relationships among all the events of these ostensibly peaceful lives, and little is categorically excluded.
    Beattie has moved away here from the laconic, cool voice of much of her early fiction, which often communicated her condescension toward the characters portrayed. In allowing the story to move in the patterns of Carol's associations, Beattie has relinquished the satirist's hold on narrative and has made possible the communication of Carol's complex responses, both willed and unconscious. As a result, "In the White Night" shows the sympathy that, in replacing satire, has allowed Beattie to portray mature adults and their existential problems. Like Carol and Vernon, Beattie has found that sometimes it is best "to stop passing judgments."

Kerry Ahearn

IN THE ZOO

Author: Jean Stafford (1915-1979)
Type of plot: Domestic realism
Time of plot: The early twentieth century
Locale: Adams, Colorado
First published: 1953

> Principal characters:
> THE NARRATOR, a young orphan
> MRS. DAISY MURPHY, her married sister, the mother of two
> children
> MRS. PLACER (GRAN), their childhood guardian
> MR. MURPHY, the town drunk of Adams, who keeps a small
> menagerie
> LADDY (CAESAR), a dog that Mr. Murphy gives the narrator and
> Daisy

The Story

Two sisters, now grown and living apart, visit each other every other year at a convenient railroad hub, Denver. There they go to the zoo and reminisce about their childhood, especially about Mr. Murphy, who kept a small collection of animals in his backyard, and their foster mother, the awful Mrs. Placer.

Mrs. Placer ran a boardinghouse, and she liked her tenants and the girls to call her Gran. She and the boarders had a favorite activity: nursing resentments. At the end of each day, sitting down to their "ugly-colored" meal, Mrs. Placer and the guests reviewed the evils, plots, thoughtlessness, sins, and slurs that they had the misfortune of experiencing that day. The girls, cowed, tried silence as a defense, but Mrs. Placer invariably managed to uncover some real or imagined slight that the two timid, unpopular orphans suffered. She would, for example, announce to her audience that the awful teacher said that the narrator could not carry a tune in a basket.

Mrs. Placer's poisonous litany continued through years of boardinghouse conversations. It was the teacher's fault that the girls could not learn fractions. A girl with braces who actually played with the girls did so only in order to lord it over them because they did not have the money to have their own teeth straightened. Steeped in this atmosphere, the narrator recalls, she and her sister grew up like worms. Despite their indoctrination, one thin filament of an impulse toward happiness survived, finding its outlet in Mr. Murphy's menagerie. An alcoholic who drank all day and played solitaire, Murphy was friendly and completely undemanding with the girls. He kept a small fox, a deodorized skunk, a parrot, a coyote, and two capuchin monkeys, which the girls spent hours watching. Mrs. Placer knew about the visits but allowed them, taking pleasure in excoriating Murphy.

Murphy gave the girls a present of a puppy. Moreover, he told them how to convince Mrs. Placer to let them keep it by pointing out that the dog would make a good watchdog. Mrs. Placer's morbid and paranoid imagination worked as Murphy anticipated. She raised a dozen objections to the girls' having a dog: It would be unhouse-broken, flea-ridden, mangy, incorrigible, and destructive. She suspected Murphy of trying to fob off a young cur that would prove to be a trial to everyone, pulling up the garden, smelling of skunk, and biting everyone. Then the girls brought up the magic word. In the eyes of Mrs. Placer and her chorus of boarders, the dog then underwent a transformation. It sat alertly beside its mistress, its ears pricked, ready to lay down its life in her defense. Surely, there were many burglars, Peeping Toms, gypsies, and Fuller Brush men with evil intentions of all kinds lurking to threaten Mrs. Placer. She told the girls that they could keep the puppy.

Named Laddy, the dog proved intelligent and genial, behaving well around Mrs. Placer and her boarders. The girls doted on his beauty and adored his company. The dog accompanied them to school in the mornings, "laughing interiorly out of the enormous pleasure of life." He enjoyed his masculine pleasures of hunting and running around with fellow dogs on outings that sometimes occupied him for three-day weekends. The girls loved him for that, too.

It was Laddy's sign of masculine independence, however, that attracted Mrs. Placer's disapproving attention. Gradually, she transformed their dog, Laddy, into her dog, which she called Caesar. She turned Caesar into an aggressive guard dog, ready to bite paperboys and door-to-door salespeople. The police officer came repeatedly to her house with complaints, finally warning her that the dog would be shot if he committed another major crime.

When Murphy learned what happened to the dog, he went, with his monkey Shannon on his shoulder, to Mrs. Placer to complain. As she opened her door, the dog leaped at Murphy, but his victim was not Murphy but Shannon, whose neck he broke with one bite. In a voice that would not have deceived an idiot, Mrs. Placer said, "Why, Caesar, you scamp! . . . Aren't you ashamed?"

Early the next morning, Murphy fed the dog poisoned hamburger, killing him. Crazed by grief, he mourned the loss of Shannon, singing at his grave every day, marking it with a plaster Saint Francis. Unable to watch his agony, the girls retreated to cry and dream of escape. Over time, they became more clever at avoiding Mrs. Placer's malicious concern for their well-being. Eventually, they grew up, got jobs, and, in Daisy's case, found a husband. They did escape.

The narrator returns her narration to the present as the two women recall more of their lives since their unhappy childhood. After Mrs. Placer died, the sisters sold the boardinghouse to the first person who came along.

The story ends with the narrator bidding good-bye to her sister and boarding a train. The sisters enjoy parodying their foster mother, speaking of the hidden immoral evil in those around them and of their certain martyrdom. On the train, the narrator begins to write a letter to her sister that is also in the voice of Mrs. Placer. She enjoys a devastating and unholy laugh.

Themes and Meanings

There are three zoos in Jean Stafford's "In the Zoo": the zoo in Denver in which the story is framed, the zoo of the boardinghouse's assortment of misfits, and Mr. Murphy's menagerie. The narrator anthropomorphizes freely, giving animals human characteristics. The human qualities that the animals take on always have emotional and moral dimensions. The narrator projects a human character on animals; they become symbolic of various states of being. For example, there are, at the beginning of the story, a pathetic bear, a fine bourgeois grizzly, and some eternally hip and satiric monkeys. Laddy, the amiable guy-dog, becomes Caesar, the mean watchdog. Reading the narrator's descriptions of animals, one may infer that she experiences, vicariously through them, various states of mind and heart that she is too timid to attempt in life.

There is also a moral dimension to the characterization of the humans and the animals of the story. Mrs. Placer's moral failings are the centerpiece of the story. She is what most influences the moral condition of the two sisters, their dog, and the boarders. Tellingly, no human in the story is described as having animal characteristics, possibly because to do so would denigrate animals. The narrator loves animals, it seems clear, precisely because they are not human.

Style and Technique

"In the Zoo" is written in the first person, and most of it is a recollection. The narrator writes of her past, adding hindsight and moral judgment to her story. In this respect, and in the detail of the girls' being orphans dominated by a horrible guardian, the story is reminiscent of the works of Charles Dickens. The story's championing of emotional and creative expression and denunciation of emotional repression and hypocrisy is also Dickensian. At the time the story was first published, such direct and explicit moralizing had long been out of literary fashion.

In the story, animals and people all serve as moral emblems. In the first paragraph of the story, a polar bear is judged, when an old farmer calls him a "back number." At the end of the story, the narrator gains bitter amusement by observing a priest as her guardian would have considered him: likely someone pretending to be a priest, up to some evil sexual design on her person. The narrator judges herself as a child, calling herself and her sister "given to tears," "Dickensian grotesqueries," and "worms." One may regard the story's somewhat anachronistic style, and its ever-present moral judgment, as having two messages: First, that Mrs. Placer refuses to die in the mental life of her foster child, and second, that the narrator wishes to point out that there are still many people lost in the hinterlands—moral, emotional, and geographical.

Eric Howard

IND AFF
Or, Out of Love in Sarajevo

Author: Fay Weldon (1933-   )
Type of plot: Realism
Time of plot: The late 1980's
Locale: Sarajevo, Bosnia
First published: 1988

Principal characters:

THE NARRATOR, a female English college student
PROFESSOR PETER PIPER, her thesis director

The Story

A twenty-five-year-old unmarried graduate student is on vacation in Yugoslavia with Peter Piper, a married professor of classical history who is her thesis adviser and also her lover. The purpose of the trip is ostensibly to recover from the past year's "sexual and moral torments" but really to let Peter decide whether to leave his wife of many years for the narrator. They have already visited Serbia and Croatia. They are now in Sarajevo, Bosnia. They plan to go on to Montenegro to swim and lie in the sun. So far, though, they have met with nothing but rain.

The narrator finds—and Peter struggles to see—the water-filled footprints incised in the pavement near the Princip Bridge in Sarajevo where the assassin Gavrilo Princip stood as he fired the shots that killed the Austrian archduke Franz Ferdinand and his wife, Sophie, in 1914 and thereby triggered World War I. The couple would have preferred to jump into their rented car, drive off somewhere in the countryside, eat a picnic lunch, and make love alfresco, but the unending downpour forces them into an undistinguished restaurant.

While they wait for their wild-boar dinners to arrive, they chat desultorily. Peter complains about the ubiquity of cucumber salad in Yugoslavian restaurants, and the narrator notices—for the first time, apparently—that she has become accustomed to his complaints. When she changes the subject to a more serious matter—whether the archduke's assassination actually triggered World War I—Peter brusquely states that the war would have occurred even without Princip and returns to extracting pepper pips from his cucumber salad. The narrator persists in trying to get Peter's attention by declaring her love with "Ind Aff" for him. "Ind Aff," short for "inordinate affection," is their private joke. (John Wesley, one of the founders of Methodism, had used the term in his diary and had made a point of stating that what he felt for a young member of his flock was not Ind Aff, but a spiritual concern.) However, Peter answers, as he has on other occasions, with a reference to their love as his wife's sorrow. The narrator recalls to herself that Peter has often started quarrels on this same subject that were never resolved but merely ended by shifting to lovemaking, so she asks him to talk about something else.

Peter's bad mood becomes progressively worse as they continue to wait for their dinners to appear. As he and the narrator bicker about the causes of World War I and about slips of the tongue, they sound more and more like an unhappily married couple. After a time, the narrator looks up to catch the eye of a handsome young waiter, to exchange brief smiles with him, and to feel unexpectedly the tug of Ind Aff. When her glance moves to an older waiter whose eyes indicate disapproval, she is brought to think of the difference in age between herself and Peter, who is forty-six years old. Peter, who has noticed these almost imperceptible interactions, asks her what she is thinking of. She responds with an automatic declaration of love, but at the same moment, she realizes that she does not love him. She makes a quick decision about their relationship. Recalling that she has her passport and traveler's checks in her purse, she kisses Peter on the top of his head, says good-bye, and leaves the restaurant immediately, thus ending their affair. She is not sorry then and is not sorry later.

Themes and Meanings

Although this is, as the narrator claims, a "sad" story because it describes how a love affair goes sour, it is also a comic tale because it describes how a young woman who thought she was in love suddenly comes to her senses and escapes from a bad and depressing situation unscathed and even triumphant.

Peter, the narrator's much older lover, seems singularly unlovable. He is irritable, petty, boring, prissy, and, it turns out, vindictive. It seems clear that he has no great regard for the narrator, whose mind he regards as second rate and whose relationship with him he characterizes as "shacking up." How could the narrator ever have fallen for him? She herself confesses that she had somehow confused ambition with love because she was a student and he was her thesis adviser, on whom her future in academia depended.

Leaving Peter not only frees the young narrator from an undesirable entanglement but also enables her to become an independent person. Rather than waiting for Peter to decide whether to abandon his wife for her sake, she takes matters into her own hands and leaves him. When Peter later attempts revenge by opposing the acceptance of her thesis, she appeals the decision and wins the appeal.

Style and Technique

"Ind Aff" is a first-person narrative that tells what happens and what is said during the last hour or so of a love affair. The narrator, who tells about her experience some time after it occurred, guides the reader through the essentials of the situation and of her own gradual understanding of it. Her manner is straightforward and barely ironic, but the reader soon knows that the story is not going to be so much about the end of love as about the beginning of self-awareness. In fact, especially near the beginning of the story, the narrator lets the reader anticipate what she herself does not yet seem to have grasped.

The description of the rainy scene near the Princip Bridge underscores the lovers' disappointment with the bad weather that has spoiled their plans. Although the narrator is not explicit on this point, the reader can attribute Peter's bad mood not so much to the missed idyll in the country as to the effect of the bad weather on Peter's own physique and psyche (he is, after all, in his forties). The reader might even think of the persistent rain as the cause of the end of the affair, which, as it turns out, is an arrangement that cannot be sustained in stormy circumstances.

As they wait for their dinner, the narrator attempts to give some content to their conversational exchanges by talking about the site near the Princip Bridge they had visited earlier and what had occurred there. There is a noticeable gap between the momentous historical events she wants to talk about and Peter's banal preoccupation with his cucumber salad. Though her questions about the shot from Princip's gun as the cause of the Great War lead nowhere with Peter, they do lead the narrator to think about the preamble to the assassin's act, its consequences, and the glory and tragedy involved. They lead the reader to try to see connections between the young woman's preoccupation with the historical event and the nonevents of what can be seen of her life. When she attempts to imagine the minute details of the scene up to the moment when Princip pulled the trigger, the reader surmises that a concern about a decision of her own underlies her effort. The decision the reader is led to anticipate—the narrator's leaving Peter—occurs simultaneously with the young woman's realization that she is lying when she declares her love for him.

At this point in the story, the perceptions of narrator and reader coincide. The young woman's newfound awareness of herself is made clear by the way she now sees her situation. She kisses Peter good-bye deliberately on his bald spot. She notices for the first time that he smells of chlorine. On her way to catch the airport taxi, she glimpses two wild-boar dinners covered with congealed fat emerging from the kitchen. She knows that they are stone cold, just like the love affair she is escaping.

The reader and the narrator are likely to interpret the significance of the assassin's actions differently, however. The reader might have seen the assassin as a hero, as the narrator's musings suggest, and might have been led to think of assassination as the act of a patriot who wanted to end tyranny. The reader might also have been tempted to draw parallels between Princip's decision to act and the young woman's decision to end her affair with Peter. However, the narrator intends a different rendering. The young woman is no poor, silly Princip, misled by an "inordinate affection" into causing a catastrophe by irrational and precipitous action. Rather, she decides *not* to do what she had previously felt inclined to do, for she had come to her senses.

Margaret Duggan

INDIAN CAMP

Author: Ernest Hemingway (1899-1961)
Type of plot: Realism
Time of plot: About 1910
Locale: Michigan's upper peninsula
First published: 1924

Principal characters:
NICK ADAMS, a young boy, the protagonist
DOCTOR ADAMS, his father, a physician
UNCLE GEORGE, his uncle
AN UNNAMED INDIAN, who commits suicide
HIS PREGNANT WIFE, who endures a difficult labor

The Story

"Indian Camp" is a story of initiation in which young Nick Adams accompanies his father, a physician, on a call to an Indian camp, where the father delivers a baby by cesarean section using only his jackknife. The violence and pain of the birth contrast sharply with the ease of the suicide of the pregnant woman's husband, brought on by her screams, and introduce Nick to the realities of birth and death.

The story begins in the dark, before sunrise, as Nick, his father, and Uncle George are rowed across the lake by some Indian men. Nick's father explains that they are going to the camp to treat an "Indian lady who is very sick." The trio follow an Indian with a lantern through the dewy grass. Their way becomes easier and lighter when they are able to walk on the logging road that cuts through the woods, and eventually they are greeted by the dogs that live at the edge of the shantytown occupied by the Indian bark-peelers. The lighted window and the woman holding a light at the doorway of the nearest hut direct the two men and the boy to the woman in labor.

Inside on a wooden bunk lies the pregnant woman, who has been in labor for two days and who cannot deliver despite the help of the other women in the camp. The woman screams as the men enter. The interior of the hut is sketchily described, except for the bunk beds, the lower berth of which is filled by the woman and the upper berth of which holds her husband, who hurt his foot with an ax three days before. The room smells very bad.

Nick's father goes into action, demanding hot water and trying to tell Nick that the woman is going to have a baby. His condensed but rather technical explanation is interrupted by the woman's scream and by Nick's asking if his father can give her something for the pain. His father explains that the screams are not important and that he does not hear them. The husband in the top bunk turns over to face the wall. While scrubbing up, Nick's father explains to Nick that he will have to operate. With Uncle George and three of the Indian men holding her down, Doctor Adams performs a cesarean section, without an anesthetic, using his sterilized pocket knife. The woman bites Uncle George, who calls her a "damn squaw bitch." Nick holds the basin for his father during the operation, which takes a long time.

The arrival of the baby breaks the tension, and Doctor Adams asks Nick how he likes being an intern. Nick turns away so as not to see his father removing the cord or sewing up the incision. The doctor assures the woman, now quiet and pale, that the nurse will drop by the next day and bring all that she needs. Exhilarated after the operation, like a football player in the locker room after a game, Doctor Adams brags that this has been one for the medical journals, using a jackknife and tapered gut leaders.

Brought back to his duties, the doctor looks at the father in the top bunk only to find that in the quietness he has cut his own throat with a razor. Although Nick's father orders George to take Nick out of the hut, it is too late because Nick has already seen the man and the pool of blood.

On their way back to the lake, his postoperative exhilaration gone, Nick's father apologizes for bringing him along. Nick, however, is full of questions, about childbirth, about the woman's husband, about death. Back on the lake, Nick's father rows in the early morning chill. Nick, sitting now in the bow of the boat, trails his hand in the water, which feels warm in the cool of the air. A bass jumps and makes a circle in the water. In the early morning on the lake sitting in the boat while his father rows, Nick feels quite sure that he will never die.

Themes and Meanings

"Indian Camp" is first and foremost a tale of initiation. During the course of the story, Nick witnesses birth and death, the difficulty of the first and the ease of the latter. In the beginning, as Nick and his father are rowed across the lake, Nick nestles, protected and warmed, in his father's arms. On the return trip, with his father in the bow, Nick sits by himself in the stern, now separated forever from his innocence and from the protection of his father by the experiences of the night at the Indian camp, even though it is obvious from the ending that Nick does not fully grasp, or perhaps cannot absorb, the harshness of what he has witnessed.

The story, on a larger plane, also deals with such themes as the conflict between the civilized and the savage. The doctor, as a man of reason and science, is plunged into a dark region of the primordial as he and his son are transported into the heart of the dark forest. Both as a man of science and as a father, the doctor fails to cope adequately with the primitive forces of death and life.

Nick Adams by his very name calls forth the tension between Adam, the first man, and "old Nick," or Satan, suggesting a combination of good and evil inherent in all humankind. "Indian Camp" is the first of a series of stories about Nick Adams, and it reflects the recurring themes of the sequence: discovery and loss, innocence and experience, good and evil.

Style and Technique

Ernest Hemingway once said that when he wrote he was trying to make a picture of the whole world but was always boiling it down. "Indian Camp" is one of his most boiled-down stories, and it occupies an important place in the Hemingway canon. It is, as noted above, the first Nick Adams story, and it was the opening story in Hemingway's first book, *In Our Time* (1924). It introduced his early readers to the "Hemingway style," clipped, pared down, exact—a style that would make the writer famous and much, too much, imitated.

The plot of the story is minimal (a simple night's experience), the images are few, and the modifiers scarcely in evidence. However, each word has been chosen with a poet's care. In 1924, it was a new kind of writing in prose; each word carried weight and seemed endowed with a meaning beyond itself. What Hemingway left out was as important for his style as what he retained. The ending of "Indian Camp" offers a good example of Hemingway's working method.

Initially the story was to end with Nick experiencing the dawn, his hand trailing in the warm water of the lake as the bass jumped, making a circle. Now, however, the story concludes with a modifying series of prepositional phrases, each of which introduces both the irony and the innocence of the moment on the lake, suggesting the motif of therapeutic forgetfulness that later formed a central part of all the other Hemingway characters. The tightness of the rolling phrases, their flow, and their association provide a useful example of how Hemingway layers so much onto his prose without the excesses of authorial intrusion or literary hyperbole.

Charles L. P. Silet

THE INDIAN UPRISING

Author: Donald Barthelme (1931-1989)
Type of plot: Parody
Time of plot: The early twentieth century
Locale: "The city"
First published: 1968

Principal characters:
UNNAMED NARRATOR, the protagonist
SYLVIA, his sometime companion
MISS R., an "unorthodox" teacher
A COMANCHE BRAVE, a torture victim

The Story

Donald Barthelme constructs "The Indian Uprising" as a battle-scene progress report. However, the narrator, clearly one of the leaders of the city forces, shows none of the tactical or organizational skills of a military officer, and his fragmented account mixes very detailed front-line news, sentimental love talk, asides directed at persons about whom the reader knows nothing, information on torture methods, and so forth. There is no story here in the conventional sense, but rather a collage of smug observations leading to a surprising reversal in the final paragraph.

The title suggests that the subject at hand is the familiar material of countless American stories: Narratives of Indian uprisings have been best-sellers in the New World since the last part of the seventeenth century, and Hollywood has made countless cinematic versions by adding the complications of romantic love to the dangers of the fight. In the first paragraph, Barthelme echoes much of that mythology by implying that the city is a kind of El Dorado, with yellow-brick streets, that its main thoroughfares are named after military heroes, and that an anguished, morally aware couple will add a sophisticated philosophical inquiry on what makes "a good life."

The coherence is soon upset. Sylvia proves at least part of the time to be fighting on the Indians' side, and the narrator himself takes part in the torture session. However, through the accumulation of detail the story creates a collage of images, and through this collage the reader comes to know not so much the individuals' motivations and fates as the general social reality.

First, there is city life itself. The scene could be any American metropolis, with its ghetto, heterogeneous population, and incredible accumulation of material goods. The list of objects piled in the barricade does much to describe an entire culture. The narrator, clearly well-off financially, defends the status quo in every sense and conveys the smugness of his urban class by his surprise that the ghetto dwellers join the insurgents, by his long list of live-in girlfriends (each of whom he has given a table made from a hollow-core door), by his preoccupation during the Uprising with his latest door project, his latest girlfriend (presumably a film star), and his personal development under the teacher Miss R. He is culturally sophisticated yet blind to the implications of the chaos around him and within him.

Second, the narrative plays with the conventional idea of the "initiation story." The narrator admits early (echoing the dying words of Montaigne), "I decided I knew nothing." His friends direct him to Miss R., who sets out to teach him the truth, "the litany," "the hard, brown, nutlike word." He fails to recognize the danger of her dress "containing a red figure," and she makes his initiation an ironic one when at the end she represents the Indians' Clemency Committee, which arrests him and presumably will torture him in turn.

Finally, the promise of a love story is withdrawn during the chaos of the narrative. Sylvia turns out to be the narrator's enemy (many of the city "girls" find the Comanches attractive, it seems), no hint is ever given about his relationship with Jane, nor is much revealed about the female "you" of whom he speaks longingly several times. The most humorous mislead is the narrator's connection with Miss R., who at times seems madly romantic, calling him "my boy, mon cher, my heart." In this regard, her final demand that he strip makes wonderful irony of the whole theme of romance.

Themes and Meanings

Barthelme's improvisation in this instance creates a typically divided piece: It is as much about the conventions of narrative fiction as it is about life, and thus it balances the ordered and chaotic, the recognizable and confusing, and the tragic and comic in an attempt both to attract and to repel the reader. The story appeared during the height of the antiwar turmoil surrounding the Vietnam War (late in the story the helicopters kill "a great many in the south," though that is the section still held by the city's forces); guerrilla warfare and memories of ghetto riots in Newark, Harlem, and Watts were fresh in the minds of everyone.

The primary issue in "The Indian Uprising" is cultural crisis both as a fact and as a literary problem. If art grows from culture, what in American culture seems to value and foster art? The first-person narrator could not say, for he seems untouched by his own sophistication—he is vicious, complacent, amoral, and self-deluded. Here Barthelme seems to offer a genuine prophetic impulse, a desire to give a warning about the chaos of this life of replaceable partners and disposable, "merely personal emotions," and the dangers of a culture that worships cold pragmatism, chooses its heroes from among its generals and admirals, and uses its technology to make war on peasants and children. Moreover, questions about what, in a social context, is "a good life," of what use knowledge is in finding such a life, and what effect art has in modifying humankind's savage instincts cast a strong shadow over the narrative.

Barthelme's humor, however, especially his mocking echoes of heavily shadowed works by Thomas Mann, T. S. Eliot, and even William Shakespeare, should make any interpreter beware. The narrator, after all, cannot with complete fairness be thought of as a "person." The same might be said of the other characters, so fragmented and chameleonlike do they come to the reader. Above all, Barthelme is a comic writer; the first-person narrator does not control the arrangement or sequence of details, but is rather controlled throughout by Barthelme's virtuosity.

Thus any discussion of ideas in Barthelme's fiction runs into the issue of his skepticism about ideas and systems. There is no commitment in his fiction, no affirmation of particular truths, and for some readers this makes Barthelme a less than major writer. His portrayal of a confused world of insatiable egos, each pursuing material goals that look unmistakably like junk when realized, suggests a pessimism that the comic impulse does not hide. However, there is also a sense of the paradoxical in this story, that the imagination (not the narrator's, but the author's, and presumably the readers' in turn) continues to supply wonderful responses to experience. "The Indian Uprising" shows such a response and hints at morality even if the argument cannot be logically and systematically presented.

Style and Technique

The coherence of the narrative comes not from plot, for that would suggest a coherence of human events, but from a repetition of images, gestures, actions, and phrases. In general, the story illustrates that from beginning to end, the situation of civilization is getting worse, but the details of the narrative are not organized to demonstrate that. Two motifs, however, run through the entire story: the torture of a Comanche brave and the narrator's preoccupation with women, including an unidentified "you" of whom he speaks yearningly. This combination of love and war in one narrative and in one person is itself a cliché, and through it Barthelme mocks popular literary tradition and also the American culture's eagerness to romanticize war.

Barthelme's methods can be summed up in two words: irony and parody. Both are forms of mimicry, commencing with someone else's prior form and statement, and both are essentially negative responses to that original statement.

Barthelme takes the forms of conventional short fiction, but not for conventional purposes. The modern short story has developed a heightened sense of the significance of repetition: events, colors, gestures, and so forth. These correspondences are usually associated with meaning. "The Indian Uprising" illustrates the patterning and follows the forms, but denies the link with meaning. The Wild West fiction that Barthelme mimics would depend on a suspenseful plot and a confrontation at the end between representatives of good and evil. Sylvia's apparent betrayal, the female schoolteacher, and the love story mimic the traditional elements: In the classic manner, all three help lead to the obligatory showdown, but not in the traditional way. That the schoolmistress should be the turncoat denies conventional expectations and mocks the idea of education as a cohesive force in a culture.

There are many examples of the use of patterns of images and repetition of gestures, but the question of meaning is made problematical very early, as when the narrator lists (he uses the term "analyze") the contents of the barricade in front of him and can conclude only that he knows nothing. A similar fate awaits anyone trying to analyze the details of the narrative. On the map, for example, the Indian-held territory is green, and the narrator's side holds the blue; the city girls, including Sylvia, wear blue mufflers that collectively seem like a blue fog; Miss R. wears a blue dress; blue ends her litany list. None of this comes to mean anything. Similarly, the narrator several times repeats the line, "See the table?" which might be a secret joke on Platonic essences, but it means nothing in the context of the narrator's intentions. The narrator notes near the end that "strings of language extend in every direction to bind the world into a rushing, ribald whole," a sentence so neatly balancing confinement and free impulse that it can stand for Barthelme's methods of irony and parody: In fact, there is no ribaldry in that world (except perhaps from the Indians' "short, ugly lances with fur at the throat"), and no unity, but the narrator unwittingly communicates Barthelme's intention to create the illusion of a whole world of fragments. To make that illusion, Barthelme beguiles his readers with sheer wackiness. The paragraph as a logical or narrative unit does not exist in this story; each is a collage of ironic and sometimes shocking juxtapositions. The details accumulate like debris and, like the objects in the barricade, might reveal much ironically by their disordered presence, but not by logic or system.

Kerry Ahearn

INDISSOLUBLE MATRIMONY

Author: Rebecca West (Cicily Isabel Fairfield, 1892-1983)
Type of plot: Psychological
Time of plot: The early twentieth century
Locale: An industrial city and the surrounding moorlands in Great Britain
First published: 1914

Principal characters:
GEORGE SILVERTON, a solicitor's clerk
EVADNE SILVERTON, his wife

The Story

As the story opens, with George Silverton, a solicitor's clerk, entering his darkened house after a day's work, there is an immediate sense of unease. George is evidently a sour, dry, secretive man who resents everything about his wife Evadne—her exotic beauty, which can sometimes change to ugliness; her quick, emotional response to things that he regards as trivial; her small, sensual pleasures; and above all her apparent refusal to respond to or even, perhaps, notice his growing irritation.

All of this might seem to be typical of the situation between an ill-matched husband and wife. As the author describes George's life before marriage, however, George emerges as a misogynist with a neurotic fear and hatred of sex. He had cherished the idea of wife-desertion as a justifiable way for a man to cleanse himself of what he called "the secret obscenity of women." He married Evadne in the belief that they shared a bond of spiritual purity but quickly came to the conclusion that her interest in the marriage was purely physical. This disgusted him.

Ten years later, he feels cheated and physically defiled. The crisis point is reached when a letter arrives enclosing a handbill announcing that Mrs. Evadne Silverton is to speak at a public meeting in support of Stephen Langton, a Socialist candidate for the town council. Although George is a radical, in the mild reformist meaning of the term, the word "socialism" and the sight of Evadne's name—his surname—on the handbill appall him. His evaluation of his wife as a woman of emotional and intellectual triviality is undermined by his refusal to acknowledge even to himself that she has become a popular and respected political speaker and writer.

Political bigotry becomes mixed up with sexual bigotry. He tells her that Langton is a man of low morals, and when Evadne tries to defend him, he accuses her of being a "slut" and threatens to throw her out of the house if she speaks at the meeting. She hides her hurt by going into the kitchen and noisily washing up. George follows her and picks up a knife, as if to throw it at her—a presage of the murderous confrontation at the climax of the story. Evadne's "weapon"—a soggy dishcloth that she decides not to use—is considerably less lethal. George repeats his threat.

When Evadne gathers her outdoor clothes and dashes out of the house, crying for the first time in their married life, he totally misreads her intention. He is convinced that she is going to meet Langton and that Langton is her lover.

As George, in slippered feet, painfully follows Evadne up a hill and into the green fields and the moors beyond, the wild thoughts of secret assignations and sexual betrayal that clutter his mind match the wildness of the countryside. The idea, expressed earlier, of purification through desertion, takes on urgent force. He is determined to witness his wife's adultery so he can divorce her and be released forever from sexual contact with her.

His humiliation on discovering that Evadne has simply come out for a swim in the lake to cool herself down after the argument leads to the most blistering thought of all: There is no adultery—and therefore no divorce and no escape. Evadne is infected by the intensity of George's emotions: The two people confront each other with murderous intent. All of their past petty misunderstandings are stripped away to reveal a profound underlying hatred. Evadne, stronger than George, seems ready to kill him, but the weaker side of her nature prevails and he strikes her first. As she falls, she drags him down with her into a raging river.

A long, agonizing description of George's struggle in the water, crashing painfully against the rocky banks, ends when he manages to grasp hold of a mooring ring. Having hauled himself out, he puts his feet into the water again and strikes a soft surface, which he identifies as the curve of Evadne's back. He pushes her under the water and holds her down.

Making his painful way home, he has several changes of mood. He is buoyed up with pride in his own strength and masterfulness; then chastened by the thought that he will be hanged for murder; then elated again as he visualizes the ultimate solution—suicide, by gas, in his bedroom. He will thus demonstrate his own strength of purpose and achieve the dignity of purification by death.

The discovery that Evadne, having escaped from what he had imagined to be his deathblow, is now sprawled asleep, wet and muddy, on the bed that he had planned for his own noble death scene, is his final humiliation. He cannot even gas himself, for Evadne has, with her customary thrift, turned off the gas at the mains. Resignedly, he gets into the bed beside her. Her arms slip around him—a warm, unaffected gesture indicating that life will go on as before. This symbol of Evadne's resilience is perceived by George as total defeat.

Themes and Meanings

At the time of publication, Rebecca West, although only twenty-one, had already won considerable recognition in British avant-garde circles for her incisive contributions to feminist and socialist journals. The story reflects not only her political and feminist preoccupations but also the emotional turbulence of her private life.

The heightened melodrama of the plot overlays a profound and biting criticism of institutionalized marriage, with particular concern for the role that women are expected to perform. Until the moment of murderous confrontation, when the pure loathing that underlies their previous petty disagreements is laid bare, neither partner knows anything of the other's true characteristics or inner thoughts. To Evadne, George is a weak but attractive man with a pleasing, albeit indecisive, intellect. She ascribes his frequent moods of irritability to pressures at work and has no inkling of the sexual disgust with which he regards her. To her, the marriage is dull, but tolerable, and gratifying to her physical needs.

George sees Evadne as a trivial, sensual creature with no inner depth or spirituality. His deliberate blindness to her public achievements demonstrates his fear of not being able to master her—an indication that his disgust with her sexuality may also be based on fear of inadequate manhood.

In a very complex and illuminating passage analyzing Evadne's hesitation at the point of murder, the author describes the contradiction that she perceives as central for most married women—on one hand, her need to maintain confidence in her own powers and capabilities, and, on the other, the "unnatural docilities" that are dictated by custom, upbringing, and habit—"a squaw, she dared not strike her lord." It is this acquired docility that prevents Evadne from striking the first blow. Her expression of utter contempt, which George observes as she falls into the river, is a humiliation that he will have to live with; paradoxically, her submission becomes part of her strength.

West's conception of Evadne as a woman with "black blood in her," although expressed variously in a vocabulary that would not be acceptable to later generations, is vital to the sharp contrast that she seeks to make between husband and wife—a physically weak white man brought up with and espousing some of the narrower and more puritanical aspects of Christianity, and a strong woman of mixed ethnic origin whose diverse cultural background has endowed her with greater freedom and flexibility. By centering her story on absolute opposites, the author is able to create a flash point explosive enough to unleash the fierce sexual antagonisms that, she implies, lie beneath the petty squabbles of most marriages but rarely come to the surface.

Style and Technique

West's rich, reverberating prose crescendos to a tumultuous pitch in the scene on the moors—a powerful evocation of elemental passions in an elemental landscape. Her style echoes some of the qualities of Charlotte Brontë's writing but without the Brontë Romanticism. West reveals herself to be emphatically anti-romantic; her story tears away at the myths of conventional marriage and exposes its raw interior nerve.

Her narrative technique is, in fact, modernist, and it is significant that the story was published in the first issue of *Blast*, which rapidly became the main organ of the vorticist movement, bringing together writers and artists who embraced the concept that its editor, Wyndham Lewis, described as "the hard, unromantic external presentation of kinetic forces."

Most of the narrative is expressed from George's viewpoint, and for much of the time Evadne's character is presented in his subjective terms. The positive quality of her actual nature is defined by occasional, definitive interventions in the writer's own voice. This duality of voice—subjective and objective—heightens the contrast between the two people. It emphasizes George's physical and intellectual weakness and his self-delusions, and it gives authority and power to the characterization of Evadne and to her function in the story as the indissoluble element in the marriage.

The story, with its passionate overtones and intricate underlying analytical structure, was acclaimed as a brilliant achievement—particularly impressive in that so young a writer was able to handle profound and difficult emotions with so much confidence and power. The story was an early indication of the qualities of West's more mature works, many of which pursue and develop this story's themes with similar stylistic intensity.

Nina Hibbin

THE INFANT PRODIGY

Author: Thomas Mann (1875-1955)
Type of plot: Sketch
Time of plot: The late nineteenth or the early twentieth century
Locale: A European city
First published: "Das Wunderkind," 1903 (English translation, 1936)

Principal characters:
BIBI SACCELLAPHYLACCAS, a Greek child pianist, the prodigy
THE IMPRESARIO, who manages Bibi and produces the concert
VARIOUS MEMBERS OF THE AUDIENCE

The Story

Bibi Saccellaphylaccas, the child prodigy, enters the packed concert hall to the applause of an audience already favorably disposed because of advance publicity. Dressed all in white silk, the eight-year-old boy, whose age is advertised as seven, sits at his piano and prepares to play a concert of his own compositions. The hall's expensive front seats are occupied by the upper class, including an aging princess, as well as by the impresario and Bibi's mother. Bibi knows that he must entertain his audience, but he also anticipates losing himself in his music.

As Bibi plays, it is clear that he knows how to work his audience. He flings his body with the music and bows slowly to prolong the applause. Recognizing that the members of the audience respond more to a show than to the aesthetics of the music, he thinks of them as idiots.

In fact, his listeners react to the performance in the context of their individual interests and experiences. An old gentleman regrets his own musical inability but views Bibi's talent as a gift from God to which the average person could not aspire. There is no more shame in falling short of Bibi's accomplishment than in bowing before the Christ Child.

A businessperson, believing art to be merely a pleasant diversion, calculates the profit from the concert. A piano teacher rehearses the critical comments that she will make after the concert concerning Bibi's lack of originality and his hand position. A young girl responds to the passion of the music but is confused that such passion is expressed by a child. A military officer equates Bibi's success with his own and applauds in smug self-satisfaction.

An elderly music critic reacts disdainfully, seeing in Bibi both the falseness and the rapture of the artist. Contemptuous of his own audience, the critic believes that he cannot write the truth because it would be beyond his readers. He thinks that he would have been an artist had he "not seen through the whole business so clearly."

As the concert nears its end, laurel wreaths are brought to Bibi. The impresario places one around his neck and then kisses him on the mouth, sending a shock through the audience and leading to wild applause. The critic sees this as a ploy to milk the audience and seems almost sorry that he can so easily see through it.

Bibi's final number, a rhapsody, merges into the Greek national hymn, exciting the Greeks in the audience to shouts and applause. Again the critic deplores this exploitation and plans to criticize it but then wonders if it is perhaps "the most artistic thing of all." After all, an artist is "a jack-in-the-box." He leaves, reflecting that criticism is on a higher level than art.

When the concert ends, the audience forms two groups, one around Bibi and the other around the aging princess. The princess meets Bibi and asks if music simply comes to him when he sits down. He responds that it does but thinks to himself that she is stupid.

As the audience leaves, the piano teacher is heard remarking on Bibi's lack of originality. An elegant and beautiful young woman and her two officer brothers go out into the street. An unkempt girl says to her sullen companion that "we artists" are all child prodigies. The elderly gentleman who had been impressed with Bibi hears the comment and wonders what it means, but the girl's companion nods his head in agreement. The final paragraph shows the girl watching the beautiful young woman and her brothers; she despises them but gazes after them until they are out of sight.

Themes and Meanings

Thomas Mann has spoken of this sketch, along with several others written at about the same time, as wearing "the impress of much melancholy and ironic reflection on the subject of art and the artist." Clearly, there is cynicism on the part of both artist and audience. The performance is not staged as an aesthetic experience but is designed to draw the greatest possible reaction from an audience composed of those whom Bibi views as idiots. Everything is calculated to appeal to emotionalism, from Bibi's dress and the misrepresentation of his age to the timing of bows and the selection of compositions. There seems to be more gimmickry than art, and the story hints that the impresario, who manages the show, may be more responsible than Bibi for its final effect. Even the title of the story calls attention to the age of the performer rather than to the artistry of the event.

Those in the audience respond in terms of their own preoccupations and needs and, thus, cannot give themselves over to the music. The piano teacher is unable to relinquish her claim to expertise, and the young girl relates all to her feelings of sexual passion. The music critic is determined to demonstrate his intellectual superiority, although at times he seems to regret his inability to participate emotionally in the concert. The performance is a social occasion, with even the seating divided by class and with the audience responding similarly to Bibi and to the aging princess. The unkempt girl sees herself, like Bibi, as an artist, but clearly she envies the beautiful socialite.

Although the sketch questions the motives of artist and audience, it leaves open the possibility that the illusion created is, as the music critic suggests, "the most artistic thing of all." Art, by definition, is contrived; it is artifice.

Style and Technique

Much of the effect of the sketch comes from the omniscient perspective of a narrator who can recount the thoughts of all characters, thus allowing the reader to see beneath the surface of the concert. This permits the ironic contrast between, for example, Bibi's condescending view toward the audience and the equally condescending view of the piano teacher and the critic toward Bibi. Nearly all the characters are subject to this ironic vision. At times, the irony is quite straightforward, as when the best seats are described as belonging to the upper class because they "of course" feel the most enthusiasm for art. At other times, the position of the narrator is more difficult to determine. When one of Bibi's pieces is called "an effective childhood fantasy, remarkably well envisaged," is that description an objective assessment by the narrator or a mocking of the rhetoric of the concert's program?

The irony is supported by Mann's precise observation and imagery. When the princess applauds, she does so "daintily and noiselessly pressing her palms together." Her companion, "being only a lady-in-waiting," must "sit up very straight in her chair." Images of water are used to contrast Bibi the performer and Bibi the artist. As a performer, he is described as "diving into the applause as into a bath." As an artist, he regards the "realm of music" as "an inviting ocean, where he might plunge in and blissfully swim."

Larry L. Stewart

INNOCENCE

Author: Harold Brodkey (1930-1996)
Type of plot: Psychological
Time of plot: The 1950's
Locale: Cambridge, Massachusetts
First published: 1973

>   *Principal characters:*
>   WILEY SILENOWICZ, the narrator, a student at Harvard
>   ORRA PERKINS, a beautiful young Radcliffe student who becomes
>   his girlfriend

The Story

Wiley Silenowicz describes Orra Perkins and begins to explain why he was so obsessed with her. She was more than merely beautiful; her looks were like "a force that
struck you." If someone were to see her in sunlight, that experience might be translated into watching "Marxism die." Whereas Orra was beauty personified and ap-
proachable only by men of money and breeding, Wiley was a young man with neither.
Although the odds were against him, however, he was not about to be frightened away
from Orra.

The story opens when Wiley and Orra are seniors in college and Wiley has figured
out how not to be invisible to her anymore. At the close of the first part of the story,
Wiley concludes that to become something more than a "sexual nonentity" to Orra he
must get her attention. Orra would be his ultimate sexual adventure. What is it worth,
Wiley asks, to be in love this way?

Wiley explains that his recounting of his relationship with Orra will not be orderly.
He does not believe that he can do his story justice by remaining calm. To understand,
he says, is to tremble. Wiley now details how he lured Orra into a sexual relationship
with him. They agreed to meet at his room before they went out to dinner, and Wiley
left his door unlocked so that Orra could enter without even knocking. On entering
Wiley's room, Orra was shocked to find him in bed. When he told her that he was naked under the sheet, she cried, "Damn you—why couldn't you wait?" Although she
was disappointed with Wiley for not letting their relationship progress more slowly,
she undressed and they engaged in sexual intercourse. Wiley regarded their sex as "really sort of poor" and was disappointed because Orra did not have an orgasm. He
imagined that all of her other lovers were too intimidated by her beauty to help her
achieve an orgasm. That first night they remained together and talked about love and
its infinite possibilities.

The third part of the story concerns Orra's inability to have an orgasm. She was convinced that having an orgasm was irrelevant, but Wiley believed that her not having an
orgasm was a barrier that set a limit on their relationship. Orra strongly disagreed and

did not want to experiment sexually in order to remedy the situation. Wiley concludes that "she was fantastically alive and eerily dead at the same time. I wanted for my various reasons to raise her from the dead."

In the last part of the story, Wiley decided that conventional sexual activity would not cause Orra to have an orgasm. Although she was reluctant to engage in other sexual acts, Wiley proceeded with oral sex. She did not want him to be solely interested in her having an orgasm. She wanted to remain distant and not give herself totally to any man. Whenever her body would "vibrate," she became "embarrassed." Eventually, however, through the experience of mutual sexual discovery, they both became more in tune with what is needed for total sexual gratification. At the end of the story, Orra finally had her first orgasm while engaged in sexual intercourse with Wiley. After screaming that she was "coming," she angrily remarked that she "always knew they were doing it wrong, I always knew there was nothing wrong with me."

Themes and Meanings

Harold Brodkey's story can be read on more than one level. "Innocence" clearly concerns itself with the evolution of two lovers discovering their own sexuality; however, Brodkey is also saying much more. Concerned with shedding light on the dark corners of a person's mind, he and his character Wiley are one and the same person. As a character, Wiley appears in several Brodkey short stories.

The beautiful young woman, Orra, in this story has been regarded as a "trophy" to the men she has known and has exerted control over them by remaining aloof. After Wiley decides that he wants more than mere sex, he is willing to go on a quest without really knowing where it will end. For her part, Orra has already made compromises in her young life. She has made herself into an icon, but in so doing has remained ignorant of her true self. As Wiley and Orra develop their relationship, sexual awakening is the story's central focus. However, as in other Brodkey stories, this focus is merely a metaphor for something larger. As college students, Wiley and Orra take a journey together toward self-discovery. Wiley may not be totally secure as a person himself, but his willingness to probe every avenue, to kick over every rock, allows both he and Orra to grow. Wiley wants more from Orra than she has been willing to give to any man in the past.

In an interview, Brodkey has said that "Innocence" is about "earning" and not just about sexual gratification. Love and sex cannot be cut off from other tools of self-discovery such as religion, philosophy, and mythology. In this story, two lovers are able to smash societal and cultural barriers and become richer for having tried. Whereas none of Orra's former lovers was willing or able fully to satisfy her sexually, Wiley is a different sort of male—one who links his own sexual satisfaction with hers by refusing to gratify himself and remain unconcerned with her needs. Even though Orra claims to believe that she is incapable of orgasm, Wiley realizes that her delusion does them both a disservice.

Because "Innocence" is sexually explicit, it has been compared to both Norman Mailer's story "The Time of Her Time" and D. H. Lawrence's *Lady Chatterley's*

Lover (1928). Brodkey has taken issue with some of these comparisons. For example, he believes that his own story is more about the re-creation of a particular moment in time, whereas the Mailer story is more concerned with the people involved. This may be a loose contrast, but Brodkey sees a clear distinction. There is a closer link between *Lady Chatterley's Lover* and "Innocence" than between Mailer's story and "Innocence." Although it can be argued that Lawrence's novel is a precursor, Brodkey's story moves beyond the force that social class played in *Lady Chatterley's Lover.* Brodkey has stated that within "Innocence" the point is made that "what happens in sex follows a certain kind of logic." Fantasies of any kind, sexual or otherwise, can run counter to the fulfillment that can be attained through the recognition of what is real. Wiley and Orra become grounded in reality by discarding the seemingly "innocent" fantasies and myths that are barriers to true gratification.

Style and Technique

During the 1960's, when Brodkey gained prominence as a short-story writer, his early stories were characterized by a sense of control. With "Innocence," he commences on a different path. The prose of this story is chatty and meanders from point to point. There is no doubt that this is an autobiographical story. In his earlier work, there was at least a pretense of separateness. However, when Wiley utters the words "I distrust summaries" and later in the same paragraph states, "I admire the authority of being on one's knees in front of the event," it is clear that the reader is in the presence of none other than the author himself.

A recollection of a real event, the story is told from every possible angle. For a story that is more than thirty pages long, the reader may well ask when will enough be enough. The author's obsessions permeate the story; what may pass as civilized prose is of no interest to Brodkey. In "Innocence" and other stories that followed, there is a certain frenzy that envelops what transpires within the stories. The author's own personal history overshadows all else in these stories.

For all the sexual explicitness of "Innocence," the story is not set up to be an erotic rush for the curious reader. At times, the sexual content borders on the clinical, reflecting Brodkey's admiration for "the authority of being on one's knees in front of the event." "Innocence" is thus the culmination of memory merged. Brodkey's self-absorption in his own past has been magnificently thrown together. The reader becomes a coconspirator with the arrogant author who has let loose the achings of his soul onto the page.

Jeffry Jensen

INNOCENCE

Author: Seán O'Faoláin (John Francis Whelan, 1900-1991)
Type of plot: Wit and humor
Time of plot: About 1915
Locale: Dublin, Ireland
First published: 1946

> *Principal characters:*
> THE NARRATOR, the father of a seven-year-old boy about to have his first confession
> THE OLD AUGUSTINIAN PRIEST

The Story

A father reminisces about what happened to him forty years earlier when, after confession, for "the first time I knew that I had committed sin." The occasion for this recollection is the sight of his seven-year-old son being prepared by nuns for his first confession: The father knows that his son does not really believe in the practice—it is "a kind of game" between the nuns and the priest. The father recognizes that his boy, who often calls his father "A Pig," is "a terrible liar," given to tantrums. However, the father's love allows him to understand and value the son's childishness.

Given hindsight, the father knows that someday his boy "will really do something wicked" and will be overcome with fear. He recalls how he experienced terror when, as a boy, he falsely confessed to an old and feeble priest that he had committed adultery. It was the priest's reaction to this confession that generated the terror that the narrator knows his son will one day feel: "Then horrible shapes of understanding came creeping toward me along the dark road of my ignorance"—the priest had mistaken him for a girl. To escape, he was ready to tell any lie: "I was like a pup caught in a bramble bush, recanting and retracting," desperately seeking the words of absolution and penance.

The father recollects vividly his fear and guilt, his sense of being polluted: "I knew that from then on I would always be deceiving everybody because I had something inside me that nobody must ever know. I was afraid of the dark night before me." He realizes now how the innocence of his son resembles "that indescribably remote and tender star" that he glimpsed in his isolation. This insight converts his son's mischief into a precious sign of a necessary but now past and irretrievable stage of spiritual development.

Themes and Meanings

As the title indicates, the story concerns the nature of innocence, sin, and forgiveness. The narrator reflects on how the Catholic Church's practice of preparing children for confession does not introduce them to the real world, especially the fear of knowing that one has done something "wicked." Confession is a game for most children, a ritual that marks the boundary between childhood and maturity.

As the narrator-father muses on his son's transparent and innocent lying, he recalls "the first time that I had committed sin." The emphasis is on knowledge, one's coming to awareness. Because the occasion is pivotal to his growth, the narrator provides a meticulous description of the setting and cultural context: The Church connotes Saint Augustine's view of the inherent sinfulness of man; the gloomy and battered surroundings evoke neglect, exhaustion, and fragility. Opposed to this bleak atmosphere is the narrator's love for the bright candles surrounding Saint Monica, the mother of Saint Augustine, and his adolescent fascination with dark nooks and "the stuffy confessional boxes with their heavy purple curtains."

If one scrutinizes the motive that made the narrator (as an adolescent) decide to play the game and confess having committed adultery, one perceives that it was the experience of "terror that crept into me like a snake," a dread like that of a criminal suddenly apprehended by a police officer, that compelled him to deviate from his usual practice of confession.

More revealing is the process of his shock at the insistent questioning by the old priest into the details of his sin, his panic at the thought of "harm" done to him. What shocks him more, spawning "horrible shapes of understanding," is the priest's mistaking him for a girl. At this point, the boy becomes desperate in wanting to escape, ready to fake anything so that the priest will desist. However, what "utterly" breaks him is when the priest, finally convinced that the narrator is a man, asks whether the woman he victimized "was married or unmarried." With this mapping of the possibilities of evil, the child is initiated into adult knowledge and practices, into the perverse delight that adults derive from the thought of prohibited or sinful acts.

Although the narrator as child does not fully grasp the nature of his discovery— which is less about himself than about adult behavior (in the person of the old priest whose feebleness blunts the satire)—he sums up the event in a double-visioned comment: First, it was "an absurd misadventure" worthy of laughter among friends; second, he compares himself to "a pup caught in a bramble bush," a deflating image. From a distance of forty years, the incident appears trivial. However, the last three paragraphs of the story explore the psychological experience of the boy who felt the world become sullen and hostile. With a feeling that "I had done something inside me that nobody must ever know," the secret transforms the adolescent into an adult. His claim, taken seriously, produces an interiority, or a double, the guilty self behind the innocent mask presented to the public; the narrator "cannot laugh" at this because it signifies the end of childhood innocence.

In the last paragraph, the narrator affirms the beneficent "fatherhood" of priests who can compassionately instruct children. However, he laments the fact that his son, "this small Adam," will grow up, his innocence transposed into an "indescribably remote and tender star." Implicit here are the traditional notions that duplicity characterizes adult experience, that because sin pervades the world, the need for confession and penance will always be felt.

Even though the narrator as father glories in his son's childish conduct, the narrative centers on the loss of his own youthful innocence as he is caught in the calculus of sins in the penny prayer book. Although the narrative alludes to the institutional or cultural framework within which innocence is lost, the narrator persists in purveying a dualistic metaphysics of innocence/guilt, of sin/childhood fantasies. The ideology of Augustinian moralizing is subtly reinforced by the attractiveness of a seemingly unpremeditated game, a spontaneous act of freedom. However, the penny prayer book and the act of confession entail a total worldview that contradicts the sentimental if dubious idealization of childhood innocence.

Style and Technique

In an anthology of short stories that he edited, Seán O'Faoláin describes one of the most intense, strange, and painful pleasures of good fiction, an experience that he calls "Moral Shock": "the excitement and challenge of being brought face to face with some way of life, apparently coherent, seemingly practical, yet disturbingly different from our own."

The central incident in this story may not be strange to a Christian audience, but what may perhaps disturb the common reader and trigger "moral shock" is the idea that the sense of guilt associated with maturity can materialize only in a discourse polarized around the categories of good and evil. The text itself is polarized between the world of childhood with its make-believe creatures (such as the Robin in the Cow's Ear) and the domain of religion.

Except for tidbits about his son's prankish temper and fits, his calling his father "A Pig" (the capitalization hints at the totemic stature of the father), the narrative elaborates on the occasion when the narrator was "primed" for his act: The "dim, wintry afternoon" inside the "old, dark, windy church" is described in full, including such seemingly insignificant details as "the heels of the penitents stuck out when they knelt to the grille." The connotative texture combines an abundant use of both adjectives and the evocation of a self-conscious, ascetic discipline: "The priests dressed in the usual black Augustinian garment with a cowl and a leather cincture." The visual imagery of light and dark; the juxtaposition of Saint Monica and Saint Augustine, of the penny prayer book and the sin of adultery; the old and feeble priest confronting the child attracted to the bright candles and the sensuous surface of the world—all these generate an allegory of two opposing but interpenetrating realms: adult sinfulness and the natural virtue of youth.

After the exposition on the father-son relationship and the impressionistic rendering of setting and atmosphere, the text begins to dramatize the exchange between the priest and the boy. This is the heart of the story, where the process of discovery occurs. O'Faoláin's technique is orthodox: He describes the boy's reactions and sensations. After capturing the priest's tired, ambiguous tone, he intrudes a distant perspective in order to comment on the whole affair, after which he resumes the effort to transcribe the boy's mood following the harrowing ordeal. The conclusion seeks to formulate a lesson to the effect that playing fables can precipitate one's passage to the real world, but the quoting of his son's monotonous litany of misdeeds tends to dissipate the serious didactic aim with a humorous note.

O'Faoláin's technique may be defined as seriocomic when it mixes the boy's fantasy world and natural outbursts of rebellion against the father's authority (lumping humans with animals) with the reflective and somewhat disabused stance of a moral observer far removed from the scene. The narrator's voice tries to convince the reader of its sincerity and authority, but it also wants to entertain and distract through the deliberately adopted tone of the solicitous and loving father who himself was once an erring adolescent. The first-person point of view is meant to convey the authenticity of the event, but it also produces an ironic undercutting of itself when the reader realizes that he is also the target of the narrator's deception: "I knew that from then on I had something inside me that nobody must ever know." In effect, the story is the narrator's act of confession to the reader, who cannot help now but share the secret that he has been trying to hide all these years.

E. San Juan, Jr.

INSTRUCTIONS FOR JOHN HOWELL

Author: Julio Cortázar (1914-1984)
Type of plot: Fantasy
Time of plot: The late 1960's
Locale: London, England
First published: "Instrucciones para John Howell," 1966 (English translation, 1973)

> *Principal characters:*
> RICE, a spectator at a play
> AN ACTOR, the man who plays the role of John Howell
> AN ACTRESS, the woman who plays the role of Eva
> FLORA, an actress who plays the role of the woman in red
> AN ACTOR, the man who plays the role of Michael
> THE TALL MAN, who gives Rice the instructions for John Howell

The Story

The title of the story, "Instructions for John Howell," is ambiguous, for the identity of John Howell is only tentative. John Howell is a fictional character in a play that Rice attends. John Howell is also the actor who appears in the role, and, during the second and third acts of the four-act play, John Howell is Rice himself.

During the first intermission of the play that Rice is attending at the Aldwych Theater, a man in gray invites him backstage, gives him a costume and wig, and instructs him to act the part of John Howell. When Rice protests that he is not an actor, the man agrees, saying that he is John Howell. Onstage during the second act, Rice finds that his lines are entirely predetermined by the words of the other characters. He has no freedom to do what he wants to do or say what he wants to say. As the act progresses, it becomes clear that the character Eva is deceiving her husband, Howell, by having an affair with another character in the play, Michael, and that the mysterious woman in red seems to be implicated in the infidelity in some way. At one point during the action, the actress who plays Eva whispers to Rice in her offstage voice, "Don't let them kill me."

During the second intermission, the man in gray and a tall man congratulate Rice on his performance and serve him several glasses of whiskey. The tall man gives Rice extensive instructions on what he is to do during the third act, and it becomes apparent that the decisive moment of the play comes at the end of this act, when the woman in red speaks a line that determines the denouement of the play in the last act.

In the third act, under the influence of the alcohol and resisting confinement to the predetermined plot, Rice begins to improvise. By the lines that he delivers, he creates problems for the actor playing the role of Michael. He is amused by the display of anger that he sees in the wings as the tall man protests what he is doing. He is disturbed by Eva's plea—again in her offstage voice—that he stay with her until the end. Rice tries to delete the last line of the third act by leading Eva offstage, but she turns around to receive from the woman in red the inevitable words that will determine the outcome of the play.

In the third intermission, the tall man and his accomplices throw Rice out of the theater. When he returns to his seat to watch the last act, he is surprised that the theatrical illusion takes over immediately, so that the audience does not protest the change of actors. The actor who played Howell in the first act is again in the role. At the crucial moment, as Eva is about to drink the tea poisoned by the woman in red, Howell startles her so that she spills the tea. In the confusion that follows, there is a sharp cracking sound. Eva slowly slips into a reclining position on the sofa and Howell runs offstage.

Rice runs out of the theater and through the streets of London. He realizes that someone is following him and turns to find that it is the actor who played the role of Howell. When Rice states that he tried to stop the irrevocable action of the play, the actor responds that amateurs always think that they can change things, but that it never works. It always turns out the same way. When Rice asks why they are both fleeing, if it always happens this way, the actor begs Rice not to leave him in his predicament of forever running away, then disappears in flight down the street. As he hears the sound of whistles in the streets, Rice runs in the opposite direction, reminding himself that there will always be streets and bridges on which to run.

Themes and Meanings

"Instructions for John Howell" is representative of the artistic and political concerns that are evident in all the fiction of Julio Cortázar. As in many of his stories, Cortázar here elaborates on a familiar theme: the juxtaposition of art and life through the device of a play viewed by a spectator who cannot distinguish the theatrical illusion from the world of real experience. The theme is primarily an artistic one, for it questions the relative authenticity of reality and art, but it becomes in Cortázar's story a symbolic representation of the conflict of individual liberty and the restrictiveness of organized social and political forces. Rice is forced into the role that he must play, is given specific instructions on how to play it, and is ostracized and then pursued by unseen oppressive forces when he exerts his individual will in an effort to change the inevitable outcome of the events.

Although Cortázar always declared himself in sympathy with socialist societies such as Salvador Allende's Chile and Fidel Castro's Cuba, he did not align himself with any particular political ideology; rather, he was committed to the principle that the exploitation of human beings is evil. It is possible to view Cortázar's political commitment as naïve, but in fact that naïveté is one of the themes of his fiction. The story of Rice is a narrative of a loss of innocence, as the character—bored with the weekend in London and then impatient with the mediocrity of the first act of the play—is confronted with the terror of the infringement of his personal liberty and the persecution that follows his rebellion against the authoritarian directorial staff of the play. The actor, who has experienced this conflict night after night with each performance, is less naïve than Rice, for he understands the system and the impossibility of escaping the oppression.

The theme of the loss of innocence in any of the many forms that it may take dominates the stories of Cortázar, particularly those published in the 1950's, in English in 1963 with the title *End of the Game, and Other Stories*, then again in 1967 as *Blow-Up, and Other Stories* after the success of the Michelangelo Antonioni film (*Blow-Up*, 1966), based on the lead story. The innocence is sexual in "Final del juego" ("End of the Game"), artistic in "Las babas del diablo" ("Blow-Up"), and overtly political in "Las armas secretas" ("Secret Weapons") and "El perseguidor" ("The Pursuer").

Style and Technique

Through the device of the theatrical illusion in "Instructions for John Howell," Cortázar develops one of the more terrifying aspects of the loss of political innocence. The actor who portrays John Howell becomes John Howell. In like manner, the tall man who gives the instructions points out that Rice is no longer Rice, nor is he an actor. Rather, he is John Howell. The transformation of the "real" person into the character that he is portraying occurs in the text through the language of the narrator, who frequently refers to the actor as Howell and, in the last moment of the story, uses pronouns ambiguously to confuse the identities of the two men: the two John Howells crouched in the alleyway to elude their unseen pursuers. Thus, the narrator's linguistic structures reinforce the theme of the effect of oppression on the freedom of the individual.

The transformation of the character into another person, or the mutation of the individual into an object with which the individual is obsessed, occurs frequently in Cortázar's stories, and it always is effected through the narrative voice. It is evident that Rice becomes John Howell onstage not so much because of what he does but because of what he says, and because of his conviction that he can alter the reality of the play by his words. The illusion of the play becomes for Rice/Howell an inevitable reality that can be changed only by the force of his linguistic resources.

The narrator begins the story with words that provide an explanation for the seemingly impossible events: "Thinking about it afterwards—on the street, in a train, crossing fields—all that would have seemed absurd, but what is theater but a compromise with the absurd and its most efficient, lavish practice?" These words not only justify the denouement of the plot but also create a symmetry in the narrative, for the reference to street, train, and fields anticipates the aftermath of the events: Rice (or Howell) fleeing his pursuers by way of streets, trains, and fields.

Gilbert Smith

INTENSIVE CARE

Author: Lee Smith (1944-   )
Type of plot: Domestic realism
Time of plot: 1988
Locale: Greenwood, Mississippi
First published: 1988

Principal characters:
HAROLD STIKES, a solid husband and owner of three Food Lion
supermarkets
JOAN BERRY STIKES, his former wife, a home-economics teacher
CHERRY (DORIS CHRISTINE) OXENDINE WESTALL PALLADINO
STIKES, his new wife
LOIS HICKEY, the head nurse in intensive care

The Story

"Intensive Care" is told by a gossipy omniscient narrator partly through flashbacks. The story begins in the Beauty Nook, where several women are having their hair styled and listening to the details from head nurse Lois Hickey about how Cherry Oxendine Westall Palladino Stikes is dying in intensive care. In the women's self-righteous view, Harold Stikes is getting just what he deserves for deserting his wife and children to marry Cherry.

The next scene shows Harold Stikes leaving the hospital, where he has been visiting Cherry, and driving indiscreetly to his old home in the suburban Camelot Hills development. While his former wife and their children are gone for the day, he lets himself in with his key, sits in the living room, and mulls over his decision to leave his family. The house is straight out of the pages of *Southern Living* magazine, with everything neat and orderly, and so was his previous life: Joan, his efficient former wife, a home-economics teacher, produced three children spaced three years apart before she got her tubes tied. However, hardworking Harold was infuriated one day when he found a magazine quiz called "How Good Is Your Marriage?" that Joan had filled out: She rated their marriage just average.

Six months later, Harold ran into redheaded, dynamite-figured Cherry Oxendine working in his own Food Lion deli, and events took their course. Cherry got cancer and had to have her breasts removed, but Harold proposed to her anyway. Now, three years later, the cancer has returned, along with pneumonia, and Cherry lies dying in intensive care. Harold had her only for "one trip to Disney World, two vacations at Gulf Shores, Alabama, hundreds of nights in the old metal bed out at the farm with Cherry sleeping naked beside him, her arm thrown over his stomach. They had a million laughs."

Disorderly and disreputable, Cherry was married twice before (not to mention her torrid adulterous affair with Lamar Peebles, her rich high school boyfriend), has two grown children, and is a terrible cook, eating tacos, chips, and beer in bed. She is also gullible, believes in astrology and unidentified flying objects (UFOs), and has wild technicolored dreams. However, Harold has admired her ever since high school, in which she was a cheerleader and Miss Greenwood High. In particular, he remembers a "close-up encounter" with her after the senior class picnic at Glass Lake, when she appeared out of the lake in her topless glory, and no questions asked, Harold helped her ashore and gave her his shirt.

The story ends late one night when Harold returns to the old farm where Cherry's parents raised cockapoos and where he has been living with Cherry for the past three years. In the kitchen, he finds lasagna and a piña colada cake, his favorite, left by his former wife, who has been bringing him food ever since Cherry went into intensive care. He eats the food, then takes a walk down a dirt road with the last two cockapoos. As he walks along, a star detaches itself from the sky, flies down, and hovers over him as big as a field: "Although Harold can't say exactly how it communicates to him or even if it does, suddenly his soul is filled to bursting. The ineffable occurs." Then the UFO is gone.

Two weeks later, Cherry dies. Harold might eventually return to his family, but he will love Cherry forever and never tell anyone what he saw.

Themes and Meanings

Some readers might think of Harold Stikes as belatedly living out his high school fantasies about Cherry Oxendine or merely going through a mid-life crisis. Apparently his sensible former wife Joan thinks so because she continues her own life without letting their breakup bother her; she just stops stocking beer in the refrigerator. However, her reaction (or lack thereof) might be seen as another symptom of what was wrong in their marriage and what drives Harold to Cherry. Sensible Joan is lacking in passion and possibly even thinks of the average marriage as ideal, another design out of *Southern Living* or *Good Housekeeping*, two of her favorite magazines, which she displays neatly on the glass coffee table in the living room.

However, for Harold, the average marriage is not enough. The author, Lee Smith, seems to side with Harold; her story seems to be saying that every life should have some great passion, love, and excitement, even if only briefly and in the disorderly and disreputable form of such persons as Cherry Oxendine, whose favorite magazines—*Parade, Coronet, The National Enquirer*—litter the floor on her side of the bed. Cherry herself, who prophetically changed her name from Doris Christine when she was in the eighth grade, seems to have no problem packing fun into her hectic life. In short, "Intensive Care" is about how one should live one's life: with verve, gusto, and pizzazz, even if it is a little messy.

The story also comments on life in the consumer culture and in a small town. All the references to consumer correctness, as exemplified in Joan's magazines and such names as Beauty Nook and Camelot Hills, critique the manufactured American Dream, which costs money but still elevates the bland, sanitized average as ideal. This ideal average becomes worse in the petty busybody confines of a small town, where conformity and perpetual adolescence rule, as exemplified in the story's opening scene. Head nurse Lois Hickey has no respect whatever for confidential medical information, and the spiteful, self-righteous women think nothing of viewing Cherry's death as fit punishment for Harold. To them, she will always be Cherry Oxendine, that fancy tart they were jealous of in high school.

Style and Technique

Smith excels at making telling use of meaningful details in her story. Besides magazines, for example, hairstyles distinguish the women, as befits a story that begins in the Beauty Nook. Lois Hickey wears her frosted hair too short, in Dot Mains's opinion. Joan Berry Stikes still wears her shiny blond hair in the same pageboy style she had in college (a Baptist school), never deviating. However, Cherry Oxendine is a naturally curly redhead, except maybe for that time she popped up from the lake with muddy, dripping hair and greeted Harold.

References to food also abound in the story, in the characters' names and other details. Harold Stikes marries Joan Berry and works his way up in the world by becoming the owner of three Food Lions. He meets Cherry Oxendine, obviously a powerful dish, in his own Food Lion deli, and she serves him up a big glob of potato salad along with the roast beef sandwich he ordered. Also, Harold's former wife apparently expects to lure him back by leaving his favorite dishes around.

Allusions to ancient mythology and contemporary popular culture also play a part. The women in the Beauty Nook are like a bunch of harpies, Cherry's rise from the lake is like Aphrodite's birth from the sea, and Joan's dishes are perhaps reminiscent of the one Medea served up to Jason. Popular culture appears in the form of UFOs. For Harold Stikes, his close encounter with a UFO is very similar to his close encounter with the heavenly body of Cherry Oxendine: "He feels that he has been ennobled and enlarged, by knowing Cherry Oxendine."

All these references tend to build up the contrasts between the two main women in the story, Joan and Cherry, and the two ways of life that they represent and between which Harold Stikes has to choose. So also do the two meanings in the title "Intensive Care." For Joan, Lois Hickey, and the girls at the Beauty Nook, life is just one enormous hospital in which the patients have to be managed with intensive care. However, for a while, Cherry Oxendine and Harold Stikes live life and love each other with intensive care.

Harold Branam

AN INTEREST IN LIFE

Author: Grace Paley (1922-   )
Type of plot: Realism
Time of plot: The 1950's
Locale: New York City
First published: 1959

Principal characters:
VIRGINIA, the female protagonist, the abandoned mother of four
children
MRS. RAFTERY, her downstairs neighbor, a busybody
JOHN RAFTERY, Mrs. Raftery's son, who visits both his mother
and Virginia every Thursday

The Story

The plot is quite simple: "An Interest in Life" offers a first-person account of a young woman, Virginia, who is deserted by her husband shortly before Christmas. Thanks to the advice of her downstairs neighbor, Mrs. Raftery, rent and food money from the Welfare Department, the amorous attentions of Mrs. Raftery's son, John, and her own sense of humor, Virginia and her four children manage quite well without her husband.

The husband's parting gifts are a new broom and a passionate, mean kiss intended to let her know what she will be missing. With only fourteen dollars and the rent unpaid, Virginia turns for help to her downstairs neighbor. Mrs. Raftery's advice: Tell Welfare, the grocer, and the cops, who will provide toys for the kids, and look around for comfort; "With a nervous finger she pointed to the truckers eating lunch on their haunches across the street. . . . She waved her hand to include all the men marching up and down in search of a decent luncheonette. She didn't leave out the six longshoremen loafing under the fish-market marquee." The tone is set; the story continues in this earthy and ironic vein as Virginia's tough-kid humor and self-mockery protect her against self-pity.

One night, Mrs. Raftery advises her son to visit his old friend, Virginia. Soon he comes regularly, bringing presents for the kids and even offering to do the dishes. He takes a special interest in Girard, Virginia's most difficult child; he gives him an erector set, signs him up for Cub Scouts, and plays the father Girard never really had. Nevertheless, Virginia rejects his first advances, fearing that the world will blame her for corrupting an upstanding member of church and community; then, too, John is not as sexy as her husband, whose "winking eyes" she still misses.

When John questions Virginia about her husband, she makes excuses about his need to do well in the world, while thinking to herself how cruel he was, trying to turn neighbors and friends against her and constantly putting her down. John listens patiently, continues to help with the kids, but finally stops coming, apparently discouraged by her cold responses.

In despair at the loss of this one true friend, Virginia decides to submit a list of her troubles to "Strike It Rich." Soon after the doorbell rings, "two short and two long meaning John." "As always happens," Virginia tells herself, "where you have begun to help yourself with plans, news comes from the opposite direction. She thinks about how easy it would be for John to walk out of their lives forever and decides "not to live without him."

John mocks her dream of being chosen for "Strike It Rich," reducing her troubles to "the little disturbances of man" as Grace Paley, the author, does to the troubles of so many of her would-be victims. Soon after, Virginia and John become lovers; Mrs. Raftery approves because now John comes to visit every Thursday; Virginia maintains her way of life, noting how remarkable it is that "a man who sends out the Ten Commandments every year for a Christmas card can be so easy buttoning and unbuttoning"; and the reader is ready for a happy ending of sorts. Instead Paley throws a curve; Virginia dreams that her husband returns, "raps her backside," and they are right back where the story started. The last line, "The truth is, we were so happy, we forgot the precautions," makes it clear that the future will repeat the perpetual cycle of passion, childbirth, and desertion. Virginia may have the spunk of a survivor, but her dependence on men and her own sexuality condemn her to a life of poverty.

Themes and Meanings

"An Interest in Life" is the central story in Paley's collection *The Little Disturbances of Man: Stories of Men and Women in Love* (1959). As the title suggests, this story demonstrates one of Paley's favorite themes, the way in which a good sense of humor and a healthy appetite for life can reduce apparent tragedies to minor disturbances. Virginia seems a survivor, whose intelligence, honesty, and street smarts mark her kinship with the picaresque heroes of J. D. Salinger and Saul Bellow. There is, however, a darker side to Paley's work—a grim picture of urban poverty, of men who are irresponsible and of women who find them irresistible, of a culture and an economy in which the poor are lulled into dreams of sudden riches rather than encouraged to find realistic ways to better their plight.

Early in the story, Virginia's self-awareness wins the reader's admiration: "I don't have to thank anything but my own foolishness for four children when I'm twenty-six years old, deserted, and poverty-struck. . . . A man can't help it, but I could have behaved better," she tells herself. However, at the end of the story, she envisions herself making the same mistake once again. This conclusion seems quite intentional on Paley's part, a warning to the reader not to romanticize the lusty life of the poor, to see Virginia for what she really is: a survivor, yes, but not a heroine.

Style and Technique

There is general critical consensus that what makes Paley so popular is the authenticity of the language that her characters speak and the wonderful irony and wit that underlie her stories. Her characters are brought to life not so much by what they do, but by how they think and talk. This is especially true of her first-person narratives. Whether it is that of an old woman telling her niece the story of her long-term relationship with a second-rate actor ("Goodbye and Good Luck") or a sexually precocious fourteen-year-old explaining how she got herself engaged to her sister's boyfriend ("A Woman, Young and Old"), the first-person voice is used by Paley to reveal the core of naïveté and vulnerability behind the tough facade that her narrators present to the world.

Paley also uses a classic unreliable narrator as a vehicle for dramatic irony. In the process of telling their stories to other people—boyfriends, mothers, aunts, nieces—Paley's narrators acknowledge the temptation to gloss over the uglier parts. They are, in fact, more honest with themselves; for example, Virginia hides some of the truth about her husband from John Raftery, yet tells the reader how cruel he really was. The implied author, whose point of view the reader understands from the structure of the story, suggests that there are deeper truths the narrator will never understand because of her limited perspective on her own life.

The typical Paley narrator interprets the ending of her story as a happy one; the implied author provides evidence of a different perspective. Thus, the reader understands that Rosie in "Goodbye and Good Luck" may get her man in the end, but only after thirty years spent without a home of her own. At this point, her lover must be close to seventy and may not have much life left in him. Josephine, the fourteen-year-old in "A Woman, Young and Old," feels proud to be engaged, yet the reality of venereal disease, adultery, and promiscuity surrounding this engagement promises little hope for a happy future.

This darker side to Paley's stories provides tension and depth but does not dampen their surface vitality. The language her characters speak expresses optimism and spunk, never self-pity. Because Paley depicts a world dominated by poverty and infidelity through the eyes of a narrator who accepts her own plight, the reader can applaud the small triumphs and hopes that make daily life possible in the ghettos of New York.

Jane M. Barstow

THE INTERIOR CASTLE

Author: Jean Stafford (1915-1979)
Type of plot: Psychological
Time of plot: The 1940's
Locale: The United States
First published: 1947

Principal characters:

PANSY VANNEMAN, a twenty-five-year-old woman injured in a
    car accident
DR. NICHOLAS, the surgeon who repairs her shattered nose
MISS KENNEDY, a nurse in her hospital

The Story

Pansy Vanneman, twenty-five years old, is in the hospital recovering from severe injuries that she received when a taxi in which she was riding had an accident that killed the driver. It is now six weeks after the accident, and Pansy has recovered enough for her surgeon to operate on her smashed nose. She has spent the previous six weeks in a kind of waking trance. She has had no visitors, because she only recently moved to the city and apparently has not formed connections there. Her behavior is so passive as to cause comment among the nurses and resentment at her indifference. She barely responds to the presence of others, sometimes not answering their questions. Pansy doesn't seem to take part in life at all, and her doctor wonders if she is suffering from shock in an unusual way. Her rich fantasy life, however, provides her with continual solace. She has one particular object of contemplation: her own brain. She thinks of her brain as a kind of flower or jewel that is deeply interior and invaluable. She has withdrawn from the world of pain to this interior castle, where she feels soothed and comforted. She has no need for anything else.

As her operation approaches, it becomes clear that the real world was uncomfortable for Pansy even before the accident. Sometimes her contemplation of the color pink, the color of her brain, brings to mind a painful scene from her past of a day on which she had gone to an autumn party wearing a pink hat. At the party, Mr. Oliver, with whom she thought herself in love, casually compared her with a Katherine Mansfield character and then invited another woman out. Her reaction to that incident was to throw away the hat and flee from other reminders of the day, going so far as to lock her door against a clam peddler whose cry had inspired the only personal comment Mr. Oliver had made to Pansy before that party. Pansy's characteristic reaction to unhappiness or unpleasantness has always been flight; it may even give her some satisfaction to be in a situation like her present one in which active participation is not required.

In his desire to repair Pansy's nose so that she can breathe properly and take part in the life of the world again, Dr. Nicholas becomes her enemy. She is afraid that he will damage her brain, and, in fact, because she has had a skull fracture, there is a possibility that he might. Her real fear, however, seems to be that he will steal her hideaway from her. The preparations for the operation cause her excruciating pain; she flees from this agony into the contemplation of her brain. At intervals, she feels threatened by robbery and recalls how her mother once was robbed of an object that was precious to her.

During the operation itself, Pansy is anesthetized, although awake. When she thinks it is all over, the doctor asks her if he can perform a second operation at this time, although it will take him beyond the anesthetized regions and cause her pain. She agrees, knowing that she cannot spend the rest of her life in isolation, and thus must be able to breathe. The second operation is incredibly painful, but as a result she has the most complete vision of her brain, as a pink pearl that grows until it contains the room and the surgeon in its rosy luster. After the operation, when she is back in her room, she feels that she has been robbed of her consolation. The pain is intense, but now it offers her no reward: she shuts herself up "within her treasureless head."

Themes and Meanings

Jean Stafford chose the title of this story for a collection of her stories, suggesting that people create for themselves interior castles that allow them to retreat from the hurts dealt them by society. Pansy has found no social space in the real world to inhabit. Her few tentative offerings of herself having been rejected, she has shut herself up like a clam. The clam motif is present throughout the story, in the clam peddler from whose cries she flees, and in the pink pearl that is her favorite image of her beautiful, fragile brain.

Pansy is unable to "close the valves of her attention/ Like stone," as Emily Dickinson's narrator does. The world, in the form of Dr. Nicholas, pushes in with pain and demands. The interior castle is invaded and cannot be defended. Dr. Nicholas's name is ambiguous, suggesting both Saint Nicholas (Santa Claus) and Old Nick. Through his skill as a surgeon, he wants to make Pansy fit to go back to society, while she wishes to remain isolated in her head. To inhabit the fantasy world permanently is not an option; Pansy must submit to him and lose her means of escape. She knows that the time will come "when she could no longer live in seclusion, she must go into the world again and must be equipped to live in it; she banally acknowledged that she must be able to breathe."

Pansy's consciousness is presented as tentative and wavering, crystallized only through her experience of extreme pain. It seems that the pain allows her to focus herself enough to seek out the escape of the interior castle. The focus on Pansy's inner life makes the setting deliberately vague. In most of her other postwar stories, Stafford uses numerous topical references to provide a realistic frame for her action. Here, to represent Pansy's mind, she gives few details of time or place. Many questions are left unanswered, such as how Pansy could have no visitors for so long, what she does ordinarily, and where she was going when she had the accident. These questions are not answered because they are not important to Pansy, whose only concern is the fate of her interior castle. The reader knows that the fantasy will not survive, for Pansy is not a decisive enough person to insist on her imagined world to the point of madness or death. Dr. Nicholas will remove it, leaving Pansy with even less of a sense of self than she had to begin with. Through its portrait of a weak and wavering personality, "The Interior Castle" makes suggestions about what qualities are needed to survive and get along in an insensitive society.

Style and Technique

Long descriptive passages and very little dialogue characterize Stafford's style in "The Interior Castle." The descriptions of painful clinical procedures implicate the reader in Pansy's pain. The details are precise, and the descriptions of how the pain feels are evocative. Long paragraphs and complicated, carefully formed sentences recall the style of Henry James; like James, Stafford reports each minute detail of a mental state.

Stafford uses flashbacks and association to show how Pansy's mind works. Pansy does not think sequentially or logically. Only a very few images in her mind are associated with names, suggesting her lack of attachments. The narrative follows the drifts of her consciousness. Thus there is little conversation—only the few remarks that are important to Pansy are recorded. She thinks of years as having particular colors. Pink is the most important color, the color of her brain; concentrating on it can bring her ecstasy. However, she also has negative real-world associations with the color pink, having to do with the inappropriate hat she wore to the autumn party. She must drown out the real-life pink, as well as the gray of the winter world outside the hospital, with the fantasy pink. The author skillfully weaves back and forth between Pansy's remembered world and the one she has created to replace it.

Stafford uses techniques of psychological realism to portray a young woman who seems to have little experience in her past and nothing to look forward to, and who clings desperately to a fantasy world that enables her to escape from a painful present.

Janet McCann

THE INTERLOPERS

Author: Saki (Hector Hugh Munro, 1870-1916)
Type of plot: Suspense
Time of plot: The late nineteenth century
Locale: The Carpathian Mountains in Eastern Europe
First published: 1919

> *Principal characters:*
> ULRICH VON GRADWITZ, a Carpathian nobleman and landholder
> GEORG ZNAEYM, a lesser landholder in the same region

The Story

This fablelike story of vendetta and reconciliation begins with a short history of conflict between two families in the Carpathian Mountains of Eastern Europe. Ulrich von Gradwitz, the local nobleman, is patrolling a narrow stretch of scrubby woodland that borders his much larger and more valuable holdings of forestland. The land that he patrols, however, acquires its value in his eyes because it was the subject of a lawsuit between his grandfather and the grandfather of a neighbor, Georg Znaeym, now his archenemy. At the origin of the conflict, each family held that the other claimed the woodland illegally; now, although Ulrich patrols the land as his, Georg regularly hunts its poor woods, simply to indicate his continued claim of rightful possession. What began as a legal battle generations before has become a personal and hate-filled conflict between the two current representatives of the families in the dispute.

On this particular night, both Ulrich and Georg, assisted by their retainers and huntsmen, have come out onto the land. Each comes nominally to defend his claim, but actually to destroy his great enemy by shooting him down in his tracks on the land over which they have disputed for so long. Despite a windstorm that would usually keep the wildlife in secure hiding, many animals are abroad, and Ulrich is sure that this restlessness indicates the presence of his enemy on the slopes.

Straying from his party of retainers and wandering through the woods, Ulrich unexpectedly comes face-to-face with Georg. Each is armed with a rifle, and each intends to use it because no interlopers will interfere, but not without some parting words of vengeance and hatred. Before either can speak, however, a sharp blast of wind tears from the ground the giant beech tree under which they stand, pinning them underneath.

After the impact and first physical shock that leaves them speechless, Ulrich and Georg realize that they are both still alive, and they pick up their conflict in words rather than rifle shots. Each threatens the other with the possibility that his retainers will arrive first, in which case it will be easy for an "accident" to be arranged in which the tree will have apparently crushed the hapless victim, leaving the survivor free of the charge of murder. Their threats made, they relapse into silence and discomfort as they stoically await the arrival of one or the other party of retainers.

After some effort, Ulrich frees an arm and reaches into his pocket for a wine flask that he carries, greatly enjoying the restorative effect of the drink as it warms his body. As he looks across at his enemy, some unaccountable change comes over him. He offers Georg a drink from the flask, which the other is barely able to reach. Under the combined effects of the situation, the shock, and the wine, Ulrich sees the similarity between him and his fellow sufferer, and a sudden transformation alters his old hatred. He tells Georg that, although the other is free to do as he pleases, if Ulrich's men arrive first, they shall be instructed to free Georg; at first surprised, Georg is then caught up in the change of attitude and makes a similar promise to Ulrich.

Each now awaits his retainers more eagerly than before, but instead of eagerness for vengeance, each feels anxious that he may be the first to demonstrate his magnanimity. Instead of raging at each other, the two now reflect together on the impact that their reconciliation will have on the surrounding countryside—how amazed the other landholders and peasants will be when they see the sworn enemies in the marketplace as friends! The two begin planning the ways in which they will demonstrate their reconciliation by sharing holidays and visits back and forth between their two houses.

During a lull in the wind, Ulrich suggests that they shout together for help. After no response, they call again, and Ulrich thinks that he hears an answering cry. A few minutes pass before Ulrich cries out that he can see figures coming down the hill, and the two shout again to attract the attention of the hunters. In the last few sentences of the story, Georg, anxious to know whose party will arrive first, asks Ulrich if they are his men. The figures are not men but wolves.

Themes and Meanings

Although Saki's design is clearly to draw as much suspense and surprise into as narrow a compass as possible, the story itself nevertheless presents abstract themes of justice in the human world and of the human relationship to the natural world.

The most obvious of these themes involves the dissection and final denial of the vendetta mentality that motivates these two figures. The early history of the conflict shows how accidental the hatred between these two men actually is. They inherit a conflict that is not rightly theirs, and it distorts their relationship not only to each other but also—as the reference to the surprise in the marketplace shows—to the community in which they live. Furthermore, the parties of huntsmen and retainers (who never actually appear in the story) represent further ramifications of injustice, wherein the dependents are also caught up in the hatred between the principals, much as the Montagues and Capulets are trapped in the conflict that leads to the death of Romeo and Juliet. The physical blow that levels both men thus paradoxically symbolizes the sudden consciousness of the distortions that the vendetta has caused: Their common plight makes Ulrich and Georg recognize, apparently for the first time, how much they have in common, and thus how much more reasonable friendship would be. Having once seen the world from this new perspective, the two are quick to correct the fundamental distortion of their relationship, and the apparent ease with which hatred and distrust dissolve indicates how insubstantial their former condition was.

The appearance of the wolves, the unexpected "interlopers" of the story's title, points out the fundamental irony of the tale as a whole and thus touches on the second great theme that the story presents. From this perspective, the story may be said to belong to the school of literary naturalism, in which fundamental natural processes are shown working themselves out in the human world, regardless of human designs or wishes. The essential mistake that Ulrich and Georg make is their assumption that this narrow stretch of almost worthless woodland is somehow theirs to possess in any real sense. They, like their fathers and grandfathers before them, have assumed that legal rights, established in human courts and supported by human institutions, actually establish true dominion over the world of nature.

The fablelike elements of this story show how mistaken such an assumption is. At virtually every turn, the plans of the human characters are thwarted or altered by the different design of the natural world: The best opportunity for settling their vendetta, when no interlopers are present, is cut off by the wind and the falling tree; after their reconciliation, their plans for the future are erased by the advent of the unexpected interlopers. Finally, the wolves themselves symbolize the utter indifference of nature to "important" human disputes and resolutions. The surprise conclusion thus reveals and summarizes this primary theme of literary naturalism with sharply dramatic and terrifying indirection, suggesting in its irony that nature may not be indifferent so much as malicious toward the proud designs of humankind.

Style and Technique

This brief masterpiece is an excellent representation of the principal stylistic and technical elements of Saki's achievement. Above all, the economy of the story's construction—the swift drafting of the background, with its elements of local color and drama; the limited cast of characters; the neat, subtle introduction and arrangement of the plot details necessary to the surprise conclusion—is typically masterful, and indeed necessary to the success of the story because readers must not have time to doubt the realism of the situation, in either its physical or psychological aspects.

The quiet, calm voice of the omniscient narrator seems initially to comfort the reader with a sense of control over the events that it narrates, yet as the disquieting details accumulate—the restlessness of the forest creatures, the "accident" of the tree's falling at just the right moment, the "success" of the men's calls for help, the alarming hysteria of Ulrich's laughter—the lack of modulation in the tones of the narrator becomes one of the principal devices by which the suspense is developed and sustained. The end of the story reveals Saki's powerful control in the fact that the surprise is held back until the very last word—a word that, in retrospect, explains and justifies all the details and arrangements made in the careful crafting of the story as a whole.

Dale B. Billingsley

INTERPRETER OF MALADIES

Author: Jhumpa Lahiri (1967-   )
Type of plot: Domestic realism
Time of plot: The 1980's or 1990's
Locale: India
First published: 1998

> *Principal characters:*
> MR. KAPASI, the tour guide
> MR. DAS, the father
> MRS. DAS, his wife
> RONNY,
> BOBBY, and
> TINA, the Das children

The Story

"The Interpreter of Maladies" chronicles a day during an Indian American family's vacation in India visiting tourist sites with their Indian guide. On this summer day, Mr. and Mrs. Das, a young Indian couple born in the United States, and their three children, Ronny, Bobby, and Tina, as well as their Indian guide, Mr. Kapasi, travel by car to the Sun Temple at Konarak. When they stop at a roadside tea stall for refreshments, the middle-aged guide Kapasi observes the young family. Though the family is of Indian heritage, their manner, attire, and interactions are American. When Mrs. Das purchases a snack from a shirtless vendor, he sings a popular Hindi love song to her, but she does not understand the language and expresses no embarrassment.

During the ride to the temple, the Das family engages in mindless activity: Tina plays with the door lock, the two boys snap their chewing gum, Mrs. Das paints her fingernails in boredom, and Mr. Das tinkers with his camera. Kapasi observes them. Mrs. Das converses with Kapasi and learns he has another job as a translator for a physician and his Gujarati patients. Intrigued with Kapasi's description of this job, Mrs. Das questions him further. Mrs. Das's interest sparks in Kapasi a sexual infatuation toward her. Kapasi notices Mrs. Das's sensuous appearance.

The group stops for lunch, after which the children leave the picnic table, and Mr. Das photographs his wife and Kapasi together. Mrs. Das asks Kapasi for his address so she can later send him a copy of the photo; he writes it on a scrap of paper, which she places in her handbag. Silently, Kapasi fantasizes how this photograph could be the beginning of an intimate correspondence between him and Mrs. Das. The fantasy continues in his mind throughout the day.

At midday, they reach the ruins of the Sun Temple, whose exterior walls are covered with sculpted erotic friezes: Naked bodies are depicted in various positions. Kapasi observes Mrs. Das studying the carvings and notices her own sexy qualities, her short skirt and tight blouse. To himself, he laments his own loveless marriage.

Kapasi suggests they detour to visit a ruined monastery. At the monastery, Mr. Das and the children exit the car to photograph the many monkeys climbing on the ruins. Mrs. Das and Kapasi remain in the car. After her family walks away, Mrs. Das gets into the front seat with Kapasi. After some small talk, Mrs. Das suddenly confides to Kapasi that her husband is not the father of her second son, Bobby. She recounts the story of her unwise marriage to her husband, her growing unhappiness, her brief infidelity, and the son she conceived with a friend of her husband. She tells Kapasi her husband is ignorant of these facts.

Mrs. Das reveals her painful secret to Kapasi because of his talent as "an interpreter of maladies"; she wants his opinion on her case. Kapasi kindly asks if she is mistaking guilt for pain. That is not what Mrs. Das wants to hear; she exits the car in a huff and goes in search of her family.

Meanwhile, hungry monkeys surround Bobby, who holds a bag of puffed rice. Bobby is frightened and injured slightly by the monkeys as his family stands by panicking. Kapasi rescues Bobby, chasing away the monkeys. The group returns to the car, consoling Bobby. Mrs. Das removes a hairbrush from her handbag to smooth Bobby's hair. As she does so, the slip of paper with Kapasi's address slips from the bag and is taken away by the wind. Only Kapasi notices it. At this moment, he observes the Das family as a tableau and knows this image of them will forever be preserved in his mind.

Themes and Meanings

Told in the third person and limited to Kapasi's point of view, "Interpreter of Maladies" depicts an epiphany regarding Kapasi's mistaken belief that love can easily cross cultural boundaries. Though he has studied several languages and is proficient in English, Kapasi is a somewhat flawed observer of the bicultural issues raised by the visiting Indian American Das family.

Kapasi observes the Das family as a cultural contradiction. Because Mr. and Mrs. Das were both born in the United States of Indian parents, one would think their Indian heritage would be strong, but it is not; they seem unmindful of their heritage, behaving stereotypically as any other vacationing American family would. Mrs. Das, for example, appears oblivious of the attention she draws with her short skirt in this place where women customarily cover themselves.

Other details mark them as stereotypically American. Obsessed with his camera, Mr. Das misses out on his vacation because he peers at it only through a camera lens. In Kapasi's view, neither of the Das parents seems at all Indian in their interaction with their children. For example, searching for his wife, Mr. Das asks his children, "Where's Mina?" using her first name. Mrs. Das seems uninterested in her children, complaining about having to take Tina to the toilet, for example. Kapasi notices that the Das family, including the parents, "were all like siblings," suggesting their customs differ significantly from those practiced in India.

Despite the "un-Indian" qualities of the Das family, Kapasi develops an infatuation for Mrs. Das, noticing her sensuousness, her bare legs, the color of her lipstick, her tight blouse. When Mrs. Das expresses interest in Kapasi's work as an interpreter for a physician and his Gujarati patients, Kapasi is flattered; her apparent interest intensifies his infatuation. He begins to think he might interest her romantically.

When Mrs. Das requests Kapasi's address so she can send him the photo of the two of them, Kapasi imagines they will develop an intimate correspondence. Kapasi's thoughts reveal details about his dull marriage: He has his job and his daily tea and newspaper, and he and his wife endure a loveless routine. Mrs. Das's sensuousness and her "sudden interest in him, an interest she did not express in either her husband or her children," has a "mildly intoxicating" effect on Kapasi. Clearly, Kapasi desires an intimacy that is lacking in his life.

The climax of the story occurs at the monastery when Kapasi and Mrs. Das are alone in the car. She climbs into the front seat, heightening Kapasi's romantic feelings toward her; instead, she confesses her husband is not the father of her second son, Bobby. His birth resulted from a brief infidelity, a secret she has guarded for eight years. She says she is tired of the pain and asks Kapasi, the "intepreter of maladies," for his opinion. Shocked by her confession, he can only ask, "Is it really pain you feel, Mrs. Das, or is it guilt?"

Troubled by her secret, Mrs. Das perhaps feels that confessing to a virtual stranger in a "foreign" country will unburden her. Kapasi's response, however, discourages her, and she leaves to join her family. When Bobby is slightly injured by the monkeys and his family panics, Kapasi rescues him. The story ends with the family consoling Bobby. The paper scrap with Kapasi's address falls out of Mrs. Das's handbag and disappears in the wind. At this moment, Kapasi knows "he would preserve forever in his mind" this tableau of the Dases.

Kapasi's concluding epiphany is sudden and ambiguous. He realizes his feelings for Mrs. Das and hers for him are a fantasy. His infatuation for her, his hope that they would develop an intimate correspondence, and his fantasy that romantic love could bridge the cultural chasm between them fade as quickly as the scrap of paper disappears in the wind.

Style and Technique

The most significant stylistic technique in this story is the tightly controlled point of view, third person and limited to Kapasi. Though Kapasi has some knowledge of Western culture, it comes from sources such as the television show *Dallas*. Consequently, his view of the bicultural Dases is skewed, and a dramatic irony develops: Though Mrs. Das's actions and language suggest she has no romantic interest in Kapasi, he cannot perceive this fact, and his fantasy about an intimate romance with her seems ludicrous and obsessive. At the moment of epiphany, Mrs. Das and her family remain a cipher.

The use of Indian tourist sites as settings for the action underscores the bicultural themes, highlighting the "Americanness" of the Das family—an Indian American family encountering their heritage for the first time.

The tone of the narration, complex and subtle, implies a negative criticism of the characters. When describing the Dases, the narrator focuses on subtle negative aspects of them: the father's fixation on his camera, his wife's apparent boredom with her family and the tour itself, and the children's irritating behavior. Though the narrator richly details the bicultural Dases, the presentation of them accents their negative qualities. The narrator's tone toward Kapasi is only slightly better. He is a more rounded character than the members of the Das family, but his foolish obsession with Mrs. Das is subtly criticized by the narrator's tone, creating a dramatic ironic tension between Kapasi's fantasy about a love affair with Mrs. Das and the real impossibility of that romance ever developing.

Sensual images run throughout the story, supporting Kapasi's self-deception that he may have a romance with Mrs. Das. The carvings on the temple of naked bodies making love and the recurring images describing Mrs. Das's sensuous attire juxtaposed with the frumpy images of Kapasi's wife serve to create sexual tension in Kapasi's mind.

Chris Benson

INTERTEXTUALITY

Author: Mary Gordon (1949-   )
Type of plot: Autobiographical, family
Time of plot: 1959-1960
Locale: Long Island, New York
First published: 1995

> *Principal characters:*
> THE NARRATOR, who recalls two incidents she witnessed as a child
> HER GRANDMOTHER, a stern, practical Irish immigrant
> HER AUNT, an unmarried daughter who lives with her mother
> HER MOTHER, a widow forced by circumstances to return with the narrator to live in her mother's house

The Story

The narrator, a middle-aged woman, frames the story with allusions to the lengthy classic novel by Marcel Proust, *À la recherche du temps perdu* (1913-1927; *Remembrance of Things Past*, 1922-1931, 1981), that are significant in interpreting the story. She begins with a brief history of her grandmother's early life as an Irish immigrant. Although she admired her, she never liked her grandmother, a practical, physically imposing woman with a strong work ethic. The narrator recalls two incidents that ocurred when she was ten years old.

The grandmother came to the United States in the late nineteenth century at the age of nineteen and worked as a domestic servant, saving her earnings to pay the passage to the United States for her own mother and six siblings from Ireland. She married a jeweler and gave birth to nine children. The family has always told entertaining stories about their collective past, but the narrator recognizes these as myths; the unpleasant realities of their lives are never discussed. This is a closed world of women, with the men seldom mentioned. These women believe that they must simply get on with life as if unfortunate events had never occurred. The grandmother is the family caretaker; in addition to raising her own nine children, she takes in three of her poverty-stricken sister's children. The narrator and her mother, destitute and homeless after the death of her father, are also taken in by the grandmother, but as recipients of charity, they are expected to go along with the grandmother's wishes. They have no part in household decisions and can only witness events as bystanders.

In the first incident witnessed by the narrator, her eighty-year-old grandmother takes the only vacation of her life, a month-long trip to Florida to visit relatives. While she is away, her unmarried middle-aged daughter collects money from the family to remodel the house, eliminating the old kitchen, buying new appliances, and getting rid of many of the household objects. This is, on the surface, a practical decision intended to make life easier for the old woman. She has lived in the house for forty years and has decorated it with mementos that have significance for her: pictures of saints, poems, lamps with French paintings, and a Celtic cross. The family gathers to celebrate the grandmother's return. When she is confronted with the surprise, she reacts with shock, bursting into tears and hiding in her bedroom, the only room that has remained untouched. She composes herself and returns to the party, saying nothing at all about the renovation of her house. This event is never discussed in the family.

The second incident occurs a year later when the grandmother announces that she wants to build a summer house as a gift to her granddaughter. She shows them the discarded screens she plans to use for this project. Her unmarried daughter mocks her scornfully, calling the idea crazy. The grandmother abandons the idea and goes to the kitchen to wash her hands. This event, too, is never again mentioned by the family.

The story concludes with the narrator describing a scene from the Proust novel. She imagines that she is drawn into the elegant nineteenth century French dinner party and, in a dreamlike sequence, has just finished her own dinner when she sees her grandmother entering the restaurant in her housedress and practical black shoes. The narrator tries to capture her grandmother's emotions. Does she view these people with contempt, judging them sinful in their indulgence and wastefulness, in contrast to her own righteous life of self-denial? Or, might she be imagined as entering the scene as the beautiful child she once was, to be invited into the summer house where she will be given a pleasurable treat and petted and indulged?

The narrator returns to her insight at the beginning of the story, her sense of loss in failing to understand her grandmother's life.

Themes and Meanings

Although Mary Gordon has elsewhere made a clear distinction between fiction and memoir, the events of this story closely parallel the circumstances of her own childhood. The incident of the renovation of the house is described in her memoir *Seeing Through Places: Reflections on Geography and Identity* (2000). Like much of Gordon's fiction, this is a story about the lives of women, with men playing subordinate roles in the narrative. Although she has been called a Catholic writer, Gordon prefers to say that she writes out of her experience as a woman. However, the Irish Catholic immigrant experience underlies the narrative.

The characters are not given names; they are known only in their roles within the family: grandmother, mother, aunt, sister, and daughter. While well-developed in their individuality, they also represent the closely guarded secrecy and self-denial of Irish Catholics. Such words as guilt, blame, and punishment permeate the text. These women, survivors of harsh experience, cannot openly express their emotions and turn to myth to describe their family past. They have learned not to dream or to expect things they cannot have. This self-denial has allowed them to succeed in a hostile world in which prejudice against Irish Catholics was common. However, the darker side of this tendency is the repressed anger that drives the daughter who deprives her mother of seemingly worthless objects that represent the small pleasures of her life.

The narrator reports these events without emotion, like the uncomprehending child she was at the time she observed them. Now middle-aged, she explores the meaning of these events and is grieved by her new insight that her grandmother's life is a mystery to her. This stern, hardworking woman, who refused to reveal the disappointments in her life, is given another chance to lead a different life in the narrator's imagination.

The story suggests that the habitual self-abnegation and secrecy of these women not only colors their own experience but also deprives the following generations of essential truths about these women's lives. Their descendants, like the narrator, inherit only entertaining myths and must reconstruct in their imaginations the unrealized possibilities and the small tragedies of thwarted desires and unrealized pleasures. At another level the story is evidence of the power of the written word to confront memory and to reinvent a past that cannot be recovered.

Style and Technique

The title of the story refers to an expanded definition of "text" to include anything to which meaning is assigned, not just the written word, but also historical events, images, advertisements, and film, among other possibilities. "Intertextuality" in this sense occurs when a relationship is created between two texts that gives new meaning to both. Proust's *Remembrance of Things Past* proposes that in moments of unconscious memory provoked by an image or object, people discover the truths of their lives. The unconscious mind links the past and present, transcending real time.

This passage from the novel invokes the narrator's unconscious childhood memories and invites her to imagine a scene that places her grandmother in the text. The unrealized possibilities of this woman's life are a minor tragedy. This sadness is extended by the narrator's recognition that she herself failed to understand her grandmother and that this possibility is forever gone, except in the imagination.

Gordon's work is notable for her vivid description of everyday events and objects. The small, sad details of the grandmother's home—slipcovers, doilies, a Celtic cross, and pictures of saints—hold the meaning of her life, revealing the emotional cruelty of the daughter who throws them away. Gordon is also noted for her startling metaphors. The daughter's laugh is an "entirely mirthless noise that sounded like the slow winter starting of a reluctant car." The silence between mother and daughter is "like a sheet of gray glass that stretched between them." In cold, mechanical terms, the author conveys the absence of love that describes their relationship.

Gordon has written novels and collections of short stories as well as nonfiction works, including memoirs and a biography. The themes of self-denial and secrecy are characteristic of several of her novels. Her first novel, *Final Payments* (1978), is the story of a young Irish Catholic woman who, tortured by guilt, nearly allows a selfish, self-denying older woman to destroy her life. Similarly, in *The Other Side* (1989), Gordon portrays the lives of four generations of Irish Catholic immigrants who prosper financially, but whose emotional deprivation results in a tragic failure of love.

Marjorie Podolsky

INVENTING THE ABBOTTS

Author: Sue Miller (1943-   )
Type of plot: Domestic realism
Time of plot: The twentieth century
Locale: Haley, Illinois, and Cambridge, Massachusetts
First published: 1987

Principal characters:
DOUG, the narrator
JACEY, his brother
THEIR MOTHER, a widow and schoolteacher
GRANDMA VETTER, the boys' grandmother
ELEANOR ABBOTT,
ALICE ABBOTT, and
PAMELA ABBOTT, sisters in a well-to-do family
JOAN ABBOTT, their mother

The Story

Doug, the narrator of "Inventing the Abbotts," is the younger of two brothers. The story begins when the brothers are teenagers in Haley, Illinois, and ends with their return to that town when their mother dies. Growing up as the sons of a widowed schoolteacher, each brother yearns in his own way for the wealth and secure social position enjoyed by the Abbott family.

Lloyd and Joan Abbott have made their daughters the center of the town's social life by hosting several elaborate parties a year for them. Because the parties are held in colorful tents in the Abbotts' yard near the center of town, everyone knows when one is being set up, and there is much talk about who has and has not been invited.

Jacey, the older brother, is impressed by the Abbotts and by what their wealth represents to him. Doug, after watching his brother worry over his invitations to the Abbotts' parties, refuses to take the parties seriously. He sometimes attends without responding to the invitation, and once he goes to a party with Elvis-like sideburns drawn on his cheeks with ink.

Jacey is attracted to the Abbott family because of the economic and social differences between the two families. The brothers' father was killed in the war when Jacey was young and a few months before Doug was born. Their mother moved to Haley where her mother, Grandma Vetter, lived. Grandma Vetter helped raise the boys until her sudden death when Doug was ten.

Jacey's interest in the Abbott family takes the form of his romantic pursuit of the Abbott sisters. The summer before Jacey leaves for college, Doug walks in on him and Eleanor, the middle sister, naked together. Later, Eleanor drops out of school and leaves her family. In rebellion against the family, she tells her parents she has been sleeping with Jacey, knowing they will be offended, especially because he is not from a wealthy family.

A few years later, Jacey falls in love with Alice Abbott, the oldest of the sisters. Alice has been married and separated. She and her two children have moved back to her parents' home. The secret romance continues for two summers, then Alice's parents learn about it and tell her to cut it off. She is not independent enough to say no.

The following fall in Cambridge, where both brothers and Pamela Abbott are college students, Jacey invites Doug to his apartment. Pamela arrives, and Jacey is very rude to her, asking her if she wants to go to bed with him.

A few weeks later, Jacey apologizes to Doug. He explains that Pamela sought him out. The two of them got drunk while Pamela told him about how unhappy she was with her controlling parents. Jacey says he had an affair with her even though he did not particularly like her. He wanted to close off the possibility that he would see Alice again. Feeling Pamela was using him as part of a family drama, he was cruel to her and invited her and Doug over at the same time to intentionally embarrass her.

After graduation, Doug moves to New York, where he sees Pamela occasionally; in his last conversation with her, he tells her that Jacey has gotten married. Pamela makes insulting remarks about Jacey's wanting to marry up. Having realized that the Abbotts are not as wealthy as he once thought and having seen how the sisters have treated Jacey, Doug questions why she thinks marrying an Abbott would be marrying up.

After their mother dies of cancer, Doug and Jacey encounter Mrs. Abbott on the street in Haley. Instead of sympathizing about their mother's death, she comments that she has no more daughters for Jacey. Jacey does not react but instead acts immediately afterward as if her comment were something that had been said years ago when he was a child; he has grown up at last.

Themes and Meanings

As the title suggests, "Inventing the Abbotts" explores how the characters endow people and events with meaning that suits their own needs. For Jacey, the Abbotts represent wealth and comfort beyond the means of his widowed mother. Although his interest in the family takes the form of romantic involvement with the daughters, what really fascinates him is the life he perceives the family to have, embodied for him in their showy parties with pretty tents on the lawn. The family conforms to his imagined ideal that contrasts with his own family's life and opportunities.

At the same time as Jacey invents the Abbott sisters to meet his ideal, they invent him to meet their needs. Eleanor uses her sexual relationship with him in her rebellion against her parents. Although Doug makes clear in his narration that he and his brother are nice, hardworking boys who are in most ways no different from their wealthier friends, Eleanor convinces her parents that Jacey is lower class and even dangerous. Pamela's perception of Jacey as being exciting and threatening because of their class difference draws her to him later in the story.

Doug, to some extent as well, as a boy has an inflated idea of the Abbotts' wealth. He realizes by the end of the story that they are not especially rich; he also is able to see the family's faults, such as the snobbery of both the parents and of Pamela and the parents' attempts to control their daughters' lives, driving them away in the process.

For the brothers, learning to see the Abbotts as they really are means that they have grown up. By the end of the story, they recognize the Abbotts' faults and no longer need to judge themselves against this family. The Abbotts are still throwing parties under tents in their backyard, now for their grandchildren, but Jacey and Doug have moved away and can no longer be hurt even by Mrs. Abbott's unkind words when she sees them in town.

Style and Technique

Doug, the story's first-person narrator, interprets the events, but most of the story's plot concerns his brother Jacey. This choice of narrator allows for the story to be told by an observer who is close to the events and has an emotional investment in them but has some distance from the central events. Further, this narrator can interpret what has happened by comparing his views of the Abbotts to his brother's. Not only does he tell Jacey's story, but he also is able to understand his own reactions to the Abbotts by interpreting what has happened to his brother.

Like many of Sue Miller's other stories and her novels such as *The Good Mother* (1986) and *Family Pictures* (1990), this story contains a fascination with how families function and why the members interact the way they do. The story reveals what Jacey and Doug find attractive about the Abbotts and what factors in their upbringing make the Abbotts fascinating for them. In addition, the story shows a great deal about the Abbott sisters—how and why they rebel against their parents and how they develop snobberies like those of their parents.

Social issues and their associated psychological components are common concerns of late twentieth century American literature, reflecting the many developments in the social sciences over the course of the century. This interest in issues of social class and in psychology is reflected in the many realistic details that evoke a small midwestern town and its inhabitants. It is made even more evident in the use of dialogue to explain the characters' motivations. In one conversation, Doug's mother tells him that Jacey needs the idea of the Abbotts for security. After her husband died, she clung to her new baby, Doug, but cut herself off from Jacey. He attached himself to Grandma Vetter instead. His mother explains that this break from her at a young age and his attachment to his strict grandmother caused him to have a special need for security, which made him desire the Abbotts. She says that if the Abbotts had not existed, Jacey would have invented them.

The mother contemplates her own motivations and feelings as well as those of her sons. She regrets losing her connection with her son and cries in front of Doug for the first time in years when she admits that he has turned out all right without a close bond to her. Through the realistic details and dialogue, the story suggests that the psychological factors within the family and the class issues of the community they live in play equal roles in forming the characters.

Joan Hope

THE INVISIBLE MAN

Author: G. K. Chesterton (1874-1936)
Type of plot: Mystery and detective
Time of plot: 1910
Locale: England
First published: 1911

Principal characters:
FATHER BROWN, a detective-priest
LAURA HOPE, a clerk in a confectionery
JOHN TURNBULL ANGUS, a suitor of Laura Hope
ISIDORE SMYTHE, an inventor and competing suitor for Laura
JAMES WELKIN, a rejected suitor of Laura who threatens Isidore
    Smythe
FLAMBEAU, Father Brown's protégé

The Story

The story begins as John Turnbull Angus pines for his reluctant, would-be fiancé, Laura Hope, outside the confectioner's shop where she works. Angus enters the shop and begins his familiar banter about marriage and the particular bliss that Miss Hope would presumably enjoy as his bride. She attempts to discourage the ardor of her young suitor by telling him the history of her past admirers.

Laura's father, she tells Angus, was the owner of an inn in Ludbury, outside London, and she often served tables there. Two of her customers, one a dwarf, the other a man with an appalling and disfiguring squint, sought her hand in marriage. Trying not to hurt their feelings and declining to tell them that the real reason she could not marry them was that they were "impossibly ugly," she told them instead that she could not possibly marry anyone who had not "made his way in the world." This white lie, however, merely encouraged further competition between the two, as both of them left to seek their fortunes and win her love.

After leaving her father's inn, Laura discovered that one of the two, Isidore Smythe, had become a success. Smythe had made a fortune with his Silent Service, providing household robots that performed various custodial chores in the home. The other suitor, Welkin, had disappeared mysteriously, but Laura had the strange experience of hearing his laughter without seeing his physical form. She now lives in fear that one or both of them will appear and that she will be forced to marry one of them.

As she finishes this strange tale, and Angus begins to make light of it, Smythe appears just in time to discover a threatening note written on stamp paper pasted to the window of the confectionery: "If you marry Smythe, he will die." Smythe declares that the note is in Welkin's handwriting, and he and Angus resolve to return to Smythe's apartment and enlist the aid of Flambeau, a local detective. While at the apartment, Angus is struck by the strangeness of Smythe's home, filled as it is with the silent robots that serve Smythe and his guest. As an air of otherworldliness pervades, Smythe shows Angus another note that he has received from Welkin: "If you have been to see her today, I shall kill you." Sensing imminent danger, Angus leaves to find Flambeau and solemnly charges the chestnut seller and the police officer outside Smythe's apartment to watch it carefully and monitor anyone who enters or leaves it.

Angus encounters Father Brown at Flambeau's house, and the three of them hasten back to Smythe's apartment only to find blood on the floor and Smythe missing. On being questioned, the chestnut seller and the police officer testify that no one has entered Smythe's apartment. Angus declares wildly that an "invisible man" is responsible for the crime. As Smythe's body is found in the canal, Father Brown takes charge of the investigation.

The priest surveys the scene and suggests that no preternatural invisible man has committed a crime, but one who has become "invisible" by virtue of his familiarity to the observers. Welkin, dressed as the postal carrier, had previously delivered the threatening notes and easily entered the apartment without attracting notice, murdering Smythe and carrying his dwarfish body away in his mail sack. The resourceful Father Brown has solved another mystery.

Themes and Meanings

By choosing to entitle this story "The Invisible Man," G. K. Chesterton was inviting comparison with the more famous novella of the same title by H. G. Wells. In Wells's tale, the invisible man is literally invisible, a young scientist who discovers the principle of invisibility and goes mad, using his new power to murder and to plunder the environs of London. Chesterton's invisible man is by contrast quite ordinary—a simple postal carrier—but invisible in his own way. Chesterton's biographer, Alzina Stone Dale, suggests that "in Chesterton's story there is no upwardly mobile young scientist exploring the outer limits of the universe for what he can gain, but a social statement that many members of society are 'invisible,' like his murdering postman, who 'has passions like other men.'"

It was Chesterton's intent in his fiction to draw attention to the "invisible" elements in society—the common, ordinary items and persons of everyday life—in order to defamiliarize them. In so doing, he hoped to force the reader to notice what would otherwise be taken for granted: the real moments, relationships, and situations that make up one's life. The selection of a common parish priest to be his detective-hero, one who outfoxes both society's criminals and society's authorities, illustrates this thematic concern.

Father Brown lives in a very concrete world; he takes note of the subtleties and ambiguities of human affairs in ways that the people he encounters do not; as a result, the world is vividly real to him. What may go unnoticed in the daily abstractions that others call "real life," Father Brown regards as the foundation of human existence. This sharpened perception makes him an excellent detective but, more than that, a shrewd observer of human behavior and its ironies. Those who read the Father Brown tales to see how the crafty detective will solve the mystery receive this bonus: an invitation to recover their childhood sense of wonder and a challenge to celebrate the splendor of the ordinary in the course of everyday life.

Style and Technique

Chesterton wrote nearly fifty Father Brown mysteries in five collections during a period of twenty-five years. Each of the Father Brown stories follows a fairly recognizable formula; toward the end of the tale, the priest unravels the chain of events that have led to a seemingly unsolvable crime—astounding the principals in the story as well as Father Brown's protégé-detective, Flambeau. In many ways, Father Brown is the prototype of the modern detective who discovers the "unfamiliar in the familiar." In "The Invisible Man," Father Brown notices what the others in the story do not: the "invisible" postal carrier working anonymously in their midst. His eye for the seemingly insignificant detail sets him apart from his fellows and heightens his deductive powers.

The remarkable Father Brown is less a typical parish priest than a spokesperson for Chesterton's own orthodox Christian social views. Consequently, the Father Brown tales often contain wry social commentary on the class structure in Britain and deflate the pomposity and pride that the intellectuals of Chesterton's culture often evinced. Chesterton was nothing if not a defender of the "common folk," and his Father Brown series consistently champions the ordinary and the commonsensical over the flamboyant and the intellectualized. The world of Father Brown is thus the idealized world that Chesterton imagined a truly Christian society would evoke.

Bruce L. Edwards, Jr.

THE ISLAND AT NOON

Author: Julio Cortázar (1914-1984)
Type of plot: Fantasy
Time of plot: The 1960's
Locale: The eastern Mediterranean and Aegean seas
First published: "La isla a mediodía," 1966 (English translation, 1973)

Principal characters:
MARINI, a flight attendant
CARLA, one of his lovers
FELISA, another flight attendant
KLAIOS, the patriarch of Xiros

The Story

Marini is a flight attendant on an airline route between Rome and Tehran. During one of the thrice-weekly flights, he sees a small island through the plane window while he is handing out lunch trays. One of the crew tells him that Xiros, the island, is one of the few places on the Aegean that tourists have not discovered yet. Although from the plane Xiros appears to be little more than a speck, a strip of white sandy beach rising into a desolate central plateau, Marini falls into the habit of looking at it every time the plane flies over, which happens around noon during each flight. Seen from a high altitude, the small, solitary island has an air of unreality, as if it exists only in Marini's imagination. For Marini, flying three times a week over Xiros seems as unreal as dreaming three times a week of flying over Xiros.

The island does indeed exist, and when Marini is between flights he gathers information about it. He locates it on maps, reads about it in travel guides, and frequents secondhand bookstores searching for books about Greece. A few weeks after first sighting Xiros, he is offered the glamorous Rome-to-New York route but turns it down because he does not want to stop seeing the island several times a week. Xiros has become the center of his life. His strange fixation not only produces a rift with his girlfriend Carla, who is not interested in listening to endless talk about Xiros, but also creates friction with the other flight attendants, who do not understand why Marini drops whatever he is doing at noon to look down at the tiny island. They begin to call him the lunatic of the island. The only one who shows any sympathy toward him is Felisa, who agrees to fill in for him at noon so that he can go to the back of the plane and gaze at his island.

Eager to see the island up close, Marini borrows money from his friend Mario and goes there on vacation. Arriving at dawn on a barge after a complicated trip, Marini is met at the dock by Klaios, the patriarch of the island's only village, and some of the other islanders. Feeling reinvigorated, Marini gets out of his city clothes, puts on shorts and sandals, and goes exploring on the island. He walks along the deserted beach, watches squid fishermen casting and taking up their nets, and swims in the emerald blue waters with Ionas, one of Klaios's sons. Lying on the beach after the swim, Marini imagines giving up his job and making his living as a fisherman, like the island's inhabitants. He begins to think that his future lies in Xiros, that somehow he would remain there forever.

At noon that same day, Marini climbs one of the cliffs and sees the Rome-to-Tehran flight in the distance. As he watches, the plane makes a nose dive and plunges into the ocean one hundred meters from the island. Hurrying down to the beach, he swims out to look for survivors. After a few minutes, he notices a hand bobbing in and out of the water. He drags the survivor to the shore and tries to keep him alive with mouth-to-mouth resuscitation, but the man bleeds to death from a gaping wound in his throat. Klaios and his children rush to the beach and surround the corpse.

Klaios looks out to sea looking for other survivors, but they are alone on the island, except for the corpse. Marini, who is the dead man, has never reached Xiros.

Themes and Meanings

The principal theme of Julio Cortázar's story is one man's longing for a simpler, less encumbered existence. Trapped in a dull, monotonous occupation, Marini spends his life on the move, without settling down or establishing permanent relationships. With lovers in several cities and no fixed residence, he lives in the air, literally and figuratively. When Carla writes to him that she is pregnant and suggests that they marry, he only sends her money to pay for an abortion. The protagonist is identified only by his last name, which is reminiscent of the Spanish word for sailor, *marino*, and Marini is indeed a modern-day mariner who travels from airport to airport without laying down roots.

Another salient feature of Marini's life is that he is separated from nature. Locked up in the plane, peering at the tiny island down below, he is imprisoned by the accoutrements of advanced civilization. The physical distance between the high-flying jet plane and the island is a symbol of Marini's—and, by extension, modern humanity's—alienation from the natural world, which in turn is symbolized by Xiros, a place of sandy beaches, rocky cliffs, and lush vegetation.

As soon as he arrives on the island, Marini undergoes a spiritual rebirth. For him, this is the dawn of a new day. No longer will he inhabit a world of fast-moving machines and ephemeral personal encounters. The island offers him the possibility of a more placid and genuine existence. On the island, he can live close to nature. Xiros is a realm of natural harmony, "a world where the aroma of thyme and sage were one with the fire of the sun and the breeze of sea." When he gets to the island, Marini takes off his watch, which is a symbol of the tyranny of time—a tyranny all the more pronounced for someone who organizes his life according to flight schedules. On the island, things are different, for its inhabitants organize their lives according to nature's rhythms rather than manmade clocks. There is also a striking contrast between the communal life of the inhabitants of Xiros, where every resident seems to be related, and the impersonality of the big-city hotels, where Marini spends most of his nights.

In the end, however, Marini cannot begin a new life on the island. Although he thinks initially that he can kill the old man within him, the denouement of the story shows that Marini ultimately cannot unburden himself from his past. His death is precipitated by his inability to sever old attachments. When he first hears the droning of the plane's jet engines overhead, he tells himself not to look up, for the plane contains his worst side. Then he thinks of Felisa and imagines that the flight attendant who has taken his place is flirting with her. These thoughts make him look up instinctively, and it is then that he sees the plane crashing into the ocean. Marini's attachment to the man that he was prevents him from freeing himself from his old life.

Style and Technique

The most striking device in this story is its surprise ending, which permits several possible interpretations. From a psychological point of view, one can read this story as the history of an obsession. With his face pressed against the plane window, Marini is a man in the grip of an obsession. As the rest of his life becomes "blurred, as if taking the place of something else," he turns into a monomaniac, a man whose whole existence revolves around the few moments each Monday, Thursday, and Saturday when he can gaze at the object of his fixation.

If this is so, then Marini's visit to Xiros may well be no more than a hallucination. Perhaps the plane does go down, and Marini dies in the crash. The story's conclusion would then be the record of Marini's dying fantasies, the longed-for but never achieved existence that flashes before his eyes in the instants before death. One can also read the story as pure science fiction, postulating that, in the make-believe world that Cortázar creates, it is possible for a character to be in two places at once.

The device of depicting characters whose lives mysteriously split in two is a recurring motif in Cortázar's stories. Indeed, some of this author's best-known tales feature protagonists who live simultaneously in two different realms. Whether Cortázar intends these stories as sheer fantasy or as allegories of psychological states is not clear. What ultimately matters is that a story like "The Island at Noon" moves the reader to question the routines and expectations that make up everyday life in the highly mechanized modern world.

Gustavo Pérez Firmat

ISLANDS ON THE MOON

Author: Barbara Kingsolver (1955-   )
Type of plot: Domestic realism
Time of plot: Probably the 1980's
Locale: Tucson, Arizona
First published: 1989

> *Principal characters:*
> ANNEMARIE, a single mother, probably in her twenties
> MAGDA, her mother
> LEON, her son
> KAY KAY, her best friend

The Story

Annemarie, a single mother, lives in a trailer park in Tucson, Arizona, where her parents moved from New Hampshire for her father's health when she was a child. Her father, whom she remembers fondly, died less than a year later, leaving his wife, Magda, and Annemarie to fight poverty alone. With all their money spent on getting to Arizona, the mother and daughter could not return to New Hampshire. It is one of Annemarie's many regrets.

Annemarie has just received a note from her forty-four-year-old mother, announcing that she is pregnant. Magda is an environmentalist and activist who wears pure cotton dresses and makes necklaces from the lacquered vertebrae of nonendangered species. Annemarie herself is also pregnant, although Magda does not know about it, and Annemarie sees her mother's pregnancy as a way to upstage her. Before receiving the news of her mother's pregnancy, Annemarie had not spoken to her mother in months, although their mobile homes are only one hundred feet from each other. Magda has been waiting until Annemarie stops sending her negative energy. She breaks her silence, however, to ask Annemarie to take her to a clinic for amniocentesis.

Annemarie's best friend is Kay Kay, a diminutive but independent locomotive driver. In the days before taking her mother to the clinic, Annemarie confides in Kay Kay. Annemarie thinks her mother is too old to be having a baby and fears that her son, Leon, will take her mother's side, and that she will be abandoned. Kay Kay reminds Annemarie that many mother-daughter relationships are problematic, citing her own mother as an example, but Annemarie feels hopeless where her mother is concerned. In these conversations with Kay Kay, Annemarie also talks about her relationship with Buddy, her former husband and the father of her son. Buddy wears braids in imitation of Willie Nelson, has flames painted on the hood of his car, and once drove off to Reno with another woman after Annemarie paid to have his car repaired. Annemarie is considering marrying him again, now that she is pregnant.

Annemarie picks up her mother on a Saturday. They immediately begin arguing about Annemarie's hair, after Magda offers her a new shampoo to try. It is apparent that Annemarie has a chip on her shoulder; anything her mother says sounds like a criticism to her. At the clinic, the doctor performs a sonogram before the amniocentesis. While the mother and daughter watch the tiny life on the television screen, Annemarie finally realizes that Magda's pregnancy is not a plot against her; it is Magda's future. This is the beginning of a change in the way Annemarie relates to her mother.

On the way to pick up her son, Leon, from Little League practice, Annemarie discovers that her mother's pregnancy is not an accident but a planned event. They find Leon at the park and head home. Distracted by a discussion between Leon and Magda about famous Leons in general and Leon Trotsky's death in particular, she runs a stop sign and there is a collision. Annemarie, who is not wearing a seat belt, finds herself lying across her mother's lap, her head out the window and Magda's arms tight across her chest. Leon has been thrown from the car but is unharmed. In the ambulance on the way to the hospital, Annemarie tells her mother that she, too, is expecting a child.

The doctor, amazed that Annemarie has escaped with only cuts and bruises, declares, "Sometimes the strength of motherhood is greater than natural laws." Annemarie is left with the feeling that her life has just been handed to her anew, and that the world is waiting to see what she will do with it. At the hospital, Annemarie and Magda finally have the talk of their lives, the one Annemarie had once believed would have no beginning and no end. They talk about the day her father died and how they have always felt about each other. Annemarie finally understands her mother. When she wonders aloud how she could have been so blind to Magda's feelings, Magda compares the two of them to islands on the moon, where there is no water, and "a person could walk from one to the other if they just decided to do it."

Later, as her mother sleeps, Annemarie lays her hand on her mother's swollen belly, accepting her new little sister.

Themes and Meanings

Barbara Kingsolver explores the themes of motherhood and relationships of children to parents in this and other stories in her collection *Homeland, and Other Stories* (1989). In "Islands on the Moon," one senses Annemarie's ambivalence about her own status as a mother. Although she undoubtedly loves her son with all of her heart and wants another child to cuddle now that he dodges her kisses, she envies Kay Kay and her lover their freedom, happiness, and courage. "Their relationship is a sleek little boat of their own construction, untethered in either direction by the knotted ropes of motherhood, free to sail the open seas."

More knotted ropes appear later when Annemarie brakes to allow three women to cross a road. They appear to be mother, daughter, and granddaughter, and their identical braids remind Annemarie again of braided rope. To the protagonist, motherhood is difficult and complicated. She worries about her son and recognizes that she is a worry to her own mother. Motherhood is also strong, however, like a strong, knotted tether, sometimes even stronger than natural laws.

Another favorite theme of Kingsolver's is the strong, unattached woman. Kingsolver's best women never need a man, although they are desirable to men and like them well enough. Annemarie has married the same shiftless man twice but has spent most of her adult life independent of him and is unattached at the time of the story.

At the other end of the spectrum are Kay Kay and her lover. They have flouted convention and spurned parenthood for an untethered existence and are described as free, courageous, and happy. The unconventional lifestyle and the character who stands out in a crowd, as Magda certainly does, are common Kingsolver themes.

Style and Technique

The story takes place in Arizona, whose landscape is described as a moonscape, dry, barren, and lifeless. Ironically, the trailer park in which the characters live is named "Island Breezes," but it is hot and dry and there are no breezes. In the beginning, the name of the place serves to underscore the hopelessness of Annemarie's life. Later in the story, the symbolism vividly illustrates Magda's comparison of mother and daughter to islands on the moon. They choose isolation from each other when there are no natural obstacles to communion.

Although this story reads like a clip from real life and its themes involve human relationships, it is rather light in tone. The characters are multidimensional, but their comical sides are emphasized. Kingsolver uses trivial things to characterize the people in the story, such as Magda's "one-hundred-percent-cotton dresses" and the flames painted on the hood of Buddy's car. The triviality increases the sense of realism. There is a tension, however, between this light tone and the unresolved conflict between mother and daughter. This tension is carried through in several literary devices. The name of the desert trailer park, "Island Breezes," emphasizes the absence of water and refreshing breezes in the Arizona desert. The "knotted ropes of motherhood" are the very image of tension.

Annemarie creates tension in her own life, resisting every overture by her mother, forcing her naturally wavy hair into short spikes. She views relationships, at least the one between herself and her mother, as if they are battlefields, in which there are opposing sides rather than reciprocity.

Joyce M. Parks

IT MAY NEVER HAPPEN

Author: V. S. Pritchett (1900-1997)
Type of plot: Satire
Time of plot: About 1917
Locale: London
First published: 1945

> *Principal characters:*
> VINCENT, the narrator and protagonist, seventeen years old
> MR. BELTON, Vincent's uncle, a partner and salesperson in a
> furniture factory
> MR. PHILLIMORE, Belton's partner
> MISS CROFT, the company secretary, slightly older than Vincent
> MR. SALTER, Belton's former partner, now a competitor

The Story

At age seventeen, Vincent is sent to work for his Uncle Belton, a dapper, dreamy man who makes Vincent believe that this job is the opportunity of a lifetime. Everyone assures Vincent that he has his foot on the first rung of the ladder, that life is now beginning for him. On his first day, Vincent takes the train to work with his uncle, who along the way gives the boy the impression that Mr. Phillimore, his partner, is the genius of the firm, a man to be feared and respected. He encourages Vincent to remember young Samuel of the Old Testament, who, when he heard the voice of God, replied, "Speak Lord, thy servant heareth." Belton thinks it would not be inappropriate to think the same thoughts when Phillimore calls.

The Beautifix Furniture Company turns out to be a modest enterprise, precariously supported by the capital Phillimore brought to the firm. In Belton's eyes, however, it was he who saved Phillimore from the clutches of a possessive mother. Phillimore is also something less than the godlike figure Belton had described on the train. Effeminate, clumsy, and dithering, his chief virtue in Belton's view is his high regard for Belton. Vincent soon learns that their partnership is like a marriage, each member of which is sustained by the weaknesses of the other. Belton and Phillimore are temperamental opposites, too. Belton is dreamy, optimistic, and idle, while Phillimore is fretful and pessimistic. One day, Belton returns to the office with a framed needlework piece bearing the motto, "It may never happen." Predictably, the two men differ on its interpretation. For Belton, it is an encouragement not to worry about problems that may never arise; for Phillimore, it means precisely the opposite, that life would be futile if one's fears were never realized. "I should die!" he confides to Vincent, who is beginning to think that Phillimore is no fool.

As time passes, Vincent increasingly realizes the uncertain future of the business. Belton's fears (when he can confront them) are focused on the competition from his ex-partner Salter, whom he regards almost as Satan incarnate. One day at lunch, however, Vincent sees this enemy, who turns out to be just as worried and dejected as Phillimore in his worst moments. Rumors circulate through the office that Belton is looking for another partner to provide a new influx of capital, and Phillimore begins behaving more strangely than usual, dropping hints that young Vincent (whom he continually calls Vernon) should be courting Miss Croft. Miss Croft regards young Vincent with the disdain a young woman always has for an adolescent boy, but he regards her as something remote, exotic, and untouchable. He believes that she is in love with Phillimore. All these tensions—commercial and romantic—come to a climax one day when Phillimore comes into the office drunk and insults Miss Croft by emptying a drawer full of papers over her head. Later that day, Phillimore also tries to kiss her, but she rejects his advances. Phillimore walks out of the office and does not return. They learn eventually that he has joined the enemy—Salter.

Eighteen months later, Vincent sees Phillimore in a crowd and overhears him say to someone, "I should die." Phillimore then sees Vincent and gives him a contemptuous look before disappearing forever into the crowd.

Themes and Meanings

"It May Never Happen" is a typical V. S. Pritchett story in dealing not with social or political issues but with character revelation. The story's satire is directed in part at the values and mores of the lower-middle classes, but its main concern is with the interactions of the characters, each of whom turns out to be at least slightly ridiculous. The most obviously humorous character is Belton, who dreams of commercial success. His persistent optimism undermines those very dreams, for it prevents him from seeing anything clearly, especially himself. He would rather daydream than work, and he habitually avoids responsibility by spending his money on luxuries when he should be devoting his time to selling the company's products. Young Vincent regards Phillimore's pessimism as more farsighted than Belton's cockeyed optimism, but Phillimore himself is weak and flighty. His clumsy attempt to win Miss Croft is typical of his inability to deal with life. Vincent and Miss Croft are typical young people, naïve and self-centered, struggling to enter the adult world yet fearful of its responsibilities. Vincent, as narrator looking back on these youthful experiences, sees all too clearly his own awkward gropings toward insight and experience while at the same time revealing the absurdities of the elders he once admired and feared.

Thus, Pritchett's humor is directed ultimately at the follies of human beings in general, at their posturings and lack of self-knowledge, their fears and weaknesses, their sexual anxieties, and their general ineffectualness. As always, however, Pritchett's satire is more compassionate than condemnatory. He sees and reveals so that readers may laugh with one another, not at one another. In his world, everyone is slightly ridiculous, and hence, everyone is joined together in common, flawed humanity.

Style and Technique

In this, as in most of Pritchett's stories, there is little emphasis on plot as normally defined. Although there is a chronological order to the events of the story, these events seem almost incidental. Pritchett's focus is on the characters and the surface details of their lives and surroundings. He presents these in a lean, uncluttered prose that deceives by its very simplicity. There are no verbal tricks or fancy literary devices in Pritchett's writing, only direct, clear language that manages, in spite of its surface clarity, to suggest much more than it appears to say. Tone of voice, turn of phrase, and implication of gesture carry the burden of the story's meaning. The reader who fails to pay close attention to these details will conclude that this is no more than an amusing anecdote about eccentric Londoners. The more careful reader, perhaps puzzled by the story's inconclusive ending, will read again, this time relishing the details by which Pritchett reveals his characters. The tone throughout is wry and sardonic, as if the author were glancing out of the corner of his very keen eye at the passing human comedy. Pritchett's art is his artlessness, his refusal to preach, moralize, or oversimplify. His broad and lasting appeal derives not from commentary on abstract issues but from his desire to reveal and understand the ordinary person and the defenses that all people erect to deal with the world and their own failures in it.

Dean Baldwin

IVY DAY IN THE COMMITTEE ROOM

Author: James Joyce (1882-1941)
Type of plot: Satire
Time of plot: The early nineteenth century
Locale: Dublin
First published: 1914

Principal characters:
MR. HYNES, a journalist
MR. HENCHY, a canvasser for the local Nationalist election
candidate
MR. O'CONNOR, another canvasser for the local Nationalist
election candidate
MR. CROFTON, a Conservative canvasser for the local Nationalist
election candidate
JACK, the caretaker of the committee room

The Story

There is much more talk than action in "Ivy Day in the Committee Room." On a rainy autumn afternoon, election canvassers drift in from the Dublin streets to warm themselves around a meager fire in the election committee room. As the story begins, there are only two people in the dimly lit room: Jack, the old caretaker of the committee room, complains to O'Connor, one of the canvassers, about his uncontrollable, ne'er-do-well son. Jack falls silent, however, as other canvassers join them, and the conversation turns to local politics. Their candidate is "Tricky Dicky Tierney," and they discuss him and his cronies, as well as one another, with varying degrees of cynicism. Another topic of keen interest is the likelihood of Tierney buying them a round of stout.

When the stout does, indeed, arrive, they become more enthusiastic in their support of Tierney. Henchy, one of the canvassers, defends Tierney's willingness to welcome a visit from King Edward VII. This discussion inevitably leads these Dubliners to the subject of Charles Stuart Parnell, the great Irish political leader who led the fight for Home Rule, meaning Irish self-government, until his fall from power and his death shortly thereafter, on October 6, 1891. The story takes place on October 6, some years later. O'Connor wears an ivy leaf in his lapel to commemorate Parnell's death.

Parnell's involvement in a divorce case led to his fall from power, and the men argue briefly about his character, but they are soon praising him with an odd mixture of sincerity and cynicism: "We all respect him now that he's dead and gone—even the Conservatives." Henchy asks the journalist among them, Hynes, to recite his poem "The Death of Parnell." After a long silence, Hynes does so. His poem condemns the politicians and Catholic priests who contributed to Parnell's downfall. The canvassers are greatly moved by this recital, except the Conservative, Crofton, who compliments it carefully as "a very fine piece of writing."

Themes and Meanings

"Ivy Day in the Committee Room" is from James Joyce's celebrated collection of stories *Dubliners* (1914), and it was the eighth of the book's fifteen stories to be written. It is included, however, in the fourth and final informal category of stories into which Joyce retrospectively arranged the collection; with "A Mother" and "Grace" it comes under the heading "stories of mature public life." These stories deal with Irish culture and society in the early twentieth century. Their emphasis is on civic institutions and public mores. Their tone, as "Ivy Day in the Committee Room" bears out, is slyly but relentlessly satiric.

Unlike the generally introspective and emotional interests of their companion pieces in *Dubliners*, these stories deal almost exclusively with the external features of their contexts, as befits their public orientation. Concentration on externals enables Joyce to vary and extend his use of epiphany, the method that he originated of endowing characters and their worlds with ostensibly complete autonomy, in order that they reveal their own typical nature.

"Ivy Day in the Committee Room" depicts a condition embodied by a small group of Dubliners but shared by a large number of people throughout the country. Their condition is one of shock, defeat, and social paralysis brought about by the eclipse of the political career of Charles Stewart Parnell, the nearly mythical figure who led the fight for Irish Home Rule. His departure from the political scene, followed by his sudden and untimely death, left Irish political hopes in a traumatized condition for a generation—Joyce's generation.

Parnell, known at the height of his powers as "the uncrowned king of Ireland," exists in the story as an ironic contrast to the impotence of his bereft adherents and as a far more desirable political option than that offered by the crowned king of Ireland, Edward VII. However, in the allusive manner of the story, such an irony has more than merely political resonance. It also points up the emotional poverty of one of the characters: Jack, the caretaker, is unable to enforce "home rule" in his own household. Even such a vehement Parnellite as Henchy is to be viewed satirically because he is a caricatured embodiment of the vehement moralism that terminated Parnell's political career.

"Ivy Day in the Committee Room" draws attention to the poverty of contemporary political activity in Ireland in a variety of ways. The bland platform of Tricky Dicky Tierney, with its apparent ability to satisfy both Nationalist and Conservative voters (who ordinarily would be at opposite ends of the political spectrum), is presented in strong, if implicit, contrast to Parnell's individual integrity. Tierney's nickname further emphasizes this contrast. To underscore the difference still further, Joyce has given his candidate a surname the Gaelic root of which, *tiarna*, means "lord." Clearly, in contrast to the noble Parnell, there is nothing lordly about the latter-day bearer of the electorate's aspirations.

Tierney's henchmen are aware of the contrast, but their inability to make anything of a public nature out of this awareness becomes clear when their criticism of him is washed away with drink. Infidelity to Tierney is replaced by infidelity to themselves, a development that is all the more graphic for being unconscious. Accepting Tierney's drink is a vivid example of the characters' undependable allegiances, lapsed idealism, and self-forgetfulness. It is also the story's clearest illustration of the discontinuity between thought and action that seems typical of the post-Parnell political world in Ireland.

Indeed, the central activity in "Ivy Day in the Committee Room" is inactivity. The characters' devotion to waiting, wondering, and killing time reveals a state of lethargy and vague regret that suffuses the story. Drawing on a general sense of ebb and aftermath, the story gives such deficiencies an authentic reality by conceiving of them as central features of the characters' public presence. Condensed in the story's brief temporal span is the history of a political generation that has lost its way. Time is the medium through which history asserts itself, but Henchy and company seem to be refugees from time. The sodden conditions outside the room, added to Jack the caretaker's difficulty in scraping together an adequate fire, connote the ungenial nature of the environment and the bleak outlook for the petty characters.

Joyce, as though to establish the terms of his own artistic integrity, is unsparing in his exposure of the venality and indifference of these lowest of the political low (foot soldiers in the petty skirmish of a ward election). Even Hynes, who is admittedly a cut above the others in the committee room, comes under the author's satiric lash. Indeed, his poem, for all the sincerity with which Hynes delivers it, is the last word in banality and bathos. A superb parody of derivative rhetoric and outmoded language, it fails literally to merit Crofton's judgment of it as "a very fine piece of writing." Its naïve and outspoken genuineness of sentiment is in brilliant contrast to the tacit, guileful satire of the story whose climax it is.

Style and Technique

If he had written nothing else, Joyce would be assured of a place in literary history because of his innovations in short fiction. His counterdramatic sense of his material, his stylistic resourcefulness, and his celebrated deployment of epiphany enable him to distill aesthetic and cultural validity from superficially unpromising raw material.

Joyce's use of anticlimax as revelation is seen to good advantage in "Ivy Day in the Committee Room." That aspect of the story's technique may be thought of, in effect, as being synonymous with its subject matter. In addition, the drifting, unpredictable flow of conversation in the story mirrors the characters' rudderless, improvised social existence. At the same time, however, without the characters' knowledge, their conversation creates a structure of thematic relationships, conceived around the issues of loss, impoverishment, and venality.

Speech and verbal utterances of all kinds are extremely important in all of Joyce's stories, and "Ivy Day in the Committee Room" is noteworthy for its talkativeness and for the witty and fastidious precision with which it mimics local Dublin usage. This emphasis on talk, its implicit contrast between talk and action, and its mocking and tacit allusion to the cliché that "talk is cheap" confer on the reader the role of eavesdropper. The intimacy thereby created between speaker and auditor, or between character and reader, is a demonstration of one of Joyce's most characteristic artistic strategies, the impersonality of his authorial presence.

This strategy, coupled with (or indeed expressed as) a rejection of omniscience, gives the reader an unmediated, though artfully contrived, experience of the material. As a result, the material achieves a definitive showing forth of itself, ostensibly on its own terms. In Joyce's terms, it attains "epiphany." Economically, unobtrusively, incisively, but above all, inferentially, Joyce lays bare the pathetic stagnation of public life in Dublin as he knew it—that unheroic, degraded present that he could neither forgive nor forget.

George O'Brien

IVY GRIPPED THE STEPS

Author: Elizabeth Bowen (1899-1973)
Type of plot: Psychological
Time of plot: 1944, with a flashback spanning the years 1910 to 1912
Locale: An English coastal town across the channel from France
First published: 1945

> *Principal characters:*
> GAVIN DODDINGTON, the protagonist, who is in his early forties,
> a youth in the flashback
> MRS. LILIAN NICHOLSON, a widowed school friend of
> Doddington's mother
> ADMIRAL CONCANNON, a neighbor of Mrs. Nicholson

The Story

"Ivy Gripped the Steps" is divided into three sections: The first and the third act as frames, being short and set in the present, 1944; the second, by far the longest section, contains a flashback to 1910-1912, when the middle-aged protagonist is between eight and ten years old. As the story opens, an external narrator describes the outside of a brick-and-stone house, which once was prominent but which has become abandoned and neglected since the war made Southstone, on the coast of England, part of the front line.

Ivy overwhelms the house, leaving a grotesque rather than a stately impression. Gavin Doddington, having a few days of vacation from the Ministry, has come to see the house where as a youth he visited his mother's school friend, Mrs. Lilian Nicholson. During his last visit, which took place more than thirty years ago, he experienced a painful awakening regarding his relationship with Mrs. Nicholson.

In the second section, three visits by young Gavin to the prominent house at the seaside resort of Southstone are presented: the first in June, a second in January, and a third in September. As an eight-year-old boy coming to Southstone to shore up his health against the damp climate of his own inland home, Gavin is impressed with the luxury and ease at Mrs. Nicholson's home. While at Southstone and under the care of the maid, Rockham, Gavin soon becomes enchanted with Mrs. Nicholson, whose life as a beautiful and charming widow of independent means seems constituted of social engagements and leisure. Her life contrasts with his own; his family struggles to make a living from the land. During his first visit, Gavin becomes aware of three important facts that he does not fully understand because of his youth: Mrs. Nicholson does not treat him like a child, he has become infatuated with her, and Admiral Concannon in conversation calls her "my dear."

During his second visit, the intimacy between Gavin and Mrs. Nicholson grows, partially as a result of Rockham's illness and partially because of Mrs. Nicholson's manner. At a dinner party at the admiral's and afterward in her conversation with Gavin, Mrs. Nicholson reveals her social nature to the reader but not to the young Gavin: She is generally self-centered and flirtatious. It is during the third visit to Southstone that Gavin experiences a painful awakening. He has been growing fonder of Mrs. Nicholson and has been treated kindly by her. He, however, overhears a conversation between Admiral Concannon and Mrs. Nicholson that makes him realize the true nature of the unlikely triangle made up of Mrs. Nicholson, Admiral Concannon, and himself. The admiral rebukes Mrs. Nicholson for being flirtatious with him and for mesmerizing Gavin. Mrs. Nicholson, not in control of this social situation, likens Gavin to a pet dog by way of excusing her behavior. When Gavin enters the room, Mrs. Nicholson attempts to retain her social veneer by speaking to Gavin as if nothing unpleasant has happened.

The last section of the story picks up chronologically after section 1: Gavin Doddington, who before the lengthy flashback has been staring at the abandoned house that once belonged to Mrs. Nicholson, notices that he has unconsciously picked a leaf of the ivy. Presumably, the flashback has been running through Doddington's mind as he faced the house. He is surrounded by the devastation of war—an evacuated town, buildings intact yet left neglected, bombed sections of buildings, barbed wire, cement barriers—and the memory of the devastation of his feelings of love. It has only been with Mrs. Nicholson, before her veneer was shattered in that overheard conversation, that he has experienced such strong emotions. Gavin Doddington after his awakening is left with no feelings, "nobody to talk to"—"not a soul." He in vain tries to pick up a young woman but is left alone amid the debris of war and emotional devastation.

Themes and Meanings

"Ivy Gripped the Steps" appears in a volume of war stories written by Elizabeth Bowen during World War II. Gavin Doddington reflects on his shattered life amid the ruin of a deserted and bombed coastal town in England. His specific loss—his inability to love—caused by Mrs. Nicholson is a microcosm for the loss felt by those who experience war. Although the war occurs some thirty years after Doddington's traumatic experience at Southstone, it is the war-torn city that calls him back to relive his experience of devastated love.

War is continually alluded to even in the flashback section of the story, which takes place between 1910 and 1912. The admiral forecasts war, warning that England will have to protect itself from Germany, and the Concannons host a meeting to promote the Awaken Britannia League. As an adult, Doddington still considers World War I to be Admiral Concannon's War, the one that the admiral predicted. He remembers the talk of war and Mrs. Nicholson's refusal to believe in it. The admiral, Mrs. Nicholson, and Gavin Doddington's diverse views on the possibility of war reflect their characters: The admiral reacts with concern, Mrs. Nicholson reacts either with unconcern or with denial, and the young Gavin reacts with confusion. Similarly, in the social triangle—including Admiral Concannon, Mrs. Nicholson, and Gavin—which was only a triangle of love to Gavin, the behavior of the three follows the same pattern. Gavin, who is too young to comprehend either the imminence of war or the mere facade of love, suffers as a result of Mrs. Nicholson's ego. She acts with insensitivity and selfishness, while the admiral shows concern for Gavin's feelings. The shallowness of Mrs. Nicholson's world has proved ephemeral. Her society, as well as her character, is only a facade; neither can survive reality. The once carefree community of Southstone—a town now in ruins—is slowly being released from the grip of war; Gavin Doddington, a man emotionally devastated, has not yet been released from the grip of the past. As the town retreats into darkness at the end of the story, Doddington is left alone with his memories.

Style and Technique

An external voice narrates "Ivy Gripped the Steps"; the voice speaks of Gavin Doddington, as well as all the other characters, in the third person. However, the narrative stance emphasizes Doddington as the protagonist because no information given in the story is foreign to him: The description of the ivy-choked house is given to the reader as Doddington looks at it, the long flashback section is presumably a memory of Doddington, and the scene outside the Concannons' home centers on Doddington. Although he does not narrate the story technically, his experience controls the narration. As an eight- or ten-year-old, he is not sophisticated enough to understand the full reality of his experience with Mrs. Nicholson, but as an adult he is: He knows that he is alone and restive at Southstone with his memory. His feelings of love, devastated at an early age, have never recovered.

Bowen begins early to establish the tone of her story through her diction. Ivy-covered houses, frequently considered stately and prestigious, are shown capable of carrying negative connotations. In the title and in the first three paragraphs of the story, the diction suggests that the ivy is a destructive image: "Gripped," "sucked," "deceptive," "matted," "amassed," "consumed," "brutal," "strangulation." The ivy that gripped the house has taken it over and made it grotesque. All other places in the story where the word "gripped" is used also convey negative connotations. The admiral grips his hand behind his back after he confronts Mrs. Nicholson with her flirtatious behavior; Doddington grips a cigarette in his mouth as he is turned down by the young woman and is left alone and desolate. Twice Gavin Doddington's being gripped by his love for Mrs. Nicholson is emphasized. The first situation occurs when Gavin at age eight has an early intuitive feeling that he can never approach Mrs. Nicholson:

> Gavin, gripping the handrail [along the cliff], bracing his spine against it, leaned out backwards over the handrail into the void, in the hopes of intercepting her [Mrs. Nicholson's] line of view. . . . Despair, the idea that his doom must be never, never to reach her, not only now but ever, gripped him and gripped his limbs.

Bowen employs the same images in a later scene describing Gavin's relationship with Mrs. Nicholson. He has just been called a child by her, and his reaction is one of anguish: "Overcharged and trembling, he gripped his way, flight by flight, up the polished banister rail, on which his palms left patches of mist; pulling himself away from her up the staircase as he had pulled himself towards her up the face of the cliff." Just as the ivy has taken over the house and turned its image from a positive to a negative one, the feelings that Mrs. Nicholson nurtured in Gavin toward herself not only have caused him pain but also have doomed him to a life without genuine feeling, to a life without love. Both Mrs. Nicholson and the leisurely, irresponsible life she led are shown to be destructive forces.

Marion Boyle Petrillo

JACKALS AND ARABS

Author: Franz Kafka (1883-1924)
Type of plot: Parable
Time of plot: Unspecified
Locale: An oasis in the North African desert
First published: "Schakale und Araber," 1917 (English translation, 1946)

> *Principal characters:*
> THE NARRATOR, a European man
> AN OLD JACKAL, the spokesperson for the pack
> AN ARAB CARAVAN DRIVER

The Story

At night in a desert oasis, the narrator, traveling with an Arab caravan, tries to get to sleep. The distant howling of jackals causes him to sit up again, and in no time the pack is swarming around him. One of them presses close against his body, then stands before him and speaks. It is the oldest in the pack, and it assures the narrator that his arrival here has been awaited for a long time, by countless generations of jackals, in fact. This sounds curious to the man, as he has only come by chance and on a short visit to the African desert.

As if to cast the newcomer in the role of a messiah or liberator, the jackal explains that he and his race are the persecuted enemies of Arabs and place all their hopes in a "Northerner," whose intelligence far exceeds that of an Arab. The blood enmity between jackals and Arabs requires the extinction of one or the other. The narrator at first thinks the jackals mean to attack the Arabs sleeping in the camp, and he warns that they themselves would undoubtedly be shot down in dozens. Meanwhile, two younger beasts have set their teeth into his coat and shirt and are holding him down.

The old jackal corrects the man's misunderstanding and tells him that jackals have only their teeth for weapons and that to attack and kill the Arabs would make the animals unclean forever—a kind of unpardonable sin. To be rid of Arabs is what they desire, to return their territory to the natural order of cleanliness: "Every beast to die a natural death; no interference till we have drained the carcass empty and picked its bones clean. Cleanliness, nothing but cleanliness is what we want." Their wish is for the man to slit the Arabs' throats for them, and to facilitate the deed they now present him with a small, ancient, rusted pair of sewing scissors.

At this point the leader of the caravan appears from downwind, cracks his whip over the jackals, and sends them fleeing. He knows what has been going on and explains to the narrator that the jackals regard every passing European as their chosen savior and entreat him to kill the Arabs for them. The rusted sewing scissors follow his people like a curse until the end of their days, he says. For the jackals it is a vain, foolish hope, and that is why the Arabs like them. To demonstrate his point, he has a dead camel carried up, and the jackals abandon every thought but that of the carrion. They approach, their fear of the whip forgotten, and soon they are swarming over the carcass. Now the caravan driver begins to lash them with his whip, bringing them to their senses and driving them off in pain and fear. However, they have tasted the blood and flesh and are drawn irresistibly back. The Arab raises the whip again, but the narrator grasps his arm. It is enough; the demonstration is clear. "Marvelous creatures, aren't they?" smiles the caravan driver, "And how they hate us!"

Themes and Meanings

For Franz Kafka and for his narrator, the world of this story is an alien one, geographically and culturally. The two sides between which he finds himself know their places and their desires, but the outsider is subjected to confusion. As in many of Kafka's narratives, he hears conflicting sides of an issue and is not in the position to know which is correct. In fact, probably both are valid in "Jackals and Arabs." The beasts and the men exist in a dual relationship of enmity and symbiosis, hating each other and needing each other to survive and flourish. Their symbiotic existence may be considered a part of the natural order of life, but not their enmity, for it relies on deception and duplicity, and these are human, not animal, traits. Thus, the jackals appeal to a noble sense of cleanliness in order to have the stranger assume the guilt of murdering their enemies. The Arabs are equally perfidious, if less sophisticated, in their treatment of the beasts. The caravan driver asserts that the jackals make finer dogs than any of the ordinary kind, yet he gives them the food they crave most and then would drive them repeatedly from it with his whip. It is a closed world that functions handsomely and is founded on age-old traditions of coexistence, yet the sum of its parts is paradoxical.

Alongside this commentary on the strange system itself is the portrait Kafka presents of the outsider momentarily caught in it. "Jackals and Arabs" is also about the "Northerner," the European, a satire on the presumed superiority of Western thought and culture. It is given to the cunning old jackal to flatter the storyteller as a savior from the North, clever and possessed of an intelligence not found in the Arabs, and it is possible that he would be taken in by the flattery. Should his European wisdom fail him, in any case, there is great persuasive force in the teeth of the encircling jackals, two of them already locked on his clothing. Luckily, however, the narrator has no time to consider the rightness of what he is asked to do, for the caravan leader's intervention relieves him of making that decision.

Style and Technique

As in many of his other stories, Kafka here employs a simple, matter-of-fact narrative style to recount a plot both realistic and fantastic. As a result of that style, one can easily overlook the logical incongruities of the mixture. Most evidently, Kafka has animals converse with men about matters normally thought to preoccupy only human beings: subjugation and liberation, sin and guilt, the upholding of cultural traditions. He has them act with a cunning and deceit of the sort also generally thought to be humankind's exclusive talent—or weakness. If the conversation at the heart of "Jackals and Arabs" makes exceptional creatures of the jackals, however, it also implies a critique of humanity. The animal chosen for this parable is not a noble one in the popular mind, but one thought of as a scavenger, unclean, ill-tempered, and cowardly.

For most northern Europeans, a desert oasis is not an ordinary and familiar place, but the overlay of Kafka's realistic description nevertheless includes occasional glances into its far-from-exotic corners, as with the references to the unbearably rank smell that the beasts emit and with the account of the jackal that sinks its teeth into the dead camel's throat, working at the artery "like a vehement small pump." Even when his purpose is serious, Kafka's essentially humorous view of events is apparent. The narrator glosses his delicate situation among a pack of unpredictable jackals with dry understatement of the dangers. Both the jackals and the Arab caravan driver are given to sarcastic opinions of each other; at a point of potentially high philosophical seriousness, the jackals resort to comic buffoonery to illustrate the uncleanness of killing.

On the subject of parables, Kafka once said that they reside in and refer to a fabulous realm and have no use in practical, everyday life. The most they can do is tell readers that the incomprehensible is incomprehensible, and they know that in any case. To follow parables one would have to abandon reality and become a parable oneself. As usual, "Jackals and Arabs" will be comprehensible to the jackals and Arabs in the story. To the "Northerner" on his brief stay in their country, and to the reader, it offers no explanation of its paradoxes.

Michael Ritterson

JACKLIGHTING

Author: Ann Beattie (1947-   )
Type of plot: Social realism
Time of plot: The 1970's
Locale: Charlottesville, Virginia
First published: 1982

Principal characters:

THE ANONYMOUS NARRATOR, a woman
WYNN, her boyfriend
SPENCE, their friend, whom they are visiting
PAMMY, Spence's girlfriend

The Story

Nicholas has died sometime during the past year from injuries incurred while he was taking a midnight ride on his Harley and a drunk, driving a van, hit him head-on. Last year, on his birthday, he was alive but in the hospital, brain-damaged from the accident. This year, on his birthday, he is dead, and the narrator and her boyfriend, Wynn, both of whom used to drive from New York to Virginia to spend Nicholas's birthday with him, have come instead to visit Nicholas's brother, Spence, who now lives alone in the house that the brothers once shared.

The first half of the story takes place on the day before the anniversary of Nicholas's birthday. It is August and hot, but Spence makes jam so the narrator and Wynn can take some back with them to New York. He stays in the kitchen cooking because he does not want to talk with them. Spence's girlfriend, Pammy, sleeps upstairs with a small fan blowing on her. She is a medical student at Georgetown and has just arrived in Virginia after finishing summer school. Wynn stands in the field across from the house, pacing with his head down. At thirty-one, he thinks that he is in love with one of his students and is going through a mid-life crisis. The narrator watches Wynn from the house as he swings a broken branch and bats hickory nuts in the field. When Spence walks through the living room, he comments on Wynn's foolishness and on Wynn's September birthday, of which he wants to be reminded. The narrator tells Spence that last year she gave Wynn a Red Sox cap for his birthday.

When Nicholas was hit by the van, he, presumably, was not wearing his helmet because he had established in it a nest of treasures—dried chrysanthemums, half of a robin's blue shell, a cat's-eye marble, yellow twine, a sprig of grapes, a piece of a broken ruler—while baby-sitting the neighbors' four-year-old daughter. The narrator realizes that the head-on collision could have happened to her or Wynn or Spence because they all had ridden on the back of the Harley without helmets. She also wonders how she and Wynn and Spence are going to feel without Nicholas—the Nicholas who saw the world, the Nicholas who taught the narrator to trust herself and not settle for seeing things the same way, the Nicholas who made her a necklace with a lobster claw hanging from it and placed it over her head.

Even though the second half of the story takes place on the anniversary of Nicholas's birthday, no one brings it up. Spence makes bread. Pammy and the narrator sit on the porch: Pammy reading the *Daily Progress* and polishing her nails, and the narrator waiting for Wynn to return from his walk. Pammy mentions that she is older than she looks but that Spence, for a "joke," tells people that she is twenty-one. She also mentions that she was once addicted to speed. During that time, she traveled the subway, watched horror films, and slept with a stockbroker for money. She considers that time of her life actually another life and feels snobbish toward other people (including the narrator, Spence, and Wynn) who have not lived this way. The narrator, in turn, feels snobbish toward Pammy because Pammy's addiction makes the narrator realize that other people are confused too.

Spence and the narrator play catch in the heat to distract her from Wynn's taking a walk. Spence suggests that next year they go to Virginia Beach, rather than smolder at his house, in tribute to Nicholas's birthday. The narrator says that she and Wynn came because they thought it would be a hard time for Spence and they did not know that Pammy would be there. Spence does not know why he failed to mention the person who is supposed to be his lover.

Nicholas's past birthdays were celebrated with mint juleps, croquet games, cake eating, and midnight skinny dips. However, there is no celebrating on this anniversary of his birthday: Wynn is sure that he is having a crisis, Spence is crying about his overdone bread, and Pammy feels both isolated from the others and unsure about continuing medical school. The narrator, depressed and drinking on the porch, remembers Nicholas as possessing imagination, energy, and a sense of humor. She realizes that she knows nothing. She remembers that the drunk in the van had thought he had hit a deer when he hit Nicholas. She sees the intense stars. She remembers that every year Spence reports people on his property who are jacklighting.

Themes and Meanings

The title suggests the story's preoccupation with hunting. Jacklighting is night hunting done with a light used as a lure. Although no actual hunting occurs in "Jacklighting," the final sentence of the story suggests that hunting has occurred on Spence's land and will occur again. More important, the reference to jacklighting connects Nicholas's death with hunting. The drunk driver, who hit Nicholas, thought that he had hit a deer. The image of a deer, stopped in the middle of the road because it is blinded by oncoming headlights, is the same image of a deer being lured with lights and then killed by hunters. Nicholas, too, being hit head-on, was presumably blinded by the van's headlights or, symbolically, hunted by the drunk driver. The suggestion that the van driver is a hunter—a killer—gives the story social reverberations, albeit subtle ones. There is no mention that the van driver was penalized for his crime, and apparently the only recourse Spence can take for his brother's death is to chase hunters off his land or stalk upstairs with a rolled newspaper to kill the wasp that is bothering Pammy.

The preoccupation with hunting expands to an abundance of animal references in the story. Other animals besides deer are hunted, if not by hunters with jacklights and guns then by death itself, which is continuously pursuing anything living. Whereas Nicholas has already been hunted down, the other characters are in the process of being hunted simply because they are getting older and having birthdays. Ann Beattie concludes the story with the narrator sitting on the porch, in the dark. The stars are shining down with the intensity of flashlights—an image that is chillingly similar to the hunters' jacklights shining from the dark—an image that, symbolically, suggests the narrator being hunted.

Hunting, on another, less malignant level, is simply a sport or game that people play on Spence's land. Other games—croquet, baseball, catch, the descriptive game Nicholas invented—function, like hunting, as a distraction from the enigma of life and death.

Style and Technique

Beattie, like other postmodernists, writes many of her short stories in scenes, rather than in a straight narrative. "Jacklighting" is written in six: the first, third, and last scenes present information from the narrator's point of view; the remaining scenes function more dramatically because of their inclusion of dialogue and action between characters. Quite tellingly, there are dramatic scenes between the narrator and Pammy and the narrator and Spence, but not between the narrator and Wynn—the man to whom she is supposedly closest.

One effect of writing in scenes is fragmentation. Each scene functions as a separate (and on one level complete) piece that, when placed with the other pieces, makes up the whole story. No matter in what order the pieces are placed, the reader must make a transition in time and space between them. Furthermore, simply because the reader must make these transitions, it is inferred that there are other fragments—other unwritten pieces—between the scenes. Ultimately, the fragmentation of the story's form complements the fragmented lives of the story's four characters.

Cassie Kircher

JANUS

Author: Ann Beattie (1947-   )
Type of plot: Psychological
Time of plot: The 1980's
Locale: An American suburb
First published: 1985

Principal characters:
ANDREA, a real estate agent
HER HUSBAND, a stockbroker

The Story

Andrea is a real estate agent who, from all appearances, is a success at life. She has a good husband, financial security, many possessions, and a job in which she excels. Part of her success at selling real estate is her ability to use tricks to make a house desirable; for example, occasionally she brings her dog, Mondo, to a house if she believes the prospective buyers are dog lovers. Her most common and successful ploy is to bring her special bowl to the house, a bowl that she says is a paradox because it is both subtle and noticeable. She sets the bowl in a prominent place, usually on the coffee table. This bowl fits anywhere, under a Bonnard still life or on a Biedermeier table. Always, she leaves the bowl empty. It sits empty at home, too; she asks her husband not to drop his keys into it.

Over time, Andrea becomes more and more attached to her bowl. She feels that it brings her good luck and wishes she could thank it. Once, she accidentally leaves it at a house and panics; as she rushes back for it, she feels like a mother who has forgotten her child. She begins to dream about the bowl and becomes more possessive toward it. Her anxieties about the bowl grow. Although she knows she would never lose or harm it, she fears that it may be lost or damaged. She has never talked to her husband about the bowl, but as her possessive feelings toward it grow, so does her unwillingness to talk to him about any of her selling strategies or successes, for she believes that they are dependent on the bowl.

Andrea and her husband have a loveless marriage. They are alike in many ways: both quiet, reflective, detail-oriented, and slow to make value judgments, but stubborn once they have come to a conclusion. They are different in other ways: Andrea likes the ironies of life, while her husband is impatient with them. They seem to have little interest in each other's lives: When they talk together, they exchange the news of the day; in bed, they murmur "sleepy disconnections." Andrea does not think about her husband when she is not with him; instead, she thinks about the bowl.

The greater significance of the bowl is finally revealed. It is not just a possession detached from any meaning; it was a gift from a lover. He tried to convince Andrea to change her life, to leave her husband for him, to know what she really wanted and act on it. Instead of leaving her husband, she tried to have both husband and lover. Her lover left, taking with him the emotional satisfaction in her life and leaving her with the financial security and emotionally dead marriage that she refused to give up.

Themes and Meanings

Janus, the Roman god of doorways, gates, and beginnings, has two faces; one looks forward, the other backward. Janus represents duplicitousness; his qualities are strikingly apparent in the character of Andrea. She too looks both forward and backward. Her life is marked by her growing success in her real estate career, and she looks forward to her next sale as she plans the techniques she will use to ensure the sale. Her whole married life has been a matter of looking forward to more possessions and greater financial success rather than enjoying the present. At the same time, Andrea looks backward more and more as the story progresses. She is not consciously aware that she is looking backward, but by the end of the story the reader is aware that her obsession with the bowl represents a longing for a past that is no longer available to her. When she has to choose between husband and lover, she continues to look both ways, unwilling to choose. Ultimately the choice is made for her when her lover departs.

Andrea is also duplicitous. Her affair is an obvious example, but there are other examples in the way she conducts her business. She uses deceptive techniques to sell houses, taking pride in her ability to make the subtle changes that appeal to buyers. She lies to her clients as well: When she forgets her bowl at one of her houses, she tells the woman of the house that it is a new purchase that she set down for safekeeping. When a buyer calls to inquire about the bowl, she pretends that it belongs to the owner of the house. Andrea even lies to herself by refusing to acknowledge the reason for her obsession with the bowl.

The bowl is clearly a strong symbol of Andrea's life. Both are empty. When she looks at the bowl, Andrea sees the "world cut in half, deep and smoothly empty." She, like the bowl, is cut in half, without the love or spiritual qualities that are components of a complete, fulfilled life. Just as the bowl seems to her meant to be empty—she puts nothing in it and rejects her husband's attempts to use it as a receptacle—she chooses emptiness for herself as well. She has refused her lover, and she is indifferent to her husband. Her childlessness, although never mentioned, serves as an implicit symbol of the sterility of the marriage. Her only "child" is the bowl that she fears to leave behind or damage. The bowl has replaced her lover and has supplanted her husband as the object of her affection.

Interestingly, it is the quality that Andrea has perfected in her business that makes her most fear the loss of or damage to her bowl. "Why not," she worries, "in a world where people set plants where they did not belong, so that visitors touring a house would be fooled into thinking that dark corners got sunlight—a world full of tricks?"

A significant quality of the bowl, to Andrea's business and to the story, is its appeal to all of her customers. Perhaps Ann Beattie is suggesting that the appeal of love, and the understanding of the inevitable unhappiness of love lost, is universal. "Janus" is a story about love, obsession, and loss with which readers can sympathize.

Style and Technique

Beattie tells the story of Andrea and her fixation on the ceramic bowl in an objective, detached way. There is little plot; the reader is shown a glimpse of a time during which Andrea's obsession grows. Details about the bowl, the day-to-day stimuli in Andrea's life, and her state of mind are given profusely and objectively, in a flat tone. Beattie does not suggest how one should react to Andrea's plight, but simply puts it forth. The story ends without resolution. The reader has more awareness of the relationship between the bowl and Andrea's loveless life, between her past choices and her present condition, than Andrea herself does.

The drama in the story is predominantly psychological. The reader is told that Andrea dreams about the bowl, that she has a deep connection with it, that it is a mystery to her, and that she loves it. She focuses her life around it, centering all of her sales strategies on the bowl and refusing to talk to her husband about it, concealing from him details about her use of the bowl and thus about her life at work, and therefore shutting him out of her life even more than she had done in the earlier years of their loveless marriage. At the end, Beattie describes the bowl just as she depicts Andrea: "still, safe, and unilluminated." Beattie provokes a certain amount of horror in her reader by suggesting a life with so little self-knowledge.

Janine Rider

JAPANESE HAMLET

Author: Toshio Mori (1910-1980)
Type of plot: Parody
Time of plot: The 1930's
Locale: Northern California
First published: 1979

> *Principal characters:*
> TOM FUKUNAGA, a Japanese American who aspires to be a
> Shakespearean actor
> THE NARRATOR, his friend

The Story

Tom Fukunaga is a Nisei, a person born in the United States of parents who emigrated from Japan. He is more in tune with the mainstream culture in the United States than with traditional Japanese culture. Fukunaga is thirty-one years old but still a schoolboy. Besides free room and board, Fukunaga receives five dollars a week from a Piedmont home where he stays, just as he had done when he was a freshman at Piedmont High School. Ostensibly, the main reason behind Fukunaga's decision to stay in school is his affection for William Shakespeare's plays and his aspiration to become a ranking Shakespearean actor. Fukunaga's relatives, however, believe that he is a worthless loafer and ought to be ashamed of himself for being a schoolboy at his age. Despite the fact that he has been disowned by his parents and is laughed at by his relatives, Fukunaga has been chasing his dream by practicing lines from *The Complete Works of William Shakespeare.*

Fukunaga often visits the narrator's house in the evening with a copy of Shakespeare's plays. Because the narrator is free in the evenings, he does not mind Fukunaga's visits and at first is willing to help Fukunaga practice his recitations. As the days go by, the narrator starts to wonder what role the prominence of his house and attention play in helping Fukunaga waste his energy and time; he suspects he has been drawn into the mock play that is Fukunaga's life. At the age of thirty-one, Fukunaga was still as far from appearing on the stage as he was when he was in high school. The narrator has reminded Fukunaga several times, to no avail, that he has to contact stage people if he wants to become an actor. Observing the discrepancy between Fukunaga's goals and the effort he puts into achieving them, and how little progress he has made toward becoming a professional Shakespearean actor, the narrator sees the validity of the criticism made by Fukunaga's relatives.

The narrator tells Fukunaga that he likes best hearing him recite Shakespeare's sonnets. Fukunaga, however, insists that Hamlet, the title role of Shakespeare's immortal play, is his forte. The narrator notices that when Fukunaga talks to other people about Shakespeare, he always starts by mentioning Hamlet. Even during the recitation practice, after playing parts in other Shakespearean plays, Fukunaga always comes back to Hamlet, for he believes that this is his special role, the role that will establish him in Shakespearean history.

Fukunaga's stubbornness and obliviousness to his own strengths and limitations make the narrator realize that by providing Fukunaga with a willing ear, he has become his accomplice, helping to prolong a dream that cannot be fulfilled. Finally, the narrator musters up enough courage to tell Fukunaga that his book of Shakespeare is destroying him; he would be better off in business or with a job. The two of them do not see each other again until some years later, when the narrator spots Fukunaga on the Piedmont car at Fourteenth and Broadway. Fukunaga's head is buried in a book, which the narrator presumes is *The Complete Works of William Shakespeare*.

Themes and Meanings

Because of their struggle with English, most Issei—first-generation immigrants from Japan—describe their experience in the United States in Japanese. Their writings were published mainly in local Japanese newspapers. Until the late twentieth century, few of those works were translated into English. As a Nisei writer, Toshio Mori wanted to introduce the Japanese American community to the general reading public in the United States. His thematic preoccupation with the sense of community, the conflict between the mainstream U.S. culture and traditional Japanese culture, and the necessity to bridge the two cultures has caused several critics, including William Saroyan, to refer to him as the first real Japanese American writer.

"Japanese Hamlet," however, is not just a story about cultural conflict. It is true that Fukunaga was apparently caught in the clash between the boundless optimism and individual freedom of choice that mark United States culture, and traditional Japanese culture, which places practicality above ideals. When there is a conflict between individual aspiration for self-fulfillment and a person's social and familial obligation, the traditional Japanese ethic would expect a person to forfeit his or her claim to individual freedom in exchange for communal harmony. The correlation between Fukunaga's experience and that of Hamlet also suggests that the thematic appeal of Mori's portrayal of collisions between dream and reality, between commitment and effort, and between individual choice and communal pressure is as specific as it is universal. Both Fukunaga and Hamlet are mediocre actors: Both are trapped in the world of inaction and procrastination, wasting time and energy in fantasizing about what might happen instead of making things happen. Both are playacting, but not acting—their self-created unreality impugns the significance of their relationship with reality. If critic Frank Kermode is right in positing that it is in the perplexed figure of Hamlet, "just because of our sense that his mind lacks definite boundaries, we find ourselves," Fukunaga's experience is indeed as Japanese as American, for the tragicomic power of the story is generated by conflicts that are as indigenous to the Japanese American community as to the United States generally.

In their introduction to *Imagining America* (1991), the collection in which "Japanese Hamlet" is anthologized, Wesley Brown and Amy Ling suggest that the story is a parody of "immigrants who for better and worse idealized an America existing only in their imaginations." Mori's accentuating the similarity between Fukunaga's experience and that of Hamlet, and his portrayal of conflicts that possess universal significance, also raise questions about a society that made it impossible for Fukunaga to become a ranking Shakespearean actor, turning the story into a social tragedy.

Style and Technique

Typical of Mori's writing style, the narrative pace of "Japanese Hamlet" is deliberate and almost leisurely. The writer effectively uses a first-person narrative. The narrator is observant and contemplative, but his professed candor does not conceal the fact that his perception is limited and subjective. This creates an ambiguity about Fukunaga's appearance in the story. Like Fukunaga's relatives, the narrator finally starts to question the practicality of Fukunaga's aspiration and the true motive behind his decision to remain a schoolboy in his thirties. The narrator recalls a conversation in which Fukunaga confides that he would not be richer if he worked for someone and had to pay for his room, board, and carfare. Fukunaga nevertheless implores the reader's admiration and sympathy, partly because the subjective propensity of the first-person narrative point of view usually creates a distance between the narrator and the reader.

"Japanese Hamlet" is a tragicomedy. Mori's use of humor in the story works expediently well with his thematic concerns. The title, for example, sounds as cacophonous as it is facetious. The seeming incompatibility of the two terms also calls the reader's attention to a painful paradox faced by many Japanese Americans in the first half of the twentieth century: Its tragic tone is accentuated by the impossibility of Fukunaga's fulfilling his dream—especially in a society that treats people according to their skin color. Mori's use of humor in the story thus fits the definition of what Max F. Schulz calls "black humor": the kind of humor used to portray "an absurd world devoid of intrinsic values, with a resultant tension between individual and universe." The fact that "Japanese Hamlet" was written two years before 120,000 Japanese Americans, two-thirds of them American citizens, were sent to relocation camps further underlines the story's apocalyptic significance, demonstrating the necessity to create a society in which tragedies similar to Fukunaga's life can be avoided.

Qun Wang

THE JAPANESE QUINCE

Author: John Galsworthy (1867-1933)
Type of plot: Social realism
Time of plot: The late nineteenth or the early twentieth century
Locale: London, England
First published: 1910

Principal characters:

MR. NILSON, a well-to-do and important London businessperson
MR. TANDRAM, another well-to-do and important London
businessperson, Mr. Nilson's next-door neighbor

The Story

Though "The Japanese Quince" has far-reaching ramifications about the main characters' lives (as does its central symbol), the story's events transpire in less than an hour in the compressed length of less than three pages. Upstairs in the midst of his early morning pre-breakfast routine, Mr. Nilson becomes aware of a disturbing sensation that he cannot identify. Downstairs, when the sensation recurs, he decides to take a stroll in the garden square surrounded by the exclusive row houses of his neighborhood.

Once outside, Mr. Nilson is charmed by an ornamental tree and a blackbird singing in it. Suddenly, he becomes aware that his next-door neighbor is nearby, also admiring the tree, and the two, who have not been formally introduced, exchange a few laudatory remarks about the Japanese quince and the blackbird. Then, both becoming embarrassed, the pair bid each other good morning and return to their houses. About to reenter his house, Nilson again gazes at the tree and the blackbird, experiences the disturbing sensation, notices his neighbor (also about to reenter his house) gazing at the tree and bird, and then, "unaccountably upset," turns "abruptly" into the house and opens his morning newspaper.

Themes and Meanings

The primary themes of the story can be formulated as a series of conflicts: emotion or spirit versus convention or habit, the aesthetic versus the pragmatic, communion versus loneliness or self-centeredness, and self-knowledge versus willful ignorance. Each of the businesspeople is jarred out of his dull, self-centered routine by the intrusion of nature and by a sudden, piercing awareness of beauty. When each businessperson becomes slightly uneasy about appearing to be romantic—an impractical admirer of beauty—in his neighbor's eyes, however, the brief communion of the pair is broken off, and each one returns to the world of practical events and financial matters reported in and symbolized by the morning newspaper each one carries. Each man resumes living within the restrictive confines of his row house, his daily routine, and his society's conventions (so restrictive that because the neighbors' wives have not met, they have not met socially, either, though they have lived next door to each other for five years).

The flight from self-knowledge to willful ignorance is suggested in the story's last sentence: Nilson refuses to analyze the unaccustomed emotions that have disturbed him, instead deflecting his attention to his morning newspaper. Failing to acknowledge that he is bothered by the thought of communing with another human being and by the recognition of an aesthetic or romantic side of himself that is mirrored in Tandram, Nilson escapes to the pragmatic world of quantification and measurement. Nilson quantifies not only in meditating on stock prices such as those of Tintos (in the story's beginning) but also in pondering the disturbing sensation, of which he seeks the exact physical location (just under his fifth rib) and physical cause (wondering whether it could be something that he ate the night before). Thus, he does not realize that what bothers him are nonmaterialistic things missing from his life: beauty, friendship, and emotion.

Style and Technique

Besides the tree and its blackbird occupant, "The Japanese Quince" has a number of other symbols. Both Nilson's mirror, at which he gazes in the story's second paragraph, and the scrolled stairs leading up to his house suggest the themes of self-knowledge and the aesthetic versus the pragmatic. When Nilson searches in his mirror to find the cause of the disturbing sensation, he mistakenly looks for the physical or superficial rather than within himself. At the story's conclusion he remains a mystery to himself, like a scroll (the shape of his stairs) that has remained wound up rather than being unrolled and read. Conversely, what he is missing from life is, at the same time, suggested by the mirror and stairs. Though his hand glass has its practical side (literally), its back is made of ivory, which is there for its aesthetic appeal. Though his stairs are eminently usable, their scrolled design is beautiful rather than utilitarian.

That the Japanese quince is enclosed in the "Square Gardens" suggests a social and human-made confinement of nature, paralleling the main characters' repression or walling off of things natural. The tree and blackbird themselves have manifold symbolic aspects. The blackbird resembles in some respects both Nilson and Tandram. They are both dressed in their business "uniforms" of formal black frock coat; they, like the blackbird singing in the tree, have been emotionally stirred by spring and the Japanese quince.

Moreover, the bird is described not only as "chanting out his heart" but also as perched in the "heart" of the tree, the repetition of the word "heart" reinforcing the ideas of emotion, passion, or romance. Lastly, the bird is in a kind of communion with the tree, each one contributing to the other: The bird gives the tree an added musical beauty and vitality, while the tree shares its fragrance and shelter with the bird. For a brief moment, Nilson and Tandram also commune and communicate with each other, though all too soon their practicality intervenes and interdicts. Their black frock coats, after all, though resembling the blackbird's plumage, are the sober, colorless badges of the sedate and matter-of-fact business world.

The tree is an exotic rather than a fruit-bearing one, a feature implying the theme of the contrast between the aesthetic and the pragmatic: It is simply beautiful to look at, though it will not provide a crop to be eaten or sold. In this respect, it resembles a work of art. While various edifying concepts can be derived from books of sociology, psychology, history, critical essays, and the like, what will be missing are the beauty, emotion, and pleasure to be gained from seeing a beautiful tree, listening to a blackbird's song, or reading a story such as "The Japanese Quince."

Norman Prinsky

JASMINE

Author: Bharati Mukherjee (1940-   )
Type of plot: Social realism
Time of plot: The 1980's
Locale: Southfield and Ann Arbor, Michigan
First published: 1988

> *Principal characters:*
> JASMINE, an ambitious young Indian woman from Trinidad
> THE DABOOS, a family of Trinidadian Indians living in Michigan
> BILL MOFFITT, a professor of molecular biology at the University of Michigan
> LARA HATCH-MOFFITT, Bill's wife, a performance artist

The Story

Jasmine, a vivacious, starry-eyed, young Indian woman from Trinidad who believes that Trinidad is too small for a girl with ambition, has herself smuggled into the United States to find a well-employed husband and forge a new life. She enters Detroit from the Canadian border while hidden in the back of a mattress truck. With her daddy's admonition that opportunity comes only once resounding in her ears, she challenges herself to use her wits and to refashion her destiny.

Being an illegal alien, Jasmine spends her first few months working as a chambermaid and bookkeeper, in exchange for meager board and lodging, at the Plantation Motel in Southfield, run by the Daboos, a family of Trinidadian Indians who helped her get there. Conscious of her social status as a physician's daughter in Port-of-Spain, she feels superior to the Daboos, thinking of them as country bumpkins who were nobodies back home. She decides to leave them soon.

The central action of the story begins when Loretta and Viola, the Daboo girls, prevail on Jasmine to go with them to Ann Arbor to the big bash of the West Indian Students' Association. The music, the dance, and the company of boys who talked with confidence about their futures in the United States stir her desires and ambition, and she decides not to return to the life of drudgery at the Plantation Motel. Instead, she thinks of trying her luck in pursuing higher studies in Ann Arbor, which seems to her the magic place to be. The next evening, she lands a job as a live-in housekeeper, cook, and baby-sitter for an easygoing American family: Bill Moffitt, a biology professor; his wife, Lara, a performance artist; and their little girl, Muffin. They do not even ask about her legal status or her social security number. She considers herself lucky to have found a nice American family like the Moffitts to build her new life around.

Jasmine's well-paying job with the Moffitts gives her a new sense of emancipation, and she starts living the American Dream. After her initiation into the American way of life, she feels she has become her own person. Even her parents become a distant memory, as she tries hard to break with her past. Her proximity to Bill Moffitt provides her subliminal stimulation. She begins to think of Bill, Muffin, and herself almost like a family, and wishes Lara were miles away.

After a few months, Lara goes on the road with her performing group. Jasmine has become more and more attracted toward Bill and his world of comfort and ease. One night, while dancing closely with Bill, she feels aroused and is half-willingly seduced by him. Her desire to assimilate into U.S. society is so overpowering that when Bill, passionately caught in the act of undressing himself and Jasmine, calls her "flower of Trinidad," she immediately retorts, "Flower of Ann Arbor, not Trinidad." As they make love in front of the fireplace, the narrator playfully and ironically describes Jasmine as thinking of herself as "a bright, pretty girl with no visa, no papers, and no birth certificate. No nothing other than what she wanted to invent and tell. She was a girl rushing wildly into the future."

Themes and Meanings

Bharati Mukherjee's major concern in her fiction is to explore the problems of emigration and assimilation, on both physical and psychological levels. In "Jasmine," she fictionalizes the process of Americanization by exploring the experiences of a young Trinidadian woman who, driven by ambition and adventure, pulls up her traditional roots and arrives in the New World to forge a new identity for herself. In her exuberance, she views her illegal entry into the United States as a "smooth, bargain-priced emigration." Thinking exclusively in economic terms, she is unaware of the real price involved in the bargain. Ironically, she is exploited by both her own countrymen, the Daboos, and her new American employers, the Moffitts. In both positions, she is nothing more than a live-in domestic servant, although the Moffitts euphemistically call her a mother's helper. She does not tell the Moffitts that in Trinidad her family also kept servants. Her adventure thus becomes a story of survival, expediency, and the losses, compromises, and adjustment involved in the process of assimilation into mainstream America. At the end of the story, her half-willingly letting her employer seduce her symbolically suggests the seductive power that the United States wields over new immigrants.

In an interview published in *The Canadian Fiction Magazine*, Mukherjee asserts that immigration is a positive act for her characters, for "the breaking away from rigidly predictable lives frees them to invent more satisfying pasts, and gives them a chance to make their futures in ways that they could not have in the Old World." Mukherjee's remarks apply to Jasmine, who first breaks away from her past by cutting herself off from the Daboos and anything too reminiscent of the island, and then conveniently reinvents a new narrative of her past for the Moffitts to make her shabby island hometown sound romantic. Her inventiveness is instantly noticed by Lara, who discerns in Jasmine the creative talent of an actor or a writer.

The open-ended conclusion of the story makes the reader wonder how Jasmine will invent the narrative of her future life in the United States. Will her instinct for survival make her try to blackmail Bill or break up his marriage so she can live with him and secure the status of a legal U.S. resident? Ironically, in Jasmine's moment of ecstasy, the narrator seems to use both the spur and the curb to simultaneously unleash and undermine her unbridled fancy by describing her as "a girl rushing wildly into the future."

As an immigrant narrative, the story shows noticeable affinities with Mukherjee's novel, *Jasmine* (1989).

Style and Technique

Written in a playful and racy style, punctuated with the vernacular of the island, the story develops an ironic perspective on the problem of emigration and assimilation. Mukherjee uses the limited omniscient third-person point of view to make Jasmine the center of consciousness in the story. Throughout the narrative, the focus is on the actions, thoughts, feelings, and inner workings of Jasmine's mind. Although she herself does not speak much in the story, the entire process of emigration and assimilation is seen from the viewpoint of this starry-eyed optimist. Through this narrative technique, the author makes the reader aware of Jasmine's class consciousness, her sense of superiority over the Daboos, her effort to deceive the Moffitts in inventing a suitable story of her home and family, and her subliminal desire to usurp the Moffitts' marriage with a view to building a family of her own.

The author also uses Jasmine's wide-eyed naïveté and her ignorance about the American way of life to develop an ironic perspective on the process of Americanization. Jasmine's knowledge about the United States is limited to stories she heard about other Trinidadian girls who had gone there. As such, even her working conditions with the Daboos seem to her like a good deal, although Loretta sees her as nothing more than her father's drudge. Similarly, she thinks that her job with the Moffitts as mother's helper is as good as anyone's, but the narrator undercuts her view by parenthetically inserting that "Americans were good with words to cover their shame." Again, when she calls herself the flower of Ann Arbor, not Trinidad, as she surrenders her body to Bill, the omniscient narrator comments that "she forgot all the dreariness of her new life and gave herself up to it." Thus, the narrative technique allows Mukherjee to celebrate what she calls "the exuberance of immigration," the process of Americanization with all of its gains and losses.

Chaman L. Sahni

JEALOUS HUSBAND RETURNS IN FORM OF PARROT

Author: Robert Olen Butler (1945-   )
Type of plot: Fantasy
Time of plot: The late twentieth century
Locale: Houston, Texas
First published: 1995

> *Principal characters:*
> THE NARRATOR, a jealous man who has been reincarnated as a
>   parrot
> HIS FORMER WIFE, now his owner
> HER LOVER, a man who wears cowboy boots

The Story

The story revolves around a compulsively jealous husband, the unnamed first-person narrator of the story. It opens abruptly, with the narrator sitting on a perch in his cage in a pet store in Houston, having been reincarnated somehow as a yellow-nape Amazon parrot. One day, his former wife, accompanied by what he assumes must be her current lover, enters the store and is drawn to him. She buys him and takes him back to their former home, where she keeps him in a cage in the den. Despite his physical and, to a degree, psychological transformation, he is still jealous of his former wife's latest lover. He is limited, however, to taking out his resentment on the bird toys in his cage.

In a flashback, the narrator reviews the circumstances that led to his death as a human. His wife had always had lovers, and after becoming suspicious that a new employee at her office had become the latest in that series, he found out where the man lived and went to his house. The narrator climbed a tree in an attempt to look through a window to catch his wife and the man together but died after falling from his perch. No explanation is offered as to the mechanism of his reincarnation.

Over time he becomes more and more birdlike, distancing himself from his jealousy as his thoughts increasingly turn to flying away and escaping. One day his wife leaves the door to his cage open, and he tries to fly to freedom. The sliding glass doors through which he sees the sky, trees, and other birds outside are closed, however, and he flies headfirst into them. When he eventually sees his wife and her new lover naked, he finds them more pitiful than beautiful or threatening, and his jealousy appears to have given way to sympathy. Already injured by flying into the doors that lead outside, he resolves to continue to throw himself against the glass. The story ends with the implication that his response to this new existence, though motivated by a desire for freedom rather than revenge, will have the same fatal result as his response to his former situation.

Themes and Meanings

The physical transformation of the narrator provides considerable opportunity for comedy, while his more gradual psychological transformation provides the primary thematic elements. As in Franz Kafka's *Die Verwandlung* (1915; *The Metamorphosis*, 1936), one of the few close literary analogs to Butler's tale, the reader is led to consider whether the transformation is really as profound as one might initially suppose. The parrot's response in the opening scene to watching the clerk in the pet store, who took his former wife aside and "made his voice go much too soft when he was doing the selling job," is similar to the vengeful rage the cuckolded human had felt: "I'd missed a lot of chances to take a bite out of this clerk in my stay at the shop and I regretted that suddenly." Similarly, he waits for the lover "to draw close enough for me to take off the tip of his finger."

The parrot and his widow—the only characters directly quoted in the story—exchange "Hello" on the first page, and their dialogue remains at the level of what might realistically be exchanged between bird and owner. However, the story suggests that even this is an improvement over their communication during his human existence. In the only instance the story provides from their marriage, the narrator never speaks at all after his wife opens a conversation with a series of references—perhaps calculated—to a male coworker: "right after the third one I locked myself in the bathroom because I couldn't rage about this anymore. . . . I was working on saying nothing, even if it meant locking myself up." As a parrot, the narrator is indeed locked up and virtually speechless, but despite this apparent intensification of his plight, his rage lessens over the course of the story. He gains insight by considering the parallels between his two lives: "I attack that dangly toy as if it was the guy's balls, but it does no good. It never did any good in the other life either, the thrashing around I did by myself."

Eventually he comes to love his wife more than he had when alive, to regret his own failures in their relationship, and even to feel pity for her latest lover. He finally realizes that his consciousness had always been divided, that he had always had another creature inside who might have felt love while he was only aware of jealousy and anger. Robert Olen Butler contrives, however, to leave it an open question as to how much of the narrator's emotional change is genuine compassion brought about by his new perspective and how much of it is merely the effect of the supplanting of his human emotional responses by his increasingly parrotlike nature. Does he become more human or less human when he is a parrot?

Style and Technique

The reincarnation of the human narrator's consciousness into the animal body is established as the opening premise with the very title and is never explained. However, once Butler makes this stipulation, the story proceeds in a rigorously realistic mode. Although many writers have told stories from the point of view of animals, few have made more than a token effort to reproduce that animal's consciousness in any species-specific way. The obstacles to such representation are evident: The true target of such fictions is almost always the tale's relevance for understanding human rather than animal behavior, and the necessity of communicating the story in a written human language automatically implies a human "interpreter" or "translator" between the reader and the animal's mind and expression, especially in first-person narratives. Butler's construction of his parrot narrator ameliorates these difficulties in novel ways.

The convention of reincarnation motivates the otherwise anomalous presence of human concerns on the part of the animal, while at the same time the location of that consciousness in a parrot results in shifts in perspective and distance characteristic of those explored in more traditional animal narratives. Rather than simply imagine a person in a parrot suit, Butler imagines the physical limitations of the parrot's brain and nervous system as constraining the narrator's behavior and thought. When his wife says "Hello," he can say it back, but when she then says "Pretty bird," he can only repeat "Hello": "She said it again, 'Pretty bird,' and this brain that works like it does now could feel that tiny little voice of mine ready to shape itself around those sounds." Butler thus provides a foundation for both the recognizably human aspects of the tale and the animal point of view that defamiliarizes them for the reader. The initial encounter with the wife exemplifies the method: "She knows that to pet a bird you don't smooth his feathers down, you ruffle them. But of course she did that in my human life. as well."

The choice of an animal that can literally speak human language works in two distinct ways. First, by limiting his human characters' dialogue just as severely, because the parrot usually reports—and repeats—only words spoken directly to him, his wife's speech is almost identical to that of the parrot, furthering the idea that human minds may not be so far removed from those of animals in some respects. Second, the parrot's simple vocabulary is delivered in contexts that bring out dramatic irony and comedy. For example, a cliché of parrot speech is transformed into an insult to upset the boyfriend with a "thick Georgia truck-stop accent": "A word, a word we all knew in the pet shop, was just the right word after all. . . . I said 'Cracker.' He even flipped his head back a little at this in surprise. He'd been called that before to his face, I realized." Another food term is adapted to similar effect when the bird later sees the man naked: "We keep our sexual parts hidden, we parrots, and this man is a pitiful sight. 'Peanut,' I say."

Butler gradually shifts the balance between the narrator's human and animal consciousnesses over the course of the story. In the beginning, the human element predominates, and the narrator's concerns, particularly the jealousy foregrounded in the title, remain much the same as they were before his reincarnation. By the end of the tale, the avian elements predominate, but the human narrator's presence, once established, cannot be forgotten, and his final desire for flight and freedom, even at the cost of his life, must be read both literally and metaphorically as a desire shared by the human and the bird.

William Nelles

JEAN-AH POQUELIN

Author: George Washington Cable (1844-1925)
Type of plot: Regional
Time of plot: About 1805
Locale: New Orleans
First published: 1875

> *Principal characters:*
> JEAN MARIE POQUELIN, the protagonist, a Creole
> JACQUES POQUELIN, his younger brother
> MR. WHITE, his American neighbor, the secretary of the Building
> and Improvement Committee

The Story

People wonder about the transformation of Jean Marie Poquelin. He had been a gregarious, successful indigo planter, but his gambling led to the loss of his fortune and all but one slave, and indigo ceased to be a profitable crop. In an effort to recoup his fortune, Poquelin turned to smuggling and the slave trade. However, there, too, success eluded him: His last voyage to Africa ended in disaster, and he came home one night without his ship or his cargo.

He also returned without his younger brother, Jacques, who had insisted on going along, and people wonder about this circumstance, too. Poquelin was devoted to Jacques, always praising his bookish brother's learning and intelligence, but Poquelin also is known for his bad temper. Did he murder Jacques in a fit of rage?

No one knows, and no one asks. The once proud estate decays, its fields reverting to marsh. Dwarf palmettos grow up as a fence around the property; in the canal alligators crawl, and in the brackish ponds snakes lurk beneath the carpet of water plants. Strange stories, like the strange flora, grow up about the house: At sunset all the windows are reputed to turn blood red; beneath the front door there is rumored to be a bottomless well to receive unwelcome visitors—and no visitor is welcome. Only an occasional hardy schoolboy ventures near to watch Jean Poquelin being rowed by his one remaining slave, an old mute.

With time, though, developers come. They want to drain the marsh, fill in the canal, and run streets through Poquelin's property. The new American government will pay Poquelin for this land, which it wants in order to provide housing for the influx of Yankee immigrants.

Poquelin, however, does not want anyone encroaching on his property. He goes first to the governor and then to the municipal authorities, where, with growing irritation, he insists on his right to keep his land, but the official is adamant. Finally Poquelin departs, bestowing a shower of French curses on the Americans and their government.

After Poquelin leaves, the official wonders aloud why Poquelin objects to having the value of his property increased through drainage and development. His interpreter tells him that Poquelin does not want neighbors because he is a witch. One evening, the interpreter had been hunting in the swamps and had returned after dark. As he passed Poquelin's house he saw the old man walking, but Jean was not alone. Beside him was something that resembled a man but could not have been because it was too white.

Despite Poquelin's objections, the street is opened, the marsh drained, and the canal filled. Snakes and alligators retreat, and in their place come new buildings and new settlers. Amid these changes, Poquelin clings to his old house and old ways, thereby increasing his reputation as a witch. If a woman dies, a child is lost, or a crop fails, Poquelin is blamed. Children taunt him in the street. A Building and Improvement Committee organizes to buy Poquelin's house.

Among the committee's members is the city official who heard the interpreter's ghost story. He suspects that the white figure is Poquelin's brother, who is being held in seclusion against his will. If the committee can prove that this is so, they can proceed against Poquelin and thereby get his property. White, the committee's secretary, is sent to spy.

The next day, shortly before dark, White steals onto the Poquelin property. He sees Jean and, shortly afterward, the white figure, from which comes the odor of death and decay. As soon as the two go inside, White prepares to leave. Then he hears voices, one belonging to Jean, the other hollow, unearthly. White flees.

Henceforth, the secretary becomes Poquelin's defender. He orders the children to leave Poquelin alone. He squelches every rumor about the old man and stands up for him at the committee's meetings. When a group of Creoles comes to taunt Poquelin with a noisy charivari, White confronts the mob and turns it away.

Hours later, toward morning, the noisemakers return, and this time White cannot stop them. However, Poquelin has escaped their jeers; when they invade Poquelin's property, they find him dead beneath a tree, attended by his African mute. Chastened, the mob wants to leave, but White insists that its members attend the funeral to discover Poquelin's secret. As they watch, the slave leads a brown bull pulling a cart with the coffin, and behind walks Jacques Poquelin, a leper. As they go off into the swamp, everyone realizes how much Poquelin suffered and sacrificed to guard his brother's secret, the discovery of which would have led to their separation.

Themes and Meanings

In the first sentence of this story, George Washington Cable establishes the time and place of his story: "In the first decade of the present century, when the newly established American Government was the most hateful thing in Louisiana . . . there stood, a short distance above what is now Canal Street . . . an old colonial plantation-house half in ruin." In addition to giving the setting, Cable here establishes his theme, which is the clash of two cultures.

Representing the old world is Jean Poquelin, the aristocratic Creole. He lives in an old house that he refuses to tear down or modernize, despite the urging of his neighbors. He can speak some English but prefers to use French, even when he confronts American officials. Believing in a government by aristocracy rather than by bureaucracy, he goes directly to the governor with his problem: "I know not the new laws. I ham a Fr-r-rench-a-man! Fr-r-rench-a-man have something aller au contraire—he come at his Gouverneur." A Creole goes to his governor because he believes in personal loyalty, in ties of community and kinship. Poquelin visits the graves of his parents every day, and this same impulse drives him to shield his brother so that no one will learn of his disease and force him to go to the leper colony.

Cable sympathizes with the plight of the Creole represented by Poquelin. He has White say that Poquelin was "a better man" than his persecutors. At the same time, though, Cable realizes that Poquelin's world is doomed. His house is decaying, and so, too, is his brother. The aggressive, industrious Americans are physically transforming the city, bringing new values with them. They cannot understand why Poquelin should resist improvements to his property, because these will make money for him. Cash, not community or tradition, concerns them, and they corrupt the native residents with their outlook. The lower-class Creoles stage the charivari, but only at the prompting of the Americans.

In the clash of cultures, the old falls before the new. Poquelin dies; the mute slave and Jacques retreat into the swamp, which is itself retreating before the onslaught of outsiders. The Poquelins have yielded to a more successful but less humane world.

Style and Technique

After the Civil War, local colorists across the country sought to preserve the landscape and habits of their section before progress erased their memory. Joel Chandler Harris, for example, recorded his "Uncle Remus" stories because he feared that black folklore would soon disappear. What Harris sought to do for black folklore, Cable did for French New Orleans. His goal was to preserve a sense of *jadis*, the world as it was in an earlier time. He paints a small, intimate city limited to "the few streets named for the Bourbon princes." Beyond are the marshes navigated by canoes paddled by slaves owned by French-speaking aristocrats.

Cable evokes a sense of nostalgia for this vanished era. However, he looks at it realistically, recording it with the accuracy of a social scientist. When the Boston Literary World objected to Cable's use of dialect in "Jean-ah Poquelin" as unrealistic, Cable replied that he heard that patois every day. He notes the Creoles' clothes, mannerisms, customs (including the charivari), and landscape with careful detail. The conflict between Creole and American is also precisely rendered, as Cable shows the innovations so hateful to the older inhabitants: "trial by jury, American dances, anti-smuggling laws, . . . the printing of the Governor's proclamation in English."

Living in a period of rapid social and economic changes brought about by the Civil War, Cable looks back to an earlier yet similar time shortly after the Louisiana Purchase turned New Orleans from a French colony into an American outpost. "Jean-ah Poquelin" stands like a wrought-iron gate that grants one admission from the busy street into a quiet courtyard of the past.

Joseph Rosenblum

THE JEWBIRD

Author: Bernard Malamud (1914-1986)
Type of plot: Fable
Time of plot: About 1961
Locale: New York City
First published: 1963

Principal characters:
HARRY COHEN, a Jewish frozen-foods salesperson
EDIE, his wife
MORRIS (MAURIE), their ten-year-old son
SCHWARTZ (THE JEWBIRD), a talking blackbird

The Story

Harry and Edie Cohen, a lower-middle-class Jewish couple, live with their ten-year-old son, Morris (Maurie), in a small top-floor apartment on the Lower East Side of New York City. Cohen, a frozen-foods sales representative, is angry and frustrated by his relative poverty, by his dying mother in the Bronx, and by the general mediocrity of his family and his life.

When the story opens, the Cohen family is sitting down to dinner on a hot August night, their recent attempt at a vacation cut short because Harry's mother had suddenly become ill, forcing them to return to the city. While this less-than-happy family is eating, a ruffled blackbird comes flying through the open window and plops down on their table in the middle of their food. Harry curses and swats at the bird, which flutters to the top of the kitchen door and amazes them by speaking in Yiddish and English. The bird explains that he is hungry and is running (and flying) from what he calls "Anti-Semeets" (anti-Semites). He says that he is not a crow but a "Jewbird," and he demonstrates this by immediately beginning to pray passionately, a prayer Edie and Maurie join, but not Harry.

The Jewbird says that his name is Schwartz and asks for a piece of herring and some rye bread rather than the lamb chop the family is eating. Harry insists that the bird eat on the balcony, so Maurie takes him there to feed him and asks his father if the bird can stay. Harry says that Schwartz can remain only for the night but relents the next morning after Maurie cries at the prospect of losing his new friend.

The uneasy truce between Schwartz and Harry is threatened by Schwartz's requests for Jewish food and a Jewish newspaper as well as by his general garrulousness. Harry resents the bird and the fact that Schwartz calls himself Jewish. Harry makes Schwartz stay on the balcony in a wooden birdhouse even though the bird much prefers being inside with the family, where he can be warm and smell the cooking. When Harry brings home a bird feeder full of corn, Schwartz rejects it, explaining later to Edie that his digestive system has deteriorated with his old age; he prefers herring.

In the fall, Maurie returns to school and Schwartz becomes his tutor, helping him with his lessons. He becomes the boy's companion and friend, urging him to do his homework, listening and coaching while Maurie struggles with his violin, and playing dominoes with Maurie when his chores are finished. When Maurie is sick, Schwartz even reads comic books to him (although the bird dislikes comics). Maurie's school grades improve (to nothing lower than C-minus) and Edie gives Schwartz credit for the improvement, but the bird denies the suggestion that he really had anything to do with Maurie's rising academic status.

Schwartz's appearance continues to annoy Harry until one night he picks a quarrel with the bird, complaining about the way it smells and its snoring that keeps him awake. Harry curses the bird and is about to grab it when Maurie appears and the argument ends. Schwartz then avoids Harry when he can, sleeping in his birdhouse on the balcony but longing to spend more time inside with the family. Edie suggests to Schwartz that there might be some reconciliation if he would bathe as Harry wishes, but Schwartz argues that he is "too old for baths." Schwartz claims that he smells the way he does because of what he eats; he asks why Harry smells.

As winter approaches, Schwartz's rheumatism bothers him more and more; he awakens stiff, barely able to move his wings. Harry wants the Jewbird to fly off for the winter, and he begins a secret campaign of harassment. Harry puts cat food in the bird's herring and pops paper bags on the balcony at night to keep Schwartz awake. As a final stroke, he buys a cat, something Maurie has always wanted, but the cat spends its days terrorizing Schwartz. The bird suffers from all this harassment, losing feathers and becoming ever more nervous and unkempt, but somehow he endures.

The end comes on the day after Harry's ailing mother dies in her apartment in the Bronx. While Maurie and Edie are out at Maurie's violin lesson, Harry chases Schwartz with a broom. Harry grabs the bird and begins swinging it around his head; fighting for his life, Schwartz is able to bite Harry on the nose before Harry furiously pitches him out the window into the street below. Harry throws the birdhouse and feeder after him, then sits waiting with the broom, his nose throbbing painfully, for Schwartz's reappearance. The Jewbird does not return, however, and when Edie and Maurie come home Harry lies about what happened, saying that Schwartz bit him on the nose so he threw the bird out and it flew away. Edie and Maurie reluctantly accept Harry's version of the incident.

In the spring, after the snow has melted, Maurie looks for Schwartz and finds the bird's broken body in a vacant lot. "Who did it to you, Mr. Schwartz?" he cries; "Anti-Semeets," his mother tells him later.

Themes and Meanings

Bernard Malamud, like many Jewish writers, frequently examines in his fiction the changing attitudes Jews display about their religion and their heritage. In this story, readers see a Jewish family that is moving away from the orthodox Jewish traditions. Schwartz, who says he is a Jewbird, represents those traditions. His black color resembles the dark clothing traditionally worn by rabbis; he instantly falls into prayer on his arrival. He eats traditional Jewish food and generally scorns the meals the Cohens serve. Schwartz's values reflect the values of orthodox Judaism, values Harry Cohen, at least, has forgotten or is trying to forget. Schwartz becomes the equivalent of an aging Jewish relative: a grandfather or uncle for Maurie, a Jewish father for Harry. Ironically, Harry's real mother (Maurie's grandmother) is slowly dying in her own apartment, ignored except when her illness interrupts Harry's life. If she were brought into their household and cared for, she would probably help Maurie in the way that Schwartz does; presumably she would also irritate Harry in the way that the Jewbird does. Schwartz tells the Cohens that he is fleeing from anti-Semites, people who persecute Jews because of their religion and traditions. Edie Cohen's remark that anti-Semites killed Schwartz points out that Harry Cohen is a kind of anti-Semite himself, although he is probably not aware of it. He has turned his back on his religion.

Style and Technique

Malamud subtly builds his story toward the climax found in the final paragraphs. The fact that Harry Cohen's mother is ill, yet living alone nearby, is mentioned in the first paragraph but allowed to remain in the background until the end of the story, when Harry attacks the bird the day after the death of his mother. Presumably Schwartz is at that point a symbol of the Jewish parent Harry has essentially ignored and allowed to die alone. By throwing the bird out the window, Harry is able to exorcise the guilt he may be feeling about his treatment of his mother.

Malamud uses dialogue to establish Schwartz's Jewishness ("If you haven't got matjes, I'll take schmaltz") and to make this talking bird seem perfectly human. The fact that Schwartz can read comic books, play dominoes, or coach Maurie on the violin seems quite plausible because of the bird's conversational abilities. By the point in the story that Schwartz is being urged to take a bath, he seems simply to be one of the family, an elderly relative, and not a bird at all. His politeness ("Mr. Cohen, if you'll pardon me") only accentuates his human qualities. Conversely, Harry's language, his profanity and his basic rudeness ("One false move and he's out on his drumsticks"), underscores his own lack of humanity. There is no logical reason for his intense hatred of Schwartz, as there is no reason to call the bird names and swear at it the way he does. Schwartz, after all, brings much to Maurie's life and asks only for a little food and warmth in return. It is through Harry's anger and his begrudging attitude toward Schwartz that Malamud displays the real character of this Jewish salesperson, a man who has lost his heritage and ignored the cries for help of his own people.

In the final paragraphs of the story, the hints Malamud has been dropping fall into place. Edie Cohen realizes that although Schwartz told them he was fleeing from "Anti-Semeets," his death was the result of an encounter with anti-Semites, the Cohen family itself. Edie and Maurie, the more sensitive members of this family, recognize and regret their failings; Harry Cohen presumably will never again recognize the lessons of his faith, whether they are delivered by humans or by birds with human souls.

Don Richard Cox

THE JILTING OF GRANNY WEATHERALL

Author: Katherine Anne Porter (1890-1980)
Type of plot: Psychological
Time of plot: The early twentieth century
Locale: The American Southwest
First published: 1930

Principal characters:
GRANNY WEATHERALL
JOHN, her late husband
HAPSY, her deceased daughter

The Story

Stricken by a sudden illness, Granny Weatherall, an octogenarian, has been confined to bed. She is being examined by Dr. Harry, much to her annoyance. Denying there is anything wrong with her that requires a doctor's care, she dismisses him in the petulance of old age—"The brat ought to be in knee breeches"—only to hear him and Cornelia, her daughter with whom she now lives, whispering about her. Granny imagines herself giving Cornelia a good spanking.

Granny's mind wanders to things that needed to be done tomorrow—dusting, and straightening, and going through the box in the attic containing love letters from George, the fiancé who jilted her, and John, her long-deceased husband, and her letters to them. She does not want the children to know how silly she had been when she was young.

Granny thinks how clammy and unfamiliar death must feel, but she refuses to worry about it now. After all, her father lived to be 102 years old. She decides that she will live just to plague Cornelia a little more. Thoughts of rationalizing that she is not too old to be self-sufficient—she often thinks of moving back to her own house where there would be no one to remind her that she is old—are intertwined with memories of all the work she has done in her long life, the meals cooked, the clothes sewn, the gardens made. Especially vivid is her memory of herself as a young widow fencing in a hundred acres, digging the postholes herself. She wished the old days could be back, with the children young and everything still to be done.

Granny is overtaken by the memory of the innocent green day with the fresh breeze blowing, when she waited to marry George, who did not come. A whirl of dark smoke covered the bright day; for Granny, that was hell. For sixty years she has fought against remembering this central trauma of her life. "What does a woman do when she has put on the white veil and set out the white cake for a man and he doesn't come?"

In her growing confusion, Granny hallucinates about her dead daughter, Hapsy, holding a baby on her arm. It is as if the baby is Hapsy and Granny at the same time, before the image becomes gauzy and Hapsy says close in her mother's ear, "I thought you'd never come." Unable now to make herself understood to her children by her bedside, Granny mistakes Father Connolly's administering of extreme unction for tickling her feet and thinks, "My God, will you stop that nonsense? I'm a married woman." Granny realizes that death has come for her and she is not ready for it. Her affairs are not in order. She hopes to see Hapsy again but fears that she may not. She asks God for a sign, but there is none. Her last thought is of the cruel pain of George's rejection.

Themes and Meanings

"The Jilting of Granny Weatherall" is primarily a character study. By being privy to Granny's death, the reader can infer much about her life. The title describes the enormous hurt and humiliation that has secretly festered in her mind and heart for sixty years. Her great pride was devastated by her jilting; although she married a good man, raised a family, and managed a farm by herself after her husband's death, she never totally got over the shock and disappointment of George's rejection. The fact that she has saved George's letters suggests how much he continued to mean to her in her heart and how the pain of her jilting remained with her for sixty years.

Over the years, Granny was transformed from Ellen, a young bride with "the peaked Spanish comb in her hair and the painted fan" to the fiercely proud old woman, living with one of her daughters, whom the reader encounters on her deathbed. She has weathered all that fate has thrown at her: serious illness, perilous childbirth, traveling country roads in the winter when women had their babies, sitting up all night with "sick horses and sick negroes and sick children and hardly ever losing one."

Through perseverance and hard work, Granny has surmounted life's obstacles and endured into old age with children who love her. However, in her most secret self, there is the evergreen memory of George's rejection. She has not been able to share this deep hurt with her loved ones, and it has cut off a central and tender part of herself from all others. Katherine Anne Porter has drawn Granny's character with such clarity and compelling force that her life story becomes a kind of prototype for everyone's, regardless of age or circumstance. Personhood is sacred, and, once violated, the scars may remain for a lifetime. There is something ineffably poignant about Granny's wanting George to know that she had her husband and children like any other woman. The sanctity of the human heart and the existential loneliness of the human condition are the enduring themes of this story.

Style and Technique

"The Jilting of Granny Weatherall" was published soon after British novelist Virginia Woolf's *To the Lighthouse* (1927) and American novelist William Faulkner's *The Sound and the Fury* (1929). Following these innovators in the stream-of-consciousness technique, Porter employs multiple points of view, combining stream of consciousness and ironic detachment. Often in the same paragraph and sometimes even in the same sentence, the omniscient author devolves into Granny Weatherall. The effect of this innovative technique is often ironic and always realistic. By tightly controlling point of view, Porter enriches Granny's persona, making it easy for the reader to empathize with her. Empathy is further enhanced by the use of dialogue, which places the reader directly at the scene. The experience of reading this story is to enter Granny Weatherall's mind, to share in her memories, and to experience the pain of her rejection.

Porter's clear and simple diction and syntax contrast with the complex point of view. Simile and metaphor are the predominant rhetorical devices. They serve largely to render Granny's death experience in recognizable terms. Dr. Harry's hand is "a warm paw like a cushion on her forehead" and he "floated like a balloon around the foot of the bed." Granny "floated around in her skin," and when her eyes closed involuntarily, "it was like a dark curtain drawn around the bed." "Her eyelids wavered and let in streamers of blue-gray light like tissue paper over her eyes." Her hallucinatory vision of Hapsy with the baby "melted from within and turned flimsy as gray gauze and the baby was a gauzy shadow." As death approaches "she saw Dr. Harry with a rosy nimbus about him," and Cornelia's voice "staggered and bumped like a cart in a bad road." It "made short turns and tilted over and crashed." The earlier floating images are replaced by images of falling. "Her heart sank down and down, there was no bottom to death, she couldn't come to the end of it." As Granny "lay curled down within herself" she grew one with the surrounding darkness that "would curl around the light and swallow it up." The light from the bedside lamp "flickered and winked like an eye." The final sentence describes her death: "She stretched herself with a deep breath and blew out the light."

Robert G. Blake

JIM BAKER'S BLUEJAY YARN

Author: Mark Twain (Samuel Langhorne Clemens, 1835-1910)
Type of plot: Tall tale
Time of plot: About 1860
Locale: The California Mother Lode country
First published: 1879

Principal character:
JIM BAKER, a California hermit

The Story

"Jim Baker's Bluejay Yarn" was first published as chapter 3 of Mark Twain's travel narrative *A Tramp Abroad* (1880). In that version, the actual narrative is preceded by an introduction, which appears at the end of chapter 2, in which the narrator of *A Tramp Abroad* introduces Jim Baker as "a middle-aged, simple-hearted miner who had lived in a lonely corner of California among the woods and mountains a good many years, and had studied the ways of his only neighbors, the beasts and the birds, until he believed he could accurately translate any remark they made." Also in the introductory section, Jim Baker elaborates on his high opinion of jays, offering the opinion that they are "just as much a human as you be," and concluding that "a jay will lie, a jay will steal, a jay will deceive, a jay will betray; and four times out of five, a jay will go back on his solemnest promise." The narrator affirms that he knows this to be true because Jim Baker told him so himself, thus establishing his own naïveté and gullibility. This beginning establishes a "frame" for the story.

Some editors print the introductory material as part of "Jim Baker's Bluejay Yarn," although others include only the material from chapter 3 of *A Tramp Abroad* that is discussed below. Because the story materially benefits from establishing Jim Baker's character and his views on jays, it is best to read a complete version.

Jim Baker's "yarn" cannot be captured in a simple summary of events, because, as Twain pointed out in an essay entitled "How to Tell a Story," a "humorous story depends for its effect on the manner of the telling," rather than on its contents. Thus, the events of the story are unimpressive unless presented with the droll style of the master storyteller. Even when read aloud, the yarn falls flat unless it is artfully presented. Being such a master raconteur, Jim Baker must be "heard" as he elaborates this tale of an excessively ambitious bluejay whose reach far exceeded his grasp.

Baker begins in a matter-of-fact way by establishing his authority as an expert on bluejay behavior by setting the story at a time in the past "when I first begun to understand jay language correctly." Being the last remaining soul in the region, Baker no doubt gained his knowledge of jays by doing just what he describes in the story: watching bluejays from his front porch. In fact, he seems to have nothing else in particular to occupy his time, so on this Sunday morning, Baker says, "I was sitting out here in front of my cabin, with my cat, taking the sun, and looking at the blue hills, and listening to the leaves rustling so lonely in the trees, and thinking of the home away yonder in the states, that I hadn't heard from in thirteen years, when a bluejay lit on that house, with an acorn in his mouth, and says, 'Hello, I reckon I've struck something.'" In this way, Twain not only establishes the "authenticity" of the story but also subtly characterizes the narrator and his way of life.

As Baker watches, the jay becomes intrigued by a knothole he has discovered in the roof of the abandoned cabin on which he is perched. After an elaborate examination to satisfy himself that it is indeed a hole that he has discovered, the jay drops an acorn into the opening and awaits the sound of it hitting bottom. When he hears nothing after a proper interval, he seems first curious, then surprised, and finally indignant. Baker is able to infer this because, as he told the reader at the outset, he understands jay language. In this context, the elaborate description given of the jay's behavior is Baker's way of describing the bird's language. "He cocked his head to one side, shut one eye and put the other one to the hole, like a 'possum looking down a jug; then he glanced up with his bright eyes, gave a wink or two with his wings—which signifies gratification, you understand—and says, 'It looks like a hole, it's located like a hole—blamed if I don't believe it is a hole.'" For the remainder of the yarn, Baker alternates between elaborate descriptions of bluejay behavior and interpretations of the meaning of the activity.

The first acorn having been lost in the recesses of the hole, the jay quickly fetches another, only to drop it in with the same results as the first. He tries to drop acorns, then quickly peep in the hole to see where they fall, but this technique, too, is unsuccessful. After a marvelous bout of cursing, he finally concludes that this is a hole of a kind that is new in his experience, but his frustration only strengthens his resolve. "Well," he says, "you're a long hole, and a deep hole, and a mighty singular hole altogether—but I've started to fill you, and I'm d——d if I don't fill you, if it takes a hundred years!"

The jay works himself into a frenzy dropping acorns into the hole, but again with no noticeable results. This time his cursing attracts another jay, and the two hold a noisy conference on the ridgepole. The second jay, unable to make any more sense of the mysterious hole than the first, "called in more jays; then more and more, till pretty soon this whole region 'peared to have a blue flush about it." All the jays offer their opinions, leading to a cacophony of disputation. This continues until one old jay eventually finds his way through the open door of the house and finds all the acorns scattered over the floor.

The other jays' curiosity and interest now turns to derision, and they join in laughing at their silly companion. Baker finishes his story by telling the reader that "they roosted around here on the housetop and the trees for an hour, and guffawed over that thing like human beings," then concludes in defense of these silly creatures, "it ain't no use to tell me a bluejay hasn't got a sense of humor, because I know better. And memory, too. They brought jays here from all over the United States to look down that hole, every summer for three years." Other birds came also, and all saw the humor except an owl from Nova Scotia who had come west to visit "the Yo Semite" and stopped by on his way home. "He said he couldn't see anything funny in it. But then he was a good deal disappointed about Yo Semite, too."

Themes and Meanings

At the beginning of *The Adventures of Huckleberry Finn* (1884), Twain threatens to shoot anyone looking for a moral in his book. He would probably say much the same about a search for themes and meanings in "Jim Baker's Bluejay Yarn." Unlike the animal fables of Aesop, Jean de La Fontaine, or Joel Chandler Harris, Twain's animal tales are not classic fables meant to illustrate some moral point. Though the bluejays are described in very human terms, and though their behavior parallels that of human beings, one should not impose some heavy moral implication on the story. For Twain, this type of narrative was an art form more closely related to performance than to serious literature. Its humor is its point, and that humor lies more in the style of telling the tale than in the material itself.

Style and Technique

In "How to Tell a Story," Twain observes that "the humorous story is strictly a work of art—high and delicate art—and only an artist can tell it; but no art is necessary in telling the comic and witty story; anybody can do it. The art of telling a humorous story—understand, I mean by word of mouth, not print—was created in America, and has remained at home." The distinction Twain makes between comic and witty stories—that is, stories depending on a "punch line" or clever play on words—and the "humorous story" is an important one for appreciating the artistry of "Jim Baker's Bluejay Yarn," as well as for understanding the high value Twain placed on humor as an indigenous American art form.

The humorous story depends for its effect almost entirely on the artistry of a master storyteller. Foremost among the techniques necessary to tell such a story effectively is the characterization of a narrative voice appropriate to the material. Such stories, Twain says, are "told gravely; the teller does his best to conceal the fact that he even dimly suspects that there is anything funny about it." Properly told, the humorous story results in "a performance which is thoroughly charming and delicious. This is art—and fine and beautiful, and only a master can encompass it."

Twain was himself such a master storyteller, as he demonstrated in his career as a lecturer. From his work on the stage, as well as from firsthand contact with other storytellers, he mastered not only the art of performing stories but also the art of writing them down as published tales. Few writers have recorded the oral tradition on the page as well as Twain did in such pieces as "Jim Baker's Bluejay Yarn." Reading the story tends to be anticlimactic unless one can, either aloud or in the imagination, read it so that Jim Baker's voice is heard. In the hands of a fine performer, this simple tale of some silly bluejays can still produce the laughter that it did when Twain himself told it to his audiences.

William E. Grant

JOHN FORD'S *'TIS PITY SHE'S A WHORE*

Author: Angela Carter (1940-1992)
Type of plot: Metafiction
Time of plot: The late nineteenth century
Locale: The prairie somewhere in the American Midwest
First published: 1988

Principal characters:
JOHNNY, a rancher's son
ANNIE-BELLE, his sister
THE MINISTER'S SON, who marries Annie-Belle

The Story

This story imagines what twentieth century film director John Ford, known for his Westerns, would have done if he had made a film adaptation of Jacobean playwright John Ford's *'Tis Pity She's a Whore* (1629?-1633).

An unnamed rancher sets up home in a remote region of the American prairie. After bearing two children—a boy named Johnny and a girl named Annie-Belle—his wife dies. The children's only human contact, apart from their taciturn and overworked father, is the minister of the nearest town, who drives out in a buggy to collect them every Sunday so that they may attend church. Isolated in a seemingly infinite plain, beneath the vast sky whose pressure (the storyteller asserts) crushed their mother to death, Johnny and Annie-Belle enter into an incestuous relationship. Johnny wants to run away to the West, but Annie-Belle is reluctant to desert their father. When the minister's son—unnamed in the text—begins to court her, she rejects him, but when she becomes pregnant it becomes politic for her to marry.

Following the wedding, the minister's wife discovers that Annie-Belle is pregnant and is enraged. Annie-Belle initially blames a passing stranger but eventually confesses the truth to her husband. The minister and his wife decide that the couple must go west to avoid the shame of local gossip, but when the couple goes to the nearest railroad station to make their departure, Johnny follows them, determined that if he cannot have Annie-Belle, no one else will. The minister's son is killed while trying, unsuccessfully, to shield his wife from Johnny's bullets. Johnny then kills himself.

Themes and Meanings

The story draws a careful comparison between a significant genre of American films and early seventeenth century English drama by envisaging what the famous director John Ford, who created a series of classic Westerns from *Stagecoach* (1939) to *Cheyenne Autumn* (1964), might have made of the most famous work by the English playwright John Ford, *'Tis Pity She's a Whore*. The playwright Ford was a key contributor to Jacobean tragedy, a melodramatic form of tragedy that flourished after the death of William Shakespeare in 1616. Although James I died in 1625, Jacobean tragedy continued to be produced—or at least published—during the reign of Charles I. Carter's supposition is fanciful, but by no means absurd. Although director John Ford never adapted plots in this fashion, other directors of Westerns did. Director William Wellman's 1948 *Yellow Sky* transfigured Shakespeare's *The Tempest: Or, The Enchanted Island* (1674) long before John Sturges created *The Magnificent Seven* (1960) using Japanese director Akira Kurosawa's *The Seven Samurai* (1954). Although such adaptations encourage the notion that certain plot forms express universal features of human existence, the emphasis of Carter's story is on the crucial differences that would inevitably arise out of the transplantation of the story's setting from the stage version of Italy that many seventeenth century English dramatists portrayed as a society of hot-blooded vendetta-pursuers to the American Midwest mythologized by filmmakers as a land of bold pioneers and gunslingers.

Although the Hollywood censors would not readily have condoned the use of incest as the pivot of a film plot during Ford's heyday, there remains a sense in which the plot of *'Tis Pity She's a Whore* is much more convincing in the mythical midwestern setting than the mythical Italian setting. The story's "punch line" is a laconic footnote in which Carter observes that although the New World John Ford could not copy the Old World John Ford's final dramatic flourish—when Giovanni makes his last entrance with Annabella's heart impaled on his dagger—such events were not entirely alien to the American heartland.

There is no logical reason why Johnny could not have killed Annie-Belle with a knife, but he would never have done so in the climax of an American Western film because the primary totemic object of the Western was the handgun—specifically the Colt revolver, or six-gun. Nor is there any logical reason why John Ford should not have remade a Jacobean tragedy as a Western, although he would never actually have done so because the Western is an essentially heroic genre and Jacobean tragedy has no heroes. One of Carter's story's underlying themes is, however, the progressive loss of innocence that affected Western films as their makers and consumers became more aware of the dark historical underside of the conquest of the West.

Director John Ford himself began the demolition of Western mythology in *The Man Who Shot Liberty Valance* (1962)—in which actor James Stewart fails miserably to dispatch Lee Marvin's villain with his six-gun, leaving John Wayne to complete the task surreptitiously with a Winchester rifle—but did not carry it much further. He left it to the Italian director Sergio Leone to continue the process of reinterpretation in *A Fistful of Dollars* (1964) and its sequels, and it was Sam Peckinpah who reimported Leone's cynicism to the United States in *The Wild Bunch* (1969). It is significant, however, that neither Leone nor Peckinpah thought it necessary or desirable to forsake climactic shootouts between fate-appointed heroes and doomed villains.

Carter's imaginary Western is by no means unique in substituting melancholy tragedy for morally problematic quasi-gladiatorial combat—Ford had produced a tragedy of sorts in *The Searchers* (1956)—but there remains something distinctly English, if not narrowly Jacobean, about its representation of violence as a wholly futile passion. Johnny's suicide, which arguably displays the only function for which handguns are uniquely convenient, is far too mundane to figure as the ending of an authentic Western; for this reason, the care lavished by Carter's narrative voice on the labor of making the Western setting seem highly appropriate eventually works to challenge the most fundamental assumptions of the Western genre.

Style and Technique

Carter's text intersperses expository narrative with excerpts from the hypothetical shooting script with which the director might be working. Occasional quotations from the script of the original play are inserted for comparative purposes. The narrative sections are lightly spiced with discreet references to the titles of classic Westerns, including—in addition to such Ford vehicles as *She Wore a Yellow Ribbon* (1949)—the 1970's TV series *The Little House on the Prairie*, exemplary of a less violent subspecies of Western, whose scenario is reproduced and subverted in the story. The fact that so many characters remain unnamed encourages the reader to think of the story as an example of a capacious set of texts rather than a self-enclosed and self-sufficient entity.

The narrative passages include a good deal of judicious authorial commentary on both versions of the story, drawing comparisons between them, but their main focus is on the way in which the story might be visualized and supported by incidental movement. Carter puts a very heavy emphasis on the landscape of the scenario, crediting it with a powerful causative force, as when she holds the pressure of the sky responsible for the death of the rancher's wife. This reflects the fact that in all the great Western films—and Ford's in particular—the landscape is a key feature, described so lovingly by the panoramic vision of the camera that it often seems overwhelming.

Although Westerns invariably feature villains who can be symbolically slain in the climactic duel, there is a sense in which the heroes' real antagonist is the terrain. Indeed, in some ways, the real heroes of Westerns are not the good gunmen whose destiny it is to slay the evil gunmen but the people on whose behalf they are acting: the ranchers and farmers who are taming the wild prairie, making it into American soil, and the ministers and schoolteachers who are shaping and fostering the American dream. Carter's narrative representation of a Western script, elaborately furnished with commentary, is by no means entirely ironic; it captures and celebrates the essence of the real artistic triumph of the film genre as well as revealing the dry rot corroding its illusions from within.

There is an authentic and sincere lyricism in Carter's descriptions, not only in their references to American geography—which include a mock-rhapsodic interpretation of the seductive shape assumed by the entire double-continent in the Mercator projection—but also in their cameos of everyday life, as when Annie-Belle washes her hair or when the minister's wife gives noisy vent to her anger while carrying out her domestic chores. Without such honest appreciation of the aesthetic virtues of the Western, the transformation of the Jacobean tragedy could not be nearly so effective or so ultimately revealing.

Brian Stableford

JOHN NAPPER SAILING THROUGH THE UNIVERSE

Author: John Gardner (1933-1982)
Type of plot: Psychological
Time of plot: The late 1960's and early 1970's
Locale: London, Paris, and the United States
First published: 1974

> Principal characters:
> JOHN NAPPER, the protagonist, a painter
> THE NARRATOR, a writer
> JOAN, the narrator's wife, a composer
> LUCY, the narrator's eight-year-old daughter

The Story

The narrator, a writer who teaches in a rural American university, is driven home from a party one night by his wife, Joan. Feeling old and perceiving death all around him, and goaded by his wife's nostalgia for John Napper, a successful painter they once knew, the narrator tells the story of his and his family's experience of the painter John Napper.

The narrator became acquainted with Napper when the latter served for a time as artist-in-residence at the narrator's university. John Napper had a commanding physical presence despite his old age: bohemian, big, and energetic. His enthusiasm for everything—including Irish music, which he sang with zest, accompanying himself on a guitar—was unflagging. No intellectual debate fazed him: To both sides he would say, "Exactly" or "Marvelous" (his favorite words), impartially, as it were. For example, the narrator believes that Welsh music is better than Irish, and Napper would find his choice "marvelous," while at the same time expressing—too jovially to be gainsaid— his distaste for Welsh music and his admiration for Irish music.

After Napper returns to Paris, the narrator's wife finds herself unable to compose music and wants to visit Napper and his wife Pauline, a mosaic artist. The narrator, who always wears a black hat and has a cynical outlook on the world, and is both repelled and attracted by Napper's optimism, as well as passionately hostile to any kind of fakery, manages to get a grant that finances his family's visit to the Nappers.

They find a young couple staying in the Nappers' Paris studio. The young man is an American, a cartoonist, and he shows the narrator and his wife some of John Napper's old paintings, which he found under the bed. The paintings are violent and gloomy, in surprising contrast to the paintings of Napper's old age, which invariably feature flowers. Learning that the Nappers are staying in London, the narrator and his family visit the Nappers in their apartment there.

When confronted by the information that the narrator has seen his old paintings in Paris, John Napper shows him a selection of similar paintings, mentioning that some of his works have been lost along the way. They are all pessimistic and foreboding. With his typical energy he judges his artistic past "Amazing!"—as though it were something from which he had miraculously escaped. At this point, the narrator's daughter Lucy asks Napper to do her portrait for seven cents, and Napper agrees. The narrator's son Joel is jealous of his sister because of this, so Napper promises to show him the armor in the Wallace Collection in London.

After he does this, Napper sketches Lucy in the courtyard of the building. That night in the pub in the narrator's hotel, Napper and the narrator drink beer and sing for the Irish clientele. The narrator sings gloomy Welsh songs and plays his banjo; Napper plays his guitar and sings sentimental Irish songs, about which the audience is enthusiastic.

The narrator has been writing an epic poem about the Greek mythic hero Jason, and he shows it to Napper in his studio. They discuss epics for a while, with Napper focusing on the destruction often featured in epics. They are interrupted by a girl—a former student of Napper in Paris—and before the narrator can read her any of his epic, the couple staying in Napper's Paris studio appear, thus effectively cutting off the narrator's performance.

The next day, the narrator does manage to read some of his epic to Napper. Napper continues to paint after this and talks about music and painting, which excites the narrator more than the Scotch he has been drinking. (The narrator drinks a considerable amount of Scotch in the story; Napper, hardly anything.) Napper has been working on his painting of Lucy, and the narrator, looking at a large seascape by Napper on the wall, is reminded of its similarity to Joseph Turner's work and of Napper once telling him that Turner led a double life as a sailor and a miserly-seeming philanthropist, with a separate wife for each role. Napper, while he and the narrator are still in the studio that evening, insists that artists are piggish, especially when they are young (that is, that they are unscrupulous in their passions), and that he is glad to be much less so now that he is old. The narrator observes a recent painting of Napper's wife Pauline. Among a profusion of light and flowers, Pauline has a funereal look, and at the edges of the painting the gaiety of its tone is vaguely sinister. Lucy's painting is also gay, but there is a sly look in her eyes, whereas Pauline's face has a hieratic quality. Quite drunk by now, the narrator understands that Napper, in searching for his own vision of light in things as they are, found darkness instead and, rather than yield to it, decided to invent the world itself in his paintings—a world of light and gaiety.

Napper and his wife accompany the narrator to a restaurant where the narrator's wife, Joan, has been waiting for her husband to arrive. She has already eaten by the time they get there, and she is angry. Napper soothes her with flattery and a story, after which the narrator gets into a fistfight with (ironically) a Welshman over Samuel Beckett, a writer famous for his metaphysical gloom. Joan runs out, followed by Pauline, and the narrator and Napper end up in a taxi together. Napper, with his usual paradoxical enthusiasm, praises the narrator's violent stupidity and his own insane optimism.

Themes and Meanings

At the heart of this story is the conflict between optimism and pessimism. How does one face a world that seems to be ruled by chaos in the end? Both John Napper and the narrator see this chaos. Napper had hoped to find a positive meaning in the world when he was young, but all he saw in his search was the destruction in the world and the violence of the search itself, both of which he embodied in his paintings. The narrator, unlike Napper, is still searching, and so far he has not gotten beyond the signs of destruction, his vision of which he expresses through his taste for gloomy things and his destructive behavior—his drinking, for example, and the songs he sings about tragedy, as well as the hostile tricks he plays on the hypocrite who replaces Napper at the university and the fight he gets into at the end of the story. The narrator, in fact, is at the level that Napper was when he was young.

To be sure, the narrator is a pessimist, and John Napper is an optimist. It is more complex than that, however, for the narrator is a pessimist who yearns to be an optimist, while Napper is an optimist who refuses to give in to his essential pessimism. He has decided that if chaos informs the world, he will re-create the world from scratch, as it were, in his art. He will make the world a mask that hides the face of chaos. The irony here, as the narrator sees, is that some of the chaos comes through the mask in innuendos, and it is this that gives his paintings an air of mystery and makes them unique. If there is something unreal, even fake, about Napper's optimism, though, the narrator is still attracted to it. Napper's passionate enthusiasm, including its ragged edges, amounts to an inspiration for the narrator and his wife, who find life boring and depressing without him near. They are able to overcome their blocks and create when they visit Napper in London—the narrator continuing an epic of search and his wife composing music for the flute.

Finally, the story is about vision and how it is acquired. All the adult characters in the story are artists, to whom vision is essential. The artist, the story says, uses art to find a vision of the world's meaning and record what he sees along the way. Napper arrives at a vision that belongs only to him, and it suggests that the artist is like God creating the world to suit his own desires, as well as his knowledge of the conflict between his personal will and the blind and sinister energy governing phenomena. The narrator, on the other hand, creates an art that dramatizes the search for a positive vision—indeed creates the story "John Napper Sailing Through the Universe," which shows his vision of all the phases of the artist's vision itself.

Style and Technique

Because vision is so important to the story, and because the protagonist is a painter, imagery is John Gardner's chief tool in projecting the story's meaning. Light and darkness figure prominently throughout. Both are used to show the two sides of John Napper's vision. Darkness predominates in his early paintings, emphasizing pessimism and the violence of Napper's search for order and the violence in the world, especially the human world. Light predominates in his later paintings, underscoring the willfulness of his optimism and enthusiasm. Light is also embedded in the image of

Napper's hair, which is wild and white and often mentioned, and is meant to suggest a light in the darkness, optimism against a background of pessimism. Light is further inferred in the narrator's epic poem, which is about the mythic hero Jason; the golden fleece he searches for corresponds to the light of a happy vision for which the narrator is searching.

There are other images in the story that belong to the contrast between light and dark, such as the bright flowers that are a staple of Napper's paintings, the black hat that the narrator wears everywhere, the dark house and landscape readers see him in at the beginning, and the tomblike hotel he is staying in at the end.

Besides its use in dramatizing the meaning of the story, imagery is a mainstay of characterization in it. It is often through imagery that the characters are revealed, with Napper's hair, bright eyes, untidy clothes, and gaily sinister paintings pointing to his mind and personality, and the narrator's hat and Scotch pointing to his.

Finally, it should be pointed out that this story is autobiographical to an unusual degree. The narrator is clearly Gardner himself, at work on the book that eventually became *Jason and Medeia* (1973). Gardner's first wife was named Joan; their children appear in the story as well. The title character, the painter John Napper, illustrated Gardner's novel *The Sunlight Dialogues* (1972). Here, as in other stories in the collection in which "John Napper Sailing Through the Universe" appeared, *The King's Indian* (1974), Gardner is playing with the conventions of fiction, testing them, experimenting with them. Only a reader with an intimate knowledge of Gardner's life—and John Napper's life—could say with authority where the autobiography stops and the "fiction" begins.

Mark McCloskey

JOHNNY PANIC AND THE BIBLE OF DREAMS

Author: Sylvia Plath (1932-1963)
Type of plot: Psychological
Time of plot: The late 1950's or early 1960's
Locale: Roxbury, Massachusetts
First published: 1968

Principal characters:
THE NARRATOR, a young woman working in a city hospital's psychological clinic
JOHNNY PANIC, her imaginary god
MISS TAYLOR, her supervisor
MISS MILLERAVAGE, an insensitive nurse
THE CLINIC DIRECTOR, a mysterious figure

The Story

The narrator, a young assistant in a large metropolitan hospital's psychology clinic, obsessively transcribes patients' dreams, which she memorizes from their hospital records, into a book that she calls her bible of dreams. In her book, Johnny Panic is the god. In order to read more of the patients' dreams, she hides in the women's room until she thinks that everyone has left the office. (Practical difficulties and fears keep her from sneaking the records home.) When she returns to the office and begins to read the medical records, she is caught by the clinic director. He ushers her to another floor in the hospital, where Miss Milleravage (the narrator cannot remember the name exactly) gleefully chases her, seizes her dream notebook, and overpowers her. With a bedside "Tch, tch," Miss Milleravage and the director chide her for believing in Johnny Panic. The narrator realizes that she is about to be given electroshock treatment. She is stunned with fear but trusts Johnny Panic not to forget his own.

The young woman sees herself as a connoisseur of dreams, which she reads, memorizes, and compiles from medical records, savoring them and playing them over in her mind. She also imagines what is in the dreams of patients whose records she does not see. She identifies the patients by their real or imagined dreams, rather than by their names.

The narrator also has her own dream—one of complete terror, in which she is suspended over a half-transparent lake that is so large she cannot even see its shores. Gigantic dragons swim on the bottom of this lake; hideous things float to its surface: swarms of snakes, human embryos, dead bodies, monsters in human form, the cutting and crushing detritus of civilization (knives, paper cutters, pistons, nutcrackers, and automobile grilles), and finally a human face rising up. The frightfulness of this dream makes her world shrink, with the sun shriveling to the size of an orange, only chillier. The narrator knows that she has something in common with the patients; both her dreams and the patients' are spun by Johnny Panic; her compilation is Johnny Panic's bible.

The story is full of gruesome and fearful accounts of the frailty of the human body and psyche. Lumbar punctures, skin problems, tumors, nerve disorders, medical students who play catch with the livers of cadavers, and the scene of the impending electroshock are among the details that contribute to the impression that the modern hospital is, in its own hygienic and scientific way, as much a chamber of horrors as its medieval counterpart. At the moment that the narrator thinks that she is most lost, facing the obliteration of her personality and memory through electroshock, Johnny Panic's face appears in a nimbus of arc lights. The story accumulates details of horror and revulsion until finally the face of the god of fear is revealed.

Themes and Meanings

Sylvia Plath's more evident theme in this story is that there is a god of fear. Moreover, there are martyrs to the religion of fear—the psychiatric clinic patients. The narrator is an impostor who pretends to be on the side of the doctors and nurses—the religion's persecutors—but she is in fact one of the doomed members of Johnny Panic's flock. When the director catches her reading from her book of dreams, she asks herself, implicitly referring to her subversive beliefs: "What does he know?" Her answer is "everything." The director does, in fact, seem to know everything; he is not surprised to find the narrator in the darkened office. Physically, he is "gray pinstripe" grotesque, with bad breath, brown shoes, a potbelly, and thick eyeglasses. Seemingly aware of everything about the narrator's mental life, he effortlessly exerts complete command over her. His voice comes "from the cloudy regions above" the narrator's head. He lifts her up out of her chair and guides her to her fate on the "indeterminate floor" without her resisting or thinking of resisting. By contrast, Miss Milleravage must use physical force and the help of two of "Johnny Panic's top priests," the big men in white shirts.

Readers who compare their own dreams and fears with those of the story's characters may feel some relief at thinking that they are psychologically stronger than the narrator. This response may be considered a weakness of the story; readers may not identify enough with the narrator to make the use of the first person entirely effective. On the other hand, readers are obliged to acknowledge that the story effectively conveys the currents of otherness, menace, and horror that flow, mostly denied or unacknowledged, through human life. The narrator is sensitive to what most people choose to ignore.

Style and Technique

The story's use of a first-person narrator may be a weakness, because the narrator is not necessarily easy to identify with. The story's strongest, most effective technique is its use of detail, specifically the overwhelming accretion of the grotesque and the frightening, such as a woman whose tongue has swollen to hideous proportions, "the dirty yellow-soled bare feet" of patients lying on their sides during lumbar punctures, a story about the bombing of London that Miss Milleravage punctuates with a smile, the soulless and depressing objects of the office, the patient who is pathologically afraid of dirt and contamination, the bare light bulbs in their wire "cages," and the neat cot where the narrator is to be held down and have electricity run through her brain.

Another effective and daring technical accomplishment of the story is its shift from ostensible realism to ostensible madness. The story begins as the realistic account of a high-strung but apparently normal young woman who has a secret hobby. She works in an office, where she happens to be fascinated with the dreams that are recorded in the medical record books. She eats lunch and reflects on the character of the people with whom she works.

Early in the story, it is daytime in a normal, recognizable world. Then the narrator waits for night to fall in the dark of the rest room, and a world of gothic horror replaces the sane one. In this other world, Johnny Panic rules people's lives and the hospital is full of horrors. Although the empty and dark office is creepy, the narrator reflects that "all's right with the world." Strange drafts and unexpected shafts of light crisscross the office. The director, godlike and grossly human, makes his appearance.

In the second half of the story, the narrator goes mad; she accepts, or creates in her madness, the hospital's night world. In the sane, normal world, hospital directors are not omniscient inquisitors (however much they may wish to be), and young clerks caught doing something suspicious are not given shock treatment. In this other world, however, the hospital director finds the narrator because—being omniscient—he knows that she is there, and that her being there after hours expresses her faith in Johnny Panic. He has been waiting for her overt declaration.

In the first part of the story, the central figure among the narrator's coworkers is Miss Taylor, who keeps the office organized and who knows where every slip of paper is. A character type with whom readers may be familiar, Miss Taylor is reassuring; she verges on being comic. Miss Milleravage and the director are definitely not reassuring and familiar personality types; they dominate the second half of the story. In the first part, Johnny Panic is a metaphor; in the second part, he is real. Panic either warps the mind of the narrator or focuses it. Whichever is the case, the first-person narration follows along naturally. This effect could not be achieved except in the first person, which is perhaps the best reason for its use in the story.

Eric Howard

THE JOLLY CORNER

Author: Henry James (1843-1916)
Type of plot: Psychological
Time of plot: The late nineteenth or early twentieth century
Locale: New York City
First published: 1908

Principal characters:
SPENCER BRYDON, the protagonist, an owner of property in New
    York City who has lived abroad for many years
ALICE STAVERTON, his old friend
MRS. MULDOON, his housekeeper

The Story

After an absence of thirty-three years, Spencer Brydon returns from abroad to New York City. He makes this dramatic move in order to oversee improvements to his property, which consists of two houses that have been the source of his financial independence throughout his life. One is in the process of being converted into apartments, while the other, the "jolly corner" of the title, is the house in which Brydon grew up and which he therefore is loathe to alter in any way.

In the course of conversations with Miss Staverton, Brydon reflects on what sort of person he might have become had he not chosen to tramp about the world for most of his adult life and had instead stayed in his native United States. Miss Staverton has her views, which do not entirely coincide with those of Brydon. It transpires that Brydon harbors a desire to confront what he terms his "alter ego," the self he might have been. Miss Staverton reveals that, somewhat incomprehensibly, she has already seen this other self—in her dreams. She, however, declines to disclose what she has seen.

Brydon is in the habit of coming to the jolly corner in the evenings after he has dined out and before retiring to the hotel where he lodges (the house itself remaining empty for the moment). In the course of his nocturnal prowlings about the premises, he hopes to encounter his alter ego, who, in Brydon's view of things, haunts the house as a ghost. While stalking the creature, Brydon one night discovers that he himself has been turned into the prey, that the ghost is following him.

The climax to the tale occurs one evening when Brydon comes once more to the house, wanders about more or less as usual, but discovers in retracing his steps that one door, which he believed he had left open, has been mysteriously closed, and another that had been closed has been opened. As Brydon retreats carefully down the staircase toward the front door and escape from the pursuing specter, he pauses on the final landing, only to become aware of a vague shape in his view. The shape assumes human form, a man with a monocle, dressed in evening clothes, whose face is hidden by white-gloved hands with two of the fingers missing. As the ghost drops his hands, revealing his face, Brydon is shocked to recognize someone or something totally other than himself—a ghost who is not, so far as Brydon can discern, his other self at all. As the ghost aggressively advances, Brydon retreats and finally faints away at the bottom of the staircase. He awakes to discover the face of Miss Staverton, who had dreamed of Brydon's confrontation and had been thus prompted to come to the jolly corner to save him. Brydon protests that the ghost was not his other self, a view that Miss Staverton reinforces with "And he isn't—no, he isn't—you!" at the tale's close.

Themes and Meanings

As the comparative brevity of the incidents indicates, the interest of "The Jolly Corner" lies primarily elsewhere than in the structure of its plot. As is not uncommon in the later Henry James, both in the novels and in the tales, the amount of incident is severely circumscribed, while the space given to reflection and elaboration on the inner states of the characters (here only one character, Spencer Brydon) is correspondingly expanded to such an extent that the story is virtually consumed by this psychological interest. If one compares "The Jolly Corner" with, for example, the earlier *The Turn of the Screw* (1898), surely James's most famous ghost story, one sees immediately how comparatively slender is the thread of the plot in the later story. All the interest and all the importance in this tale reside in its disclosure of Brydon's thoughts, his fears and anxieties, his inability to confront the ghost of his former, or other, self.

The two major symbolic figures in the story are the house—Brydon's "jolly corner"—and the ghost. Both are described in some detail, and it is in the intricacy of their symbolic resonance that the key to this story lies. The house is of several stories and contains many rooms, each of which possesses a door. The psychoanalytic dimension of this feature is surely not inapposite (regardless of whether James knew about psychoanalysis proper—and there is some evidence to indicate that he did). Entering a closed room, according to psychoanalysis, symbolizes unlocking previously suppressed memories of one's mental life. The fact that James himself, in one of his autobiographical volumes written not long after "The Jolly Corner," recounts a dream in which he recovers the world of his youth by passing through a locked door suggests that he was perfectly aware of the psychic implications of this aspect of his story. Brydon's search for his other self, what he might have been had he remained in the United States and pursued, as he likely would have done, a career in business, is a search into previously unexplored corners of his own mind and self.

The other major symbol is simply that self that Brydon does finally confront near the end of the tale—despite the fact that he stubbornly refuses to recognize himself in the visage of the ghost. The figure's opulent dress (white gloves, evening clothes, monocle—all indicate his wealth, the fact that, as Brydon observes to Miss Staverton; this figure is a millionaire), along with his damaged extremity, does not at first put Brydon off. He has already observed that by abandoning New York City, he blighted or stunted the proper development of his other self. However, when the specter lowers his hands to reveal his face, Brydon not only is appalled at the sight (the details of what he sees are never given) but also steadfastly refuses to acknowledge the ghost's identity with himself. It is not he, but, as the story pointedly puts it, "a stranger." This refusal to recognize the other, to admit that what one might have been (or indeed, in strict psychoanalytic terms, what one invariably is), constitutes a classic example of repression, a symptomatic defense of the integrity of the self against the threat of its dissolution, the alternative being classic schizophrenia, the splitting of the self into two (and possibly more) warring and irreconcilable parts. James's choice of an ending reasserting the mental health and wholeness of his hero (in contrast to the rather different handling of this motif by his friend Robert Louis Stevenson in *The Strange Case of Dr. Jekyll and Mr. Hyde*, 1886) signifies what has often been noted as characteristic of his writing and his project as a man: the necessity for some level of repression and control over the darker impulses of the psyche if human society is to continue to function, possibly even to prosper. James's faith in the power of the imagination to maintain its balance in the face of threatening influences and disruptive forces is nowhere more apparent than in Brydon's shutting out of the ghost he cannot recognize as himself if he is to remain who he is.

Style and Technique

The other notable feature of this, one of James's last completed stories, is its characteristic density of syntax. "The Jolly Corner" provides an excellent example of that "late style" that has captivated James's admirers and infuriated his critics. Several explanations have been offered for this gradual shift in James's stylistic practice toward greater and greater intricacy and attenuation. (One of the least convincing is Leon Edel's assertion that this shift was caused by James's change from composing in longhand to dictating to a secretary.) Whatever the reasons for the markedly increased difficulty of James's writings from the turn of the century onward, one thing is indisputable: The attenuation of direct statement, the endless qualification and hedging around a point, serves to reinforce one's sense of the tentative and uncertain quality in the thinking of James's characters.

The whole point about Spencer Brydon is that by leaving the United States he has abandoned that life of active and vigorous intervention in the world (figured here in the possibility that he would have pursued a career in business) in order to live more or less freely (if narrowly) and unencumbered by the necessity to act directly or decisively. James's stylistic practice thus motivates and effectively realizes a character whose *raison d'être* is precisely not to be decisive, powerful, or direct. Brydon's incapacity to decide who he is or might have been, his tentativeness in confronting his alter ego (despite his manifest desire to meet this creature) is in part the result of the very circumlocutions, the syntactic irresolution of James's style. Whatever may have been the motivation of James's later style, it would seem that here at least the fit between thematic focus and linguistic practice is most intimate.

Michael Sprinker

JORDAN'S END

Author: Ellen Glasgow (1873-1945)
Type of plot: Ghost story
Time of plot: The 1890's
Locale: Virginia
First published: 1923

> *Principal characters:*
> THE NARRATOR, a young doctor, called to Jordan's End to
>   examine the master of the house
> JUDITH YARDLY JORDAN, the wife of Alan Jordan, mistress of
>   Jordan's End
> FATHER PETERKIN, a gnarled old man who helps his son
>   sharecrop land on Jordan's End

The Story

As the story opens, the narrator, a young doctor beginning practice in an isolated section of Virginia near the turn of the century, is on his way to Jordan's End, a country estate at some remove from a small town. He has been sent for to examine Alan Jordan, the owner of the place. As he goes along in his horse and buggy, he encounters a fork in the road: One branch of its gives indications of having been well traveled; the other, deeply rutted but covered with grass and overhanging leaves, appears to have been little used. As he ponders which road to take, a voice from the bushes by the side of the main trail advises him to take the well-traveled road if he is going to the country store. Emerging from the woods, a stooped old man appears in the road, and when the doctor inquires the way to Jordan's End, the fellow points to the less used trail and says that if the doctor is going in that direction he would like to ride along.

As the two travel the road to Jordan's End, Father Peterkin, in response to the young doctor's questions, provides information about the ill fortune that has beset the master and mistress of the place. It appears that ever since the Civil War the fortunes of the Jordan family have been in severe decline. Now, according to Father Peterkin, young Alan Jordan has been taken ill and the management of the place is in the hands of his wife, Judith, the mother of their nine-year-old boy. Aside from a few black field hands, the only other personages at Jordan's End are three old women related to Alan by blood or marriage.

When the doctor arrives at the Jordan place, he is seized by a kind of foreboding, a feeling that is intensified by the appearance of the house itself—a crumbling Georgian manor house, with rotting eaves and windows without panes. Everywhere there is evidence of deterioration, of decline. His conversation with Father Peterkin provided him with information about the history of insanity among the male members of the Jordan family, but nevertheless he is unprepared for the sight of this relic.

Receiving no answer to his knock on the main door of the house, he proceeds toward the rear and encounters there Judith Jordan, the mistress of Jordan's End. He is very much taken by her haunting beauty. She welcomes him and acquaints him briefly with the recent illness affecting her husband. Alan Jordan is confined in an upstairs room of the house and is being watched over by two of the few remaining field hands. Implicit in her depiction of the trouble afflicting the master of the house is that he has lost his mind and must be watched constantly. The doctor accompanies her to the room, where Alan Jordan sits aimlessly in a chair, flanked by the two servants, playing listlessly with the fringe of a plaid shawl that has been draped around his shoulders. At a glance, the doctor sees that Jordan is "helplessly lost in the wilderness of the insane."

Informed that a famous alienist, Dr. Carstairs, is coming from Baltimore the next day to examine Jordan, the young doctor provides an opiate for use in sedating the patient should he become violent. He leaves Jordan's End, indicating to Judith Jordan that he will come again after Dr. Carstairs has made his visit.

On the following day, he encounters the doctor in the town as the celebrated alienist is about to board the train. In a brief conversation, he learns that Jordan's situation is hopeless; Jordan will not recover his faculties. Later that day, an old black man from Jordan's End comes to town and asks the doctor to return with him. When he arrives at Jordan's End, one of the old women greets him at the door and sends him upstairs, where he encounters the body of Alan Jordan, attended only by his wife and son, and being prepared for burial by two old women. Still young, handsome, and in his physical prime, the corpse of Alan Jordan moves the doctor emotionally. He realizes that Judith Jordan has administered the sedative in a dose sufficient to end the life of her husband and to end her own suffering.

The young woman who had come to Jordan's End as a bride only ten years ago and who had watched the result of generations of intermarriage destroy her beloved husband, as it had destroyed his father and his father's father and beyond, must now go on alone. The doctor, torn apart inside by the agony he knows the lovely, still young woman must feel, asks her if she wishes him to come back to Jordan's End again. She demurs, and he knows that she will never send for him. As the tale ends, the doctor drives off in his buggy through the gloomy woods.

Themes and Meanings

The title of this story is deliberately ambiguous: Jordan's End is both the name of the house and a declaration about the fate of its owners. As does Edgar Allan Poe's House of Usher, the condition of the physical place wherein resides the latest in the line of Jordans mirrors the condition of that line, and by extension, the decline of a way of life. (This theme was taken up by William Faulkner a few years after the publication of this story.) However, Ellen Glasgow holds out some hope for the future in the person of Judith Jordan. Judith tells the doctor, "I must go on." The reader believes she will, heartrending though her plight may be.

It was narrow-mindedness born of pride, ethnocentrism born of ignorance, that led families such as the Jordans to the kind of inbreeding that produced insanity in generation after generation. The way of life, the way of thinking, and the refusal to admit that things had changed—all were causes for the decline of southern aristocracy. These two young people, so much in love, had come to Jordan's End full of hope and had seen that hope dashed by the onset of Alan's mental illness. It is not, however, the house that destroys these young lives; rather, they are destroyed by their unswerving allegiance to a belief system that is false at its very base. In some sense, then, this is really a kind of ghost story. It is the ghost of the past that haunts the corridors of Jordan's End. It is a belief in this ghost that deranges succeeding generations of Jordan males.

Style and Technique

The use of the first-person narrator, a young, impressionable physician who is just starting out in life, provides the author with the opportunity to reveal to her readers a tale that affects the doctor's sensibility. He is both sobered and saddened by what he encounters at Jordan's End, and because he represents a new generation, a kind of new southerner, his "getting of wisdom" makes a statement about the future as well as the past. Moreover, Glasgow's use of the physical description of the road leading to Jordan's End and of the house and the grounds—and of the dimly lit room in which young Alan Jordan is confined—contributes to the sense of foreboding, and to the picture of decay. Adding to this is the raw autumn weather in which the story takes place. Although the story is a flashback with the narrator in the present recollecting something that happened some thirty years ago, Glasgow trades on the reader's awareness that there are many old houses at some remove from towns everywhere—houses that would yield, if they could only speak, similar tales of decline and fall.

Dale H. Ross

JORINDA AND JORINDEL

Author: Mavis Gallant (1922-   )
Type of plot: Psychological
Time of plot: The early twentieth century, probably the 1920's
Locale: A lake not far from Montreal, Canada
First published: 1959

>   *Principal characters:*
>   IRMGARD, the protagonist, a seven-year-old girl
>   FREDDY (ALFRED MARCEL DUFRESNE), a poor French Canadian
>   orphan boy
>   BRADLEY, Irmgard's cousin from Boston, who is ten years old
>   MRS. BLOODWORTH, a drunken wedding guest
>   GERMAINE, Irmgard's French Canadian nursemaid
>   MRS. QUEEN, the English cook

The Story

In the course of a summer at the lake, Irmgard, a rather spoiled child of an upper-middle-class Canadian family, loses some of the innocence and charm of early childhood. In doing so she becomes, regrettably, more like her smug parents and her rather unpleasant cousin Bradley.

Like most children, Irmgard is a secret observer of adult life. Her parents have parties that sometimes drag on into the next day. The most curious leftover guest at a recent wedding party was a drunken woman named Mrs. Bloodworth, who spent a noisy night practicing the Charleston and possibly getting incorporated into the little girl's dream as a witch—that is, the witch that in the dream captured Jorinda and reached out to turn Jorindel into a bird.

The child is a bit confused in her folklore because in the Grimms' fairy tale, it is Jorinda, the girl, who is turned into a bird, while Jorindel, the boy, stands paralyzed as a stone. When her cousin Bradley, who visits all during August, goes back to Boston, he is said to have "fallen out of summer like a stone." At the beginning of the story, it is Bradley whom she identifies with the Jorindel of her dream. By the end of the story, however, she has decided that it was probably her local friend Freddy who was spirited away by the wicked witch of the forest.

Freddy is a poor French Canadian orphan who works on his uncle's farm for food and shelter. He was reared in an orphanage until age seven, when he was considered old enough to work. He was never taught to read or write or even to eat politely, but he has visions of the Virgin Mary. Freddy is quite entranced with Irmgard, who taught him to swim and knows intuitively what he is thinking.

When Bradley, the ten-year-old cousin, shows up for a visit, all that is changed. The inarticulate Freddy stands on the sidelines waiting for an invitation to join the two children. When Bradley asks who he is, Irmgard disclaims knowing him, not once but three times.

Freddy disappears and Irmgard does not even think about him until Bradley leaves almost a month later. Bradley has proved to be a rather unsatisfactory companion because he is very self-centered and contemptuous of girls. He is big, healthy, and stubborn, however, quite like Irmgard herself in that regard, and claims officiously that he is going to be a mechanical and electrical engineer when he grows up. Irmgard has only aspired to be a veterinarian or a nun. By comparison to the pair of them, Freddy looks old, undersized, and undernourished.

When Irmgard at last remembers Freddy again and goes to find him, the rapport they once knew is gone. She no longer knows what he is thinking, and he has discovered that he can live without her. He agrees to go swimming with her, not at her place but at the dirty public beach where she has been forbidden to go. Because they have no swimming suits, he swims naked and she with bloomers on.

Mrs. Queen, the cook, says that Freddy will be sent back to the orphan asylum. Irmgard remembers her dream, however, and says that Freddy was sent on an errand into the forest and got lost. After all, there is a witch there who changes children into birds.

Themes and Meanings

On one level, this story reveals the peculiar combination of fact and fancy that constitutes the mental life of children. On another level, it is social criticism of a class society that perpetuates callousness and prejudice. Although Irmgard may project the idea of witch on the outsider, Mrs. Bloodworth, because of her bizarre behavior, the real witches who destroy childhood are the adults who perpetuate pride and prejudice and who condone neglect.

Differences in language conveniently underline the distinctions between British Canadians and French Canadians. Irmgard unconsciously learns this distinction close at hand in the kitchen, where she is more at home, no doubt, than in the drawing room with her parents. Mrs. Queen, the chronically complaining cook who used to serve the upper classes in England and has absorbed some of their snobbishness, disdains to learn French. Germaine, the loving but somewhat simple nursemaid, speaks nothing but French. Though the two servants are necessarily much in each other's company, they do not communicate. Irmgard, as a small child who unconsciously learns to understand French from her nurse, simply accepts this odd situation among grown-ups as a matter of course. Her experience of losing the ability to communicate with her friend Freddy further suggests the consequences of such class divisions.

The relationship between Germaine and Irmgard is also changing, and that link with the "other world" of French Canadians will soon be broken. Irmgard will outgrow the need for a nursemaid and become more like her cousin Bradley, who never sees visions and explains everything with the formula, "Well, this is the way it is." The imaginary world, shared to some extent by Irmgard, Germaine, and Freddy, will fade away into the seemingly factual but severely limited perception of middle-class society.

The implied criticism of the adult generation is not, however, exclusively directed against the middle class. Freddy's uncle appears only once in the story, but surely he must bear some kind of responsibility for the almost barbaric state of little Freddy. He gives him shelter only when the child can work for his keep, and apparently makes no effort at all to educate him. When Irmgard shows up at the uncle's farm to renew her acquaintance with Freddy, the boy's uncle curses her in obscene language. Both children are shocked, Irmgard because she does not understand these words, Freddy because he does. Although Freddy's return to the orphanage in Montreal may have something to do with disapproval of the children's swim at the public beach, that was apparently the pattern of his days, anyway. The uncle obviously does not care to be burdened with a child when his services are not valuable. Freddy, in any case, is the loser because he has had a glimpse of a gentler life that is denied him.

Nevertheless, this is not an exercise in social realism where all evil derives from social structures. Irmgard's triple denial of her friend, vaguely suggestive of Peter's denial of Christ, is a flaw not directly attributable to social conditioning. To some extent, at least, it is a fall from grace, when the child "advances" from the innocent blend of fact and fancy to deliberate lying and betrays a sacred bond.

Style and Technique

Though the deeper implications of this story are grim and unsentimental, the style is light, sometimes humorous, and perceptive about childhood experience. After all, no one really expects children to be especially angelic. When Irmgard is asked if she still likes Freddy now that Bradley is here, she offers some rationalization that even she suspects is not adequate:

> "Oh, I still like Freddy, but Bradley's my cousin and everything." This is a good answer. She has others, such as, "I'm English-Canadian only I can talk French and I'm German descent on one side." (Bradley is not required to think of answers, he is American. . . .) Irmgard's answer—about Freddy—lies on the lawn like an old skipping rope, waiting to catch her up. . . . "I like Freddy," Irmgard said, and was heard, and the statement is there, underfoot. For if she still likes Freddy, why isn't he here?

Nevertheless, at this stage of limited sophistication, Irmgard is only subliminally aware of moral or emotional implications. Although Freddy is forgotten for a while, Irmgard becomes convinced that she has left something behind in Montreal. She goes over her personal belongings to see what is missing, even getting up in the night to see if her paint box is still there. Not until Bradley leaves does she account for this unexplained vacuity as Freddy's absence.

Mavis Gallant is especially perceptive about this limited or selective awareness that makes childhood a private place where witches turning children into birds may adequately explain an unpleasant fact for which she and others may share some guilt. Grown-ups make more sophisticated rationalizations.

Irmgard's father and mother do not figure prominently in the story, but close to the end Irmgard, observing their reaction to Mrs. Bloodworth, interprets their expressions in the light of her own experience.

> They weigh and measure and sift everything people say, and Irmgard's father looks cold and bored, and her mother gives a waking tiger's look his way, smiles. They act together, and read each other's thoughts—just as Freddy and Irmgard did. But, large, and old, and powerful, they have greater powers: they see through walls, and hear whispered conversations miles away. Irmgard's father looks cold, and Irmgard, without knowing it, imitates his look.

The last episode returns to the dream that Irmgard remembers at the breakfast table. She remembers that it was Freddy who was sent on an errand.

> He went off down the sidewalk, which was heaving, cracked, edged with ribbon grass; and when he came to a certain place he was no longer there. Something was waiting for him there, and when they came looking for him, only Irmgard knew that whatever had been waiting for Freddy was the disaster, the worst thing. . . . But she does not know exactly what it was.

Nor is she sure whether it was Freddy, Bradley, or herself who encountered "the worst thing."

In an effective closing, the author suggests how far the parents have come from even the limited insight their daughter demonstrates. Irmgard starts to tell them about her dream, but her father cuts her off impatiently with "Oh, no dreams at breakfast, please." Her mother agrees: "Nothing is as dreary as a dream." The reader may intuit that the dream is, after all, no drearier than reality.

Katherine Snipes

JOSEPHINE THE SINGER
Or, The Mouse Folk

Author: Franz Kafka (1883-1924)
Type of plot: Animal tale
Time of plot: Unspecified
Locale: Unspecified
First published: "Josephine die Sängerin: Oder, Das Volk der Mäuse," 1924 (English translation, 1942)

> *Principal characters:*
> JOSEPHINE, a mouse and singer
> THE NARRATOR, an anonymous member of the mouse folk

The Story

The narrator, a philosophizing mouse, reflects on the powerful effect that the singing of his fellow mouse Josephine has on the unmusical community of mice. Among the practical, sly, and care-laden mice, Josephine is an exception. She alone loves music and knows how to supply it. However, there are some mice who do not find anything extraordinary in Josephine's singing. The narrator partly includes himself in this opposition group that finds nothing artistic in her song, which seems to be nothing more than common mouse squeaking. The narrator adds, however, that one must see her as well as hear her in order to understand her art, which derives its uniqueness from the way she stands before the assembled mice and does with great ceremony what every other mouse does without thinking. The fact that she is somewhat less proficient in squeaking than the average mouse seems only to heighten the effect of her performance.

It is times of trouble that Josephine deems most fitting for her recitals, for at such times the restless and anxious mice are eager to come together for mutual support and comfort. "Quiet peace is our most beloved music," the narrator notes early in the story, and when the mice fall silent in her auditorium, it is as if they were participating in this longed-for peace. Thus, the narrator asks himself: "Is it her song that delights us, or perhaps rather the solemn stillness, with which her weak little voice is surrounded?" In order to gather the scurrying mice, Josephine usually needs only to assume her singing pose, with her head tilted back, mouth half open, and eyes turned to the heights. If the number of listeners is too few, she will stamp her feet, swear, and even bite until a suitable audience is found.

Why do the mice go to such lengths for her, the narrator asks. He suggests that the community sees itself as Josephine's protector, as a father for this fragile, needy child. Josephine, on the other hand, believes that her role is to protect the mice from their daily troubles. Her song supposedly saves them from their serious economic and political situation. However, it is all too easy, the narrator insists, to pose as the savior of the mouse folk, who are accustomed to suffering and capable of overcoming on their own any challenges to their survival.

Josephine's singing profits from a childlike quality that characterizes the mouse folk. Life is too difficult for the mice, their enemies too many, and the dangers facing them too incalculable for a prolonged, carefree, and playful childhood. In contradiction to their practical intellect, their underdeveloped childish side causes them to behave foolishly for the sake of a little fun. However, they are also grown-ups for too long, which leads to a certain tiredness, despondency, and lack of musicality. "We are too old for music," the narrator claims.

During Josephine's concerts, only the young mice pay attention to the nuances of her delivery. In these brief moments of rest from their struggles, the older mice withdraw dreamily into themselves: "It is as though the limbs of each individual were loosened, as though the restless one were permitted for once to relax and stretch out pleasureably on the great warm bed of the people." Josephine's staccato squeaking resounds in the dreams of her listeners and liberates them from the fetters of their daily lives: "Something of our poor brief childhood is in it, something of lost, never to be recovered happiness, but also something of the active life of today, of its slight, incomprehensible cheerfulness that lasts in spite of everything and is inextinguishable."

This is not to say, though, that Josephine herself gives new strength to the mice in times of danger, which is what she and her adherents like to believe. Nor does the power of her singing justify the demands for special privileges that she makes, especially the demand to be freed from all daily work, which she claims damages her voice. What she really wants, according to the narrator, is unequivocal and lasting public recognition of her art. This is precisely what eludes her.

Recently Josephine has stepped up her struggle for recognition, threatening to overwhelm her opponents with her singing or, failing that, to cut her coloratura arias. The narrator dismisses these notions as empty rumors circulated by her followers. She is unrelenting, however, claiming to have injured her foot or to be indisposed. Her concerts have turned into theatrical performances. After her adherents flatter and coax her into singing, she still breaks down and eventually leaves, but not without first checking the crowd for the least sign of their understanding of her music.

The latest news is that she has disappeared on an occasion when her singing was expected, and that the search for her has turned up nothing. Although she may go into hiding and destroy the power of her song, the mouse folk are strong and can overcome even her death. They will not have to forgo much, for the memory of her squeaking will live on in future assemblies, perhaps with greater vitality.

As for Josephine herself, she will be delivered from her earthly torment and happily lose herself among the countless heroes of the mouse folk. As the mice do not practice history, she will soon be forgotten "in heightened redemption like all her brothers."

Themes and Meanings

Written only a few months before his death, Franz Kafka's last tale depicts the conflict between an artist seeking proper recognition for her work and a community that has only limited understanding of her artistry. As the title indicates, Josephine, a name that echoes that of Joseph K., protagonist of Kafka's novel *Der Prozess*

(1925; *The Trial*, 1937), and the mouse folk exist in a reciprocal relationship, one in which, however, neither side can comprehend the truth of the other. Because Josephine is seen through the eyes of one of her critics, albeit one who tries hard to be as objective as possible, it is hardly surprising that the outcome of the narrator's reflections is the downfall of the artist and the triumph of the superior wisdom of the mouse folk.

The narrator ascribes the powerful effect of Josephine's singing not to any vocal talent—her squeaking is clearly substandard—but to the gestures and style of her performance and, more important, to the receptivity of her audience. The mice appear to be particularly moved by the silence that precedes her singing as well as by the opportunity it provides for a communal respite from their labors and worries. Josephine's insistence on special privileges and recognition of her exceptional status, however, eventually undermines any claims she might have to be a protector of the mouse folk.

At the end of his life, Kafka thus seemed to condemn the artist's claim to autonomy and radical individuality and affirm instead the artist's function within a responsive community. Neither Josephine's personality nor the quality of her art will be remembered by this ahistorical folk, but rather the liberating power of her performances in the midst of danger, worry, and haste. Paradoxically, her redemption will come about only when she as a heroic individual is forgotten, leaving nothing but the collective memory of the dreams and the sense of well-being that her singing induced.

Style and Technique

The mouse-narrator presents his observations, analyses, arguments, and counter-arguments with careful precision and in a tone of utmost seriousness that sharply contrast with the quaint world of anxiously scurrying mice. Even when he states that Josephine's auditorium was "still as mice," the pun is not consciously his. Similar incongruities—mention of the dispersion of the mice out of economic considerations (which some commentators take as a veiled reference to the Diaspora of the Jews), their neglect of history and lack of a musical tradition, their serious economic and political circumstances—demonstrate both the breadth and the limitations of the scholarly mouse's vision.

Kafka leaves the boundary between the mouse and human worlds deliberately fuzzy. The mouse writes in an impeccable German, records his observation of Josephine and her effect on the community from a number of angles, and qualifies his generalizations and judgments for the sake of clarity and objectivity, yet he is an integral member of the mouse folk and shares their hopes, desires, cares, and disappointments. The result of this dual aspect is a sharpening of the contrast between the grand seriousness of the subject of the narrator's meditations (the relationship of artist and community) and the slightness of their context within the mouse world. This ironic interplay between human and mouse, great and small, serious and comic, produces a marvelously rich text that further trivializes Josephine's meager performances. The true artist is Kafka in the guise of his philosophical mouse.

Peter West Nutting

JOURNEY BACK TO THE SOURCE

Author: Alejo Carpentier (1904-1980)
Type of plot: Fantasy
Time of plot: Unspecified
Locale: A Latin American or Caribbean country
First published: "Viaje a la semilla," 1958 (English translation, 1970)

Principal character:
DON MARCIAL, MARQUES DE CAPELLANIAS, a nobleman

The Story

This story traces the life of Don Marcial from his death back to his birth. It begins with the impending destruction of his house some time after his death. In twelve more sections, noted by roman numerals, the reader is escorted backward through the stages in Marcial's life. Each section provides details that typify these stages.

Marcial has already died when an old manservant literally opens the door into the house and the time frame moves to Marcial's funeral. Continuing to move backward in time, the story tells about his life as an old man, a middle-aged man, married man, young man, teenager, young adolescent, young child, toddler, crawling baby, an infant and, finally, a fetus.

At each stage, several essential characters are introduced who either are appropriate to that stage or serve to indicate the kind of man that Marcial is. For example, at his deathbed is Father Anastasio, his priest and confessor. As a young adult, Marcial makes bold love to Señora de Campoflorido. As a toddler, he plays with his father's African groom, Melchor.

The totality of the information creates an image of a lusty man who has led a relatively uneventful life. Each rite of passage is celebrated, such as the party given when he becomes an adult. Because the story is told in reverse order, the party is disbanded as he achieves nonadult status or minority.

In the last section, Marcial enters his mother's womb to become a fetus, and everything surrounding Don Marcial undoes itself into its original form. For example, wool blankets unravel and once more become sheep fleece. Even the grounds where the house once stood return to their original desert state or—as the title indicates—go back to the source.

Themes and Meanings

The title of the collection in which this story was first published in English, *The War of Time* (1970), illuminates Alejo Carpentier's ideas. Many of his other works are also studies in time. They often show the relentlessness of time on human beings, and one way to look at this particular story is the way in which time works in the life of Don Marcial.

Carpentier has created Don Marcial as an unexceptional person, which allows him to become an allegorical figure. Marcial moves from death to birth undergoing the same experiences of all human beings. These experiences include the anxiety of the teenage years as well as the decrepitude of old age when he signs away his possessions to the attorneys. Interest is sustained because everything is in reverse. The action flows like a film set for rewind, so even the most common event is seen from a different point of view. This is one of Carpentier's goals—to see the common events of human lives from a fresh, new perspective.

Additionally, Carpentier believes that both history and time are cyclical and even unreal. As a revolutionary, both as an artist and in his politics, he considers that events create effects that result in causes that create effects, over and over again. This lack of any unusual quality in Don Marcial's life makes him an Everyman. These same kinds of events can occur an infinite number of times in an infinite number of lives. Nothing suggests a finality to this story. If there is a journey back to the source, then the very existence of a source implies everything can begin all over again; the cycle continues.

Dividing the story into thirteen parts is another way to examine time. Conventional time is told on a clock divided into twelve parts, so the existence of a thirteenth part suggests there is something beyond conventional or normal time. That thirteenth hour, the time before normal human time, is what fascinates Carpentier.

For Carpentier, a Latin American writer, time takes on a special significance. The significant time is that before Europeans came and conquered Mexico, Central and South America, and the islands of what is now the Caribbean. Carpentier, like Pablo Neruda, Jorge Luis Borges, Gabriel García Márquez, and many other Latin American writers, wants to come to terms with and write about what these lands were like before European structures, both physical and societal, were imposed.

Carpentier was certainly influenced by Indigenism, a school of thought to which he was introduced on a trip to Haiti in 1943. In Haiti in 1928, a strong cultural and intellectual movement began in an attempt to resist occupation by the United States or any European country. This attitude was expressed by the Indigenist writers as an attempt to recover, among other things, the African roots of the area, and to hold on to their particularly Latin American cultures.

"Journey Back to the Source" can readily be seen within this context. Carpentier may not have discovered all the indigenous characteristics of the region, but he has succeeded in destroying the house and all the European trappings around Don Marcial. Carpentier shows how the search must be begun, and that with the European surroundings gone, knowledge is now possible.

The fact that Melchor, his father's groom, is African becomes more significant in this light. Melchor is introduced in section ten, when Marcial is a toddler. Carpentier praises Melchor lavishly. Melchor is considered greater than God and capable of skills as varied as taming wild horses with two fingers, stealing sweetmeats for his young friend, and tormenting the police. This noble, beautiful creation of Carpentier's mind is part of the source, because the Africans, too, were torn from their traditional world when they were forced to the New World by Europeans.

Melchor may also be the "old Negro" in sections one, two, and thirteen. This old Negro is the one who watches and listens to the initial destruction of the house, which is being accomplished with the tools of Western civilization. He is also the one with the magical stick. When he whirls it above the paving stones of the courtyard, time begins its backward journey to the source, as if by magic. Whether or not he is Melchor, he is an old man of African descent and is, therefore, capable of helping the peoples of Latin America discover their own history.

Style and Technique

Because this story was written originally in Spanish, the style of Carpentier's writing is not so transparent in English. His techniques, however, are more readily available. The influence of the surrealists, resulting from his spending time in Paris from 1928 to 1939, is evident. There is a nightmarish, unreal quality as everything begins to go backward, including the hands on the clock. It is the physical descriptions of the house and its furnishings, paralleling the physical description of the man, that make the story so interesting to read. The whirlwind quality of the final section is particularly frightening. One example of his use of physical description is the lengthening of the candles back to their freshly cut wicks as Don Marcial's dead body turns into that of a sick old man. For another example, as Marcial goes from being a teenager to a prepubescent adolescent, the furniture grows taller.

An interesting allusion used by Carpentier is a statue of Ceres, the Greek goddess of agriculture. The statue is used twice in the story, in the first and last sections. The statue witnesses the destruction of the house in the first section and is sold off to an antique store in the last section. Ceres is an appropriate allusion in this story about cycles, causes, and effects. Her counterpart in Latin mythology is Demeter. Because of the cyclic nature of agriculture, a cult grew up around her that, among other things, featured the Elysian Mysteries. These were dramas enacting life, death, and resurrection. "Journey Back to the Source" begins with death, goes backward through life, and awaits a resurrection at the end.

Judith L. Steininger

JOURNEY THROUGH THE NIGHT

Author: Jakov Lind (Heinz Landwirth, 1927-   )
Type of plot: Psychological
Time of plot: After World War II
Locale: A train traveling through France
First published: "Reise durch die Nacht," 1962 (English translation, 1964)

> *Principal characters:*
> AN UNNAMED TRAVELER
> HIS FELLOW PASSENGER

The Story

Between three and four o'clock in the morning, on a train traveling between Nice and Paris, two Austrians are seated opposite each other in a locked compartment, to which the narrator's fellow passenger has somehow obtained a key. Describing his un-expected companion, the narrator uneasily likens him to a seal and wonders why he does not show his tusks. His partly comical, partly anxious description grows menac-ing when he pictures the contents of the other's small black suitcase. He correctly con-jectures that it contains carpenter's tools, a hammer, saw, chisel, and drill. What he guesses earlier has now become undeniable: The owner of the black bag is a cannibal, intent on murdering and eating him.

Although the friendly cannibal appears sure that he will accomplish his aim, the protagonist expresses his determination to thwart him. Having gotten fair warning, he insists that he will remain awake through the night's journey. The cannibal persists in his confidence, however, and matter-of-factly describes how he will dismember and consume his fellow traveler. The narrator's resistance yields to curiosity, and he asks if the ears can be digested or if they have bones in them. Soon convinced that his life truly is endangered, he attempts to ward off the threat by maintaining a stream of con-versation. This leads to a detailed account of dismemberment by the cannibal as he opens his black bag.

The narrator slowly succumbs to his companion's perverse logic and mentally ac-cepts the inevitability, even the reasonableness, of the violent end that awaits him. Only hesitantly and feebly does he manage to express his will to live, asking that he be spared long enough to go for a walk in Paris. The cannibal asserts himself still more sardonically and reopens his bag of tools. The narrator instinctively leaps to his feet and pulls the emergency cord. The train screeches to a halt, the cannibal speedily dis-embarks, bitterly chiding his intended prey for the foolishness that will now cost him a huge fine, and several upset passengers crowd into the compartment. Still shouting invectives, the cannibal disappears into the darkness.

Themes and Meanings

"Journey Through the Night" is the second of seven stories in Jakov Lind's debut book *Eine Seele aus Holz* (1962; *Soul of Wood, and Other Stories*, 1964). Although only three stories deal directly with the Holocaust, the collection immediately gained its Austrian-born author international fame as a savagely inventive, often grotesquely humorous portrayer of the Nazi extermination of the Jews. Given the atmosphere of horror that pervades the book, along with Lind's biography as a survivor of Nazi persecution, a sweeping view of his early stories as Holocaust parables was widely espoused, and "Journey Through the Night" was often cited as such a parable. Lind himself appeared to suggest reading the story in this vein. Writing on the annihilation of the Jews in his native Vienna as a result of Nazi racism, he expressly linked the central motif of the story with the Jewish catastrophe. "Vienna died," he said, "when it destroyed its [Jewish] spirit in an act of autocannibalism."

An analogy with the Holocaust will, however, appear less evident to readers unacquainted with Lind's larger work and the forces that motivated it. If the Nazi universe of industrialized genocide can be imagined at all, it is only in terms of its own singular realities. These, however, were so enormous as to defy both objective historical portrayal as well as literary representation through metaphor or symbol. However Lind may have intended his decidedly elusive tale, it is bare of any reference to the Holocaust. Thus, the reader may legitimately view its central theme in more universal terms: as humanity's endless capacity for evil or, alternately, as the insanity of a world in which evil has seemingly become normal. Lind's success in conveying his theme depends, in turn, on the psychological plausibility of the story's uneventful plot, the morbid interplay of victimizer and intended victim as developed through the motif of cannibalism.

Within the locked train compartment, Lind's narrator discovers that the social codes that regulate interpersonal behavior and guard human society from physical assault have been suspended. His fellow passenger claims the right to commit the unthinkable, to murder, dissect, and consume him. His Paris vacation trip, which promised some degree of civilized enjoyment, turns into a nightmare of brutality. At first disbelieving his would-be killer, or perhaps in order to shield himself against believing him, the narrator attempts to dismiss his evil intent jokingly. This can be accepted as the normal, if anxious, response of a person educated to respect the sanctity of human life and thereby to expect the safety of his own. When the cannibal tauntingly opens his black bag, the mere sight of the tools seems to convince him that he is hopelessly trapped. He capitulates intellectually to the immorality of brute power and, without prompting by his captor, begins to accept his impending gruesome death as reasonable: "Every animal eats every other just to stay alive, men eat men, what's so unnatural about that?" Although comically distorted, this sympathy on the part of the victim with the aims of his tormentor validly reflects a psychological phenomenon well documented in the literature on captivity and imprisonment. Only at the last second, when the cannibal wields his mallet, does the succumbing narrator almost miraculously spring to his feet and pull the emergency cord.

In his autobiographical writing, Lind has spoken of his own deep shame at the helplessness and, as he saw it, the passivity of the Jews as they were rounded up by the

Germans and deported to their deaths. Possibly he wished, in "Journey Through the Night," to provide a moral corrective to the depravity that holds sway in the train compartment by having the narrator overcome his psychological torpor and save his own life. Nevertheless, it is the embodiment of evil, the cannibal, who has the last word in the story. Although his murderous hand was stayed, his potential to wreak evil remains undiminished; and the irate passengers who crowd into the compartment— among them, as representatives of public order, a conductor and a police officer—will hardly believe the narrator's unlikely tale. As the cannibal charges as he scurries off, his intended victim has made a fool of himself for life.

Style and Technique

Lind's story is slightly more than six pages long. Narrated in the first person by the protagonist, it primarily consists of his thoughts and descriptions and the dialogue between him and his fellow passenger. To the extent that the story can claim a plot, in the sense of a series of connected events rising to a climax, the plot is skeletal. It consists entirely of a few key actions and gestures: the cannibal's opening of his black bag to reveal its contents, his wielding of the mallet, the protagonist's last-second tug on the emergency cord, and the appearance of other travelers as the cannibal escapes. Lind has reduced the setting and time of his story to the barest minimum. Such drastic reduction places the burden of artistic success on the persuasiveness of the psychological conflict that unfolds between the two characters within a single hour and a space whose sole attribute is its seemingly inescapable confinement.

It testifies to Lind's artistry that he has rendered believable a situation so utterly bizarre as the one around which his story is constructed. In large part, this results from the subtly disquieting atmosphere that he creates at the very outset. The eerie bluish light of the train compartment, the view into a darkness relieved only by a few scattered lights of unclear origin, the nocturnal hour between half-wakefulness and deep sleep, and the unidentified hovering voice of the first lines dissolve reality and allow the presence of a cannibal to become plausible. What remains problematic, however, is the narrator's quick acceptance of his doom. Rather than motivate this submission through a genuine contest of wits between the two characters, with its own clear and compelling logic, Lind relies for narrative effect on the grotesque humor of the dialogue and what soon appears to be savagery for its own sake. As a result, the message of the story becomes muddy. The reader is left unsure of the significance inherent in the narrator's finally awakened will to live, while—despite momentary defeat—the murderous immorality of the cannibal appears to triumph.

Sidney Rosenfeld

JUDAS

Author: Frank O'Connor (Michael Francis O'Donovan, 1903-1966)
Type of plot: Psychological
Time of plot: Probably the late 1940's
Locale: Unspecified; probably Cork, Ireland
First published: 1947

> *Principal characters:*
> JERRY MOYNIHAN, the narrator and protagonist
> KITTY DOHERTY, the nurse of whom Jerry is enamored
> PADDY KINNANE, his friend
> MOTHER, his mother

The Story

Jerry Moynihan says goodnight to his mother before he leaves for the evening to meet Kitty Doherty, whom he has not seen for three weeks. Jerry is clearly infatuated with Kitty, although he is painfully shy and awkward. Although warned by office-mates that nurses are trouble, he regards Kitty as a well-educated, superior person from the best side of town. He finds excuses to show up wherever she is and then walk her home.

When he does not see Kitty for a few weeks, he convinces himself that she is dying to see him but then concludes that she is actively avoiding him because of some unspeakable indiscretion. He fears that he has said something obscene and yearns for a knife with which to take his life.

One beautiful summer evening, distracted to the point of madness, Jerry tries to catch Kitty's tram and is forced conspicuously to chase it down the street. He finally waits outside her house until a comrade, Paddy Kinnane, approaches and asks what he is doing. Paddy wonders if Jerry has a date with a woman. Embarrassed, Jerry lies that he is waiting for a male friend and soon slips away from Paddy.

Jerry quickly takes up a post elsewhere on the street and, when Kitty approaches, frightens her by calling to her from the shadows. In the conversation that follows, she tells him she has been staying home with her mother, who is suspicious of Jerry because he will never come to the door and introduce himself. The mother is convinced that his intentions are untrustworthy, and Jerry is chagrined to learn that Kitty has had other boyfriends and that others have noticed his interest in her. Kitty admits her attraction to Jerry and insists that he kiss her, which he reluctantly does in spite of finding it "a very sissy sort of occupation."

When he arrives home late and his mother questions where he has been, Jerry resents the intrusion and stomps off to his room. Lying in the dark, wracked with guilt, he goes into his mother's room to apologize and breaks down sobbing; his mother consoles him with endearments he has not heard since his childhood.

Themes and Meanings

A favorite character type of Frank O'Connor is the naïf, a figure unlettered in the ways of the world and always a step or two behind everyone else, who seems sophisticated and aware. Usually these characters are children, but Jerry Moynihan is an adult, probably in his twenties, who, as he understatedly admits, was not exactly knowledgeable about females. Because of his inexperience, Jerry is very much like a young person; he is shy, awkward, and tormented by his feelings for Kitty.

Not surprisingly, Jerry jumps to wild, comic extremes in his view of their relationship. He is especially prone to hyperbole, thinking that Kitty is above going to the cinema with him and hoping that she would be imperiled with drowning or slavery from which he could save her. These notions of chivalry are reminiscent of a boy who has read too many tales of King Arthur and the Round Table. When he fails to see her, he convinces himself that he has said something unpardonable that stems from a deep carnal impulse and that he is actually "a volcano of brutality and lust. 'Lust, lust, lust!' I hissed to myself, clenching my fists."

His reactions to his mother's innocent questions also reveal exaggerated emotions. When she asks where he has been, he snaps that he has been out drinking and carousing, and then, when he tries to apologize, he begins to cry like a child. Emotionally and experientially, Jerry is a child, and his sense of guilt is disproportionately strong. As the title suggests, Jerry regards himself as a Judas for choosing a younger woman's company over his mother's.

O'Connor took every opportunity to explain that one of his major literary influences was Anton Chekhov, whom he praised for the verisimilitude of his characterizations and the depth of his psychological investigation. The quality of loneliness he saw in Chekhov's characters struck a respondent chord in his own experience and most deeply influenced his own writing. In story after story, O'Connor portrays characters who must live with some essential loss or deprivation and who, in spite of any evidence to the contrary, must make their isolated or alienated ways through the world. Jerry Moynihan is just such a figure, although on the surface he may seem little more than a stunted adult.

Not only is Jerry ill at ease with women, he is not especially comfortable with other men, and the character of Paddy Kinnane is used to reveal this aspect of his character. To the reader, Paddy is little more than a harmless, perhaps undeservedly self-assured, tease. To Jerry, Paddy is intolerably annoying and perhaps even a moral reprobate. Jerry is outraged at Paddy's referring to women as "dolls," and questions, "What could a pure-minded girl think of a chap who naturally used such a phrase except— what unfortunately was quite true—that he had a mind like a cesspit."

Jerry is actually a very lonely person, and his social isolation becomes subtly apparent in his conversation with Kitty. She recounts her argument with her mother in which she defends Jerry and admits having "spooned" with other young men in the past. He is shocked that she not only has known other men but also has spooned with them. Kitty is no longer angelic to him, he is no longer a knight saving a damsel in distress, and his world seems suddenly changed, "It was another door opening on the outside world." At this moment Jerry has an epiphany about his sheltered existence, and will never again view life in the way he has.

Style and Technique

"Judas" is another example of O'Connor's penchant for subjective narrators who comment, often comically and unwittingly, on their own experiences. In his study of the genre of the short story, *The Lonely Voice* (1962), O'Connor made the now-famous complaint that the modern short story "no longer rang with the tone of a man's voice speaking." By way of correction, he always gave his stories a quality of human speech, a sense that an actual person, rather than a disembodied voice, was bringing the tale to the reader. Nowhere is this more evident than in "Judas."

The story begins clearly enough with Jerry's saying good-bye to his mother and her asking if he will be late, but then the first full paragraph begins, "That was all we said, Michael John, but it stuck in my mind." The reader pauses, rereads the passage, and wonders who Michael John may be. The inquiry is never answered, but the name appears again out of nowhere on the last page when Jerry reviews his life with his mother, "I remembered all our life together from the night my father died; our early Mass on Sunday; our visits to the pictures, and our plans for the future, and Christ! Michael John, it was as if I was inside her mind while she sat by the fire waiting for the blow to fall." Michael John is obviously Jerry's immediate audience, and the story is a pointed monologue directed to a boon companion. Time has clearly passed since the events narrated, but by Jerry's addressing a particular someone, the reader is allowed an intimate sense of acquaintance with the central character.

The story is also noteworthy for O'Connor's subtle manipulations of tone. Through much of the story the tone is gently comic, as the reader witnesses Jerry's amusing overreactions and his oddly distorted notions of the world and other people. When he returns home, insults his mother, and then apologizes, however, there is no hint of humor, and the story ends on a decidedly somber note, "I couldn't bring myself to tell her what I had done, nor could she confess to me that she was jealous: all she could do was to try and comfort me for the way I'd hurt her, to make up to me for the nature she had given me. 'My storeen bawn!' she said. 'My little man!'"

The irony in this scene is especially penetrating. First of all, Jerry is still a little man, an immature creature who amuses the reader throughout the story. More tellingly, Jerry is more profoundly lonely than ever before. He is left without conversation, with waves of guilt, and with the certain knowledge that one phase of his life with his mother is forever over. Perhaps the story's most bitter irony is that to gain the thing he wants most desperately, a romantic relationship with a woman, he must lose an important aspect of his relationship with his mother.

David W. Madden

JULIA AND THE BAZOOKA

Author: Anna Kavan (Helen Woods Edmonds, 1901-1968)
Type of plot: Psychological
Time of plot: 1910-1940
Locale: London, England
First published: 1970

Principal characters:
JULIA, an adventurous young woman and heroin addict
HER BRIDEGROOM, "a young man with kinky brown hair"
THE TENNIS PROFESSIONAL, who first introduces Julia to drugs
A DOCTOR, who helps Julia get her heroin

The Story

"Julia and the Bazooka" is the story of a young girl who grows up to become a heroin addict, but who dies, not because of her addiction, but as a victim of World War II. The story is narrated in a nonsequential manner and overlaps and doubles back on itself, but even in its convoluted form, it is a simple and powerful narrative.

The story begins directly enough—"Julia is a little girl with long straight hair and big eyes"—but the chronological order is soon abandoned and past and present mix together without temporal value, and readers must piece together the chronology themselves. Rearranging the elements of the story into sequence, the narrative of Julia's life would look roughly like this: She has never known her father, and "her personality has been damaged by no love in childhood so that she can't make contact with people or feel at home in the world." As a child she loves flowers, but she has "sad" eyes and does not share the "enthusiasm for living" of her classmates. "She feels cut off from people. She is afraid of the world."

Drugs change all that. A tennis professional introduces Julia to heroin—or at least, he gives her a syringe to "improve her game"—and with her "bazooka," as the tennis professional jokingly calls the drug apparatus, she wins a tournament and a silver cup. By the time she gets married to "a young man with kinky brown hair" (and there is no way of telling the exact distance between events), the syringe has a permanent place in her purse. "Now Julia's eyes are not at all sad," and "she no longer feels frightened or cut off now that she has the syringe."

Julia lives for twenty years as a heroin addict, and the reader catches glimpses or fragments of her life. She travels "with her bridegroom in the high mountains through fields of flowers." Later she drives "anything, racing cars, heavy lorries. . . . Julia always laughs at danger. Nothing can frighten her while she has the syringe." Still later, she befriends a doctor, "understanding and kind like the father she has imagined but never known," who sees that the syringe "has not done Julia any great harm" and who tells her "'you'd be far worse off without it.'" Indeed, the narrator explains, "Without it she could not lead a normal existence, her life would be a shambles, but with its support she is conscientious and energetic, intelligent, friendly."

It is suddenly wartime. Julia has a rooftop garden—in London? space is as vague here as time—and as the bombs are falling, "Julia leaves the roof and steps on to the staircase, which is not there." She is covered by a blanket and dies alone, although she appears to retain consciousness for some time and to continue to recognize people. At the same time, her bridegroom of years before is killed in a battle at sea and dies because of the selfishness of another.

The last part of the story is even more dreamlike, as Julia passes through cold and then heat, pursuing the specter of death. She is cremated; her ashes are put in her silver tennis trophy and placed in a niche in a wall by a winter sea "the colour of pumice." There are no flowers. "There is no more Julia anywhere. Where she was there is only nothing."

Themes and Meanings

"Julia and the Bazooka" is an apologia for heroin addiction, but, beneath this story of drugs, there is a portrayal of the essential isolation and cruelty of twentieth century life. Anna Kavan was herself a drug addict for thirty years, but she did not fulfill the popular image of the drug addict, for, as she says about Julia, she did not "increase the dosage too much or experiment with new drugs." Much of Kavan's writing is autobiographical, and "Julia and the Bazooka" mirrors Kavan's own immersion in and simultaneous escape from the world, through drugs.

The story is, first, the narrative of a woman and her attachment to her syringe, her "bazooka," and the relief she gets from it. Her syringe helps her to compensate for childhood deficiencies and provides a barrier against the coldness and ugliness of the modern world. "She hardly remembers how sad and lonely she used to feel before she had the syringe." In the end it is not drugs that kill her, but the bombs in wartime London, which are a perfect symbol for human isolation and hatred.

This is the deeper level of the story that, for at least a quarter of its length, describes the cold isolation of Julia's ashes in the wall. The syringe has been a weapon itself against the cold inhumanity of the world, a cold she can no longer feel in death, as in drugs. Certainly Julia plays with death, tempts it, in her drug addiction. However, drugs also help Julia avoid the death-in-life that Kavan portrays as inherent in modern life.

Style and Technique

"Julia and the Bazooka" is slightly longer than two thousand words, yet much is packed into it—a whole life, in fact, a life of adventure, of addiction, and of death in wartime. It is a short, powerful story whose effect is based, in large part, on Kavan's precise and beautiful prose.

Much of the power of the story comes from Kavan's language and imagery, which are simple and direct. A typical sentence in the story ("Julia is also dead without any flowers.") is simple in structure, spare in language, and present in tense. Within those limits, though, her imagery is rich: "Snow is Julia's bridal veil, icicles are her jewels." The dominant imagery in the story is flowers: Julia is picking red poppies in a field ("the front of her dress is quite red") at the opening, and she dies amid her pots of geraniums (she lies beneath the blanket "in her red-stained dress") at the end. However, the flower imagery contrasts starkly with the other dominant imagery of military weapons in the story—both the "bazooka" and the "flying bombs" that will kill Julia. The story is also highly symbolic, in the sense of dreams, and the bazooka stands not only for the syringe, but also for the weapon Julia uses in her fight against the isolation of modern life, as a bomb is a weapon in the wars of that life.

Aside from language and imagery, the most notable element in the story is its structure. The story is told in a continuous, overlapping present, and events are linked not by clear temporal causation, but by some discontinuous order only the narrator knows. Similarly, characters and events are not described in any great detail in the story (often they are not described at all), and the cumulative effect of this structure is to render accurately the isolation and fragmentation of contemporary life. Certainly, a number of other writers have used Kavan's fictional methods (compare the American writers John Barth and Donald Barthelme), but Kavan put her own spare stamp on this style. Kavan's prose does not call attention to itself, yet it has a powerful sensory effect, from the colors of Julia's flowers through the cold and heat of her death. The story leaves a lasting impression.

David Peck

JULIA CAHILL'S CURSE

Author: George Moore (1852-1933)
Type of plot: Social realism
Time of plot: The early nineteenth century
Locale: Western Ireland
First published: 1903

Principal characters:

THE NARRATOR, an unnamed cart driver
JULIA CAHILL, an attractive, spirited, unmarried Irish woman
FATHER MADDEN, the new parish priest

The Story

A cart driver in a small Irish village has a passenger from outside the village. The passenger asks about a young woman named Margaret, who recently has given birth to a child out of wedlock. Because she and her child were forced to emigrate to the United States, an association is made between her experience with the community's moral intolerance and that of Julia Cahill. The latter was forced to leave Ireland twenty years previously but cursed the parish before she left.

The listener's implied incredulity about the effectiveness of Julia's curse on the village arouses the driver's vehement insistence that Julia's powers came from her association with the fairies. To impress his passenger, he recounts the circumstances that precipitated the lethal curse.

Although he describes Julia Cahill as tall and lithe with fine black eyes, the village narrator especially emphasizes her high-spirited character. The daughter of a well-to-do shopkeeper, one day she listened at one counter while, at another counter, her father and a suitor, a prosperous farmer named Michael Moran, bargained over the dowry that she would receive when she married Moran.

The deciding factor in the arrangements was the interference of Father Madden, a new priest in the parish. Father Madden supported arranged marriages because he believed that the usual means used by young people to get to know each other—dances and walks—foster premarital sex and illegitimate children. He particularly wanted the free-spirited and attractive Julia to be kept away from single young men.

Julia refused to accept the arranged marriage and insisted she would find her own husband. Her rejection of Father Madden's directive and her continued attraction to the young men of the county inspired Father Madden's Sunday sermon, which denounced her power to attract others as coming from the devil. As a result of this clerical censure of his daughter, Julia's father turned her out of his home. Then the parishioners, including the young men, refused to have anything to do with her. Only the kindness of a blind woman, Bridget Coyne, who offered Julia shelter, kept her from resorting to the poorhouse.

After two years, Julia decided to leave the village and emigrate to the United States. Before she left, she went to a mountaintop and raised her hands and expressed her curse on the parish: "That every year a roof must fall in and a family go to America." The narrator says that not only one but two or three roofs collapse each year. After twenty years, only Bridget Coyne remains to receive communion from the priest, and she is leaving for America soon, as is the cart driver himself.

Themes and Meanings

Many of the stories in George Moore's *The Untilled Field* (1903) analyze the effect on the individual when a community, sharing a common religious belief and social needs, experiences repressive measures that discourage the development of both. Moore believed the spiritual and physical fertility of the Irish people was atrophying because the Roman Catholic Church, in its zeal to promote the Heavenly Kingdom, was stifling earthly life. The stories in this anthology portray an ironic situation: spiritual deterioration resulting from an overconcern with spiritual well-being. In Ireland, the people's deep faith caused them to accept the guidance of the church in all aspects of their lives, temporal as well as spiritual. In many of the stories, and in "Julia Cahill's Curse" in particular, clerical domination is so overpowering that individual members have no latitude for self-expression. As a result, the people are forced to move away; both the church and the community cease to exist.

The central conflict is that between humanism and orthodox religion. The protagonist, Julia Cahill, is a spirited, lively young woman who attracts the young men in this Irish village. In defiance of the traditional authority of the father to arrange a suitable marriage for his daughter, she insists on her prerogative to enjoy the company of young men at dances and eventually to choose her spouse based on her own feelings. In other words, she intends to enjoy her earthly life and make her own decisions.

Cahill probably would not have insisted that his daughter obey him if the parish priest had not interpreted Julia's attractiveness in moral terms. Father Madden sees Julia's spirited individualism as a power given her by the Devil. In other words, if a woman attracts men, she is bewitching them to forget their duty to God.

The credulity of the villagers is equated with a vacuity of personal development. Unlike the self-actuated Julia, who suffers social ostracism rather than concede her right to choose a marriage partner, the male villagers obey the priest's injunctions to have nothing to do with her. The people's spiritual emptiness is expressed in the broken-down, deserted houses left as the villagers, unable to develop personally, leave the village and go to the United States, the land of free personal development. The priest, the cause of this human atrophy, is left saying the Mass for one parishioner who is also leaving the village.

Style and Technique

Moore's use of dialogue moves the account of Julia Cahill's curse from the format of a tale to that of a dramatic exposition of the problem. The narrator of the story, the cart driver, represents the uneducated, credulous Irish peasants who populated Julia

Cahill's history, implicitly supporting the theme of the story. The speech patterns of the person listening to the cart driver reveal someone who is educated; his comments and questions indicate a skeptical worldview. This contrast between narrator and listener heightens one of the author's main points: Because of clerical domination, the people in these backward Irish villages have lost contact with the intellectual development of the rest of the world.

The title of the story, "Julia Cahill's Curse," also symbolizes the spiritual malaise of the Irish people living in the village. The narrator believes the legend that twenty years earlier someone witnessed Julia Cahill raising her hands to the sky and calling down a curse. The listener's incredulity, however, represents the reader's understanding that people are emigrating from the village not because of a curse but rather to find freedom of growth and development. Although the narrator apparently still does not recognize that self-destruction, not the curse of the woman who was ostracized for insisting on self-determination, is responsible for the village's deterioration, he too is emigrating to the United States and superstitiously looks forward to meeting an unchanged Julia Cahill, retaining her youth through the power of the fairies.

As the narrator looks over the abandoned houses, he rejects the listener's suggestion that they are the result of eviction. Indeed, the landowners would welcome the return of workers and tenants. The untilled fields he laments remind the reader that Moore called this collection of short stories by that title. That title suggests that the theme of this short story can be found, perhaps less directly stated, in all the short stories. The untilled fields represent the undeveloped minds, imaginations, and feelings of a people who have given up their human development in exchange for spiritual guarantees of eternal happiness.

That Julia Cahill is atypical of these villagers is expressed in a classical allusion when the erudite listener describes her as an outcast Venus, the embodiment of physical love. She undoubtedly represents beauty and life in the form most threatening to communal religious stability: sexual attractiveness. Her curse is really her departure, for the people of the village are losing love. On the other hand, her departure is the beginning of the people's salvation as they follow her into an exile in the United States that will permit them to develop their own potential and enjoy their earthly lives.

Agnes A. Shields

A JURY OF HER PEERS

Author: Susan Glaspell (1876-1948)
Type of plot: Domestic realism
Time of plot: The early 1900's
Locale: Dickson County, in the American Midwest
First published: 1927

Principal characters:
MARTHA HALE, a farmwife
LEWIS HALE, her husband
HENRY PETERS, the sheriff
MRS. PETERS, the sheriff's wife
GEORGE HENDERSON, the county attorney

The Story

Martha Hale is baking bread one cold March morning when the county's most extraordinary scandal forces her out of her kitchen. She has been asked by Sheriff Peters to assist his wife in gathering personal belongings for Minnie Wright, whom he has jailed on suspicion of murdering her husband. Martha approaches the Wrights' isolated farmhouse with her husband, Lewis, Mr. and Mrs. Peters, and George Henderson, the county attorney. She pauses before crossing the threshold, overwhelmed with guilt because she had never visited in the twenty years Minnie, her girlhood friend, has been married. She nervously listens to her husband describe coming to the Wright place on their isolated country road the night before, because he wanted to convince John Wright to get a telephone and share the installation costs. Martha hopes her husband will not incriminate Minnie, but his remarks imply the Wrights were not happily married.

George Henderson takes notes as Mr. Hale tells how Mrs. Wright sat unemotionally rocking in her chair and responded oddly to his request to see her husband. She calmly replied that although he was home, he could not talk because he was dead. Pleating her apron, she said he died of a rope around his neck while he was sleeping in bed with her; she did not know who did it because she was sleeping on the inside and she slept soundly.

That Minnie has murdered her husband seems clear to the attorney, but without her confession, he knows that a jury will want definite evidence, especially when trying a woman for murder. Seeking evidence of a motive, the sheriff looks around at the kitchen things, and Mr. Hale comments with a tone of superiority that women worry over trifles. Reacting defensively to the men's condescension, Martha and Mrs. Peters instinctively move closer together and defend their neighbor as if she were a close friend. After Mr. Hale questions whether the women would even know a clue if they came on it, the men leave the kitchen to solve the mystery.

Now alone to piece together the puzzle, the two women deduce from small details, such as spilled sugar not cleaned off the table, what must have happened the day John

Wright was killed. They conclude that John was stingy because of Minnie's broken stove and much-repaired clothes. Martha suddenly understands that Minnie, once a lively girl who wore pretty clothes and sang in the choir, kept to herself after marriage because she was ashamed of her shabby appearance. Mrs. Peters realizes that a person gets discouraged and loses heart after years of loneliness. Turning their attention to Minnie's unfinished quilting, Martha asks Mrs. Peters whether she thought it was to be quilted or knotted. At that moment, the men come in. Laughing at the trifling question about the quilt, Mr. Hale mockingly repeats it.

When the three men leave for the barn, the women discover more clues. Mrs. Peters sees erratic stitches, so different from the even sewing of the other pieces. Martha immediately pulls out the uneven stitches, despite Mrs. Peters's warning about touching anything. They recall how Mrs. Wright once sang so beautifully, and they think she no doubt had a canary because they see a birdcage. While looking for Minnie's sewing things to bring to her in jail, they find her canary wrapped up in a piece of silk with its neck wrung. Just as they figure out that John must have violently ripped off the birdcage door hinge and silenced the chirping canary by wringing its neck, the men return. Without plotting any collaboration, the women instinctively conceal the dead bird in the sewing basket and make excuses to divert the men's attention. When she is again alone with Mrs. Peters, Martha describes her rage when a boy once took a hatchet to her kitten when she was a girl. Then Mrs. Peters admits her loneliness while homesteading in remote Dakota after her baby died. How the men would laugh to hear their talk about such trivia as a dead canary, she says.

The story concludes as Henderson, who has failed to come up with incriminating evidence, facetiously remarks that at least they found out Mrs. Wright was not going to quilt the material; he asks the ladies to repeat the exact quilting technique mentioned earlier. With her hand against her coat pocket, hiding the dead canary, Mrs. Hale responds, "We call it—knot it, Mr. Henderson."

Themes and Meanings

Adapted from Susan Glaspell's popular one-act play, *Trifles* (1920), "A Jury of Her Peers" is about sisterhood. Women's roles as wives, mothers, and homemakers do not make them totally passive, unintelligent, or subordinate to men. Mrs. Peters, for example, being small, thin, and soft-spoken, did not strike Martha Hale as a sheriff's wife when they first met; however, Mrs. Peters reveals her inner strength in defying her husband by suppressing evidence that would surely convict Minnie Wright of murder. Because they understand how John's killing the canary must have been the last straw in killing his wife's love of life, Martha and Mrs. Peters "knot" the criminal investigation. They shift their loyalty from their husbands, and the male-dominated legal system, to a woman who mirrors their own lives. As Martha wistfully says of her regret in abandoning her neighbor Minnie, "We live close together, and we live far apart. We all go through the same things—it's all just a different kind of same thing!" Because the legal defense of justifiable homicide by an abused wife might not have succeeded in the early twentieth century, the women take matters into their own hands.

They also retaliate against the men's arrogant air of superiority. The men's supposedly logical, intelligent methods of investigation lead to naught, whereas the women's intuitive, emotional responses to their "sister" probably will save Minnie's life. A climactic moment occurs when the attorney laughingly says that the ladies would not gather dangerous things to take to Mrs. Wright in jail, unaware that they are concealing crucial evidence. When Henderson says that Mrs. Peters does not need supervising because "a sheriff's wife is married to the law," she responds that she does not think of it that way. Rejecting the way the men think about Mrs. Wright's guilt, the women also reject the men's control over their lives. This assertion of power to think and act independently reiterates a strong feminist theme: Their allegiance to sisterhood is stronger than that to marriage.

Style and Technique

Glaspell uses rich verbal and dramatic irony to show that women's intuitive powers can be superior to men's analytical skills. Aware of the details of daily household chores, the two women grasp the overall scenario: an enraged husband killed by an even more enraged wife. Besides showing how women know that trifles are not insignificant, Glaspell dramatizes gender differences to foreshadow the women's rebellion. The women, for example, respond sympathetically on seeing the mess from broken jars of fruit, upset at the futility of a woman's hard work in the intense summer heat. On the other hand, the men berate Mrs. Wright for sloppy housekeeping, as if she could have prevented the cold weather from bursting the jars while jailed overnight.

The descriptive narration, interwoven with insightful dialogue, skillfully reveals a sense of place, characterization, and plot events. For example, Glaspell sets the Wrights' farmhouse in a hollow, suggesting the emotional emptiness of their lives. She compares John Wright's hardness to "a raw wind that gets to the bone," and Minnie is like a bird herself—"sweet and pretty, but kind of timid and—fluttery." Although caged up, small, and defenseless like the canary, Minnie becomes enraged enough to murder John.

As the pieces of a patchwork quilt are sewn together, Glaspell slowly stitches together details that reveal the pattern clearly. She makes clever use of the quilting term of "knotting" to suggest that the women have joined to block the prosecution's case against Minnie. Quilting points to another key metaphor in defining the importance of women's work as sisterhood. Whereas women in a community have traditionally gathered for quilting bees to finish the tedious work of stitching the patchwork top layer to the stuffing and backing, the solitary Mrs. Wright, having to rely on herself, would have chosen the faster method of knotting (pulling yarn through the material at perhaps twelve-inch intervals and tying it off in a knot). Although Minnie Wright's community of sisters neglected her in the past, they now rally together to save her life. A jury of her peers has reached its verdict: not guilty.

Laura M. Zaidman

JUST LATHER, THAT'S ALL

Author: Hernando Téllez (1908-1966)
Type of plot: Suspense
Time of plot: The 1940's
Locale: Colombia
First published: "Espuma y nada más," 1950 (English translation, 1971)

> *Principal characters:*
> AN ANONYMOUS BARBER, the narrator
> CAPTAIN TORRES, a military officer

The Story

In a barbershop in a small Colombian town, the proprietor, the narrator of the story, is shaving a man. This is no typical customer, however; the barber recounts that he began to tremble when he recognized him. The barber's detailed description of Captain Torres hanging up his military cap, bullet belt, and holster highlights the man's authority and his potential for violence. During the course of the shave, the two men engage in brief but revealing dialogue. The captain has just returned from capturing a band of revolutionaries and takes pride in his success on a difficult mission. The barber encourages Torres to give details on the number of men apprehended and their fate, because he is a clandestine member of that faction. To add to the barber's anxiety, Torres asks for acknowledgment of his treatment of revolutionaries. His brutality is confirmed when he reminds the barber of the previous week's event when he summoned the town to view target practice on the bodies of hanged rebels.

The barber's monologue reveals the moral dilemma that he faces while shaving the captain. On one hand, he is an informant for the revolutionary party and has the opportunity to kill his enemy. Allowing the man to leave unharmed would compromise the barber's credibility as a rebel. Given his expertise with a blade, the barber contemplates how easy it would be to slit Torres's throat while he reclines, with his eyes closed, and his face covered with lather. Killing the captain would mean avenging the death of many of his comrades and perhaps even saving those recently captured. Fate has presented him with a rare opportunity to become a hero.

On the other hand, the barber considers that killing under such circumstances not only could be interpreted as a cowardly act, but also would make him as much a criminal as Torres. "Murderer or hero?" the protagonist asks himself. He realizes that the crime would eventually lead to his capture and execution. The barber also reflects on the result of revolutionary armed conflict. Although he recognizes Torres's inhumanity, murdering him would contribute one more link to a never-ending chain of violence. "Others come along and still others," the rebel in barber's gown thinks to himself, "and the first ones kill the second ones, and they the next ones and it goes on like this until everything is a sea of blood."

He finishes the shave and must determine what to do before the captain rises from the chair. The story's climax is reached with the barber's decision. "I don't want blood on my hands," he says to himself, "Just lather, that's all." As Torres leaves the barbershop he says, "They told me that you'd kill me. I came to find out. But killing isn't easy. You can take my word for it."

Themes and Meanings

Several aspects of Hernando Téllez's personal background peer through his story's narrative. Christian morality, crime suspense, and political circumstance are key elements in this story. Téllez was educated by clerics at the Christian Brothers school in Bogotá and worked at a newspaper as a crime reporter. As a journalist, he later covered politics. His liberal political activity led to various government appointments abroad, which gave him a vantage point for his journalistic essays on social, political, and literary issues.

Political upheaval is the most apparent theme in Téllez's story. Given the author's political partisanship, its historical context points to the period of civil unrest known as "La Violencia" in Colombia. The Liberals had been in power for sixteen years when the Conservatives won elections in 1946. The assassination of Liberal party leader Jorge Eliécer Gaitán in 1948 unleashed an equally brutal feud between Liberals and Conservatives that lasted more than a decade. Torres and the barber personify these feuding parties in Colombian politics.

Christian morality influences the barber's decision not to kill Torres despite the numerous deaths the man has orchestrated. As if his values were being tested, the barber is put in a situation where a man's life is literally in his hands. The emphasis on his hands is notable because, given their expertise with a razor, they can be lethal, but they also know exactly how much pressure to exert in order to attain a smooth shave without the tiniest nick. The barber reiterates in various ways that he is, above all, excellent at his trade. Tempted to play God, he ultimately rejects the opportunity to kill his enemy: "You are an executioner and I am only a barber."

Along with Christian morality, the cult of virility or "machismo" is prevalent in the socialization of boys in Latin America. Demonstrating courage and settling conflict by fighting is part of the macho culture. Both Torres and the barber show signs of internalized machismo. Torres epitomizes the macho who gambles his life by allowing a rebel to put a razor to his throat. The barber's thought process suggests an inner struggle between religious and cultural indoctrination.

A characteristic of crime fiction is that a criminal is apprehended and brought to justice for the good of law-abiding citizens. Such an accomplishment means the resolution of the conflict. As history has shown repeatedly in Latin America, in situations in which the criminal is a government official with power over the community, citizens may be forced to procure justice themselves. Regardless of the political ideology, the story portrays the disregard for human rights, including persecution, incarceration, torture, and death, perpetrated against civilians by an oppressive regime.

Style and Technique

Téllez's writing is distinctive for its economy of words. Descriptions and explanations are kept to a minimum, and superfluous adjectives are eliminated. Suppressing information is a technique used to hold the reader's attention. For example, the remarkably short opening sentences establish several unknowns: Who came in? Where is he? Why does he inspire fear? Who is sharpening a blade, and why? As one reads on, some questions are answered as new ones emerge.

The conversation between Torres and the barber consists of scant, but key, facts. The reader must play close attention not to miss any important clue. After building interest with just enough information about the two characters, the author introduces suspense as another technique to hold the reader's attention. At first, only limited knowledge is granted. Then an abundance of detail is supplied, thus suggesting its importance to the plot. For example, minute focus on the captain's hair growth and texture, his cheeks, chin, neck, the consistency of the lather, and even the angle of the blade as it is maneuvered over the customer's face creates expectations in the reader.

Throughout the narration, the barber reiterates just how good he is with a razor while he reminds himself of this customer's crimes. The reader is thus convinced of both the barber's ability and motive to kill Torres. "And how easy it would be to kill him," thinks the barber, "he deserves it." The barber also repeatedly expresses ambivalence, highlighted by his fear, nervousness, and profuse sweating. The following sequence illustrates the protagonist's wavering, which keeps the reader in suspense: "I could cut this throat just so, zip! zip! . . . But I'm trembling like a real murderer. . . . I'm sure that one solid stroke, one deep incision, would prevent any pain. . . . But what would I do with the body?" This inscription of self-doubt keeps the reader guessing and interested in the resolution. Another ingredient that maintains suspense in the story is the race against the clock. Considering his skill at shaving, it should not take the barber long to finish his task.

The surprise ending is another technique that prevents the plot's intrigue from dissolving. The ending paradoxically eliminates the possibility of an end to the story. There is no closure to the situation, as there seems to be no end to the violence in Colombia. As if coming full circle, the captain's exit from the barbershop arouses as many questions for the reader, and as much fear for the barber, as does his arrival at the beginning of the story.

Gisela Norat

JUST LIKE A TREE

Author: Ernest J. Gaines (1933-   )
Type of plot: Social realism
Time of plot: The 1960's
Locale: Rural Louisiana
First published: 1963

> *Principal characters:*
> AUNT FE, an elderly black woman
> AUNT LOU, her closest friend
> LOUISE, her kin
> EMMANUEL, a young black man

The Story

Aunt Fe, an elderly woman known and loved throughout her small community in rural Louisiana, is leaving the place where she has lived all of her life. Louise, her kin, has come with her husband, James, to take her north. On this day, members of the community, all of whom feel as though they are kin to Aunt Fe, gather to say farewell. No one wants to see her leave, and those who know her best are sure that she would rather stay where she is. Aunt Clo, one of the old ones, thinks that moving Aunt Fe is like uprooting a tree and finding you did not get the taproot. You destroy the tree and you create only holes: one in the ground and the other in the air, where the lovely branches used to be. Louise, however, believes she has no choice.

Louise's main motivation for taking Aunt Fe away is fear for the old woman's safety. There has been a recent bombing, in which a black woman and her children were killed. There is little doubt that the bombing was the work of white racists opposed to the nonviolent struggle for justice waged by blacks involved in the Civil Rights movement, which promises (or threatens) revolutionary changes to a region resistant to change of any kind.

Even benign whites such as Ann-Marie Duvall, whose love for Aunt Fe is genuine, cannot quite understand what black people want. Ann-Marie's visit to Aunt Fe, in spite of the barriers of sleet, mud, and darkness that must be overcome, indicates her willingness to meet her obligations to these people, as had her father, her grandfather, and her great-grandfather. An irony that escapes Ann-Marie is that her great-grandfather's relationship to black people had been that of master to slave.

Few of the blacks who have gathered to say good-bye to Aunt Fe are involved in social agitation. They are more directly involved in the timeless battles of families, neighbors, and generations. Elias, for example, suffers under the commanding eye of his mother, Aunt Lou. He wants to get rid of the useless mule, Mr. Bascom, but Aunt Lou promised her late husband that she would look after Mr. Bascom, and Aunt Lou does not make promises lightly.

Louise's husband, James, does not know what to make of these country folk. He does not understand why Louise, whom he calls "Baby," insists on taking Aunt Fe north. The people of the community, in turn, have their doubts about James. Leola finds his practice of embracing and nuzzling his wife in the presence of others distasteful and more: A man who carries on that way in public, Leola believes, has something to hide.

A leader in the civil rights struggle is Emmanuel, a young man who has known Aunt Fe since his boyhood. It was from Aunt Fe that he learned the gruesome details of his father's lynching. He also learned from her that he must not respond to the violence and hatred that killed his father with violence and hatred of his own. Now, Emmanuel finds himself the target of resentment from some members of his own community; they believe that people like him, stirring up the resentment of the whites, are ultimately responsible for outrages such as the bombing and the deaths that result.

Emmanuel understands the feelings that drive people to say such things and sympathizes, but he believes that unless the struggle goes on, those who have already died will have died in vain. Louise says that what Emmanuel does is up to him, but she is taking Aunt Fe away before it is her house that is bombed. As Emmanuel takes his leave, Aunt Fe utters a prayer that God will be with him.

Aunt Fe does not leave after all. During the night she dies. Her friend Aunt Lou, who is with her at the end, asks her to tell the others that Lou is not far behind.

Themes and Meanings

The source of the story's title is a black spiritual that also served as an anthem of the Civil Rights movement. The spiritual celebrates a determination to remain firm in the way of salvation. In its secular application, it expressed a resolve to remain firm in the struggle for justice. Both aspects of the spiritual's significance are relevant to this story.

The title's allusion to African American folk Christianity suggests the deep spiritual roots of the community depicted in the story. These roots are linked to religion, but they are not merely religious in the narrowest sense of that word. This is what an outsider such as James cannot understand. As a white woman, Ann-Marie is also an outsider, but her life has touched that of the black community at a number of points; she does not fully understand the community, but, unlike James, she appreciates how much there is to understand.

The metaphor of the tree extends to Aunt Fe as well. It turns out that she will not be moved. From one point of view, her death on the eve of her scheduled departure is mere coincidence, but one senses that her will is involved, even if there is no conscious decision on her part. When she says that she will not leave, in a last conversation with Aunt Lou, her assertion seems to combine awareness and determination; certainly Aunt Lou is not surprised at her friend's death.

The themes generated by the tree metaphor come together in the person and situation of Emmanuel. Although his cause is a secular one, he bears the name of the Redeemer and is moved by a sense of mission, driven by the force of the spirit. Aunt Fe has been an inspiration to him: Both her personal character and what she represents of the community's past have led to his commitment to the community's future. He seems to need something from Aunt Fe before he takes his leave. Perhaps, in her prayer, he hears her blessing. Having received it, he will not be moved.

Style and Technique

The most striking technical feature of "Just Like a Tree" is the author's use of multiple narrators. Each narrator speaks with a distinctive voice, and each has something to contribute to the narrative. Even the outsiders, James and Ann-Marie, with their limited understanding, point to deeper levels of insight.

It is Aunt Fe's departure that is most on the mind of these people, but their thoughts are not limited to this one event. They have their own lives, their own concerns, illustrated by the tensions, observed with understated humor, between Emile and Aunt Lou. Through multiple narrators, the author provides not only multiple perspectives on what is happening to Aunt Fe, but also a wider and deeper acquaintance with the community as a whole.

Aunt Fe and Emmanuel stand at the moral center of the story, and it is significant that neither assumes the role of narrator. Readers see them as the others see them. They hear as the others do their words and their silences. The responsibility of understanding what to see and hear remains the reader's. One may assume that Gaines supports the Civil Rights movement, but the emphasis in this story is not on the didactic but on the dramatic.

This is the emphasis that motivates the technique. On first reading, there may be some difficulty in keeping straight who is who, and who is related to whom. By demanding the reader's active involvement in the narrative process, Gaines encourages one to bring to bear on the story the power of one's own moral imagination.

W. P. Kenney

KEELA, THE OUTCAST INDIAN MAIDEN

Author: Eudora Welty (1909-2001)
Type of plot: Fable
Time of plot: The 1930's
Locale: Cane Springs, Mississippi
First published: 1940

> *Principal characters:*
> LITTLE LEE ROY, a clubfooted black man who was once in a
> carnival sideshow
> STEVE, a young man who was Lee Roy's barker for the sideshow
> MAX, the man who takes Steve to see Lee Roy at his home in
> Cane Springs

The Story

Practically the entire story "Keela, the Outcast Indian Maiden" is presented as a dialogue between Steve, a young man who once was the barker for the sideshow in which Little Lee Roy, a clubfooted black man, was presented as Keela, the Outcast Indian Maiden, and Max, a man who runs a café near Lee Roy's home and who brings Steve to see him. Occasionally, Lee Roy himself enters into the conversation, but primarily the story focuses on Steve trying to explain to Max why he continued in the barker's job. Ostensibly, Steve has come to find Lee Roy and give him some money, or something, and thus expiate his sin against the humanity of the clubfooted black man. Once he finds him, however, he takes little note of him at all, directing his attention primarily to Max, ignoring Max's repeated question about whether this man is the same as Keela. The only thing on Steve's mind is to tell his story.

Steve has come to find Little Lee Roy, the story soon makes clear, not to make any reparation but, like Samuel Taylor Coleridge's Ancient Mariner, to implicate someone else, to force Max to understand the meaning of the situation and to make him care. In horrified accents, Steve tells of Keela/Lee Roy biting chickens' heads off, sucking their blood, and then eating them raw. In his anxious state, Steve says, "I was the one was the cause for it goin' on an' on an' not bein' found out—such an awful thing. It was me, what I said out front through the megaphone."

Steve then tells how one man came to the show and exposed the fraud and freed Lee Roy. He insists, however, that he himself did not know the show was a fraud, that he did not know Keela could tell what people were saying to "it." He says he has been feeling bad ever since and cannot hold on to a job or stay in one place. The fact that he still refers to Keela/Lee Roy as "it," however, and that he does not see that his continuing to work for the show was immoral regardless of whether the so-called freak was an outcast Indian maiden or a clubfooted black man, indicates that Steve still has not faced the nature of his guilt. He seems puzzled that the man who freed Lee Roy could have studied it out and known something was wrong. "But I didn't know," Steve says. "I can't look at nothin' an' be sure what it is. Then afterwards I know. Then I see how it was." He insists that Max would not have known either, that he, too, would have let it go on and on just as he did.

When Max says he bets he could tell a man from a woman and an Indian from a black person, Steve hits him in the jaw and knocks him off the steps. Max makes no attempt to fight back, and Steve explains his action by saying, "First you didn't believe me and then it didn't bother you." Then, without ever admitting that he has actually found Lee Roy, Steve says that he has to catch a ride someplace. The anticlimactic conclusion of the story is reached when Lee Roy's children come home and he tells them that two white men came to the house and talked about "de old times when I use to be wid de circus," to which his children reply, "Hush up, Pappy." The final irony—that what for Steve has been a horrifying experience of his own guilt is for Little Lee Roy a memory of the days with the circus when he was the center of everyone's attention—does not erase the responsibility of the white man for setting up the freak show and exploiting the black man. It is, after all, such moral indifference—Steve's, Max's, and even Lee Roy's—that is at issue here.

Themes and Meanings

The most obvious thematic point of the story depends on the gap between Steve's need to exonerate himself and Lee Roy's seeming incomprehension of the moral crime that the white men have perpetuated on him. The related theme of moral blindness is reflected by Steve's inability to accept the fact that this black man before him is indeed the same as Keela, who was made to act as a freak in a sideshow, and by Max's seeming indifference to the moral crime that has been committed. Eudora Welty has said that she got the idea for the story one day on assignment at a fair. A man building a booth told her a story about a little black man in a carnival made to eat live chickens. It is the only real-life story she ever used, she says, for it was too horrible for her to have made it up.

Certainly the actuality of the story is horrible enough, but Welty sees more in the case of Little Lee Roy than one example of humanity's cruelty to others. Lee Roy also surely catches her imagination as a real-life example of the mythical outcast figure forced to serve as scapegoat for the bestiality of society itself. She transforms the little black man into one of her holy innocents, exploited and elevated into a mythical figure.

Steve's inability to look at things and know how they are and his insistence that this probably had to happen suggest that in some ways the story is a kind of parable of the guilt of the southern white man about his responsibility for slavery. Just as the white slave owner insisted that he did not know how bad things were for the black man or argued that he was meant to live in servitude, Steve attempts to justify what happened to Little Lee Roy. The fact that the geek, or sideshow freak, in the story is black also allows Welty to suggest the broader and more complex sources of the white man's exploitation of the black man: as a scapegoat figure for his own dark nature.

The black-man-as-scapegoat theme is amplified by the explicit focus of the side-show freak functioning also as scapegoat. Although the human desire to view a freak can partially be attributed to the curiosity to see abnormality, curiosity alone does not explain the phenomenon. Desire to see freakishness is a basic, and perhaps base, cathartic need. That people pay money to see such acts as someone biting the heads off chickens can be explained in typical scapegoat fashion, that seeing such abnormality makes one more comfortable in his own normality. The fact that people frequent such shows, even when they know that the Outcast Indian Maiden or Lost Swamp Woman is actually a destitute local, further indicates that the geek show is a primitive ritual of scapegoat significance, complete with grotesque disguises, audience suspension of disbelief, and communal catharsis.

Style and Technique

The basic technique of "Keela, the Outcast Indian Maiden," typical of Welty, is the imposition of a mythic framework on a seemingly realistic situation. Welty draws on her knowledge of ancient myth to create around Little Lee Roy an aura of archetypal significance. The first clue to this is the name Little Lee Roy, which (given the French words for "the king," le roi) suggests "little king." Moreover, because Lee Roy is club-footed, he suggests the maimed king, a variation of the Fisher King of the Holy Grail story. As such, he fulfills the role of scapegoat described in anthropological studies of myth. Steve, as the outsider who comes into his kingdom to do something about the king's injured condition, becomes the Quester of the myth. One primary task of the hero in the ancient myth is to ask the king the important question, "What aileth thee, mine uncle?" Steve's failure to pose the liberating question to Little Lee Roy while he was in the freak show and his further failure to inquire of him now that he is back home in Cane Springs make Steve's guilt the same as that of the Quester in the myth who fails to pity the king.

Welty's creation of such a figure that embodies so many subtle aspects of the social scapegoat implicates the reader in Steve's guilt for letting it go on and on and not being found out. It is not only the concrete image of a disguised little black man biting chickens' heads off in a carnival sideshow that horrifies the reader, but rather the realization that he or she has always paid his money to see such things and then tried to deny their reality. The story's impact cannot be attributed solely to the physical horror it depicts, although that indeed is shocking enough. Like any good short story, "Keela, the Outcast Indian Maiden" presents a moral dilemma that has the power to involve the reader directly, but that does so through the symbolic power of the language of the story itself.

Charles E. May

THE KEPI

Author: Colette (Sidonie-Gabrielle Colette, 1873-1954)
Type of plot: Psychological
Time of plot: About 1897
Locale: Paris
First published: "Le Képi," 1943 (English translation, 1959)

Principal characters:
COLETTE, the narrator, a young wife
PAUL MASSON, her friend
MARCO, a forty-five-year-old woman who ekes out a living as a
    ghostwriter
LIEUTENANT TRALLARD, Marco's young lover

The Story

Colette's good friend Paul Masson senses her loneliness and visits her frequently to cheer her up with his "lies." One day he tells her about the lady of the library, who has never had a lover. Once she had a husband, but he mistreated her and she left him; nowadays she makes a living ghostwriting cheap novels for a sou a line. This, however, is not another of Masson's lies—Marco really exists.

Colette is intrigued by the tale of the struggling, middle-aged writer and accompanies Masson to Marco's dilapidated apartment. There she finds a thin, graceful woman with beautiful eyes and elegant manners. Marco's clothing is threadbare, yet she entertains her guests with dignity and tact.

The two women become good friends. Although their friendship is not one of great intimacy, Marco makes a rare confession one day.

> To be perfectly frank with you, I'm convinced that fate has spared me one great trouble, the tiresome thing that's called a temperament. No, no, all that business of blood rushing into the cheeks, upturned eyeballs, palpating nostrils, I admit I've never experienced it and never regretted it.

On her part, the twenty-two-year-old Colette plays the role of fashion mentor, giving her friend hair and makeup tips. Because of Marco's poverty, she cannot afford new clothing and toiletries, yet she suddenly receives a minor windfall: Her husband, apparently prospering in America, sends her fifteen thousand francs. Marco accepts her good fortune with composure and prudently uses the money to move to an apartment only slightly larger and more comfortable; she also allows Colette to help her choose a smart new wardrobe.

One evening, Masson, Marco, and Colette compete to see who can write the best response to a letter in the newspaper's lovelorn column from a "warmhearted, cultured" lieutenant. Marco's letter piques the lieutenant's interest, and a correspondence begins between the two. When Marco shows one of Lieutenant Trallard's letters to Colette, the young woman obliquely criticizes its banality, but Marco is only half listening—her response is to ask Colette for a toothpaste recommendation.

The correspondents eventually meet and quickly become involved in a passionate affair. Marco develops all the symptoms of a "belated, embarrassing puberty": She describes her lover (who is apparently much younger than she) in idealistic terms, blushes easily, and is dreamily absentminded. At the beginning of the affair Marco is nervous and drawn, but as she comes to accept her new sensuality she begins to gain weight, her plumpness reflecting her now sated, even surfeited, appetites. However, one day eight months later, she announces to Colette that the affair has abruptly ended.

She recounts that while lying in bed with the lieutenant during a rainy afternoon of lovemaking, she playfully placed his hat—the round, flat-topped kepi—on her head in a waggish move. As she did so, she saw something change in the man's eyes as he viewed his middle-aged lover in her post-coitus dishabille striking the pose of a flirtatious teenager, suddenly setting off her own age in conspicuous relief. She has not seen him since: The affair was terminated as expediently as it was begun.

Colette does not hear news of Marco for some time, until one day Masson mentions that she is back at the library. "So she's taken up her old life again," remarks Colette.

"Oh no," said Masson. "There's a tremendous change in her existence!"
"What change? Really, one positively has to drag things out of you!"
"Nowadays," said Masson, "Marco gets paid two sous a line."

Themes and Meanings

In many of Colette's stories, love, or a semblance thereof, leads to disappointment—not because love is naturally disappointing, but because people mismanage it. In "The Kepi," the innocent Marco pursues love in the wrong way from the beginning when she refuses to see the distressing usualness of the lieutenant's letters that Colette perceives. Colette further hints at the problem when Marco pops in one afternoon shortly after first meeting the lieutenant. Because Marco is in high spirits, Colette believes that she has control of the situation and is keeping the liaison in its correct perspective. This is not the case, though, for Marco's emotions are out of control to the extent that she half-seriously believes her lover has cast a spell on her. This lack of control is symbolized in her weight gain and in her final imprudence with the kepi. Colette intimates that vigilance, perspective, and a measure of self-control, both physically and emotionally, are necessary to maintain love, even more so when one of the parties can no longer rely on youthful attractiveness to gloss over infractions. If Marco's response to unlooked-for love had been the same gracious equanimity with which she received her financial good fortune, then she may still have lost her love, but not her dignity, Colette seems to say.

Masson's closing comment, that payment of two sous per line constitutes a "tremendous change" in Marco's life, reminds the reader ironically of the other "tremendous" (that is, trite) change that Marco underwent, from poised woman to foolish soubrette. Although the narrator implicitly criticizes Marco's behavior, Colette herself contributes to her friend's downfall. Fashionable details ("the new 'angel' hairstyle," "more nipped-in waistlines," and "a rosier shade of powder") preoccupy both the narrator and the character Colette. Becoming more attractive under Colette's care not only makes Marco more alluring to the opposite sex but also primes the austere and dignified woman to see herself as romantic heroine. The narrator's tone implies that Marco's misadventure is the result only of Marco's poor judgment; Colette never acknowledges her own complicity.

Style and Technique

Colette is not only misleading in suggesting that she had nothing to do with Marco's downfall, but also deceptive in another way. Autobiography does not simply creep into "The Kepi"; it leaps in. The first four paragraphs, for example, could be culled directly from Colette's autobiography. As in many of her stories, the line between fact and fiction is blurred, the distinction between author and first-person persona negligible. Because of this, Colette is at once the most honest writer of fiction and the most deceptive. She is honest in that she does not attempt to disguise herself and speaks candidly about her life and the people she knew, such as Paul Masson. She is deceptive because "The Kepi" remains, nevertheless, a work of fiction. Having introduced herself as Colette, a real person with a real life, her implicit message is that everything she relates must be true, too, which is not the case. Her daring and unashamed mixture of fact and fiction provides her work with a tantalizing realism to some readers, and a measure of frustration to others who like their genres more clear-cut.

In the end, the kepi is a powerful symbol because of the antithesis developed by Colette's scattering of feminine details throughout the story. Even her digressions relate to style; for example, when she moves to a new apartment, Colette relates that she purchased "white goat skins, and a folding shower bath from Chaboche's" to decorate it. More important, Marco and Colette's relationship is founded on and solely nourished by feminine concerns: hair, clothes, makeup. These details establish the effectiveness of the kepi as the vehicle of Marco's debasement, the irony being appropriately struck by the introduction of the sole item of masculine fashion in the story.

Susan Davis

THE KERCHIEF

Author: Shmuel Yosef Agnon (Shmuel Yosef Czaczkes, 1888-1970)
Type of plot: Lyric
Time of plot: Probably the early twentieth century
Locale: Galicia (a former province of southern Poland)
First published: "Ha-mitpahat," 1932 (English translation, 1935)

> *Principal characters:*
> THE NARRATOR, a small boy
> HIS FATHER
> HIS MOTHER

The Story

"The Kerchief" is a lyric memory of a pious, naïve childhood in a traditional Jewish household in Galicia. In a series of thirteen episodes, or chapters, requiring from one to a very few paragraphs each, the first-person narrator recalls his relationship with his mother and father, the background of the kerchief, which was a gift from his father to his mother, and the time of his Bar Mitzvah at age thirteen, when he gave away the precious kerchief to a beggar.

The first ten sections of the story focus on the emotional effect on the family of the father's yearly weeklong visit to the Lashkowitz fair, where Jewish merchants gathered together from all over the district to sell their wares. The narrator remembers especially the sadness of his mother in his father's absence, during which she refrained from rebuking the children severely and spent much time standing at the window looking out. These absences of the father are likened to the week of the Ninth of Ab, observed in memory of the destruction of the Jerusalem Temple.

While his father was gone, the narrator slept in his father's bed. He used to meditate about the promised Messiah who would reveal himself suddenly in the world and lead them all to the Land of Israel, where his father would not have to go to fairs and he himself would not have to go to school, but would walk all day in the courts of the House of God.

The child would sometimes dream of this fabulous event of the future, when the precious gifts of God would seem like a heaven of many-colored lights. However, often a great bird would come and peck out the lights. One night the dreamer tied himself to the wings of the bird and commanded it to take him to Father. The bird took him instead to the gates of Rome, where he saw a miserable beggar suffering from many wounds. The dreamer turned his eyes away so as not to see the beggar's suffering, but where he directed his eyes a great mountain arose covered with thorns, thistles, and evil beasts. He was terrified, but he did not scream lest the creeping things on the mountain should enter his mouth. Then Father appeared, wrapped him in his prayer shawl, and returned him to his bed.

The father always brought gifts for everyone when he returned from the fair. The child thought that the Master of Dreams must have informed the father of their most secret desires, for the presents were always something for which each had been longing. One day Father brought for Mother a lovely silken kerchief adorned with flowers. She wore it on her head thereafter on all the most sacred occasions of family ritual and religious festivals. The narrator remembers, "I used to look at Mother on the Day of Atonement, when she wore her kerchief and her eyes were bright with prayer and fasting. She seemed to me like a prayerbook bound in silk and presented to a bride."

The eleventh section concerns an unlucky beggar who arrived in town sick with running sores. Children used to throw stones at him. Even the grown-ups, who were not by nature cruel and who generally were hospitable to the poor and suffering, rejected this particular beggar and drove him away.

The twelfth section recalls the day of the narrator's Bar Mitzvah at age thirteen, "when I entered the age of Commandments and was to be counted a member of the congregation." He was very happy and pleased with himself and dressed "like a bridegroom." Best of all, his mother had tied her precious kerchief around his neck before he went to the House of Study. As he walked home alone, he came suddenly on the despised beggar sitting on a heap of stones. The boy was terrified, "as a man who sees in waking what has been shown him in dream." Overcome, however, by an unaccountable sweetness he had never experienced before, he untied the kerchief from his neck and gave it to the beggar, who took it and wound it around his sores.

The last section tells of his confrontation with his mother when he had to beg forgiveness for having given away her most precious possession. His mother accepts the deed with love and affection, apparently as evidence of obedience to the Holy Law.

Themes and Meanings

Shmuel Yosef Agnon, who was born in Galicia, then called Austria-Hungary, in this story celebrates some of the most endearing of traditional Jewish values, especially the sacredness of the family and its implied reflection of the love between God and his children. Seeing this idyllic vision through the eyes of a child allows the writer to present it simply and reverently, without any tinge of whatever frustration or disillusionment adult experience might bring. In his later stories, Agnon is just as adept, with a Kafka-like awareness of disorder, doubt, and alienation that seems, perhaps, more typical of modern Jewish experience. The confusion and ambiguity of such stories as "A Whole Loaf" stand in stark contrast to this more transcendent vision of wholeness and spiritual integrity, rooted in family devotion and compassion for those who suffer.

According to Hebrew legend, the Redeemer awaits the time of his coming by sitting among the beggars at the gates of Rome, binding his wounds. In his dream, the child first imagines the deliverance of the Israelites as the receiving of gifts, like the delightful return of his father with toys for all the children. However, when he gains enough courage to tie himself to the great overshadowing bird that dims that vision, he is taken to the gates of Rome and confronted with the suffering Redeemer as beggar.

He is, at that point, unequal to this confrontation and turns away to the ominous mountain, which probably represents the inherited burden of human guilt that makes redemption necessary. His father rescues him in his dream from a situation he is not yet mature enough to bear.

When, on the day of his Bar Mitzvah—an appropriate time to accept moral responsibility—the boy comes face-to-face with the despised beggar, he accepts him as the Redeemer of his dream, and this time he does not turn away. Transfixed with mingled compassion and joy, he offers the most valuable thing he has: his mother's kerchief, a symbol of the sacredness of the home.

Only later, when he must account for its absence to his mother, does he realize that he has incurred some debt of guilt for giving away her property. The fact that the mother accepts his action confirms the idea, demonstrated elsewhere in the story when the father's gifts are broken or wear out, that material things are only temporary, but the spirit of the giving lives on in the heart.

Style and Technique

This story succeeds through a lyrically rhythmic, lucid style that reflects the uncluttered, trusting perception of the naïve boy with just a touch of the older, wiser understanding of the man who looks back nostalgically at his childhood:

> When my father, of blessed memory, went to the fair at Lashkowitz for the first time, my mother was once standing at the window when she suddenly cried out, "Oh, they're strangling him!" Folk asked her, "What are you saying?" She answered, "I see a robber taking him by the throat," and before she had finished her words she had fainted. They sent to the fair and found my father injured, for at the very time that my mother had fainted, somebody had attacked my father for his money and had taken him by the throat; and he had been saved by a miracle. In later years, when I found in the Book of Lamentations the words "She is become as a widow," and I read Rashi's explanation, "As a woman whose husband has gone to a distant land and who intends to return to her," it brought to mind my mother, peace be with her, as she used to sit at the window with her tears on her cheeks.

This episode, with its suggestion of clairvoyant sensitivity in the mother, is one of several that suggest the invisible bond of family love that transcends time and space. At one point, the narrator's little sister puts her ear to the dinner table and listens intently, then announces with joy, "Father is coming! Father is coming!" and it was so. The periodic separation and joyful reunion establish a rhythm in the story, in the boy's childhood, and, by analogy to the Old Testament relationship between God and his chosen people, in the religious understanding of history.

The encounter with the beggar has a speechless, almost surrealistic quality. The presence of the brilliant sun suggests that Heaven alone witnesses and approves the deed. Whether the beggar is literally the Redeemer does not matter in the purity of symbolic action.

The sun stopped still in the sky, not a creature was to be seen in the street; but He in His mercy sat in Heaven and looked down upon the earth and let His light shine bright on the sores of the beggar. I began loosening my kerchief to breathe more freely, for tears stood in my throat. Before I could loosen it, my heart began racing in strong emotion, and the sweetness, which I had already felt, doubled and redoubled. I took off the kerchief and gave it to the beggar. He took it and wound it around his sores. The sun came and stroked my neck.

The author's use of Hebrew legend and ethnic customs and rituals precludes a judgment of sentimentality that might otherwise arise when childhood experience is somewhat idealized. One realizes that such a story transcends realism, expressing the archetypal dreams of a devout people.

Katherine Snipes

THE KEY

Author: Võ Phiên (1925-   )
Type of plot: Social realism, frame story
Time of plot: 1975
Locale: Guam; Fort Indiantown Gap, Pennsylvania; and Saigon, Vietnam
First published: 1985

> *Principal characters:*
> THE NARRATOR, a Vietnamese refugee
> A FELLOW REFUGEE, a man about fifty years old
> HIS FATHER, a ninety-three-year-old man, who was left behind

The Story

    The story opens with the reflections of an unnamed narrator, a former refugee who muses that it is strange that the first picture in his memory is that of a shower. He tells how the ship he was on, carrying nine thousand refugees from Vietnam, anchored at the American island of Guam at about 3:00 A.M. on July 5, 1975. After leaving the boats, the refugees first headed to the showers, where they washed after their long journey. The showers, the narrator explains, then became an important part of their daily lives. Every day, as they would line up before the showers, they would socialize and exchange news.

    The narration then shifts to a refugee camp in the mainland United States, at Fort Indiantown Gap in Pennsylvania. The showers there were also important but cruder than those in Guam. The Pennsylvania camp was divided into sections, with each section of about one hundred people assigned to a small, dark shower room, with three showers so that three people of the same sex could wash at the same time. Because the shower rooms were airtight, some people used them as steam baths to cure colds. Many people went into the shower to tape Vietnamese songs and the voices of their friends.

    While showering one day, the narrator hears the confessional story of one of his fellow refugees. Described as shy and in his mid-fifties, the man had his wife, his daughter, and two sons with him in the camp. His family was more complete than most of those of the other refugees, who had been forced to leave family members behind. Despite this, he and his wife always seemed sad.

    The fellow refugee became unusually talkative during the shower. He told the narrator that he had a father who was ninety-three years old and senile. The father had asked him to buy a coffin, a common practice in rural Vietnam. Living in the city, the refugee had not followed the old custom of buying his father a coffin in preparation for death but had promised to buy him a good one after the old man died.

    As it became evident that all of South Vietnam would fall to the forces of the north, the refugee and his family made preparations to flee. However, the father was too old to take along, so the family hid all of their money and valuables, including an ounce of gold for the coffin, in a locked wardrobe for any friend or neighbor who would take care of the elderly father. The middle-aged man and his family had a difficult escape on an overcrowded boat and barely survived until they were rescued by an American ship. Immediately after the rescue, though, he put his hand in his pocket and realized that the key to the locked wardrobe was still in his pocket.

Ever since then, the man has been tormented by thoughts of the friends and neighbors searching for the valuables. He worries about robbers breaking in to look for the hidden wealth and possibly beating his father. Full of guilt, he wears the key around his neck, like a Christian religious symbol. The story reminds the initial narrator of all that he himself had failed to do and all that he had left behind him. He never gets a chance to tell the fellow refugee about the metaphorical key around his own neck, though, because the man seems to avoid him and the two never meet in the shower again.

Themes and Meanings

Although "The Key" is only a few pages in length, it tells one of the epic stories of the late twentieth century. In the years following the fall of the South Vietnamese capital of Saigon to North Vietnamese forces on April 30, 1975, more than a million people fled from the southern part of unified Vietnam and resettled in other countries, mostly in the United States. The first great flood of refugees, generally referred to as "the first wave," left just as the forces of the north were achieving their victory. The United States government established a half-dozen camps inside the mainland United States to receive and hold this first wave of refugees until they could be resettled around their new country.

Leaving a homeland and plunging into a radically different culture was traumatic for most Vietnamese refugees, who carried with them a longing for the land and people they had left behind them. Life in the refugee camps was particularly difficult because the refugees were between homes they had abandoned and homes that they had not yet established.

The first part of the story, in which the narrator tells of his own arrival in Guam and of life in the Pennsylvania refugee camp, may be Võ Phiên's own experience or it may be based on his observations of other refugees. This portion is the kind of anecdote that many Vietnamese people in the United States can tell about their own backgrounds. As editor of a Vietnamese-language literary journal in California, Võ has undoubtedly heard and read repeated accounts of the hard journey from Vietnam to the United States. Still, these accounts remain vivid for most first-generation Vietnamese Americans because the versions of the same story make up the Vietnamese American epic, the tale that summarizes their foundation and their history.

Style and Technique

The strategy for the tale is that of a story within a story. The narrator starts by telling about his own arrival in American territory. He remembers almost exactly the time that his ship dropped anchor in Guam, emphasizing how important this event was for him and how vivid it remains in his memory. He draws the reader's attention to small details. He remembers the appearances of individuals leaving the ship and the sight of the old Christian bishop on the deck of the ship carrying them into the harbor in Guam. He remembers the sound of splashing water in the showers.

These realistic details give the story its sense of being immediately present in the memory of the teller, but they also help to enable the author to make use of symbolism without reducing the fiction to thin allegory. Although this type of anecdote is common among Vietnamese refugees, "The Key" is also symbolic in character. Võ expresses the movement from the old country to the new and the burden of the memory of the old through the symbols of the shower and the key. A shower is a place in which people attempt to wash off old soil and begin anew. The Pennsylvania shower room in this story is a wet, dark, airtight place, a small chamber similar to a womb. Showering is a kind of new birth.

In the shower, people remove their clothes before they begin to try to cleanse themselves of their pasts. The shower, then, is a place of honesty and of unadorned truth because people who shower together are naked together. Only in the shower can the shy middle-aged man unburden himself to the narrator.

A key is a common symbol for anything that can open secret places. Here the secret places are the unspoken sadness that refugees have for their homeland, their uneasy consciences about having survived when others did not, and the feeling of guilt caused by leaving people and unresolved problems behind. The narrator remarks that the middle-aged refugee wears his key around his neck, like a Christian religious emblem. Although Christianity is a minority religion in Vietnam, Catholicism has deep roots in the country, and even non-Christians are familiar with the faith and with its symbolism. As the Christian carries the reminder of Christ everywhere, the Vietnamese refugee carries the memory of ancestors left behind and of customary obligations unfulfilled.

The fact that the key represents an unfulfilled obligation to a parent is especially meaningful. Traditional Vietnamese society places great importance on respect for elders in general and for parents in particular. To have failed to fulfill a duty toward a father, especially the duty to prepare the father's funeral, is to bear a burden similar to the religious burden of guilt.

Carl L. Bankston III

KILL DAY ON THE GOVERNMENT WHARF

Author: Audrey Thomas (1935-   )
Type of plot: Psychological, domestic realism
Time of plot: The 1980's
Locale: The coast of Canada
First published: 1981

Principal characters:
THE WIFE, pregnant for the second time
TOM, her husband
ROBERT, their son

The Story

"Kill Day on the Government Wharf" unfolds from the point of view of a young wife expecting her second child. She, her husband, and their young son are enjoying a vacation at their recently purchased cabin on an island. The cabin is rustic, although it does have basic plumbing and electricity. The year-round residents of the island are predominantly aboriginal Indians who fish for a living.

The story covers events on a late spring day on the island before the summer residents and tourists have arrived. The wife, her husband, Tom, and son, Robert, have been in their cabin for ten days. She is a city person, yet she is enjoying the simplicity and challenges of the country more and more. She wishes, in fact, that the cabin were more primitive and that she could remain on the island through her pregnancy and delivery, living as close to nature as possible. Tom was born and raised in the country. He is extremely self-reliant and competent in the woods. However, he is more than content with as many amenities as possible and looks forward to their return to the comforts and security of home in the city.

In the morning, the husband and wife are having breakfast, talking about their son and about their quite different feelings regarding country living. Tom says that he would like to go fishing before it rains and try to catch something for their dinner. His wife encourages him, enjoying the unfamiliar image of him as frontier provider.

She has another cup of coffee, does the dishes, and wonders whether she could really go through the pregnancy and delivery on the island, with none of the supports and safeguards of contemporary hospitals. Part of her yearns to do just that, but she wonders whether she genuinely wants to live closer to nature or whether, as her husband would think, she is indulging in romantic daydreaming.

Nevertheless, she recognizes that her competency, assurance, and independence are increasing the more she lives in the country. She has learned how to make and light a good fire, how to cook on a wood-burning stove, how to recognize edible and poisonous plants, and how to treat stings, burns, and injuries. She has planted an herb garden. Somewhat reassured by her accomplishments, she does some baking and then takes Robert to the government wharf to watch the fishermen bring in their catch.

Several men are working intently, scooping the cod fish out of the boats, tossing them on the wharf, clubbing and filleting them, and then packing them in garbage cans so they can be weighed. The men go about their work with great intensity, concentration, and proficiency. At first, the wife feels disoriented, even dizzy, owing to the sights, sounds, and smells; yet she is also deeply engaged by this timeless scene of humanity harvesting the sea.

The wife and her son return to the cabin, and the boy takes his afternoon nap. With the scene at the wharf still vividly in her memory, she dreamily imagines how readily she would choose to live such a simple, even primitive life away from the complexity of the city. Then, one of the young fishermen from the wharf knocks on her door and asks to use the telephone. She lets him in.

The young man makes his call and then notices that he has left blood stains on the telephone. He apologizes and asks for a rag to clean it. The wife looks at his hands and notices myriad shallow cuts on them, some recent and many scarred over. He tells her that they are inevitable given the sharpness of the knives they use. She startles him by dipping her fingers into the blood on his hands and drawing lines across her forehead and down her cheeks. He takes the rag from her, spits on it, and wipes the blood from her face. Then he leaves.

That evening, Tom returns to the cabin. He tells his wife that although he did not catch any fish, he nevertheless has a beautiful cod for their dinner that was given to him by a young man in gratitude for her allowing him to use the telephone. Later on they make love, and Tom is surprised by the directness and intensity of his wife's desire. Then they sleep, as Sunday night turns into Monday morning.

Themes and Meanings

"Kill Day on the Government Wharf" is the story of a woman's awakening to her most profound and elemental desires and needs. When the story opens, she tells her husband how increasingly vital and independent she feels since they have left the comforts of the city for a much more strenuous life on the remote island. Tom notices many positive changes in her but suggests that her notions of rustic living are sentimental and would not withstand the reality of prolonged experience. She too wonders if this is not true.

After Tom leaves to go fishing, the wife begins a day of chores and activities, which seem to confirm her feelings that she is growing more independent as a result of the challenges of the island environment. Remote from familiar amenities, she finally has the opportunity and need to acquire knowledge and develop skills that city living renders unnecessary. She is becoming increasingly self-reliant, closer to her husband in this regard because he grew up in such an environment.

When she takes her son to watch the activity on the wharf, she is initially queasy and disoriented, but soon she finds herself watching with deep interest and something more. The ritual of killing, cleaning, packing, and storing the fish has a timeless reality and significance that one cannot experience in the world of supermarkets and packaged meals. The wife is surprised by how profoundly satisfying she finds the scene.

When the young man appears at her door, he asks to use the telephone. The telephone is a modern convenience, and its ready availability and usefulness would seem to support Tom's argument in favor of city life and modernity. However, when she responds to the young man's masculinity, marks herself with his blood, and is in turn cleansed with his saliva, she seems to assert a complete acceptance of the ritual she has just witnessed and the world that it represents. In other words, the act signals her recognition and acceptance of her own deepest instincts to live much closer to the rhythms of nature than city life allows. She has made a profoundly significant choice; and the conclusion, with its emphasis on love, fulfillment, and peace indicates that the consequences of that choice will be positive for her and her family.

Style and Technique

Beginning with breakfast and ending in sleep, the story moves from surfaces to depths in its portrayal of the main character. It opens with a conversation between a husband and wife that is entirely natural and realistic. The reader sees and hears a young couple who obviously love each other and are somewhat amused by how differently they are responding to their rustic environment. The opening scene is so dramatic and realistic that the reader hardly notices the few authorial glimpses into each character's mind or the stage-setting comments that indicate time and place.

When Tom leaves to go fishing, the narrative focuses on the wife's thoughts and feelings as she goes about her routine activities for the day. The transition to her interior state of mind is smooth and deepens the reader's interest in her. It provides crucial insight into the depth of feeling that underlies her earlier comments to her husband about city and country life. The reader recognizes that despite the wife's doubts, her attraction to the elemental in her surroundings is genuine and deep.

The excursion to the government wharf on kill day focuses predominantly on the wife's physical and psychological reactions to the scene unfolding before her. Initially disoriented by the sights, sounds, and smells of kill day on the wharf, the wife soon feels like a participant in the ritual, responding deeply and positively to its assertion of the elemental connection of life with death. Returning to the cottage, she is in a dreamlike state.

When the young man comes to her cottage and asks to use the telephone, the wife seems almost hypnotized by his sudden presence, and by the aura of masculinity and primal energy that envelopes him. She seems to be carried along by profound psychological and emotional currents into a ritualistic demonstration of her embrace of the elemental. Symbolically, with the young man's blood, she links herself with his world, so much closer to the rhythms of nature than the world of the city. That all this occurs on a Sunday subtly reinforces the ritualistic aspect of the wife's action.

Michael J. Larsen

KILLED AT RESACA

Author: Ambrose Bierce (1842-1914?)
Type of plot: War
Time of plot: The American Civil War
Locale: Resaca, Georgia, and San Francisco, California
First published: 1891

> *Principal characters:*
> THE NARRATOR, a topographical engineer during the Civil War
> LIEUTENANT HERMAN BRAYLE, a recklessly brave aide-de-camp
> THE GENERAL, a Union Army brigadier
> MARIAN MENDENHALL, Brayle's lover, who lives in San
> Francisco

The Story

The topographical engineer of a Union brigade during the Civil War, the narrator recalls campaigning in Georgia. He particularly remembers Lieutenant Herman Brayle, a recently added officer in the geographically heterogeneous unit, who came from an Ohio regiment. Tall, handsome, with blue-gray eyes and blond hair, Brayle displayed foolhardy courage during the Battle of Stone River. He did such things as sitting like a statue on horseback, exposed in the open air, and standing like a rock without cover. Mindless of hissing bullets when he carried messages to front-line commanders, he would hand his much-valued horse to an orderly and quietly walk on his perilous errands without ever even stooping down for safety. Once, when his puzzled admirers remonstrated, he smiled amiably and said that if he were mortally wounded, he hoped that the captain would whisper in his ear, "I told you so."

At Resaca, Brayle's brigade was part of a Union arc protected by trees. Beyond an open field, Confederate earthworks formed a chord to the Union arc. The general ordered Brayle to go from one end of the Union arc to the other in order to tell a certain colonel to move closer to the enemy. The general advised Brayle to leave his horse behind, implying that it would be safer for him to go through the woods on foot. Instead, Brayle galloped straight into the open field, proceeding parallel to the enemy line two hundred yards away. He made a dramatic picture with his hat blown off, his long, yellow hair rising and falling rhythmically, erect in the saddle, reins in his left hand, his right arm dangling at his side. Enemy rifles began to spit at him, triggering a spontaneous, thunderous, and deadly but inconclusive artillery duel.

The narrator spotted a gully at right angles to the enemy line in which Brayle might easily have taken refuge after his horse was killed. Instead, he merely stood beside it, declining to move. Riddled with bullets, he soon fell. Marveling at him, both sides ceased firing, and his corpse was honorably removed—to the accompaniment of a fife-and-drum dirge from behind the awestruck enemy lines. Afterward, when the general distributed Brayle's effects, the narrator received a leather pocketbook.

It is now a year after the end of the war and the narrator is on his way to California. He idly inspects the contents of Brayle's pocketbook and finds a letter to Brayle written by a woman named Marian Mendenhall from San Francisco that is dated July 9, 1862. Signed "Darling," the letter alludes to a soldier wounded at a battle in Virginia who told the writer that he saw Brayle taking cover behind a tree during the battle. The woman adds that she could stand learning that her "soldier lover" has died, but not that he was a coward.

The narrator calls on Marian Mendenhall at her San Francisco home, confirms that she knows of Brayle's death, and returns her letter. Telling the narrator that his errand is unnecessary, the woman accepts the letter indifferently, but blushes when she sees a stain on it. The narrator tells her that it is the heart's blood of a true and brave man. Recoiling, she says that she cannot stand the sight of blood, tosses the letter into her fireplace, and asks how Brayle died. Noting that the woman is both exceptionally beautiful and "detestable," he replies that Brayle was bitten by a snake.

Themes and Meanings

This story has such important autobiographical touches that it is worthwhile to outline Ambrose Bierce's wartime activities. Bierce was born in Ohio and was living in Indiana when the Civil War began. Within days of the war's outbreak, he volunteered as a private in an Indiana infantry company. Two months later, he was in combat. Assigned to the brigade of General William Babcock Hazen in March, 1862, he fought in several high-casualty engagements—including Shiloh, Stone River, and elsewhere. In April, 1863, he became a topographical engineer and saw more action at Chickamauga and Chattanooga. He was shot in the head at Kenesaw Mountain. After returning to duty three months later, he participated in engagements through Georgia, including one at Resaca, which he mapped for General Hazen. Because of his courage and efficiency, he steadily rose in rank.

It is also relevant to note that Bierce was disappointed in love at least twice. While recuperating from his head wound in Indiana, he argued ruinously with his fiancé for her flirtatiousness. In 1871 he married another woman and had three children by her but later left her after finding a love letter to her from another man.

Bierce's purpose in "Killed at Resaca" is to dramatize the meaninglessness of military heroism, the occasional valor of wartime opponents, and the folly of love. To satisfy his lover's needs, poor Brayle makes it the business of his life to die heroically. With good looks, useful soldierly qualities, a genial nature, and a nice sense of humor all going for him, he still seeks and meets his death—deliberately and vainly. His suicidal gallop not only draws a hail of enemy bullets, it provokes the premature charge of his comrades, leading to a hundred deaths altogether.

The dirge played by Confederate fifes and drums as Brayle's corpse is retrieved is admirable but silly. Silly, because after a momentary pause, the two sides will resume trying to tear each other to bloody shreds. Through all this, Bierce's central aim is to satirize romantic love. Brayle apparently wants to prove that he is brave enough to merit his darling's commendation—by risking his life until he is killed. Is another reading possible? Perhaps Brayle actually wants to wreak revenge on Miss Mendenhall by demonstrating that it is wiser for him to prefer death in combat to life with any woman who could write such a callously challenging letter.

Style and Technique

"Killed at Resaca" displays both Bierce's realistic descriptive powers and his cynical, sarcastic language. His narrator photographically describes the area into which Brayle rides and in which he is then killed: enemy earthworks, slight crest, woods, curving fringe of forest, and an open field with its sinuous gully. For naturalistic irony, Bierce also notes that the ensuing firefight occurs under a sunny sky.

Bierce's bitter diction regularly seeps into his more neutral passages. Examples abound: men with gray-blue eyes associate courage with men similarly "gifted"; the general's mind is too preoccupied to consider his staff officers' lives, "or those of his [enlisted] men, for that matter"; bold dispatch riders are the "object . . . of admiring marksmen." Bierce is almost vitriolic when he says that soldiers' lives are "precious to their country." Occasionally, when Brayle returns from another reckless display of bravado, he is "about as good as new"—that is, wounded only slightly. When the captain to whom Brayle jocosely whispers is himself killed, Brayle adjusts the corpse's limbs "with needless care." When Brayle stands erect near the end, "death . . . did not keep him long waiting." A splendid bit of understatement comes at the end of "Killed at Resaca." Asked by Miss Mendenhall how Brayle died, the narrator closes his account thus: "'He was bitten by a snake,' I replied." The final pair of words conceal, rather than reveal, the narrator's seething disgust.

Bierce lets his readers complete the closure of this narration. Why this reply? The narrator does not want the "detestable" woman—whose love bite was indeed venomous—to feel proud that she armed her lover with courage and be able to remember that he died for her. Curiously, the narrator concludes earlier in his account that Miss Mendenhall's letter caused the death of a hundred men, and adds, "Is woman weak?" This is Bierce the misogynist writing, not Bierce the former soldier. If those hundred men had not been killed then at Resaca, most would certainly have been killed later that day or soon thereafter. After all, historical casualties during the furor at Resaca included roughly six thousand Union men and five thousand Confederates killed, wounded, or missing. Given such figures, who could much care about a lone casualty named Brayle?

Robert L. Gale

THE KILLERS

Author: Ernest Hemingway (1899-1961)
Type of plot: Social realism
Time of plot: The Prohibition era
Locale: Summit, Illinois
First published: 1927

> *Principal characters:*
> NICK ADAMS, a young boy traveling on his own
> OLE ANDRESON, a former prizefighter who has incurred the
> enmity of the mob
> GEORGE, a counterman in a small diner
> SAM, a black cook in the diner
> AL, a gangster
> MAX, another gangster

The Story

The story begins abruptly with two gangsters, Al and Max, entering a small diner in the town of Summit, Illinois, near Chicago. They try to order dinner, but George, the counterman, tells them that the dinner menu will not be available until six o'clock. After asking for eggs with ham and bacon, the two gangsters order the only other customer in the place, Nick Adams, to go behind the counter with George. Next they ask who is in the kitchen, and they are told that the only other person there is Sam, the black cook. They tell George to have him come out. Al takes Nick and Sam into the kitchen, where he ties and gags them; then he props up the slit where dishes are passed through from the kitchen and positions himself with a sawed-off shotgun aimed at the counter, while Max remains at the counter talking to George. He tells George that they are going to kill Ole Andreson, a Swede who usually comes into the diner at six.

They wait until after seven for Ole Andreson, who never comes in, and they finally leave, with Al concealing the shotgun under his coat. George goes into the kitchen and unties the other two. He tells Nick where Andreson lives and advises him to go and warn him. Nick goes to Andreson's boardinghouse, and, after speaking to the woman who looks after the place, he goes to Ole's room, where he finds Ole lying in bed. When Nick asks Ole if he should go and tell the police, Ole tells him not to, that it would not do any good, and he rolls over in the bed toward the wall, saying he "got in wrong," and that there is nothing he can do to save himself.

Nick then returns to the diner, where he tells George and Sam what Ole said. Sam says that he does not want to hear it and shuts the kitchen door. George says that Ole must have double-crossed someone from Chicago, and Nick says that he "can't stand to think about him waiting in the room and knowing he's going to get it," and that he is going to get out of town. George tells him that that is a good thing to do, and that he had better not think about Ole's dilemma.

Themes and Meanings

Ernest Hemingway's style gives the clue to the real meaning of the story. On their first reading, most readers think that the killers and Ole Andreson are the central figures, but the reader never learns what Ole did or what will ultimately happen to him. Instead, the story simply ends with the three bystanders back in the restaurant discussing what has happened. Although the tone of the story is objective throughout—indeed, the story consists almost entirely of dialogue, with little interpretation or judgment by the author—the focus is clearly on the three bystanders, especially Nick Adams.

Of the three, Nick Adams is the only one whose last name is given, and he is the one who goes to warn Ole, so the narrative follows him throughout. In addition, one of the few interpretative comments on the action by the author concerns Nick. When Nick is untied by George, Hemingway mentions that Nick has never had a towel in his mouth before and that his reaction is one of "trying to swagger it off." At the end of the story, it is only through simple dialogue that the reader learns the reactions of all three. However, Nick's reaction is most important, as the other two are from the area and are apparently more accustomed to violence. Their reaction is less out of shock than an attempt to avoid involvement. Nick is more impressed by what he has witnessed and decides that he does not want to have anything to do with the kind of town where such things happen. It is an initiation for Nick into the evil that exists in the big city. This is one of many stories by Hemingway that deal with the experiences of Nick Adams. Most of the Nick Adams stories appear in the collection *In Our Time* (1924, 1925).

That the story is set near Chicago during the Prohibition era, when lawlessness was rampant, further adds to the realization of evil to which Nick comes. The gangsters are described in an almost comic way as stereotypical mobsters; both wear overcoats and derby hats, and gloves that they do not remove when they eat. As they talk with George, they openly discuss their plan to kill Andreson, and they remain in the diner for more than two hours, having George tell the other customers that the cook is not in. They show very little concern about being apprehended. As they leave, with Al only partially concealing the sawed-off shotgun, they further flaunt their disdain for the law. All this to Nick is a rude awakening to the acceptance of violence by those who live in and near the larger cities.

Style and Technique

The typical Hemingway style is evident in this story. Almost entirely narrated in an objective style, with very little interpretation by the author or any but the most rudimentary descriptions, Hemingway's story makes the reader interpret the significance of the action. Those descriptions that are given are sparse and designed only to establish the mood, such as the few details about the gangsters wearing tight overcoats, derby hats, and gloves. The story is developed through dialogue in a series of short dramatic scenes.

In the dialogue, Hemingway uses a spare, terse style, typical of conversation. Much of the dialogue is concerned with trivial things, with the result that the seriousness of the central incident is consistently undercut. For example, the two gangsters order dinners, and George tells them that dinners will not be available until six o'clock. They then haggle over what time it is and haggle more before they decide to order eggs and bacon and eggs and ham. Ultimately, this conflict between the reality of murder and the casual, matter-of-fact attitude toward it that typifies both the killers and the citywise bystanders is central to the story: Although the other characters, even the doomed Andreson, accept this state of affairs, Nick struggles against it.

Roger Geimer

THE KILLING OF A STATE COP

Author: Simon J. Ortiz (1941-   )
Type of plot: Social realism
Time of plot: The 1950's
Locale: Acoma Reservation, New Mexico
First published: 1974

> *Principal characters:*
> FELIPE, a Native American former marine
> ANTONIO, his younger brother
> LUIS BACA, a sadistic, Indian-hating police officer
> THE UNNAMED NARRATOR, a young reservation boy

The Story

The twelve-year-old narrator retells a story that his friend Felipe told him shortly after Felipe and his brother Antonio shot a New Mexico state police officer. The narrator says that Felipe was not a bad person, but was a little wild. Several years older than the narrator, whom he has taken hunting and fishing, Felipe is a former marine who served in the Korean War and has now returned to the reservation.

Felipe tells his story within a story in a serious, sad manner, because he wants the narrator always to remember it. He blames the shooting on the wine he and Antonio had been drinking. They had come to town and were accosted by Luis Baca, who patrolled the state highway near the reservation and who had previously arrested and beaten Felipe. Baca tells the brothers to get out of town, although they are causing no trouble. As they drive back to the reservation in their pickup, Baca passes them in his patrol car and laughs at them.

After following Baca for some distance, Antonio suddenly speeds up and forces Baca's car off the road into a shallow ditch. While Baca struggles to get his car back on the road, Antonio makes a U-turn and passes back by the patrol car. After another U-turn, they pass by again, taunting Baca. By now, Baca has managed to get his car back on the highway, and he follows the brothers with siren blaring. While Felipe gets out his rifle and cartridges, Antonio turns off the state highway and onto a dirt road running through the reservation, Indian land where Baca has no jurisdiction. That does not stop his pursuit. Antonio drives to a remote area of the reservation near Black Mesa with Baca following, although now at a considerable distance.

The brothers park the pickup behind junipers, which shield it from the road. They get out, find a place where they cannot be seen, and wait in ambush. When Baca slows because of a narrow spot in the road, Felipe begins firing. Although he cannot see Baca because of the sun's glare in the windshield, he aims at the windshield where the steering wheel would be. Felipe fires four times, hitting the windshield with three of the shots. The car stops and Baca gets out slowly. "He called something like he was crying. 'Compadre,' he said. He held up his right hand and reached to us. There was blood on his neck and shoulder." In a gesture of surrender, the wounded Baca tries to unbuckle his pistol belt, but Felipe fires again, hitting him in the belly and knocking him back a step against his patrol car. A final shot to the head drops Baca to the ground.

The brothers approach Baca, who is still alive and moving. Antonio removes Baca's service revolver from its holster and shoots Baca with his own pistol. As Felipe describes it, Baca made a feeble gurgle like a sick cat and then went to hell.

Felipe tells the young narrator that he knows he will be caught and that he will probably die in the electric chair at the state prison near Santa Fe. He has no doubt that Antonio will be caught too. The narrator does not really believe Felipe's story until a few days later when he hears his parents talking about it and is convinced that it is true.

Themes and Meanings

Simon J. Ortiz has written that what he does as a writer, teacher, and storyteller is to "demystify language," making it "familiar and accessible to others, bringing it within their grasp and comprehension." One way that he does this in "The Killing of a State Cop" is by using the twelve-year-old narrator as the means of telling the story and thereby as the sensibility through which the events are transmitted to the reader. The narrator is unmoved and matter-of-fact about the brutal and tragic events he is retelling. He registers no emotional reaction, and the events raise no questions of either a practical or a philosophical nature in his mind. The narrator's concluding statement that "for quite a while, I prayed a rosary or something for him" represents only a perfunctory response to the events he has described.

Ortiz has written elsewhere that language is a "way of life" and that he does not regard it merely as a mechanically functional tool, but as "a way of life which is a path, a trail which I follow in order to be aware as much as possible of what is around me and what part I am in that life." Ironically, in this story the language of the narrator is a gauge of his limited awareness, of his inability to grasp the significance or the tragic implications of the events. The narrator, as created by the language he uses, is no part of the life around him.

In a broader perspective, the story deals with characters with whom it is impossible to sympathize. Luis Baca, although the victim, is a despicable human being, brutal, racist, and ultimately contemptible. When wounded, he addresses his plea for mercy to "compadres," "friends," a hypocrisy that robs him even of the dignity of an honorable death. Felipe deserves no sympathy either. Although persecuted by Baca, he needs wine to find his courage and then shoots from ambush, taking revenge far in excess of the provocation and showing no mercy for his victim or remorse for his crime. He has no understanding of himself or the murder beyond the wine and the simplistic motives he cites—a long-standing hatred of Mexicans, a particular fear of Baca, and a desire for revenge for the beating Baca gave him. The younger brother, Antonio, is seen only at two removes, through what the narrator tells the reader that Felipe said; therefore, his personality and motivation remain too vague to gain sympathy. Even the narrator, although young and innocent, remains passive and devoid of emotion or understanding, thereby failing to elicit sympathy.

The hopelessness of the situation Ortiz describes is intensified by the accessibility of alcohol. Even though it is illegal for Indians to have alcohol, Felipe hated the law and broke it whenever possible. Making it illegal for Indians to buy liquor does not prevent them from drinking, but it leads to a resentment—a hatred—of authority, so when they do drink that hatred is intensified by a sense of the injustice and discrimination of which they are the victims.

The pervasive sense of fatalism that dominates the story comes from these sources. Felipe never imagines that he can get away with killing Baca, and he tells the narrator that he had "better learn to be something more than him, a guy who would probably die in the electric chair." The narrator, however, gives no indication that he has learned anything from the story that will enable him to be something more. The meaningless cycle of brutality and hatred will be perpetuated in the lives of the young, who have nothing to shore them against it but the perfunctory response of "a rosary or something."

Style and Technique

The conversational tone and diction of the young narrator and of Felipe are consistent throughout the story; they create a style that is deliberately antiliterary. Sentences are short, syntax is simple, and clarity is never sacrificed for effect. The visual qualities that have made Ortiz an acclaimed poet are also present in this story; description is spare but made vivid through the use of precise detail. Ortiz also effectively uses the framing device of the young narrator who repeats the story that his older friend had told him.

Major details of plot and character are drawn from an actual murder that occurred much as Ortiz describes it on the Acoma Reservation in 1952. Two brothers, Willie and Gabriel Felipe of Acoma, ambushed a New Mexico state police officer named Nash Garcia. Ortiz would have been the same age as his nameless narrator when Garcia was murdered, and he must have heard the case discussed when he was growing up at Acoma, where he lived until he was twenty.

Dennis Hoilman

KILLINGS

Author: Andre Dubus (1936-1999)
Type of plot: Domestic realism
Time of plot: The 1970's
Locale: A small town in Massachusetts
First published: 1980

> *Principal characters:*
> MATT FOWLER, a fifty-five-year-old businessperson
> RUTH, his wife
> FRANK, their son
> RICHARD STROUT, the man who shot Frank
> MARY ANN STROUT, Richard's estranged wife
> WILLIS TROTTIER, Matt's friend

The Story

In August, Matt and Ruth Fowler buried their twenty-one-year-old son, Frank, who had been murdered. The next month, Matt tells his friend Willis how distressed he is that his wife, Ruth, keeps running into Richard, the man who killed their son and is out on bail until the trial. Willis, who owns a restaurant, says that Richard has come there with a date and tends bar in a nearby town. Matt admits that he has started carrying a gun, hoping that Richard will do something that gives him an excuse to shoot him. Ruth knows about the gun and does not believe that he keeps it at his store because of crime in the area.

Richard, a spoiled, bad-tempered man, had married young and had two children. Frank, home from college for the summer, met and began dating Mary Ann Strout a month after she and Richard had separated. Shortly after Frank and Mary Ann had begun dating, Richard came to Mary Ann's house and assaulted Frank. Ruth already disapproved of her son dating an older woman with children, and her concerns were deepened by rumors that Mary Ann had been unfaithful to her husband. After the assault, Ruth became even more concerned that Frank was too involved with Mary Ann.

Matt enjoyed seeing Mary Ann with Frank, admiring her beauty and the couple's youth and passion. However, he knew that his son was planning to start graduate school in the fall and doubted that Frank was serious about Mary Ann. One night, when Frank was having dinner with Mary Ann and her sons, Richard came to the house and shot Frank in the face and chest.

After a lifetime of being protective of his three children, Matt's grief at his son's murder overwhelms him, and his anger that Richard walks through town where Ruth can see him becomes unbearable. One night, Matt and Willis wait outside the bar where Richard works. When the bar closes and Richard leaves, alone, Matt realizes that part of him has hoped that Richard would be with friends, and he and Willis would have to abandon their plan. They intercept Richard, aim guns at him, and order him into his car. Matt sits behind Richard, with his gun cocked and pointed at his head; Willis follows them in his car. Matt warns Richard to be silent and to drive so as not to attract attention. When they get to Richard's duplex, Willis parks away from the house, and Matt walks in with Richard. Matt observes the tidy home, the picture of Mary Ann and the children, and the neatly made bed, and thinks of Richard's new girl-friend. He instructs Richard to pack his suitcase with clothes for warm weather, say-ing Richard is going to jump bail. Richard is afraid and pleads with Matt, arguing that he was trying to reconcile with Mary Ann, but Frank was in the way. Richard insists that he will spend many years in jail, but Matt is convinced that Richard will be out in a few years if convicted. He tells Richard that the trial would be too much for Ruth to bear so they have bought him a plane ticket out of town, but he feels guilty for having given Richard this false hope.

Telling Richard that someone will pick him up and take him to the airport, Matt in-structs Richard to drive into the woods, take his suitcase, and get out of the car. Rich-ard drops the suitcase and runs, but Matt shoots him in the back. As Richard tries to crawl away, Matt kills him with a shot to the head. Willis and Matt drag the body to the grave they had dug earlier, bury Richard and his suitcase, cover their tracks, and toss the gun into the river. Matt drives Richard's car to Boston and leaves it on a busy street, throws the keys in the river, and returns home with Willis.

Matt has not discussed his plan with Ruth and hopes she will not wake up when he gets home. However, he finds her smoking a cigarette in their darkened bedroom, and she immediately asks him if he did it. She holds him while he tells her the whole story, and both agree that although it will hurt their other children to think that Richard has gotten away free, it is best not to tell them what happened.

Themes and Meanings

Many of Andre Dubus's short stories concern working-class families, and several have characters who work in bars. In "Killings," the catalyst for the plot is a bartender, but the main characters are the middle-class family that is forever shattered by the ap-pearance of the bartender's estranged wife in their lives. Dubus, who spent the last thirteen years of his life in a wheelchair after a freak accident, often uses his fiction to remind readers just how suddenly and unalterably their lives can be changed.

In this story, Dubus invites his readers to ponder the disparity between people's eth-ical responsibility to society and the primal urge to protect and avenge their loved ones. Matt, a gentle and devoted family man, tenderly watches his youngest son's re-lationship with Mary Ann deepen. When her estranged husband kills Frank, Matt's grief is intensified by his wife's pain whenever she sees Richard in town. Matt's agony that Richard walks free and seemingly unconcerned is compounded when he and Wil-lis talk about the short sentences they have heard of other killers getting. Matt says he has to take care of the situation because it is too hard on Ruth, but the reader may won-der if that is just his excuse. It is also unclear how much Willis is only an accomplice and how much he fuels Matt's anger.

At the end of the story, Matt tells Ruth what happened, but it is clear that he hardly comprehends his responsibility for it. He, Ruth, and presumably Willis, will be marked forever by the secret of the cold-blooded murder. Nevertheless, Dubus does not judge Matt and label him either a hero or a sinner—he simply presents the ethical problem to the reader.

Style and Technique

"Killings," one of Dubus's best-known and most respected stories, was the basis for the film *In the Bedroom* (2001). Although the story revolves around passion and violence, Dubus tells the tale in a flat, calm way. The first two acts of violence are dropped into the story unexpectedly and without emotion. The story opens with Frank's funeral, then moves on to the conversation between Willis and Matt about how Matt wishes he could kill the man who murdered his son, but the reader does not know who killed Frank, how, or why. Next, in a long descriptive paragraph, Richard is introduced. He is first connected to Frank by the flat opening line of the next paragraph: "One night he beat Frank." Only then does the reader learn about Mary Ann, and Matt's and Ruth's differing feelings about her.

In a lovely, lyrical scene, Mary Ann joins the Fowlers for a barbeque after a day at the beach. Matt's love for his son is mixed with a wistful attraction to Mary Ann. She is beautiful, but Matt sees in her eyes a sadness and pain that he and his family have been spared, and he wishes he could help and comfort her. The next paragraph starts with, "Richard Strout shot Frank in front of the children." Such jarring shifts of mood are used to emphasize how quickly life can turn from sunny to violent and how swiftly the good things in life can be taken away.

The story's point of view is that of the limited omniscient narrator. The reader sees the events through Matt's eyes only, so Ruth's and Willis's roles in the tragedy are only implied. There is little dialogue; instead, Dubus paints vivid descriptions of the small details of life: the sights that the men pass on their way to Richard's home and to the place of his execution, the way Richard's socks and underwear are folded in the drawer when Matt makes him pack his suitcase, and Matt's memory of his children climbing trees.

Irene Struthers Rush

THE KIND OF LIGHT THAT SHINES ON TEXAS

Author: Reginald McKnight (1956-   )
Type of plot: Psychological
Time of plot: The mid-1960's
Locale: Waco, Texas
First published: 1989

> *Principal characters:*
> CLINT, an African American boy who lives in Waco, Texas
> MARVIN PRUITT, his classmate, a dark-skinned African American
> AH-SO, his classmate, a large silent African American girl
> KELVIN OAKLEY, an older student, a white bully
> MRS. WICKHAM, his white teacher

The Story

"The Kind of Light That Shines on Texas" is told in first person by Clint, an African American boy in a predominantly white elementary school in Waco, Texas, who must deal with his own racism before he can see his African American classmates as fully human. The first line of the story indicates Clint's active dislike for one of his African American classmates, Marvin Pruitt. His reasons for this dislike are too clear: Marvin epitomizes certain negative stereotypes of African American males. Marvin is dark-skinned, smells bad, is two grades behind, and is hostile. Clint largely ignores a second African American classmate, Ah-so, a heavyset girl, who is also behind in school, but obviously not stupid; she simply refuses to speak.

Their sixth-grade teacher, Mrs. Wickham, makes little effort to hide her racism. She ignores Marvin, who sleeps away most of the day, she narrows her eyes in disapproval whenever Clint answers a question correctly, and she badgers Ah-so with questions even though this girl steadfastly refuses to speak. Mrs. Wickham frequently regales her students with *harmless* racist jokes. Clint even laughs at her jokes.

The white children, when not outright hostile, show little understanding of their own racist attitudes. One boy assumes that Clint should feel ashamed of Marvin because they share the same skin color. Clint does feel ashamed: ashamed of Marvin and ashamed of himself for feeling the way that he does about Marvin.

One white boy, Kelvin Oakley, proves to be real trouble for Clint. Oakley constantly refers to Clint with racist slurs and expresses a desire to kill him on a nearly daily basis. Clint does his best to ignore Oakley's slurs and to avoid the older, bigger boy. One day the school coach gives Oakley the chance he has long awaited to hurt Clint. Following a relatively innocent game of murderball, the coach replaces the large, squishy red rubber balls with hard-pumped volley balls.

He sets the boys to play against each other; the usual rules of the game are suspended. Surprisingly, Clint wins this game with a hit on Oakley's nose, leaving the older boy flat on his back and bleeding profusely.

Clint, however, knows that retribution will follow. Shortly afterward, Clint faces Oakley in the locker room. Oakley now threatens to get Clint after school. Marvin Pruitt is standing innocently by, combing his hair. Clint demands, "Why not him? . . . How come you're after *me*, not *him*?" Clint manages to escape Oakley that afternoon, but he cannot escape the implications of his own words. That evening, Clint keeps trying to reassure himself that he did not mean his words *that way*, but Clint knows in his heart that he did mean those words, exactly the way that they sounded.

The next day, Oakley predictably picks a fight with Clint. Clint demands that Oakley call him the worst of racial epithets, "nigger." Marvin Pruitt sees what is going on, disdainfully brushes Clint aside, and proceeds to pound Oakley. After the fight is all over, Marvin simply stares down Clint. The school morning goes on as usual with the pledge of allegiance and the songs of Texan pride. However, a chastened Clint now looks at and sees Ah-so for the first time as a girl with a pleasant face and a pretty smile.

Themes and Meanings

Many of Reginald McKnight's stories deal with the theme of internalized racism. McKnight, like the narrator of "The Kind of Light That Shines on Texas," grew up in a military family that moved often. No doubt, he draws from his personal experiences of being one of only a handful of African American children in predominately white schools. His protagonists are often isolated in an environment in which their ethnicity is highlighted and they are denied the support of an African American community.

Living in a predominately white culture, Clint absorbs the racism of many of his white peers. This internalized racism makes Clint eager to distance himself from his African American classmates. His greatest fear is that the white children will lump all African American children together; they will not see that Clint is different from the dirty, dark-skinned Marvin or the silent, heavyset Ah-so. His skin color, however, is impossible to escape. Even in seemingly innocent questions about how Clint combs his hair, the white children constantly remind him of his racial difference. Clint is painfully aware of racism in all its guises; he sees through Mrs. Wickham's preferential treatment and her *harmless* racist jokes, yet he continues to do his "Tom-thing." Clint is extra careful to always be neat in his appearance, to perform well in school, and to follow all the rules.

However, Clint's diligent efforts cannot save him from being singled out for viciously racist treatment: first, by Oakley, and then by Coach Gilchrist. Clint's internalized racism surfaces in the locker room scene when he demands to know why he, rather than Marvin, is being singled out. Clint implies that African Americans like Marvin deserve to be singled out because they fit the negative stereotypes of African Americans as held by many whites.

As in most good short stories, the protagonist has a moment of self-realization. Clint, alone in his room, realizes the import of his words about Marvin in the locker room. He has this revelation as the sun shines through his window, changing the color of his own skin to orange. He begins to meditate on a classroom experience in which Mrs. Wickham demonstrated the relativity of color by shining first a white light, then a black light, through a prism. Perhaps Mrs. Wickham is incapable of understanding the metaphorical implications of this demonstration, but Clint begins to understand.

He realizes more fully the implications of his revelation the next day when Marvin intervenes on his behalf. Marvin, rightfully so, treats Clint as if he is beneath Marvin's contempt. Marvin, thought to be dumb, knows how Clint meant his earlier racist slur, but he still fights for a member of his own race. Later that morning, an enlightened Clint is able to look at and really see Ah-so for the first time.

Style and Technique

McKnight's stories seldom lack external action, but the internal action of the characters is often his central focus. His stories often use first-person narration, and some are obviously drawn from personal experiences. However, McKnight writes convincingly in the voices of a range of African American males, drawn from various backgrounds, social classes, and occupational choices. One of the most distinctive qualities of McKnight's fiction is the trueness of voice for each individual narrator.

As one might expect from McKnight's life, the settings of his stories vary. Several of his stories are set in West Africa, where McKnight spent a year teaching and writing. Most of his stories are set somewhere in the United States. One common factor in the latter stories is that the protagonist is typically isolated in a predominately white environment, which is often openly hostile.

Although McKnight's African stories are boldly experimental, he more often opts for a plain, unpretentious style. His narrators sound like real people; they are never forced into articulating epiphanies beyond the realistic range of perception established for their ages, classes, or occupations. However, his stories have their moments of poetry, as when Clint finally sees the light on his own racism. McKnight gently leads Clint to this point of self-realization, with plenty of digressions along the way.

One factor that distinguishes McKnight from the African American protest writers who precede him is his political reticence. It would be easy enough to demonize the whites in this story, but McKnight deftly forces the reader to confront the more difficult truth of this story: The narrator has learned to despise his own race. Readers, regardless of skin color, are forced to re-examine their own racial biases. His stories, as McKnight says that they should, tend to get under one's skin.

Nancy E. Sherrod

KINDRED SPIRITS

Author: Alice Walker (1944-   )
Type of plot: Realism
Time of plot: The early 1960's
Locale: Airplanes in flight and Miami, Florida
First published: 1985

Principal characters:
 ROSA, a recently divorced writer
 BARBARA, her sister
 IVAN, her former husband
 SHEILA, Ivan's second wife
 AUNT LILY, Rosa and Barbara's mother's sister

The Story

Rosa and her sister Barbara are flying to Florida to visit their Aunt Lily's household, in which their grandfather has recently died. Still traumatized by her recent divorce, Rosa wonders about her former husband's character, the nature of their relationship, and how love and affection can be transformed or disappear. She and her husband are one of a series of sets of kindred spirits that emerge from the story.

Rosa wonders about the closeness that she and her husband shared despite the fact that he is white and she is black, how that intimacy and commonality changed over time, and how quickly she has been replaced by a new woman who is white and Jewish like her former husband—someone who can offer him a different kind of kindredship than she can. Still deeply pained by the dissolution of her marriage, Rosa believes that her trip to Florida is a kind of penance that must be paid to her family. When her grandfather passed away, she felt unable to face her family and chose not to attend his funeral, instead traveling on her own. Having returned from Cyprus and other travels, she has now recruited her older sister to go to Florida with her to make the process of facing her aunt less difficult.

At the Miami airport the sisters are met by Aunt Lily, who stands tall and dignified. She runs a foster home for a living, creating a home environment and pseudo-family for children separated from their biological kin. Rosa is struck when she sees Lily waiting in the airport that the older woman is what she herself may be like when she is older. She feels alienated from her relatives because her own sense of politics and history, which so much informs the way she sees the world and assigns value within it, is very different from their own. At the same time, she realizes that they share a common worldview based on lifelong experiences of institutionalized racism. Rosa recognizes yet another kindred spirit in her thoughts of her dead grandfather, whom she realizes had a temperament and habit of observing the events around him similar to her own, and at the same time, did things to women that offend her personal feminist convictions.

As Rosa's visit progresses, she comes into conflict with both her aunt and her sister, in part because of her emotional neediness, which they find at odds with her past lack of responsibility to family obligations, and in part because of her need to decipher meanings from her family's life—a process of attentiveness and documentation that she uses in her profession as a writer.

The story ends with Rosa and Barbara back on a plane, their visit ended. Rosa again contemplates her strained relationships with her former husband, grandfather, aunt, and sister. In her continuing depression, she feels cut off and alone. This feeling is alleviated at the last moment by Barbara, who puts on one of their grandfather's old fedoras—like the one Rosa is already wearing—and takes Rosa's hand, reaffirming their status as kindred spirits and their common link to the man who has passed away.

Themes and Meanings

"Kindred Spirits" is infused with the politics of the Civil Rights, women's, environmental, and New Left movements. Race, class, and gender analysis are clearly at work in the way that Alice Walker has Rosa look at the world. In addition to having a writer's astute powers of observation that make her look for visual as well as verbal clues to interior meanings and personal motivations, Rosa has a highly politicized way of critiquing the urban landscape around her, of assessing world events of her generation (such as the Cuban revolution and the conflict between Greeks and Turks in Cyprus), and of placing her own family members in context within that world.

Themes introduced through Rosa's thinking and looking at the world around her include the insidious nature of racism; the destructiveness of male violence against women; the pervasiveness of sexism and misogyny across classes and cultures; the political economy of urban development; the clash of gender, class, and race as interacting elements in personal identity and relationships; and privilege and repression as flip sides of the same phenomena. There is also the personal theme of self and family, and of the closeness or remoteness and cross-identification that exists between family members. Physical and psychic dislocation is a primary theme, accented by the statement on the first page of the story that the protagonist "was at a place in her life where she seemed to have no place." With the house where she lived during her marriage no longer available to her, she travels abroad, rootless, feeling compelled to move and go. Further, her place within her family has become unclear and ill-defined.

Walker also deals directly with the personal politics involved with a writer who draws her material from her own life and that of her family members. In displaying Rosa's sister's and aunt's discomfort she asks to what extent the writer's habit of assessment and reuse of family matters in developing characterization and plot in her work violates her relatives' privacy or is a kind of voyeurism that they have a right to resent.

Style and Technique

"Kindred Spirits" is strongly informed by the dictum of the women's movement that the personal is political. Walker's Rosa thinks about people in her life in a historical context, both in the sense of their (and her own) place in their family's history and in the sense of them as players in a larger process of societal change. Although revolutions serve as the backdrop of the protagonist's consciousness, her visions of her aunt, her grandfather, and her sister are each set against a backdrop of personal or social history from which a moral or political lesson can be drawn. Her aunt's regal demeanor belies the Jim Crow practices of racial segregation and defamation that have framed most of her adult life; her sister's marriage raises the issue of domestic violence; and her own marriage and its dissolution raises questions about interracial relations.

The story is strongly autobiographical. Rosa is in many ways an alter ego for Walker, with the fictional persona having experiences that parallel the author's own marriage and divorce, her child, her travels, her political concerns, and her profession. Walker uses the device of the rhetorical question implicitly and explicitly to examine the larger theme that gives her story its title: kinship. This theme is wrought through the story line of the protagonist finding bits of her own identity in her grandfather (whom she loves despite his imperfections, particularly his attitudes about women) and in her aunt (whom she admires and identifies with physically, but whom she ultimately dislikes), and in her ruminations about the changing loyalties of her husband. These family matters are magnified into fundamental universal concepts of kinship. By examining sister and mate, grandfather and aunt, and recognizing the deeply complicated mix of motivation and standpoint for each individual, Walker asks by extension what elements unite and divide all people.

Though again flying in a plane at the conclusion of the story—flight being the metaphor for displacement with which the story begins and ends—the main character is "grounded" by her trip to Florida. In the midst of accepting an abstract life of loneliness lived much in the mind and through which other people are often objectified, she is, through her sister's gesture of donning their grandfather's hat and reaching for her hand, reassured of her commonality and connection within her family and with the family of humankind.

Barbara J. Bair

KING OF THE BINGO GAME

Author: Ralph Ellison (1914-1994)
Type of plot: Social realism
Time of plot: The mid-twentieth century
Locale: New York City
First published: 1944

Principal characters:
THE PROTAGONIST, a young southern African American
THE ANNOUNCER, the director of the bingo game

The Story

A young black man sits in a movie theater in New York waiting for the featured film to end. He has come to the big northern city from North Carolina but has been unable to find work because he does not have a birth certificate. His wife is ill, and he is hoping to win the bingo game that is played at the end of the feature so that he can take her to a doctor. He has not eaten all day, and the smell of the peanuts that another viewer is eating increases his hunger. Two men near him are drinking liquor, and he wishes that he had some, remembering how people used to share with one another down south. He drifts off to sleep but has a nightmare, which causes him to shout. The men who are drinking ask him to be quiet and offer him some whiskey, which he takes.

After the feature ends, the lights come on, a curtain hides the screen, and an announcer and an attendant come out to preside over the bingo game. Players who get "bingo" climb onto the stage and spin a large wheel by means of an electric switch. If the wheel stops at double zero, a player wins the jackpot, which is now $36.90. The young man plays five bingo cards, wins, and mounts the stage.

He finds being on stage confusing. The lights are blinding, he does not understand the jokes and comments of the announcer, and the crowd laughs at him. Even the smell of the announcer's hair oil unsettles him. As he presses the button that controls the wheel, he is drawn into its whirl of light and color. He realizes that so long as he presses the button that makes the wheel spin, he controls it—that he is the "King of the Bingo Game." So long as he keeps spinning the wheel, he controls his fate; his wife will be all right.

The young man's thoughts are unknown to the announcer and the audience, who grow impatient. The crowd wants him to finish his turn, and the announcer tells him that he is taking too long, but he brushes the man away, then calls him back and explains that he is going to show everyone how to win the bingo game. He shouts, urging his wife to live, and the audience, thinking him crazy, quiets for a moment, then begins to taunt him again.

Two men in uniform approach him from the side of the stage, wrestle him to the floor, and take the button and cable away from him. The wheel stops on double zero.

One of the men signals to the other, who hits the young man on the head. Just before he loses consciousness, he realizes that his luck has ended.

Themes and Meanings

Ralph Ellison's story combines themes familiar from modern literature with a theme that was common in the literature of the ancient world. The modern themes are the alienation of the individual from society and the criticism of that society as crass and materialistic; the ancient theme is the inability of the individual to control fate.

The protagonist is not part of the industrial North's society in which he now lives. In the North Carolina from which he came, one could live by the effort of one's body and hands. In the big city, documentation is needed before one can get a job, and the main character is cut off from the money that he needs to help his ailing wife because of this circumstance. The elaborate procedure by which one wins the bingo game mimics the maze of requirements of the urban world; it is not enough to get five bingo numbers in a row—one must also spin the wheel and have it stop in the right place to win even a small jackpot.

The black protagonist is a person amid a largely white society, another element that keeps him from getting a job and being accepted in the city. The bingo announcer makes fun of his rural origins and calls him "boy," emphasizing the difference between him and the society in which he lives, while holding him up as a figure of fun for the audience to laugh at.

Even the black members of the audience deride the protagonist; their behavior establishes the point that he is not being ridiculed solely because he is black, but because he is an individual alone in the spotlight when he steps to the stage. The members of the audience are a crowd that belittles his personality and actions, just as the larger society will not let him get a job. When he senses that the black members of the audience might be ashamed of him and his blackness, he thinks that he will keep pressing the button, making a spectacle of himself, to give them something really to be ashamed about. By insisting on his own individuality and freedom, even the freedom to make a fool of himself and embarrass fellow African Americans, he becomes not only a black person, but a person.

Finally, however, the protagonist's efforts to free himself and assert his own individuality, to save himself and his wife economically, must fail. The jackpot is too small, the technology and procedures arrayed against him are too formidable. In order to win, he must make the wheel stop on double zero. He realizes that so long as the wheel is spinning, he controls fate—neither winning nor losing. Fate is larger than he or the wheel. Life cannot remain suspended, and the "uniformed men" who represent the power of society overwhelm him and end his attempt to control his destiny.

Style and Technique

"King of the Bingo Game" is written in a naturalistic style and from a third-person, limited point of view. The first technique reinforces the gritty, realistic quality of the story, and the second puts the reader in the place of the protagonist and helps the reader to experience the confusion that he feels.

A naturalistic style dictates that a writer describe the physical reality of a scene, such as the first detail noted in the story, the smell of the peanuts that makes the protagonist hungry. Throughout the story, physical details predominate—the feeling of whiskey moving through the protagonist's body, the blinding lights, the odor of the announcer's hair oil, all compel the reader to see, feel, and even smell what the protagonist is experiencing.

The third-person, limited point of view conveys information about the story as it is seen by only one person, but allows Ellison to use language that that character himself would not use, unlike the first-person point of view, in which the vocabulary of the story must be that of the main character. The use of this technique means that the reader experiences the same feelings of bewilderment and excitement that the protagonist does, but they are presented in language more vivid than he himself might use. Because the protagonist does not feel himself to be a part of the world that he inhabits, the movie house, its patrons, and the procedure of the bingo game are a welter of disconnected fragments that puzzle and finally overwhelm him—and the reader.

Two dream, or hallucination, sequences further frighten and confuse the protagonist. In one, he imagines himself back in the South, jumping from a railroad trestle as a train is about to run him down and scrambling down an embankment to apparent safety; instead the train leaves the tracks and follows him down a street as white people laugh at him. The other sequence, a hallucination, occurs as he stands on the stage pressing the button controlling the bingo wheel. This time he imagines himself pursued by a subway train while he carries his wife in his arms. If he stops, they will be run over by the train; if he jumps to the other tracks, he will be electrocuted by the rail that powers the train. This dream reflects his plan of continuing to press the button that activates the wheel; so long as he keeps doing what he is doing, he reasons, he will be all right. These sequences tell the reader more about the protagonist's psychological state, but even though they differ greatly from the rest of the story, they are reasonable even in naturalistic terms. The protagonist has not eaten all day, so it is possible that he might fall asleep and dream; after he wakes he drinks straight whiskey, which, coupled with an empty stomach and the disorientation of being on the stage, might well induce a hallucination.

James Baird

KING SOLOMON

Author: Isaac Rosenfeld (1918-1956)
Type of plot: Parody
Time of plot: The twentieth century and the time of the biblical Solomon
Locale: Jerusalem
First published: 1956

> *Principal characters:*
> SOLOMON, at once king of ancient Israel and a successful modern
>   Jewish old man
> THE QUEEN OF SHEBA, a guest
> THE COUNSELORS

The Story

A man of great eminence and amatory prowess is entering old age with powers undiminished. The women still flock to him, and he periodically publishes books of deep thought. However, there is nothing impressive about him physically, and his aphorisms seem remote from reality and from the life he leads.

The great man's counselors are at once his audience, before whom he disports himself and his achievements, and his severest critics—among themselves. They decry his taste; they are jealous of and voyeuristic about his love life; they try in vain to ascertain the source of his success. As the old dictum has it, no man is a hero to his valet.

The climax of the story is the visit of the queen of Sheba. She may be merely another woman drawn to this charismatic man, but she stands out by being a queen, by coming from afar, and by injecting herself into Solomon's life as perhaps no other individual, certainly no woman, ever did. The consequences of her visit are no less ambiguous than her personality is. On the one hand, she turns out to be as unromantic and self-absorbed as Solomon. She is middle-aged; she eats too much and is overweight; she is indecorous, exhibitionistic, and vulgar. At last, she virtually throws herself at him and succeeds only in embarrassing him.

On the other hand, she has some insight into Solomon's main defect. Though neither saint nor sage, she presents in her parting speech a keen analysis of Solomon as a man who lives for a love that takes rather than gives, a self-absorbed man who arouses love in others but has little of it himself, who mistakes sexual adventurism for something tender or spiritual.

The climax of their affair or relationship is the climax of the story as well. The affair neither draws Solomon out of himself nor ends with a marriage. The last section of the story is therefore a sorry coda, bringing Solomon into late old age, with all of its attendant indignities. He grows more obsessed with possessing women, strays from God, quarrels with his priests, grows out of touch with the people he governs, and becomes bogged down in bureaucratic procedures.

The story closes poignantly with glimpses of Solomon as a doddering old man. He loses what little hold he has on reality. Approaching death, he, like all human beings, becomes overwhelmed by the mystery of existence, the absence of the meaning of life, the transience of all achievements. Sleep becomes elusive, the body falls apart. Even animal sensual gratification becomes elemental, as a hot water bottle replaces wife or mistress.

Themes and Meanings

The classic pieces of early literature—the Bible, Homer, Greek and Shakespearean tragedy—deal with heroes who are larger than life and who, whether they be good or evil, grapple with important philosophical and moral issues. The heroes of modern literature, by contrast, are swamped by the trivia of daily life. Getting through each day with a modicum of dignity is their task as much as wrestling with God, Fate, or mystery was that of the earlier heroes.

The difference in literary presentation is attributable to a host of cultural factors. Just as writing about Achilles' or Hamlet's laundry lists would have been incomprehensible to Homer or Shakespeare, so too would a story written today that presents a hero in the antique mode be dismissed by the sophisticated reader as hopelessly naïve and one-dimensional. Isaac Rosenfeld's story is an attempt to cross the great divide between the archaic heroic vision and the modern mundane one. How could the romantic, semi-legendary figure of the ancient Israelite king be made comprehensible and relevant to the modern reader? What would result from a juxtaposition of the heroic mode and the quotidian? What would Solomon be like were he alive today or were modern readers transported, with their modern sensibility, to ancient times?

Rosenfeld's Solomon moves in a world of telephones, newspapers, kosher markets, radio, stamp albums, pinochle, overtime pay. The biblical Solomon, or the historical figure on which he is based, must have relaxed with the ancient version of pinochle or stamp collecting, but such activities, not part of the heroic dimension, are excluded from the Bible.

The biblical Solomon is one of the great Israelite heroes. A man who ruled over the ancient Judaic kingdom at its zenith, he was especially renowned for his wisdom and amatory powers. However, he was human enough to transgress at last, by worshiping false gods at the prompting of his pagan wives. Rosenfeld's Solomon, by contrast, is seen mainly in his declining years. He is a seedy, idiosyncratic old man whose charisma is incongruous. His thoughts on everything, himself included, are inscrutable. His famous sayings are remote from experience, hardly remembered by him, and seem to be part of a pose. The stories he tells children do not amuse them. Even his physical presence does not impress: He is a sloppy, overweight, bespectacled old man often seen in an undershirt, with glasses and cigar. His counselors are not reverential but, as they would be in life and in modern literature, envious, carping, and exasperated. The advent of the queen of Sheba, a glorious event in the Bible, is here merely the occasion for further signs of his decline. He does a poor job of impressing her, and their relationship is a pathetic and vain attempt by two aging persons to understand each other.

The central vision of the story is the modern one—that a king is merely another human being; that greatness in human affairs is enigmatic and fortuitous; that a man, even if a famous achiever, is reduced by time to the grim animal level; that life, even at its best, is sad and not at all what it is made out to be in idealizing literature and chronicles. God and redemption are—given the biblical material—glaringly absent.

Style and Technique

This is less a conventional short story, with dialogue and dramatic climax, than a chronicle presenting an overview of events and characters. Important are not only the literal events but also the biblical version of them in the back of the reader's mind. The telling, tone, and manner are as much a part of the meaning as is the matter. The biblical version is dismissed as the "official chronicle" commissioned by a king concerned with his "image." Rosenfeld's story presumes to show the reader the way things really were, which in modern times means the unsavory underside. The narrator even irreverently describes the Scriptural version as "a bit thick," evasive, unreliable, and sycophantic. One of its most famous anecdotes is called an "abominable invention."

This approach makes the omniscient narrator one of the main characters of the story. His style is that of a debunker, an investigative reporter or revisionist historian who is getting behind the formal, official, solemn canonical version of events and setting the record straight, no matter how unsavory the results. A biblical passage is even quoted in order to establish the contrast in styles and in visions of reality and in order to subject it to sardonic questions. In fact, Rosenfeld's Solomon is often a comic figure; a biblical epic has become a Jewish anecdote about a schlemiel—a fool.

Manfred Weidhorn

THE KING'S INDIAN

Author: John Gardner (1933-1982)
Type of plot: Fable
Time of plot: The early nineteenth century
Locale: Boston, Nantucket, and the Atlantic and Pacific oceans
First published: 1974

> *Principal characters:*
> JONATHAN UPCHURCH, a nineteen-year-old Boston schoolmaster
> DR. LUTHER FLINT, a mesmerist
> MIRANDA FLINT, his daughter
> CAPTAIN DIRGE, the captain of the whaler *Jerusalem*
> AUGUSTA, his daughter
> JEREMIAH, his blind companion
> MR. KNIGHT, his first mate
> BILLY MORE and
> WILKINS (SWAMI HAVANANDA), seamen
> JIM NGUGI, an African harpooner
> KASKIWAH, an American Indian harpooner
> WOLFF, a mutineer

The Story

John Gardner's "The King's Indian" is told by an ancient mariner to his "guest," later revealed to be Gardner himself. The tale is about hoaxes, according to Jonathan Upchurch, its narrator, as well as "devils and angels and the making of man." Upchurch promises to answer the question, "Ain't all men slaves, either physical or metaphysical?"

Upchurch begins with his boyhood infatuation with beautiful seven-year-old Miranda Flint, the stage foil to her mesmerist father, Dr. Luther Flint. Nine-year-old Jonathan experiences visions of birds during one of Flint's exhibitions, and Miranda's sharing his screams makes the boy even more obsessed with her. A decade later, Upchurch, a schoolmaster in Boston, saves his money so that he can fulfill his dream of moving to southern Illinois and starting a farm, but some sailors get him drunk and exchange his savings for a sailboat. Impulsively, he decides that "in landlessness alone lies the highest truth, shoreless, indefinite as God!"—a line borrowed from the greatest of sea narratives, Herman Melville's *Moby Dick* (1851)—and he sets sail, only to be overrun by the Nantucket whaler *Jerusalem* and taken aboard.

Upchurch soon learns that the ship is no ordinary whaler, that—in violation of all New England beliefs—it is carrying slaves, though the crew denies their existence. A second mystery, also denied, is the presence of a woman whose voice "haunted me as once Miranda Flint's eyes had done." The mystery is only intensified when Upchurch finally sees the beautiful girl with the humpbacked Captain Dirge and his constant companion, the blind and mysterious Jeremiah.

Upchurch becomes acquainted with the crew, especially the red-bearded Billy More, who rescues him from falling from the rigging of the mainmast. Upchurch suspects that the entire crew, including the taciturn first mate, Mr. Knight, and the garrulous "multi-breed" Wilkins, are mad, perhaps infected by the brooding Dirge. The captain discovers Upchurch's learning and appoints him tutor to his seventeen-year-old daughter, Augusta. Already in love with her, Upchurch falls even deeper, becoming enraptured by her "unearthly" eyes. Their relationship develops quickly, and soon this "fleshed ideal" kisses her walleyed tutor.

Captain Dirge boards every ship that the *Jerusalem* encounters, and Augusta grows exceedingly distracted each time. Pretending to be one of the slaves after blackening his skin with burnt cork, Upchurch goes along on one of these trips, only to discover Augusta in the same disguise. A sailor on the ship that they are visiting tells Upchurch that Captain Dirge is an impostor, that the real captain is dead, but the sailor is killed before he can say more.

Back on the *Jerusalem*, Kaskiwah, an American Indian harpooner, gives Upchurch two mushrooms to eat, causing him to have a vision of a ship that appears from beneath the sea bearing a white-bearded man issuing cryptic epigrams. After the man returns to the sea, a huge "pigeon-like thing" also delivers a message to Upchurch: "Fool, retreat!"

Billy More then tells Upchurch the secret of Captain Dirge's quest. Four years before, three American ships saw the *Jerusalem* go down near the Vanishing Isles in the Pacific Ocean with only a portrait from the captain's cabin surviving. When Dirge and his ship arrived in Nantucket to learn that they had been reported dead and to see the painting exactly like the captain's own, the captain vowed to solve the mystery. Dirge consulted experts in the "praeternatural," one of whom took special interest because the portrait was of him: Dr. Flint. Dirge's objective is not whales but "a crack in Time." Later, Augusta tells Upchurch that their quest is no less than to "understand . . . everything."

Upchurch begins to complete the puzzle, realizing that Augusta is really Miranda Flint. Wilkins and a seaman named Wolff then lead a mutiny to uncover the rest of the deceit, killing Mr. Knight and Billy More along the way. Jim Ngugi, an African harpooner, saves Upchurch from the same fate, but Miranda is not so lucky, being beaten and raped by Wilkins. Upchurch discovers that Miranda's magnificent beauty is yet another trickster's fraud.

Wilkins takes complete control by killing Wolff and reveals the depth of the knavery. The "ghost ship" story is nothing but a hoax arranged by the *Jerusalem*'s owners with the help of Swami Havananda, Flint's rival and Wilkins's true identity. Flint, unaware of the hoax, killed the real captain and Augusta and replaced Dirge with a ventriloquist's dummy, which he operated in the guise of Jeremiah. Wilkins/Swami Havananda, after revealing his part in all this, kills himself.

Upchurch and Ngugi take charge of the ship and their destiny. After eighteen days of calm near the South Pole, surrounded by icebergs, singing whales, and huge white birds, Flint comes out of hiding. Upchurch sees his antagonist as nothing but "an impotent old goof hardly better than the puppet he scared me with before." Flint challenges Upchurch to a chess match: Should Upchurch lose, he will become the old hoaxer's disciple, and if Flint loses, he will give up Miranda. Upchurch, who has claimed not to know the game, surprises Flint with the King's Indian, an expert's opening, and the mesmerist bursts into flames, the victim of spontaneous combustion and of his own villainy.

Following a debate about truth, innocence, and similar issues, Upchurch and Miranda make love. The wind finally rises, and so does a giant sad man in white from the sea. Ignoring this vision, Upchurch and his crew set sail for "Illinois the Changeable!"

Themes and Meanings

"The King's Indian" is in the tradition of narratives using journey motifs and naïve young protagonists to explore initiations into the worlds of self-discovery and values. Dr. Flint may intend his quest to reveal one kind of truth, but for Jonathan Upchurch, it is a voyage of faith and love. Such themes are fitting for a story by the author of *On Moral Fiction* (1978), who insists that writers should create in their art an affirmation of life.

Mr. Knight, as his name suggests, sees only darkness around him; his faith ended by science, he wonders if the world is merely mechanical. The real Captain Dirge loses his life because he misplaces his faith, believing in the brimstone demon Flint. After saving Upchurch from annihilation, Billy More warns him to "banish all thought of Nowhere by keeping yer mind from belief in it. . . . If ye must think, think of Faith itself. . . . Faith, that's the secret! Absolute faith like a seagull's." Upchurch decides that one is the slave either of some purposeless power or of "some meaningful human ideal." He can discover that ideal, and therefore faith, only through love.

"Human consciousness," Upchurch explains, "is the artificial wall we build of perceptions and conceptions, a hull of words and accepted opinions that keeps out the vast, consuming sea." Melville's Captain Ahab wants to smash through this wall by conquering a giant whale; Flint plans to do the same by finding the time warp; Upchurch has a simpler solution: "A mushroom or one raw emotion (such as love) can blast that wall to smithereens."

Flint bursts into flames because his only vestige of humanity, his love for his daughter, has been consumed by his own overwhelmingly evil nature. Upchurch's victory seems ironic because Miranda has lost her beauty, but such is mere appearance, like the stage magic of her father. Faith must go beyond mere surfaces: "no more illusions, no more grand gestures, just humdrum love." Miranda also recognizes the power of love. "You're so wall-eyed!" she exclaims to Upchurch. "Jonathan, I love you. . . . You're grotesque." Armed with love and faith, Upchurch ignores the "solemn white monster" who appears out of the sea, and he implores his crew of ruffians, "We may be the slime of the earth but we've got our affinities!"

Style and Technique

In *On Moral Fiction*, Gardner criticizes writers who create elaborate verbal palaces with no life inside, and he has Billy More issue the same complaint: "Words, whatever their sweetness and juice, turn prunes at last, and eventually ashes." However, there is still pleasure in an elaborate, self-conscious style when the writer has confidence that he is creating more than the sand castle that Jonathan Upchurch says this story is.

The novella-length "The King's Indian" is full of grandiose, usually comic, celebrations of figurative language. Upchurch experiences "the smell of unlimited futurity stinging" his "nosedrills." He sees a sperm whale with "teeth that would serve as Plato's form for the fall of civilizations." Billy More—all the characters are philosophers and poets—describes Captain Dirge's house as "so crammed with brass and silver and gold it would keep a dead Eskimo sweating for fright of thieves."

More important, "The King's Indian" is a virtual catalog of allusions to past masters, especially the literature of the sea. The story's mariner-guest frame and its albatrosses come from Samuel Taylor Coleridge's *The Rime of the Ancient Mariner* (1798). Miranda is named for the heroine of William Shakespeare's *The Tempest* (1611), her father is Gardner's version of Shakespeare's Prospero, and Wilkins is his Caliban.

Most of the time, Gardner pays homage to American masters. Flint the mesmerist and ventriloquist and his spontaneous combustion come from Charles Brockden Brown's *Wieland* (1798). Gardner reminds the reader of the debt that his moral tale owes to Mark Twain's *The Adventures of Huckleberry Finn* (1884) when Miranda refers to Ngugi as "Nigger Jim." The mad captain's quest for knowing the unknowable is obviously inspired by *Moby Dick*. Gardner's primary homage, however is to Edgar Allan Poe's *The Narrative of Arthur Gordon Pym* (1838). Both Upchurch and Pym make unplanned, nightmarish voyages toward some mystical whiteness near the South Pole, accompanied all the way by screaming white birds. Numerous specific references to Poe's novel appear, including Pym's initials carved on the *Jerusalem*'s bulkhead.

When the guest identifies himself as Gardner, he acknowledges "the help of Poe and Melville and many another man," and he says that his tale is "not a toy but a queer, cranky monument, a collage: a celebration of all literature and life." Most of all, perhaps, it celebrates the storyteller as one who gives shape and meaning to existence while entertaining his audience as well.

Michael Adams

THE KISS

Author: Anton Chekhov (1860-1904)
Type of plot: Psychological
Time of plot: The 1880's
Locale: The village of Mestechki and various small towns in Russia
First published: "Potseluy," 1887 (English translation, 1915)

>   *Principal characters:*
>   LIEUTENANT RYABOVICH, a timid artillery officer
>   LIEUTENANT LOBYTKO, a boastful womanizer
>   LIEUTENANT MERZLYAKOV, a coldly analytic intellectual
>   LIEUTENANT GENERAL VON RABBECK, Mestechki's leading
>   landowner

The Story

The setting of "The Kiss" is a Russian village on a May evening. The officers of an artillery brigade encamped nearby are invited by a retired lieutenant general, von Rabbeck, who is the leading landowner in the village, to spend an evening dining and dancing in his residence. After describing a panoramic scene of aristocratic society, Anton Chekhov focuses on one of the officers, Ryabovich, who characterizes himself with the diagnosis: "I am the shyest, most modest, and most undistinguished officer in the whole brigade!" He is an inarticulate conversationalist, a graceless dancer, a timid drinker, and an altogether awkward social mixer. During the evening he wanders away from the activities he is unable to enjoy and strays into a semidark room that is soon entered by an unidentifiable woman, who clasps two fragrant arms around his neck, whispers, "At last!" and kisses him. Recognizing her mistake, the woman then shrieks and runs from the room.

Ryabovich also exits quickly, and soon shows himself to be a changed man: "He wanted to dance, to talk, to run into the garden, to laugh aloud." He no longer worries about his round shoulders, plain looks, and general ineptness. He begins to exercise a lively romantic fancy, speculating which of the ladies at the dinner table might have been his companion. Before falling asleep, he indulges in joyful fantasies.

The artillery brigade soon leaves the area for maneuvers. Ryabovich tries to tell himself that the episode of the kiss was accidental and trifling, but to no avail: His psychic needs embrace it as a wondrously radiant event. When he tries to recount it to his coarse fellow officers, he is chagrined that they reduce it to a lewdly womanizing level. He imagines himself loved by and married to her, happy and stable; he can hardly wait to return to the village, to reunite with her.

In late August, Ryabovich's battery does return. That night he makes his second trip to the general's estate, but this time pauses to ponder in the garden. He can no longer hear the nightingale that sang loudly in May; the poplar and grass no longer exude a scent; he walks a bridge near the general's bathing cabin and touches a towel that feels clammy and cold; ripples of the river rip the moon's reflection into bits. Ryabovich now realizes that his romantic dreams have been absurdly disproportionate to their cause: "And the whole world . . . seemed to [him] an unintelligible, aimless jest." When the general's invitation comes, he refuses it.

Themes and Meanings

This is a masterful tale, as Chekhov demonstrates his vision of life as a pathetic comedy of errors, with misunderstanding and miscommunication rooted in the psychic substance of human nature. Lieutenant Ryabovich, the least dashing and romantic of men, is transformed by the kiss meant for another into a person with a penchant for an intense inner life that runs its dreamy course virtually separate from the dreariness of external reality. He inflates an insignificant incident into an absurd cluster of fantasies centering on ideal love and beauty. All the more embittering, then, is his plunge from ecstasy to despair as he recognizes, in the story's anticlimactic resolution, the falseness of his hopes, the frustration of his yearnings.

Chekhov dramatizes two of his pervasive themes in "The Kiss." One is the enormous difficulty, often the impossibility, of establishing a communion of feelings between human beings. Ryabovich discovers that he cannot communicate to his fellow officers his happiness "that something extraordinary, foolish, but joyful and delightful, had come into his life." Lieutenant Lobytko regards Ryabovich's experience as an opportunity to parade and exaggerate his own sexual adventures. Lieutenant Merzlyakov dismisses the lady in the dark as "some sort of lunatic." The brigade general assumes that all of his officers have his own preference for stout, tall, middle-aged women.

The other great Chekhovian theme (which he shares with Nikolai Gogol) is the contrast between beauty and sensitivity, and the elusive characteristic best expressed by the Russian word *poslost'*. The term is untranslatable, but it suggests vulgarity, banality, boredom, seediness, shallowness, and suffocation of the spirit. Ryabovich, surrounded by the coarseness of his comrades, depressed by the plodding routine of artillery maneuvers, poignantly tries to rise above this atmosphere of *poslost'* by caressing an impossible dream.

Style and Technique

The story's structure is contrapuntal, with Chekhov using unobtrusive symbolism and situational irony to contrast the two worlds of romance and drabness. After his kiss, Ryabovich soars on wings of joy, exhilarated by "a strange new feeling which grew stronger and stronger." After dining and dancing, he and the other officers walk through their host's garden on their way back to camp. Chekhov bathes the scene in an atmosphere of lyric romanticism, as stars are reflected in the river's water, sandpipers cry on its banks, and a nightingale trills loudly, "taking no notice of the crowd of officers"; they admire its self-absorption. The nightingale serves to symbolize Ryabovich's state of sensibility. Like the bird, his soul is singing loudly and is indifferent to its surroundings.

The counterpart to the nightingale is the ass, Magar, which paces ploddingly at the end of the dusty procession of the brigade's cannons, horses, and men, with Chekhov describing the dullness of artillery life precisely and minutely.

When Ryabovich returns to Lieutenant General von Rabbeck's garden in late summer, "A crushing uneasiness took possession of him." His exultant mood has disappeared as he confronts the prospect of a nonexisting reunion with a nonexisting beloved. Again, Chekhov symbolizes Ryabovich's feelings of rejection and disillusionment: "there was no sound of the brave nightingale and no scent of poplar and young grass." As Ryabovich touches the general's cold, wet bathing towel and observes the moon's reflection, this time torn to bits by the river waters, he has a shattering epiphany of heartbreak: "How stupid, how stupid! . . . How unintelligent it all is!" he exclaims, interpreting the endless, aimless running of the water as equivalent to the endless, aimless running of his life—of all lives. "What for? Why?"

Gerhard Brand

KLEIST IN THUN

Author: Robert Walser (1878-1956)
Type of plot: Biographical
Time of plot: 1802
Locale: Thun, Switzerland
First published: 1907 (English translation, 1957)

> *Principal characters:*
> THE NARRATOR, a former clerk in a brewery in Thun
> HEINRICH VON KLEIST, a Prussian writer
> KLEIST'S SISTER

The Story

The narrator imagines to himself how the Prussian writer Heinrich von Kleist, then twenty-five, might have lived during the spring and summer of 1802 in a villa on a small island in the Aar River near the town of Thun. Kleist's arrival was probably unspectacular: He walked over a short bridge, rang the bell, and someone lazily answered. It was the charming Bernese girl who would become his housekeeper. He is satisfied with the rooms she shows him, but he feels a little sick and wonders why, especially in the midst of such beautiful natural surroundings.

He writes—it is the beginning of his writing career—and occasionally reads from his work to friends in nearby Bern. However, he is dissatisfied with what he produces, among other things, his comedy *Der Zerbrochene Krug* (1808; *The Broken Jug*, 1930). The lazy spring weather is maddeningly distracting: "It is as if radiant red stupefying waves rise up in his head whenever he sits at his table and tries to write." He had intended to become a farmer after arriving in Switzerland.

He often sits at the window and muses on the stunning yet unsettling landscape of the lake, fragrant fields, and bewitching mountains. Lonely, he longs for a nearby voice, hand, or body. By gazing intently on the beauty around him, he tries to forget himself, but memories of home and his mother disturb him. He runs out into the garden, rows a boat onto the open, sunny lake, swims, and hears the laughter of women on the shore. Nature, he thinks, is "like one vast embrace."

His enjoyment of the scene is never without pain and longing. Sometimes it feels like the end of the world here, and the Alps seem like the unreachable gates to a high, distant paradise. The light at dusk is spellbinding, yet its beauty is tinged with sickness. Kleist deems himself superfluous and longs for a heroic life. Pursued by a vague uneasiness, he climbs up the castle hill, then races back to his room, resolute on writing, which unfolds once he at last forgets where he is.

Rainy days are intolerably empty, dark, and confining. Sunny Sundays and market days, on the other hand, he likes, for they are full of life, movement, sounds, and aromas. He feels almost as if he were in Italy. Normal workdays, though, seem still and lifeless. On a fragrant summer evening he looks down on the lake, whose fiery, sparkling surface conjures up the image of jewels on the body of a vast, sleeping, unknown woman. He wants to drown in the image of the alluringly beautiful depths, and soon the thought of shimmering breasts and lips chases him down the mountain and into the water, where he laughs and cries.

Insisting on perfection in his work, he tears up several manuscripts, but keeps on writing, only to be defeated again: "The good fortune to be a sensibly balanced man with simple feelings he sees burst into fragments, like crashing and thundering boulders rolling down the landslide of his life." He resolves to accept his self-destructive nature, "to abandon himself to the entire catastrophe of being a poet."

In the fall he becomes ill, and his sister comes to bring him home. His inner suffering is reflected in his haggard face and matted hair. She asks what is wrong, but he is unable to tell her. His manuscripts lie strewn over the floor, and he gives her his hand to stare at.

They leave Thun behind on a bright autumn morning. Dejected, Kleist sees nothing of the landscape passing by the coach. He dreams instead of clouds and images and caressing hands. His undefined pain seems to ease. His sister urges him to take up a practical activity, and he agrees.

"But finally one has to let it go, this stagecoach," the narrator concludes. Last of all, he wishes to mention the marble plaque on the villa indicating that Kleist lived and worked there. Time and interest permitting, anyone can read it. The narrator says he knows the area around Thun a little, for he once worked there as a clerk in a brewery. There was a trade fair there a little while back; he is not exactly sure, but he thinks it was four years ago.

Themes and Meanings

In this early masterpiece of biographical description, Robert Walser clearly identifies with the struggles of the young Kleist to establish a writing career. Writing, the text suggests, was a painfully difficult process for both writers, particularly in their respective foreign environments (the Swiss Walser wrote his Kleist story near the beginning of his eight-year stay in the Prussian capital of Berlin). Bordering on madness, yet seductive in its images, writing was no longer a romantically innocent activity or a matter of simple inspiration. For Kleist, artistic ambition and the drive for expressive perfection were undermined by longing for physical contact, on the one hand, and a vague heroic idealism, on the other. The lush and sensual natural surroundings of the Bernese Oberland stirred up the images of desire that were so detrimental to his writing. Thus, nature, instead of being an idyllic model of creative simplicity, took on a foreboding quality and caused the numerous radical shifts in his mood. His rescue by his sister implied that only a life of mundane routine could save him from the catastrophe of the madness of the solitary writer, but few things could have been more threatening to his creative energy than the example of normalcy held up to him by his sister's life and education. In contrast to the simple marble commemorative marker, Kleist's brief visit to Thun was, at least for Walser, an occasion for the complex manic-depressive turmoil that would later tear Kleist apart.

Style and Technique

The narrator relates the intensity of Kleist's emotional instability with remarkable coolness and ironic detachment. There is a playfulness in the framing of his narrative: He begins by trying to picture in his mind Kleist's visit to Thun and ends with the almost frivolous remarks on tourists and a trade fair that deserves to be forgotten. In between, the grimness of Kleist's agitation is greatly alleviated by the light touch with which the narrator tells his story. By mentioning casually at the end that he is a former clerk in a brewery, he tries to trivialize his role, yet his story is filled with poetic figures and betrays a high degree of literary consciousness.

Although the persistent use of the present tense and the occasional sentence of quoted monologue bring an immediacy to Kleist's perceptions and experiences, the reader is constantly made aware of the narrator's own voice. The vividness of his imagery and poetic language remain in the foreground as a reminder of the narrator's loquacity in contrast to the silence of Kleist's destroyed manuscripts. The narrator's ironic distance from his subject undercuts the temptation to identify Walser with Kleist. Kleist would never have written and published a work of such poetic intensity on an incident so slight and lacking in dramatic conflict. Walser obviously delights in the sound and rhythm of his sentences and the brightness of his imagery. Nevertheless, the tragic consequences of the drive for self-expression are easily discernible beneath the alluring poetic surface of Walser's text.

Peter West Nutting

KNEEL TO THE RISING SUN

Author: Erskine Caldwell (1903-1987)
Type of plot: Psychological, regional
Time of plot: The 1930's
Locale: On and near a southern plantation
First published: 1935

> *Principal characters:*
> LONNIE NEWSOME, a poor white sharecropper
> MARK NEWSOME, his elderly, deaf father
> ARCH GUNNARD, the owner of the plantation
> CLEM HENRY, an African American sharecropper

The Story

"Kneel to the Rising Sun" focuses on the poor white sharecropper Lonnie New-some, as he struggles to cope with psychological abuse and physical deprivation at the hands of the plantation owner and with the death of his own father, which was directly related to this deprivation.

Initially, Lonnie agonizes about how to conquer his fear and request more rations from plantation owner Arch Gunnard for himself and his starving family. His agony is intensified by the proximity of Clem Henry, an African American sharecropper who confronts Arch for more rations in a seemingly fearless way when he and his family are in need. Lonnie's hesitance provides Arch Gunnard the opportunity to further terrorize Lonnie and possibly Clem Henry and the other sharecroppers who are present. Arch cuts off the tail of Lonnie's groveling dog with his jackknife, adding it to his large collection of tails. Overwhelmed by the abuse of his dog and his own fear, Lonnie fails to ask for more rations despite his father's assessment that the entire family will starve to death within three months without an increase in rations.

Late that evening, because of hunger, Mark Newsome, Lonnie's deaf father, wanders off in search of food. Lonnie and Clem discover Lonnie's father dead and partially devoured in the pen in which Arch Gunnard fattens his savage hogs. With difficulty, they extract what remains of the elder Newsome, and at Clem's urging, Lonnie wakes up Arch Gunnard and brings him to the hog pen. There, Clem courageously confronts Arch with the fact that Mark Newsome's death is directly due to Arch's starving of his sharecroppers, which prompts Arch to attack Clem, who resists. Arch goes for help from his white neighbors, and Clem hides in the nearby woods. Although Clem helped Lonnie find his father and confronted Arch about the skimpy rations that led to the elderly man's death, at the white mob's insistence, Lonnie not only tells where Clem has hidden but also joins in the search party. In fact, Lonnie is one of the most energetic searchers, although he does not participate in the actual murder of Clem.

Traumatized by the death of his father and by the murder of Clem and aware that his cowardice had significantly contributed to both, Lonnie trudges homeward, struggling to verbalize what he had never thought of before. However, when his wife asks about all the shooting, he tells her that nothing is the matter, and the story ends with his wife again asking him to obtain more rations from Arch Gunnard because Lonnie's father was going to be famished when he returned.

Themes and Meanings

Thematically, Erskine Caldwell's "Kneel to the Rising Sun" operates on several levels. It is a graphic depiction of the worst aspects of the sharecropping system that followed (and in many ways continued) the slavery system of the American South. Throughout, emphasis is placed on Arch Gunnard's hatred of African Americans and his fanatical desire to debase or, failing that, destroy them. After cutting off the dog's tail, Arch comments that he wished that African Americans had tails because there would be more to cut and, therefore, more satisfaction. He also repeatedly refers to Clem Henry as needing to be taught a lesson or at least chased out of the area, and when the opportunity arises, he and his vigilante neighbors murder Clem for even minimally opposing the existing system. Thus, the most prominent theme of the story is the racism pervading the American South even seventy years after the demise of slavery.

On a more subtle level, "Kneel to the Rising Sun" is a profound study of the psychological dilemma of the poor white southerner, both before and after the Civil War. Lonnie has to deal with the racism he has been taught and his pride in being white, which links him to the plantation owner, as well as his economic equality with and therefore natural emotional bond with the African American sharecroppers. Thus, Lonnie is in psychological agony throughout the story. He admires Clem's bravery in defying Arch Gunnard but also resents it, even though the bravery is expressed in the form of support for Lonnie's own father, because of his belief that Clem, an African American, should not be so brave and should therefore be punished (especially since Lonnie himself lacks such bravery).

Lonnie loves his father, but joining with Clem in criticism of Arch Gunnard conflicts with the loyalty that he has been trained to feel toward his fealty lord, a fellow white. Given these conflicts and Lonnie's dilemma of either defending his family and economic class against Arch Gunnard and thus becoming a symbolic "nigger" (in the language of the system) or defending Arch and the system and rejecting African American Clem Henry (and by extension his own friends and family), Lonnie illustrates the fundamental psychological transference underlying the poor white's obedience to the southern caste system. Lonnie's betrayal of Clem and participation in the search for him becomes a transferred search for his own father and an outlet for anger and frustration against the oppressive system that killed his father. For example, during the search for Clem, Lonnie forgets that it is not his father, Mark Newsome, who is being sought. Therefore, thematically, the story presents the southern poor white's rage and violence against African Americans as transformed, transferred rage from its actual target and genesis, the deprivation and brutality of Arch Gunnard and the southern caste system.

This psychological dilemma also generates the story's naturalistic theme, the message that if there is hope for improvement in this southern world of race and class hatred and oppression, it is a desperate hope that will not be fulfilled soon. After the brutalizing that he suffers, Lonnie has thoughts that he has never had before, but he never clearly expresses them or acts on them. He tells his wife nothing is wrong. The message is that the southern caste system is still safe from attack by Lonnie and his kind, despite the death of Lonnie's father and of Clem Henry, his only real friend. Thus, the major forces—the plantation owners, their ideological system, and the transferred anger of the poor white sharecroppers—remain intact, with very little hope for freedom or change.

Style and Technique

Caldwell's "Kneel to the Rising Sun" employs several important literary techniques, including the third-person focus on the consciousness of Lonnie, whose psychological struggles are Caldwell's primary concern. A technique that enhances this psychological portrait is Caldwell's use of hyperbole, particularly as to the sharpness or leanness of Lonnie's face. Clem Henry says to Lonnie that any sharecropper who stays with Arch Gunnard long enough would have a face so sharp as to split boards for a coffin, and Lonnie's consciousness repeatedly returns to this idea. After Arch kills Lonnie's dog and the sharecropper fails to ask for more rations, he rubs his chin and feels the exposed jawbones and tendons. Again, after Arch and the others leave, the defeated Lonnie feels his pointed chin hurting his chest. This latter hyperbole, particularly, conveys Lonnie's lack of pride and manhood, in his inability to hold his head erect after his dog (and symbolically he and his family) is mutilated by Arch Gunnard. The mutilation theme is repeated when Arch's hogs kill and partially eat Lonnie's father, symbolizing the greed of southern plantation owners who devour their sharecroppers.

Another technique in generating the naturalistic powerlessness and psychological pessimism of the story is Caldwell's use of similes that dehumanize and desensitize by association. For example, Arch Gunnard uses the dog's tail as a razor strap, seeming to sharpen his knife on it, demonstrating Arch's lack of empathy for or recognition of the living, feeling nature of the animal he is about to torture. To the same effect, Arch cuts the dog's tail as if he is cutting a willow branch to use in driving cows. Equally dehumanizing are Caldwell's likening of the savage hogs devouring Lonnie's father to hounds devouring a dead rabbit and his comparison of the white hunters nearing discovery of Clem Henry to a group of fox hunters nearing their prey.

Probably most effective technically is the story's repeated irony, which emphasizes Lonnie's psychological dilemmas and inability to recognize reality. For example, Lonnie tells Clem that Arch Gunnard did not have any more to do with his father's death than Lonnie did (although both had much to do with it). Also, Lonnie becomes the foremost searcher in the effort to find and kill Clem, his friend. Conveying the same ironic message are Lonnie's denial to his wife that anything is wrong after his father and Clem have been killed and his wife's final request that he obtain more rations for when his father returns. The irony effectively conveys the idea that irrationality and distortion control events and people in the naturalistic world of this graphically powerful story.

John L. Grigsby

THE KNIFE THROWER

Author: Steven Millhauser (1943-   )
Type of plot: Impressionistic
Time of plot: The 1990's
Locale: A small town
First published: 1997

> *Principal characters:*
> HENSCH, the knife thrower
> HIS BEAUTIFUL ASSISTANT
> SUSAN PARKER,
> THOMAS, and
> LAURA, audience members who agree to be marked with a knife

The Story

The first-person plural narrator, "we," begins by recounting when the townspeople first learn that the renowned knife thrower, Hensch, would be giving a single performance at 8 P.M. on Saturday night. The ambiguity of the townspeople's response to the news is based on the reputation of Hensch, who is a skilled artist but is surrounded by strange rumors. Although the townspeople know that Hensch is a knife thrower, they are not certain exactly what he does. Some say Hensch has crossed the line and has built his reputation from disreputable acts because he has introduced the element of an artistic wound into the simple discipline of knife throwing. Young women particularly have willingly let themselves be wounded by him, and the townspeople acknowledge that without this hint of the forbidden and sadistic, they would not have been drawn to the performance.

Precisely at 8:00 P.M., Hensch walks on stage. He begins with simple knife throwing and the pinning of objects that have been tossed in the air. His beautiful female assistant, wearing a flowing white gown, releases six hoops that his knives catch against the wall in a complicated pattern. Hensch successfully completes a number of throws but he ignores one hoop that she releases. Tension begins to grow in the crowd as the audience wonders why Hensch ignored the hoop. Did he not like the throw? Was he displeased with his assistant? Was he losing his skill? The crowd takes a deep breath as the hoops are tossed again, and suddenly, he fixes three hoops against the wall with a single knife.

Following this act, the assistant brings out a live fluttering butterfly in a bowl. She releases the butterfly, and it ascends. So fast that the audience almost does not see him do it, Hensch throws his knife and perfectly impales the innocent and beautiful butterfly against the boards. The audience marvels and wonders what Hensch could possibly do next to exceed that feat.

Hensch places his own hand, palm up, on a table. He tosses a knife in the air, and the audience cries out as the knife lands, tip down, on what appears to be his palm. However, Hensch shows the audience his hand, uncut, and wiggles his fingers in the air.

The knife throwing takes an increasingly dangerous and suspenseful turn as Hensch's assistant stands against the wall while he throws the knives, one after the other and they strike nearer and nearer to her flesh. After a series of throws, the assistant tells the audience to be very quiet as the master knife thrower is going to mark her with a knife. She removes her long white gloves and stands against the wall. The knife strikes the wood beside her neck. The audience, the narrator says, feels a twinge of disappointment—had the master missed his mark? Then they see the trickle of blood down her neck, and they applaud as she takes her bow.

When she returns after leaving the stage for a few minutes, she is dressed in a long black gown with long sleeves and a high collar that conceals her wound. The narrator reports that the audience imagines the white bandage beneath the collar and imagines her body scarred by similar, equally concealed wounds. Then the assistant asks for volunteers from the audience who wish to be marked. A girl, Susan Parker, steps forward, and while the assistant holds Susan's arm in the air, the knife thrower slightly marks her forearm with a knife. The assistant leads her off the stage and tells her she has been very brave but tells the audience that the knife thrower can mark more deeply, but the sacrificial person must show himself or herself to be worthy. A young man, Thomas, comes forward and he, too, is marked, though more deeply.

The assistant then asks if there is anyone who is willing to make the "ultimate sacrifice" and be fatally marked by the master. Silence prevails in the audience until finally a young woman named Laura steps forward. Amid awe in the audience, she ascends the stage. The knife thrower tosses the fatal knife, and Laura falls to the ground. The audience gasps, and the curtain falls. The story begins to come to an end with a description of the girl and her look of surprise, and then the audience departs, everyone believing it was a setup, just a show. However, there is enough doubt in their minds that they begin to see themselves as implicated in the wrongdoing, guilty and outraged at a man such as Hensch who, although he had the right to make his living, did so by going too far.

Themes and Meanings

The style and storytelling method used in "The Knife Thrower" is consistent with that used in other works by Pultizer Prize-winning author Steven Millhauser. Millhauser tends to select simple, realistic yet improbable subjects and to invest them with a quality of Magical Realism or, as in the case of "The Knife Thrower," a kind of "satanic realism." The power of the story is achieved through the suspense created by the general dangers of knife throwing and the specific peril of the artistic wound that Hensch inflicts. The use of the first-person plural narrator not only adds an element of mystery and collective implication to the story as it unfolds but also makes the reader part of the audience in a very intimate and complicated way. Just as the audience is both fascinated and repelled by Hensch's audacity, so is the reader both drawn into the story by means of the author's spellbinding skill and made to feel voyeuristic and implicated by continuing to read though the story moves toward a dire outcome. On reading the story, the reader, like the audience, comes to see his or her own dark side, the side of human consciousness that is fascinated by the forbidden, and is also relieved, as well as outraged, to find that the collective nature of human behavior may mitigate but does not absolve responsibility. Yet, the fact that Hensch's final act is part of a performance leads the audience and the reader to take comfort in the fact that it was all a show, both Hensch's knife throwing and the story itself. That comfort, however, is very measured as the reader and the audience are left to wonder if what took place before their eyes was real or fake.

Style and Technique

The language used in the story is deceptively plain and simple and thus underlines the mounting horror and wonder. The fact that Millhauser does not name the assistant although he names each of the volunteers makes Hensch and his assistant seem to be a single, outside unit, in contrast to the volunteers, who are members of the community. The story suggests that a community can be spellbound temporarily by influences that are simply passing through; however, as the outcome of the story indicates, the community will be forever changed as a result. The story bears a resemblance to Shirley Jackson's "The Lottery" in its mythic yet specific setting. However, in "The Knife Thrower," the reader comes to realize that the evil in which a community partakes is often invited in and acts as a scapegoat for the community's inability to face its own dark side. The community leaves the scene affirming the need for making a living but blaming Hensch for going too far. What this last line reveals is that the audience, even after such a terrifying performance, refuses to accept that Hensch himself does not go too far; rather, the audience not only encourages but also needs Hensch to perform for them so that they may be reaffirmed in their provincialism and may persist in their righteousness.

Susan M. Rochette-Crawley

THE KUGELMASS EPISODE

Author: Woody Allen (Allen Stewart Konigsberg, 1935-   )
Type of plot: Parody
Time of plot: The 1970's
Locale: New York City and Yonville, France
First published: 1977

Principal characters:
> SIDNEY KUGELMASS, a professor of humanities at City College of New York
> DAPHNE KUGELMASS, his unappealing second wife
> DR. MANDEL, his psychoanalyst
> PERSKY, a magician/inventor
> EMMA BOVARY, the heroine of the novel *Madame Bovary* by Gustave Flaubert

The Story

Psychoanalysis is incapable of curing the civilized discontent of Professor Sidney Kugelmass. He feels frustrated in his second marriage—to a woman whom he regards as an overweight oaf—and pressured by the alimony and child support that he must pay his first wife. He longs to transcend the banality of his existence and fantasizes doing so in an adulterous affair with a glamorous woman.

His opportunity comes with an unexpected phone call from a tinker in Brooklyn who dubs himself "The Great Persky." Persky has constructed a cabinet that can somehow transport its occupant into the world of a literary work. All Persky need do is toss in a book, tap three times, and whoever is inside will find himself within that book's fictional universe.

Kugelmass decides that he wants to pursue a romance with Emma Bovary. He pays Persky twenty dollars, and soon after getting inside the cabinet with a paperback of Gustave Flaubert's novel *Madame Bovary* (1857; English translation, 1886), finds himself in the Bovary house in provincial Yonville. Kugelmass and Emma spend a romantic afternoon alone together in the French countryside, which ends when he must return to meet his wife Daphne at Bloomingdale's. Kugelmass goes back to nineteenth century Yonville many times during the next several months. He and Emma become passionate lovers.

Fascinated by Kugelmass's tales of the world from which he comes, Emma is eager to visit it. Persky manages to transport both of them back to New York City, where they pass a rapturous weekend at the Plaza Hotel. On Monday morning, Kugelmass must return to his wife and his job, and he brings Emma to Persky's house to have her dispatched back to Yonville. This time the cabinet does not work, however, and Emma must spend the week ensconced at the Plaza Hotel, while Persky desperately attempts to repair his invention and Kugelmass, afraid that his liaison will be discovered, begins to panic. By the time Emma is able to return whence she came, her relationship with Kugelmass has disintegrated. He is now reconciled to a banal life with Daphne in twentieth century America.

Nevertheless, three weeks later he returns to Persky to seek another romantic adventure, an affair with one of the beautiful women in Philip Roth's sexually explicit *Portnoy's Complaint* (1969). The cabinet malfunctions, however, killing Persky, and substituting an old Spanish textbook for *Portnoy's Complaint*, so that a terrified Kugelmass finds himself pursued at the end by the irregular verb *tener* ("to have").

Themes and Meanings

Like the Flaubert novel whose main character it appropriates, "The Kugelmass Episode" examines the futility of the quest for personal happiness. Although it is cast in a comic key, Woody Allen's story, like *Madame Bovary*, is organized around a logic of disillusionment. Each stage of transcendence is a disappointment, and the more that Kugelmass, who has already been through two marriages at the outset of the story, reaches for something exotic that is beyond his grasp, the more miserable he becomes. It is appropriate that he is last seen hounded by the verb *tener*, a graphic reminder of the elusiveness of the heart's desire: People cannot have what they want and do not want what they have.

Allen is best known for his achievements in film—as a prolific director, writer, and performer. Many of his cinematic works explore the complex relationship between art and life by being playfully metafictional; when characters mug to the camera or are themselves artists, the medium becomes aware of itself. "The Kugelmass Episode" is a similar fiction about fiction. Its interaction between "real" and invented characters anticipates the premise of Allen's film *The Purple Rose of Cairo* (1985), in which a film character walks off the screen and into a romance with a woman in the audience.

As a professor of humanities, Kugelmass is a professional reader of literature. Like Flaubert's Emma, whose addiction to extravagant love stories ultimately leads to her depression and suicide, Kugelmass is more stimulated by literary images than by the people and situations he encounters outside books. The simple diagnosis of his skeptical psychotherapist, Dr. Mandel, is that he is "so unrealistic." Kugelmass is unable to reconcile the realities of his ordinary existence with the enchanting plots and persons he has encountered in his reading. Neither Flo, his first wife, nor Daphne, his second, could possibly be more exciting than Sister Carrie, Hester Prynne, Ophelia, or Temple Drake. Literature has spoiled him for life.

Allen assumes that his readers will catch these and other literary allusions, that his readers, like Kugelmass, are intimately acquainted with the most prominent works of Western literature and will pride themselves on their ability to follow the learned references, but, even more so, on their privileged detachment from the pathetic professor in the story. They may share his enthusiasm for books, but they have a redeeming awareness that undercuts the kind of uncritical absorption that undoes both Emma and Kugelmass—at least, such an awareness is assumed by Allen's mocking text.

Even after discarding Emma, Kugelmass has not learned his lesson. He is soon lusting after another literary figure and deprecating his life outside of books. It is a futile, destructive cycle of desire and deceit, one that the story's conclusion suggests must be broken: The eternal quest for happiness yields only eternal dissatisfaction. Persky's extraordinary machine is destroyed, and the wizard himself dies. As the story approaches its final words, abjuring its own rough magic, it seems to be endorsing Dr. Mandel's insistence on confronting the ordinary and coming to terms with it. The story does so, ironically, through Allen's farfetched fictional contrivance.

Style and Technique

"The Kugelmass Episode" is a very amusing story, and its humor is that of a network of incongruities. There is a striking disparity between anxious, balding Kugelmass and the glamorous life that he would lead. The reader laughs at his pretensions and groans for his frailties. Kugelmass is yet another version of the distinctive Allen persona, familiar from other stories and from Allen's film roles. He is a contemporary American reincarnation of the Yiddish schlemiel figure: the hapless man who, according to the Yiddish proverb, falls on his back and breaks his nose. Though Sidney Kugelmass, whose very name ludicrously undercuts his romantic aspirations, has failed at everything, including freshman English, he naïvely keeps returning for more.

After Emma and Kugelmass exchange their first remarks, the reader is told, "She spoke in the same fine English translation as the paperback." By the end of the relationship, Emma is complaining to Kugelmass that "watching TV all day is the pits." Much of the humor in this story results from juxtaposing the florid style of a literary classic—about a woman steeped in literary rhetoric—with the casual vernacular of a modern, irreverent New Yorker. Kugelmass holds a respected social position and is in awe of Emma Bovary, but his speech is laced with outdated proletarian slang: "sock it to me," "scam," and "jitterbug." His streetwise talk is as affected as are provincial Emma's aristocratic airs. Although Emma covets elegant formal clothing, she is fascinated by the marked-down leisure suit that her new lover wears. It is difficult to imagine an odder, and more appropriate, couple than Emma Bovary and Sidney Kugelmass. One is a French heroine and the other an American antihero, but both are in love with a narcissistic idea of love.

As its title suggests, "The Kugelmass Episode" is more a sketch than a fully realized fictional universe of three-dimensional characters. It is an essay in narrative form, an inventive meditation on *Madame Bovary*. Much of its charm derives from its self-mockery and its awareness of its own artifice. One of the more remarkable moments in the piece occurs when a professor at Stanford who is a specialist in Flaubert suddenly discovers a strange character named Kugelmass in his familiar novel. He rationalizes that it is the mark of a classic always to surprise on each reading. In depicting a nineteenth century literary character visiting the urban American culture of television, films, and football, Allen's brief, perceptive fantasy delights on each reading.

Steven G. Kellman

LADY MACBETH OF THE MTSENSK DISTRICT

Author: Nikolai Leskov (1831-1895)
Type of plot: Realism
Time of plot: The mid-nineteenth century
Locale: Mtsensk District, Russia
First published: "Ledi Makbet Mtsenskogo uezda," 1865 (English translation, 1922)

> Principal characters:
> KATERINA IZMAYLOVA, the protagonist, a merchant's wife
> ZINOVY BORISOVICH IZMAYLOV, her husband
> SERGEY, her lover
> BORIS TIMOFEYEVICH, her father-in-law
> FEDYA LYAMIN, her nephew
> SONETKA, a convict

The Story

Nikolai Leskov's storyteller begins his tale with a description of the oppressive boredom of the provincial Russian merchant household, where the men leave to conduct their business and the women are left in a latter-day harem, to look after the children—if there are any—and the larders. Katerina Izmaylova, the young wife of Zinovy Borisovich Izmaylov, is attractive, spirited, and quite unprepared by her poor but free and simple childhood for the stultifying narrowness of her husband's way of life. Her five-year marriage has brought no children, and despite the fact that Zinovy Borisovich's first wife bore no children either, Katerina is reproached for her barrenness, for "ruining her husband's life." Passive, languid, Katerina wanders the silent house, sleeps, watches the servants from her attic window.

It is from that attic window, her bedroom window, that Katerina looks out on the spring garden in the sixth year of her marriage and decides to go for a stroll. She hears laughter near the barns and finds her father-in-law's clerks teasing the fat cook by hoisting her into a flour vat to weigh her. The chief culprit is Sergey—young, handsome, insolent, and more than ready to test Katerina's boast of her strength. In doing so, he embraces her—and a flustered Katerina leaves but not without finding out that Sergey is a newcomer, fired by his last employer for carrying on with the mistress.

That evening, Sergey appears at Katerina's door, complaining of loneliness and boredom. He has little trouble sweeping Katerina off her feet and into bed, and the two lovers spend every night together for the week thereafter. Then Boris Timofeyevich, Katerina's father-in-law, catches Sergey sliding down a pillar beneath the attic window and takes the unrepentant sinner to the storeroom, flogs him brutally, and locks him in. He sends for his absent son, and in the face of Katerina's pleas and brazen lack of shame, decides to send Sergey to prison.

On the day of his decision, however, Boris Timofeyevich falls ill after eating his porridge and mushrooms, and toward evening dies "just like the rats in his granaries."

No one is particularly suspicious, because mushrooms are a tricky thing, and Boris Timofeyevich is an old man—and the mistress's affair is the mistress's business. Zinovy is delayed, Sergey recovers in the master's bed, and all appears to be going well. Katerina and Sergey make love and go through rituals of jealousy and reassurance. One night, however, Katerina dreams twice of a huge cat, and the cat speaks with the voice of her murdered father-in-law. She awakes from the nightmare to hear her husband's key turning in the locked gate outside.

Sergey hides, and Zinovy confronts his wife. She at first denies everything but then loses her temper and calls Sergey out of hiding to taunt Zinovy. Enraged, he strikes her, and at this point Katerina's vaunted girlhood strength returns. She throws her husband to the floor, and she and Sergey, hands entwined, strangle him. To make sure, Katerina finishes him off with a heavy candlestick and then carefully wipes the cherry-sized drops of blood from the floor. Sergey buries Zinovy in the cellar, and no one is the wiser. Everyone assumes that the master has mysteriously disappeared before reaching home.

Katerina, pregnant, is about to assume control of her husband's properties, but another heir appears on the scene, Zinovy's young nephew Fedya Lyamin. Now it is Sergey who is uneasy, the "unhappiest of men," and he constantly hints, insinuates, and suggests to Katerina that Fedya's continued existence is an obstacle to their happiness. Fedya falls ill and is forced to stay home from an evening holiday church service. With the entire household gone, Katerina sees her chance. She and Sergey smother the child with a pillow. This time, however, there are witnesses. A group of young men returning from the church service, curious about the mistress's "amours," decide to peep through the window to catch the lovers in the act—but the act they catch them in is murder.

The two are tried, flogged, and sentenced to hard labor and exile in Siberia. They begin the long trek together, in the same gang of convicts. Katerina's baby, still the legal heir, is given to Zinovy's relatives to rear, but as long as Katerina can be near Sergey, she has no thought for anything else. Sergey, however, tires of her passion and her devotion now that she is no longer a wealthy merchant's wife, and he takes up first with one female convict, then another. He and Sonetka, his new love, humiliate and taunt Katerina, finally tricking her into giving Sergey her last pair of warm stockings—which end up on the devious Sonetka's feet.

As the gang is herded onto a barge to ferry across a turbulent river, Katerina seems numb to the jibes and laughter of her tormentors, but as the ferry reaches midriver, she acts. She leaps into the water, taking Sonetka with her. Sonetka emerges from the waves to grasp for the boat hook, but Katerina, in her last show of strength, pulls her down, and both disappear for good.

Themes and Meanings

"Come you spirits that tend on mortal thought, unsex me here," says William Shakespeare's Lady Macbeth as she steels herself for Duncan's murder. There are no such words from Leskov's merchant murderess, Katerina Izmaylova, as she dispatches first her father-in-law, then her husband, then her nephew—and finally her ri-val and herself. She neither reflects, nor rehearses, nor suffers remorse. No abstract notions of power or kingship rule Katerina's actions—her lover Sergey can bring her nothing in the way of authority or status—nor, until the third murder, does she show any trace of greed. When the authorities ask her why she has committed these crimes, she answers simply, nodding at Sergey, "For him." The source of Katerina's newfound strength of will, so murderously directed, is passion itself—purely physical, sexual passion, inseparable from her femaleness.

Leskov had originally intended his Katerina to be one of a series of female types from the area along the Oka and Volga rivers, types to be taken from the peasant, mer-chant, and gentry estates. His series of sketches never materialized, but "Lady Mac-beth" has become one of Leskov's best-known, most powerful tales. This "dark king-dom," the patriarchal, superstitious merchant milieu, was mined by other Russian writers of the mid-nineteenth century, such as Aleksandr Ostrovsky in his plays and Fyodor Dostoevski in *Idiot* (1868; *The Idiot*, 1887), but Leskov's treatment is unsur-passed—all the more so, because, unlike Ostrovsky, he does not set out to draw a genre picture or an expose of this pious and ignorant but shrewd and pragmatic class, a class whose domestic customs and habits date back to Byzantine books of instruction on the proper conduct of households, wives, and children. That Katerina is unjustly reproached for her childlessness, that her relatives inspect her every move for signs of waywardness or impropriety, that her husband threatens to torture the truth out of her—these things Leskov presents as a matter of course, as givens. What interests him and what interests the reader is not so much sociology or psychology as character—human nature, Katerina's nature.

Leskov does not sentimentally justify Katerina's crimes, but it is clear that she is neither fundamentally evil, nor weakly corrupt, nor cruel. Like many another Leskov character, she seems a potentially heroic figure somehow gone wrong. Fate may mas-querade as society but really fools no one. In her energy, vitality, and sensuality, she is far more appealing than either her victims or her partner-in-crime; her obsession, her "possession," is an honest one, which she herself neither rationalizes nor justifies. The instincts that Sergey awakens in her are not all murderous—for the first time in her married life she really sees, hears, and smells the beauty around her. The very strength of her feeling leads to her downfall.

It is no accident that Sergey and Katerina's first bantering exchange is a challenge of strength. The old peasant weighing the flour says, "Our body . . . counts for nothing on the scales. It's our strength that weighs, not our body." In the end, it is Katerina's tragic strength, not inert weight, that pulls both herself and her rival beneath the waves.

Style and Technique

In "Lady Macbeth of the Mtsensk District," Leskov eschews his much-used *skaz* narrator—the chatty, distracted, half-educated storyteller who reveals more about himself than about his tale—in favor of a more detached voice. Although the narrator here is an insider, referring to the Mtsensk District as "our part of the country," he no longer seems a part of the life there. Far from making the story of Katerina Izmaylova a dry, judicial account of crime and punishment, this detachment gives it a straightforward, inexorable movement. Like any good storyteller, the narrator wants his listeners to pay attention, to wait for what happens next; in his very first paragraph, he promises a story and a character that none can remember "without an inward shudder." Thereafter, he ends each short chapter—there are fourteen—with either an obviously temporary resolution or a tantalizing hint at events to come: "This was what the old man decided to do; but he was not given the chance to carry out his decision"; "But time was passing not only for them: after his long absence, Zinovy, the wronged husband, was hurrying home."

The narrator's deliberate hints are not the only device that lends this tale its concentrated forward motion. Although Leskov's narrator avoids dialect and folksy locution, he still creates an air of folklore and myth. The young, beautiful wife kept under lock and key by an old, miserly husband and his tyrannical father, the saucy suitor with his swagger and his black curls—these are the stuff of folktale and magic. Magical, too, is Leskov's description of the lovers' night in the moonlit apple orchard, but the magic becomes more ominous in Katerina's vision of the snub-nosed cat in her bed—once there to wake her in place of her lover, once there to remind her of her sins.

The dreamlike, trancelike quality of Katerina's obsession leads her onward, hypnotizing both her and the reader. The dream turns into a nightmare on the march to Siberia, when Sergey's betrayals and mockeries come as fast as his flattery and blandishments came before. Animal imagery and prophetic vision come together at the end of the tale when Katerina, staring fixedly at the waves, sees the heads of her victims rising from the water, and when she herself rises up one last time to throw herself on her rival "like a strong pike on a soft little perch."

Jane Ann Miller

THE LADY OR THE TIGER?

Author: Frank R. Stockton (1834-1902)
Type of plot: Fairy tale
Time of plot: The distant past
Locale: A semi-barbaric land
First published: 1882

Principal characters:

A SEMI-BARBARIC KING
HIS SEMI-BARBARIC YOUNG DAUGHTER, who is in love with a
young courtier at her father's court
A YOUNG COURTIER AT THE KING'S COURT, who is in love with
the princess

The Story

In "the very olden time," a half-barbaric king, who was also half-civilized, because of the influence of his distant Latin neighbors, conceived a way of exercising justice on offenders against his rule. He placed his suspect in a Roman-like arena and had him choose to open one of either of two doors that would open into the arena. Behind one of the identical doors lurked a ferocious tiger that would leap out and devour the accused; behind the other door awaited a lovely maid who would, if her door was the one opened, come forth and be married at once to the opener. (It mattered not that the man may be married or otherwise committed, for the whimsical king would have his justice.) The fate was to be decided by chance alone, and no one who knew of the placement behind the doors was allowed to inform him which to elect.

All of this was popular among the audience, and even their thinking members could not deny that it was a fair test. The public experienced pleasing suspense and an immediate resolution. Best of all, everyone knew that the accused person chose his own ending.

Now it happened that a handsome young courtier dared to love the king's daughter, who was lovely and very dear to her father. The man, however, though of the court, was of low station; his temerity was therefore an offense against decorum and the king. Such a thing had never happened in the kingdom before. The young lover had to be put into the arena to choose a door, a lady or a tiger. However, the princess loved the young man; clearly and openly that was the case. She did not want to lose him to a ravenous tiger, but at the same time, could she bear to lose him to another woman in marriage?

The king searched the kingdom for the most savage of tigers. He also searched for the most beautiful maiden in all his land. No matter which door the young man selected, he would have the best that could be offered. The public could hardly wait, and as for the king, he reasoned that chance would have its way, and in any event the young man would be disposed of.

The princess achieved something no one had before: She knew which fate was behind each door. She worked hard to learn the secret, using the power of her will and gold to secure it. Moreover, the princess knew who the woman was, a lady who had directed amorous glances toward the young man at court, glances that—or so the princess fancied—he had sometimes returned. For her interest in the princess's lover, the princess hated the woman behind the door.

In the arena on the fatal day, the young man looked at the princess, expecting her to know which door hid what fate. The princess made an immediate and definite motion toward the right-hand door, and this door her lover opened directly.

Did the tiger or the lady come out of the doorway? The princess loved the young man, but she was also a barbarian and she was hot-blooded. She imagined the tiger in horror, but how much more often did she suffer at the thought of his joy at discovering the lady? In one fulfillment, she would be forced to see him torn to pieces before her very eyes; in the other, she would be forced to watch him marry and go off forever with a woman she hated. The story stops exactly at the point at which the young man opens the door. It does not tell his fate.

Themes and Meanings

Frank R. Stockton said of this story, "If you decide which it was—the lady or the tiger—you find out what kind of person you are yourself." He pretended that he himself did not know, that although he had planned a decided ending, he could not write one, "for I had not the advantage of being either semi-barbaric or a woman." Thus, interpretation of this story relies on each reader's decision, depending on how the reader views the world and human nature in it. The amount of faith the reader has in love and how much the reader believes that jealousy, hate, and pride may alter one's love will affect that decision. What the reader imagines "semi-barbarism" (that of the princess) to be, as well as its opposite, will also affect his or her own interpretation of the ending.

However, certain points about the story are not open to interpretation. The princess does take the trouble, great trouble, to find out which door is hiding what. She is not her father's daughter; she does not leave things to chance, for her heart is engaged. She does not hesitate to give direction, nor does her lover hesitate to rely on her. If he trusts her so, would she trust him less? Still, this is a fairy tale, with a fairy-tale way of presentation. Are such complexities of motivation that would lead the princess to indicate the door to the tiger right for such a tale? One may answer no, yet the course of true love is here pointedly crowned with hate and jealousy. A possible theme of "The Lady or the Tiger?" is the necessity of trust in another person's humanity and love in a world where one never knows for certain what that person will do. The reader may wonder: "Which door would I have chosen?"

Style and Technique

This is a tale rather than a story. There is no dialogue; no one speaks to the reader but the narrator, who spins the yarn and asks the questions of interpretation at the end. He knows the story, but one senses that he does not have omniscience, that he is not there himself. He knows more than the populace and king, yet he does not know and will not reveal the outcome. That seems unfair—he leaves his readers dangling—but that is his purpose from the beginning. The story is a tour de force, hinging on a gimmick. What is annoying is that the narrator seems to know the ending but will not tell it.

However, the tale may be saved for the reader by the distance the author keeps from his material and the atmosphere of mystery that he maintains. He has heard the story, and it has amazed him with its mixture of the humane and the barbaric. If the plot is a teaser, are its psychological concerns also? In not letting the characters speak, in not even naming them, and in having their motivations generalized, the author approaches allegory—the allegory of logical human emotions. He turns the tale into a matter of "what would you do?" He turns outward from the story to the reader directly, thus placing emphasis on theme rather than on plot.

In not deeply developing his characters, holding them at arm's length, he has made it impossible for one to know what they will do. One is told their motivations in general terms, but one does not experience the characters having them: One does not hear their words or glimpse their process of thought. Hence, the reader is not involved in the story. The characters in the tale are but once-upon-a-time people, representative but not real. When readers are asked at last to decide, on the basis of their personalities, what they will do, they are unable to respond but can say only what they would do or what people they have known would do. If the tale fails, it is in this aspect.

One can see that the king turned his fancies into facts, simplified them with his court of chance. He avoided the complexities of responsibility in the decisions by chance. His daughter turns facts into fancies (gold into information, and that information into what she fancies or wants—the right door). In other words, while the father simplifies, the daughter complicates, or takes on responsibility. With what ultimate intent does she do this? How cold or warm is she in her heart? One cannot know. The story lacks the nearness that readers require to answer the question Stockton asks them.

This story works the way a mystery story does, yet the necessary clues are not there. Hints are but hints, for they are canceled out: They do not add up or point in any direction. If "semi-barbarism" is to be looked to for a clue, it fails, because one does not know what "semi-barbarism" means. Not only are explanations of motivations lacking but also a corpse or an action that would shed light on the characters' motivations.

Without its brevity and fast pace this story would have failed miserably. One moves directly from what the king is like to his testing procedure to the young couple's affair to preparations for the trial and finally to the critical—and incomplete—choosing of the door, all in eighteen medium-sized paragraphs. One remains on the surface of the story, which is really a summary of events and the reasons for them. In place of dramatization there are posturings, as if the story were a slide show with lecturer—except that the lecturer wants the listener to finish for him.

William E. Morris

THE LADY WITH THE DOG

Author: Anton Chekhov (1860-1904)
Type of plot: Psychological
Time of plot: The 1890's
Locale: Yalta and Moscow
First published: "Dama s sobachkoi," 1899 (English translation, 1917)

Principal characters:
Dmitrii Dmitrich Gurov, a banker
Anna Sergeevna von Diederitz, a married woman

The Story

The story begins with a description of a bored banker, Dmitrii Gurov, on vacation in the southern Russian city of Yalta. Idly attentive toward the other vacationers, Gurov takes special interest in a recent arrival to the resort town, a young woman named Anna Sergeevna von Diederitz, who strolls along the embankment with her little dog. Judging from her appearance, Gurov decides that she is a married woman alone and bored on her vacation. Although he too is married, he has had many affairs, and he becomes excited by the prospect of having a brief affair with this stranger. Beckoning her dog toward him, he uses the pet as an excuse to strike up a conversation with her, and within a short time they develop an easy air of companionship.

Anton Chekhov next depicts the pair after a week has passed. It is a warm, windy day, and the two go down to the pier to watch a ship come in. As the crowd around the ship gradually dissipates, Gurov asks Anna Sergeevna if she wishes to go for a ride. Suddenly, on an impulse, he embraces her and kisses her. He then suggests that they go to her room. The next scene portrays Anna Sergeevna and Gurov in her room; they have just made love for the first time. She is distraught because she feels guilty, not only because she has deceived her husband but also because she has discovered that she has been deceiving herself for a long time. She tells Gurov that she was twenty when she married her husband and has since realized that he is nothing but a flunky. Anna Sergeevna, on the other hand, wants to live, to experience life. Now she believes that her infidelity has proved her to be a petty, vulgar woman and that Gurov will not respect her. Gurov listens to this confession with an attitude of boredom and irritation. He feels that her repentance is unexpected and out of place. Nevertheless, he comforts her, and within a short time her gaiety returns.

They leave the hotel and drive to Oreanda, a scenic spot outside Yalta. There they gaze in silence at the sea and listen to its incessant, muffled sound. Chekhov writes that in the constancy of this noise and in the sea's calm indifference to human life and death there perhaps lies a pledge of eternal salvation, of uninterrupted perfection. Listening to this sound in the company of an attractive woman, Gurov gains a new insight into life. He perceives that everything in this world is beautiful except that which people themselves do when they forget about the highest goals of existence and their own human worth.

After this moment of transcendent reflection, the two return to Yalta, and for the next several days they spend all of their time together, indulging in the sensual pleasures of Yalta and the joys of their new relationship. At last, however, Anna Sergeevna receives a letter from her husband asking her to return home. After she bids Gurov farewell at the railroad station, presumably forever, he, too, thinks that it is time for him to return home to Moscow.

Back in Moscow, Gurov tries to return to his familiar routine of work, family life, and entertainment. He assumes that his memories of Anna Sergeevna will fade, just as the memories of his other lovers always have. He discovers, though, that he cannot stop thinking about Anna Sergeevna, and soon he begins to regard his present life as nonsensical, empty, and dull. Impulsively he decides to travel to Anna Sergeevna's hometown, hoping to see her and to arrange a meeting with her. After arriving in her town, he seeks out her house but does not enter it. Instead he decides to attend a premiere at the local theater that night in the hope of seeing her there. When he confronts her at the theater, she is shocked yet thrilled, and she agrees to meet with him in Moscow.

Now begins an agonizing time for Gurov. Meeting with Anna Sergeevna once every two or three months, he finds that he is living a double life. His everyday life is routine and conventional, but he regards it as being full of lies and deception. His other life, the one involving Anna Sergeevna, is of necessity kept secret, but it contains all that is important to him, and indeed it represents the core of his being. In the final scene of the story, Chekhov depicts the two lovers trying to come to terms with their difficult situation. Anna Sergeevna is in tears; she believes that their lives have been shattered by their love and the deceit that it requires to survive. He too recognizes that he cannot tear himself away from her, and he perceives a fearful irony in the fact that only now, when he has begun to turn gray and to lose his good looks, has he found true love. The anguished pair talk about the necessity of changing their lives, of breaking through the walls of deception around them, but they cannot see a solution to their dilemma. Chekhov concludes his tale with the comment that it seemed as though a solution would be found shortly and that a new, beautiful life would then begin but that it was also clear to the couple that the end was still a long way off, and that the most complex and difficult part was just beginning. With this moment of unresolved uncertainty, Chekhov brings to a close his penetrating study of human love and human destiny.

Themes and Meanings

In "The Lady with the Dog," Chekhov provides a masterly portrayal of human psychology, demonstrating how one's expectations of life can be overturned by unpredictable reality. At the outset of the tale, Gurov is shown to be rather cynical and an egocentric opportunist in his attitude toward women. Coldly analytical about his own emotions and his numerous relationships, he has categorized his lovers into three types—the carefree, the intellectual, and the predatory. However, he discovers in his relationship with Anna Sergeevna something new and unexpected. Love for the first time becomes an emotional experience that is deep, sincere, and touching. Significantly, the woman who created this effect on him is not depicted as being a dazzling beauty; he himself realizes how strange it is that this small woman, not distinguished in any way, has become the center of his life. Love, Chekhov suggests in this story, can transform even the most ordinary people and lives into something unique and extraordinary.

Chekhov's exploration of the process by which Gurov discovers that his preconceived notions about women are illusory illustrates one of the writer's broader concerns. Throughout his career, Chekhov emphasized the necessity of exposing falsehood or hypocrisy in society and of espousing the truth, honest and unconditional. Thus, he highlights Anna Sergeevna's despair over the hypocrisy of her marriage to her husband and Gurov's indignation over the falsehood permeating his regular existence in Moscow. Chekhov often articulated his belief in humanity's inalienable right to absolute freedom, and he has instilled this ideal into his two protagonists. In their longing to break free from the fetters of deceit marring their relationship, Chekhov's characters aspire to the kind of beauty and dignity glimpsed by Gurov as he sat with Anna Sergeevna by the sea outside Yalta. Chekhov's narrative illuminates both the value of this ideal and the difficulty of attaining it.

Style and Technique

Like most of Chekhov's late tales, "The Lady with the Dog" reveals the careful touch of a consummate craftsman. Constructing his story out of a small number of selected vignettes, Chekhov managed to evoke the full complexity of an intimate relationship between two sensitive human beings in a concise, almost laconic fashion. One technique that helped the writer achieve such conciseness is the use of minor yet significant detail to suggest emotional states. For example, as Gurov listens to Anna Sergeevna lament her situation when they first become lovers, Chekhov indicates the man's insensitivity to her agitation by depicting him slicing a watermelon and eating it without haste. Similarly, Chekhov's nature descriptions echo or shape a character's emotions: The sensuous sound of the Black Sea at night facilitates Gurov's recognition of the timeless beauty present in the world around him.

To underscore the subjective nature of his characters' perception of events, Chekhov often uses such passive and impersonal constructions as "it seemed" and "it appeared." Perhaps the most striking feature of the structure of "The Lady with the Dog" is the air of uncertainty with which it ends: Chekhov provides no definitive resolution to his lovers' problem. Such an inconclusive ending was not typical for nineteenth century Russian literature. Chekhov seems to imply here that life, unlike the tidy fiction that his predecessors liked to create, does not conform to neat patterns or boundaries but rather continues in a way that defies human control or manipulation. Chekhov pioneered the use of this kind of "zero ending" in his fiction, and it has since become a staple of the modern short story.

Julian W. Connolly

THE LADY WITH THE PET DOG

Author: Joyce Carol Oates (1938-   )
Type of plot: Psychological
Time of plot: The late 1960's or early 1970's
Locale: Nantucket, Massachusetts; a town in Ohio; the road to Albany, New York
First published: 1972

Principal characters:
ANNA
HER LOVER
HER HUSBAND

The Story

"The Lady with the Pet Dog" covers the major phases of Anna's adulterous affair with a married man. Anna, a married woman, meets her lover for the first time at a beach. After they decide to terminate the relationship, he drives her to Albany, and she eventually returns to her husband in Ohio. In the central scene at a public concert, the lover secretly confronts her; the next day, they resume their affair, meeting in hotels. Finally, Anna has a vision of happiness that remains ambiguous. This chronology of events, however, is broken up into three overlapping sections, and each narrates successively more events.

The first section consists of the central scene at the public concert. By beginning in the middle of events, the story challenges the reader to discern who the characters are and how they are related. The silent encounter between Anna and her lover goes unnoticed by everybody else; it seems so unreal that she feels as if she had imagined him. Her husband notices that she is not feeling well, takes her home, and they make love clumsily, symbolizing their unhappy marriage.

The second section goes back six months, starting with the car ride to Anna's sister in Albany, New York, leading up to the central scene, and ending with the resumption of the affair. Although Anna feels the car ride bonds her to her lover, her emotions are confused and conflicted. She rehearses significant conversations in her mind but is capable of only trivial utterances. She knows that she and her lover do not have a future together, yet she does not want to return to her husband. When she does, she feels like a "nothing" and contemplates and attempts killing herself.

Because the next key events of Anna's encounter with her lover at the concert and of the clumsy lovemaking with her husband are repeated in the second section, the reader now knows that the characters in the first and second sections are indeed the same and what the chronological relationship of these two sections is. Anna's lover calls her the morning after the concert. He persuades her to meet him, and they begin to see each other in hotels when he is in town. However, she remains unhappy, even suicidal, because she realizes that he will not leave his wife.

The final and third section tells the entire story, this time from beginning to end. Anna is spending some time away from her husband at her family's old beach house in Nantucket, Massachusetts. There she meets a man, his nine-year-old son, and their dog. The boy is blind, something the man later claims his wife uses against him. As they begin a conversation, the man makes several sketches of Anna, one of which shows her with his dog (hence the story's title). Although both are married, they eventually begin an affair.

Confused and insecure, Anna decides to end the affair and to visit her sister in Albany, where her lover takes her. Then events already contained in one or both of the previous sections are recounted: the drive, the concert, and the resumption of the affair. Section three continues with Anna again feeling suicidal because her life is stuck in repetitions. The section ends, however, with Anna's joyous vision of her affair as a true marriage; her resulting happiness surprises her lover.

Themes and Meanings

The main thematic concerns that Joyce Carol Oates shows in this story can be summarized in a phrase that is the title of the 1972 collection that contains "The Lady with the Pet Dog": *Marriages and Infidelities*. The themes work on the levels of literary tradition and social commentary.

On the level of literary tradition, the story reveals influences on Oates's writing. In *Marriages and Infidelities*, the author re-imagines stories from seminal authors of world literature. This process metaphorically represents the marriage of two autonomous stories, as well as infidelities, that is, more or less subtle changes that may turn the narrative basis upside down. "The Lady with the Pet Dog" is based on Anton Chekhov's short story of the same title. In addition to moving the plot from late nineteenth century Russia to 1970's United States, two significant narrative changes affect the meaning of the story.

First, Chekhov's novella arranges the same basic plot elements in chronological order, in keeping with in the classical dramatic structure of exposition, climax, and resolution. In sharp contrast, Oates's version breaks up the chronology into a boxlike structure with three partially overlapping segments.

Second, Chekhov's focus is on the development of a woman-hating womanizer who, for the first time in his life, finds true love. His story ends with the lovers' mutual affirmation of their love's power, although their love needs to remain hidden because of constraints of czarist Russian society. Oates shifts the focus to the woman, Anna. The confusion of marriages and infidelities is in the tradition of nineteenth century realism, not just in Chekhov's writing but, above all, in French author Gustave Flaubert's *Madame Bovary* (1857; English translation, 1886). Like Emma Bovary, Anna experiences marriage and adultery as equally unsatisfying; thus, the boundaries between what society considers right or wrong become blurred.

Both narrative changes affect the level of social commentary. Anna's struggle in the male-dominated society of the United States is shared by other female protagonists in Oates's early work: their self-images depend on men, not on themselves or other women. Although she also considers it absurd, Anna feels she needs men to save her, and she behaves accordingly. Like an addict, she looks for salvation in the very things that hurt her.

The ultimate question about the meaning of the story centers on Anna being able to sustain her self-generated happiness. The question is connected to the general issue of the extent to which Oates's writings during the 1970's present powerless women going mad or to which she explores new options for women's empowerment. The story's ending is usually interpreted as Anna accepting her lover in all his imperfections. Although this reading is supported by the ending of Chekhov's novella, it is debatable whether Oates's Anna will be able to remain true to her newfound positive emotions. In fact, it is worse than before because this happiness depends on a man she only imagines.

Consequently, her real lover is stunned by the happiness she radiates and asks her what is wrong. The lovers have never connected on a profound level; therefore, it remains doubtful that their suggested intuitive understanding is more than second guessing.

Style and Technique

The short story is a third-person narrative but is limited omniscient, meaning that the reader experiences events from Anna's perspective and is directly aware of only Anna's emotions and thoughts. This technique underscores Anna's emotional isolation because her ups and downs suggest manic-depressive behavior, as well as an obsessive desire to find fulfillment in a relationship with a man, all driving her to suicidal thoughts.

The narrative perspective also emphasizes that her marriage and affair have the same effect on Anna. With her husband, she feels like a shadow of a woman, strangely detached from life and lacking boundaries, giving way to suicidal thoughts and an abortive attempt at her own life, revealing how little she relates to her own body. After a particularly disappointing meeting with her lover, she splashes water on her face, first leading briefly to suicidal thoughts of drowning but then shifting to homicidal thoughts about her lover and his family. She feels insignificant. Anna fails to realize that, for her happiness, neither man matters, as is symbolized by both remaining nameless.

The metaphor of water plays a central role. Generally a symbol of the unconscious, water is connected to emotional breakthroughs for Anna. She experiences water as something that drowns her and, therefore, triggers suicidal thoughts. In the final scene, she again has suicidal thoughts but then feels flooded by her joyous realization that her affair is a true marriage. In the context of her mood swings and the previous negative connotations of water, her final vision remains ambiguous, because flooding implies the danger of violent drowning.

The most striking technique that Oates uses in this story is the plot structure. The narration does not simply alternate between past and present, nor is it circular; rather, it is linear in a complex way. The story is told by rewinding to an earlier time and then covering a wider range of events. In this boxlike structure, events narrated in one section are embedded in the following section. As a result, the narrative "boxes in" the crucial moment of choice. When her lover secretly confronts Anna in public, she could break free, for example, risking a scandal; however, she chooses to remain silent and be defined by the two men in her life.

Consequently, Anna can be seen as "boxed in" by the repetitions of her life. The plot's boxlike structure, then, supports the interpretation of the story's ending as an emotional high point that is likely to be followed by new low points. Anna appears to be trapped in the repetitions of marriage, adultery, and narrative.

Ingo R. Stoehr

THE LAGOON

Author: Joseph Conrad (Jósef Teodor Konrad Nałęcz Korzeniowski, 1857-1924)
Type of plot: Symbolist
Time of plot: The late 1890's
Locale: Malaysia
First published: 1898

> *Principal characters:*
> TUAN, the white man
> ARSAT, the protagonist, a Malayan

The Story

Toward dusk in a tropical lagoon, a white man arrives by boat at the hut of Arsat, a Malayan whom he had befriended years earlier. Arsat greets him at the doorway with an anxious, fearful look and asks the white man, whom he calls "Tuan," if he has brought some medicine. Tuan asks who is sick, and Arsat brings him to the bedside of Diamelen, his woman. She has been stricken with fever and is seriously ill. Fearful that she will die, Arsat and Tuan keep watch by the fire outside the hut. As night arrives, plunging the lagoon into an unquiet darkness, Arsat begins to tell the white man the tale of how he and Diamelen came together, a story of love and betrayal.

Arsat and his brother were brave young warriors, sword bearers to the ruler, Si-Dendring. By chance Arsat met Diamelen one day, and from then on he could "see nothing but one face, hear nothing but one voice." By day he waited on the path to see her, and by night he crept along the hedges of the women's courtyard to steal a glance at her. Often they would whisper longingly to each other in the leafy shadows.

However, Diamelen was forbidden fruit, the wife, or concubine, of Inchi-Midah, a noble chief. Nevertheless, Arsat longed for her all the more, and she for him. Baring his heart to his brother, Arsat was at first advised to wait. Patience, his brother told him, was wisdom. However, as time passed, Arsat grew gloomy, and his warrior blood impatient.

One night, the tribe having gone down to the river to fish by torchlight, Arsat and his brother made their move. Courageously, they paddled their canoe past the tribesmen and waited quietly by the shore for Diamelen. She came running to them, and Arsat took her into his arms and swept her into the boat. Quickly, soundlessly, they made their way downriver, paddling through the night and arriving by afternoon of the next day at a little beach, close by the safety of the deep jungle. Here the men slept while Diamelen kept watch.

Suddenly Arsat and his brother awoke to Diamelen's cry of alarm. The ruler had sent a war party after them, and now the warriors were in sight, drawing toward them in a large boat. Escape by water was thus impossible, so Arsat's brother urged him to take Diamelen and run. The brother would hold off the party as long as he could and then catch up with them. Arsat and his woman ran, hearing the shots from the brother's gun. Making their escape, Arsat looked back and saw his brother surrounded by the enemy. He heard his brother's cries as the men fell on him, but Arsat did not go back. Instead, he and Diamelen went on to safety and a new life together.

After his tale, Arsat rises from the dying fire and returns to the bedside of Diamelen. It is almost dawn. From the doorway, the white man hears a loud groan and sees Arsat stumbling out. "She burns no more," Arsat tells him.

The white man prepares to leave, urging Arsat to come with him, but the grieving lover refuses. He tells Tuan that because he has now lost his world, he is resolved to go back to his enemies. He will fight them on behalf of the brother whom he had deserted. As the white man pulls away from the hut, he sees Arsat standing motionless in the sunshine above the cloudy waters of the lagoon.

Themes and Meanings

"The Lagoon" is a story of love, courage, and cowardice and of their complex interweaving in the fabric of human behavior. Arsat is acknowledged a great warrior. The rank that he holds in the tribe attests his courage and skill; his daring first escape with Diamelen is further proof that he is a man unafraid to risk his life. However, he is also a man capable of love.

The story he tells the white man is, on the surface, a tale of high romance and adventure, but like the lagoon itself, it is deeper and more mysterious than it appears. The nature of his love is brought into question when he sees his brother fall amid the enemy. At that moment Arsat is faced with a choice. If he goes back to help his brother, he acts with the proper courage of a warrior and a man. However, his courage would be purchased at the risk of losing what he most cherishes—not only his life but also his world, his Diamelen. He must therefore choose between love and honor, fidelity and betrayal. In effect, he can carry off his love only at the price of cowardice. In choosing love, that noblest attribute of man, he has paradoxically bought dishonor, and it is only at the end, when Diamelen dies, that Arsat decides to seek a form of redemption, to regain his honor and courage by returning to his enemies. The problem is that his resolution comes too late. With Diamelen dead, Arsat has nothing to lose. The choice now becomes irrelevant, for his return can be seen not as the pursuit of lost honor and bravery but as an expiation of guilt, an easing of the conscience, even a form of suicide—the ultimate cowardice.

Thus, at the very end of the story, Arsat is motionless, staring beyond the sunlight "into the darkness of a world of illusions." What is illusory is not love or courage or cowardice, but human beings' ability to act purely, to conduct their lives without contradictory emotions or damnable choices. Significantly, Arsat's love of Diamelen allows him to see nothing but her face, hear nothing but her voice, and after her death he tells the white man that he can see nothing. "There is nothing," the white man responds—nothing but illusion, uncertainty, and the darkness of an impenetrable lagoon.

Style and Technique

The complexity of "The Lagoon" is heightened by Joseph Conrad's use of the frame narrative, the story-within-the-story. Arsat's tale of love and fraternal betrayal is framed by the arrival and departure of the white man, who is at once an observer and a participant. As in a later story, "Youth," in which the narrator provides a frame for Marlow's tale of adventure, this sort of double narrative and double point of view pushes Arsat's tale out of its personal focus and forces it to be seen in more cosmic terms. Arsat's tale has affected the white man, who understands that he, too, has become part of the world of illusions. He shares complicity in the love, bravery, and cowardice. (The brother's gun was a gift from the white man, for example.) Arsat's tale, like the lagoon itself, stirs ripples in the mind and experience of the white man and in the reader as well. The white man is the bridge between the personal agony of Arsat and the universal tragic experience of humanity, in which one's choices can lead to inescapable ruin.

Finally, the setting of the lagoon is the perfect embodiment of the illusory world of man's actions. As the dominant image, the lagoon exists on three levels of interpretation. Precisely and intensely described, the lagoon has literal, palpable reality. It is a place immersed in the sounds and dark shadows of the tropical wilderness.

On a second level, the lagoon is a symbol of evil, a malign force, aggressive and alive, like a predator. It is not a personal malignity, something that lies within the responsibility of Arsat or the white man, but a menace that exists independently of human beings' actions—in the manner of an ancient Greek chorus chanting of fate and destiny.

Finally, the lagoon is a metaphor for the human condition, a symbol of the dark uncertainty of motive. It is a psychological entity, suggestive of a confused state of mind.

Edward Fiorelli

LAMB TO THE SLAUGHTER

Author: Roald Dahl (1916-1990)
Type of plot: Suspense
Time of plot: The mid-twentieth century
Locale: A town or city, probably in England or the United States
First published: 1953

> *Principal characters:*
> MARY MALONEY, a devoted housewife
> PATRICK MALONEY, her husband, a police detective

The Story

This story begins with the most innocent of domestic scenes. Mary Maloney, a housewife in her sixth month of pregnancy, is waiting for her husband to return home. It is a Thursday night, and they usually eat out. When Patrick Maloney does come home, he is strangely moody and takes a stronger drink than usual. Mary tries to divert him with the usual domestic comforts but to no avail. Patrick asks her to sit down, announcing that he has an important matter to discuss with her. Though the reader is never told, it is clear that Patrick is going to divorce Mary. He ends his speech by saying that he will see that she is provided for and that he hopes that there will be no fuss because it might reflect badly on his position in the police department.

The announcement that she will lose the man around whom her world revolves puts Mary into a daze of unbelief. Instead of arguing with Patrick, she goes on as if nothing has happened, hoping that this will somehow cause her problem to go away. She prepares to make supper and goes down to the deep freezer. She chooses a frozen leg of lamb for the meal. Moving like a somnambulist, she walks into the living room. When Patrick tells her that he does not want dinner, Mary moves behind him and hits him over the head with the leg of lamb.

Patrick falls to the floor with a crash, and this brings Mary to her senses. Mary realizes that she has killed Patrick, and though she is willing to take the legal consequences, she fears for her unborn child, who might die if she is executed. Her mind is now working clearly, and she devises an elaborate deception for the police. She prepares the leg of lamb and puts it in the oven. She then goes to her room and gets ready to go out. As she does so, she rehearses the conversation that she will have with the grocer, trying to get the voice tones and facial expressions as close to normal as possible. This deception is put into operation. She goes to the grocery and uses the exact words that she has rehearsed, so that the whole scene at the grocery appears to be the everyday act of a wife picking up food for her husband's dinner and chatting with the grocer. She then returns home, telling herself that she must remain natural and to expect nothing out of the ordinary when she enters the house. Thus, when Mary does arrive, she calls out to Patrick as if he were still alive. Her shock at actually finding Patrick's body is almost completely unfeigned, as if she really did not know that she has already killed him.

Mary then calls the police and reports that Patrick Maloney has been killed. Two police officers, one of whom is Jack Noonan, arrive at the house. Both men are familiar to Mary, who knows most of Patrick's friends on the police force. They begin the investigation into Patrick's murder by recording Mrs. Maloney's story about going out to get food for supper and coming back to find Patrick's body. Noonan, completely taken in, comforts Mary, asking if she would rather go to her sister's house or stay with his wife. Mary, however, stays throughout the investigation. When a doctor and other specialists arrive to examine the body, the police conclude that Patrick was killed by a blow to the head with a blunt instrument, probably made of steel.

The police begin searching the house for the murder weapon but with no success. Mary asks Noonan for a drink, then invites him to have one himself. Soon all the police are having a drink, and the investigation has become a consolation scene. Finding that the lamb is now cooked, Mary asks the police officers to eat it because she owes it to Patrick to extend the hospitality of his home to his friends. She finally persuades them to eat the meal as a favor to her. As they do so, they remark that the murder weapon would be very difficult to conceal. One man says to Noonan that the weapon is "probably right under our very noses," which causes Mary to giggle.

Themes and Meanings

The story of the woman who murders her husband with a frozen leg of lamb and then has the murder weapon eaten by the detectives is one of the most famous examples of the "perfect crime" story. However, this work's value lies, not simply in the originality of the murder method but in the way that Roald Dahl ties this to larger themes. The use of a leg of lamb as an instrument of death reveals the hidden and sinister meanings that lie in seemingly innocent objects. Dahl, like many modern suspense writers, weaves his stories around trivial, everyday events that suddenly take on frightening aspects revealing the danger and uncertainty that underlies modern life, rather than reviving medieval settings and horrors in the manner of the earlier gothic writers.

Mary Maloney lives the life of a devoted housewife almost until she actually murders her husband. The news of her divorce causes no outward change in her behavior. She goes on, as if pretending that nothing has happened will make it so. The murder seems almost an unconscious and unwilled act. However, after the murder, Mary becomes a deliberate and clear thinker. She now artificially creates her alibi for the murder by consciously returning to her innocent state before Patrick's death. She practices her lines, voice tone, and facial expressions before she goes to the grocery so that they will appear perfectly natural and arouse no suspicions in the grocer's mind. When Mary arrives home, her shock at seeing Patrick's body is so spontaneous that she almost seems to have fooled herself. Mary's deception grows as she manipulates the police, reaching its peak when Patrick's friends destroy the evidence of his murder as a favor to his wife, who is his killer.

Dahl creates a series of bizarre metamorphoses in this story. A leg of lamb becomes a murder weapon. Mary Maloney, the victim of her husband's insensitivity, makes him her victim. Patrick, an investigator of crimes, becomes the subject of a criminal investigation. A dead man's friends console his murderer. The police destroy the evidence needed to trap the criminal. The best hiding place for the murder weapon turns out to be right under the officers' noses. Dahl reveals how much of "normal" existence is actually a contrived appearance that can be easily manipulated. Mary moves outside the predictable by turning the lamb into a weapon, then overcomes the police by turning the weapon back into a lamb. Having experienced what lies beneath the surface, she can now arrange appearances to her own advantage.

Style and Technique

As befits a story dealing with appearances and reality, much of "Lamb to the Slaughter" is told through details that Dahl carefully selects and arranges into various patterns to cause the reader to go below the surface to find the meanings in the story. Reference is made to Mary's large, dark, placid eyes early in the story, indicating her harmless, domestic personality; they are referred to again when she persuades Patrick's friends to eat the leg of lamb, revealing this time how deceptive Mary's appearance is. Throughout the story, words such as "simple," "easy," "normal," and "natural" acquire an ironic overtone, for the reader perceives the complex, artificial, and abnormal state of the world. Patrick's announcement of divorce and the police officers' dismissal of Mary as a likely murder suspect are never actually depicted; the reader is left to deduce these events from snatches of dialogue.

Dahl's technique reaches a hilarious crescendo in the dinner scene, in which the police officers eat the leg of lamb and discuss the possibility of finding the blunt instrument used to kill Patrick. The officers' complacence, their belief that as soon as they finish eating they will easily be able to track down the murder weapon, and their actual behavior as unwitting accessories to their friend's murder reveal the polarities on which the story is built. On the surface, the story depicts a world that is orderly, rational, and easily understood, but beneath this world are strange forces that can invest even the most innocent and everyday scenes with grotesque meaning.

Anthony J. Bernardo, Jr.

THE LANGUAGE OF CATS

Author: Spencer Holst
Type of plot: Fantasy
Time of plot: The 1970's
Locale: West Virginia and Washington, D.C.
First published: 1971

Principal characters:
THE SCIENTIST, a code-breaker
HIS WIFE
HIS SIAMESE CAT

The Story

A thirty-five-year-old scientist is a brilliant breaker of codes whose skills saved the world during a recent war. However, although his wife is extremely neat, the scientist is a slob who leaves his clothes lying about and accidentally starts fires in wastepaper baskets. She nags him constantly, but because he is a gentleman who will not argue with her, he leaves her, moving into a cottage in West Virginia with a Siamese cat.

The beautiful blue-point Siamese hypnotizes its owner. Soon the scientist loses all interest in people, even in books, and the cat becomes the center of his life. Deciding to communicate with his companion, the scientist buys and steals a thousand cats, which he places in cages. He records their sounds and files them systematically until he masters their basic vocabulary.

After the scientist begins talking to his cat, the animal is eager to tutor him in the subtleties of the cat language. The Siamese eventually begins explaining the history of cats. Thousands of years earlier, he says, they had an advanced civilization that included space exploration and mental telepathy. When they realized their way of life had grown too complex, they decided to simplify it by creating a race of robots to take care of them. These robots evolved into humans. Now the scientist understands why cats seem so contemptuous of their owners.

The Siamese explains that cats, fearing an atomic war, have chosen the scientist to learn their language and transmit to the human leaders these rules: Do not kick cats; no atomic wars; no mousetraps; kill the dogs. If the rules are not obeyed, humans will be eliminated. To demonstrate their power, cats will release a gas in Washington, D.C., and Moscow that will drive everyone insane for twenty-four hours. The scientist opens his thousand cat cages.

Unable to decide to whom in Washington he should try to present the cats' demands, the scientist wanders back to his former home. When his estranged wife begins shouting, he starts breaking up the furniture that she loves more than she has ever loved him. His violence cleanses them both, and they fall in love again and run off for a second honeymoon. When she suggests that he retrieve his cat, the scientist says the animal can take care of itself.

Hundreds of miles away in the mountains, they spend two months in solitude. Eventually, the scientist tells his wife about the cats and his decision that humanity is not worth saving. She thinks he is insane, especially after he claims to have encountered Santa Claus in the forest, but she loves him even more.

Finally returning to civilization, they discover that Washington and Moscow have not been attacked. The wife is surprised to learn that the cat, having starved to death, was the insane one, not her husband. All Siamese, it turns out, are crazy, making grandiose claims about the race of cats.

Themes and Meanings

Spencer Holst's satirical fable encompasses topics ranging from the dangers of scientific experimentation to the perverse natures of love and communication. Rather than explore a large issue such as the moral insanity of scientists creating a weapon capable of destroying all life, Holst compresses this theme through his scientist's need to turn everything into an experiment and then flee the consequences of his actions.

Rather unsubtly, Holst points out his protagonist's insensitivity in the name of experimentation. His fascination with his cat would seem to imply fondness for all cats, but this is disproved when he systematically records their sounds: "He carefully compared the shriek when a *right* front foot was being amputated, to that made when a *left* front leg was being cut." He just as casually records their sounds when mating, giving birth, fighting, and dying. The result, communication, is much more important than the means of obtaining it. Communication, whether by human or animal, expresses emotions, but the scientist is consumed by the process while ignoring the emotional side. For him, morality never enters the equation.

The same holds true when the scientist's cat warns him of the attack on Washington and Moscow. Although brilliant as a scientist, he is, as his wife can attest, ineffectual as a human being. Unable to decide how to communicate the cats' message, he runs away. Science is supposed to impose order on chaos, but Holst shows how the opposite also can be true. The scientist's effort to understand the language of cats is potentially valuable, but it can also have negative results. His eagerness to accept all the results of his experiment blinds him to the possibility that his Siamese, armed with intelligence at least equal to that of humans, may share human weaknesses, such as a joy in lying. That a man capable of saving the world can be fooled by a cat underscores the absurdity of Holst's satire.

The scientist's propensity for chaos extends to his marriage. His self-absorption overwhelms his affection for his wife, and when she responds with hostility, he simply runs away, foreshadowing his relationship with his Siamese. The perverse nature of love is shown by the wife's responding positively to his anger when they meet again. She had thought she knew him, and the man she knew was a messy bore. His violence, ironically, reveals his humanity. His flight with his wife also destroys something else he seemingly loves—his cat. Holst cunningly juxtaposes the lying cat, the scientist absorbed in theories, and the too-easily forgiving wife to question the limits of reason.

The marriage originally broke apart because the couple could no longer communicate, and it reassembles itself not through language but violence. When the scientist wanders into his old home, the narrator relates that he has not communicated with his wife since he had left, but he did not communicate with her even when he was with her. It is ironic that a man who can speak a hundred languages cannot talk to his wife, and just as ironic that he can talk more easily with cats. When under pressure, as with the cats' demands, the scientist cannot communicate at all. Language is a means of imposing order on chaos, but the user of language must have the will to enact this order. The scientist decides that the human race is not worth saving, not because of any of its obvious defects but because of his own ennui.

Style and Technique

Most of Holst's stories are brief; they are written in a deceptively simple style, and many have been performed by the writer in Greenwich Village coffeehouses. As a typical Holstian celebration of the essence of storytelling, it is appropriate that "The Language of Cats" begins, "Once upon a time there was a gentleman." Like such self-conscious postmodernists as John Barth and Donald Barthelme, Holst's primary concern is the nature of narrative and language.

The simple style is appropriate for Holst's moral fables, but his stories are hardly didactic. Far from attempting to preach on the dangers inherent in scientific experimentation, Holst, in "The Language of Cats," merely pokes fun at intellectual hubris. The short sentences and paragraphs draw the reader easily into a seemingly placid universe in which the unexpected packs an extra punch:

> Then he quit his government job and began to study in earnest the thousands of shrieks and caterwauls he had recorded, and after a while the sounds began to make sense.
> Then he began to practice, mimicking his records until he mastered the basic vocabulary of the language.
> Toward the end he practiced purring.
> He had never experimented on his own cat. He wanted to surprise it.

Holst even calls attention to his awareness of the reader's awareness of his style by dropping a 398-word sentence into the middle of his story. This atypical sentence, which digresses into description for its own sake, ends, "imagine how the world would appear to a person after finishing such a ridiculously lengthy, pointless sentence." Holst makes clear that he, as creator, is manipulating this digression by including three times the first-person pronoun that appears nowhere else in the narrative. Like the Siamese, he creates and plays for the sheer joy of the experience while observing, through the lying cat's death, the possibility of the story consuming the storyteller, ending the story with the Siamese's vision of a race of supercats degenerating into impotent meows.

Michael Adams

THE LAST CLASS

Author: Alphonse Daudet (1840-1897)
Type of plot: Social realism
Time of plot: About 1873
Locale: A town in Alsace, France
First published: "La Dernière Classe," 1873 (English translation, 1900)

> *Principal characters:*
> FRANZ, the young boy, the narrator
> MONSIEUR HAMEL, the teacher

The Story

"The Last Class" is the tender story of a young Alsatian boy and his last French lesson. The setting is an unnamed town in Alsace, and the story takes place near the beginning of the Prussian occupation of Alsace and Lorraine, about 1873. Little Franz is the narrator of the story. Having gotten a late start on this beautiful warm morning, Franz rushes to school. He is fearful that Monsieur Hamel will scold him because he is late and has not prepared his French lesson on participles.

On his way to school, Franz passes through the town square, and in front of the town hall he sees a small group of people reading notices posted on a grating. These are notices posted by the Prussians concerning orders issued from headquarters. While Franz is running across the square, Wachter, the blacksmith, calls to him that there is no need to hurry. Franz thinks that Wachter is teasing him.

Out of breath, he arrives at school. To his dismay, there is no noise or confusion to cover his entrance. Instead, this day, there is the silence and stillness of the Sabbath. Frightened and red-faced, he enters the classroom; instead of giving Franz a harsh scolding, however, Monsieur Hamel gently directs Franz to his seat.

Once settled in his seat, Franz begins to notice the differences that this day has brought. Monsieur Hamel is all dressed up in his Sunday best, the clothes that he wears when prizes are given or on inspection days. Franz's classmates are especially solemn this day. Then his attention is drawn to the back of the room, where villagers are seated, and to Hauser, there with his old primer spread across his knees. Everyone has an air of sadness and anticipation.

Monsieur Hamel gently announces that orders have come from Berlin that beginning tomorrow, German only will be the language of instruction. Today, he tells them, is the last lesson that they will receive in French. Franz regrets the time that he has wasted. The villagers are sorry that they have not visited more often and now wish to express their gratitude for Monsieur Hamel's forty years of service.

It is Franz's turn to recite, but, unprepared, he struggles to express himself and fails. Monsieur Hamel does not belittle or scold him. Instead he expresses the regret that Franz and all the children should have for not having learned when the time was at hand. He points out that it is not Franz who is chiefly at fault. He blames himself and the parents especially for not having been sufficiently concerned with their children's education.

With great patriotic fervor, Monsieur Hamel speaks of the French language as the best language in the world. He continues by reading their lesson to them. The grammar lesson is followed by the writing lesson, with the model provided by Monsieur Hamel's beautiful handwriting of "France, Alsace! France, Alsace." Every student in the class is intent on his work, and nothing but the scratching of pens can be heard.

From time to time, Franz observes Monsieur Hamel, who is studying every detail of the room in which he has taught for the past forty years, and sorrow for this man fills Franz's heart. The writing lesson is followed by history. Hauser joins with the little children to spell out the letters. Then the Angelus and a trumpet blast of the Prussians sound at the same moment. Monsieur Hamel rises from his chair and, in a choked voice, tries to address the class, but he cannot. Taking a piece of chalk, he writes on the blackboard in his largest hand, "Vive La France," and then dismisses them with a motion of his hand.

Themes and Meanings

Alphonse Daudet expounds the themes of freedom and patriotism in his short story "The Last Class." Courage, the importance of education, and the preciousness of one's own language are interrelated themes.

The people of the town and of Alsace have already had their freedom taken from them. A reminder of this loss appears in the second paragraph, where mention is made of the Prussians drilling in Rippert Meadows. Another reminder is the posting of news on the grating in the town square in front of the town hall. Here the townspeople come to learn of any new regulations that are to be imposed on them. Even as Franz sees the people reading the notices, he expects more bad news, battles lost, requisitions made. There is an aura of helplessness that comes with this loss of freedom. The atmosphere of this day, however, is not like that of other days even under the Prussian occupation. The sadness, solemnity, and quietness of the classroom seem to forebode something worse to come. The gentle tone of Monsieur Hamel is not the usual voice that has instructed these young people. His is usually the confident, commanding voice of self-assurance, scolding, prodding, and encouraging his students to learn. Today the sense of defeat and loss of freedom is even greater than that usually evoked by the simple presence of the Prussians and their initial occupation of the country that Monsieur Hamel loves.

Monsieur Hamel announces that today will be his last day to teach. Tomorrow the students will have a new teacher, and tomorrow all instruction will be given in German. With that, he implores them to be especially attentive because this will be the last lesson that they will have in French. Suddenly, Franz is struck with the realization that he is about to lose something priceless, a part of his life. At this moment too, he regrets the time that he has wasted, the classes that he has missed. The very things that the townspeople cherish, they have taken for granted; now the loss of freedom has robbed them of their precious language. The cut is even deeper when Franz's turn comes to recite because he has not studied, he is unprepared. However, Monsieur Hamel does not lay the blame on Franz. He states that he as well as the students' parents must be faulted for their indifference to their children's education. The language for which they have so much pride and feel such great love is to be taken from them. Language, the mark of one's heritage, is their key to personal freedom. By refusing to allow the Alsatians to teach in French, the Prussians have taken one more step to enslave them. The loss of national identity is especially cruel when one is denied expression in one's own language. This loss is driven home, by the presence of old Hauser with his old primer, spelling out the letters with the children in the merging of generations with a common bond.

The proud Monsieur Hamel embodies at the same time the courage and frustration of a subjugated people. There is hope still in his demeanor, dressed as he is in his finest clothing on this sad day. His determination to teach once more comes as a rallying cry to those present not to forget who they are, not to give up their heritage and what they hold dear to them. In defiance, he has lifted the flag by writing in his finest hand, "France, Alsace! France, Alsace!" With one last courageous gesture, standing straight and tall, Monsieur Hamel assures his friends that freedom will be theirs once again by boldly writing the words "Vive La France" on the blackboard.

Style and Technique

The language that Daudet uses in "The Last Class" is straightforward and earthy, depicting with poetic simplicity the setting of the story and the people who are the heart of it. The tone and mood blend into a tender sadness yet maintain the intensity of purpose intended by the author. The reader is immediately drawn into and made a part of the story through Daudet's skillful realism.

It is easy to visualize the scene and feel as Franz must feel on this beautiful, warm day. The temptation to enjoy the outdoors and the call to responsibility at school are so humanly portrayed that the reader can easily identify with Franz. The descriptions of the outdoors and of the interior of the school are indeed tableaux, but tableaux that radiate the warmth of the sun and encourage the reader to participate in the last lesson. One can share Franz's embarrassment at not knowing his lesson, and one can participate in the emotional distress that marks Monsieur Hamel's testimony to courage and patriotism. The reader is both an observer looking through the window and a student or villager sitting on a bench in the classroom.

An almost spiritual quality is felt when the Angelus rings—a sense of freedom. This is countered, however, by the trumpet blast of the Prussians—enforcing the realization that freedom must be won again.

David J. Quinn

THE LAST DAYS OF A FAMOUS MIME

Author: Peter Carey (1943-   )
Type of plot: Absurdist, existential
Time of plot: The 1970's
Locale: Australia
First published: 1979

> *Principal characters:*
> A MIME, a talented, unnamed performer
> A WOMAN, his companion

The Story

A mime arrives in an Australian airport for a performance tour of the country. The mime is famous throughout Europe for his ability to invoke terror in his audiences, but little is known about him in Australia. Members of the media greet him at the airport and ask him what is in the package he is carrying. He replies that it contains a blue string and explains that "The string is a prayer I am always praying." The Australian media fail to understand the significance of his answer: that the blue string helps him overcome his despair, a personal condition familiar to his audiences in Europe but not to those in Australia. They photograph the package anyway and record the enigmatic response. The next day, the mime's comments and pictures of the package appear in the newspapers. The novelty of the prayer string captivates the public, and soon packages of blue string are sold as souvenirs before the mime's performances.

At the beginning of the tour, the mime draws large and enthusiastic audiences. Using only movements and facial expressions, the mime creates such terror that audiences panic, frightened by his uncanny ability to imitate life in its most harrowing state. During the performances, they leave their seats and rush into the outside world for reassurance, but they always return for more of his art: They devour "the terror like brave tourists eating the hottest curry in an Indian restaurant." When a critic in a provincial town questioned the purpose of terrorizing an audience, the mime decided to devote concerts to the celebration of love and laughter. These efforts to lighten his performances were disasters because the audiences did not want to be uplifted. At his agent's insistence he returned to his specialty in a program titled "TWO HOURS OF REGRET," which terrified and therefore pleased everyone.

The mime's private life, like his public performances, was dominated by terror. He often attracted women who wanted to help him overcome the emotional pain he suffered, but he was unable to establish a successful relationship and was accused of merely miming love. One of the women told him that his art consisted of nothing more than an expression of his "neurosis," that he was capitalizing on it "like someone exhibiting their club foot, or Turkish beggars with strange deformities." This woman cut his prayer string into tiny pieces.

Worn down by the heavy schedule, the mime gave into depression and the nagging doubts that had plagued him for years. Facing his own disintegration, he questioned why his audiences longed to experience the terror that he wanted to overcome in his private life. So he called a press conference and announced that there would be no more concerts. Instead he would offer his skills to the general public, who could call on him to mime whatever they wanted to see. He then fulfilled requests to describe through his art such things as death, marriage, and flying, but did so in such an obscure manner that his popularity declined. Finally, when asked to mime a river, he drowned himself. The drowning was the only one of the famous mime's performances to be filmed. However, the film does nothing to explain how he once had exerted such power over his audiences.

Themes and Meanings

On one level, "The Last Days of a Famous Mime" examines the nature of art and the role of the artist. Although the story is abstract, its disjointed narrative suggests that it is a self-reflection on the writer's own art. Peter Carey chose a specialized and rather obscure kind of artist to express his ideas about writing. However, a familiarity with Carey's fiction helps to clarify the narrative, which can be read as a coded guide to his work before and after the story's appearance in 1979. Carey has never celebrated love and laughter, as the mime attempted to do and failed.

In 1974 when his first collection of short stories, *The Fat Man in History*, was published, some Australian critics hailed the book as a daring departure in Australian fiction, and others found the violence and absurdist technique offensive. *War Crimes*, which appeared five years later, offered the same kind of narrative, as did his first novel, *Bliss* (1981). The novels that followed continued to practice the art of terror and to do so in an absurdist fashion. In particular, *The Tax Inspector* (1991) could be compared to the mime's performances that drove people out of the theater, only to return for more horror. The narrative brims with incest, senseless violence, corruption, cruelty, depravity, and madness. Like the critic who questioned the need for the mime's performance, many literary critics asked when *The Tax Inspector* appeared if vivid accounts of such base human behavior were appropriate material for fiction. The same holds true for *The Unusual Life of Tristan Smith* (1994), which traces the preposterous adventures of a grossly deformed central character.

To use a mime as a symbol for the writer is not altogether farfetched, for the writer mimics life through the limitation of words just as the mime does solely through movement and expression. For example, the idea of the writer as mime is strikingly apparent in Carey's *True History of the Kelly Gang* (2000). In this novel, Carey imitates Ned Kelly by telling the story of the noted Australian folk hero in Kelly's voice. The spelling, punctuation, vocabulary, and grammatical elements mimic the style that the unschooled Kelly might have used if he had actually written his history.

"The Last Days of a Famous Mime" can also be separated from the artist and read as an account of an existential hero's disintegration in a meaningless universe. Several of the companion stories in *War Crimes* and in *The Fat Man in History* take up this theme in varied forms. Certainly a troubled and desperate mime, who merely imitates being in silence, serves as an appropriate symbol for the existential hero adrift in a terror-filled emptiness in which he mimics life in vain.

Style and Technique

The story of the famous mime's last days is told in sixteen numbered sections that cover about seven pages. Some of the sections contain only one or two sentences. As the fragments of action unfold in a formalized manner, the narrative takes on the quality of a mime's performance. The language is stripped to the barest essentials, just as the famous mime controls his art so that each movement and expression are absolutely essential to the story he is telling.

Because the media figure prominently in the narrative, at times the style assumes the quality of a news report. Facts about the mime's public life are presented in a detached and objective manner, as though the perfunctory account appeared in a newspaper and was written by an indifferent reporter. Only two of the sections contain brief dialogue that relates the conflict between the mime and the woman. Otherwise, the numerous events are simply summarized. No matter how illusory the action, it is presented as fact. For example, when the mime has resorted to fulfilling requests from the public, one of his exploits is described as follows: "Asked to describe an aeroplane he flew three times around the city, only injuring himself slightly on landing."

Carey's skillful use of the absurdist technique makes the mime's last days memorable, no matter how implausible the action. Each time the story is read, it takes on new dimensions. From the outset of his writing career, Carey has proved himself a brilliant stylist and has worked effectively in a variety of forms. This early story remains one of the finest examples of a controlled narrative that abounds with meaning.

Robert Ross

THE LAST JUDGMENT

Author: Karel Čapek (1890-1938)
Type of plot: Parody
Time of plot: Around 1929
Locale: Heaven
First published: "Posledni soud," 1929 (English translation, 1932)

Principal characters:
FERDINAND KUGLER, a recently deceased thief and murderer
PRESIDING JUDGE, a deceased judge
GOD, a witness

The Story

Ferdinand Kugler dies in a gunfight with a police officer. Numerous warrants for his arrest are outstanding, and at the time of his death, he is a fugitive from an army of police officers and detectives. In Heaven, an overworked network of courts faces the chaotic task of delineating which souls will be allowed to remain and which will be sentenced to Hell. As a result of the number and severity of his crimes, Kugler must wait an indeterminate period until his case can be judged. For the same reason, his case is reserved for a special panel of three judges rather than a jury.

The defendant must state his name, occupation, and the dates of his birth and death. Kugler's inability to remember the date of his death bodes poorly with the judges, intensifying his own naturally contentious attitude. Without further formalities, the presiding judge summons the sole witness in Kugler's case: God. Before God testifies, the presiding judge explains why God need not swear the oath and then instructs him to avoid particulars that have no legal bearing on the case. The judge also warns Kugler against interrupting the witness, pointing out that it would be useless to deny any part of God's testimony.

God begins with a brief statement on Kugler's unruliness as a child. The defendant's first crime was his failure to express his love for his mother. When God describes Kugler's first act of larceny—stealing a rose from the notary's garden before he was ten—Kugler recalls having stolen the flower to give to a young girl, Irma, the daughter of the tax collector. The witness satisfies Kugler's curiosity about Irma's fate, explaining how she went on to marry the son of the man who owned the factory that employed Kugler's father. The witness adds that Irma contracted a venereal disease from her husband and subsequently died of a miscarriage.

Despite the presiding judge's persistent reminders to avoid such digressions, Kugler is irrepressibly curious as to the outcomes of the lives he touched. He discovers how his family suffered for his crimes. He was a drunkard and runaway by fourteen, bringing the dishonor to his home that would force his father to die of grief, and his pretty sister, Martika, to live a poverty-stricken life and remain unmarried.

The testimony goes down the list of Kugler's murders. The defendant is often genuinely surprised by the resonance of his actions, at times remorseful, and at others amazed. After an accounting of Kugler's murders is finished, the judge asks the witness to explain the defendant's motives. "For the same reasons others do," is his response, "From anger, from greed, deliberately and by chance."

After Kugler turns down his only opportunity to speak in his defense, the judges withdraw to make their decision, leaving him alone with God. Kugler takes advantage of their absence to ask God several questions. God explains that the judges were also judges on earth, making Kugler wonder why God himself takes no part in passing judgments. God explains that because he knows everything, it would be impossible for him to judge, adding that "the only justice people deserve is human justice."

After the judges return, the presiding judge pronounces Kugler guilty and sentences him to Hell. He then summarily calls the next case.

Themes and Meanings

Karel Čapek's brief, simple tale is surprising in its reversal of conventional wisdom that it is for God alone, not humans, to judge. Presumably, the judicial system of Čapek's Heaven is ultimately of God's design. His apparent refusal to take more than a secondary role in judging souls presents a God who values impartiality as highly as mercy. It seems as though God's assumed capacity for mercy would only lead him to violate his own code of sin and retribution. One might ask who better to judge than he who knows all? However, God's all-knowing view seems to dictate that the strain of mercy would only contaminate the fair rationing of justice. He explains to Kugler that if the judges knew everything, they too would not be able to judge fairly: "They would understand everything, and their hearts would ache."

Kugler's crimes fall into two distinct categories, felonies and misdemeanors. The crimes of his youth hardly strike one as extraordinary or heinous. It is in maturity that he commits his numerous felonies. In fact, several of Kugler's earlier crimes take their motives from basic human impulses or frailties, for which the average reader may feel sympathy. Although it is God's place to tell the complete story, it is the judges' to view the crimes and not the criminal. Čapek implies a kind of original-sin theory, suggesting that everyone is capable of the kind of misdemeanors that Kugler has committed, and that everyone is vulnerable to judgment. The number of Kugler's felonies merely intensifies the question.

The judges' disinterest in Kugler's few good points presents them as less than impartial. Their desire is to keep their court running smoothly, to hear only about the defendants' crimes, only those matters that have "a legal bearing on the case." In his testimony, God discusses the good and evil sides of Kugler's character, as though both aspects do indeed have a bearing on the case, but even he defers to the judges' instructions. He finally explains, not without irony, that humans "deserve each other," a sad note on human failure to make better use of the free will that he has given them.

Style and Technique

"The Last Judgment" is one of forty-eight short tales that Čapek wrote expressing his interest in crime fiction. Looking to the Bible and earlier, crime narratives have remained a popular and entertaining method for exploring the diverse capacities of human nature. Čapek's interest in the genre may not be unique or innovative in itself, but his unabashed irreverence brings a refreshingly humorous flavor to the form.

The courts in Čapek's Heaven are the same in appearance and protocol as those on Earth. This parody of judicial protocol works with very little actual exaggeration of the basic court system but merely by transposing the system into a sublime context; though exceptions, as is the wont of parody, do exist. Rather than stating a predetermined list of charges, the presiding judge asks Kugler what he considers himself to be guilty of, to which the defendant claims total innocence. The use of God as Kugler's trial witness, in knowing more about the defendant than the defendant himself does, is Čapek's method of pointing out the more natural predilection for believing in one's guilt until proven innocent.

The portrayal of the system is basic enough as to be immediately recognizable in nearly any culture, during nearly any period of the twentieth century. Placing the panel of judges, human souls, in a position of authority causes them to appear bumbling and officious, even, and perhaps especially, during the story's more poignant moments. In the presence of God, it seems absurd that they should hold any greater importance than any other human soul. God enters the court without fanfare but with an impressive, "stately" bearing. Kugler's fascination at seeing God is the first sign that there may be any softness in his character. Even when the presiding judge gestures impatiently at God's seeming digressions from matters of bearing, one cannot forget where the true and highest power present in court is sitting.

The ensuing testimony is not so much a testimony as a dialogue between witness and defendant, through which a more rounded vision of Kugler's life and career is evidenced. Čapek has created the image of God as observer, present but not interfering, objectively allowing humans to impose their own sense of justice in his domain. As a piece of crime fiction, the story operates as a medium of scrutiny rather than suspense: a "why-done-it," rather than who.

Jon Lavieri

THE LAST MOHICAN

Author: Bernard Malamud (1914-1986)
Type of plot: Adventure
Time of plot: The 1950's
Locale: Rome
First published: 1958

> *Principal characters:*
> ARTHUR FIDELMAN, an art scholar
> SHIMON SUSSKIND, the beggar who pursues him

The Story

As the story opens, Arthur Fidelman, artist manque, arrives at the Rome train depot for a stay of some weeks as part of his yearlong project to pursue research for a critical study of Giotto, only one chapter of which rests in his briefcase. Instead, he meets a refugee named Shimon Susskind, a beggar-peddler, who pursues Fidelman through a series of scenes. In the first scene, Fidelman, responding "Shalom" for the first time in his life, refuses to give Susskind a suit but grudgingly gives him a dollar. The next encounter takes place about a week later, after Fidelman has "organized" his life—working in libraries in the morning and studying in churches and museums in the afternoon. Returning to his hotel, he is surprised by a visit from Susskind, who again importunes him for the suit but settles for five dollars. The next day at lunch, Fidelman again glances up to see Susskind, who once more pleads for some investment money so that he can sell ladies' stockings, chestnuts, anything. Rebuffing Susskind, Fidelman continues his research, returning to his hotel late that night to discover that his briefcase is missing. The pursued now becomes the pursuer.

However, before that event takes place, Fidelman dreams that he is pursuing Susskind through the Jewish catacombs under Rome, by the light of a seven-flamed candelabra. Elusive Susskind, who knows the ins and outs, escapes; the candles flicker; and in his dream Fidelman is left "sightless and alone."

Next Fidelman postpones his trip to Florence, reports the theft to the police, and moves to a small pension, where he broods and attempts to write but feels lost without something solid—his first chapter—on which to build. Then begins his search through the markets, through lanes and alleys of transient peddlers, throughout October and November, for Susskind. Although he truly knows Rome now, his "heart is burdened with rage for the refugee." One Friday night, Fidelman strays into a synagogue and hears about the tragic loss of life during the Holocaust, then wanders through the ghetto, tracking Susskind, who, he now knows, also makes money by saying prayers for the dead at the cemetery. Fidelman visits the cemetery the next day and sees grave markers lamenting those killed by the Nazis, but he does not find Susskind.

In mid-December, visiting St. Peter's to see the Giotto mosaic again, he sees Susskind selling black and white rosaries on the steps and confronts him but is told nothing. Furtively, he follows Susskind to his "overgrown closet" in the ghetto but does not talk with him. In his dream that night, however, he does confront him, seeing him in the context of the Giotto painting that shows Saint Francis giving an old knight his gold cloak. The next day he hurries, bleary-eyed, to Susskind's room, taking a suit to him. Susskind admits that he burned the chapter because, although the "words were there . . . the spirit was missing." Fidelman experiences a triumphant insight and runs after the fleeing Susskind shouting, "All is forgiven," but the refugee is last seen still running.

Themes and Meanings

Arthur Fidelman, the Jew from the Bronx, makes a journey to Italy to discover its rich history and thus complete his study of Giotto. In a sense, what he actually does complete is the study of himself. His quest becomes transformed when he meets the mythic, archetypal trickster-beggar Shimon Susskind, who challenges Fidelman to recognize suffering—his own and that of the Jewish refugees of World War II—indeed, to recognize his own Jewishness and responsibility to his fellowman. In an early scene, Susskind asks, "You know what responsibility means?" Fidelman replies, "I think so." "Then you are responsible," says Susskind, "Because you are a man. Because you are a Jew, aren't you?" This exhortation comes to mind at the end of the story, when Fidelman achieves his revelation and willingly gives the suit to Susskind.

When Fidelman, after the theft of his briefcase, must stay in Rome to pursue Susskind, he immerses himself in the real life of Rome, casting off the veneer—replacing his oxblood gumsoles with light Italian shoes—burrowing beneath the surface of art in the churches and museums to the bedrock question posed in one of his dreams: "Why is art?" He begins to understand the real meaning of Giotto's work showing the saint bestowing a cloak on the old knight.

The scholar becomes a real human being rather than a superficial observer. As his dreams reveal, he begins to acknowledge his own Jewishness (the dream of the catacombs and candelabra) and his own larger humanity. The richness of his insight reverberates beyond simple statement, but one senses that in gaining understanding of the suffering of Susskind, he is beginning to understand the root of all suffering—his own included.

Style and Technique

Bernard Malamud's key framework involves the use of the journey-quest motif joined with pursuit and then reversal, so that Fidelman, initially the one hounded by Susskind, becomes the pursuer. The episodes consist of sharply focused encounters between the two key characters, though some critics find Susskind to be the central character of the story. In review, however, the reader will sense the balance between the mythic characterization of Susskind, the survivor, and Fidelman—the man who would have faith—learning through their interaction. When Fidelman begins the pursuit of Susskind, he enters Susskind's life, and Fidelman's quest for knowledge shifts from "static" words in the libraries and the scrutiny of the pictures on the walls to an awareness of the hidden life that generated Giotto's compassion. For Fidelman, this hidden life is found in the synagogue, in the reminders of Auschwitz, and in the freedom-seeking connivance of Susskind.

Within this journey-quest framework, Malamud sets dream sequences that show the reader the subconscious awareness growing in Fidelman. Susskind, the magical, appears and vanishes in dreams as he does in Fidelman's conscious life. In the dream of Jewish catacombs, Fidelman acknowledges his "sightlessness" without the seven-flamed candelabra. His final "vision" rests on the last dream, which interprets the gift that Giotto portrays in the mosaic—the compassion, the awareness of suffering that can thus lead to Fidelman's final epiphany.

Content and construction blend in this story to make the conscious and subconscious accessible, to make Susskind at once a schnorrer and a savior, to render Fidelman capable of an act of faith, one that links him with humanity, not with mere scholarship.

Eileen Lothamer

THE LAUGHER

Author: Heinrich Böll (1917-1985)
Type of plot: Social realism
Time of plot: The mid-twentieth century
Locale: Unspecified
First published: "Der Lacher," 1955 (English translation, 1963)

Principal characters:
THE NARRATOR, a man who works as a professional laugher
HIS WIFE, a quiet woman who has forgotten how to laugh

The Story

In the opening line, the narrator admits to his embarrassment when anyone asks him his profession. He makes a good living as a professional laugher, but he envies people with professions that require no explanation, such as barbers, bookkeepers, and writers. He explains that he has avoided calling himself a laugher for a long time, instead referring to himself as an actor. Gradually, however, the infrequency of other sorts of work, such as mime and elocution, and his love of the truth have forced him to admit that he is a laugher.

He explains that the sorts of laughter that he can produce span centuries, continents, social classes, and even age groups. He can laugh like a Roman emperor or like a sensitive schoolboy. His diversity in laughing has made him indispensable to recording companies and television directors and to third- and fourth-rate comedians, who need someone in the audience to help start other people laughing at their mediocre jokes. Despite his admitted excellence at laughing, the narrator finds his profession to be not only embarrassing but tiring. He acknowledges that he does not actually make people happy but merely fakes happiness.

At this point, the narrator begins to sketch how his work influences his private life. He comes home exhausted, unwilling to laugh or to hear laughter when he is off-duty or on vacation. The desire to get away from work, he believes, is common enough among all workers who do too much of one thing, such as bricklayers, confectioners, and boxers. He recalls that during the first years of his marriage, his wife encouraged him to laugh for her. Eventually, as she came to understand his aversion to laughter, both the sight of it and the sound of it, she stopped asking him to laugh and even gave up laughing herself because other people's laughter made him nervous. He concludes that his wife has forgotten how to laugh, even though they both smile occasionally. Their marriage is quiet and peaceful; they converse in low tones.

The narrator concludes with a view of himself from the eyes of the outside world; others view him as taciturn and serious. He recalls that even his brothers and sisters have known him as a serious boy, and he doubts that he has ever heard, or could even recognize, his own natural laughter.

Themes and Meanings

In *Understanding Heinrich Böll* (1992), Robert C. Conard convincingly argues that understanding Böll involves knowing his history. Böll grew up in Germany during the tumultuous years following World War I. His liberal Roman Catholic parents opposed Adolf Hitler and Nazism, and Böll was in fact the only boy in his class who was not a member of the Hitler Youth. He chose not to join because he did not like the marching and the uniforms. Because of the unstable government and economy following World War I, Böll's parents struggled from day to day to support themselves and their children.

As an adult, Böll was recruited to fight in World War II, but he repeatedly tried to get out of Hitler's army. He refused to be promoted to an officer, thinking it wrong to distance himself from the common troops. After being injured four times over six years, he felt relieved when he was captured by American soldiers. His experiences left him strongly prodemocratic and anticapitalist and skeptical of politics and politicians in general. In his later years, he became a member of Germany's Green Party because he shared their views on disarmament, the environment, and capitalism. He won the Nobel Prize in Literature in 1972. Böll contended that the day-to-day misery of his early life in Germany—not the war—convinced him to be a writer. He believed that the writer was duty-bound to blend art with political and social commentary.

The narrator of "The Laugher" exemplifies Böll's blend of art and social realism: Embarrassed by his profession, the laugher is stripped of his dignity. He realizes that he makes a good living and seems unable to imagine alternatives, so he never really questions his meaningless life. He never talks of quitting or of changing professions. He has become what Böll would consider a typical capitalistic laborer, sacrificing the quality of his life for economic security. The laugher becomes increasingly disconnected from his work, his laughter, and ultimately he can even discuss his work rationally and, seemingly, accept its inevitability. In addition, the nameless narrator has turned into himself, unable to reach out with his imagination or to be influenced by those around him. His brothers and sisters simply recognize that he was a serious child, and his wife acquiesces to his professional needs, supporting his absurd career by giving up laughing herself.

Style and Technique

The laugher is typical of the characters in Böll's later satires. Written in the first person and confessional in tone, these satires allow their narrators to relate the details of their odd occupations or unusual ways of life; their work is usually beneath human ability and unrewarding. Perhaps the best known of this genre is "The Thrower-away" (1957), which like "The Laugher" begins with the narrator expressing discomfort about telling what he does for a living. Through such characters, Böll exposes social realities.

Böll's satires generally have a nameless, unemotional narrator, starkly realistic description, and exaggerated details. "The Laugher" has all of these characteristics but it differs from much satire in being stripped of a specific historical context. Details such as the thriving television and film industries help place this story loosely in the mid-twentieth century, but the narrator himself could be in almost any society with a capitalistic economy. "The Laugher" relies on the exaggerated details to reveal the plight of meaningless work and superficial lives. The laugher has no national history and no connection to his government. Böll sees a danger in this sort of life in that such disconnection of the citizenry of Germany allowed Hitler to come to power. Through "The Laugher," Böll both analyzes and criticizes social reality.

In his critique of Böll's satires, Conard says that Böll carries out details to "their ultimate self-parodying conclusion." Once Böll mastered this technique, Conard contends, the form ceased to interest him and he drifted away from the genre. Böll himself once explained his formula for satire as "nothing but the development of a very simple mathematical formula . . . A basic idea consistently exaggerated until it can't be exaggerated any more, then you have a satire. To do that you need imagination, not information." Böll uses this technique in "The Laugher."

Once one accepts that someone might laugh for a living, might even earn a living laughing, then all else follows logically. Readers can see the narrator planted in the audience and watching a third-rate comedian sweat out a bad joke, hoping that the laugher will come through at the precise moment with an infectious laugh that will save it. They can see him drag himself, exhausted, from the nightclub, gather up his coat from the coatroom, happy to be going home, only to find a telegram awaiting him, urgently requesting his services as a laugher somewhere else. Böll lets readers feel the hectic, meaningless, unexamined life of the anonymous narrator and makes them contemplate how different and yet similar the narrator's odd life and work may be to their own lives and work.

In all, the style of Böll's "The Laugher" is pleasant to the ear, both in German and in Leila Vennewitz's English translation. The style rests on an articulate narrator, candid though not introspective, analytical but disconnected, who reveals the details of his embarrassing and unfulfilled career and his peaceful but, presumably, unpassionate marriage.

Carol Franks

THE LAUGHTER OF MY FATHER

Author: José Antonio Villarreal (1924-   )
Type of plot: Domestic realism
Time of plot: The Great Depression of the 1930's
Locale: Santa Clara, California
First published: 1992

> *Principal characters:*
> RICHARD, the narrator, a Mexican American
> JUAN MANUEL, his father, a Mexican
> CALIBAN, a reclusive Chilean known as el Brujo (the warlock)

The Story

Richard, the narrator, recalls something that happened during his boyhood, adding comments that come from an adult's perspective. His story is about what he learned one Sunday about his father and about a mysterious man from Chile. Initially, Richard was so afraid of this mysterious Chilean that when the man approached him and his friends, he and his buddies would run off in all directions.

Worried that this man, who was known as "el Brujo," might be the devil, he mentioned this fear to his parents one Saturday evening, after the man had frightened him and his friends. His parents only laughed, however. Richard was offended because his mother had told him about the devil and his cunning. Being devout Roman Catholics, all three knew the theological implications of Richard's charge. In trying to convince his parents that the Chilean was the devil, Richard used the religious teachings that his mother had given him as a basis for his reasoning. These led him to wonder aloud if God can control the devil. The heretical implications of this remark prompted his mother, and Richard himself, to stop the argument.

After the mother changed the subject by pointing out that the Chilean was, after all, rather odd, Richard's father, Juan Manuel, revealed that he knew more about him; he had even visited the strange man's house. El Brujo used cosmetics, such as pomades and perfumed lotions, and lived in a cluttered house with incense burning in every room. When the mother asked Juan Manuel why he never told her that he knew el Brujo, he replied with a look and a voice conveying the message of her "transgression," and asked her when he ever told her everything that he does. Never, she replied.

The next day, Richard discovered that the family's Sunday routine was to vary somewhat. On most Sundays, his hard-working father bathed, dressed, and went into town to the pool hall, hoping to find a Mexican with whom to discuss what he most loved: his native country. Although he was a desperately poor laborer, Richard's father received *La Opinión* by post. On that Sunday, however, Richard saw that his father was in his work clothes and wondered whether he and his father would do agricultural piecework. Ever mysterious, his father simply told him to eat and get ready.

Richard also remembers another mysterious job that he went on with his father—one involving what his father called an alembic, or, in plain English, a still. On that particular Sunday, their work involved searching for the leaves and fruit of cactus for the family to eat. Richard and his father looked for the food along the dry riverbed of Guadalupe Creek, where they found a man who had just died of hunger. Juan Manuel shut the dead man's eyes and guessed that he was an Okie who had arrived the night before. Richard went to the nearest house to call the sheriff.

Later, Juan Manuel searched among the smooth stones of the riverbed for a particular type of stone: "Oblong, but not flat. A bit thick, but not round." He and Richard found three, which he smoothed with sandpaper before they left. Richard wondered what all the business with the stones was about but said nothing, knowing that he would soon find out. They then went to el Brujo's house, where Richard's father told the Chilean that the three rocks were the most powerful "stone magnets" that he found after scouring miles of riverbeds and beaches. Impressed, el Brujo was eager to buy the magic stones. While his father and el Brujo haggled over a price, Richard noticed that el Brujo's house was cluttered with expensive furniture and grim religious artwork, including tapestries covering the windows. The house was pungent with incense, exactly as Juan Manuel had described it.

After Richard and Juan Manuel left, Richard became angry with his father for cheating el Brujo, but his father only laughed. With his usual self-confidence, Juan Manuel told Richard that the high price he charged for the stones was an honest trade. The seven and a half dollars he received would buy two sacks of flour, a sack of much-needed beans, some apple pie and ice cream, two gallons of gasoline, and a trip for Juan Manuel and his wife to the cinema. Not only did the family profit, so did el Brujo, who bought the stones in order to attract women. Having faith in the "attracting" stones, the lonely el Brujo would gain the confidence he needed to attract a woman. Juan Manuel argued that the stones would perform as advertised. Richard did not think el Brujo would attract a woman because he was so strange; however, Juan Manuel replied that women were also strange. That, Richard observes, is the mystery of el Brujo. The father and son laughed together.

Themes and Meanings

José Antonio Villarreal calls "The Laughter of My Father" a sketch. A sketch captures a moment; it may lack the unified, finished look of a less spontaneous portrait. The story has many themes, including family life, discovery of adult ways, and the powers and limits of reasoning. These themes are all part of the narrative sketch of one weekend in a Mexican American boy's life. The story's themes may, however, be unified under two categories: survival and "the other."

Richard, the boy, is at first concerned that el Brujo may threaten the survival of his soul. Next, more serious threats to his survival are implied in the revelation that the family is in difficult financial straits (his father works six or seven days a week to put food on the table), and in the discovery of the man who has starved to death (ironically, in the midst of food). El Brujo, in turn, is looking for a woman; he is entirely alone, an effete, Europeanized Chilean among Mexicans and English-speaking Anglos. Without a wife and children, his kind (he being the only one of his kind) will die out. Being alone is clearly dangerous; it is difficult to survive even with the help of others.

Not to be alone, however, means to deal with the other. Richard, despite his keen intelligence, is overcome by fear of el Brujo. He is aware, despite his familiarity with his parents, of their otherness. There are things they know that he does not; they think and act according to rules he does not fully understand. The dead man and the sheriff also represent the other; they belong to the Anglo world in which Richard feels uneasy.

Style and Technique

Readers are likely to notice the story's highly formal diction. There are many examples of this. El Brujo uses "pomades," Juan Manuel and he "converse," the "alembic" is an "apparatus," and so on. This formalized diction is, however, peppered with common vocabulary (four-letter words, epithets). One explanation of this technique is that Villarreal is exploiting the effect of Spanish translated directly into English. Based on Latin, Spanish sounds ornate when translated directly into English. When characters speak, they speak Spanish, and the narrative is reflective of Richard's thinking, which often is in Spanish. Thus, a character says "because of the manner in which he dresses," rather than "because of the way he dresses," or "because of the clothes he wears." Villarreal intends the reader to remember that the characters are speaking and thinking in a "foreign" language, one that separates them from the Anglos, and that is—in their relative poverty and isolation—their greatest cultural inheritance.

Eric Howard

LAURA

Author: Saki (Hector Hugh Munro, 1870-1916)
Type of plot: Wit and humor
Time of plot: The early twentieth century
Locale: England and Cairo
First published: 1912

> *Principal characters:*
> LAURA, an English woman who is reincarnated
> AMANDA, her confidante
> EGBERT, Amanda's irritating husband

The Story

"Laura" is a story in three parts. The first part consists entirely of a conversation between Laura and her friend (or possibly relation) Amanda, in which Laura expresses her belief that once she has died—which she expects to happen in about three days—she will be reincarnated in some shape appropriate to her nature and her behavior in previous lives. She thinks that her present life has probably earned for her demotion to the status of an animal, but an attractive animal, such as an otter; and that her behavior as an otter may earn for her promotion back to a "primitive" rank of humanity, such as being "a little, brown unclothed Nubian boy."

Amanda is reluctant to believe any of this, but the first part of Laura's prediction comes true, in that she dies on time, indeed slightly early. In the second stage of the story, Amanda is brought to complete belief in Laura's theory by the depredations of a marauding otter, which does exactly the kind of irritating things that Laura did when she was alive, and which seems to be conducting a vendetta against Amanda's husband, Egbert, with human skill and foreknowledge. This stage ends with the killing of the otter by an imported pack of hounds, and Amanda's collapse from nervous prostration—evidently caused by her guilt at having taken part in a kind of murder.

The third stage of the story functions almost as a coda. Amanda has been taken on a holiday to Egypt and has recovered, now dismissing the otter episode as mere coincidence. Then she hears her husband yelling in rage at some malignant prankster who, like Laura and the otter, knows exactly how to irritate him most. Who is the culprit? "A little beast of a naked brown Nubian boy." With that Amanda relapses.

In a sense, the center of the story is Amanda's growing conviction, which the reader is invited to share. She moves from utter doubt of Laura's theory (in itself mildly preposterous), to fear that it may be true, to total and crippling belief. Around this center, though, there are several unexpected questions. The reader is told that Laura's motivation in all of her shapes is dislike of Amanda's husband Egbert. Egbert, however, is never more than irritated by the killing of his hens or the spoiling of his shirts. Laura's true victim is Amanda, who appears to be, if not her friend, at least someone to whom she talks. Why is Amanda singled out? How are the two ladies connected? They do not seem to be related, for Amanda can ask cautiously if there is madness in Laura's family, like someone who does not know, but Laura certainly lives in Amanda's house. Conceivably they are relatives by marriage, in which case the animosity of Egbert and Laura could be familiar, familial, even that of brother and sister, while the handling of Amanda would contain a touch of scorn or contempt. This is left unexplained, however, like so much in the story—the nature of Laura's illness, the mechanics of the metamorphoses, and the source of Laura's insight.

Themes and Meanings

As a story, "Laura" functions mainly as an assault on the comfortable certainties of the English upper class in the last few years before World War I, which was to shatter that class's power and kill so many of its members (including the author, who was shot by a German sniper in 1916). The main vehicle of the assault is Laura, who projects from the start an air of total superiority. Her belief in the transmigration of souls most obviously contradicts central tenets of Christianity—Laura scornfully wonders if she could be imagined as an angel—but Laura also rises above fear (the thought of death causes her no emotion), above the doctor (whom she mentions only with sarcastic deference), and above all forms of social convention (even, in otter shape, exploiting the opportunities presented by her own funeral). Most of all, though, Laura rejects all forms of moral judgment. She does confess that "I haven't been very good," but immediately qualifies this by listing all of her failings without interest and then claiming that they are excused by circumstance. She furthermore goes on unrepentantly to repeat them all in future existences, and at all times takes a positive delight in mischief. The thoughts that she projects are that sin is fun, that virtue is so boring as to be provocative, and that dash and elegance are the most important qualities that a person can possess.

Amanda and Egbert function by contrast as images of sober rectitude and orthodoxy. Egbert's passions—such as they are—center on country hobbies and on keeping up a social front; there is a kind of significance at the very end in the disturbance of his highly imperial ritual of dressing for dinner. Amanda seems less hidebound but also views the death of her friend primarily as a nuisance, interrupting her plans for golf and fishing and preventing full enjoyment of her rhododendrons. In this she evidently represents her class. During a brief conversation, her uncle-in-law Sir Lulworth shows that he takes a similar view of Laura as "unaccountable" and "inconsiderate." The settled routine that all three of these characters imply is so rigid as to make every reader sympathize with Laura's defiance and disturbance of it.

Nevertheless, there is an ambiguity in Saki's story. For one thing, his original audience was drawn largely from the class that the story attacks. For another, Laura and Sir Lulworth at least share a quality of lordly open-mindedness, very much an upper-class quality. If "Laura" is a satire, it is an insider's satire that accepts much of what it pretends to reject. Possibly the key to its meaning lies in the fact that Amanda suffers so much more than the other characters in her social circle. The reason for this is, surely, that the others remain armored in certainty, like Egbert, or in self-confidence, like Sir Lulworth. Amanda, however, is fatally weak. At the very beginning she refuses to believe that Laura is dying. Once convinced, however, she wants Laura to take it more seriously. Then she rejects Laura's idea of reincarnation, apparently simply because it is unfamiliar, only to be talked into it later by Sir Lulworth. She continually oscillates between doubt and belief and is never capable of cool detachment. The narrator in fact passes judgment on her: "She was one of those who shape their opinions rather readily from the standpoint of those around them." In a word, she lacks individuality. She exists only as a member of society. To Saki this is an unforgivable flaw.

Style and Technique

Most of the force of "Laura" is generated by its style, and especially by the sardonic tone of its privileged speakers, Laura and the narrator. Both exploit a deliberately inappropriate ceremoniousness of phrase. "I have the doctor's permission to live till Tuesday," says Laura, implying that survival until Wednesday would be a breach of etiquette. "As a matter of fact Laura died on Monday," reports the narrator, with equal calm. Laura also repeatedly demonstrates a sort of literal-mindedness that challenges the unstated ethics of English conversation. "How could you?" asks Amanda when Laura confesses setting all of Egbert's hens loose—and by this Amanda means, evidently, "How could you be so irresponsible?" Laura, however, chooses to take the question as a mere "matter of fact," like her own death, and answers that it was easy. In the same way, when Amanda says "today is Saturday; this is serious," she clearly means, again implicitly, that what is serious is the fact that Laura has only three days to live. However, Laura again takes the statement only at face value, as if what is serious is today being Saturday. Both exchanges, tiny in themselves, nevertheless reinforce the story's basic point that moral responsibility is no virtue and that being serious does no one any good.

Other devices within the story include the narrator's repeated indications that the moral attitudes of his orthodox characters are hypocritical, and the careful and studied use of verbs describing speech. It is noticeable that in the story's first section, Laura's speeches are followed by neutral or detached words, such as "said," "observed," and "admitted." Amanda, however, gasps, protests, exclaims, and sighs, though all this is created far less by grief than by indignation. Amanda, too, is almost the only character in the story incapable of using the highly dispassionate and class-bound English pronoun "one," so clearly demonstrated by Laura: "When one hasn't been very good in the life one has just lived, one reincarnates in some lower organism." Both Egbert and Sir Lulworth, however, use "one" at critical moments, to distance themselves or to indicate offense. The absence of this word from Amanda's armory is one more pointer to her vulnerable emotional status.

It is ironic that a woman so lacking in individuality cannot use a nonindividual form. However, the truth behind the detail is that self-possession is necessary for detachment. In this as in other matters, Saki is remarkable for his close observation and for his power in packing complex satire into scenes of great brevity and simplicity.

T. A. Shippey

LAWNS

Author: Mona Simpson (1957-   )
Type of plot: Coming of age
Time of plot: The 1980's
Locale: Berkeley, California
First published: 1985

Principal characters:
　　JENNY, a freshman at the University of California
　　LAUREN, her roommate
　　GLENN, her boyfriend
　　HER FATHER, a successful businessperson
　　HER MOTHER, a successful lawyer

The Story

Jenny, a college freshman, begins her narration by bluntly confessing that she steals. Her narrative monologue then moves loosely from present to past as she shares her feelings about several major areas of her life. Jenny works Saturday mornings sorting mail in her dormitory, where she has been stealing letters and packages. She has received a letter from the campus police saying they suspect that some of the mail sorters may be throwing out mail, and there is a meeting about it that she must attend.

She recalls the day that she came to the University of California at Berkeley. Her mother and brother had not come with her and her father. She was upset and embarrassed when her dad cried as he said good-bye, and was afraid someone would see him acting like that. Later, she took a long walk across campus and saw a man riding a lawnmower. The image made her happy and stayed with her. That night at dinner, she again saw the man, whose name is Glenn. She thinks that she is in love, for the first time. She worries that Glenn will find out about her but does not explain exactly what it is that she does not want him to know. She describes the night that they got together and how glad she was, because she wanted it to happen. Memories of her father intrude, but it turns out all right.

She says that she never steals Glenn's letters and describes what she knows about his family and a former girlfriend, who apparently is failing chemistry at school in San Diego. Jenny herself, who is enrolled in pre-med classes, got an A+ in Chemistry 1A.

On the day of the meeting with the police, Jenny has to skip Chemistry 1C for the first time. She lies to Glenn, saying she has a doctor's appointment. The students are questioned, but nobody says anything. The police officer's body reminds her of her father's. One student sticks up for all of them, and Jenny is grateful. After they are dismissed, she promises herself that she will not steal again.

She says that she lies all the time and struggles over which things she should tell

Glenn. She describes the development of her intimacy with Glenn by recounting some of the personal things he has told her: That he used to spin tales as a child until his parents took him to a psychologist to make him stop, that he has imagined what it would be like to stand at her funeral, no one knowing who he is, and that he loves her. She says sometimes she cries.

Her mother has just phoned, and Jenny describes her as a proud, self-absorbed woman who went back to law school some years earlier and believes that she has done it all without any sacrifice on the part of her family. Jenny says her mother "should know about me."

Jenny's father pays her a surprise visit. He hopes to spend the weekend with her, and she is clearly anxious and inwardly hostile. She talks herself into going with him on the condition that he return her in time for her date with Glenn. Later that night, she wakens to her father's molesting her in their hotel room, and it is clear this is not the first time. Her relief at returning to the dorm to visit with her roommate, Lauren, and get ready for her date ends when her father calls, jealous that she has other plans. Afraid he will ruin her new life, she tells her mother.

Her mother feels personally affronted, then comes to be with her, kicks her husband out, and says she is on Jenny's side. She says she is going to therapy and wants Jenny to go too. Jenny declines, deciding to rely on her friends instead. Jenny relates that she has told Glenn, and their relationship is now over. She feels as if her father has cost her everything. She remembers an ordinary morning, waking up with Glenn, and how later he took her for a ride on the lawnmower while he worked because he did not want to say good-bye, and how she sat on the handlebars and laughed. Lauren is supportive when Jenny tells her. They go out to breakfast, stopping on the way to watch the children on an elementary school playground.

Jenny sees Glenn, who has a new girlfriend, while he is working on a lawn. He congratulates her on an academic award she has won. She still loves him but sees him as one of those things she can never have.

Jenny starts stealing letters again but only one each Saturday. One Saturday she sees a little white envelope addressed to her. She throws it out, thinking it cannot be from Glenn, and finishes her shift. As she leaves, she changes her mind, retrieves the letter, and puts it in her mailbox so she can go to get mail like everyone else.

Themes and Meanings

Mona Simpson's twist on the conventional loss-of-innocence or coming-of-age theme not only focuses on this experience from a first-person female perspective but also shows the young woman who is telling the story struggling with being as calculating, manipulative, and pathological as the adult world that caused her loss of innocence. The story dramatizes the psychological complexes that can occur when sexual taboos are violated as a matter of course, and paints such an accurate slice of middle-class life that the reader is hard put to keep such ramifications of violating those taboos at a safe distance. Simpson relentlessly traces the effects of self-absorbed parents on daughters who are caught in circumstances that force them to grow up too fast, and who become disillusioned with and wistful about the values and safety of growing up in a middle-class nuclear family.

Jenny's resulting emotional reality becomes a kind of gamesmanship designed to keep the outside world in check. The conventional treatment, of emphasizing the loss of innocence, is radically transformed into an emphasis on seeing whatever happens merely as something that has happened, and going on from there. The resulting paradox of wanting to get on with life at the same time that the present is a creation of past violations is simultaneously heartbreaking, unromanticized, authentic, and compelling.

Style and Technique

The primary stylistic technique for articulating these issues is the narrative voice of Jenny. Author Joan Didion has maintained that style is character; the same aesthetic tenet holds true in this story. Simultaneously hardened, scared, and hopeful, the tone with which Jenny tells her story actually creates the story. She stops herself when she thinks that she is off track; when she feels it is important to the story, she comments freely in a clipped, authentic teenage conversational manner replete with such believable verbal tics as the rueful, "I just know, OK, I'm not going to start fooling myself now. Please," or, "He says they're not going to do anything to the person who did it, right, wanna make a bet, they say they just want to know, but they'll take it back as soon as you tell them." On the other hand, out of Jenny's own colloquial conversational style and experience comes an occasional sparingly lyrical perception that beautifully articulates her pain at feeling vulnerable, imprisoned, or apart, as well as her need to reach for a chance of happiness.

The narrator's powerful autonomy moves her beyond the sentimentality one might be tempted to ascribe to someone who has lived through circumstances such as hers. This is achieved primarily through brilliant irony of tone that allows her to confess that she steals and lies. It is precisely because of her description of these behaviors, combined with the disjointed flow of time throughout the narrative, that her story seems honest and believable.

The somewhat elliptical title of the story is subtly reinforced throughout the narrative by images of lawns on campus and at home, and the care it takes to keep them green and well-trimmed. These images provide ground cover for the story, and allow the sexual innuendo implied in the phrase "reaping what one sows" to resonate throughout the narrative. There are subtle but consistent descriptions connecting lawns and games—the astroturf football field at Berkeley, the baseball diamond back at home—and, in stark contrast, the beautiful lawns in front of various university buildings that Glenn, Jenny's first love, is paid to manicure. Such images further emphasize the weariness Jenny feels with the calculated mental strategies she uses just to keep herself in the game—whether it be as a perfect student with A-pluses in chemistry or as a hardened child one step ahead of her father's pathology—and underscore her need for more chances to sit on the handlebars of a lawnmower and laugh.

Maria Theresa Maggi

LAZARUS

Author: Leonid Andreyev (1871-1919)
Type of plot: Social realism
Time of plot: The first century C.E.
Locale: Jerusalem and Rome
First published: "Eleazar," 1906 (English translation, 1917)

> *Principal characters:*
> LAZARUS, a man raised from the dead
> AURELIUS, a famous sculptor
> CAESAR AUGUSTUS, the emperor of Rome

The Story

Lazarus has just returned home after being dead for three days. Sumptuously dressed, he is surrounded by his sisters Mary and Martha, other relatives, and friends celebrating his resurrection. His three days in the grave have left marks on his body; there is a bluish cast to his fingertips and face, and there are cracked and oozing blisters on his skin. The deterioration of his body has been interrupted, but the restoration, his return to health, is incomplete. His demeanor, too, has changed. He is no longer joyous, carefree, and laughing, as he was before death. Now he is silent, neither laughing at the jokes of others nor offering such play himself. It is some time before those around him begin to notice these changes in him. No one asks him about his experience of death for a time. His friends and relatives are celebrating him as a symbol of life; their emphasis on his resurrection overshadows the other awful truth: His return to life has also made him their surest connection to death and its mysteries.

When one of the men asks Lazarus to tell them what he saw in death, he does not answer. The question is repeated, but still Lazarus does not answer. It is at this moment that the people notice the bluish cast to his complexion and his death sores, as well as his bloated body. They notice these things as Lazarus sits silent, and they feel his gaze on them as one of "destruction." One by one the guests—and eventually Mary and Martha—depart.

Lazarus does not embrace his second life as he did his first. He is silent, cold, and indifferent to all that is around him. Those who fall under his gaze lose their own interest in life and slowly waste away. Those affected by his gaze feel no reason to do anything: There is no reason to eat, to play music, to go anywhere. Having broken the trail from death back to life, Lazarus is now the conduit through which death reaches humanity.

Gradually the desert envelops Lazarus's life and enters his home. As his friends and family leave him, there is no one to care for him. Shunned by all, he finds that life contains no meaning at all.

As word of Lazarus and his spectacular return to life spreads, visitors travel great distances to see the man who spent three days in the grave. All these visitors meet the same fate as those who have visited Lazarus before them: Their lives become empty and meaningless. It is as if a great shadow passes over everything. In everything, even the newest, youngest, and most hopeful, these people see death and destruction.

The sculptor Aurelius of Rome has created works that others claim to be of immortal beauty, but he himself is unsatisfied, feeling that something elemental eludes him. Determined to visit Lazarus in the Holy City, he will not be dissuaded by his friends' protestations against the trip. He fears neither Lazarus nor death. Aurelius approaches Lazarus surely and proudly, then asks to pass the night with him. Lazarus tells Aurelius that he has no bed, no light, and no wine, but the sculptor shrugs these details aside as inconsequential. When Aurelius begins to talk, he boldly refers to Lazarus's death, his time in the grave, and his ugly appearance. As Lazarus invites him into his house, the night shadows fall across the earth. When Aurelius's servant enters the house the next day to meet his master, he is shocked and disheartened by Aurelius's countenance. The sculptor, too, has fallen victim to the gaze of Lazarus, and he loses forever his ability to create beautiful works of art.

Eventually the emperor Augustus summons Lazarus to Rome. When he arrives, the emperor is not yet ready to receive him, so Lazarus waits seven days to be called. During this time he wanders the streets of Rome, the Eternal City, where he meets a drunkard who invites him to drink with him. After looking into Lazarus's eyes, however, the drunkard loses all joy in drinking. Then Lazarus meets a young couple, deeply in love, who invite him to look on their beautiful love. They, too, come under his curse of emptiness and mournfulness. Finally Lazarus meets a wise man who claims to know even the horrors of death. Falsely secure in his knowledge, the wise man soon realizes that knowledge of something is not the thing itself, that death is greater and more horrible than mere knowledge of it. Under the curse, the sage can no longer think.

Lazarus's final meeting is with the proud Augustus himself, who defies Lazarus's power of destruction. Augustus proclaims his own power, authority, and greatness. Feeling impervious and invincible, he looks into Lazarus's eyes. What at first seems a soft and loving gaze seduces Augustus, pulling him into the abyss of despair and shadow. Augustus orders Lazarus's eyes burned out and sends him home, where the blind Lazarus stumbles across the desert in the direction of the setting sun. One day he follows the sun and never returns.

Themes and Meanings

Leonid Andreyev uses the biblical account of Christ's resurrection of Lazarus as the seed of this story, which explores life, death, and illusions of human immortality and invincibility. By presenting Lazarus's five encounters—with an artist, a drunkard, two lovers, a sage, and a ruler—Andreyev argues that even the most revered of human accomplishments are futile against death.

Attitudes in Western civilization have long held that artists achieve immortality through their work. The story of Lazarus presents an opposing perspective. Although Romans claimed that the work of Aurelius was so beautiful that it achieved immortality, Aurelius himself was dissatisfied. He felt that something was eluding expression in his work. The "supreme beauty" that eludes reproduction is life or soul. When he first meets the sculptor, Lazarus sees not a man but a visage that resembles bronze. Already Aurelius has been diminished from man to work—that is, the sculptor is himself likened to a work of art.

Humans also use wine to mask pain and horror, the ultimate pain and horror being death. Lazarus forces on the drunkard a realization of all that he drinks to avoid, shattering his illusions. After this fateful meeting, the drunkard's pleasant wine-induced dreams give way to fearful visions. Drink no longer has the power to dissolve death.

Likewise even love, though a powerful, celebrated human emotion, ultimately fails to triumph over death. Even learning, philosophy, wisdom, understanding—all of these, personified in the sage, are powerless against death. The final challenge comes from the great Caesar Augustus, the emperor of the Eternal City. His power, pride, courage, and authority are inconsequential against death, represented by Lazarus. In his rage at having to confront and accept this truth, Augustus orders Lazarus to be blinded. Augustus dares not kill this messenger of death, so he exercises his power only to this limit of maiming Lazarus.

Style and Technique

Andreyev relates his tale simply and directly, using clean and honest language, even to describe the most distasteful details of Lazarus's appearance and stench after his three days in the grave. Much of the power of this story lies in Andreyev's skillful use of allegorical motifs and archetypal images to express the idea of death's ultimate power. These give the story of "Lazarus" breadth and timelessness. Lazarus's five meetings can be read in such allegorical and archetypal terms. In each instance, Andreyev uses characters as representations of concepts. Rather than explore their psychological workings, feelings, and motivations as characters, Andreyev uses them as types. The lovers, for example, represent the concept of love in all of its implications and complexity. The sage, too, is archetypal and allegorical rather than a unique character is his own right. Andreyev is less interested in this particular character than he is in the larger ideas of knowledge and wisdom and their cultural significance.

Adding an interesting twist is the irony suggested by the role of the sculptor in the story. Although Andreyev argues the ultimate futility of art in the face of death, he himself is an artist and "Lazarus" is a work of art. This gives the story an added layer of tension that makes possible a more complex reading.

Julie Thompson

THE LEADER OF THE PEOPLE

Author: John Steinbeck (1902-1968)
Type of plot: Social realism
Time of plot: The early twentieth century
Locale: California
First published: 1936

Principal characters:

JODY TIFLIN, a sensitive and tolerant young boy living on a ranch
CARL TIFLIN, his intolerant father
RUTH TIFLIN, his mother
GRANDFATHER, Ruth's father

The Story

As Jody plays aimlessly near his family's ranch house, his dog's behavior causes him to look up and see his father coming down the road toward home carrying an object that appears to be a letter. Once inside the house, Carl Tiflin hands his wife, Ruth, a letter from her father, informing them that he will be coming to visit later that day. Noticing the unpleasant expression that appears on Carl's face, Ruth scolds him for his apparent resentment of her father's visit. He simply explains that the old man "talks." Ruth tells her husband to be patient and at least pretend to listen to his repetitious tales. Jody, on the other hand, is excited by the prospect of hearing the often-repeated tales of his grandfather's leading pioneers across the plains to the west and of their encounters with the Indians. Uncharacteristically, he does his chores carefully, then goes to meet his grandfather. After his happy greeting, Jody invites his grandfather to hunt mice under haystacks with him the next day.

Supper reminds Grandfather of the buffalo that he so often ate during his "crossing" to the west, and he recalls a story that the Tiflins have heard many times. Carl looks for opportunities to interrupt; later in the evening, when the old man predictably starts to say, "I just wonder if I ever told you . . . ," Carl assures him that they have all heard his tales many times, while avoiding his wife's angry eyes. Only Jody lies by saying that he has not heard his grandfather's tales.

The next morning, before Grandfather appears for breakfast, Carl complains about having repeatedly to listen to accounts of the "crossing"—a time that is now over and finished. As Grandfather nears the kitchen, he overhears Carl's complaints. As he sits down, Carl asks the old man if he heard what he said and apologizes, saying that he was just joking. Grandfather acknowledges that those days are over and that perhaps his stories are no longer relevant.

His spirit now broken, Grandfather confides to Jody that perhaps he should not stay any longer, feeling as he does. He suggests that it is not the stories themselves that matter, but the act of "westering" and of knowing that once the Pacific Ocean was reached, it was over. Jody offers his grandfather some lemonade as his way of offering him solace.

Themes and Meanings

"The Leader of the People" is best known as a chapter in John Steinbeck's novella *The Red Pony* (1937), in which Jody Tiflin comes of age on his parents' ranch. Considered on its own, "The Leader of the People" is an initiation story. Early in the story, for example, Jody utters "those damn mice" in front of a hired man, then turns to see if the man has noticed his "mature profanity." From his grandfather, Jody learns that human beings are fallible and have limits. In the course of this story, he develops a more mature sensitivity, expressing it in the simple act of offering his grandfather lemonade. He has learned to feel and to reach out beyond himself to try to deal with the feelings and needs of others. For the first time, his request for lemonade is not just an excuse to get some for himself.

A second major theme developed in the story concerns the concept of the spirit of "westering." Through the grandfather, Steinbeck explores the place and meaning that the nation's pioneer heritage—the western movement—has for later generations. The old man's repetitious accounts of leading the "crossing" merely irritate Carl, but Jody—who is of yet another generation—can sense what his grandfather is really talking about. Jody understands that the important thing is not that his grandfather led a group across the plains—someone else could have done that—but the whole concept of "westering," participating in a mass movement eager for new experiences that forever changed the course of national history. The western frontier was not merely a geographic line but a mental outlook. The closing of the frontier signaled an end to a spirit of possibility and a view of humankind as a vital moving force. As a "leader of the people," Grandfather concludes that the spirit of "westering" has died and that, for those without that spirit, all is indeed "finished." It may be that Jody's generation will recapture something of that vision that his father's generation has lost.

Style and Technique

Although the message of "The Leader of the People" is complex, its story is simply told. Steinbeck fuses form and content so thoroughly that his narrative never seems strained. As in all the stories that make up *The Red Pony*, dozens of unobtrusive details are imbedded in "The Leader of the People." The style is well suited to the story's themes and subject matter; it uses vivid images and symbolism to convey profound meaning in such a way that the story is perceived as natural and appropriate to the ages and the personalities of its characters. Skillful word choices are especially notable. The hired man, Billy Buck, for example, speaks "ominously" to Jody about securing permission to kill mice in the haystack: He knows what a strict disciplinarian Carl is. Ruth "entangles" Carl in her "soft tone" when she tries to make him understand that when the "crossing" ended, so did her father's life. Grandfather himself, however, can only convey this thought to the young Jody, when he expresses his feeling that the vibrant frontier spirit of his generation has died.

The Pacific Ocean and the physical setting of the Tiflin ranch are important symbols in this story. The ocean is a literal, physical "end" to the frontier, leaving no more land to discover or acquire. In contrast to its past history, the land occupied by the Tiflins no longer supports Indians and large game. In their place are such small animals as mice, snakes, squirrels, pigeons, and the like. By comparison to the vast herds that once roamed the west, these creatures seem small, insignificant, perhaps even petty. The mice that Jody is at first so excited about hunting and killing ultimately seem unimportant compared to the human lives that have been taken on that land in the earlier days. Grandfather asks, "Have the people of this generation come down to hunting mice?"

The offering of the glass of lemonade marks a mutual understanding between Jody and his grandfather. The old man almost declines, but when he "saw Jody's face," he realizes that Jody needs this chance for an unspoken expression of sympathy and compassion. Likewise, when Jody suggests having lemonade, it is not because he necessarily thinks that Grandfather is thirsty; it is his way of showing his grandfather that he understands his sadness about "westering" being finished.

The idea that vital, progressive movement such as Grandfather had experienced in the days of "westering" has come to an end is suggested in the motions of the animals on the ranch. A flock of white pigeons flies out of a tree only to circle the tree and land again; the cat leaps off a porch only to cross the road and "gallop back again." Neither ever really goes anywhere.

Victoria Price

THE LEANING TOWER

Author: Katherine Anne Porter (1890-1980)
Type of plot: Coming of age
Time of plot: 1931
Locale: Berlin
First published: 1941

Principal characters:
CHARLES UPTON, the protagonist, an American art student in
Berlin
KUNO HELLENTAFEL, his boyhood friend from Texas
ROSA REICHL, his landlady
OTTO BUSSEN, a German mathematics student
TADEUSZ MEY, a Polish music student
HANS VON GEHRING, a young German student from Heidelberg
suffering from a dueling wound

The Story

This lengthy story opens in Berlin in late December of 1931 as Charles Upton, a young, poor art student, the son of a farming family in Texas, is seeking new quarters because his hotel is unpleasant, oppressive, and expensive. On Christmas Eve his thoughts turn to Kuno Hallentafel, a childhood friend from Texas and the son of a prosperous merchant. Kuno, whose family came from Germany and later returned for visits, spoke so glowingly of the beauty and grandeur of Berlin that Charles decided to study art there. Charles "in his imagination saw it as a great shimmering city of castles towering in misty light."

Much of the rest of the plot is devoted to showing how Charles's early romantic perceptions of Berlin are contradicted by the reality of his life there. In this sense, it is an initiation story common in American literature, in which the protagonist, usually a young person, is disabused of earlier beliefs, or loses his innocence, as he comes to a sobering new awareness or understanding brought about by his travels or encounters with different types of people. Charles's disillusionment with Berlin comes most dramatically at the hands of the hotel owners and landlords he encounters, in general a base, grasping, and ill-tempered group who have little sympathy for the people who need to rent their ghastly and uncomfortable furnished rooms. When Charles tries to move earlier than expected, one landlady even summons a police officer, who treats him with disdain as she cheats him of some of his meager resources. The most important landlady is Rosa Reichl, a once-wealthy, affected, overbearing, and intrusive woman. During their first meeting Charles accidentally breaks a small plaster replica of the Leaning Tower of Pisa, a treasured memento of her honeymoon in Italy. In

Rosa's furnished rooms, Charles comes to know three other young men who also are instrumental in his initiation.

The first of these young men is Otto Bussen, a very poor German mathematics student from Dalmatia. Bussen speaks Low German, an indication of his inferior social status. Under the guise of trying to improve him, Rosa continuously criticizes his manners and behavior. At one point he appears to try to commit suicide by poison, but he is saved by the efforts of Charles and the other boarders. The second boarder is Tadeusz Mey, a Polish student of music, also harassed by Rosa, who brings to Charles the perspective of an intelligent non-German who understands the larger cultural contexts of European history. The third boarder is Hans von Gehring, a student from Heidelberg who has come to Berlin for treatment of an infected dueling wound on his face, of which he is proud. Hans, at times a contemptuous and disdainful incipient Nazi, harbors notions of the superiority of the German race.

The last part of the story shifts from Rosa's rooms to a Berlin cabaret for a New Year's Eve celebration. Here again, the conflict between the three boarders is evident as they discuss women, social classes, racial distinctions, and World War I; for Charles, however, as the evening wears on and midnight approaches, the animosities dissolve into song and drunken camaraderie. The good will generated at the cabaret continues as the boarders return to their lodgings to find Rosa also happy from drinking champagne. At this point, Charles notices that the broken Leaning Tower of Pisa has been mended and is now behind glass in a corner cabinet. Charles's drunken jollity fades, however, as he begins to feel "an infernal desolation of the spirit." He expects that a good cry is all that is needed to complete the evening's adventure, but the concluding sentence indicates his deep and ultimate disillusionment: "No crying jag or any other kind of jag would ever, in this world, do anything at all for him."

Themes and Meanings

The principal theme of initiation already noted in Charles's disillusionment with Berlin through his encounter with landlords and through his association with Otto, Tadeusz, and Hans is reinforced by his perceptions of Berliners as surly, resentful, and hostile to outsiders. The lengthy December darkness of Berlin also increases his sense of alienation: "The long nights oppressed him with unreasonable premonitions of danger. The darkness closed over the strange city like the great fist of an enemy who had survived in full strength, a voiceless monster from a prehuman, older and colder and grimmer time of the world."

Charles's disillusionment extends beyond Berlin to Germany itself, a country still showing the effects of defeat in World War I, evidence of which he sees in the blinded and mutilated veterans on the street. The rise of Nazis to power and the coming of World War II is suggested by Hans's remark that Germany will win the next war. Charles, in other words, is coming to understand some important aspects of German culture in the 1930's.

Still another dimension of Charles's growing sensibility concerns Europe's relationship to the United States. He comes to understand through his conversations with his fellow roomers that the nations of Europe mistrust and stereotype one another. Tadeusz, the cosmopolitan Pole, who is Charles's mentor in these matters, tells him: "Europeans hate each other for everything and for nothing; they've been trying to destroy each other for two thousand years, why do you Americans expect us to like you?" Tadeusz's question points to still another aspect of Charles's education. Even though he is poor, he comes to realize that all consider him a rich American, regarding him with a mixture of scorn and envy.

Charles's trip to Europe is really, then, a journey into understanding. This innocent boy from Texas, with images of Berlin as a "shimmering city" dancing in his head, comes to know something about the dispiriting darker aspects of life. This disillusionment in the context of international travel has been a favorite theme in American literature, and it reflects the clash of cultures that accompanied America's rise to prominence as a world power in the early decades of the twentieth century.

Style and Technique

The dark and unpleasant atmosphere of Berlin and its impact on Charles is made vivid through Katherine Anne Porter's use of animal imagery, which sometimes borders on caricature. Repeatedly, she turns to various animals to help her characterize the people of Berlin whom Charles finds so distasteful. They are often compared to pigs who waddle down the sidewalk or who have enormous rolls of fat across their backs. In one remarkable scene, porcine Berliners gather to gaze longingly at a shop window full of hams, sausages, and bacon, next to another window displaying various pigs made of candy, wood, or metal. Porter then describes these Berliners as "shameless mounds of fat" standing "in a trance of pig worship, gazing with eyes damp with admiration and appetite." A description of the landladies of the city brings forth a torrent of unpleasant animal comparisons: "They were smiling foxes, famished wolves, slovenly house cats, mere tigers, hyenas, furies." In addition to animals, Porter focuses on the furnishings of rooms and the decorations of Berlin to emphasize the essential grotesquerie of the city. Charles at one point closely examines a dozen repulsive pottery cupids on a steep roof and speculates on the unrefined taste of their owners.

The season of the year also helps to underscore symbolically Charles's psychological state. Besides the darkness of late December, the dying year is an appropriate time for the demise of Charles's illusions about Berlin, his disappointment coming to a climax, ironically, after the New Year's Eve celebration. The one note of hope in this final scene can be inferred, again, from the season. It is going to be a new year soon, and perhaps for Charles this symbolizes a new beginning, free of previous misconceptions.

Another symbol, the most important one in the story, is the small replica of the Leaning Tower of Pisa. It is not well integrated and clear, but it does suggest several things important to the story. Its vulgarity is clearly associated with that of its owner, Rosa, and with the German nation as a whole. Its breaking by Charles, an American, brings to mind the chaos and breakdown of German culture in the aftermath of the defeat of World War I. In this connection, it is noteworthy that Rosa has put the repaired replica behind glass, safe from Charles. In addition, Charles's final thoughts about the tower suggest a personal symbolism for him, reflecting his state of mind at the conclusion of the story: The precariousness of the leaning structure reminds him of threats and danger and, ultimately, death.

Finally, the intrinsic symbolism of the journey itself corresponds to the main theme of initiation. Charles's travels to Berlin represent a journey into awareness. The naïve boy from Texas has been initiated into knowledge that leaves him sadder and more somber but also more sophisticated and mature.

Walter Herrscher

THE LEAP

Author: Louise Erdrich (1954-)
Type of plot: Autobiographical
Time of plot: The late twentieth century
Locale: New Hampshire
First published: 1990

> *Principal characters:*
> THE NARRATOR, a woman returning to her mother's home
> ANNA, her mother, a former trapeze artist

The Story

The narrator's mother, the surviving half of a blindfold trapeze act, has lost her sight to cataracts. She navigates her home so gracefully, never upsetting anything or losing her balance, that the narrator realizes that the catlike precision of her movements may be the product of her early training. The narrator rarely thinks about her mother's career in the Flying Avalons, however, because her mother preserves no keepsakes from that period of her life.

The narrator owes her mother her own existence three times. The first occurred well before she was born, when her mother, then Anna of the Flying Avalons, was performing with her first husband, Harold Avalon, in the same New Hampshire town in which she still lives. The narrator got the story from old newspapers. In contrast to the West, where the narrator has lived, New Hampshire weather can change dramatically without warning. On that pleasant June day, the local people came to the circus and enjoyed the various acts while awaiting the Flying Avalons, who gracefully dropped from nowhere, like sparkling birds. Unbeknownst to the audience that day, Anna was seven months pregnant.

The finale of the Avalons' blindfold trapeze act always had them kiss in midair. On that fateful day, however, a powerful electrical storm arose at the very moment that they began their finale. While they were in midair, their hands about to meet, lightning struck the main tent pole and sizzled down its guy wires. As the tent buckled, Harry fell, empty-handed. Realizing that something was wrong, Anna tore off her blindfold. She had time to seize her husband's ankle and fall with him, but she instead grabbed a guy wire, superheated by the lightning.

Anna burned her palms so badly on the wire that there were no lines on them after they healed; she was not otherwise injured until a rescuer broke her arm while pulling her from the wreckage. She was then confined to the town hospital for a month and a half, until her baby, a daughter, was born dead. Although her husband was, at his own request, buried at the place from which the family came, Anna had her child buried in the New Hampshire town. When the narrator herself was a child, she often visited the grave of her stillborn sister, whom she considered not so much a separate person, but a less-finished version of herself.

The second debt that the narrator owes to her mother goes back to her mother's hospital time, when she met her second husband—a doctor, who became the narrator's father. While he taught Anna how to read, they fell in love. In learning to read, Anna exchanged one form of flight for another; since then, she has never been without a book. After her husband's recent death, no one remains to read to the blind woman, which is why the narrator—whose own life has failed—has returned home to her.

After marrying, the narrator's parents settled on a local farm that her father had inherited. It was her mother who insisted on living there.

The narrator owes her existence to her mother, a third time, because of an event that occurred when she was seven. The farmhouse caught fire—probably from standing ashes—while she was home under a babysitter's care. The sitter telephoned the alarm, but the narrator was already trapped by flames in her upstairs bedroom. When her parents arrived, volunteer firefighters were surrounding the house, but because an extension ladder was broken, there appeared to be no hope of reaching the narrator's bedroom. A tall elm tree near the house had a branch that brushed its roof, but it appeared too slender to support even a squirrel. Nevertheless, the narrator's mother stripped off her outer clothes and used the broken extension ladder to climb the tree, into whose branches she vanished. She reappeared, inching her way along a bough above the branch touching the roof. After standing on the branch momentarily, she leapt toward the edge of the roof, breaking off the branch with a loud crack.

On hearing a thump, the narrator looked out her window and saw her mother hanging from the rain gutter by her heels, calmly smiling. After entering the room, her mother clutched her daughter tightly against her stomach and jumped to the safety net below.

Themes and Meanings

The clearest theme in "The Leap" is presented by the title itself, that of bridging gaps, making connections between things. Physical, temporal, and emotional connections provide a thread that runs through the story. The most obvious are the two physical leaps made by Anna, as a trapeze artist, to save herself and her children from fire. In each leap she bridged a physical gap, but she also made an emotional leap. When lightning struck and her first husband fell, she clearly chose where her loyalties lay. Instead of grasping his ankle and going down clutching him, she chose to save her own life and that of her unborn child.

Anna's final leap also involved an emotional jump, a leap of faith. The narrator says that her mother saw that there was no rescue for her, yet she stripped off her clothes to make the attempt. Anna's again choosing life for her child manifested her continued connectedness with the future.

Another temporal bridge to which the narrator refers is that of her feeling of oneness with her mother's stillborn child, whom she considered a "less finished version" of herself. In her youth she sat at the child's grave, watching her tombstone, which seemed to grow larger with time, "the edge drawing near, the edge of everything," closing, then, the gap between her and the child.

This theme can also be seen in the various circular implications that permeate the story, such as the narrator's own return from her "failed life, where the land is flat," to her childhood home, and in her mother's return to a more dependent state. Anna's blindness in old age is reminiscent of her blindfold trapeze act of her earlier years, as well as her leap onto the burning house. In an act of redemption, perhaps for the first child who had died, she provided onlookers with the kind of spectacle that she had once performed for crowds—an impossible feat that she made look easy by hanging by her heels from the rain gutter and smiling after she landed. This time she succeeded where earlier she had failed, and she saved her child.

A more pervasive but less obvious theme is that of preparation and anticipation. Throughout the story the narrator is preoccupied with harbingers, ignored warnings, and signs of impending doom, as well as with the choices that people make to prepare for the future. She couples this theme with that of acceptance of fate, recognizing that individual choices are often lesser evils, and bring with them negative consequences that must be endured.

During the fateful circus performance, the images of the approaching storm, unperceived but deadly, are vivid. The narrator contrasts the way that New England storms can come without warning to those in the West, where one can see the weather coming for miles. She also emphasizes the circus crowd's ignorance of the signs that could have been seen—"the clouds gathered outside, unnoticed." The thunder rolled, but it was drowned out by the circus drums.

During the trapeze leap and the fall itself it is clear that Anna had time to think, consciously to decide what her future would contain. Her grasp on the hot metal wire burned all the lines off her palms, leaving her with "only the blank scar tissue of a quieter future."

The other idea that runs through the story is that of gratitude. The narrator is clearly grateful for what her mother has given her: Saving her own life to allow her later to bear another child; life itself through birth; and life again, through her rescue from the fire. It is her gratitude that pulls the narrator home to read books to her mother, "to read out loud, to read long into the dark if I must, to read all night." Although it is implied that her return comes at a crucial juncture in her own life (implied by her reference to her failed life), it is a rare child to show a parent such self-sacrificing gratitude. She returns to fulfill the function that her father initiated in the hospital, that of reading aloud.

Style and Technique

Louise Erdrich's smooth-flowing narrative makes for deceptively easy reading. The story can be read on several different levels. On its most basic level, it is a pleasant story of a daughter doing her duty by an aging parent whom she loves and respects. On a deeper level, it is a commentary on to what one owes one's existence and what one makes of it. On yet another level, it speaks of the moments of decision in each person's life, and the ways in which one uses these moments to change the courses of one's own and others' lives.

Such multiple-depth interpretation is typical of short stories in general, but the simplicity of Erdrich's prose makes her story both more accessible and more obscure. The cleanness of language and vivid beauty of her images make the deeper meanings easier to understand once they are perceived, but the romantic voice relating the tale belies the more profound messages.

Similarly, the repetitive use of key words such as "preparation" and "anticipation" makes her themes easy to follow, but her matter-of-fact storytelling seems to imply a naïveté that is not the case. The addition of prosaic detail and conjecture on the events being told lends credence to the fantastic.

Margaret Hawthorne Doty

LEARNING TO SWIM

Author: Graham Swift (1949-)
Type of plot: Psychological
Time of plot: The 1970's
Locale: Seaside in Cornwall, England
First published: 1978

> *Principal characters:*
> MRS. SINGLETON, a wife and mother
> MR. SINGLETON, her husband and a civil engineer
> PAUL, their six-year-old son

The Story

"Learning to Swim," told in the third person, describes the dysfunctional Singleton family's holiday in England's Cornwall. As Mr. Singleton teaches his young son Paul to swim, his wife reflects on her past and her relationship with her husband. She recalls that she had first considered leaving Mr. Singleton while vacationing on a Greek island before they were married. She had enjoyed the holiday, but while she lay on the beach, he remained in the sea, afraid, she believed, of the land. After they were married, she again thought about leaving him. He had become professionally successful but was personally distant, preferring his engineering accomplishments to her.

Their love life, or lack of it, also has led Mrs. Singleton to consider ending the marriage. Her ideal lover is an ethereal artist, but Mr. Singleton is an athletic swimmer and engineer. She claims she has taken the lead in their sexual relations throughout their marriage, but their lovemaking has been almost nonexistent. In her opinion, her husband simply does not want to be happy. In spite of the infrequency of sexual intercourse, she did become pregnant and bear a child. In reflecting on their past arguments, she thinks that she has always forgiven him, as a mother would forgive a child. However, Mr. Singleton has rejected her mothering and, she feels, her sexuality. After Paul's birth, she had wished to put her husband into her womb, and she believes he had desired the same thing.

Mr. Singleton, too, has thought about leaving Mrs. Singleton, once after she had taken him to a classical music concert in London. No lover of music, he suspected that she simply wished to humiliate him. At school he had been a competitive swimmer, and his success established in his mind that he needed no one else, and he pursued physics and mathematics with single-minded dedication. He often dreams about swimming to an empty distant shore, and when he makes love to Mrs. Singleton, he thinks about swimming through her to that pristine land.

From the shore, Mrs. Singleton watches Paul's swimming efforts. She hopes he fails. Success will mean victory for Mr. Singleton and break the thread between her and Paul, an erotic thread wherein Paul will grow up, slender like her idealized artist lovers, and she will pose nude for him. When she calls to them, saying that it is time to come out of the sea and have some ice cream, Mr. Singleton ignores her, urging Paul to try again. While waiting, she fantasizes about making love to other young boys who, she believes, are avidly admiring her figure. From the sea, Mr. Singleton, after appraising his wife's attractive figure, reflects that in his dreams there is no one on the further shore, and if Paul swam, Mr. Singleton could leave his wife.

Unlike his father, Paul loathes the water and fears his father's gripping hands as he fears his mother's engulfing embrace with the towel when he returns to the shore. With no exit from the opposing demands of his parents, Paul begins to swim, away from his mother on the beach as well as away from his father's reaching hands, swimming toward the open sea.

Themes and Meanings

Graham Swift's works are often rooted in history, but in the private history of individuals rather than the public history of politics and wars. In "Learning to Swim," it is through the subjective memories of their private histories that the characters must work out their conflicted destinies. On the beach, Mrs. Singleton reflects back on her younger self and her expectations, and the history, as she understands it, of her relationship with Mr. Singleton. For Mr. Singleton, success as a schoolboy swimmer was the defining event in his life. When attempting to swim in the ocean, Paul remembers his past fears when taken to the local pool by his father. For all three characters, history is not something to transcend but to be endured, at least until Paul swims away from both his parents at the end.

Water is a frequent theme in Swift's writings, and in "Learning to Swim," the characters respond to water in varying ways. Mr. Singleton was a competitive swimmer in school and spent his Greek holiday in the sea. He dreams about swimming to distant shores and attempts to teach his son to swim. Mrs. Singleton, however, lies on the beach both in Greece and Cornwall and never accompanies her son or her husband in their swimming efforts. She recollects that at the time of Paul's birth, her husband's face was clammy. The birth process itself was a watery experience, and she wanted to put Mr. Singleton into her watery womb. Paul fears water, both in the pool and in the ocean, but at the end of the story, the sea provides the means to escape from both his mother and his father.

Many of Swift's writings describe the destructiveness in marital relationships, often when a child is involved. "Learning to Swim" is no exception. From the vantage point of the Cornwall holiday, it is obvious that the relationship between Mr. and Mrs. Singleton was doomed from the beginning. Self-sufficient to an extreme, Mr. Singleton views his life only through himself: Even his attempt to get Paul to swim is related to his desire to escape from his wife. In contrast, Mrs. Singleton sees herself as being at the center of her relationships with others. She imagines herself having affairs with artists, playing the role of the initiator in sex with her husband, and wresting Paul away from Mr. Singleton. Her desires and her husband's isolation are impossible to reconcile.

"Learning to Swim" is a study in sexuality. The title has sexual implications as in the swimming of sperm, as exemplified by Mr. Singleton swimming in the school pool, in the Greek sea, and in his dreams. Mrs. Singleton's sexuality is much more obvious and violates traditional taboos. She fantasizes about artistic lovers, she feels that the young boys on the beach desire her, and she hopes to pose in the nude for her son. Her maternal feelings are sexual in nature. She imagines putting her husband into her womb, and when he rejects her mothering him after their arguments, she interprets this as a rejection of her sexuality. Although she envisions posing in the nude for her son Paul, he fears she will mother and smother him with a towel when he emerges from the sea.

Style and Technique

Swift wrote "Learning to Swim" in the third person instead of the first person that he uses for most of his short stories and novels. However, he does not use the third person to create distance between the author and the reader or to speak through an omniscient narrator. While using a third-person approach, Swift allows the plight of the three Singletons to be told through sequential interior monologues. In the story, little takes place in present or real time: Mrs. Singleton sits on the beach and Mr. Singleton and Paul swim in the nearby sea. Rather, the reader enters into their present lives through the memories and recollections that make up their private histories and individual pasts. Most of "Learning to Swim" takes place in the past, and the major action is internal.

The author's decision to refer to his adult characters as merely Mr. and Mrs. Singleton with no first names is appropriate given the relationship—or lack of one—between the characters. Although husband and wife have widely different interests and disparate personalities and desires, both are portrayed by Swift as isolated and alienated figures, "singletons" in reality. The personal alienation and present isolation of his characters is pronounced in many of Swift's works, but the third-person approach in "Learning to Swim" lets the reader enter the characters from the outside in rather than from the inside out.

Swift's vocabulary and use of language is undramatic and straightforward, but as in most of his novels and short stories, there is no simple linear narrative for the reader to follow. Past events and historical memories are jumbled together, as they are in real life. "Learning to Swim" is a story of the singularity of ordinary people living outwardly normal lives who are actually plagued by extraordinary internal frustrations and desires. At the end of the story, there is no obvious conclusion to the Singletons' dilemmas, not even for Paul. He swims away from his parents, but he is only six years old, and there can be no permanent resolution for him, just as there are no permanent resolutions in most lives.

Eugene Larson

LEAVES

Author: John Updike (1932-   )
Type of plot: Psychological
Time of plot: The 1960's
Locale: New England
First published: 1964

Principal characters:
A WRITER, a man reflecting on his life
HELEN, his former wife

The Story

Gazing out the window at grape leaves, a writer reflects on their beauty, and on the relation of the recent crises of his life to nature. The effortless creativity of nature and its freedom from guilt contrasts with the artifice of his writing and with his experiences of shame and fear. As he contemplates his natural surroundings, he is beginning to sort through the memories of his divorce, trying to make sense of his feelings of pain and love. He is also contemplating his own activity as a writer, drawing the reader into the processes of capturing the images of life on a leaf of paper:

> A blue jay lights on a twig outside my window. Momentarily sturdy, he stands astraddle, his dingy rump toward me, his head alertly frozen in silhouette, the predatory curve of his beak stamped on a sky almost white above the misting tawny marsh. See him? I do, and, snapping the chain of my thought, I have reached through glass and seized him and stamped him on this page. Now he is gone. And yet, there, a few lines above, he still is, "astraddle," his rump "dingy," his head "alertly frozen." A curious trick, possibly useless, but mine.

The writer of this passage continues to enter in and out of descriptions of the natural beauty around him, drawn back from entering fully into its profusion by images of his wife's departure. Sunlight playing through the grape leaves casts shadows in menacing shapes, yet the intricacy of the colors and patterns among the leaves suggests innocence, shelter, and openness as well. Drawn outward to the embracing leaves of surrounding trees, he is suddenly cast back inward to his sorrow.

Others have told him that he acted badly, but he is yet unable to feel the appropriate guilt. He is trapped between his inability to organize the events and tuck them safely into the past, and his inability to leap forward into his unforeseen future. When his wife left to get the divorce, the familiar patterns of their existence—searching for car keys, calling the baby-sitter—were broken along with their love. Driving along the familiar tree-lined streets became an act of moving back through the events of their life together, reinterpreting them in the light of their divorce. Meeting Helen in Boston, he sees her in her dual aspect of remembered "wife-to-be" and current ex-wife. He feels the darkness within him burst out and drown their love, and feels as if that world is now gone forever. "The natural world, where our love had existed, ceased to exist. My heart shied back; it shies back still. I retreated." Now he waits fearfully for each new stab of pain brought by letter or phone. Hidden away in a cottage to write, he discovers that he is unable to escape the past and sink into nature. The pages that he writes are no more able to join him and his guilt to nature than the dead leaves he has tracked into the cottage have the power to evoke the beauty of the living sunlit leaves.

However, for the first time in a while, he is really able to see a low hill in the distance. Gazing at the lawn strewn with the fallen leaves of an elm, he recalls his first night at the cottage when he had gone to sleep reading Walt Whitman's *Leaves of Grass* (1855), certain that he was leaving his old life behind.

> And my sleep was a loop, so that in awaking I seemed still in the book, and the light-struck sky quivering through the stripped branches of the young elm seemed another page of Whitman, and I was entirely open, and lost, like a woman in passion, and free, and in love, without a shadow in any corner of my being.

After this awakening, he still must return home, but for him the shadows on the leaves have shifted with the changing light. "I imagine warmth leaning against the door, and open the door to let it in; sunlight falls flat at my feet like a penitent."

Themes and Meanings

John Updike, in this brief but intricate story, evokes the complex tissue of relations and events that connect a person to others, to nature, and to the human spirit. Human beings find themselves in an awkward position between the natural world and their supernatural spirits, between earth and heaven. Nature itself exists without morality or guilt. It simply happens and need not search for meanings in all of its actions. Humans exist within nature yet they must struggle to find meanings and standards beyond nature in order to fulfill the urges of their spirits. They cannot act solely by nature, but must be responsible and self-conscious of their behavior. Thus, humans are in-between, drawn by the instincts of their natural bodies yet commanded by the rules of their supernatural spirits. Often, they are confused by this duality and torn between the two poles of their existence.

The writer in "Leaves" feels this split with painful clarity. He longs to be able to merge into nature in order to free himself from the agonies of guilt and sorrow that trouble his existence, yet he also desires to fulfill his ability to draw meaning out of events and shape his own future. He is able to capture in words enduring images of natural beauty, yet he feels unable to bring order out of the images of his own life. He wrestles to rediscover his place in the pattern of existence after the disaster of his divorce; his attempt to find meaning in his past actions still brings him great pain.

Although his guilty humanity is the ultimate source of his discomfort, it is also the means through which he may begin to overcome his distress. Through the processes of writing and reflection, he begins to recognize his participation in both nature and humanity, and to realize the strength of the human spirit despite the fragility of the human situation. The mute pain of life can be lessened by the ability to give it words, to capture it and organize events into patterns that can be partly understood. The art of writing is a form of the spirit's struggle to harmonize itself with the natural world through which it lives. People are able to see events in new ways, turn them around, and partially rewrite the way these events affect the rest of their lives. This freedom of self-creation compensates for the spiritual pain and guilt that only humans suffer.

Style and Technique

Though written as prose, Updike's "Leaves" borders on poetry with its dense layering of meanings into a concise and rich imagery. The primary metaphor of leaves refers to the leaves of grape vines and trees, the pages on which the author writes, and the action of leaving each other. It brings together nature, spirit, and the events that bind them. The image also gradually draws the reader into the emotional process of a man taking leave of his past life and entering into the unknown patterns of a new stage of his existence.

The multiple meanings of this story's words and images suggest the inability of people to find clear and simple interpretations of their actions. Helen, the writer's wife, represents the naturalness their love once had, but as a participant in creating and maintaining the break in that love, she also represents the current pain and confusion of its loss. The sun shining on the leaves symbolizes life, love, and the guilt-free abandon of nature; it is also the image used for the guilt that casts shadows within the writer's soul and burns through his memories, changing them in the light of his sorrow. Updike's interweaving of this writer's reflections on nature, human nature, the art of writing, and his memories and emotions shows the complexity of the ways in which a person's life is shaped by, and shapes, the world around him.

This man is in the middle of his world in all ways. He is in the middle of sorting out his divorce, which has broken his life into two parts, lost past and unattained future. He exists in the midst of his friends and family, bound to them by the ties of their mutual experiences, yet he is unable to see himself as they do: as unequivocally in the wrong. The writer's difficulty in understanding his own life and feelings is so realistic that it catches the reader up into the center of the story as well, uncertain of this man's past or future but sharing in his present pain. Finally, the writer also exists, along with all humanity, in the middle between heaven and earth, both of which offer him comfort and cause him pain. He can never exist solely in either but is always a participant in both, and this "in-between-ness" is his damnation as well as his salvation.

Mary J. Sturm

LEAVING THE YELLOW HOUSE

Author: Saul Bellow (1915-   )
Type of plot: Psychological
Time of plot: 1957
Locale: Sego Desert Lake in the American West, perhaps Utah
First published: 1958

> *Principal characters:*
> HATTIE WAGGONER, the protagonist
> THE ROLFES, a retired couple
> THE PACES, the owners of a dude ranch
> DARLEY, the ranch foreman
> WICKS, Hattie's former lover
> INDIA, Hattie's dead friend

The Story

Hattie has lived in her yellow house at Sego Lake for twenty years. She arrived at the beginning of the Depression and lived a vagabond's life with a cowboy named Wicks. When Wicks left, she moved in with a woman of small but independent means named India, the original owner of the yellow house. As the story begins, Hattie is living alone in the small house, which was left to her by India. She has become something of a snob, preferring the society of the Rolfes and the Paces—who, like herself, are landowners and therefore worthy—to that of her former companions.

Into this fairly tranquil life, trouble intrudes. One evening, driving home drunk from the Rolfes, Hattie loses control of her car and ends up stuck on the railroad tracks. Darley, who works on the Paces' dude ranch, reluctantly agrees to tow Hattie's car, but he carelessly leaves the tow chain too long. Hattie, who is climbing over the chain as Darley jerks his truck into reverse, is knocked to the ground, her arm broken.

As she slowly recovers, Hattie wonders about the significance of her injury. Perhaps it is a judgment against her for her drunkenness, her laziness, her procrastinations. For the first time in her life she concerns herself with the past as fact, rather than as self-justifying fiction.

However, admitting the truth has never been Hattie's style; about the accident, she always says she lost control because she sneezed, not because she was drunk. As Hattie proceeds in her quest for truth, her old self-deceiving patterns constantly impede her. Although the old Hattie is bent on surviving, the new one is bent on knowing.

As a survivor, Hattie is a practical, social being. She must somehow pay her hospital bills, replace the blood she required during surgery, exercise her arm to regain its full use, keep the house in repair. Initially she assumes that her friends will be there to help her, as she would help them, but is the community really a safety net for the individual? Gradually she discovers that there are limits. The Rolfes are leaving for Seattle, the doctor will not buy her house, Amy (a neighboring miner and widow) will care for her only on condition of inheriting her house, and Pace offers a small monthly stipend if she will leave the house to him.

Growing confusion and isolation lead Hattie the survivor to yield more and more time to Hattie the seeker of truth. She scrupulously examines the past, focusing on her life with India, her life with Wicks, and the death of her dog, Ritchie.

An earlier version of Hattie's life with India casts her companion as an ill-tempered, foul-mouthed, helpless, drunken woman who ordered Hattie about and blamed her when things went wrong. Eventually, Hattie admits that she endured the abuse in order to inherit the house and concedes that India was basically kind and good to her.

Her memory of Wicks undergoes a similar revision. Earlier Wicks was the romantic cowboy who eventually drifted off into the sunset. Now she admits that she refused to marry him because she did not want to give up the distinguished Philadelphia name of her first husband. Among her recollections of their days as trappers is that of him kicking to death a beautiful white coyote. Their relationship ended prosaically at a remote hamburger stand they owned, when the lazy Wicks complained of the food. Hattie cooked a steak for him and threw him out. Now Hattie realizes that Wicks, like India, was a real friend.

However, the vision of Wicks's killing the white coyote leads to another admission. Hattie has lamented the death of her dog, Ritchie, but at last she admits that it was she who killed Ritchie with an ax-blow to the head when he turned wild and sunk his teeth into her thigh. Her instincts for survival led her to shed blood; her guilt led her to blame her neighbor, Jacamares; her new commitment to truth leads her to confess the whole.

This confession of her own violent impulses intensifies her feeling of being alone, dependent now only on herself for survival. Her attention shifts away from reconstructing the past to planning for the future. She hurries out to her car to see if she is now able to drive, to maintain her independence, but she cannot shift or steer; her arm is all but useless.

Because she can no longer function in this life, she must prepare to leave it. She must make a will. A brief survey of her surviving relatives leaves only one likely heir: Joyce, the orphaned daughter of a cousin. However, would leaving her the yellow house really be a kindness? Like Hattie, Joyce might become a lonely old drunk.

In a drunken blend of pain and joy, she decides to leave the yellow house to herself. Ironically, reconstructing the past has validated Hattie's sense of self and intensified her commitment to survival.

Themes and Meanings

Hattie discovers how to depend on herself when she is forced to depend on others. Like many aging people deprived of their former physical capabilities, Hattie begins to relive the past. She wants perspective on her life, an impartial view missing while she was actually caught up in events and in self-justification. This new vision helps Hattie accept herself as her own history, the sum total of her actions and her friendships. To some extent she acknowledges responsibility for her life, thus signaling a developing acceptance of death. She has come to understand that bodies, like houses, are "on loan."

Style and Technique

This story is remarkable for its unusual point of view, moving back and forth from a third-person central intelligence to a first-person confessional. The effect suggests that sometimes the author speaks and sometimes Hattie. The authorial voice, although sympathetic, tends to be more objective, whereas Hattie's voice is often lyric and subjective to the point of falsehood. Hence, the flickering point of view reflects Hattie's own vacillation between honesty and self-deception.

When readers are in Hattie's mind they find the world described in terms of simile and metaphor. For example, when Hattie is preoccupied with her dog Ritchie, the sofa cushions look like a dog's paws. Life itself is a "hereafter movie" recording a person from birth to the grave. The camera angle is always from behind, suggesting that one cannot falsify this record. As one lives, there is less and less film available, and as one prepares to die, one must watch the whole film.

The story's mixed chronology reflects Hattie's thoughts in like manner. One leaps back and forth among different layers of the past, then ahead to the future, the reader's confusion a strategic double to Hattie's own perplexity.

The symbol of the house unifies a fiction that might otherwise seem as disjointed as Hattie's mind. To Hattie the house symbolizes social position, achievement, and security. This meaning broadens when Hattie faces losing the yellow house, either by selling it to pay her medical bills or by dying and bequeathing it to someone. These are both ways in which she might have to "leave" the yellow house. In this sense, the material house becomes the outward sign of her tenuous hold on life.

Sheila Ortiz Taylor

LEAVING THIS ISLAND PLACE

Author: Austin Clarke (1934-   )
Type of plot: Social realism
Time of plot: About 1950
Locale: Barbados
First published: 1971

> *Principal characters:*
> THE NARRATOR, a high-school athlete and prominent cricket player
> CYNTHIA, his girlfriend, the daughter of the middle-class rector
> HIS FATHER, a former star athlete and cricketer, now dying in an
> almshouse
> HIS GODMOTHER, who reveals some of the narrator's family
> background
> MISS BREWSTER, the head nurse at St. Michael's Parish almshouse

The Story

The narrator, who is from a typical lower-class Barbadian family, has gained a reputation as a track athlete and cricketer at Harrison College (a high school). He is in love with Cynthia, the attractive daughter of the local middle-class rector and a student at Queen's College. Aware that Barbados holds no future for him, he is preparing to leave the island to attend a university in Canada. Before he leaves, he feels compelled to visit his dying father in the local almshouse. His father is in the section used as a hospice for the terminally ill, a ward that smells of decay and death and whose inhabitants are gaunt and skeletal.

Miss Brewster, the elderly head nurse, berates the narrator for not having visited the dying man previously and for not having brought even some fruit as a gift and, perhaps inadvertently, calling him a "bastard" for acting too proud. Nurse Brewster apparently knows the life stories of most of the home's residents and repeatedly refers to the dying man as the young athlete's father. The narrator cannot reconcile the two lives he has led: a favorite of the wealthy, middle-class social set and the scion of a lower-class family of uncertain parentage. His godmother has confused him by telling him that the man his mother had said was his father was not, but had been blamed for his birth, and that "that man was a man"—presumably, in West Indian terms, a sexually active man when younger. The narrator's discomfort is aggravated by his mother's refusal to have the putative father's name mentioned in her house.

The narrator has visited his father surreptitiously in his small shack at Rudders Pasture, on the outskirts of town, where he lived for twenty-four years. The father gave him small gifts of money on these visits, and the narrator discerned his true compassion during these encounters—although he also noticed the nude photographs of both black and white girls on the walls beside pictures that had been torn from the local newspapers, showing the narrator winning track events. The father, described by family members as having had no family and no background, appears to be what the godmother suggests, part madman and part genius, but father and son have—despite the son's superficial rejection—maintained a close bond, even to the extent of the narrator giving him a track trophy. Theirs is clearly a love-hate relationship, although the father repeatedly asserts his paternity in his maturity, dotage, and decline.

On his last visit to his father at the almshouse, the narrator wonders what the relationship was between his father and his mother: Was she pregnant when she slept with him in his shack? Did he rape her? Had she slept with several men—for payment? All that he knows is what his godmother has said, that his mother still hates him and that at school the father's name has never been recorded. Officially the narrator has been illegitimate and, although among the best in academics and athletics, "only a bas——."

Although the father, in his delirious state, requests that the son get Sister Christopher from the Nazarene Church to pray for him, the son says that there is no point in listening to a dying man's talk. His thoughts are with the Saturday afternoon cricket matches, the wealthy middle-class girls who attend them, the theater matinees, the walks in the park—with the life that he aspires to rather than that from which he has come. He would like to play at the Garrison Savannah Tennis Club as a member rather than work as a ballboy there or a gardener for some white family. He sees emigration and education as the only solution to his situation, for he has been unable to rise in the island despite his obvious strengths: Just as his father has been tormented and repeatedly imprisoned by Barrabas, the police officer, the narrator has been imprisoned by the island society.

Amid the small talk at a farewell party for him, the narrator recalls his reception at the rectory when he went to ask that a canon perform the burial service for his pauper father: Doors were closed and slammed. He finds no pleasure in the small talk and realizes that there has always been a gulf between him and his acquaintances: Legitimacy and class create impenetrable barriers in small societies.

After the party, the narrator and Cynthia proceed to Gravesend Beach, where they enjoy moonlight and love. She asks that he write regularly, but to her aunt's address rather than to the rectory, and says that she will tell her father of their love and intent to marry—even that she would like to leave Barbados because it stifles her. In the middle of their conversation, he mentions that his father has been at the almshouse; Cynthia insists she did not know that he had a father and that he must be joking to say that he was indigent and in the almshouse. Before he can praise the old man's kindness, Cynthia walks away, and they drive off in the rector's Jaguar.

Although Cynthia pledges to see him off at the airport, she does not come; although she gives him a briefcase as a going-away present and hopes to have her picture in the island newspaper's gossip column, she does not show up. He hears others' farewell conversations but has none himself.

Themes and Meanings

Austin Clarke's "Leaving This Island Place" follows an honored tradition in West Indian fiction initiated by V. S. Naipaul in 1959 with the final chapter of *Miguel*

Street, in which the central character explains his reasons for leaving the Caribbean. Clarke elaborates the theme of the search for greater opportunity abroad by introducing the conflict between the traditional family unit and illegitimacy, and the insincerity of the religious middle class with its pretensions, hypocrisy, and duplicity. As a result, the story is more than one young islander's search for personal satisfaction by attending a university abroad rather than a local university; it is a search for personal identity, an investigation of self and conscience, and ultimately a search for the meaning of love and responsibility.

The mother never tells the eighteen-year-old protagonist who his father really is; the godmother assumes that her intuition is correct but seems to be motivated by animosity rather than love; Barrabas clearly takes pleasure in punishing a simple man and a community hero for simple pleasures such as drinking heavily—a common indulgence in the West Indies; and Cynthia, although she protests her great love, is intent on deceiving her father and did not love the narrator enough to admire his rise from poverty, illegitimacy, and social marginality. The clergy love not the poor and despised, but the affluent and socially acceptable. Only Miss Brewster, the old and knowing nurse, seems to comprehend the real nature of love: She sees it in the old man and exhorts it in the young one. For her, love is demonstrated by a visit, by the gift of a piece of fruit, not by an expensive briefcase, sexual pleasure on a beach, or a ride in a fashionable car. The death of the old man, whose name the narrator has never borne, represents the death of love for and from people and the death of attachment to Barbados. Seawell Airport is the end and the beginning.

Style and Technique

The anonymity of the narrator suggests that this story is representative of the experience of many young West Indians. The characters fit neatly into two groups: the young, who will either stay in Barbados and try to assume positions of power or emigrate and achieve self-satisfaction, and the old, who are adjusted to the limitations and oppressions or perquisites of island life. Together, they suggest that there is no viable middle way. Some readers may find the constant repetition of "I am leaving" too repetitive (it occurs seventeen times, and there are five additional variations of the same idea); however, it clearly is intended to convey the narrator's obsession with departure. It becomes a leitmotif.

There are several vivid expressions that suggest Clarke's skill at both characterization and description, for example, "the smell of stale urine and of sweat and faeces whipped me in the face," and "The two large eyeballs in the sunset of this room are my father." The inclusion of snippets of the godmother's conversation throughout the story indicates that her remarks, unsettling rather than comforting, are a constant irritant. Most of the dialogue is void of the idiosyncracies of Barbadian dialect; as a result, the story becomes more than a single-island story and can be seen as a metaphor for all islands or small, isolated communities.

Marian B. McLeod

LECHERY

Author: Jayne Anne Phillips (1952-   )
Type of plot: Character study
Time of plot: The 1970's
Locale: Near Pittsburgh
First published: 1979

> *Principal characters:*
> A FIFTEEN-YEAR-OLD GIRL, the narrator
> UNCLE WUMPY, her father figure
> KITTY, her coworker at the luncheonette
> NATALIE, her friend from the orphanage

The Story

The narrator, an unnamed fifteen-year-old girl who knows she was abandoned when she was fourteen months old, in December, 1960, begins her story by saying that although she has no money, she must give herself what she needs. In between being arrested and being homeless after running away from the state-operated Children's Center, she survives by stealing food from the butcher shop and by enticing boys and young men, stimulating them with pornographic pictures and then feeling gratification through her power over their sexual release. She describes her "lovers"— one may be nervous, another may be mean, one blond, another dark. She offers whiskey to all of them. The pictures she shows them are of young girls, girls such as herself. She describes the acts she and the boys perform and says the boys sometimes get teary-eyed.

She recalls the ugliness of the dolls that she was given at the foster homes in which she was placed. Most of them had no clothes, and one had a hand missing. The girl identifies with these maimed and ruined playthings. Life treats her the same as others had treated the dolls.

The memory of the dolls reminds her of when Uncle Wumpy, her sugar daddy and father figure, gave her a doll. Uncle Wumpy was called that because of his pocked face, rabbit ears, and soft gray flesh. She recalls an outing during which she and Uncle Wumpy won cowboy hats, a rubber six gun, and a stuffed leopard for their cohort, Kitty. Drunk and wild, they shot ducks at a carnival shooting gallery until Uncle Wumpy won her the three-foot bridal doll with a bird in its hair. With Uncle Wumpy's lighter, she burned the bird and later buried it in a hole in a place she would never forget.

That memory leads her to remember that she first met Uncle Wumpy, who worked for the state road commission, while she worked at a luncheonette. She cleaned tables and was mistreated and degraded by the forty-year-old Minnie, who cursed the miners who came to eat there. Uncle Wumpy told Minnie and Kitty that the narrator needed some new clothes. He and Kitty took the young girl to Pittsburgh for some new dresses. In a motel there, the narrator vomited from the drugs she was given. Kitty and Uncle Wumpy had sex and involved her in their scene, but Uncle Wumpy never had sex with the narrator. Instead, he gave her pictures to sell. Uncle Wumpy prostituted the narrator, watching as the narrator performed oral sex, choking, gagging, and tasting the salty semen.

Natalie, the narrator's friend from the Children's Center whom the narrator believes is dead because the girl believed she would die at age twelve, comes to her in a recurrent dream. The narrator sees Natalie standing in the sand, holding herself, and calling to the narrator for help. The narrator remembers Natalie watching her all the time. Once, the narrator tipped back a box of salt into her mouth. Though she choked and screamed, Natalie only watched, staying in her chair and leaving the narrator to sleep alone in her bed.

At the Children's Center, the narrator would get cards sent to her by a jokester, someone who had been given her name and address. The cards were always inappropriate: at Christmas, a "To Daughter from Mother" card; at ten years old, a card "For Baby's First Birthday"; and at seven, the card said "Debutante." Though she was placed in home after home, she always returned to the Children's Center at holidays, which is when she would receive the cards. There, she would lock herself in the bathroom late at night and hold a candle under her chin, staring at her shadowed face in the mirror. Lying down on the cold tile floor, she would please herself, and in a moment of self-expansiveness she would see herself running from stall to stall, flushing all the toilets and refusing to let anyone in.

Believing Natalie to be dead, the narrator remembers an autumn night when they played make-believe together. In their fantasies, a black-booted man unbuckled his belt and switched Natalie with it, telling her, as he unzipped his pants, to touch his genitals. However, Natalie said she could not because her hands were poison.

The story ends with the narrator, Uncle Wumpy, and Kitty keeping house together. Kitty is on probation, but she obtains some heroin and they all shoot up. In the quiet after she has taken the drug, the narrator listens to the click of the outside neon sign. When she sees someone move, she is afraid. She thinks that if Natalie were alive, she . would find her.

Themes and Meanings

In "Lechery" and the rest of the stories that appear in Jayne Anne Phillips's collection *Black Tickets* (1979), the primary themes are home, family, loss, and degeneration. "Lechery" is a typical Phillips story in that her characters are usually outcasts, drug addicts, prostitutes, and street people who try to create makeshift family arrangements that, while often perverse, nevertheless function as a unit. Though the narrator in "Lechery" remains nameless—reinforcing the anonymous quality of so many rejected people—Phillips selects details and creates events that make the narrator both universal and unique at the same time. The author is never shy about closely examining and finding dignity in the lives of people that the average reader does not want to examine too closely.

As with all the stories in the collection, this story's principal theme is also the theme of language and how character is formed in relation to the stories being told and the words being chosen. There is a hallucinogenic quality to the language of the story that suits both the characters' circumstances and the dualistic story, which is a tale of abuse and meaninglessness and of characters finding comfort and meaning, if a bit unusual.

Style and Technique

The story is told from a first-person point of view by a fifteen-year-old girl who has been abandoned and abused. The language reflects the narrator's world and experience and yet has a youthful, almost innocent, aspect to it that suits her young, though experienced, age. The sentences are straightforward, simple, and evocative. However, the associative manner in which the story is told compels the reader, rather than the narrator, to find the sense and meaning in this young girl's life. Although not much attention is paid to the physical location of the story, words and phrases commonly used by outcast people of the southern Pennsylvania and northern West Virginia region often are employed. The date that narrator was abandoned and references to heroin as "smack" situate the story in the mid-1970's.

When the story first appeared, the term "minimalism" was emerging as a contested literary style in American literature. Authors as diverse as Ann Beattie and Raymond Carver were considered to belong to the new group of minimalist writers, writers whose style and narrative technique made use of sparse language, simplified plot constructions, and condensed imagery. Phillips, who began her career as a poet and whose most successful early work was in the genre of the prose poem, has been counted among the minimalists. "Lechery" reflects traits of minimalism in that its action and character delineation are drawn from the fringes of social and economic class and the plot, such as it is, depends less on unified action and more on its reflection of life's fragmentary and disassociated inconclusiveness. However, from this early piece, Phillips, in her imagery and her deep compassion for her maimed and marginal characters, shows literary traits that she will develop in more complicated and effusive form in her novels, *Machine Dreams* (1984), *Shelter* (1994), and *Motherkind* (2000). Making use of poetry's tradition of evocative tropes and concentrated imagery, Phillips's work is minimalist only to the extent that employing these techniques efficiently and effectively frequently results in much shorter, more lyrical fictive forms.

Susan M. Rochette-Crawley

THE LEDGE

Author: Lawrence Sargent Hall (1915-1993)
Type of plot: Realism
Time of plot: The 1950's
Locale: The Maine coast
First published: 1959

Principal characters:
>THE FISHERMAN, a veteran outdoorsman on both land and sea
>HIS SON, a thirteen-year-old boy
>HIS NEPHEW, a fifteen-year-old farm boy from inland

The Story

On Christmas morning before sunup, a fisherman wakes up keen with anticipation of a day of hunting sea ducks with his son and nephew. Their destination is a tiny ledge, Devil's Hump, near Brown Cow Island, on the Maine coast.

The fisherman is known as a "hard man," given to bragging and expressing his contempt for others less ambitious, but his forceful way achieves success in the only world that he recognizes—a world of outdoor activities focusing on hard work and hunting and fishing. His insensitivity has long made his wife yearn for a different kind of life, but on balance she has decided to stick with him despite his "incurably male" intransigence. She is thus not surprised to hear the roar of the outboard motor on the skiff that carries the fisherman and the two adolescents out to their larger boat before daylight on Christmas morning.

With the skiff and the outboard secured across the boat's stern, the three make their way to Brown Cow Island, where they anchor their boat and motor another three hundred yards in their skiff to Devil's Hump. They plan to arrive at about the same time the tide has receded enough so they can land and begin shooting around half-tide. The fisherman has it figured exactly: They will have about four hours before the ledge is completely submerged by high tide again. After finishing their "gunning" in late afternoon, they will go home with a skiff full of sea ducks—many more than their legal limit, a fact that does not ruffle the fisherman's ethical sense in the slightest. With the three is the fisherman's black retriever, too old to swim in the icy water but happy at being in on the fun.

The fisherman's mood blackens when he discovers that he has left his pipe tobacco at home. Even though he snaps at the boys, he refuses to return home, because to do so would throw his plan "out of phase." Because he is a man who persists through temporary setbacks, he merely clamps his teeth on his dead pipe and contents himself with the thought of the whiskey bottle he has packed with their lunches.

Everything goes as planned. They land their skiff on Devil's Hump, they eat sandwiches and drink coffee, and in an orgy of shotgun salvos they load the skiff with ninety-two birds. By this time the tide begins to come back in, and the fisherman, his belly warmed by whiskey, leisurely prepares to take the skiff back to the boat and head for home. A feeling of horror strikes him, however, when he discovers that the skiff has drifted away; he knows in a flash that they are dead once the ledge is again submerged by the tide.

The three hundred yards to Brown Cow Island may just as well be three hundred miles in the frigid water. In a desperate attempt to attract someone's attention, the hunters fire their remaining two and one-half boxes of shotgun shells into the air but nobody answers from the pitching sea.

The dog succumbs first. His eleven-year companionship with the fisherman ends when the hapless creature swims aimlessly off into the water, now dark with night. The fisherman's grit fortifies him to the end. He braces himself against the rock and has his son climb on his shoulders. The nephew disappears into the blackness of the encroaching waters, and the drama fades out the only way it can. The boy rides his father's straining back with faith that whatever can be done, his father will do, but nothing avails.

The skiff is found early the next morning, half full of ducks and snow. Two hours later the bigger boat is discovered five miles out to sea. At noon, at ebb tide, the fisherman is found with his right foot wedged into a crevice in the ledge, the three shotguns beside him, and under his right elbow the right boot of his son. The boys' bodies are never found.

Themes and Meanings

"The Ledge" dramatizes the events of a tragedy that actually occurred on the Maine coast, where hunting sea ducks can be extremely dangerous. The power of Lawrence Sargent Hall's story derives from its focus on the fisherman and his tenacious grasp on life until the tide overwhelms him. The account of the victims' last minutes harrows the reader with its grim depiction of the tide rising inch by inch until the boys and the dog just slip away and the fisherman drowns with his foot pinned in the rock crevice. Hall does not indulge in pathetic fallacies. The ocean is never "cruel" or "pitiless" or sentient in any way; it is mere matter subservient to the forces of lunar gravity, and God help those who are careless in its presence.

The fisherman might be judged a victim of his own pride. He has always mastered the physical world, marching through it contemptuous of the timid. Gender stereotypes intrude as he is compared to his wife, sensitive to nuances of feeling and experience that do not register in the fisherman's consciousness. She even daydreams about being a widow. Her ambivalence toward the fisherman generates a special poignancy in the final paragraph when she stares at his body on the frozen dock, seeing him as "exaggerated beyond remorse or grief, absolved of his mortality."

The boys are not developed at length, but the nephew is captured as an alien from inland when he develops a case of "ledge fever" and cannot fire at the first flight of ducks. The son's touching faith in his father speaks of what all such relationships should be, and this tie emerges vividly in the son's rubber boot found clutched under the elbow of the dead father, who holds on to the boy to the last.

The fisherman's forgetting to bring his pipe tobacco humanizes him effectively while foreshadowing his later, fatal carelessness in letting his skiff drift away. His anger at himself for leaving his tobacco is but a shadow of the stomach-emptying anguish that overtakes him when he realizes that by letting the skiff get away, he has doomed them all. His character emerges as he faces the challenge on the ledge: He may have been an arrogant man, deficient in tenderness and sympathy for the less capable, and this pride may have condemned him ultimately; but these same qualities enable him to die with dignity while hoisting his son above his head to breathe as long as possible. In all of these respects, there is a heroic completeness and humanity to the man. No one knows, of course, how the real persons who died on that ledge spent their last minutes, but they are well memorialized in Hall's fictional re-creation.

Style and Technique

Hall's refusal to give his characters names universalizes them and keeps them at a distance that avoids sentimentality. This point is made deliberately when in their last moments the boy refers to the dog only as "the pooch," and the fisherman realizes that he would have wept at the use of a familiar, personal name. Fathers and sons, husbands and wives, fishermen's sons and farmers' sons—these relationships show up in familiar archetypes in "The Ledge."

The story shows an easy familiarity with the vocabularies of coastal island life and the artifacts of that existence: yellow oilskins, outboards, skiffs, tollers (to bring in the ducks), and shotguns, as well as weather phenomena and physical features of the land and sea. In this respect, the story has all the density of detail expected of the best realistic fiction.

This tale of men against the sea follows a conventional narrative pattern. The fisherman wakes before dawn and the third-person narrator sketches his character and reveals how he is seen by others, especially by his wife. He goes about his business frying bacon, and then he and the boys take the skiff to the boat and then on to the ledge. The middle section follows the three through their successful hunt and to the discovery that the skiff has drifted away. In the powerful denouement, they brace themselves for their fate and die one by one. The story moves relentlessly to its end with no adornment and no sentimentality, and in doing so it achieves a genuine catharsis.

Frank Day

LEFTY
Being the Tale of the Cross-eyed Lefty of Tula and the Steel Flea

Author: Nikolai Leskov (1831-1895)
Type of plot: Fantasy
Time of plot: 1815-1826
Locale: London, St. Petersburg, and Tula
First published: "Levsha (Skaz o tul'skom kosom levshe i o stal'noy blokhe)," 1881 (English translation, 1906)

Principal characters:
LEFTY, the protagonist, a gunsmith of folksy ways but
    consummate skill
PLATOV, a Don Cossack of patriotic bent who accompanies
    Alexander I abroad
CZAR ALEXANDER I, the ruler of Russia from 1801 to 1825
CZAR NICHOLAS I, the ruler of Russia from 1825 to 1855

The Story

The Don Cossack Platov sets the tone for this whimsical tale by keeping the English off balance from the beginning. Alexander I's faithful but grumbling companion, in London with the czar, refuses to acknowledge English superiority in anything. When the czar exults over a gun in a museum, Platov pulls out a small tool, disassembles the gun, and proves that the mechanism was fashioned in Tula by a Russian craftsman. While the Englishmen stay up late endeavoring to come up with something the Russians cannot surpass, Platov sleeps soundly. In fact, each of the first two chapters ends with the Englishmen unable to sleep and Platov slumbering contentedly. When in need of guidance, the czar's man quotes a Russian proverb, and when in need of sleep, he prays in the Orthodox manner, downs a shot of vodka, and drops off forthwith. However, the result of his behavior is that the English hosts are frustrated, and the czar is embarrassed. Thus, Alexander is pleased when the Englishmen present him with the gift of a miraculous steel flea. There could be nothing finer than this, he says; his own workmen could make nothing like it. The flea is wondrous in its workmanship, for, despite its exquisite daintiness, it has a key that winds up a motor within. Activated by the key, the mechanical insect executes kicks and dance steps and twitches its minuscule mustache. When Alexander praises the object lavishly, Platov must retreat for a time and accompanies the czar home in obstinate silence.

In a short time, Alexander dies and is succeeded on the throne by his brother Nicholas I. After settling in to the job of being czar, Nicholas one day notices the flea, which has been passed on to him, and wonders what it is. None of his courtiers can tell him, but Platov soon appears and explains the matter to him. He also suggests to Nicholas that it would be a fine idea to allow the czar's craftsmen in Tula to examine the piece and determine whether they might be able to design something better and outdo the English. Nicholas agrees, expressing faith in his men of Tula, and puts Platov in charge of the undertaking.

Wasting no time, Platov whirls into Tula with Cossack aides and negotiates with the workmen there, charging them with upholding the honor of Russia. Lefty and two other workmen promise to do their best but are vague about what they will do and how. As Platov's warnings not to bring shame to their native land still hover in the air, the three craftsmen set off for a nearby workshop. They take a few belongings with them because they will be sequestered there for days on end. Once they are locked in and hard at work, their complete secrecy begins to intrigue those outside, who can hear them laboring but can see nothing. The townspeople even resort to trickery, shouting that the building is in danger because of a fire next door, but Lefty and the others inside ignore them and remain steadfast in their purpose, laboring feverishly up to the very moment of Platov's return.

Platov, who discerns no change in the flea, makes no effort to hide his chagrin but pulls out some of Lefty's hair, expresses his outrage, and departs posthaste for St. Petersburg, dragging Lefty with him. When they arrive in the capital in two days, Platov leaves Lefty under guard and goes to report to the czar. Nicholas asks expectantly what has been accomplished by his workmen and refuses to believe Platov's report that the men have done nothing. The flea, however, will not work when wound up by the czar's daughter. Platov is furious and threatens to exact a dear price from the unfortunate Lefty. Nicholas still believes in his men, however, and asks that Lefty be brought in to explain, though he is shabbily dressed and knows no court manners. Lefty is unabashed in the czar's presence and does proceed to explain the whole matter to him. Instructing the ruler to view one foot of the flea at a time under a powerful microscope, Lefty shows him that the Tula men have, indeed, done something even more remarkable than the Englishmen—they have put shoes on the flea. The czar is delighted, and Platov asks Lefty's forgiveness. Lefty goes on to explain that each artisan has signed the pieces he has made, except that he himself has made the nails for the shoes, and the nails are too minute to be signed.

It remains for Lefty to act as the czar's emissary and deliver the flea back to London, showing the foreigners what Russian craftspeople can do. Accompanied by an interpreter, Lefty speeds across Europe and to the English capital with the newly shod flea. When the Englishmen see what the Tula craftspeople have done, they are indeed impressed and give Lefty no respite from their questions. Because he has outdone their own workmen, they try to persuade him to wed an English lass and move to their country. Lefty, though not so blunt as Platov, is just as Russian and meets their suggestions with firm rebuttals, agreeing only to stay for a short visit. The English hosts reluctantly give in and shift their efforts to impressing Lefty with a round of visits to museums and factories, just as they had done with Alexander and Platov. Lefty takes in the sights with only mild interest—until he comes across a superior English method of cleaning rifle barrels. Immediately, the crafty Lefty recognizes this secret as something of potential military value to his country, and he demands to be taken home to St. Petersburg.

The English ship on which Lefty sails takes a long time to reach Russia, and to pass the time, Lefty engages in a drinking contest with an Englishman. As a result, he is in a deplorable condition on reaching home shores, and he is taken to the police and finally to a lowly hospital. Although Lefty pulls himself together sufficiently to make his report, various petty officials fail to recognize him or his mission and eventually conspire to keep the report from the czar. Lefty thus dies among the poor and insignificant in the hospital, a victim of ignorance, suspicion, and exceedingly rough treatment.

At the tale's end, the narrator observes that Lefty's real name is long since forgotten and that machines have taken over the work formerly done by such skilled artisans. There are no more master craftsmen such as Lefty, and therefore the legends that revolve around him continue to grow in the popular imagination.

Themes and Meanings

An abiding belief among the Russian folk of the nineteenth century was that the czar was a benevolent man with their best interests at heart. It was believed that, although there were bureaucrats who came between the czar and the people and intervened in the natural processes of trust and cooperation, if one could circumvent these petty officials and appeal directly to the czar, everything would be fine. The narrative illustrates this idea well and shows it to be a two-way proposition, with Nicholas sticking firmly to his faith in the men of Tula, and Lefty, as their representative, feeling perfectly at his ease in the presence of the sovereign. Russian peasants referred to the czar as "dear little father," and it is that feeling that is reflected in Lefty's behavior at court rather than any feeling of awe.

Russian nationalism and folk wisdom are blended in another theme in the text. Lefty and Platov are the chief fonts of the wisdom of the people, but Czar Nicholas also plays a role therein, thus intertwining the ideas of nationalism and folk wisdom and the bond between czar and folk. Platov, whose name probably alludes to Plato and thus to great wisdom, is the immediate reference point for the superiority and correctness of Russian ways. It is he who first deflates the English by behaving like the quintessential Russian nationalist while in London with Alexander. Platov is a Don Cossack, a fact that alone puts heavy stress on his Russianness. Beyond that, however, Platov considers Alexander too smitten with Western ways, so he does his best to steer the errant czar back to his native roots and values. It is in this connection that Platov's Russian qualities are strengthened: He drinks Caucasian vodka, carries a folding icon with him and says his prayers before it, crosses himself in the Orthodox manner, quotes Russian proverbs, and points out that Russian soldiers defeated Napoleon without any of the fancy military paraphernalia that he views in the museums of London. Platov is also the one who suggests (later, when Nicholas is on the throne) that the matter of outdoing the steel flea be put in the hands of the craftsmen of Tula, a town much renowned for its master workmen, especially its metalworkers.

Lefty is much like Platov as a carrier of nationalism and folk wisdom. Both make a trip to London on behalf of the czar, consume vodka, are connected with Russian icons, speak the folk idiom and make use of its rhyming aphorisms, and, most of all, prefer Russia to anywhere else. Defenders of Russian ways and of the Russian Orthodox faith, both remain steadfast in their service of God, czar, and country. Both shrewdly outwit the English. When Platov takes apart the marvelous gun in the English museum, demonstrating that its most intricate part was fashioned in Tula, it is a clear foreshadowing of the work that Lefty and his Tula brethren subsequently do, which is even more wondrous than the original work done by the English in creating the flea. Finally, both become homesick in England and long to go home to Russia.

Leskov's work, although highly nationalistic, is not without some barbs aimed at Russia as well. Foremost among these are two that are highly noticeable. The first is that, no matter how fine the quality of the Russian work on the flea, the fact remains that blind national pride and lack of technical knowledge have caused them to overtax the mechanism and partially disable the original creation. The second is that stupid bureaucrats not only prevent Lefty from getting his message to the czar but also unnecessarily cause his death. Only in a backward nation could such things occur, and Leskov puts considerable stress on their happening in Russia. Lefty, after all, dies fruitlessly trying to reach Nicholas. The death, though, reminds one that it was this same Nicholas who was wonderfully constant in his faith that the men of Tula would not let him down—even when it appears that that is what they have done. Nicholas holds firm and gives orders that Lefty be allowed to explain in his own words. Thus is Lefty exonerated, and his passing marks the end of an era, enhancing the legends about him and bringing the story full circle, back to the wisdom of the Russian folk and their ways.

Style and Technique

The long, convoluted title of Leskov's work serves a dual function. It gives the tale a comic tinge at the outset, causing the reader to chuckle and to suspect that the narrative will be colored by fantasy. At the same time, its inclusion of such a detail as the protagonist's left-handedness is an indication of the humorous but intense nationalism of the story. Both expectations—the fantastic and the nationalistic—are realized during the unfolding of the plot. It would be impossible for Lefty and his coworkers, merely by "sharpening" their eyesight, to see details with the naked eye that ordinary mortals are able to view only through a powerful microscope. However, one accepts this miraculous incongruity in the spirit of the work, an air of purest whimsy despite the historical background. Similarly, the fact that the hero is left-handed adds much to the story's effect. Indeed, Russians emphasize this aspect by commonly referring to the tale simply as "Lefty." The author's purpose is well served because the resultant feeling on the part of Russians is that even a left-handed, scruffy, admittedly uneducated Russian can surpass anything that the supposedly civilized, urbane English can do. Prejudice about left-handers being what it is, this seemingly insignificant characterization becomes a vital symbol at work for the author, and the fact that Lefty has no other name known to the reader underscores its importance.

Much of the humor inherent in the work derives from the author's remarkably creative use of language. Using a device known as *skaz*, from the Russian for "tell," or "narrate," Leskov painted such a deceptive verbal landscape that one must read it very carefully for full appreciation of its merits. *Skaz* involves the use of fictitious narrators with highly original peculiarities of language, and the linguistic distortions, puns, and malapropisms of the tale, particularly those uttered by Lefty and Platov, are virtually untranslatable. The story's enjoyableness even in translation is the result in large part of its fancifulness and cleverness.

Edgar Frost

LEGAL AID

Author: Frank O'Connor (Michael Francis O'Donovan, 1903-1966)
Type of plot: Psychological
Time of plot: The 1940's
Locale: A provincial town in County Cork, Ireland
First published: 1946

> *Principal characters:*
> DELIA CARTY, a nineteen-year-old, working-class girl
> TOM FLYNN, her young lover, a farmer's son
> NED FLYNN, his father
> FATHER CORCORAN, their parish priest
> JACKIE CANTY, the Cartys' solicitor
> MICHAEL IVERS, the Cartys' council
> PETER HUMPHREYS, the Flynns' solicitor
> DAN "ROARER" COOPER, the Flynns' council

The Story

Delia Carty, until the age of nineteen, had always been a "respectable" girl, but working as a maid for the O'Gradys proved to be her ruin, mainly because of the bad example they set for her. Within six months she was smoking and within a year she acquired a young lover named Tom Flynn, the son of farmer Ned Flynn. The narrator says that Tom is no great catch, being a big, uncouth galoot who loves to drink and chase the girls. After a two-year love affair, Delia becomes pregnant.

This is very bad news for Tom, who knows that his father "would first beat hell out of him and then throw him out and leave the farm to his nephews"; in this section of Ireland, no laborer's daughter is considered suitable for a farmer's son. Delia has to tell her mother, who persuades their parish priest, Father Corcoran, to talk to Tom's father about a possible marriage. As expected, however, Ned Flynn will not hear of it; in fact, he will not even agree to a small financial arrangement. This leads the narrator to remark, "Then, of course, the fun began."

When Delia Carty's father is told, he beats his daughter. Then he broods and grows angry about this blemish to his family name. He says, "Justice is what I want," so he brings Delia to Jackie Canty, the solicitor in town. Delia, although reluctant about bringing any kind of legal action against the man she loves, tells Canty that she has nothing in writing from Tom. She is upset when Canty informs her that Tom and his father will certainly claim that someone else is the father. Delia maintains that "Tom could never say that," but she is wrong. This is exactly the charge that Tom and his father decide to levy during the court case.

After Delia's baby is born, the court action begins. The Flynns' solicitor, Peter Humphreys, does not like the case at all, remembering "when law was about land, not love." He arranges for the Flynns to have as their council "Roarer" Cooper, a man who would normally rather fight than settle and one who has the reputation of always commanding attention—even as a first-class variety act.

On the day of the hearing, the court is crowded in order that the townspeople might hear whatever gossip is to be gained. Delia's council, Michael Ivers, approaches Roarer Cooper, asking for a settlement. Although Cooper is prepared to decline, he is sympathetic to the plight of poor Delia. After all, as Ivers knows, Cooper has daughters of his own. Ivers assures Cooper that Delia has never slept with anyone else because she was too much in love with Tom. Ivers also tells Cooper that it is the two respectable fathers that are behind this court action, not Delia. As Ivers says, "The trouble about marriage in this country, Dan Cooper, is that the fathers always insist on doing the courting." Cooper then asks why the priest did not make Flynn marry Delia. Ivers responds, "When the Catholic Church can make a farmer marry a laborer's daughter the Kingdom of God will be at hand."

Ivers is asking for a high cash settlement: £250. Cooper agrees to tell the Flynns to settle that amount on Delia, hoping that when she has that much money Ned Flynn will agree to Tom's marrying her. After lying about the judge, Cooper persuades Flynn to settle. He then acts as marriage broker, telling Ned Flynn that he would be a fool to let all that money get out of the family. When asked by Cooper, Tom says of Delia, "Oh, begod, the girl is all right." Making his way over to Delia, Cooper learns that she still loves Tom and asks her if she wants to marry him. With tears in her eyes, "as she thought of the poor broken china of an idol that was being offered her now," Delia says yes. Cooper tells her she "might make a man of him yet."

The two lawyers, Cooper and Ivers, make the match themselves in Johnny Desmond's pub; Desmond later remarks that the proceedings resembled a church mission, with Cooper threatening hellfire on everyone concerned and Ivers "piping away about the joys of Heaven." So the marriage is settled. The narrator, however, humorously observes, "Of course it was a terrible comedown for a true Roarer, and Cooper's reputation has never been the same since then."

Themes and Meanings

One of the main ideas in "Legal Aid" is that mature, reasonable adults can correct the serious errors that other adults commit out of silliness, prejudice, or plain stubbornness. As Frank O'Connor often does in his stories, he shows that social prejudice can cause serious personal problems for everyone, especially, in this case, for the young. Delia Carty and Tom Flynn would have married happily early in the story except for the prejudice his father Ned has against allowing Tom to marry beneath his station in life. Fortunately, the social prejudice that prevents the marriage is overcome by the cleverness of the two lawyers.

A second theme closely accompanying the first is that people need to understand others—particularly the young—and treat them with the kindness they would like shown to themselves. Certainly Roarer Cooper realizes that Delia Carty is a nice young girl, not much different from his own daughters. Delia may have been led astray, but her truthfulness and her obvious love for Tom persuade Cooper that he should work on her behalf. This, then, is one of O'Connor's optimistic stories, for in it he shows that human experience and humanity can lead responsible people to do the right thing and to help others who are in need.

Style and Technique

"Legal Aid" is precisely what this story is about. In keeping with O'Connor's use of humor throughout the story, it is Roarer Cooper, the council for the Flynns, who works hardest to help Delia Carty and to arrange her marriage with Tom Flynn. One would expect the parents to work out the marriage, or the parish priest, but when all else fails, it is the legal profession that straightens out this matter. O'Connor uses his frequent humor to remind readers that the human situation indeed is often comic. Delia might never have gotten into trouble if she had not been exposed to the O'Gradys, for, as the narrator comments: "The whole family was slightly touched." Of Tom Flynn's attempts to justify himself to God, the narrator says: "Between lipstick, sofas, and tay in the parlor, Tom put it up to God that it was a great wonder she hadn't got him into worse trouble."

As he often does, O'Connor makes skillful use of dialogue to convey the action and the characterization in the story. Readers are allowed to sit in on a variety of revealing conversations among each of the principal characters. Delivered in the charming, everyday speech of the Irish countryside, these conversations reveal all the key points of the story. Arranged in simple, chronological order, the story proceeds swiftly to the courtroom scene, followed by only one brief paragraph of epilogue. It is because O'Connor has characterized his people so clearly that the reader can accept the happy ending without finding it implausible.

A. Bruce Dean

THE LEGEND OF ST. JULIAN, HOSPITALER

Author: Gustave Flaubert (1821-1880)
Type of plot: Didactic
Time of plot: The early Middle Ages
Locale: Medieval Europe
First published: "La Légende de Saint Julien l'Hospitalier," 1877 (English translation, 1903)

> *Principal characters:*
> JULIAN, the protagonist, the only son of a noble couple, an
>   adventurer and hermit
> HIS PARENTS, a prototypical lord and lady
> HIS WIFE, the daughter of the emperor of Occitania
> THE LEPER, an incarnation of Jesus

The Story

In this tale, Gustave Flaubert chooses to re-create the vision of the world of medieval faith, and tells a venerable story as seen through the eyes of the twelfth century, even as such a story might be told in stained glass. The hero is followed through the twists of a plot where his predestined place as a saint is proven through the testings of life and sin, repentance and redemption. The world of Julian's birth is a perfect realization of the ideal manor life. Julian himself is the answer to his mother's prayers, and his christening is attended by the appearance of two divine messengers, each with a different prophecy. To Julian's mother appears the shadow of a holy hermit, predicting that her son will be a saint; to his father comes a Bohemian mendicant who predicts military glory, much blood, and an emperor's family. Both parents keep their visions secret and Julian grows surrounded by every fond hope. His underlying fault, an unconquerable lust for killing, is unleashed by his trapping of a white mouse that has disturbed him at Mass. From this point, at first encouraged by his parents in the medieval art of venery, Julian pursues a path that reduces him to the most savage of beasts, killing for the sake of killing, returning home matted with gore. One day, after a hallucinatory sequence of killings, Julian mortally wounds a great stag that turns and curses him in a human voice, predicting that he will kill his own parents. Again, the prophecy is kept as a secret, but Julian's fears make life at home impossible and he must forsake the world of his childhood. Thus ends the first segment.

The second part of the tale sees Julian as a mercenary soldier, killing in battle rather than in the hunt, as he gathers an army and reputation about him, finally saving the emperor of Occitania from the caliph of Cordova. The emperor rewards this fairy-tale hero and slayer of dragons with the hand of his daughter in marriage. A true Arabian Nights princess, she brings a handsome dowry and castle with her. Julian attempts to adopt domestic happiness, but his blood lust and his fear of killing his parents torment him, and one night he runs out of the palace to hunt, pursuing a host of animals that he cannot wound, until they surround him and through the pressure of their bodies force him to return to his castle. In his absence, his wife welcomes a pair of aged pilgrims who prove to be Julian's parents. She gives them her own bed, and Julian, returning in the dark, supposes them to be his wife and a lover and slaughters them, thus fulfilling the second of the prophecies. There remains only the third, of sainthood, to be realized as this second part of the tale ends.

Julian, having forsaken his wife and lands, becomes a wandering mendicant, forced by guilt to recount his sin of patricide and cast out by all men. He fears scenes of domestic happiness, the crowds in towns frighten him, and at the end of many wanderings he settles as a ferryman on the bank of a wide river. Profoundly repentant, he accepts the poor treatment accorded him by his passengers, lives on the most meager fare in a small hut, and attempts to atone for his sin by service to humanity. One stormy night, he ferries a hideous leper across the river. The leper demands shelter, food, Julian's bed, and eventually the very warmth of his body. When Julian has given all these things, without shrinking, the leper is transformed into the radiant Lord, Jesus, and rises to Paradise, bearing the transfigured saint with him. This, the author tells the reader, is more or less the story of Saint Julian, Hospitaler, as it was told in the stained glass windows of a church in his home region.

Themes and Meanings

Flaubert exploits a seemingly naïve tale to explore his own concerns of meticulous artistry and individual faith. The great lines of the story are determined for the writer even as Julian's life is prescribed for him in the prophecies of his youth. It is how the individual moves within the preordained limits of his fate that determines his final triumph. Julian is not a man of doubts, and in all of his actions he is shown as the perfect type of whatever role he fills: the perfect son, the consummate huntsman, a general and soldier without peer. His fault is imposed from without, yet it is wholly his own, and he both recognizes it, under the fear of the stag's prophecy, and agonizes under his inability to completely control it. However, he does not question the right of God to impose such suffering on him. He combats his fate by what means he can command; abandoning hunting for warfare, yet obeying the strictest rules of chivalry, giving up both warfare and hunting as a kind of penance to avoid killing his parents. However, when the actual deed is done, Julian's sorrow and repentance drive him into penitence, not rebellion. The omniscient narrator of "The Legend of St. Julian, Hospitaler" tells the state of Julian's mind, his agonies and angers, and it is through the narrator's posing of Julian's story that the reader himself may question the justice of a divine predestination that forces the individual to such glory through such suffering. Although Julian is given a name by the narrator, the other characters remain at the level of their narrative function: mother, father, wife, old monk. The only other named character is Jesus, in his apotheosis at the culmination of the story. Thus, each mark of individuality, each change in Julian's motivations is set in relief by the nameless, static quality of his companions. The continuity of the name is needed to preserve the continuity of this individual who is in turn a model child, enraged huntsman, warrior, fairy-tale prince, murderer, penitent, and saint.

Style and Technique

Flaubert is generally recognized as one of the greatest stylists of the nineteenth century. In "The Legend of St. Julian, Hospitaler," he deliberately adopts the naïve colors and simplistic story line of a twelfth century stained glass window, a tour de force of hidden effort and sophistication. Perhaps his greatest accomplishment lies in his transposition through words of the visual imagery of his supposed model. The tableaux emblematic of the stages of Julian's life are set within the narrative frame of the story as glass medallions are set within their lead strips. In the opening pages, the reader sees Julian's parental estate, serene and perfect in its sunny beauty, complete even to the pots of heliotrope and basil on the windowsills. The prophets appear before Julian's parents in carefully set-off scenes, parallel and balanced, as if two medallions were set side by side. Julian's hunting days bring careful presentations of emblematic animals, beavers, and stags. His battles are shown with red donkeys and golden Indians, colorful combatants drawn from exotic lands. Even his princess and her fairy-tale castle are drawn with the same brilliant colors and endowed with the same clearly defined static unity. The reader feels the effect of these visually composed scenes long before the final paragraph explains them in its identification of story and church window. It is Flaubert's triumph to unite the themes of faith and redemption with a narrative technique capable of bringing his scenes clearly before the eye, to enable his reader for a short time to walk with Julian in the sunlit Age of Faith.

Anne W. Sienkewicz

THE LEGEND OF SLEEPY HOLLOW

Author: Washington Irving (1783-1859)
Type of plot: Folktale
Time of plot: The early nineteenth century
Locale: A Dutch village in the Hudson Valley, near Tarrytown, New York
First published: 1820

> *Principal characters:*
> ICHABOD CRANE, the protagonist, a ragged, impoverished
> schoolteacher of Connecticut Yankee stock
> KATRINA VAN TASSEL, the daughter of a prosperous Dutch
> farmer, Ichabod's desired bride
> ABRAHAM (BROM BONES) BRUNT, a strong, handsome local boy,
> Katrina's suitor

The Story

Ichabod Crane is a newcomer to the Hudson Valley; unlike the generations of Dutch settlers that have preceded him, he has neither the strength nor the means to become a farmer and landowner. His single marketable skill is teaching, and in the isolated hamlet of Sleepy Hollow this pays meager rewards. His schoolhouse is decrepit, one large room constructed of logs; its broken windows have been patched with the leaves of old copybooks. Ichabod's quarters are whatever rooms the neighboring Dutch farmers who board him for a week at a time are willing to provide. Ichabod thus makes the rounds of the neighborhood, and his small salary, combined with his constantly changing address, allows him to store all of his personal possessions in a cotton handkerchief.

Because he comes from Connecticut, a state whose major product is country schoolmasters, Ichabod feels both superior to the old Dutch stock of the valley and frustrated by his perpetual state of poverty. He compensates for the former by regularly caning the more obstinate of his little charges and for the latter by doing light work on the neighboring farms. He further supplements his income by serving as the local singing master, instructing the farm children in the singing of psalms. Never missing a chance to curry favor with the local mothers, Ichabod always pets the youngest children "like the lion bold" holding the lamb. In short, his single goal is self-advancement, and though he has merely "tarried" in Sleepy Hollow, he clearly will remain if his prospects improve.

Ichabod cannot rely on his looks or strength to advance him, so he cultivates a circle of farmers' daughters, particularly those from the more prosperous families, and impresses them with his erudition and vastly superior tastes. He has, indeed, "read several books quite through," among them Cotton Mather's account of witchcraft in New England. He believes even the strangest of these tales; indeed, he frightens himself so much when he reads them that he is startled when he hears a bird or sees a firefly. He is, in other words, completely naïve and suggestible. The local tale of the Galloping Hessian who rides headless through the woods of Sleepy Hollow particularly alarms him. A snow-covered bush in the half-light is enough to convince Ichabod that he has seen the headless horseman.

One of Ichabod's music students is Katrina Van Tassel, the eighteen-year-old daughter of a prosperous Dutch farmer. She is "plump as a partridge; ripe and melting and rosy-cheeked as one of her father's peaches." She also, as her father's only daughter, has "vast expectations." Though she is also something of a coquette, the prospect of her inheritance makes her seem to Ichabod a desirable bride, and he determines to win her.

Ichabod's mouth waters when he contemplates the fruits of old Baltus Van Tassel's land. He dreams of the fat meadowlands, the rich wheatfields, and the rye, buckwheat, fruit, and Indian corn that will be his if he can win Katrina's hand. Once married to Katrina, he could invest in large tracts of land. He can even imagine Katrina with a whole family of children, setting out with him for promising new territories in Kentucky or Tennessee. It is, however, the sumptuous comfort of the Van Tassel home that makes him realize that he must have Katrina.

Winning Katrina, however, presents a problem in the person of her rugged, rough-edged Dutch boyfriend, Abraham Brunt, nicknamed "Brom Bones" because of his Herculean size and strength. Brom, who has long considered Katrina his, immediately recognizes Ichabod as his rival, and with his gang of roughriders plays a series of practical jokes on the Yankee schoolmaster. However, his pranks—stopping up the singing-school chimney, upsetting the schoolhouse, even training his dog to whine whenever Ichabod sings—do little to thwart the progress that Ichabod believes he is making in his campaign to win Katrina's hand. Indeed, Ichabod is encouraged when he receives an invitation to a "quilting frolic" at the Van Tassel home.

Ichabod spends extra time dressing and even borrows a horse so that he can arrive in style. The horse, somewhat inappropriately named Gunpowder, is as gaunt and shabby as Ichabod, but this does not prevent him from thinking that Katrina will be impressed. Ichabod continues to imagine the Van Tassel wealth that he will have if he can make Katrina his, and he quickly becomes the center of attention when Katrina dances with him. Brom, meanwhile, looks on with helpless jealousy. Brom enjoys himself only when telling of his close encounter with the headless horseman. Ichabod counters with extracts from Cotton Mather and stories of his own close calls with Connecticut and local ghosts.

An interview between Ichabod and Katrina follows the party, and Ichabod leaves, crestfallen. Could Katrina merely have been trying to make Brom jealous? Ichabod's anger, frustration, and sudden obliviousness to the rich Van Tassel lands seem to answer this question.

The midnight quiet of the countryside, the gathering clouds, and the ghost stories that Ichabod has heard do not improve Ichabod's mood. Indeed, he becomes increasingly uneasy as he approaches the tree from which Major Andre had been hanged. Ichabod knows that he will be safe if only he can cross the church bridge, but just then the goblin rider appears on his black horse, closing in fast behind him. Instead of disappearing in a burst of fire and brimstone as he has always been said to do, the rider throws his head at Ichabod. It strikes Ichabod's own cranium, and the rider passes on like a whirlwind.

Though Ichabod's borrowed horse reappears the next morning, Ichabod does not. The executor of his estate, Hans Van Ripper, burns Ichabod's copy of Cotton Mather and the scrawled fragments of a few love poems to Katrina. Ichabod himself becomes part of Sleepy Hollow's folklore. Some say that he was snatched by the Galloping Hessian, but others say that Ichabod is still alive, that he was afraid to return from fear of the goblin and Hans Van Ripper (from whom he had borrowed the horse) and was mortified by Katrina's refusal. Brom Bones appears soon after such discussions, always wearing a knowing smile whenever the goblin's pumpkin head is mentioned.

Themes and Meanings

In a postscript appended to the story in the handwriting of Diedrich Knickerbocker (Washington Irving's gentle burlesque on old Dutch New Yorkers and the fictive annotator of *The Sketch Book of Geoffrey Crayon, Gent.*, 1819-1820, in which this tale was published), the Dutchman records his having heard this story from an old, "dry-looking" gentleman described as possessing features strikingly like those of Ichabod Crane. When pressed for a moral, the storyteller replies: "[H]e that runs races with goblin troopers is likely to have rough riding of it." This, indeed, sums up a recurring theme in Irving's sketches: the results of the culture clash between industrious and poor but to some degree unscrupulous Yankees and the hardheaded and prosperous but also wily Dutch.

Neither the Dutch nor the Yankee newcomers possess a clear moral superiority. Here, for example, Ichabod has only a slightly better education than the Dutch children he teaches, and he would marry Katrina not from love but for her father's wealth. Similarly, Brom recognizes the threat to his interests and in his own rough way thwarts his Yankee opponent. Because Katrina does not appear especially attractive or faithful, Brom's motives hardly seem purer than those of Ichabod.

Style and Technique

Irving's version of this folktale features an effective series of starvation images that begins with his lengthy description of the gaunt, cadaverous Ichabod and extends to the almost physical hunger that his protagonist feels when he sees the rich produce of Van Tassel's land. Indeed, Ichabod's mouth waters as he contemplates this wealth and dreams that it might be his.

Complementing the starvation imagery is Irving's choice of names. Ichabod is tall and as gaunt as the crane whose name he shares. Like the biblical Ichabod, Irving's protagonist is as much an outcast as is his Old Testament namesake. Similarly, Brom, whose given name is Abraham, is as much a patriarch of his people as is the father of the tribes of Judah.

Robert J. Forman

LENA

Author: Mavis Gallant (1922-   )
Type of plot: Psychological
Time of plot: The late 1970's or early 1980's
Locale: Paris
First published: 1983

> *Principal characters:*
> EDOUARD B., a sixty-five-year-old French writer
> MAGDALENA ("LENA"), his Jewish-born first wife, formerly a
> actress, now a woman of eighty

The Story

The story begins in a hospital at the northern edge of Paris, which has made a bed available to Magdalena. To everyone's surprise, this frail, elderly woman not only has remained alive but also has remained spirited enough to ply her troublesome roommate with tranquilizers and even to hit her with a pillow. Although Magdalena has visits from an assortment of upper-class Hungarian women, it is Edouard who comes dutifully to the hospital, bringing along magazines to amuse her, allowing her to tease him, and reminiscing with her about the past.

Though Magdalena insists that she does not remember ever seeing Juliette, who eventually became Edouard's second wife, Edouard can recall every detail of that day in September, 1954, when the three had lunch together. Juliette thought the outing would be a good time for Edouard to ask Magdalena for a divorce. However, after he made a comment about Auschwitz, Edouard noticed that Magdalena had placed her left hand on his arm so as to display her wedding ring. Edouard did not mention divorce that day, and when Juliette did so, Magdalena pretended not to hear her. Magdalena never gave in. It was much later, after the Catholic Church had changed its rules, that Edouard and Juliette were married.

Edouard thinks back to how devastated he was when Juliette died. From Magdalena, he got no sympathy, just demands that he come immediately to the hospital and take his true wife home with him. Eventually, the faithful Edouard went to see her, carrying a bottle of champagne so that they could celebrate his being decorated with the Legion of Honor. Though Magdalena did comment on his ribbon, as usual she immediately turned the conversation to herself. What she really wanted to know, Magdalena said, was whether Edouard had ever loved her. When he could not assure her that he had, she began to complain about old age and death, and Edouard became furious. It was Magdalena's fault, he said, that Juliette had not been able to marry him for so long and so had been deprived of children. In essence, Magdalena had ruined her life.

After his angry outburst, Magdalena stopped begging Edouard to take her away. When he visits her, Edouard now tries to avoid meeting her eyes, in which he would see her unfailing but demanding love.

Themes and Meanings

"Lena" is one of four connected stories, all initially published in 1983, that concern three characters, Edouard B., his first wife, Magdalena, and his second wife, Juliette. In the first of these stories, "A Recollection," Edouard marries Magdalena to save her from death at the hands of the Nazi invaders of France; in the second, "The Colonel's Child," Edouard meets Juliette in a London hospital, where she is his nurse, and becomes engaged to her; in the third, "Rue de Lille," Juliette dies, her dreams of children unfulfilled. Throughout the series, Magdalena has been shown as a totally self-centered woman, and throughout most of the final story, "Lena," which like its predecessors is narrated in the first person by Edouard B., she is shown as even more selfish and more demanding in old age than she was in her youth. However, at the end of "Lena," Edouard sees that she does have one redeeming quality.

Like the three stories that preceded it, "Lena" deals with love, honor, and commitment. However, the real theme of this final narrative is how differently people view these values and how their various perspectives affect their lives.

To Edouard, "honor" means what it meant in the age of chivalry. A knight was supposed to rescue a lady in distress. It followed, then, that when a young Jewish actress was in danger, Edouard would save her, even if he had to swear vows he did not mean to keep. He did not love Magdalena, nor did he consider their arrangement a marriage. However, he felt he had a continuing commitment to her. The love of his life was Juliette, and though he does not admit to second thoughts about what he did for Magdalena, he did finally charge her with the responsibility for Juliette's unhappiness.

Like Edouard, Juliette lived by a code of honor, in her case the rigid morality of her Calvinistic upbringing. Once she and Edouard were engaged, she did bend her principles enough to live with him, assuming that they would soon be married. When it became evident that Magdalena had no intention of releasing Edouard, Juliette loved him too deeply to face life without him. However, until they were married, she would not bring children into the world. It was not only her religious commitment that stopped her, but also a sense of duty toward the children she hoped to have, children who were so real to her that she had already chosen their names, children she loved too much to let them bear the stigma of illegitimacy.

To Magdalena, such scruples made no sense. Magdalena did not live her life in accordance with abstract principles, though she was perfectly willing to make use of those who, like Edouard, did so. Her rule of life was to see that Magdalena was happy. Thus though she would not give up Edouard, with whom she had never lived, she took all the lovers who caught her fancy. Her Roman Catholicism was never a deeply felt faith but merely a convenience. As Edouard comments, Magdalena pretended to piety in order to assure the elderly women who visited her of her respectability. In much the same way, for decades she utilized her church's doctrines in order to keep Edouard.

Although it has been argued that Edouard is just another of Mavis Gallant's overly romantic male characters, it seems obvious that the author admires him for his commitment to the values he holds dear. Although a training injury made it impossible for Edouard to become a war hero, his lifetime of commitment to Magdalena surely qualifies him as a hero of private life. Juliette, too, demonstrates a quiet heroism, both in her selfless devotion to Edouard and in her continuing dedication to her principles. By contrast, as Gallant once admitted in an interview, there is not much to admire about Magdalena. She is a frivolous woman, whose only commitment is to herself. However, as Edouard finally sees, she is capable of one form of love: constancy. Throughout the years, Magdalena has remained unmoved in her belief that she is Edouard's one true wife.

Style and Technique

The fact that Gallant is often called a "writer's writer" suggests that nothing in her works is accidental. Even the titles of her stories are carefully chosen. It is interesting, for example, that this one is entitled "Lena," instead of "Magdalena," though Edouard refers to his first wife by her full name throughout his narrative. It is the elderly widows who call her "Lena" as a term of affection. To them she is a pious old lady much like themselves. Edouard's view of her is very different. Therefore it is significant that he calls her "Lena" only after their argument about Juliette, when Magdalena says she would have left all she had to any child of Edouard. On subsequent visits, Edouard begins to call her "Lena," suggesting that what was once only a sense of duty on his part has now developed into something that, if not love, is at least affection and a certain respect.

Gallant is just as meticulous about the colors she uses in her works. According to her, this series was inspired by something she saw in the Marseilles railway station, a woman in a white hat leaning out of a train window toward a man below. In "Lena," Magdalena is always draped in white, which is not meant to symbolize purity but to suggest her adamant impracticality. In her apartment, with its white sofa, the only spots of color were her red nails, her red lipstick, the red eyes of her little dogs, and the red Legion of Honor ribbons worn by her admirers. In her final days, the glamour is gone. It is now Magdalena's hair that is white. However, she still has one visitor with a Legion of Honor ribbon, her faithful Edouard. In fact, at the very end, she can count him as an admirer, for he has at last found something in her worthy of admiration.

Rosemary M. Canfield Reisman

LENZ

Author: Georg Büchner (1813-1837)
Type of plot: Biographical
Time of plot: Late January and early February, 1778
Locale: The Vosges Mountains southwest of Strasbourg, France
First published: "Lenz: Eine Reliquie von Georg Büchner," 1839 (English translation, 1960)

> *Principal characters:*
> JAKOB MICHAEL REINHOLD LENZ, one of the principal dramatic
>   writers of the German Sturm und Drang period
> JOHANN FRIEDRICH OBERLIN, a philanthropist and social
>   reformer, the pastor in Waldbach, and Lenz's host for a brief
>   period

The Story

"Lenz" is a fictionalized account of an episode in the life of the troubled dramatist Jakob Michael Reinhold Lenz (1751-1792) which was recorded by Johann Friedrich Oberlin, a pastor in whose care Lenz was placed when he began showing increasing signs of mental disturbance in 1778.

The beginning of Georg Büchner's account finds Lenz traveling on foot across the hills and valleys of the Vosges Mountains toward the village of Waldbach. As he walks, he passes in and out of a state of anxiety. He sees fantastic images in the wet, snowy landscape, in the cloud formations, and in the shifting sunlight. Like one hallucinating, he imagines that he must absorb the whole of creation, and he throws himself to the ground; "It was an ecstasy that hurt him." At other times, he feels very much alone and pursued by some unbearable thing, "seized with a nameless terror in this nothingness: he was in the void!" Then, each time, the terrifying attack passes, and he regains his calm and continues on his way. When he finally arrives at the vicarage in Waldbach—where he is quite unexpected but is hospitably received by Oberlin and his family—the domestic serenity of the place calms Lenz and recalls to him familiar images of contentment from earlier times at home.

He is given lodging in an upstairs room of the village schoolhouse, but before he can sleep, the anxiety of being alone and in darkness returns. Lenz rushes downstairs and into the street, bruising and cutting himself on the stone walls. He leaps into the water of the fountain and soon comes to his senses. Oberlin and other villagers come to his aid, and Lenz is ashamed of his bizarre behavior. Exhausted, he is finally able to sleep.

In the days following, he accompanies Oberlin on his pastoral rounds through the valley and is comforted by the man's acts of charity and sensible practicality, as well as by the affection that the rural people feel toward their benefactor. With nightfall Lenz's anxiety returns, however, and he continues his nocturnal baths in the village fountain, though more quietly, so as not to alarm his hosts and the other residents.

One day, after a solitary walk in new-fallen snow, he tells Oberlin that perhaps he might deliver a sermon in the church. Oberlin asks him if he is a theologian, and Lenz answers that he is. His request is granted for the next Sunday. Lenz preaches the sermon, and its effect on him is euphoric. With a sense of cosmic communion and self-pity, a "voluptuous crisis" suggestive of the late-medieval mystics, he passes the night in profound sleep. The following morning, he tells Oberlin of having dreamed of his mother's death, and their conversation turns to reports and experiences of clairvoyance and premonitions.

A man, Christoph Kaufmann, with whom Lenz is already acquainted, comes with his fiancé to visit Oberlin and his family. Lenz is troubled by this intrusion into his relatively anonymous life in Waldbach. At a dinner conversation about literature, Lenz argues for the honest, simple representation of life, and against the artificial idealism currently becoming fashionable. Kaufmann tells him that he has received letters from Lenz's father and tries to persuade him to return home, but Lenz is angered by the suggestion that he should leave the place where he has found peace.

When Kaufmann departs, Oberlin goes with him to visit a colleague in nearby Switzerland. Lenz is apprehensive about the separation and accompanies the pastor for a part of the way. On his way back to Waldbach he comes to the cottage of an old woman and a girl who is subject to mysterious convulsions and appears to possess visionary powers. He passes a strangely restless night there. During the days that he spends with Oberlin's family in the pastor's absence, Lenz's religious and emotional torments become more intense again. He hears of a young girl who has died in another village, and he decides to go to the place in sackcloth and ashes. He prays over the corpse and implores God to revive the child by a miracle. When no miracle occurs he flees in terror. He is seized with a fit of blasphemous anger.

Oberlin returns from his trip and tries to restore Lenz's faith in Christ's redeeming love, but Lenz is convinced of his irreparable sinfulness and falls once again into the pattern of violent nighttime seizures and garbled discourses during the day. He attempts suicide. He wanders off, insisting that he be arrested as a murderer, and is brought back by two shopkeepers. His behavior, even in Oberlin's presence, becomes more and more irrational, and his speech becomes more and more fitful and incoherent. The attacks that he formerly suffered only at night now occur during the day as well. Lenz struggles with himself, complains that the silence of the valley is unbearably loud, seeks physical pain to deny the emptiness that he feels, and again throws himself into the street from an upstairs window. Finally even Oberlin's patient faith in a recovery is exhausted, and he has Lenz taken under close surveillance to Strasbourg for his eventual return to the care of friends in Germany. The account breaks off with a terse description of the momentarily subdued but empty man.

Themes and Meanings

The Lenz whose twenty or so days in the village of Waldsbach are depicted in this story interests Büchner in at least two ways: as a fellow literary artist and as an intensely sensitive fellow human being. His personal sufferings are clearly the more important of the two concerns. Although madness and art may go hand in hand, "Lenz" is not a very strong example of the artist-novella, for it does not speculate on the nature of artistic creativity or the social role of the artist. Even though Lenz holds forth on the subject of literature in his conversation with Kaufmann, his discourse stands in isolation and only recalls—somewhat poignantly—his earlier literary successes. It is part of the story's realism, not a true theoretical digression.

Lenz's humanity, the subject of greater interest for Büchner and his readers, has several facets. At the center of Lenz's story is his struggle with himself, the schizophrenia in which "he seemed to be split in two, with one part of him trying to save the other and calling out to itself." Self-destructive and self-preserving instincts conflict within him. At the level of the individual, Büchner is crucially concerned with this kind of derangement, one perhaps common to all humankind, but visible only in the intensified form called insanity.

Lenz turns to the hope that religious faith seems to offer him, but his faith, like his instincts, oscillates between visions of preservation and destruction, salvation and damnation. He imagines himself alternately as his own prophet-savior and as the sinner rejected by God. He tries to appropriate a religious faith like Oberlin's, but it becomes distorted and threatening in his mind. Lenz encounters the traditional, integral Protestant faith of the age before Europe's great revolutionary upheavals but as interpreted by the politically radical Büchner of the postrevolutionary 1830's.

Style and Technique

As noted above, the principal basis for the story was the account that Pastor Oberlin gave in his journal entries from January 20 to February 8, 1778. Büchner's version does not correspond strictly to Oberlin's inclusions and emphases by any means, although there are sections in which the pastor's careful observations are clearly reflected in the language of Büchner's text. Private journals and creative narrative are two different things, however, and the modernity of "Lenz" lies in its emergence from personal observations into a psychological portrait conceived as literature. In the twentieth century (which saw the first appreciation of Büchner), such psychological realism would not be considered unusual, but in 1839 it surely was.

The persuasiveness of Büchner's realism in "Lenz" owes much to his combination of narrative points of view, especially the alternation between the third-person narrative, in which Lenz's visible actions and audible words are recorded, and the indirect interior monologue, through which his states of mind are conveyed (a style of narration rarely exploited in German literature for another half-century). The latter mode especially does what no journal entry could, and it has a frightening power that marks "Lenz" as a revolutionary work. The hallucinatory visions of this tormented man are gigantic and violent, even cosmic in their size and force. Thus too, through the drastic imagery, language, and gesture for which the literature of Sturm und Drang was known in the 1770's, Büchner has re-created the mind of one of its chief exponents.

Michael Ritterson

THE LESSON

Author: Toni Cade Bambara (Miltona Mirkin Cade, 1939-1995)
Type of plot: Domestic realism
Time of plot: The 1970's
Locale: New York City
First published: 1972

Principal characters:
SYLVIA, an African American girl
SUGAR, her cousin and closest friend
MISS MOORE, an adult who helps neighborhood children

The Story

Sylvia, who narrates the story, is a young girl living in a poor area of New York City. She and her friends are developing their strategies to cope with life as they know it. She has adopted the pose of a know-it-all who can figure out things for herself, and she tells herself that she resents and has no use for Miss Moore, the college-educated African American woman who frequently serves as a guide and unofficial teacher for the local children.

Miss Moore arranges a trip for Sylvia, Sugar, and six other children to go to the F. A. O. Schwarz toy store at Fifth Avenue and Fifty-seventh Street. Miss Moore knows that this will be a new experience for the children, who have been isolated in their neighborhood, and that they will encounter items they have never seen, items that are far beyond their economic means. She wants the youngsters to learn that there is much more to the world than the slum area they know, and particularly for them to realize that wealth is unfairly and unequally distributed.

The emphasis on the relative value of money begins for Sylvia when Miss Moore gives her a five-dollar bill to pay the taxi fare to the store. Sylvia is told to include a 10 percent tip for the driver and return the change to Miss Moore. Sylvia gives the cab driver the fare of eighty-five cents but decides that she needs money more than he does and keeps not only the tip but the remainder of the money.

At the toy store, the children feel uneasy and out of place. Looking through the window, they are stunned by the products offered and by their high prices. Ronald sees what he recognizes as a microscope, for three hundred dollars, but neither he nor the others know what a microscope is used for or how it might fit their academic education or their future jobs. Rosie spots a chunk of glass with a price tag of $480. None of them knows what it is, even when Miss Moore says it is a paperweight. Only one of the children has a study area at home where she might have papers to scatter, so they do not understand the concept, much less why someone might want, or be able and willing to pay $480 for, a fancy glass paperweight. Another boy interrupts Miss Moore's explanations when he sees a toy sailboat priced at $1,195. The children cannot imagine who could spend so much money on the boat, especially because they think it would probably break or be stolen when they played with it. Even Sylvia is stunned at the price. She hesitates to go inside the store, feeling ashamed somehow, as though she does not belong here, despite her bravado that she can do anything she wants.

Inside, Sylvia becomes angry at the high prices. She wants to know who are these people who could spend a thousand dollars on toy sailboats and why she and her friends cannot. As Miss Moore takes the youngsters home, she asks them to think of what kind of society it is in which some people can spend more on a toy than others have to spend on food and housing. Sugar responds that it must not be much of a democracy because some people obviously do not have an equal opportunity to earn money. Sylvia feels Sugar has betrayed her by giving Miss Moore the satisfaction of an answer, and she walks away.

Sugar catches up with Sylvia, glad that they kept the rest of the money Miss Moore gave them for the taxi, and she suggests they spend it on sweets and potato chips. She starts to race Sylvia to the store, but Sylvia intends to go elsewhere in the city to think about what she has seen that day. Sugar and the others can do what they want, Sylvia concludes, "But ain't nobody gonna beat me at nuthin."

Themes and Meanings

Toni Cade Bambara does not specify what Sylvia plans to do with her newfound insight into social and economic inequality, but Sylvia is clearly angry and uneasy. Rather than spend the money on food treats as Sugar wants, Sylvia wants to ponder the lesson that she pretends not to learn, that disadvantaged groups need to think about the inequitable distribution of wealth in the United States. Sylvia knows that Miss Moore hopes that poor people will wake up and demand their fair share of economic resources, and Sylvia's vow at the end of the story suggests that she is determined eventually to have more money than is typical of the adults in her slum neighborhood.

Style and Technique

The theme of the story is reinforced by several aspects of style that make it delightful instead of didactic or preachy, despite the fact that its central message calls for a revolution in attitudes and actions by both individuals and social institutions. Because the story focuses on the children, readers see how social and economic disadvantages are perpetuated and have lasting effects on future generations. Most important is the use of Sylvia as the narrator, because of her attitudes and her language. Sylvia has developed a smart-aleck, tough, self-centered stance to survive in the slum area. She is quick to think up or be involved with mischief, such as the time she accepts a dare to run into a Catholic church and do a tap dance at the altar. When she enters the church, however, with "everything so hushed and holy and the candles and the bowin and the handkerchiefs on all the drooping heads," she cannot go through with the plan. She has a sense of rightness, which she believes she is above or does not need, but her sense of decency and fairness is a major part of her character. Although she initially brags that she is keeping the money from the taxi fare, by the end of the story she is not eager to go with Sugar to spend it. The fact that Miss Moore does not ask Sylvia for the change suggests that Miss Moore trusts that what Sylvia is learning is more important than a few dollars.

The most noticeable and significant aspect of style in "The Lesson" is its use of language. Sylvia's speech patterns are lively and colorful, such as her comment when Miss Moore suggests she check the cost of a real yacht, that such an assignment "really pains my ass." Her way of talking is realistic for someone who lives where she does. Her slang and wit show her to be a bright, observant, believable, and interesting character, someone the reader can like and care about. By the end of the story, it is clear that Sylvia is realizing that there is more to the world than her neighborhood, and that she will have to develop new knowledge and new strategies for dealing with that world, including, probably, learning more formal patterns of English used by people outside her immediate environment.

Lois A. Marchino

THE LESSON OF THE MASTER

Author: Henry James (1843-1916)
Type of plot: Social realism
Time of plot: The 1880's
Locale: London, English countryside near London, and Switzerland
First published: 1888

Principal characters:
 PAUL OVERT, the protagonist, a young novelist
 HENRY ST. GEORGE, the Master, a famous, elderly novelist
 MRS. ST. GEORGE, his first wife
 MARIAN FANCOURT, love interest of Overt and the second wife of
  St. George
 GENERAL FANCOURT, Marian's father

The Story

Henry James's "The Lesson of the Master" focuses on Paul Overt, a young novelist with three or four novels to his credit, who is caught up in the dilemma of choosing the time-absorbing business of living or the isolation of art. Henry St. George, whose reputation as an artist remains high though his later work is inferior, is the master of the title, with Overt his pupil.

The tale begins with Overt arriving at Summersoft, an old country house near London, to find, to his delight, that St. George, whose early works played an important part in forming Overt as a novelist, is a member of the party. Before meeting St. George and within minutes after meeting Mrs. St. George, Overt determines that the cause of the decline of St. George's work is without doubt Mrs. St. George. She is, in his opinion, more suitable a wife for a keeper of books than for a literary master.

St. George joins the party but is preoccupied with the beautiful young Marian Fancourt, who has recently arrived in England from India and is very fond of literature and writers. From Marian, Overt learns all that he can about St. George. He tells her that if he were to be brought together with his idol he would be prostrate.

Prostrate is what Overt is when St. George expresses admiration for his work and special esteem for Overt's latest novel, *Ginistrella*. St. George advises Overt to learn from the example of the failure of his later works and not let his old age become a "deplorable illustration of the worship of false gods." The false gods are, in St. George's view, all that is associated with having an active social life, "the idols of the market—money and luxury and 'the world,' placing one's children and dressing one's wife—everything that drives one to the short and easy way."

Back in London, Overt is tempted by one of St. George's false gods in the form of Marian Fancourt. As Overt and Marian's relationship becomes serious, St. George sends for Overt to come to him. St. George says that his life is that of the successful charlatan who, having everything for personal happiness, has missed the real thing. He has missed "the sense of having done the best—the sense, which is the real life of the artist and the absence of which is his death, of having drawn from his intellectual instrument the finest music that nature has hidden in it, of having played it as it should be played." The master's confession of his mistake and his desire to save Overt from making the same one overwhelm the younger man, and he agrees to give up Marian and all pursuit of personal happiness.

The converted Overt exiles himself to Switzerland, where he learns from Marian by letter that St. George's wife is dead. When Overt writes in sympathy to St. George, he receives a bewildering reply: Earlier St. George had told Overt not to marry, but now he writes that he would not be at the head of his profession if it had not been for his wife. All that St. George has advocated seems a bad joke, and Overt thinks of returning to London, giving up his ambitions; instead, however, he recommits himself to his art.

After two years in Switzerland, Overt returns to London, where he is told by Marian's father that St. George is engaged to marry Marian. Overt feels betrayed and confronts St. George, who assures him that he was always sincere; the knowledge that he is saving Overt as an artist adds greatly to the pleasure of marrying Marian. He also informs Overt that he is through as an artist and will not write again.

Later in the year, Overt's new book is published and considered "really magnificent" by the St. Georges; the narrator of the tale adds that Overt is "doing his best but . . . it is too soon to say." The narrator goes on to say that the proof that Overt is dedicated to his art and not to personal happiness is that he would be the first to appreciate a new work by St. George should there be one.

Themes and Meanings

James wrote many times, as he does here, about the relationship of the artist to the social world and the conflicting obligations of life and art. "The Lesson of the Master" is one of the stories that James wrote during his middle years about the artist's relationship to the world. James struggled for three decades with the theme, from "Benvolio" (1875) to "The Great Good Place" (1900).

The conflict between life and art was central to James's own experience, as is clear in Leon Edel's five-volume biography *Henry James* (1953-1972). James himself chose a life wholly dedicated to his art, the life that St. George advocates and Overt comes to live.

The other characters in the tale seem intended only to bring Overt to terms with the realization that art is the only life for him. However, James's treatment of this decision is not unambiguous: The reader is not sure if James agrees entirely with St. George's lesson, Overt's decision, or the narrative voice when it says, "St. George was essentially right and . . . Nature dedicated him [Overt] to intellectual, not to personal passion."

Style and Technique

"The Lesson of the Master" is told in the characteristic manner of James's middle years, without the notorious complexity of his late style. The sentences are relatively short, and the plot, on the surface, is easy to follow. However, nothing is straightforward in James. Indeed, the tale is steeped in irony and ambiguity; one might apply a statement that Overt makes about St. George's work to James and this tale: "For one who looks at it from the artistic point of view it contains a bottomless ambiguity."

The point of view is that of a third-person, omniscient narrator who concentrates on Overt's thoughts and actions. The use of the narrator allows James to explore the relationship between the artist and an active social life without passing judgment on any of the primary or secondary characters. This technique alone casts a shadow of ambiguity over every aspect of the tale.

The plot is ironic and ambiguous in that St. George tells Overt not to marry Marian because it is clear that his decline is attributed to his marriage; then St. George, on the death of his first wife, marries Marian himself. The twist is that although St. George seems to have betrayed Overt, he has, in effect, sealed Overt's future. Point of view is all-important here; it is not the events themselves that are important but how they are perceived.

Brenda B. Adams

LET THE OLD DEAD MAKE ROOM FOR
THE YOUNG DEAD

Author: Milan Kundera (1929-   )
Type of plot: Psychological
Time of plot: Probably the mid-twentieth century
Locale: Czechoslovakia
First published: "At ustoupí starí mrtví mladým mrtvým," 1969 (English translation, 1974)

> *Principal characters:*
> AN UNNAMED MAN, thirty-five years old
> AN UNNAMED WOMAN, a widow in her mid-fifties

The Story

An unnamed divorced man, thirty-five years of age and handsome, is resigned to his rather dull lot in life but becomes depressed on noticing a bald spot developing on the top of his head. This sign of approaching old age causes him to think about his accomplishments in life. He concludes that he has experienced little, especially in relation to women, who—he believes—provide the only true fulfillment in life.

As he is walking home from work one day, oblivious to his surroundings, he almost passes by a former lover. The woman, however, recognizes the man immediately. Both are pleased by the chance meeting and go to his apartment, avoiding the overcrowded cafés, to wait until it is time for her to catch the train back to Prague. As he prepares coffee, he decides that fate has played a trick on him by bringing this woman, with whom he was once madly in love, back into his life now that he is middle-aged.

The woman was beautiful in her youth. Although fifteen years older than when she last saw him, she is still attractive and still places tremendous value on physical beauty. Just as some find utmost importance in moral law, so she finds importance in beauty. To confirm her beauty when she was younger, she had extramarital affairs but was careful not to let them turn into ugly habits. One of these affairs was with the man she is now visiting.

She has returned to the small Czech town to renew the lease on her husband's grave, only to discover that the lease has been canceled and someone else's marker is where her husband's used to be. The cemetery administrator's only comment was "the old dead ought to make room for the young dead." She tells her host none of this, however, but bombards him with questions in an effort to keep him from noticing how much she has aged.

Nevertheless, he notices her wrinkled face, withered neck, and manlike hands marked by blue veins. The pity he feels for her makes him feel closer to her. He launches into a long, melancholy monologue, filled with maxims about the shortness of life, which he thinks about because of his bald spot. Although he expects her to empathize, she states she does not like such shallow talk. Discussions of aging and death evoke for her disturbing, unattractive images.

Ironically, the woman argues with the man's ideas by stating that one's body is not as important as one's work. She suggests that everyone leaves something behind, a sort of memorial. She mentions her own work and her son. She is happy to give her son everything she can and then slowly disappear from his life. Although she does not say it aloud, she thinks about how her son is pushing her toward her grave by insisting that she give up everything in herself that suggests youth, especially her sexuality; he can only love a mother who is old. She also feels anxious about admitting to her son that she has let the lease on his father's grave expire.

Finding the woman's ideas as shallow as she found his, the man suddenly strokes her hand and begins detailing for her their one night together. He was twenty, shy, clumsy, and inexperienced; she was almost forty and very patient. At that time, the man had vainly tried to imagine how the woman's face would look distorted by ecstasy. When they made love, however, the light was off, and he was too shy to get up to turn it on; therefore, he could see only shadows. Not only could he not see her clearly, but he also could not hear what she was whispering, even when he drew her to him. For the last fifteen years, he has considered her the woman who eluded him. He asks her, but she cannot remember why she never saw him again after that night. Both decide the present is more important.

The man now longs to see what he missed fifteen years ago. He pulls her to him and caresses her, and she responds, elated to discover that she has retained her ability to feel passion. The man notices that her body is extremely soft because her muscles have become flabby. He also remembers, from fifteen years ago, that the woman had some teeth missing, but now she is missing none. Although he finds these changes unappealing, he manages to ignore them to some extent.

When he tries to kiss her, she suddenly freezes, realizing that he will feel the denture in her mouth. She tells him that she is older now, that he will be disgusted if they make love, that the beautiful memory he has of her will be destroyed. He argues that she is still beautiful, that he will not be disgusted; even though he knows he will be disgusted, he is still filled with desire.

As she continues fighting him, she remembers the cemetery administrator's comment. She visualizes her son's reaction when she tells him that memorials are worth nothing compared to life. She concludes that memorials are outside oneself, and therefore make no difference in life. She confirms the man's statement that it is silly to fight him, and begins to undress.

Themes and Meanings

In "Let the Old Dead Make Room for the Young Dead," Milan Kundera examines the separation of body and soul. This is evident in the thoughts and actions of the two characters. The woman has aged considerably since she last saw the man; however, he recognizes her by a certain quality in her gentle smile that was familiar and attractive to him before. The same phenomenon occurs in his apartment when she waves her hand to refuse the alcohol her host offers: The man realizes that the grace and charm that filled him with love for her before still exists in her, even though it is covered by layers of age.

After considering the idea that "the old dead ought to make room for the young dead," the woman realizes that even though monuments disappear, nothing changes. Her husband's monument is gone, but he is no less dead nor has his existence been erased. If she makes love with her host, she knows he will be disgusted by her aged body and therefore his memorial to her—his fifteen-year-old memory—will crumble. She, however, will be unchanged by this crumbling because it is not part of who she is, of the young woman who still lives inside her old body. Similarly, the man knows that the physical act of making love to the woman will be unpleasant. Nevertheless, subconsciously he wants the unpleasantness because it will prove that all of his perceived missed opportunities would have been meaningless encounters resulting in no change in his personality or perspective. Through these characters, the reader sees that the body ages, memorials are lost, but the soul is indomitable.

Style and Technique

Many of Kundera's works share the elements of humor and the intrusive narrative voice. In "Let the Old Dead Make Room for the Young Dead," the author creates humor with irony. The story appears to be a love story, but instead of the physical beauty one might expect in a love story, one sees flabby muscles, dentures, wrinkles, a withering neck, a scar, and a bald spot. This physical decay, however, encases the more youthful emotions of desire and strong will, pointing up the separation of body and soul.

The intrusive narrative voice is evident throughout the story as the author-narrator makes comments directly to the reader in parenthetical statements, using such words as "you," "we," and "let's." Critic Ann Stewart Caldwell argues that Kundera uses the device to achieve an "anti-poetic posture," the destruction of romantic illusions of reality. The intrusions close the gaps between what is real and what the characters believe to be real. In this story, the intrusive narrative voice reveals characters' thoughts, thus advancing the theme by showing the characters thinking through ideas about youth and age that result in permanent changes in their lives.

Wilma J. Shires

THE LIAR

Author: Tobias Wolff (1945-   )
Type of plot: Psychological
Time of plot: The 1950's
Locale: Northern California
First published: 1981

> *Principal characters:*
> JAMES, a sixteen-year-old boy who prefers to lie and exaggerate
> MARGARET, his mother, a strong, deeply religious woman
> HIS FATHER, an irritable and frightened man who dies
>   prematurely of cancer
> DR. MURPHY, the family physician and friend

The Story

"The Liar" of the title is the teenage James, whose morbid lies are a cause of concern to his mother. When she discovers that James has written a friend with the false news that she is suffering from a mysterious illness, she feels compelled to call on Dr. Murphy, her friend and the family physician, to help cure James of his tendency to invent things and embellish on reality. James at this point begins an inner, psychological journey triggered by his conversation with the doctor. He begins to remember various incidents in his past that will lead to memories of his father's death from cancer. This death is connected to the morbid lies James tells, but before he confronts his father's death, he recalls other episodes in his past, especially a visit to Yosemite Park, one of the defining moments of James's childhood.

His mother's strength of character is brought home most cogently to James during this episode. When a bear wanders into camp, it is his mother who successfully drives it off by shouting and throwing rocks. Although he admires her straightforward way of dealing with crisis, James realizes he is more indirect and eccentric when coping with stressful situations. James identifies this style and his morbid lies as allied with his father's neurotic temperament. Although his mother is active in the church and the community, James's irritable father will not take up causes or join groups, remaining home as if afraid of the outside world. However, even though he realizes his mother is a better family manager and the more loving parent, James feels he has much in common with his father. Returning to the Yosemite incident, he recalls that the rest of the children become angry with his father because he made them leave the camp and then had joked in a silly way about the bear on the way home. James, on the other hand, feels he was the only one to truly understand how frozen and frightened his father was at the campsite. James especially identifies with his father's use of word play as a way to cope with the fear and anxiety to which he feels both he and his father are especially prone.

Having faced these memories, James apologizes to his mother for writing lies to his friend. Soon afterward, at dinner, Dr. Murphy describes another patient of his as essentially dishonest, self-absorbed, and unlikable. These comments lead James to realize he does not want to be like Dr. Murphy's other patient. Later James enjoys listening to his mother sing and is especially impressed with the spirituality of her rendition of a hymn, "O Magnum Mysterium." When, at the end of the evening, he and his mother discuss one of his mother's difficult friends, James is impressed with her compassionate attitude and realizes that, unlike his own, her imagination is not simply morbid and fear-laden but able to imagine good possibilities. Before she even says the words, James knows she will tell him she loves him.

In an effort to encourage him to think more about other people, James's mother sends him to stay with his older brother, who lives in Los Angeles where he works helping the unfortunate. When the bus in which James is riding breaks down on the road during a terrible rainstorm, James returns to his old habit of lying. This time, however, his lie is beautiful and helpful rather than morbid—he soothes and fascinates the passengers by pretending he works helping Tibetan refugees. When, amid the rain and thunder, he invents his own imaginary version of the Tibetan language and begins singing in what he himself is convinced is somehow a holy and ancient language, the moment becomes a magical one that is helpful to the passengers and gives James's capacity for make-believe a higher and spiritual purpose.

Themes and Meanings

The most important theme of this story concerns James's identity as an inveterate liar and the metamorphosis of this identity into that of an imaginative storyteller very like the author himself. James's final lie, which, significantly, is uplifting rather than morbid, confirms his identity as an artist whose capacity for invention can contribute something to others. The final image of James singing something ancient and holy suggests that he has achieved an almost mystical transcendental state, beyond the fear and negativity he associates with his father.

Ironically, it is his capacity for make-believe that has allowed him to secure his true identity and destiny. As he tells his Tibetan story on the bus, he creates a community of listeners, affirming that his skill as a storyteller has a social function that serves to enhance the inner lives of others. As the bus seems to magically suggest a kind of cathedral, it is as if James enters a state of grace, a transformation that redeems him from his previous identity as a pathological liar.

As the magic of his inner life lifts him off the ordinary level of reality, the pessimism James associates with his father also seems to melt away. Although James continues to tell stories, in the end it is James's mother who has begun to shape the stories he tells. The spiritual and life-affirming story James tells on the bus suggests that his good-hearted mother has become his inspiration and that his cynical father's influence is fading. This aspect of the story connects to Tobias Wolff's own life, in that his father, known as "The Duke of Deception," was a notoriously unreliable con man, whereas his mother was a deeply religious and empathic woman whose strength kept the family together. As Wolff himself has suggested, all of his stories have an autobiographical core and refer on one level to his own personal life and struggles. This story can be interpreted as a portrait of Wolff himself as an emerging artist.

A final theme explores what happens when there is a death in the family. This story explores how family survivors deal with the death and loss of a loved one and how they summon up the resources to go on with their lives. For example, James's mother devotes herself to looking after her family and to creating its spiritual center after her husband dies. Similarly, James overcomes the grief and fear that threaten to overwhelm him in the wake of his father's death by using his own imaginative skills in a manner that emulates his mother's generous, confident, and life-affirming perspective.

Style and Technique

Using an unassuming and often humorous style, Wolff is often considered a "minimalist" writer because he eschews plot-driven stories with traditional beginnings, middles, and ends. Although he writes stories that seem to end before they reach closure or are arranged as a series of fragments, Wolff is not an experimental writer, preferring instead narratives that illuminate character and the behavior of people in believable and realistic settings. In "The Liar," Wolff places his psychological study of his major character in a context of credible, everyday family details.

This story is grounded in realistic detail, but one of its important aspects is its psychoanalytic structure. Soon after the narrative begins, it moves away from ordinary reality and operates in a way that suggests the therapeutic experience, with its emphasis on free association and memory. James's consciousness moves back in time and begins to operate in an associative way as he weaves together important memories involving the stark differences between his mother and his father. Through this inner journey, the reader comes to understand how James's family has acted on him emotionally and thereby is able to experience a deeper level of empathic identification with him.

Although this story is a realistic one, its ending builds to a mode of consciousness less mundane than magical. Wolff prepares the reader for this picture of James singing in a holy language by an earlier reference to his mother's singing the words *magnum mysterium*, meaning "great mystery" in Latin, an ancient language that is also associated with religious experience. The linking of the heretofore unmusical James to his mother's spiritual song encourages the reader to see James's lying not simply as dysfunctional but as a meaningful and mysterious linguistic activity. Although this story does not obviously culminate in the surprise ending of the traditional short story, this final, surprising turn of plot points to an inner world of fantasy and feeling that suggests dimensions to reality beyond the ordinary and the everyday.

Margaret Boe Birns

LIARS IN LOVE

Author: Richard Yates (1926-1992)
Type of plot: Domestic realism
Time of plot: 1953
Locale: London
First published: 1981

> *Principal characters:*
> WARREN MATTHEWS, an American Fulbright scholar in London
> CAROL, his wife
> CATHY, their two-year-old daughter
> JUDITH, Carol's aunt and the couple's landlady
> CHRISTINE PHILLIPS, a prostitute
> GRACE and
> ALFRED ARNOLD, Christine's landlords

The Story

Warren Matthews, an American Fulbright scholar, and his wife, Carol, move into a basement flat in London owned by Carol's aunt Judith. Carol soon finds she hates London, and the new living arrangements do nothing to cement an already crumbling marriage. She announces that she will return to New York with Cathy, their daughter. She will get an apartment and a secretarial job. She suggests that she and Warren use their months apart to think over the future of their relationship. The couple agree to tell Aunt Judith that Carol is returning to the United States because of an illness in her family. Warren offers no resistance to Carol's plans. After a party at Cathy's nursery school at which the child is given a cheap music box that plays "Happy Birthday," mother and child depart.

Warren is lonely. He cranks the music box backward, listening to its formless tune, then goes in search of female companionship. He recalls his reluctance as a soldier on furlough in 1945 to engage the services of the prostitutes who frequented Piccadilly Circus. He takes a bus to Piccadilly and makes a quick choice among the women there. He accompanies one, Christine, to her room in a house where she plies her trade while her six-month-old daughter sleeps. Warren enjoys the sex, and the following morning, he enjoys breakfast and casual conversation with Christine, another prostitute, and Grace and Alfred Arnold, who own the house. Christine invites Warren to stay, without charge, and he accepts. That night, during sex, each declares love for the other. Christine gets drunk and complains that everything she ever wanted was taken away from her. She tells an elaborate tale of a dashing American army officer who she claims fathered her baby but refused to provide support for her or the child when he returned to the United States.

Warren goes back to his flat, but he cannot get Christine out of his mind. He returns to her bed for several more nights, postponing his decision to rescind his avowal of love for fear of her wrath. When Christine begins to telephone his flat, he worries that Aunt Judith will discover his infidelity.

Christine tells Warren that Grace was once a Piccadilly girl, too. She was pregnant by one of her clients when Alfred married her. He took her off the streets and adopted her child. Christine's implication is clear to Warren, and he vows to prepare for an "orderly withdrawal" from the life of this "strange girl." He cannot seem to find the right time or approach, however, and continues to see Christine and the Arnolds.

Warren makes several half-hearted attempts to end the affair, but it is Christine who finally takes the initiative, telling him that she cannot see him because she must earn money. Later, when Warren calls at the Arnolds' home, Grace makes the excuse that Christine has gone to Scotland because of an illness in her family. It is the same lie that Carol used with Judith. Warren tells Grace he does not believe the excuse, and Christine calls him later to report that Alfred is angry because Warren called Grace a liar. Warren finds Alfred to apologize, only to learn that the man was never angry at all. Alfred warns against paying too much attention to what women say.

Back at Warren's flat, Judith overhears a telephone conversation between Christine and Warren. She admits to him that she has known all along that Carol's story about a family illness was untrue. Carol writes to Warren affirming her love and stating her desire to re-establish their marriage. As Warren packs to leave London and return to New York, he once more plays the music box backward, then he drops it in the trash.

Themes and Meanings

This story, like Richard Yates's other stories and novels, is a tale of loneliness, fatalism, and despair. Purposeless—lacking either comprehension of the present or vision for the future—Christine and Warren are like windup toys. They move randomly about their universe, bouncing off obstacles in unpredictable directions, only to encounter still new barriers they neither expected nor planned for. Warren is weak willed, exploitative, and self-absorbed. Although no admirable hero, he is no villain either. Rather, in Yates's world, Warren is a victim of not loneliness but the fear of loneliness, and Christine seeks only a security she has never known. Their actions are no more self-determined than those of automatons.

The theme of the story is prevarication in all its forms. Most of the characters lie most of the time about almost everything. Alfred's supposed citation for heroism in the war is actually a commendation from his enemy captors for being a cooperative and industrious prisoner of war. Christine lies to achieve the role of romantic motion pictures heroine that real life has denied her. Grace's image as a faithful wife and doting mother veils the truth of her streetwalking past.

Little in the way of genuine feeling occurs among the characters. They are less concerned about the substance of things than about appearances. Warren evaluates Christine as one might a mannequin: hair dyed, legs short, knees thick, but "all right," and "certainly young." Warren finds Christine's offer of free sex flattering not because he likes her but because the offer feels like a "triumph of masculinity." He even evaluates a potential rival for Carol's affections in New York by appearance. He asks her not what a new lover might do or be but what he might look like.

The story is not about emotion so much as about what happens in its absence. Warren, for all his initial rhapsodizing about Christine's face and form, ends up dismissing her as nothing more than a "dumb little London streetwalker, after all." The reader suspects that Carol's desire to reunite may arise more from her failure to find love and happiness in New York than from any genuine rekindling of affection for Warren. Although Yates never moralizes or judges, Christine alone emerges as a sympathetic character. She is sorely flawed, but she keeps her dignity and has the courage to fight for what she believes.

Yates's stories paint landscapes of detachment and despondency. That Warren and Christine can achieve such physical intimacy—yet remain separated from each other by a tangle of lies—is consistent with Yates's view of destiny. People do not understand what they do. They do not make choices. Lacking commitment to a goal or to a person, these characters blunder their way from one misery to another. Their lives are like the played-backward music box Warren eventually discards: cheap, meaningless, and worthless.

Style and Technique

Yates prided himself on capturing his characters in revealing secrets about themselves they would have preferred to keep. He achieves that in this story through his selection of vivid sensory images. For example, Carol's dislike for London is epitomized by the yellow, foul-smelling fog that seeps in through windows and stings eyes. Aunt Judith has a face as pink and fresh as a child's as she emerges from the shower in a billow of steam. Christine's room smells of cosmetics and urine, and her droopy cotton underpants strike Warren as "pitifully cheap."

The form of the story is consistent with Yates's fatalistic theme. There is action but no plot. The ups and downs are the rhythm of real life, with attractions waxing and waning and conflicts dissolving as quickly as they materialize. The plodding banality of the language matches the plodding banality of the character's lives. "Well, but wait a second. Listen a minute, OK? Because I really do want to tell you something," Christine says—wasting two lines of dialogue in the same way she has wasted years of her life. With equal ineptitude, the characters' lies are thinly told. They lack substance in language as they lack substance in fact. "Wouldn't it be better if we could sort of try to tell each other the truth?" Warren wonders. The phrase "could sort of try" divulges more about Warren than he would ever openly disclose.

The word "nice" is used repeatedly throughout the story. It is an appropriate word choice, as all who use it desire vaguely positive approval granted in the absence of any stringent criteria. Carol hates London because she rides the bus "for miles without seeing anything nice." Casual conversations with Aunt Judith are deemed "nice," a lie that hides the strain of their shared living arrangements. Yates reveals that "They both made frequent use of the word 'nice' all afternoon," as Christine and Warren kindle their affair.

The music box is the story's central metaphor. At best, it is a cheap and useless thing, neglected and forgotten by Carol and Cathy when they depart for the United States. Played backward, it symbolizes Warren's lack of direction. He is committed to nothing: neither work, nor family, nor illicit lover. At the story's end, Warren cranks it backward once more. Nothing has moved forward in his life, but Warren lacks the introspection needed to learn his lesson. He discards the toy just as he discards human relationships. Part of him, the reader suspects, is abandoned along with it.

Faith Hickman Brynie

THE LIBRARY OF BABEL

Author: Jorge Luis Borges (1899-1986)
Type of plot: Fantasy
Time of plot: Unspecified
Locale: An imaginary library
First published: "La biblioteca de Babel," 1942 (English translation, 1962)

Principal character:
THE NARRATOR, unnamed

The Story

The setting of "The Library of Babel" is not only the story's most important characteristic, it is, in a way, everything. Much of the narrative consists of descriptions of an imaginary library that is so large that no one has seen the top, bottom, or end of it. It is so old that the recorded history of its librarians stretches back for many centuries and still one cannot account for the library itself or for its architects. It houses so many books that the most accepted explanation for its collection is that it contains all possible books; that is, it contains all the infinite variations on every book whose pages could be generated by random strings of letters, words, or phrases without duplication. The narrator of the story asserts that, "like all men of the Library," he traveled in his youth, journeying from cubicle to cubicle searching for a book or "a catalogue of catalogues" that might explain where he was and why he was there. He anticipates dying without finding that knowledge, only "a few leagues from" the bookshelves by "which I was born." "Once dead there will not lack pious hands to hurl me over the central banister of the vast building," he claims; "my sepulchre shall be the unfathomable air. . . . My body will sink lengthily and will corrupt and dissolve in the wind engendered by the fall, which is infinite."

The story turns on the narrator's and the librarians' attempts to make sense of the infinite building in which they find themselves, a building that has been neatly divided into hexagonal rooms that open on to one another while surrounding a grand central staircase. Generations are born and die within these rooms without understanding the mysteries of their universe or their place in it. Apparently, an increasing number seem to resolve such questions by committing suicide.

The theories that others concoct to explain their situation are like the theories men have traditionally concocted to fathom their own sense of the infinitude of the world. Some believe it their duty to eliminate useless books, books filled with nonsense syllables or unknown languages. Others believe that it is useless to read or write or study in such an environment. Knowledge, they claim, will be more likely produced by chance. They roll dice. Some believe in the superstition of "the Man of the Book." They argue that because there must be some one book on some one shelf somewhere that is the "perfect compendium to all the rest," at least one person must have read it.

Such a librarian, they hope, has found the knowledge that would make him "analogous to a god." They search for him. Others search for books that foretell their own futures. The librarians spend their lives looking for such volumes, never knowing whether they have found a meaningful fiction or an absolute fact.

The history of their theories, discoveries, and disappointments, as summarized and evaluated by the narrator, moves the plot along. Like many of Jorge Luis Borges's narrators, however, this one claims that no one theory seems persuasively better than the others. The story ends without accounting for the mysteries it has raised, the narrator himself claiming to have settled on his own solution to the nature of his universe: The library is "limitless and periodic." The same volumes repeat themselves "in the same disorder (which repeated, would constitute an order: Order itself). My solitude rejoices in this elegant hope." However, his hope is a purely personal one. When confronted with a world too big and too complex to explain, men must settle on an idea that satisfies their own personal natures and that plausibly explains what data they have. In "The Library of Babel," this seems to be the closest the inhabitants will come to achieving absolute truth.

Themes and Meanings

Most stories by Borges do not "mean" something in the sense that this word is usually used. The narrator of "The Library of Babel" reminds his readers that even the word "library," which to him means "ubiquitous and everlasting system of hexagonal galleries," also means many other things in many other languages. It can mean "bread" or "pyramid" or "almost anything else." "You who read me," he addresses his audience directly, "are you sure you understand my language?" With such warnings, it is often foolhardy to close too quickly on one explanation of a Borges story and claim that it "means" one thing. He conceives of his stories more playfully and, often, more seriously than the quick application of a "meaning" would allow. "The Library of Babel" summarizes many different solutions to one intellectual puzzle: How do small, autonomous, and thinking men coexist with a world that is unimaginably large and complex? Where is their significance in such a world?

Although "The Library of Babel" clearly raises this question, it does not clearly resolve it. The story offers not one but a variety of hypothetical answers. Borges's theme seemingly has more to do with how all men address such problems than with recommending one or the other of their solutions as the correct idea or meaning. He explores the variety of ways in which men grapple with understanding themselves and their world, fascinated by the "fiction" they are forced to create to survive. If the story does not have simply one meaning, it does, like many of his narratives, resonate on different levels of associations. It places imaginary characters in a fictive world as large and as mysterious as the world usually posited by twentieth century science, and it provides a structure or a pattern that can be used to apprehend both the marvels of modern astrophysics and the troubling psychological problems that contemporary cosmology often raises. Like many of Borges's stories, this one duplicates the familiar in an unfamiliar way, playing tricks with readers' normal or expected patterns of perceptions to expand their frames of reference so that the familiar is seen in an unexpected, but more comprehensive way.

Style and Technique

"The Library of Babel" is typical of Borges's style. It has little plot, little characterization, and little conflict. It presents, rather, an intellectual challenge or puzzle to the reader. Borges often aims at getting his readers curious about a novel idea and then urging them to reevaluate their own experiences and conceptions with a fresh new perspective. Frequently, he avoids complex characterizations and plots to put more emphasis on these new ideas, moving his stories along with a prose style borrowed from the essay form. He takes his bizarre ideas and then underplays them with a spare, matter-of-fact style that makes them seem more plausible. Like many of his stories, "The Library of Babel" has a mock scholarly tone that belies its sensational and fantastic conceptions. The narrator uses a calm, dispassionate voice, which is dry, but occasionally witty. Such a tone creates the impression of a monograph hidden in some obscure scholarly journal. The narrator summarizes the second axiom of what is known about the library, saying "the number of orthographic symbols is twenty-five. . . . This bit of evidence permitted the formulation, three hundred years ago, of a general theory of the Library." The passage even includes a mock footnote that purports to theorize about why precisely twenty-five letters were enough to form all the different words in the library's infinite collection of books.

This essay style, stripped of vivid description and running commentaries about the interior states of characters' minds, lets Borges cover a wide range of ideas quickly. It also jostles many readers' prior experiences with reading literature: Most readers do not anticipate that fiction will be presented as fact.

Philip Woodard

LIFE IN THE AIR OCEAN

Author: Sylvia Foley
Type of plot: Psychological
Time of plot: 1955
Locale: Carville, Tennessee
First published: 1999

> *Principal characters:*
> IRIS MOWRY, a twenty-eight-year-old woman who has recently
> given birth to a daughter
> DANIEL MOWRY, her husband, a refrigeration engineer who plans
> to move with his family to South America
> RUTH, their daughter

The Story

Iris Mowry spends her days sitting on the edge of the roof of her home drinking wine and keeping an eye on her newborn daughter, Ruth, in a carriage below. Her husband, Daniel, a refrigeration engineer, was once in the military and stationed at the nearby missile base. Now, he occupies himself with building the cellar in their home in his free time and with thoughts of moving to Colombia, where his expertise in refrigeration would be well received. Meanwhile, Iris drifts in an emotional and spiritual limbo, preoccupied with the birds that represent to her flight and freedom and with the meat that she has purchased at the local supermarket and packed into the baby's carriage. When she presses the meat with her finger, it turns gray. The image stays with her all day as she sits on the roof drinking wine. It returns to her thoughts along with strains of Mexican music and thoughts of going to Colombia. When Daniel comes home from work, she realizes that he now has gray teeth and is gray on the inside, like the meat. He tries coaxing her from the rooftop, but she leaps onto the lawn below, breaking her arm.

Relaxing beside the pool at a neighbor's home a few days later, her arm now in a cast, Iris continues to be preoccupied with thoughts of helplessness, aimlessness, and failure. She leaves her baby with her neighbor and goes to return some overdue books to the library. Finding herself beside the tar pits that lie at the edge of her neighborhood, she is overcome with dark thoughts; bubbles rising to the surface remind her of little mouths trying to suck in air. On an impulse, she throws the library books into the tar pits, one of them the volume of the *Book of Knowledge* that contains an entry on Colombia. As she peers into the black tar pit, she seems to see the medical team that aided her when she leaped from the roof, only now it is rushing past her to another emergency.

Themes and Meanings

This brief glimpse into the life of a new mother is a study in pessimism that borders on despair. Iris once dreamed of being a medical doctor, but now she cannot even nurse her new baby without pain, and the meat that she buys at the supermarket and that she craves also disgusts her, reminding her of the way flesh turns gray and rots. The passion her husband once had for flight when he was in rocketry has turned to a preoccupation with refrigeration and moving to Colombia; his passion for her has chilled, too, and he is no longer interested in her or the baby. His blustering authority masks a feckless mediocrity. To Iris, even his eyes look like marble.

When she was younger and in love and Daniel was in rocketry, she felt the romance of imaginary flight. Now, she can only envy the birds, imagining that they can fly into the stratosphere, above the air ocean; by contrast, humans live under this ocean like bottom feeders, incapable of soaring like the birds. For Iris, flight symbolizes freedom from responsibility, motherhood, supermarket shopping, listening to the dismal dreams of her gray husband, and reading books that no longer inform or inspire, that only become overdue and burdensome. Dangling her feet from the roof of her house is as close as she can come to flight. She escapes by drinking wine on her rooftop and watching birds fly, and she maintains a tenuous hold on her responsibility as a mother by keeping an eye on her baby daughter in a carriage parked under the roof. The supermarket meat alternately attracts and repels her. It is the flesh of her mortal self, that which bleeds, grows gray, and ultimately dies; yet it sustains life and is life. Her leap from the rooftop is a foolish attempt to float above the earth, to regain the freedom and joy of living she once had. Her fingers fluttering at the end of her new cast remind her of birds, and she imagines cutting the strings that hold them so that they can fly above the air ocean like the birds.

The tar pits symbolize the primordial bog out of which humanity rose into the air, but Iris has come to feel that all humans live at the bottom of the tar pits, where darkness prevails. Throwing the *Book of Knowledge* into this oozing pit symbolizes her giving up her faith in knowledge and expresses her attitude toward her husband's dream of going to Colombia. Leaving the baby with a neighbor hints at a rejection of motherhood as well as the extent of her despair. In the end, peering into the blackness of the tar pit, she retreats into her imagination. Her actual life is lifeless and depleted of passion and flight; yet her imaginary life is undergoing an emergency, too. Iris is brought to the edge of a tar pit and to the edge of her own ability to survive.

Style and Technique

Sylvia Foley heightens Iris's psychological state by focusing on details in the environment that reflect the new mother's mental state, such as black crows, the blue stamps on library books, and her neighbor's gold rings flashing in a mirror. Her world comes to her in fragmentary details, shards of significance that reflect her own sense of hopelessness and disconnection from Daniel, her baby, and ultimately her environment. For example, an overlooked package of meat in the carriage next to her daughter Ruth makes it appear to Iris that the child and the pork loin are the same. Iris imagines that Daniel's flesh would turn gray like the meat if it were pressed. She becomes disconnected even from herself, drifting into a wine-induced haze, seeing her hands as birds, and feeling her feet float away. When she beckons Daniel to join her on the rooftop, his response is to ask whether she has lost her mind. In return, her vision sharpens, and she sees only his gray teeth and pervasive grayness.

Her maternal instinct also blurs. As Ruth gnaws on the package of pork loin forgotten in the carriage, Iris appears unconcerned and focuses on the child's bubbled lips, providing an image, and connection, that returns at the end when the bubbles in the tar pit looked like little mouths. Paradoxically, the blurred distinctions reflect Iris's increasing disconnection as well as her mental deterioration and emotional withdrawal from her husband and child. A wall disappears at one point, and another time her thighs go to sleep as they dangle from the rooftop.

At the edge of the tar pit, Iris is overwhelmed by a feeling of hopelessness that up to this point has been reflected in the images of meat, metal, and the flight of birds. The tar pit symbolizes the way she sees the world at this point in her life. She is on the brink of darkness, and when she looks into it for some kind of direction or help, she sees only an emergency medical team rushing by. The tar pit signifies not only mental darkness but Iris's sense that she is physically hampered by circumstance: Her baby daughter offers no emotional pleasure or fulfillment, and her husband dreams only of moving to Colombia and ceaselessly fiddles with his mechanical devices. Her dream of becoming a doctor has drowned in the obligations and meaningless chores that thicken the air about her, preventing flight.

By relating the events of the story in the past tense and from the third-person point of view, Foley deliberately maintains a distance between Iris and the reader, who is led to see Iris's plight with little emotional involvement. Foley's matter-of-fact tone flattens Iris's own emotions and reinforces the impression of emotionlessness. Foley allows Iris very little display of motherly love; at least, none is recognized in her behavior and in the contents of her mind, where everything seems uniformly significant: the flash of a gold ring, the grass, a black bird. Iris at times seems to be sleepwalking, and Foley underscores this impression by focusing on blurred distinctions, disconnected details, and rambling thoughts, minimizing emotional expression. The reader's own feelings thereby become a correlative of Iris's dissipated, enfeebled, and vapid existence.

Bernard E. Morris

LIFE IN THE IRON MILLS

Author: Rebecca Harding Davis (1831-1910)
Type of plot: Social realism
Time of plot: The late 1850's
Locale: American industrial city
First published: 1861

Principal characters:

HUGH WOLFE, a tubercular immigrant ironworker who sculpts
DEBORAH WOLFE, his cousin, a cotton mill worker
FIVE OR SIX AFFLUENT MEN, visitors to the ironworks
A QUAKER WOMAN, Deborah's spiritual guide

The Story

A first-person narrator relates the story of ironworker Hugh Wolfe to an auditor. The narrator lives in a house whose two cellar rooms thirty years earlier had been home to the Wolfe family—Hugh, his father, and his cousin Deborah.

Deborah returns home after a twelve-hour shift at the cotton mill and prepares to eat a supper of cold boiled potatoes. She learns that Hugh is still working, and she gathers bread, salt pork, and her share of ale to take to him, walking through hellish scenes of smoke and flame at the iron mills to deliver his meal. Although Hugh is not hungry, he eats to please Deborah. Taking pity on her, he suggests that she sleep on the nearby ash heap. Deborah loves Hugh but also acknowledges that he is repulsed by her hunchback. An outsider among the ironworkers, the artistic Hugh feels compelled to create; his passion prompts him to sculpt. .

Before the midnight shutdown, a group of affluent men survey the ironworks, discussing the heat and the rough-looking workers. Attracted to the promise of the visitors' lives, Hugh draws closer to them but realizes that the gulf between him and them can never be breached. The visitors see a large sculpture of a woman, carved from what the workers call korl, the material that remains after the iron ore is smelted. At first, the visitors mistake the sculpture for a real woman and soon are captivated by the work's poignant power. They call Hugh over to ask what emotion he intended to portray with the sculpture. He replies that the figure is hungry not for meat, but for life. Although they acknowledge Hugh's potential greatness, none of the visitors respond when he asks for help. One suggests that Hugh can make of himself anything he chooses.

After fetching the visitors' coach driver, Hugh understands the squalid reality of his life. Despairing, he returns to the cellar with Deborah, who confesses that she picked one of the men's pockets. Although Hugh initially intends to return the money, as he wanders the streets in search of the man, he begins to envision the possibilities of a different life offered by the stolen money. For the first time in his life, he becomes aware of the power of money and yearns for the freedom to create. Unaffected by a sermon he happens on, Hugh yields to temptation. He is eventually arrested, convicted of grand larceny, and sentenced to nineteen years in prison. Also prosecuted, Deborah receives a three-year term.

Having begged to see Hugh in jail, Deborah tells him that she is responsible for their plight, but her actions were prompted by love. When she sees specks of blood on Hugh's clothes, she realizes that his tuberculosis has worsened and that he is seriously ill. She pleads with him not to die. Observing the contrast between his cell and the bustling marketplace below, Hugh ponders what his life might have been. He suddenly calls out to a passer-by on the street and slashes his veins with a piece of tin. Arms outstretched, Hugh feels stillness creeping over him, and he dies. A Quaker woman tends Hugh's body, promising Deborah that she will bury him in a pleasant place and vowing to guide the woman when she is released. After leaving the prison, Deborah lives a pure and loving life among the Friends.

At the close of his story, the narrator draws back a curtain, revealing the korl statue. The woman seems to hold out her arms as dawn breaks.

Themes and Meanings

Born into the upper middle class in the nineteenth century in the industrial city of Wheeling, Virginia, Rebecca Harding Davis witnessed huge influxes of immigrants and a corresponding rise in nativist movements. In "Life in the Iron Mills," Davis responded to these social conditions by excoriating affluent classes for the oppression of factory workers and confronting readers with the grim conditions endured by laborers who produced the materials that helped build the new nation.

Davis vividly illustrates class separation in antebellum America. Protections of the gentle life insulate the middle and upper classes from learning how immigrants live. Prosperous citizens live in separate areas of the city, communing with a nature unknown to laborers who are restricted to dank cellars and suffocating factories. The narrator repeatedly cajoles his auditor, and therefore the reader, to look at and digest the horrors. Even when they witness these realities, wealthy Americans cannot understand. The factory visitors, for example, exude a sense of superiority, embodying a well-deserved privilege. To them, the factory is a nightmarish inferno, and its workers are nothing more than brutes.

Davis contradicts notions that the United States welcomes newcomers and guarantees them limitless opportunity. The nation has long been described as a melting pot. By subjecting immigrants to a metaphoric smelting process, the United States purportedly removes Old World impurities, creating a finer metal. According to this model, men and women who possess ambition and drive will invariably prosper. Adherents to the American Dream are excused from any social obligation to help those in need because they are convinced that the poor have created their own miseries by falling short in their efforts to succeed. The factory visitors voice this philosophy; one proclaims that Hugh can make anything of himself. When Hugh asks for help, the men feel no responsibility for his condition and no need to provide assistance. As a result, the ironworker cannot succeed despite his remarkable talent and drive. Such portraits imply that the United States denies true justice to its people and that its wealthy citizens lack compassion.

People in nineteenth century America believed that capitalism was beneficial to all under the system, an idea that Davis negates. The workers labor almost ceaselessly, yet they barely survive. The overseer, a representative of industry, repeatedly calls the laborers "hands," reducing them to the only parts that matter to a system that devours its workers. Davis's indictment of capitalism is most apparent when Hugh sits in jail and observes a thriving marketplace below. The bustle of affluence contrasts sharply with the forced inactivity of his cell. Always excluded from the benefits of American commerce, Hugh is now literally barred from participating. His anguish over lost opportunities is compounded as he witnesses the tantalizing possibilities. Hugh's efforts to escape life in the iron mills have resulted in condemnation to a real cell, with his legs shackled. Davis argues that Hugh has been trapped by conditions beyond his control, within an economic system that benefits the affluent, not the workers.

In addition to offering didactic social commentary, Davis presents a timeless theme of wasted talents and thwarted lives. The korl sculpture, a symbol of artistic hunger and longing, reveals the intensity of human desire. She is an extension of her creator, imprisoned yet struggling to express inner feelings. Hugh's gifts reveal themselves despite his mean existence; his obvious talent increases the poignancy of his story as his efforts are squelched and his life is surrendered. The hunger and longing expressed in both the statue and in the portrayal of Hugh could also be found in aspiring female writers of the nineteenth century, such as Davis herself. These young women yearned to create, yet social convention often circumscribed their ambitions. Even when their families endorsed these women's passions, their subject matter and techniques were limited by cultural expectations. As a result, the established writing community openly ridiculed their efforts. In various private writings, Davis noted that she was among the few who flourished and lamented the suppression of others.

Style and Technique

Although "Life in the Iron Mills" predates the emergence of American realism, the story includes some of the features of realism, including a stark portrayal of urban existence. Davis portrays industrial America in vivid detail, beginning with grim descriptions of the smoke and stench dominating the mill town. The factories invoke images of hell. Furious engines clamor incessantly, producing fiery pools of metal. Workers, exhausted after twelve-hour shifts, return home to dark cellars, slimy with moss. Davis confronts readers with the dreary and demeaning realities of immigrant life, acknowledging the poverty, disease, and substance abuse.

Adopting a narrative structure reminiscent of Robert Browning's dramatic monologues, Davis frames Hugh's story with scenes of an affluent man talking to an auditor. Like Browning's poetry, readers not only learn about the people being discussed but also come to know the narrator and his auditor and to discern injustices implicit in urban America. The narrator acknowledges that he is separated from the immigrant world and insulated from the grime, but he points out possessions tainted by smoke and soot. Driven to share his knowledge, he offers insights that would otherwise never be acquired. Davis interrupts Hugh's story several times, returning to the narrator who challenges the auditor to enter the laborer's world, to dare to learn the truth.

Davis additionally suffuses the work with biblical allusions, surrounding Hugh with images of Christ-like suffering. When the factory visitors see the korl statue, they instinctively recognize its creator's genius but refuse to nurture that talent. One of the men openly states that he washes his hands of all social obligations, suggestive of Pontius Pilate's denial of responsibility for Christ. Although Christ withstood Satan's temptations in the wilderness, Hugh, a flawed human being, does not have the strength to reject temptation. His blood flowing and life ebbing, Hugh positions his body with his arms outstretched as if he is being crucified and his life sacrificed to an unjust system. When the Quaker woman tends his body, the scene conjures up images of Michelangelo's sculpture *La Pieta*, in which the Madonna holds Christ's head in her lap. Like the Madonna, the Quaker woman mourns the loss of human potential and life.

In this overwhelmingly dark piece, Davis nonetheless suggests that the future can hold promise. The korl statue has long waited behind the curtain, hidden from view, cordoned off from middle-class comfort. The narrator suggests that people can understand the reality of laborers' existence and that this knowledge can make a difference. He reveals the statue to his friend as the dawn breaks over the korl woman's face. Her yearnings could be fulfilled in a new day, and others like the Quaker woman can facilitate redemption through love, gentle understanding, and kindness.

Donna J. Barbie

LIFE-STORY

Author: John Barth (1930-   )
Type of plot: Absurdist
Time of plot: 1966
Locale: Anywhere in the United States
First published: 1968

> *Principal characters:*
> THE NARRATOR, an unnamed writer of stories and novels
> THE NARRATOR'S WIFE
> AN IMAGINARY MISTRESS, who may be real
> THE READER

The Story

The narrator of "Life-Story" says that his greatest desire is to be "unself-conscious" as a writer. The irony is that his every comment, including this initial one, points to exactly the opposite. He worries in an acutely conscious way, for example, that his story contains no "ground situation" (a coherent, trenchant plot and conflict), and he agonizes over a prose style that he fears is "fashionably solipsistic" and unoriginal. What is even more frustrating to the narrator is that his artistic impulses are directly contradictory; he prefers "straight-forward tales of adventure" to the "experimental, self-despising, or overtly metaphysical characters of Samuel Beckett's or Jorge Borges's," but he can muster only self-conscious, solipsistic stories in which the story's artistic processes are conspicuous and cumbersome—such as in the "theatre of absurdity, black humor or allegory." He thus prefers, like his wife and adolescent daughters, real life to literature, and he reads only for entertainment. He concludes that the medium in which he desires to write is "moribund if not already dead . . . along with society."

He even suggests that his increasing preoccupation or obsession with pattern and design for their own sakes is a manifestation of schizophrenia. Later, one of his literary characters, whom the reader can see is merely a replica of the narrator (a writer writing a story about a writer writing a story), worries that he can produce no stories of "passion and bravura action," detailing further the traditional elements of fiction that seem to elude him, such as "heroes they can admire, heroines they can love, memorable speeches, colorful accessory characters, and poetical language." At one point, the writer in the narrator's story asks gloomily, "Why must writers choose to write such stuff (self-conscious introspection) when life is so full of people and places and situations to write about?"

The narrator then begins to develop his proposition that his own life might be a fiction in which he is the leading character, whereupon he decides to write about just such a phenomenon. In a sense he makes this proposition come true by writing a story about a man writing a story about a man writing a story, ad infinitum, all of whose existences are indisputably fictional. Adding to his frustration, the narrator suspects not only that he is a fictional character but also that the fiction that he is in is the sort that he least prefers. Following this line of thought, one of the narrator's fictional narrator-authors, identified as "C," suggests that to get his story moving, he must expunge the writing of "overt and self-conscious discussion of the narrative process," which is exactly what the original narrator is doing, or rather, trying to do. The original narrator says that he would like to write a story leading to an exciting climax and denouement, if he could. He is, after all, dependent on his reader for his existence.

Following up the premise that his own life is a fiction like the ones that he detests, written by an author who might resemble himself, the narrator wonders if he could not appeal to his own author to change the tone and style of his boring and colorless tale to one in which "the outmoded virtues of courage, fidelity, tact, restraint, self-discipline, amiability, et cetera" would occur. He wonders too if he could not make his own life apart from the design of his author—"to achieve factuality" or at least to be a more positive hero, but he admits the futility of such a proposal. However, ironically, the narrator's mistress, real or imagined, shows her contempt for the dullness and passionlessness of her life with the narrator by withdrawing from his life—or story. He then confesses feelings of creative and sexual impotence—the very substance of his fiction. Only the need to move his story along—paying attention to the needs of the immediate sentence before him—keeps him going.

Additional problems occur when the narrator wonders whether the story he is in might be "a roman a clef," whether it might not be a film or theater piece rather than a novel, or whether, in fact, his story might not focus on someone other than himself—his wife, for example, or his daughter, or his mistress, or even the man who once cleaned his chimney. He speculates that his childhood might not even have been real—that the part of the story that he is in might be mere background, mere forced exposition. He concludes that at this advanced stage of his story, the absence of a ground situation means that his story is "dramatically meaningless." Is that, then, he inquires, the meaning of his life as well?

The narrator brings his story to a close by arguing that in a sense he is his own author and that therefore his life is in his own hands. The old analogy between Author and God, novel and world, has broken down. Reality and creative illusion are one. Rather than being bound to and directed by an omniscient Lord or Author, one's existence as author-character necessitates the authoring of one's own life-story. At this point, the narrator's "real wife and imaginary mistresses" enter his study unannounced and unsummoned by him, confirming the notion that people as fictional beings are free from an author's dictates.

Themes and Meanings

The major technical development in early twentieth century fiction was the artist's attempt to objectify his material—to get as much distance between himself and the work of art as possible, to refine himself out of existence, as James Joyce said. Henry James said that the author's voice should never be heard lest the illusion of real life be disturbed. However, in Barth's "Life-Story," the narrator intrudes himself conspicuously between the reader and the work of art, writing about the writing process itself. It is not verisimilitude but the very artificiality of fiction that Barth wishes to convey.

On the one hand, Barth's narrator appears to sympathize with the elements of traditional fiction and to eschew the artistic tendencies of postmodern literature. Getting inside the artistic consciousness of the narrator, one sees that his sense that traditional fiction has run its course prevents him from emulating the literary forms of his predecessors: the well-made novel with a bold story line and characters who are interesting and powerful. Instead, he writes just like those contemporary authors he supposedly dislikes, such as Samuel Beckett and Jorge Luis Borges. He has no use, he says, for the absurdist fiction of these writers—metaphysical, solipsistic, antiheroic, and radically experimental.

If not before, the narrator's sarcasm (Barth's, certainly) becomes clear when he aligns his literary tastes with those of his wife and adolescent daughters, who prefer sentimental romances and read, when at all, strictly for entertainment. He is making fun of such escapist, fraudulent drool and is drawn to fiction of the absurd because it represents the world that makes the most sense to him, a world without cause, direction, or coherence. He bodies forth the absurd in a story that is relatively plotless, fragmented, and incoherent—devoid of essential meaning or action—because these are the forms that most honestly portray his own life-story. Traditional artistic conventions would be contradictory to Barth's and his narrator's true vision. It is from this understanding that the narrator concludes that his story is "dramatically meaningless," and that the absence of a ground situation is in fact the proper ground situation of his tale. The meaninglessness becomes the drama—whether the narrator will kill himself in despair or find sufficient purpose in the act of creativity to continue his story, his life-story.

Herein lies the essential affirmation of a story that could easily be read as pessimistic. At the heart of the absurdist vision is the absence of an all-knowing, caring God whose design gives purpose and direction to existence. The narrator would seem to believe that without such a God to whom to appeal for assistance, his life is fated to be barren and insignificant. At best, the Creator is an Author like himself who is relatively helpless in controlling and directing his creation. However, if this is true—if the relationship of God to mankind is analogous to that of author to novel—then, just as the narrator's characters come and go as they please in his story, so he, too, may be free to direct—to author—his own existence. Life is a fictional narrative, a work-in-progress whose only meaning is that which the author-character has the courage and imagination to provide.

Style and Technique

As seen from the previous discussion of theme, it is impossible to discuss theme apart from style and technique in the case of absurdist fiction. The vehicle becomes the message. In short, the view that life is essentially meaningless and incoherent is dramatized by a plot, characters, and actions that embody that vision. There is no

gradually ascending series of events that leads to "an exciting climax and denouement," but there is instead a kind of interior monologue that seems to end where it begins, static or circular in its movement. Even the tone of the story is mechanical and
sterile, capturing the narrator's announced feelings of sexual and creative impotence.
The repetition of "et cetera" and the use of multiple narrators and stories within stories, all of which are replicas of the initial narrator and story, suggest life without variation, life that is dull, monotonous, and endlessly repetitious.

The essential technique of the story is the purposeful attack on traditional mimesis.
The narrator's cumbersome and painfully self-conscious manipulation of text focuses
the reader's attention on fiction as artifice, not as a reality fixed and determined by a
Supreme Creator. Similarly, by establishing parallels between life and art as similar
creative ventures, the narrator leads the reader to see, as he says, that "I'm an artifice,"
author of his own life-story. By addressing the reader at numerous points, the narrator
forces readers to become cocreators of his story, even further establishing the oneness
of life and fiction.

Lawrence Broer

THE LIFE YOU SAVE MAY BE YOUR OWN

Author: Flannery O'Connor (1925-1964)
Type of plot: Psychological
Time of plot: The mid-twentieth century
Locale: Rural southern United States
First published: 1953

Principal characters:

MRS. LUCYNELL CRATER, the toothless owner of a desolate, small
    plantation
LUCYNELL CRATER, her childlike daughter, nearly thirty years old
    and completely deaf
TOM SHIFTLET, a drifter

The Story

Tom Shiftlet, a drifter, wanders onto the farm of Lucynell Crater and her deaf, re-
tarded daughter, also named Lucynell. Mesmerized by the beauty of the sunset,
Shiftlet raises his arms to the sky, forming a crooked cross with his body, and holds
this saviorlike pose for nearly a minute before introducing himself. Mrs. Crater can
see from a distance that Shiftlet is a tramp and is not afraid of him. While the daughter
looks on innocently, Shiftlet and Mrs. Crater converse seriously. He asks her many
deep questions that she does not answer, such as "What is a man?" and makes procla-
mations such as "The world is almost rotten." During this entire philosophical conversation, Shiftlet cannot keep his eyes and thoughts off an old automobile parked in the
shed, which he would love to have; likewise, Mrs. Crater is sizing him up as a handy-
man for her farm and a potential son-in-law.

Shiftlet ingratiates himself, teaching Lucynell her first word, "bird," and performing fix-up duties, including repairing and painting the late Mr. Crater's automobile
and roofing the garden house. Mrs. Crater slyly offers Shiftlet the car, some money,
and a home if he will marry her daughter. In their first conversation, Shiftlet tells Mrs.
Crater that he would not marry unless he could find an innocent woman among all the
trash. Mrs. Crater points out that Lucynell, in her deaf, childlike state, is as innocent as
one can be. After haggling over such issues as how much money Mrs. Crater will give
him for a honeymoon, Shiftlet finally agrees when the old woman offers to buy the
paint for the car, which is now running. The three of them head to town the following
Saturday for the wedding. Shiftlet is left cranky and dissatisfied with the civil ceremony, although it is uncertain whether Lucynell has any idea what is taking place.
Mrs. Crater is pleased at the success of her plan to acquire a son-in-law to work
around the place but appears to have some misgivings saying good-bye to Lucynell as
she departs with Shiftlet for the two-day honeymoon.

The fact that he has acquired the coveted car fails to cheer Shiftlet as Lucynell picks the wooden cherries off her Panama hat and tosses them out the window as they drive to Mobile. Shiftlet abruptly leaves Lucynell at a roadside eating place called The Hot Spot, after she falls asleep waiting for her food. Seeing himself as an honorable man, Shiftlet pays for the food and instructs the counterboy to give it to her when she wakes up. Before Shiftlet leaves, the counterboy comments that the sleeping Lucynell "looks like an angel of Gawd."

Back on the road, and still depressed, Shiftlet picks up a young male hitchhiker, to whom he delivers a dramatic monologue about mothers, especially his own who, he says, was "an angel of Gawd." The young man only glares, suddenly tells Shiftlet to "go to the devil," and jumps out of the slowly moving car. Shiftlet feels like "the rottenness of the world was about to engulf him," and he asks God to "break forth and wash the slime from this earth!"

An ominous, turnip-shaped cloud, which matches the color of the hitchhiker's hat, appears before Shiftlet's car. There is a peal of thunder behind him and huge raindrops begin pelting the back of his car as he races toward Mobile.

Themes and Meanings

"The Life You Save May Be Your Own" was part of Flannery O'Connor's book *A Good Man Is Hard to Find* (1955), a collection that demonstrates her skill at using irony, violence, and the grotesque to create opportunities for redemption in the lives of characters who are often comical and always spiritually adrift in a realistic, yet highly symbolic world. O'Connor demonstrates humankind's need for the mysterious grace of God, a gift that is offered suddenly in ordinary settings. Violence is a means to wake up characters to their own moral deficiency, to burn away their virtues so that there is nothing left but a humbled self, standing in perfect readiness to accept redemption.

Shiftlet indeed becomes a savior to Mrs. Crater by fixing up her farm. He also unintentionally delivers a moment of grace to her when she seems to acknowledge her feelings for her daughter for the first time, as Shiftlet is about to drive away with her. She says tearfully, "I ain't ever been parted with her for two days before." It is too late for Mrs. Crater: In her ambition to acquire a son-in-law, she seals Lucynell's fate by marrying her off to Shiftlet.

Shiftlet's own spiritual redemption is still a possibility. Throughout much of the story, he seems harmless, amiable, cheerfully performing his tasks on the Crater farm; however, his preoccupation with the automobile makes it easy to guess at his ulterior motives. His need and potential for redemption is even greater than Mrs. Crater's. After the story was published, O'Connor herself described Shiftlet as a comic character, but still "of the Devil because nothing in him resists the Devil."

The hitchhiker's violent outburst shocks Shiftlet and renders him momentarily vulnerable, a device frequently used by O'Connor to demonstrate that a character is at a crucial moment and ready, if he or she chooses, to accept God's grace. Does Shiftlet really see the ominous, turnip-shaped cloud in front of him, which is surely a symbol for his moment of potential redemption? It is difficult to know Shiftlet's reaction because the story ends with him racing the storm to Mobile. All the reader knows is that Shiftlet has been offered a chance at self-recognition; he may choose to accept or reject it.

Style and Technique

The story is filled with irony and symbolism. Shiftlet's name is appropriate because he could certainly be considered shiftless or shifty. His saviorlike pose at the beginning of the story is surely symbolic, but the title, taken from a road sign that he later sees as he drives, suggests that Shiftlet should be concerned more for his own redemption than for being anyone else's savior.

O'Connor often uses peacocks as symbols of the unrecognized beauty and mystery of grace; it is thus significant that innocent Lucynell's eyes are described as "blue as a peacock's neck." The turnip-shaped cloud must also hold some significance: Turnips grow in the ground, conceivably among that slime of the earth with which Shiftlet is so obsessed. The fact that the cloud is exactly the color of the hitchhiker's hat emphasizes the hitchhiker's role as deliverer of Shiftlet's moment of grace.

When Shiftlet speaks to the hitchhiker about his mother, he uses the same phrase that the restaurant boy uses to describe Lucynell: "an angel of Gawd." Indeed, Shiftlet's next tearful comment about his mother, that "he took her from heaven and giver to me and I left her," could be describing exactly what has just taken place with Lucynell. Perhaps Shiftlet is becoming aware, if only slightly, of the weight of his transgression.

This story exemplifies O'Connor's gift for ironic humor and her ability to capture the natural speech patterns of the inhabitants of her South. Because of the humor in her stories, the violence seems unexpected and the reader is unprepared for it, the same way that O'Connor saw humankind as usually unprepared for the grace of God.

The final irony in "The Life You Save May Be Your Own" occurs after Shiftlet's prayerful outburst in the car. A few minutes later, large raindrops begin pelting his car. The ironic message for Shiftlet is that his own actions have made him exactly the kind of slime he wishes to have washed from the earth.

Bonnie Flaig

LIFEGUARD

Author: John Updike (1932-   )
Type of plot: Impressionistic
Time of plot: The early 1960's
Locale: An American beach
First published: 1961

> *Principal characters:*
> THE LIFEGUARD, the narrator and a seminarian
> THE CROWD AT THE BEACH

The Story

No action takes place in this short story, only the musings of a divinity student pondering the purpose of life while gazing on swimmers and sun worshipers at the beach. A summer lifeguard, he is proud of his tanned, "edible" body. Transformed from the pallid seminarian who for the past nine months has pored confusedly over "handbooks of liturgy and histories of dogma," he mounts his white wooden throne (with a red cross painted on the back) as though he were climbing into "a vestment."

There is no contradiction, the lifeguard asserts, between the desires of the spirit and those of the flesh. To shine in the sun is man's goal. Love is like the ministry, the lifeguard ruminates, like being rescued. Beauty is personified in the curvature of a nymph's spine, the "arabesque" between back and buttocks.

Sunday mornings on the beach depress the young lifeguard because so few people are in church. No longer do the masses have a palpable terror of the unknown; people "seek God in flowers and good deeds." The sea seems more a "misty old gentleman" than an ominous "divine metaphor." However, it has meaning for the lifeguard. In the water, he believes, "we struggle and thrash and drown; we succumb, even in despair, and float, and are saved."

The day unfolds like a backward cinema. First come the elderly, who "have lost the gift of sleep." The women smile and search for shells; their mates, whose "withered white legs" support "brazen barrel chests, absurdly potent," swim parallel to the shore at a depth "no greater than their height." Next come middle-aged couples burdened with "odious" children and aluminum chairs. Bored women gossip and smoke incessantly. Finally come young people, maidens and boys, infants in arms and toddlers "who gobble the sand like sugar" and "wade unafraid into the surf."

Assaying this immense "clot" swarming around him, the lifeguard believes them unworthy of redemption. They are "Protestantism's errant herd," a "plague" deserving of oblivion. He is different, both a seducer and a savior, capable of providing rapture and grace. Absurdly, he speculates whether women will be eternalized "as maiden, matron and crone" and "what will they do [in Paradise] without children to watch or gossip to exchange."

On Sunday afternoon, the lifeguard experiences an Edenic vision of the beach, cast back in time just prior to "the gesture that split the firmament." A revelation comes to him, a commandment to be joyful, to "romp; eat the froth; be children." Atop his station, alertly awaiting his calling, the lifeguard listens for a cry for help. So far, he has not heard one.

Themes and Meanings

Critics have hailed John Updike as a magician with words, but he has been criticized, perhaps unfairly, for shallowness of theme. Here, without frills, he tackles important issues. In this meditation, the central question is not "What happens?" but "What is felt?" As Arthur Mizener concluded about *Pigeon Feathers, and Other Stories* (1962), the collection that contains "Lifeguard," Updike's "fine verbal talent is no longer pirouetting, however gracefully, out of a simple delight in motion, but is beginning to serve his deepest insights." There are interesting similarities between "Lifeguard" and two other stories in this collection, "A&P" and the title story, "Pigeon Feathers." In the former, the fascination is with three girls, including one described as a queen. In the latter, the fascination is with death and immortality. Compared with "Lifeguard," the other two stories are more situational and the characters less passive. In "Pigeon Feathers," a fifteen-year-old shoots a half-dozen birds; in "A&P" a nineteen-year-old quits his job at the supermarket when his boss insults three barefoot female customers.

The lifeguard is fascinated not only with religion and sex but also with aging, not unlike Harry Angstrom in Updike's Rabbit trilogy and Piet Hanema in *Couples* (1968). As in many of the other short stories contained in *Pigeon Feathers, and Other Stories*, the Protestant ethic of individual responsibility is quite pronounced, and the lifeguard suffers spiritual tensions of a neo-Calvinist nature. Seeking atonement in an unfathomable world, he believes that expiation comes through love. He has studied "with burning eyes" the bewildering, terrifying attempts of theologians to "scourge God into being"—only to "sway appalled on the ladder of minus signs" by which others "would surmount the void."

Clearly, for the seminarian, the beach is a more palatable environment for celebrating life and seeking ontological assurance than dusty library shelves. The insight provided by the sea (and the crowd) is that "the tides of time have treacherous undercurrents." Although one should seek the joy of the moment, the current of life inevitably pulls toward death's horizon.

Turning the concept of original sin on its head, the lifeguard-seminarian's philosophy implies that human beings are never so innocent as at birth. Only children and eunuchs truly love, he quips; virtue is otherwise corrupted by an "encumbering biological armor." Like the characters in tawdry biblical films, "we are all Solomons lusting for Sheba's salvation." Withdrawal from the world is no solace, for "the stony chambers need jewels, furs, tints of cloth and flesh, even though, as in Samson's case, the temple comes tumbling."

The lifeguard's references to women, even from the perspective of the early 1960's, are hostile and condescending. Women are stereotyped as old crones, bored matrons, and sexy maidens whose function is to rear children and fulfill men. Although little is revealed about the lifeguard's past, the strong implication is that he is a lonely virgin casting envious eyes around him for a meaningful relationship.

Alone and somewhat alienated, the lifeguard pontificates about the "hollow heads" below him, but he is not a particularly somber fellow—more like a bored adolescent daydreaming during an interminable church service. His eyes are open, his mind alert, but despite his preparation and sacrifice, nobody needs him.

Thus, Updike ends on a note of ambiguity. Is the lifeguard heroic or merely pompous, a callow fool or a sincere pilgrim, worthy of grace or a deluded egotist? Is his summer raiment ludicrous or compatible with his spiritual yearnings? The enigma is distinctly existential, reminiscent of Søren Kierkegaard's concept of the crowd as collective anonymity. Against a blackened beach, the individual must set himself apart, venture forth from the shallow waters, and, risking everything, cry for help. That "unheard cry" is what haunts "Lifeguard."

Style and Technique

In contrast to some of the other stories in *Pigeon Feathers, and Other Stories*, this narrative essay is bereft of any real plot, action, or dialogue. The technique is well suited to Updike's tone and accentuates the protagonist's dualistic nature. The diction of the story runs the gamut from stilted and monastic to lusty and sensuous; some antiquated phrases (memento mori) suggest the pedantic seminarian, others the efficient healer armed with "splints, unguents and spirits of ammonia." Then there are phrases descriptive of his temporal side, as when he observes the "dimpled blonde in the bib and diapers of her Bikini, the lambent fuzz of her midriff shimmering like a cat's belly."

First published in *The New Yorker* magazine, "Lifeguard" is almost a parody of a sermon—sensitive and urbane, short and bittersweet, a parable about balancing piety and spirituality. For Updike it was a tour de force, demonstrating a continued mastery of style while expanding his thematic horizons. It is clever, if not hilarious, and thought-provoking without being overly ponderous.

James B. Lane

LIGEIA

Author: Edgar Allan Poe (1809-1849)
Type of plot: Fantasy
Time of plot: The indefinite past
Locale: A castle on the Rhine and an abbey in a remote area of England
First published: 1838

> *Principal characters:*
> THE PROTAGONIST, an unnamed first-person narrator
> LIGEIA, the narrator's strangely beautiful first wife
> LADY ROWENA TREVANION OF TREMAINE, his unloved and
> loathed second wife

The Story

The narrator-protagonist recalls with obsessive longing the nature of the love that he felt for Ligeia, his first wife, who has died. Her beauty had about it the strange attractiveness of antiquity. She had the radiance of a Delian Muse; her hair was Homerically "hyacinthine" in color, her nose Hebraically aquiline. Her eyes were those of the black-eyed houri, nymphs of the Muslim paradise; they were the twin stars Castor and Pollux and shone like the truth at the bottom of Democritus's proverbial well. They recalled the timeless change found in the contemplation of a moth, a butterfly, a chrysalis, running water.

Ligeia's physical presence had an equally strange beauty. Her outward calm complemented an inner intensity in thought, action, and volition. Her intellect was as profound as her beauty. She knew well all the physical and mathematical sciences, was gifted in the classical and the modern languages. Still, Ligeia's immense and varied gifts could not vanquish death, the "Conqueror Worm" whose arrival Ligeia anticipated in the poem she had written shortly before her death.

The narrator records his lonely destitution of spirit after Ligeia's death. In an attempt to forget, he changes his castle on the Rhine for an equally desolate abbey in a remote and unpopulated area of England. He takes a new bride, the fair-haired, blue-eyed Rowena, a woman of a noble but haughty family. Their bridal chamber is an elaborate, octagonal turret of the abbey, semi-Gothic and semi-Druidical. Its furniture is massive, and the heavy canopy over the bridal couch seems to emphasize the pall cast over the marriage from its outset.

Indeed, after a month, the narrator becomes moody and sullen. He begins to loathe Rowena, for his memory flies back to the dead Ligeia. He wonders if the force of memory, directed by a strong enough will, might restore her. The narrator pursues these fancies even as Rowena is suddenly taken ill. Though she recovers briefly, Rowena's relapses are periodic and increasingly serious. She speaks with increasing frequency of the slight sounds and motions that she believes come from behind the tapestries of the bridal chamber. Though the narrator at first attempts to convince Rowena that the wind has caused these, he himself realizes that some invisible object has passed him; then he notices a faint "angelic" shadow on the golden carpet beneath the censer. He wonders whether these are opium-induced hallucinations and does not mention them to Rowena. Then he hears light footsteps and believes that he sees several ruby-colored droplets fall into the goblet of wine that he gives the dying Rowena.

Four nights after this, the narrator is sitting beside the shrouded body of the dead Rowena. He notes his recollection of the angelic form, looks at the dead Rowena, and remembers Ligeia with all the intensity that his willed concentration can muster. By midnight, he believes that he "felt" a sound coming from the ebony bed on which Rowena's corpse lies. As he directs every ounce of psychic energy that he can on the corpse, he perceives the slightest tinge of color come to its cheeks. He believes Rowena still lives and continues his conjurings, but he can think only of Ligeia. The corpse's lips seem to part for a moment, then relax in death. No conventional procedures reverse the condition, but when the narrator returns to his thoughts of Ligeia, he hears a sob come from the bed.

By dawn, the figure stirs, and the narrator wonders whether Rowena could actually have returned from the dead. He notices that the figure is suddenly taller than before. When the narrator loosens the cerements which cover the head, he finds huge masses of black hair, long and disheveled. It is only when the wild black eyes open that the narrator knows. His first love, his dear Ligeia, has returned to the world of the living.

Themes and Meanings

Edgar Allan Poe filled this story with allusions that he could hardly have expected the average reader to recognize. The story's primary theme, the incalculable potency of the directed will, derives from Joseph Glanvill, the seventeenth century English philosopher and clergyman. Glanvill held that will could survive the body if determined to do so, that God's immortality proceeded from the perfection of volition, and that humanity yielded itself to the angel of death only when weakness of will could no longer sustain life.

Ligeia has all the prerequisites to test Glanvill's thesis. Poe's detailed character sketch gives her the timeless, strange, and ancient beauty of Egypt, Greece, and Israel. Her eyes, which Poe describes in vivid detail at the beginning and end of his story, combine the immortality of the twin stars Castor and Pollux and that of the Turkish houri, nymphs of the Muslim paradise. She is universal intellect, Psyche, and a true child of Apollo, and her broad and deep erudition implies her privileged place in the order of creation.

Rowena is, by contrast, mediocre. Her beauty, though genuine, is conventional and superficial compared with that of Ligeia. It is this mediocrity, not Rowena herself, which the narrator loathes. Correspondingly, it is the force of Ligeia's will, still alive after her death, which directs the narrator's own volition to Ligeia's rebirth in Rowena's body. Poe has, therefore, elaborated on a traditional love-death theme to make a statement on the regenerative nature of the human spirit and the indomitable, irrepressible nature of the intellect.

Style and Technique

Ligeia is a woman whom Poe's readers have often encountered; she is Lenore, whose spirit hovers behind "the silken, sad, uncertain rustling" of the purple curtains in "The Raven"; she is Ulalume, whose spirit calls the narrator to her tomb to live in love-death; she is Annabel Lee in her "sepulchre . . . by the sea"; she is Annie, who has conquered "the fever called 'living.'" She is, just as likely, Poe's own mother, whose slow death from tuberculosis remained always in the poet's memory, or Virginia Clemm, Poe's child bride who died at the age of twenty-three.

Poe's special gift, which "Ligeia" well illustrates, is his ability to combine these intensely personal motifs with gaudy, arcane, and intentionally cryptic imagery, which he does not require his readers to unravel. To do so, however, is to appreciate the care with which Poe fashioned his works and to see that he did not strive merely for the sensational and the strange.

Robert J. Forman

LIGHT ACTION IN THE CARIBBEAN

Author: Barry Lopez (1945-   )
Type of plot: Realism
Time of plot: The 1990's
Locale: The Caribbean
First published: 2000

>
> *Principal characters:*
> LIBBY DALARIA, a young woman
> DAVID, her companion
> ESTEBAN, a boatman and diving guide

The Story

"Light Action in the Caribbean," a story about the inexplicable nature of evil, begins routinely with Libby Dalaria preparing to go on vacation with her companion, David. The only background the reader is given about the couple is that they have not known each other long and that Libby has recently broken up with a man named Brad after a two-year relationship.

David, a young professional, has made all the arrangements for their trip to the Caribbean; he prides himself on being competent and cool. Libby is impressed with his abilities and is determined to follow his lead. On their flight from Denver to Miami, David spends most of his time working on his laptop computer, and when they land, he makes a number of calls on his cell phone. However, he resents it when Libby reads a magazine and momentarily neglects him. He tells her he purposely screwed up things in his office before he left to make his coworkers think they cannot get along without him.

At dinner David continues to control everything, ordering the meal for both of them and acting like an expert with the wine list. Libby, on the other hand, feels stupid, with nothing to say. David advises Libby on everything from the nature of her job to what dessert to order. He often ignores her when women with large breasts pass by them. The first night, she worries about sex with him because he has wanted to tie her to the bed and spank her with a grade-school ruler.

The next day at the docks, David tries to get Esteban, their boatman and guide, to take them places where no one else has dived, flashing his money around, doing what Libby calls his Robert De Niro imitation and then his Kevin Costner imitation. She thinks Esteban is the most handsome man she has ever seen and hopes he will make things somewhat difficult for David, for she is growing tired of David's egotism. She feels euphoric diving in the Caribbean water and thinks she could have done this without David.

David continues his cocky attitude, advising Esteban about his business and telling him that he needs to evolve to get ahead and should buy more boats and get a Web site.

Esteban says that he has inherited the boat from his father and that he has his own plans for evolving. When a strange boat appears, Esteban thinks it is the military, who are stationed on one of the islands, and says that David may have to buy them out of this, warning him to hide most of his money. David says, "I'm cool" and takes $500 out of an envelope, hiding the remaining $4,500 in his life vest.

When the boat comes alongside, one of the men shoots Esteban with an automatic weapon. The men then come aboard, beat David, and ransack the boat. When one of the men asks if there is more money, Libby opens the life-vest pocket and gives him the remaining $4,500. One of the men knocks Libby unconscious and rapes her. Another man chokes David to death with a fishing line while he rapes him. They tie the three bodies to concrete footings and dump them in the water and then head toward an island with Esteban's boat in tow. After this abrupt and shocking climax, the story ends with an idyllic scene of a local man fishing a few miles away, thinking how he likes bringing fish back and selling them to the hotel.

Themes and Meanings

While working on the short-story collection *Light Action in the Caribbean* (2000), Barry Lopez told his editor that he wanted to write a book "leavened by unmitigated evil." With its horrifying ending, the title story seems to embody that attempt most clearly. In an interview, Lopez said the story began in his imagination as about a couple who are so superficial and materialistic that they are irritating. He wanted to create a woman who could not imagine her life without a man in it and an arrogant man who thought that he was so brilliant that he was superior to everyone around him.

Lopez creates a satire of such a man, the kind of person who wears tailored suits and wide suspenders, who acts as if he knows everything and who generally irritates almost everyone around him with his sense of superiority and condescension. There is absolutely no redeeming quality about David. He is selfish, self-centered, cocky, sadistic, and amoral. However, because he is such an unlikeable character, the reader is placed in an uncomfortable position at the end when he is so brutally killed. On one hand, the reader has a tendency to think David got what he deserved. However, at the same time, the reader is shocked with the extremity of his punishment for being rude and arrogant.

Lopez said in an interview that if a maître d' kicked David out of a restaurant because of his rude behavior, the reader would feel that was good, but "if he's going to be killed that's way too much of a price to pay for the life he's leading." David does not die because he is rude and arrogant; he dies simply because he is at the wrong place at the wrong time. However, the abruptness and brutality of the attack at the end of the story seems poetically just; David has acted as if he is in complete control throughout the story, but when the pirates come aboard, he is absolutely helpless.

What gives the story its poignancy is the death of Libby. Although she begins the story subservient to David, as the story progresses, the reader begins to sympathize with her because she grows tired of David's arrogance. As the reader silently urges her to dump him, she indeed begins to feel she does not need him at all. Then, just at the point of her growing independence, she dies a violent and undeserved death. None of the three deaths are deserved: They just happen. Indeed the action in the Caribbean is one in which there is no justice, just the blind violence that lurks in the world.

Style and Technique

If Lopez's purpose in "Light Action in the Caribbean" is to set up a situation in which the reader wants punishment for a character and then feels horrified when the punishment takes place, his stylistic method in the story is calculated to achieve this effect. Lopez once said that a lot of what he does in fiction is about language and rhythm. The story begins with the stylistic rhythm of ordinary, even banal, reality as Libby prepares for a quite common vacation trip with David. When the focus shifts to David, the rhythm shifts to one of satire for a character who is obviously arrogant and overbearing, a man who feels he can control everything and everyone around him. David's dialogue, his behavior, and his attitude are described in such a way as to make the reader increasingly dislike him. Indeed, the description of David has no other purpose.

The rhythm of the story shifts when the strange boat appears, as dumb and indifferent as an attacking animal, bearing down on them like a barracuda. When a man on board the second boat shoots Esteban, Lopez makes it clear how indifferent and how horrifying the act is by being quite specific about the trajectory of all nineteen of the bullets the man fires from his automatic weapon. The rape and murder of David and Libby is told in the same detached and objective fashion. There is no sense of anger or hatred in the killings, just cold brutality. The horror the reader feels is directly proportional to the indifference with which the murders are described.

The rhythm shifts again in the last few paragraphs in a coda in which Lopez describes a man in a fishing boat a few miles to the east. Although this bucolic description seems out of place after what has just occurred, it suggests the ordinary rhythm of everyday reality, a reality that continues unaffected by the horror that takes place nearby.

Charles E. May

LIGHTNING

Author: Donald Barthelme (1931-1989)
Type of plot: Psychological
Time of plot: The late twentieth century
Locale: New York City
First published: 1982

> *Principal characters:*
> EDWARD CONNORS, a freelance writer
> EDWINA RAWSON, a black fashion model, part-time student, and
> mother of a two-year-old boy
> PENFIELD, an editor of *Folks* magazine

The Story

The protagonist of "Lightning," Edward Connors, is introduced as he begins to interview people who have been struck by lightning, an assignment given him by Penfield, an editor of *Folks*. He instructs Connors to interview at least nine people, including one "slightly wonderful" person to be featured in the article.

Connors begins his research by advertising in *The Village Voice*. From the many responses he learns that many people have great-grandfathers or great-grandmothers who were struck by lightning in 1910. (Variations on this factual detail, as on others, will recur later in the story.)

Before the interviews begin, the reader learns of Connors's past, especially his earlier jobs. He was "a reporter for ten years and a freelancer for five, with six years in between as a PR man for Topsy Oil in Midland-Odessa." As a reporter, he covered business news, so his moving on to public relations with an oil firm was a logical change (urged on him by his wife, for financial reasons). He had been "in love with his work" as a reporter. The PR job paid three times as much but was dull, so when his wife left him for a racquetball pro at a country club, he left Topsy Oil and Texas for New York City and freelance work: "To each assignment he brought a good brain, a good eye, a tenacious thoroughness, gusto."

The first man interviewed, Burch, reports that being struck by lightning was the best thing that ever happened to him. After the event he became a Jehovah's Witness, and he describes his life since then as "Serene. Truly serene." Connors is impressed. The next interviewee, a woman named MacGregor, reports that being struck led to "some important changes" in her life: She married the man she had been seeing and quit her job, which had necessitated tiring commuting.

Still seeking a feature subject for his article, Connors then arranges to interview Edwina Rawson. She is reluctant but consents, and she turns out to be young, black, lovely, and charming, "not only slightly wonderful but also mildly superb." The reader watches Connors fall in love with her. The reader also learns much about her life, including her two-year-old son Zachary and her departed husband Marty, who gave her mouth-to-mouth resuscitation when she was struck by lightning. (She connects his ability to do so with "his cautious, be-prepared, white-folks' attitude toward life.")

Edwina is unsure about the effect of being struck by lightning. When Connors, who has fallen for her, asks if it changed her life, she says, "yes and no." It removed her eyebrows and "got rid of Marty," she says. Now she models to support Zachary and herself.

Hearing her story, Connors reacts unexpectedly. He thinks that the soul burns when struck by lightning, he connects lightning with music—"Lightning an attempt at music on the part of God?"—and he wishes that he had a song to sing to Edwina. Having none, he tells her odd facts about armadillos, facts more and more fanciful. Calling him "sentimental" and "crazy," Edwina goes to the movies with him.

The story shifts abruptly to Connors's next interviewee, a man named Stupple, who after being struck by lightning joined the American Nazi Party in Newark, New Jersey, and who passes on to Connors "pages of viciousness having to do with the Protocols of Zion and the alleged genetic inferiority of blacks."

Returning from that interview, turned down by Edwina for a dinner date, and "vexed by his inability to get a handle on the story," Connors talks to Penfield, the editor. He tells Penfield that he does not yet understand how being struck by lightning changes people. Penfield is not interested, but he is pleased to hear that Edwina is beautiful and will provide him with a good illustration for the cover of *Folks*.

The next day Connors interviews a Trappist monk in Piffard, New York, who received a Sony Walkman tape player from his community after he was struck and who listens to rock music on it. Connors is moved by the monk's happiness. Dining with Edwina and Zachary that night, Connors raises yet another question about the experience: "What effects the change . . . ?" Edwina is not interested, but she offers to give him a back rub. The last paragraph of the story summarizes Connors's interviews with five more people. One of them, dumb from birth, speaks perfect French after being struck. Connors's finished article is reported as containing a passage on the religious quality of the experience, which Penfield properly deleted, and as having devoted extra space to Edwina, who looked "approximately fantastic."

Themes and Meanings

Donald Barthelme's stories recurrently take up the theme of the incomplete life. Usually the life is incomplete because the protagonist lacks someone to love and be loved by. The story either develops that kind of life or, as in "Lightning" finds for the protagonist the woman he has sought. Barthelme, however, seldom has in mind a long-term relationship. The emphasis is put, rather, on the excitement, the novelty, and the anticipation evoked by awakened desire and the sense of unspecified possibilities.

Connors is characterized as deserving and ripe for such a discovery. He is enthusiastic, hardworking, and open to change. He was a good reporter in the old days and brought those qualities even to the reporting of business news. Though the public relations job dampened his enthusiasm, he was still "very fond" of the company's amiable chief executive officer. The reader sees him eagerly doing research on his struck-by-lightning project and sympathetic to the kindly people he encounters but not to the Nazi bigot.

Edwina is presented as Connors's ideal woman. Of his wife, the reader learns only that she complained about the low pay of his reporter's job and that the public relations salary permitted him to enjoy "briefly" his wife's "esteem." On the other hand, Edwina is beautiful and amusing and undemanding. Her first name suggests that she is Edward Connors's counterpart, while her black femininity complements his white masculinity. Best of all, perhaps, their relationship has progressed only to the hopeful moment of the offered back rub when the story ends; there is no suggestion of any letdown or boredom to come.

Style and Technique

Barthelme prefers a mixed mode to pure comedy or tragedy, admitting that he thereby sacrifices the opportunity to move his readers' emotions. He keeps his readers intelligently alert by shifting from level to level of diction, by finding colloquialisms and clichés to which an odd twist or application can be given, and by including unexpected topics and concerns. In a brief speculation about lightning, for example, Connors thinks: "Lightning at once a coup de theatre and career counseling?" Here the comic juxtaposition of two very different interpretations is reinforced by the dramatic and sociological jargon. When Edwina generalizes from her marriage to a white man, one reads, "She had nothing against white folks, Edwina said with a warm smile, or rabbits, as black folks sometimes termed them, but you had to admit that, qua folks, they sucked." The sentence is a comic hash of mixed terms where "white folks" and "warm smile" suggest geniality that is cooled by the amusingly denigrating term "rabbits," is then altered completely by the mixture of a bookish Latin word and the colloquial in "qua folks" (which sounds silly), and is brought to a sharp ending with an insulting slang verb. (The thrice-repeated "folks" is a reminder that Connors is writing for the magazine *Folks*.)

The most obvious comic device is the story itself. This odd exploration of an odd subject, being hit by lightning, is a typical Barthelme literalization of a common notion. As his story "Falling Dog" acts out the common phrase "struck by a new idea," so "Lightning" develops the common image of a life-changing event as "like being struck by lightning."

Because Barthelme likes to surround any positive idea with ironic alternatives and doubts, several of the characters struck by lightning experience negative or less than profound results—adherence to Nazi ideas, ability to speak French, the end of a tiring job. On the other hand, two of them achieve serenity and happiness. However, the central experience of being "struck by lightning" is that of Connors, and it takes place when he meets and falls in love with Edwina. For her, the results of an actual bolt of lightning were ambivalent ("yes and no"), and the story ends so quickly that one is left to wonder which of these terms will apply to Connors's new love—perhaps both.

J. D. O'Hara

LIKE A WINDING SHEET

Author: Ann Petry (1908-1997)
Type of plot: Social realism
Time of plot: The 1940's
Locale: New York
First published: 1946

> *Principal characters:*
> JOHNSON, a frustrated African American factory worker
> MAE, his wife, who also works in a manufacturing plant
> MRS. SCOTT, his white supervisor

The Story

Johnson, an African American man, is lounging in bed, savoring the last moments of rest before a busy shift at the factory. His wife, Mae, affectionately jokes that he looks like a huckleberry in a winding sheet. Although he protests that that is no way to talk early in the day, he smiles in spite of himself. As Johnson dresses for work, he nurses his aching legs that never seem to get enough rest from one shift to the next. Noting that the date is Friday the thirteenth, Mae considers staying home, but her husband gently urges her to go to work because it is payday—a good-luck day everywhere. By the time he convinces her to leave for work, he has already made himself late.

If this were his own plant, Johnson thinks, he would make many changes, eliminating jobs that are hard on the legs and figuring out ways people can work sitting down. As he pushes his cart up and down the assembly line, he comes close to the foreman. He finds it odd to have a white woman for a boss in a plant, and can never remember to refer to her as the forelady, even in his mind. He tries to avoid her slit-eyed stare, but just as he passes her, she shouts at him over the roar of the machines.

After a tense confrontation with the bigoted Mrs. Scott, during which she humiliates him for again being late and calls him "a nigger," Johnson feels his fists clench and the veins in his forehead swell. He restrains himself from smashing her face, but afterward wishes that he had acted, because the queer, knotted tension stays in his hands for the entire shift. Still, he cannot bring himself to hit a woman. As the hours drag on and fatigue overcomes him, he notices the women workers starting to snap and snarl at one another.

Finally the workday ends, and, with his paycheck in his pocket, Johnson stops at a diner for a cup of coffee to soothe his aching body and tense nerves. He does not pay attention to the white girl serving his coffee until she tosses her hair and says to him, "No more coffee for a while." Again he feels his hands begin to clench into tight, hard fists. He wants to hit her for refusing him a cup of coffee, assuming she has done so because he is black, but he does not. In his hurried and angry exit, he fails to see that the coffee urn is empty, and she is making a fresh pot. His anger continues to build, running through his body like poison. Everyone, it seems, degrades and belittles him.

This realization fills his mind when he returns home to Mae, who greets him with a cheerful greeting and a toss of her hair. He cringes at her gesture and ignores her attempts at humor. Affectionately trying to coax him to eat, she says, "You're nothing but an old hungry nigger trying to act tough and—" Before she can finish, Johnson feels his fists clench, rise, and smash into her face, again and again and again, as if he were entangled in a winding sheet.

Themes and Meanings

Ann Petry, who first published "Like a Winding Sheet" in the National Association for the Advancement of Colored People magazine *Crisis*, has treated several themes in an honest and brutal work of social criticism. Her story suggests that racial discrimination both in the workplace and in society at large is a significant cause of the breakdown in African American family life and marital relationships. Her description of the story behind the Johnson family violence illuminates the devastation caused by such racial injustice.

At the beginning of the story, Johnson is shown to be a caring man who plans to get up early to surprise Mae with breakfast. He savors her sweet giggle and avoids quarrels because they have been married too long and gotten along too well. Despite his apparent love for Mae and his usual nonviolence—he cannot bring himself to talk roughly to her or threaten to hit her, as many other men do to their wives—Johnson is transformed into a violent man. His hatred of society's oppression becomes a horrifying anger at Mae, which ultimately leads to her beating.

Petry explores both physical and spiritual violence in "Like a Winding Sheet." It is only after Johnson suffers repeated spiritual abuse himself, both real and imagined, that he adopts a negative image of himself. This is the horrifying realization at the heart of the story, for as one moves painfully from the first scene of degradation to the last, one knows that Johnson's frustration cannot be repressed indefinitely. It will soon explode.

Style and Technique

Petry writes in a low-key, subtle way about the overwhelming indignity and anger that discrimination against African Americans can cause. Particularly compelling is Petry's examination of where and how the African American woman fits into this deadly cycle of abuse. The characters' language and dialogue may be examined closely to see how words change meaning throughout the story, both foreshadowing and causing the horrific ending. One example of this narrative strategy is the title, with which Petry begins and ends the story.

As Mae jokingly notes in the opening paragraph, Johnson is wrapped in a winding sheet, and although he does not know it, he is spiritually dead from repeated encounters with oppressors such as Mrs. Scott. Before going to work, he smiles as he sees his black arms silhouetted against the white of the sheets and tries to shake off the negative connotations of a winding sheet, a shroud. The oppressive mood never lifts, however, as the racially charged dialogue between Mrs. Scott and Johnson at the factory intensifies his hatred of whites, and the chatter of the women workers increases his misogyny.

Gestures are symbolic also, and change meaning within the context of the story. At the coffee shop, the white girl who refuses Johnson a cup of coffee "put her hands up to her head and gently lifted her hair away from the back of her neck, tossing her head back a little." Petry uses almost the same words to describe Mae's actions later: "She patted a curl in place near the side of her head and then lifted her hair away from the back of her neck, ducking her head forward and then back." Wincing at her gesture, Johnson complains, "What you got to be always fooling with your hair for?" When Mae then lovingly calls him a "hungry old nigger," the word explodes in his head, and he responds to it the way he had wanted to when Mrs. Scott used it in a very different context earlier. As he strikes his wife over and over, Johnson realizes that something inside is "binding him to this act, wrapping and twisting about him so that he had to continue it." As he pounds her face again and yet again, he finds the word to describe it—like a winding sheet.

The chronological organization of the story creates a relentless yet subtle momentum. By the end, Johnson has been wrapped tightly in many layers of prejudice and discrimination, all compounded by his frustrated efforts to be punctual and accepted in white society. He cannot tend to his physical aches and pains in the beginning of the story, because he must not be late for work. He wastes valuable minutes in convincing Mae to go to work, eventually causing his own lateness. At the diner, he pauses outside watching the other workers savor their coffee before joining the line in front of the coffee urn. His hesitation puts him too far back to get a cup. Chronicling one frustration after another, Petry moves the story ominously forward until the winding sheet—white society—smothers both Johnson and Mae.

Carol F. Bender

LIKE THE NIGHT

Author: Alejo Carpentier (1904-1980)
Type of plot: Magical Realism
Time of plot: From the Trojan War through World War II
Locale: Greece, Spain, and France
First published: "Semejante a la noche," 1958 (English translation, 1970)

> *Principal characters:*
> THE NARRATOR, the unnamed protagonist, a young soldier about
>   to leave by ship for warfare
> HIS FIANCÉ, unnamed

The Story

The events of the story occur in a single day, but it is a day that takes more than two thousand years to be completed. The main character, who is also the narrator, is going through an ancient ritual for young men: leaving his homeland for war and conquest. In this traditional situation, the narrator undergoes several obligatory encounters. He says farewell to each of his parents, his fiancé, and friends; gets drunk on his final evening at home, then boards the boat in the cold light of day to leave his country.

Alejo Carpentier divides the story into five numbered sections, each of which advances the action while transposing it to a different place and time. The movement of the story is circular, however, beginning with the preparations for the Trojan War in section 1, moving to phases of the Spanish exploration and conquest of the New World in sections 2 and 3, and to a sort of hybrid of World War I and World War II in sections 4 and in section 5 returning to the initial scene.

A note blown on a conch announces the arrival of King Agamemnon's fifty black ships, come to take the Achaean troops to Troy. Instantly, as if that note were the beginning of a vast symphony, the scene comes noisily to life. Those who had been waiting for many days begin to carry the wheat toward the ships, the ships scrape the sand with their keels, the Mycenaean sailors try to keep the Achaeans away from the ships with poles, and children run about, hindering the soldiers' movements and stealing nuts from under the oarsmen's benches.

The narrator finds the scene disillusioning. He expected a solemn ceremony celebrating the meeting of two groups of warriors, not this pandemonium in which the leading citizens could not make their speeches of welcome. He withdraws from the beach and sits astride a tree branch because it reminds him of a woman's body. The sexual theme, here a consolation for his vague sense of disappointment, will later become a source of frustration for him. The suggestion of disappointment is readily dispelled, however, by attributing it both to fatigue from waiting all night and to a hangover. His pride and sense of superiority return when he reflects that he and the other soldiers are the occasion of all this activity. He scorns the peasants for spending the day looking "at the earth over the sweating backs of their animals," or working the earth hunched over like cattle themselves. He tells himself that they will never see Troy, the city he and his comrades are about to "surround, attack, and destroy."

His ferocity is fueled by messages—which will ultimately be revealed as lies and propaganda—sent by Agamemnon about the Trojan King Priam's "insolence," the taunts that the Trojans have made against the Achaeans' "manly way of life," and the cruelties that the abducted Helen of Sparta suffered in Troy. He believes that to rescue Helen will be a "manly undertaking and the supreme triumph of a war that would give us prosperity, happiness, and pride in ourselves forever." His optimism is tempered only by the thought of giving grief to his mother and father.

In section 2, the noise about the ships changes to music from guitars and cymbals, and the sound of people dancing the zarambeque and singing coplas. The wheat being loaded in the previous section is now accompanied by wine, oil, and a wooden pipe organ to help convert the Indians of the New World. The narrator is about to depart to conquer a new empire for Spain, and the soldiers' arrogance infects him as it did previously. He feels that he and his fellows are men different from ordinary men by nature and capable of deeds unimaginable to them. His father's praise of a peaceful and prosperous life, then, is to no avail, and though he again feels a sense of disillusionment when his father warns him that such expeditions were the "madness of many for the gain of a few," he takes leave of his father and mother with the buoyant promise that, by freeing the Indians "from their barbarous superstitions our nation would win imperishable glory and greater happiness, prosperity, and power than all the Kingdoms of Europe." His idealism is undercut, however, in the scene with his mother, in which she warns him to have no sinful dealings with the Indian women but then realizes that her son is already dreaming of trying what she has warned him against. The base motives for his adventure give the lie to the narrator's idealism even before he articulates it.

Ultimately he sees through the propaganda, his own false idealism and sexual bravado. That disillusionment takes place in the final three sections of the story, in which he argues with his fiancé (section 3), angrily leaves her to visit his mistress (section 4), and returns to his fiancé, who is ready to give herself to him (section 5). By then he is sexually exhausted and filled with a tremendous fear of failure. Insulted by his weak refusal of her body, she flees. He is left emasculated and demoralized, his soldier's pride changed to self-reproach and disgust. His motive for heroism is debased. He is in the end merely a foot soldier, traveling on a slow, overloaded boat, and he will not see his loved ones for many years, if ever.

Themes and Meanings

Carpentier's work frequently expresses an incisive criticism of modern society. His best-known novel, *Los pasos perdidos* (1953; *The Lost Steps*, 1956, 1967), chronicles the efforts of a man to rediscover his humanity after being alienated from a society devoted to ambition and greed. A Cuban writer, Carpentier criticizes postcolonial and capitalist society not through preaching but through storytelling, allowing his

Everyman characters to experience the depths of their victimhood and discontent in order to find a way out.

The narrator of "Like the Night" is at such a crucial point. He is about to take on warriorhood for the good of his society, but beneath the public promises lies economic self-interest, such as the possibility of a better trade with Asia after the Trojans are eliminated as competition. For the narrator, his adventuring involves more than merely expending his youthful energy. It has consequences for his parents, of whom he begins to be mindful, and for his fiancé, whose real passion exposes the confusion and doubt beneath his bravado. The narrator's relations with women—with his mother, fiancé, and mistress—are determined by the same false idealism and baseness that have moved him to go to war. He departs at exactly the wrong moment, when he begins to realize his victimhood and loses all heart for the ordeal he has chosen.

Style and Technique

The narrator is not the victim of a single ideology or historical movement but is a kind of Everyman (hence his namelessness) leaving for war, as it were, simultaneously from several countries thousands of years apart. The significance of the departure is deepened by the layering of history. The falsehoods stretch thinner and thinner until they can no longer provide supportive ideology for the narrator. The Trojan War is a matter of honor and manhood, the Spanish conquest begins in order to win souls, and modern war promises eternal brotherhood. None of those promises is kept, as history has proved, but in the story they keep reappearing as new heads on an old monster.

Although it debunks the narrator's idealism, Carpentier's technique of movement through time also magnifies the human pain his folly causes those who love him. His parents suffer, certainly, though the main focus is on his fiancé being left unfulfilled, the promise of their future together hopelessly ruined. The central section is given to their argument about his enterprise in the West Indies among the local people. She has no faith in the European claims of uplifting the Indians, who, according to Michel de Montaigne (whose *Essais*, 1580, 1588, she is reading), have been corrupted by the example shown them in the behavior of the explorers. The duplicitous European treatment of the Indians is but one example of a cyclic historical process, a pattern of exploitation that has been repeated for thousands of years.

Robert Bensen

LIONS, HARTS, LEAPING DOES

Author: J. F. Powers (1917-1999)
Type of plot: Allegory
Time of plot: Probably the mid-twentieth century
Locale: A Franciscan monastery in the northern United States
First published: 1943

Principal characters:
FATHER DIDYMUS, an aging Franciscan friar
BROTHER TITUS, Didymus's devoted companion

The Story

The striking title, "Lions, Harts, Leaping Does," is from a passage in Saint John of the Cross: "Birds of swift wing, lions, harts, leaping does, mountains, valleys, banks, waters, breezes, heats and terrors that keep watch by night, by the pleasant lyres and by the siren's song, I conjure you, cease your wrath and touch not the wall." Titus, who is a devoted but slow-witted Franciscan brother, reads this lovely prose to the companion whom he attends in the monastery, the octogenarian priest Didymus. The lines well suggest the plangent lyrical tone of this narrative of the aged Didymus's struggle to find grace.

When the story opens, Titus is reading to Didymus from Bishop John Bale's *Pageant of Popes' Contayninge the Lyves of all the Bishops of Rome, from the Beginninge of them to the Year of Grace 1555* (1574), an idiosyncratic and splenetic chronicle to which Didymus refers as "Bishop Bale's funny book." Titus also quotes from memory fragments from Thomas a Kempis's *The Imitation of Christ* (fifteenth century), silently challenging Didymus to identify the source in an "unconfessed contest." This introductory scene fixes the characters of the two Franciscans and reveals their warm relationship. Titus is a saintly innocent, full of childlike glee as he spars mildly with Didymus in an attempt to please. Didymus is a geometry teacher who is always alert to impulses of spiritual pride in himself and feels ashamed at impatiently patronizing Titus.

As they walk the monastery grounds together at the close of a frigid day, Didymus ruminates on the life of poverty, chastity, and obedience that he has led. He concludes that "it was the spirit of the vows which opened the way and revealed to the soul, no matter the flux of circumstance, the means of salvation," and this realization saddens him with a sense of having sinned against his older brother, Seraphin. The dying Seraphin, also a priest, had asked Didymus to visit him in St. Louis, but Didymus had refused out of what he now judges to have been a false interpretation of his duty to obey God. Didymus ruefully admits that "he had used his brother for a hair shirt," an admission that sets up the crucial question of Didymus's grace, around which the story revolves.

As the two return to the monastery, they meet the rector, who speaks to Didymus of a telegram for him, and it turns out that Titus has forgotten to give the message to Didymus. The abashed Titus produces the telegram, which announces the death of Seraphin.

In the short second section, Didymus falls asleep in the chapel and dreams of himself and Seraphin walking on a serpentine river. The two brothers talk of their parents and of their own lives until two crayfish surface and grab Didymus, who then awakens to find himself prone on the floor. Didymus is helped to his feet by Titus and starts to walk away, only to collapse from an apparent stroke.

The next day Didymus sits in a wheelchair, bundled in blankets and struggling to focus on the cold, inert landscape visible through his window. He hears Titus enter the room and move around mysteriously, gradually learning that the quietly gleeful Titus has brought him a canary in a cage: "one of the Saint's own birds," as Titus puts it. Didymus spends his long days at the window, the canary his silent companion, with Titus reading to him on occasion. His life is dreary. "They were captives, he and the canary, and the only thing they craved was escape."

In his meditations on his condition, Didymus wonders if his incapacitation is God's punishment of him for not having "gloried too much in having it in him to turn down Seraphin's request to come to St. Louis." He cannot decide if he has erred, and his uncertainty puts him in a moral predicament. If he is being punished, then praying for recovery would suggest that he has missed "the divine point." Didymus finally concludes he is not man enough to see "the greatest significance in his affliction," and wants only to walk again and eventually die a normal death. So, he copes with his situation, prays for good health, and watches the canary, identifying in his misery with the forlorn bird trapped in the cage.

One day Didymus sends Titus on an errand, and with an exhausting effort he reaches up and opens the canary's cage, then falls face down on the floor. That night in his room, having received the last sacrament, Didymus waits for death, free from desire but "beset by the grossest distractions." After Titus reads to him from St. John of the Cross, Didymus has a vision of his life as "tied down, caged, stunted in his apostolate, seeking the crumbs." At this moment he asks Titus to open the window, and as Didymus prays to lose himself in God the canary flutters through the open window into the snowy night outside. As Titus stares out the window seeking the lost bird, "the snowflakes whirled at the window, for a moment for all their bright blue beauty as though struck still be lightning, and Didymus closed his eyes, only to find them there also, but darkly falling."

Themes and Meanings

Critics disagree over the question of whether Didymus achieves grace, and each reader will have to decide the state of Didymus's soul in the light of his own interpretation of the way to religious salvation. Didymus himself is in doubt, and just before the end can find no "divine sign within himself." His own evaluation of his condition cannot be taken as definitive, however, even if his judgment of his sin against Seraphin is accepted as accurate—as it probably should be. His faults proceed not from desire but from an earnest desire to follow the will of God, and the genuine human anguish he suffers must count in his favor.

Perhaps most significant of all the evidence is the moving Nunc Dimittis with which the story ends, contributing significantly to the compassionate tone that suffuses the story of Didymus's tormented self-questioning and death. Didymus dies as the canary flees to "the snowy arms of God," and it is difficult to believe that the two of them, who want most of all to escape, do not come to the same resting place. If not, the canary is reduced in meaning to a symbol of the peace that comes in the annihilation of death, and if that is J. F. Powers's intent, then Didymus's ordeal seems greatly diminished and the allegorical elements emerge as little more than literary ornamentation.

Style and Technique

The two most salient features of Powers's direct, simple style in "Lions, Harts, Leaping Does" are his effective use of weather and landscape and the development of the allegory represented by the bird in the cage. The "angular winter daylight" proves to be a pathetic fallacy that complements the somber spiritual considerations of Didymus's inner life: The first scene, with Titus reading from "Bishop Bale's funny book," is bathed by the dying light of a cold winter day, and as they emerge from the buildings into the outdoors, the "freezing air" bites into their bodies and they pace a walkway littered with shards of ice. Didymus's face becomes "a slab of pasteboard" and his eyes water. Such imagery suits the climate of Didymus's soul as he pursues his solitary quest for an answer to his spiritual fate. Nowhere is there any greenness, any fullness of life. Even the canary is mute and joyless, enduring its alien habitat with resignation and longing for freedom.

When Titus first brings the canary to Didymus's room, the bird chirps cheerfully, and for a while it enjoys the swing that Titus provides for it. Gradually, though, the creature tires of looking out the window on the bleak snowscape, and its sadness reflects the weariness in Didymus's heart. The two of them share a tacit fellowship: "Nothing was lost of the communion he kept with the canary." As a symbol of Didymus's soul, the canary matches its moods to the priest's. As Didymus lies dying, "the canary perched in the dark atop the cage, head warm under wing, already, it seemed to Didymus, without memory of its captivity, dreaming of a former freedom, an ancestral summer day with flowers and trees." When the bird flies to freedom, the soul of Didymus makes good its escape as well.

Frank Day

LISPETH

Author: Rudyard Kipling (1865-1936)
Type of plot: Satire
Time of plot: The nineteenth century
Locale: Northern India
First published: 1886

> *Principal characters:*
> LISPETH, the protagonist, a Hill-girl
> THE CHAPLAIN OF KOTGARH, Lispeth's guardian
> THE CHAPLAIN'S WIFE
> THE ENGLISHMAN, the man Lispeth wants to marry

The Story

A Hill-girl christened Elizabeth, but known as Lispeth according to local pronunciation, grows up in the Kotgarh valley in Northern India. Her parents, having become Christians out of destitute poverty, bring their baby daughter to the Kotgarh chaplain to be baptized. When both her parents die of cholera, Lispeth becomes half servant, half companion to the wife of the chaplain then residing in Kotgarh. She grows tall, vigorous, and as lovely as a Greek goddess. Unlike other Hill-girls, when she reaches womanhood she does not give up the Christianity she has accepted. She is happy playing with the chaplain's children, taking Sunday school classes, reading all the books in the house, and taking long walks in the hills. When she is seventeen, however, an event takes place that completely changes her attitude toward the English. Interaction with them at a deeper level reveals to her that the ways of her people are more congenial and acceptable to her than the supposedly superior culture represented by the chaplain of Kotgarh, his wife, and an Englishman.

One day at dusk, Lispeth returns home from her long walk in the hills carrying a heavy burden: a young Englishman who is unconscious from a cut on the head. She falls in love with him and announces that she intends to marry him when he is well again. Horrified, the chaplain and his wife rebuke her for the impropriety of her feelings, but she is firm in her resolve.

The Englishman is a traveler in the East who lost his footing and fell while hunting for butterflies and plants in the Simla hills. Lispeth discovered and saved him. Recovering coherence after two weeks, he spends two more leisurely weeks regaining his strength. While doing so, even though he is engaged to a girl in England, he finds it very pleasant to walk and talk with Lispeth and say sweet, endearing words to her. All this means everything to her but nothing to him, for he finds Lispeth's love for himself merely amusing and romantic. Even when he takes leave of her, he puts his arm around her waist and repeatedly promises to return, knowing all the time that his promises are false. He acts, in fact, according to the advice of the chaplain's wife, who wants to avoid a scandal. After Lispeth waits in vain for three months, the chaplain's wife tells her the truth. Lispeth is incredulous, for the Englishman had professed love and the chaplain's wife had assured her of his return. She wants to know how what they told her could be untrue. When the chaplain's wife self-righteously explains their strategy to keep her quiet, Lispeth realizes that they lied to her deliberately. She leaves in silent indignation, and comes back in the garb of a Hill-girl with braided hair to make a twofold announcement: that she is returning to her people as a devotee of Tarka Devi, and that she thinks the English are all liars.

Thereafter, Lispeth takes to her people with great ardor and soon marries a wood-cutter who beats her in the manner of the Hill-people. Her beauty fades, and she grows very old. However, she may be persuaded, when drunk, to recount in perfect English the romance of her first love affair. It is hard to believe that this very old, wrinkled, and withered woman is the formerly beautiful Lispeth.

Themes and Meanings

The satiric purpose of the author is achieved by an accumulation of ironies. The epigram at the head of this story begins, "Look, you have cast out love! What Gods are these you bid me please?" Because the central ethical value of Christianity is love, casting out love is the most unchristian of acts. This is exactly what Christian missionaries and imperialists do. In the name of superior faith and breeding, they substitute deceit and untruth where all-embracing love should be. As a result, the gods that the Englishman, the chaplain, and the chaplain's wife worship become questionable, a "tangled Trinity" to a simple Hill-girl.

Ironies abound. Not only are Christians and imperialists unchristian and ordinary, but it is Lispeth—the heathen, the savage, the one guilty, according to the English, of shameless folly—who demonstrates a love that is unalloyed devotion and trust.

By baptizing Lispeth, the missionaries hold out the promise of a new and better life of the spirit. Instead of keeping that promise, they kill her, as she declares; they kill her faith in their God; they kill her trust in their way of life; they abandon her to social evils; and indirectly they ruin her unspoiled beauty. They try to put a free and innocent Hill-girl with the beauty and poise of Diana, a pagan goddess, into their own kind of garb—gaudy floral prints—that in this context may well be a metaphor for ostentation and lack of sensitivity.

When Lispeth returns to her people, the chaplain's wife is shocked at her conversion, as though it were an unnatural act. She attributes it to the innate savagery of the girl's race and finds no blame whatsoever in the deceit of the Englishman or herself. In the presence of such self-righteous superiority, no true human relationship can flourish.

When Lispeth returns to her people's way and marries, she has to endure the beatings of her husband. Her faith is strong, though, for she thinks of herself as the servant of Tarka Devi, the goddess who saves. As for her first romance, the memory of it is hers for life, clean, uninhibited, and unshackled by falsehood.

"Lispeth" is an unequivocal indictment of racist, religious, and imperialist attitudes of superiority. Rudyard Kipling shows how absurd and inhumane the outcome is when people who lack integrity and sensitivity take it on themselves in their self-satisfied stance to improve others whom they have not even tried to understand, let alone appreciate.

Style and Technique

For success at satire, the writer must engage the interest of the reader in the narration itself, and then almost imperceptibly make an about-face from lightness to depth, from pleasant entertainment to pungent import. This is exactly Kipling's technique; he tells a romantic tale set in the hills of Northern India that has the allure of distance and strangeness. Even a familiar name such as Elizabeth is changed to Lispeth in the hills, and names of places—Simla, Kotgarh, Narkunda—add to the romance. Kipling's narrator takes on the easy, purposeful tone of the fireside storyteller, step by step piling irony on irony, up to the climax, when the reader feels the full thrust of the satire.

Apart from the skillful management of content and style, Kipling uses the two notable techniques of contrast and irony. Lispeth is the only character who is individualized. She is, therefore, the only one of the principal characters who is mentioned by name—and a distinctive one at that—to show how extraordinary she is in beauty and character. In contrast, none of the English characters is mentioned by name, and they accordingly share a stereotyped attitude of superiority. Lispeth's depth of feeling, her forthright character and conduct, stand in ironic contrast to the superficial proprieties and deviousness of those who pride themselves on being her betters. The contrast helps pinpoint the irony that assumed superiority is pathetically hollow, altogether incapable of uplifting the so-called "savage," who in this story is the only one possessed of redeeming nobility. Instead of helping to save her soul, her would-be benefactors reduce her to poignant misery.

Contrasts work throughout in subtle as well as obvious ways. When Lispeth comes down the hill carrying the Englishman, her burden is both literally and symbolically heavy, and unconscious of her vigor and purity. Lispeth's strenuous effort and devotion contrast with the chaplain's wife's indolence of body and spirit, for when Lispeth comes in exhausted from her tremendous lifesaving effort, the chaplain's wife has been dozing in the living room. Lispeth saves by her own effort; the English promise to save by conversion to the Church of England. Lispeth walks twenty or thirty miles; English ladies walk a mile and a half into the hills and return by carriage. Lispeth is referred to as a child, and she has a child's innocence and lack of knowledge of the world; she cries and tries to see in a jigsaw-puzzle map where her beloved might be.

The Englishman, on the other hand, much traveled and educated, forgets the girl who loves him and to whom he owes his life. In a book he writes on the East, her name does not appear. The contrast of devotion and opportunism, of innocence and manipulation, highlights the irony of the white man's "burden," which consists not of improving but of exploiting other people. Contrasting perceptions reveal the gap that separates the characters. What is honorable passion in Lispeth's eyes is shameless folly according to the English. The relationship between them remains within the confines of racial and religious prejudice instead of growing into a richly human interaction.

Among the many ironies strung into the narrative, Kipling includes the Englishman's pledge of discretion, which is nothing short of irresponsibility, and the chaplain's wife's concern for morality, which is little more than an effort to avoid scandal. Christians in the story lack charity, and the "savage" displays sensitivity. Through a maze of paradoxes, the reader finally arrives at a point where both sides reveal their generalized prejudice. Lispeth concludes that all the English are liars. The chaplain's wife declares that no law can explain the vagaries of the savage. Lispeth's perfect English is no passport to communication; the distance between her and the English increases. Her beauty fades and her one-sided romance is only a memory. Kipling observes the misery that those human beings in power inflict on other human beings, and he writes about it in "Lispeth," a very moving satire.

Sita Kapadia

A LITTLE CLOUD

Author: James Joyce (1882-1941)
Type of plot: Symbolist
Time of plot: About 1900
Locale: Dublin
First published: 1914

Principal characters:
THOMAS MALONE ("LITTLE") CHANDLER, a thirty-two-year-old
law clerk
IGNATIUS GALLAHER, a Dublin-born London journalist

The Story

Thomas Malone Chandler, known as "Little Chandler" because of his boyish appearance and delicate manner, works as a legal clerk. On this particular fall evening, he has an appointment with an old friend named Ignatius Gallaher. After eight years abroad, during which time he has become a self-confident and successful journalist, Gallaher has returned to visit his native Dublin.

The prospect of an evening with Gallaher arouses certain conflicts in Little Chandler. On one hand, he is proud to have a talented and successful friend; on the other hand, he is reminded of the drudgery of his own work, which he associates with the drabness of his native city. When such melancholy moods strike him, he thinks of the books of poetry that he bought before his marriage. Remembering some of their lines, he is often consoled.

When his work day ends, he sets out for his appointment. His anticipation of the evening out causes him to ignore the squalor of the city slums. His rendezvous with Gallaher is to be at Corless's, a fashionable restaurant patronized by the upper classes. He has always viewed their lives from a distance, with envy and apprehension. However, thoughts of Gallaher's dash, talent, and resources buoy him up and make him feel equal to the occasion. He reflects that the contrast between the brilliance of Gallaher's career and his own prosaic job is explained by the lack of opportunity in Dublin.

He considers himself a poet of moods, now perhaps reaching emotional maturity. His melancholic temperament, he believes, would be seen by outsiders as typical of the work of the Celtic Twilight, the Irish literary movement led by William Butler Yeats. He conjectures that Gallaher may be able to advise him on publication strategies.

In Corless's bar, Gallaher greets him jovially, joking about the signs of his approaching middle age. As they order drinks and reminisce, however, Chandler begins to recognize Gallaher's crude and patronizing manner as he boasts of the pressures and prestige of his job, his adventures in "immoral" Paris, his taste for neat whiskey, and his acquaintance with the corruption of the religious orders and the aristocracy of the Continent.

Then Little Chandler tells Gallaher of his marriage and baby son and invites him to visit. Gallaher declines, however, and as they drink their final whiskeys, Chandler's resentment against his own humble life and Gallaher's condescension begins to grow stronger. Emboldened by the effects of the alcohol, he predicts Gallaher's own marriage. Gallaher insists that he is liberated from all romantic illusions about women: He is too worldly-wise for that.

When Little Chandler gets home late for tea, he has an argument with his wife. She goes out on an errand, leaving him in charge of their sleeping infant. As he awaits her return, he reflects on their dull marriage, his timidity, and his mean and domineering wife. From these doleful reflections on his domestication, he turns again to thoughts of poetry. However, when he opens his volume of Lord Byron's poems, the first verse that he reads sends him into another melancholic reverie.

This is broken by his child, who wakes and begins to cry. As he tries to read while rocking the child, a resentment against all the circumstances of his life wells up in him. He shouts at the child, driving it into hysterics. His wife rushes in on the scene, snatches the child from him, and soothes it. Little Chandler stands by, helpless before her hatred and conscience-stricken by his outburst.

Themes and Meanings

Like each of the *Dubliners* (1914) stories (this is the eighth of fifteen), "A Little Cloud" develops the theme of the paralysis of intellect and spirit in Dublin. In this story there are two specimens: Little Chandler the legal clerk and Gallaher the journalist. Through their occupations, they share a common professional interest in language as well as a Dublin background. Further, Gallaher has the reputation of success, and Little Chandler has ambitions as a poet. However, it is clear from the story that Chandler is emotionally limited. Gallaher is unsympathetic and crude, and each is self-deceived about his talents. Chandler's thoughts and Gallaher's conversation betray conventional attitudes in derivative, cliché-ridden language that belies their individual pretensions.

From the very outset, the story establishes Little Chandler's physical, emotional, and social immaturity. He has the appearance of a child, takes his own fantasies much too seriously, shows no capacity for original thought or expression, and views the social and artistic life of Dublin from a private distance. At the same time, he pins some hopes on his reunion with Gallaher to help him break out of this condition, as Gallaher's reputation and his invitation to Corless's seem to promise. However, as their conversation progresses, it is clear—clearer to the reader than to Chandler—that these expectations are not to be fulfilled.

Despite his disappointment, Chandler is inclined to ignore Gallaher's insulting behavior, and he allows the gaudy images of Gallaher's life abroad to disconcert his own fragile self-image. Thus, at the conclusion of the story, Chandler's rebellion against his domestic responsibilities is no wiser than was his vague discontent at the beginning.

The main focus of the story is Chandler: His life is circumscribed by his dull job, his passionless marriage, and his general insularity. The secondary focus is on Gallaher, who, for all of his vaunted talents and experience of the world, brings home nothing more than vulgarity and materialism. He makes no effort to understand or sympathize with Chandler, and finally has nothing to offer him but further reason to doubt himself. It is a measure of Little Chandler's lack of perspective that he allows the conversation to disconcert him: Another person might just as easily have found in the example of Gallaher's manner and values good reason to restore his faith in his workaday Dublin life.

Noting that both Little Chandler and Gallaher are significantly lacking in powers of observation, given to trite expression, yet claim to have linguistic talent, another theme of "A Little Cloud" may be observed. Each of them is more interested in the effect that he might have on others than in developing an individual perception of the world around him and a respect for language to represent that world. Moreover, the impression of Chandler's mental life does not lead to any degree of confidence in his spiritual powers.

Because of the moody, impressionistic, and allusive poetry that he thinks he might write, Chandler considers himself as a potential member of the Irish Literary Revival. Without explicitly admitting it, therefore, he imagines himself as a follower of William Butler Yeats, whose poetry of the 1890's was marked by similar qualities and was at the turn of the century much imitated by Irish writers of meager talent. From this historical perspective, then, like Yeats's poem "A Coat," "A Little Cloud" is Joyce's satire on these writers.

Style and Technique

This story, like all those in *Dubliners*, displays a high degree of realistic exactitude while at the same time maintaining a firmly controlled sense of design and symbol. The narrator's point of view, moreover, is nicely poised between the idiom of the characters—which verges on caricature—and the language of subtle irony.

First, it reports accurately the geography, architecture, and atmosphere of turn-of-the-century Dublin: the details of Chandler's route to his meeting with Gallaher (he is, in fact, literally drawing nearer to London), the townhouses of the former aristocracy that have become shabby tenements, and the exclusive reputation of Corless's. On this level alone, Joyce's and Little Chandler's notions of artistic integrity are a world apart.

Second, the story is told in a dialectical progression of three scenes: the first, presenting Chandler's eager anticipation of Gallaher; the second, the unhappy reality revealed at Corless's; and the third, the conflict in Chandler's feelings set up by the contrast between these perspectives. Each of these scenes follows a consistent progression in subject: from particular considerations of Gallaher, to Chandler himself, to general reflections on "life," ending with a retreat to "art." The rhythm of this development suggests Chandler's inability to draw any coherent or expressible conclusion from his actual experience.

Third, the language and symbology of the story suggest the theme of false feeling and forced manner. Both characters think and speak in clichés, as can be seen, for example, in the quality of mind attributed to Chandler in the opening paragraph and in the way in which Gallaher, in the middle scene, greets the news of his friend's marriage. A pattern of symbols and allusions suggests Gallaher's exaggeration and vulgarity: his orange tie, his ordering "whisky," and his ostentatious use of Gaelic and French expressions. Finally, these images are complemented in the concluding paragraphs as Little Chandler hears his wife's soothing words to their child: They remind him that he is a man of little consequence.

Coilin Owens

LITTLE HERR FRIEDEMANN

Author: Thomas Mann (1875-1955)
Type of plot: Symbolist
Time of plot: The 1890's
Locale: Lubeck, Germany
First published: "Der kleine Herr Friedemann," 1897 (English translation, 1936)

Principal characters:
JOHANNES FRIEDEMANN, the protagonist, a hunchback and
    dwarf
FRAU GERDA VON RINNLINGEN, a femme fatale, both beautiful
    and cruel
FRIEDERIKE,
HENRIETTE, and
PFIFFI FRIEDEMANN, Johannes's unmarried sisters
COLONEL VON RINNLINGEN, Gerda's husband and the district
    commander

The Story

Johannes Friedemann, as a month-old infant in Lubeck, had taken a bad fall while in the care of his drunken nurse. As a result, he is destined to live out his life as a hunchback and a dwarf. Remarkably so, Friedemann as a young adult has made an accommodation with his plight. At sixteen he had fallen in love with a blond girl his age, but one summer afternoon he saw her embracing and kissing a boy while hiding behind a jasmine bush. Friedemann made an instant vow: "Never again will I let myself in for any of it. To the others it brings joy and happiness, for me it can only mean sadness and pain. I am done with it." As a consequence, the dwarf teaches himself to revel in the changing splendors of the natural world: He learns to love music (in fact, he plays the violin passably), literature, and especially the theater, his real passion. In a substantive way, then, he has made his private peace with the world. Indeed, his surname in translation can mean "the man who seeks or finds peace."

In June of his fateful year, Friedemann happily celebrates his thirtieth birthday. Taking inventory of his life, Friedemann considers that he has boldly renounced that which he will never have, has successfully established himself in business, lives happily in the family home with his three unmarried sisters (Friederike, Henriette, and Pfiffi), and can optimistically anticipate ten or twenty more years of the good life: "And I look forward to them with peace in my heart."

In July, little Friedemann has five encounters with a voluptuous married woman, Frau Gerda von Rinnlingen. Her husband, who is forty years old (Gerda is sixteen years his junior), is a military officer (Colonel von Rinnlingen) and is the newly appointed district commander of the Lubeck area. Strangely enough, almost from his first sight of her, Friedemann instinctively recognizes and accepts Gerda as the agent of his doom; that is, she will bring about his death in a most direct way.

On a Tuesday noon, Friedemann has his first glimpse of her. While he is strolling with a business acquaintance, they see her in a yellow car being drawn by a pair of thoroughbreds. In a few words Thomas Mann describes her. Gerda's hair is red-blond; her face is "oval, with a dead-white skin and faint bluish shadows lurking under the close-set eyes." Friedemann fixes his gaze on her as she goes by. She in turn nods at him. While his companion chatters on, Friedemann stares stonily at the pavement.

Three days later he comes home for lunch and is informed that the district commander and his wife have arrived for a courtesy visit. Ignoring protocol, Friedemann without explanation retreats to his room and refuses to meet them. When his sisters announce to him that they will be returning the visit on Sunday, Friedemann says nothing: "He was eating his soup with a hushed and troubled air. It was as though he were listening to some strange noise he heard."

The dwarf's third encounter with Gerda, on the following night, is a most unsettling one. Attending the opera, he finds that he is seated next to her. His inner turmoil now begins in earnest. Little Friedemann is overwhelmed by the physical presence of the woman: her imposing height, her striking red-blond hair, her low-cut gown and full bosom, and the warm, alluring scent of her body. They do not speak, but after intermission his eyes become locked with hers. She continues to stare until he turns away. Friedemann is humiliated because he thinks that she has compelled him to cast his eyes down before her steadfast gaze.

Toward the end of the opera, Gerda drops her fan in what he interprets as a coquettish ruse. They both bend to retrieve it and their heads momentarily touch. Without a word he flees the theater and heads home, absolutely convinced that her eyes glittered at him with "unholy joy." Once he calls out her name; twice he murmurs, "My God, my God!"

Friedemann is ill the next day as his sisters go off early on their visit to the von Rinnlingens. Late that morning he finds a reservoir of strength and impulsively decides to seek out Gerda at her home. Ushered into a half-darkened room, he converses rather pleasantly with her about their mutual health and about his violin playing. Suddenly, without warning, her expression changes from one of real concern about him to one of genuine cruelty. Again she stares at him until he submits and begins to look at the floor. As he prepares to leave, she invites him and his sisters to her home the next week for an informal dance.

Friedemann goes home by way of the river, which is adjacent to her property. He knows now that his fate is in her hands. There is a scenario to be acted out, and he will submit to his role. Even though he has always yearned for peace, it cannot be his until she has had her way with him, whatever that might be. Prior to her arrival in Lubeck, he had held the sensual world at bay with his formidable gift for sublimating his sexual drive. Her presence has changed all that now. She is simply too powerful a force for him to resist.

The final episode with Gerda is an obligatory scene. Little Friedemann is prepared for the end. At her home that Sunday night the guests have gathered. A resigned Friedemann quietly sits and looks at Gerda with a gaze of unwilling adoration. In time she invites him into her garden. A subservient Friedemann follows her beyond the garden into a little park by the river's edge, leaving all the other guests behind. Seated on a bench they chat once more about their health. He admits to her that those years of sublimation had been unhappy ones. The kindness in her tone apparently causes him to stand up abruptly, to emit a loud wail, and then to take her hands in his as he kneels before her with his face buried in her lap. With his diminutive body trembling, he gasps: "You know, you understand . . . let me . . . I can no longer . . . my God, oh my God!"

Scornfully laughing at him, Gerda pushes him away and then flings him to the grass. In supreme disgust at having lost control of himself, the self-absorbed hunchback drags his body to the water's edge as she runs up the path to her husband and the other guests. Little Friedemann lets his upper torso immerse itself in the river.

Themes and Meanings

Two of Mann's themes are to be found in this story: the fate of the unhealthy artist and the destructive power of the femme fatale. The former theme is often found in his early fiction; the latter is not so prevalent. When Mann incorporates them into one tale such as "Little Herr Friedemann," the result is a work of rather unsettling power. Few Mann stories from the 1890's achieve the weight and dramatic thrust of this one.

As a typically doomed Mann male, Friedemann is one who is "marked out" from society by his deformity. Despite whatever derision he must endure because of his boy-man appearance, Friedemann has become part of the mainstream of Lubeck society: He is an entrepreneur; he leads a gainful, productive life; he is a member of a respected Lubeck family; and he is a rather visible member of the local artistic scene in that he plays the violin and is an avid patron of the arts.

Counterbalanced against all these achievements, however, is the fact that Friedemann has deliberately renounced the sensual life (love, passion, and sex). For Mann, that is unhealthy; in fact, it is for him a form of decadence in its own way. Thus, as an artist of sorts, Friedemann is considered by Mann to be typical of that class. That is, notwithstanding Friedemann's relative bourgeois stability, he leads an unhealthy and by extension an unhappy life. His fate in the river, Mann suggests, is the culmination of such a life.

The other theme has to do with Gerda as femme fatale and the deadliness of her relationship with the harmless invalid. Her motivation may be beyond the reader's understanding given that Mann does not go into her mind. Friedemann, however, most assuredly sees her as one whose actions cannot be misinterpreted: She is determined to be the cause of his destruction, as she is. He is positive that she has with great calculation brought him to the point in his life at which he must take his own life. After all, she is the one who invites him to her party. She is the one who entices him to the isolated bench by the river's edge. Gerda, finally, is the one who seduces him into passionately confessing his desire for her—and then physically rejects him. Her mocking laughter on the way back to her guests is the last sound little Herr Friedemann hears, along with the chirping of the crickets.

Style and Technique

One of the primary characteristics of Mann's style is his frequent use of leitmotifs. The particular images and verbal patterns that recur throughout "Little Herr Friedemann" serve as reinforcement of Mann's emphasis on the vulnerability of Friedemann and the strength of Gerda. For example, there are numerous references to small birds and bird sounds. Several times Friedemann is described as being pigeon breasted. Taken all together, they remind one that Friedemann is much like a frail bird, the prey of a far larger, predatory creature.

The numerous references to Gerda having a dead-white face, arms, and skin not only stress the connection she has with the femme fatale (who is almost always described in those ways) but also portray her as an emissary of death itself. Further, the motif of the jasmine bush recurs at critical points in the narrative: when Friedemann at sixteen sees his first love embracing behind that bush; when he sits on a bench near a blossoming jasmine by the river as he tries to make sense of Gerda's ambiguous attitude toward him when he visited her at home; and, finally, again on that last night on the bench as he pours out his stumbling protestations of desire to her. The jasmine is white and is heavily scented. Clearly Mann wants it to be identified with Friedemann's youthful sexual awakening and later with his several tormenting encounters with the only woman in Friedemann's adult life, Frau von Rinnlingen.

Gerald R. Griffin

A LITTLE LEGEND OF THE DANCE

Author: Gottfried Keller (1819-1890)
Type of plot: Parody
Time of plot: The early Christian era
Locale: Earth and Heaven
First published: "Das Tanzlegendchen," 1872 (English translation, 1911)

> *Principal characters:*
> MUSA, a dancer who renounces dancing on Earth in preparation
> for better dancing in Heaven
> DAVID, a dancer and messenger of the Virgin
> THE NINE MUSES FROM HADES, whose song makes all in Heaven
> homesick for Earth

The Story

The story opens with a quotation from the Old Testament that associates dance with happiness: "O virgin of Israel, thou shalt . . . go forth in the dances of them that make merry. . . . Then shall the virgin rejoice in the dance." (Jer. 31:4,13).

The legend itself takes place after the Christianization of Europe. The young girl Musa is a born dancer who dances on all occasions, with others and by herself. One day, as she is dancing alone in the sanctuary, a man wearing a royal purple gown and a gold crown appears and dances with her to music provided by small cherubs. He is David, the messenger of the Virgin.

Because more dancers are wanted in Heaven, David has come to ask Musa to spend eternity in a never-ending, joyous dance. The dancing in Heaven, he assures her, is vastly superior to that on Earth. One condition imposed on the invitation gives Musa pause: She must renounce the dance and all worldly pleasures for the rest of her time on Earth. Only when David begins playing an exceptionally sweet dance does Musa acquiesce, recognizing that her earthly body is too cumbersome for such a melody.

Musa then has her ankles chained and wastes away in a hermit's cell, living as a penitent and a recluse. Many come for advice and prayers, and a touch from Musa makes awkward girls graceful. After three years, Musa clothes herself as a bride and dies. Although it is an autumn day, her death is accompanied by sweet music, green leaves, and flowers, and the chain binding her ankles snaps with a silvery sound. Throngs of the faithful who have come to watch see her lifted up by a glorious king into Heaven, where she is lost in the ranks of thousands of shining dancers.

As always on high holidays in Heaven, the nine Muses from Hades are invited to help in the ceremonies. Musa and Saint Cecilia sit with the nine Muses; Musa sits next to Terpsichore, the Greek goddess of the dance. Our Lady herself whispers that she will not be content until the Muses are brought to Paradise forever.

In seeking to ingratiate themselves, the Muses inadvertently make themselves unwelcome in Heaven. They have prepared a song of praise, grouping themselves into two quartets, with Urania as the leading voice for both. Their misfortune is that the song they have rehearsed in the Lower World sounds very different when performed in Heaven, where it seems uncouth, almost defiant, and causes all in Heaven to burst into a torrent of tears of homesickness for Earth.

Finally, the Most High silences the Muses with a peal of thunder, and they have not been invited again to enter the sacred portals.

Themes and Meanings

Gottfried Keller's dance legend supports two opposite interpretations. As the story progresses, there is a shift in emphasis from Musa and dance to the Muses and song. The question is how the two parts relate to each other. One analysis may see the Muses' uncouth song as supporting evidence for David's statement that dance in Heaven is more refined and exquisite than the best dance on Earth. By extension, the same would be true of all the arts. Thus, in comparison with the blessed who enjoy eternal life in Heaven, the Muses appear as crude misfits who deserve to be expelled. Creatures of Greek mythology do not belong in the Christian Heaven.

Additional information indicates an alternative reading, in which Musa's self-denial is a tragic waste of her talent, and the worldly art of the Muses contains heights and depths of mortal aspiration not accessible to those in Heaven.

Keller was a nonbeliever whose thinking was influenced by the materialistic philosophy of Ludwig Feuerbach. A Swiss scholarship enabled Keller to study in Heidelberg in 1848 and 1849, where he attended Feuerbach's lectures and developed a close friendship with him. Feuerbach believed that because life on Earth is all humans have, people should devote all of their energies to leading a natural and moral life. Life should not be passed in preparation for an uncertain reward in Heaven. When seen in that light, the Christian requirement that Musa renounce dance and all worldly pleasures seems wrong.

The strongest argument for interpreting the dance legend as a criticism of Christian abstinence and self-denial is that the dance legend is the last in a set of seven legends, all of which stress the importance of experiencing life to the fullest. Most of these legends show the Virgin acting in compliance with people who seek fulfillment in this life.

The first legend, for example, is about Sister Beatrice, a nun who feels compelled to leave the convent, marries a knight, and has eight sons. Almost twenty years later she returns to the convent and finds that she has not been missed. The Virgin has impersonated her and performed her duties all that time. The Virgin's approval of Beatrice's secular life in this legend is comparable to the Virgin's remark in the dance legend that she will not be content until the Muses are taken into Paradise forever.

Keller portrays the Virgin throughout as sympathetic to human needs and desires, but he also indicates that she does not have the authority to install the Muses in Heaven. Regardless of whether one sees the Muses' performance as inferior or superior to the heavenly choir, common to both interpretations is the insight that the two worlds are irreconcilable.

Style and Technique

Keller's source for the subject matter of his seven legends was a rather poorly written book of legends published in 1804 by the pastor Ludwig Theobul Kosegarten. Keller gently parodies the pastor's portrayal of the saints by shifting the emphasis from the divine to the worldly. Although Keller's legends are short and apparently simple, they underwent many revisions between the first version of the late 1850's and the version presented for publication in 1872.

The parodistic element in the dance legend lies in Keller's subtle mockery of the heavenly figures, who are not to be taken seriously. Martha "had donned her prettiest kitchen-apron, and the sweetest little spot of soot adorned her white chin." By elaborating on the trivial, Keller implies that there is nothing of substance in Heaven. Sugary appearances are matched with frivolous behavior: The cherubs use flattery to obtain fruit, and David flirts with lovely Erato.

In contrast with such superficial entertainment, the Muses' song, full of longing and sorrow, evokes a profoundly emotional response. They sing not of shining rewards but of "the burden of earth-woe." The vicissitudes of life are real and vastly preferable to the monotony of an eternally pleasant Heaven. The Muses themselves are portrayed as serious and ambitious musicians, in contrast to David's band of little fellows with dimpled little legs.

Keller's criticism is unmistakable, yet the playful tone of the legends ensures that the devout will be astonished more than offended. There is no biting satire. Keller is not seriously attacking God and the angels, only their humorous caricatures. In fact, the Most High who silences the Muses with a long peal of thunder is not the Christian god at all, but the Greek god of thunder, Zeus. Such eclectic casting precludes a pointed attack.

The main intent of Keller's dance legend is not so much to disdain the concept of Heaven, a place in which he did not believe, as to demonstrate the unique opportunity of a life on Earth. This he accomplishes by means of a rather disconcerting shift in narrative approach.

Formal analysis may find fault with the ending of the story. It loses sight of the main character, Musa, and reads like an afterthought, as indeed it was. Keller had already sent his final version to the publisher when he attended an excellent organ concert. Inspired by the music, he telegraphed the publisher to wait, and wrote the concluding part about the Muses' song. It is the atheist's ironic commentary on the legend of Musa. The poor girl dies prematurely in her haste to get to Heaven, only to find that everyone in Heaven longs to be back on Earth.

Jean M. Snook

LITTLE WHALE, VARNISHER OF REALITY

Author: Vassily Aksyonov (1932-   )
Type of plot: Domestic realism
Time of plot: The 1960's
Locale: Moscow, Russia
First published: "Malenkii Kit, lakirovshchik deistvitelnosti," 1964 (English translation, 1965)

> *Principal characters:*
> TOLYA, the narrator
> IVAN, his son
> HIS WIFE

The Story

Little Ivan cheerfully greets his father, Tolya, coming home from work. Father's new leather cap intrigues him, and he asks whether one can fly with it. The father immediately catches on and stokes the boy's imagination by telling him that they can fly to the White Sea to see the polar bears and walruses. The boy adds whales and "limpeduzas"—a furry animal he has invented. When the father adds sharks, the boy rejects them as evil beasts.

The cheerful boy, nicknamed Little Whale by his father because he resembles a little whale in the bathtub, is not the only one greeting Tolya. His wife offers a contrasting welcome by asking him repeatedly whether he has called "him"—an influential person on whom their future depends. Tolya is bombarded by the insatiable curiosity of the boy and the persistent nagging of his wife, with the boy taking his father's side. When the wife tells them to leave the house for a walk, they happily oblige.

On the way to an amusement park, Ivan continues to ask all kinds of questions. The father answers them not only out of duty but also because he is amused by his son's alertness and curiosity. He realizes that his son lives in a wonderful, strange world unlike that of the grown-ups, and he wishes to enrich it by going along with it rather than destroying it. He also senses that the boy gropes to find an answer to everything and to create order whenever things seem to be out of the ordinary. For example, when his father shows him the moon and the Great and Little Bear constellations (which are feminine nouns in the Russian language), the boy wonders aloud where the papa bear is and concludes that he must have gone out to hunt and provide for his family.

In the Dream World amusement park, they see figures from famous fairy tales, such as the Tom Cat, the Prince, the Swan, and the Little Humpbacked Horse. Ivan wants to take them all home. When his father explains that his wish is impossible to carry out, he touches every figure and tells them and himself that he is taking them home; that is enough to satisfy his wish.

Back at home, when the father reads Ivan a story in which a crocodile grabs a little elephant by its trunk, the boy throws the book away, complaining that it is a bad book that does not tell the truth. When he hears the story in which a wolf eats seven kids, he refuses to believe it is a wolf, firmly convinced that instead the papa goat will take care of his seven kids.

When the day finally comes to a close and Ivan falls asleep, the father calls the person his wife has been urging him to call, only to hear a litany of half-truths, empty promises, and false assurances of sincerity and goodwill. Afterward, he stands over his sleeping son, who is sleeping like a little valiant knight of Russian folklore, smiling in his dream. The picture of his son fills him with joy, and he wants to drink to the health and happy life of the seven kids.

Themes and Meanings

Vassily Aksyonov began to write in the early 1960's, at the time of significant changes in the Soviet Union a decade after Joseph Stalin's death. Although full artistic freedom was three decades away, the writers of that time were able to express themselves more freely than their predecessors. They were able to get away from prescribed topics and writing methods, and they were much bolder in using allegory, irony, and satire. "Little Whale, Varnisher of Reality," although a fascinating human story, is also a subtle allegory about the Soviet way of life and thinking.

The story is built on a different way of looking at things. The protagonist is facing two worlds, each having its own rules and ways. On one side is his unhappy wife, who takes her dissatisfaction out on him because he is seemingly unwilling to assert himself adequately in the rough real world. He is having difficulties with his superiors at work as well, much of which is not his fault. He has had an affair with a beautiful aunt, as Little Whale calls her, who is pestering him now that the affair is over. His friends are not always sincere and helpful. On the other side, he sees the world of his little son, which is a world of innocence and instinctive goodness. His son's world, although replete with fantasy and make-believe, appears to be more truthful, and certainly more wholesome and nourishing, than the adult world.

The dichotomy of these two worlds can be seen from two angles, philosophical and political. The question of what is real—a dilemma that many a Soviet writer has had to face—imposes itself. Is the world of the grownups, with all of their lies, hypocrisy, insincerity, and merciless struggle for survival, the only real world, the one to which a person has to devote all of his or her time? Does Ivan's world, with its innocence, make-believe, and seemingly deliberate changing of what seems to be real, deserve at least to be treated equally, if not preferably? Because Aksyonov is not primarily a contemplative writer, it is unfair to expect Tolya to solve this age-old dilemma, nor does he try to. It is clear, however, which world he prefers—that of his little son.

The political aspect is evident in Aksyonov's taking on one of the mainstays of the Soviet official aesthetic canon concerning the approach to reality. For years the literary dogma in the Soviet Union had been to approach reality not as it was but as it ought to be. Marxist aesthetics demanded that writers accept the law that everything is based on superstructure (class struggle and means of production) and suprastructure (every other human endeavor), and depict the typical aspects of a situation. Consequently, because everything is preordained, the outcome is predictable. Although there are always exceptions—for example, there were some good feudal lords and some bad paupers—the duty of a true artist is to depict what is typical, such as a bad capitalist, no matter how many exceptions there may be. Therefore, a writer must change or varnish reality in order to be true to the Marxist thinking. This is the dilemma Soviet writers faced in the first three and a half decades after the revolution.

Aksyonov uses the innocent world of Little Whale and his varnishing of reality to question the validity of the official approach. Although he wrote the story at a time when the official approach was on its way out, it was still topical in the early 1960's. Many a writer has suffered because of his or her dissidence; some chose to leave the country, such as Aksyonov himself, while others were forced to do so, for example, Alexander Solzhenitsyn, because they refused to varnish the reality.

Aksyonov goes beyond a political discussion. For him, the position he takes in the story not only is more correct but also corresponds to human nature and is much more beautiful and, consequently, artistically truthful. He not only presents Little Whale's world as refreshing, colorful, and more credible, but he also shows that Little Whale's way is the only way toward regeneration. Ivan has an uncanny ability to ask the right questions and to reject the answers that do not satisfy his childlike sense of justice. One of his most common questions is who is good and who is bad. He rejects sharks because of their beastly behavior. He wants to hear his father say that whales are good. He angrily throws away the book about a crocodile attacking a little elephant. He also deliberately changes the wolf into a goat protecting his kids. In this way, Little Whale has a beneficial effect on the people around him. It is not surprising, therefore, that he wants his father to read him a book at a very difficult and stressful moment for the father.

It seems that Aksyonov does not reject the varnishing of reality when it is done for a good cause, rather than for political aims. Little Whale grows in stature into a role model, wiser than others much older than he.

Style and Technique

Stylistically, "Little Whale, Varnisher of Reality" shows an interesting mixture of approaches. On one hand, it is straightforward and realistic; on the other hand, there are enough elements of psychological nuances, dramatic features, and fast-paced action to brand the style neorealistic, even neoromantic. The crisp dialogue and the abundant use of modern and slang expressions render the story into a pulsating piece of fiction, resembling a film scenario. The building of characters is sketchy but convincing; the story comes out as a gemlike miniportrait. Aksyonov has succeeded in writing a story about his time and for his contemporaries, with abundant artistic qualities to make it a lasting work of art.

Vasa D. Mihailovich

THE LITTLE WIFE

Author: William March (William Edward March Campbell, 1893-1954)
Type of plot: Psychological
Time of plot: The early 1920's
Locale: A train traveling from Montgomery to Mobile, Alabama
First published: 1930

> *Principal characters:*
> JOE HINCKLEY, a traveling hardware sales representative
> MRS. THOMPKINS, his mother-in-law

The Story

"The Little Wife" is the account of a five-hour train trip, during which the protagonist, Joe Hinckley, attempts to postpone facing an almost unbearable grief by chatting with his fellow passengers. There is little external action in the story and seemingly no real tension. However, writing as an omniscient author, William March reveals the two conflicts on which the story is built: that between the passengers and their talkative companion and that between Joe's rational and emotional selves.

The story begins as Joe is boarding the train in Montgomery, Alabama, which will take him to his home in Mobile. After he is settled, Joe looks at some of the people near him. There are a couple of giggling young girls just ahead of him, and across the aisle sits a stern-faced country woman with a goiter. Again Joe looks at the telegram he had found waiting for him when he went back to his hotel after lunch. In it, his mother-in-law had informed him that his wife, Bessie, had borne him a son but that she was not expected to live through the day. As he thinks about how happy he and Bessie have been during their brief year of married life, Joe cannot help noticing the tender concern of a nearby elderly woman for her own husband. Then, hearing a porter calling his name, Joe claims a telegram that has just been sent on by his hotel. He does not open this second telegram. Instead, he goes to the back vestibule, tears it up, and tosses the pieces off the train. Immediately, he feels a great sense of relief and returns to his seat in a jubilant mood.

Joe begins visiting with everyone around him. He tells the conductor that he has just become a father. He goes over to the young girls, persuades the old lady to join them, and for two hours tells his captive audience about his meeting Bessie, their courtship, and their engagement. After the girls leave the train, Joe has a cigarette, then moves in on the elderly couple. They listen politely while he talks about the wedding, the honeymoon, and their joy when Joe and Bessie learned that she was pregnant. Joe is so wrapped up in his story that the porter has to tell him they are pulling into the Mobile station. Joe keeps smiling even when he sees his mother-in-law, Mrs. Thompkins, beyond the fence, dressed in black. It is only when she asks whether he has received the second telegram that he realizes he can no longer hide from the truth. His legs give way, and he has to sit down. After a while, he asks exactly when his wife died, and Mrs. Thompkins informs him that she had dispatched the second telegram immediately after Bessie's death. The story ends with Joe and his mother-in-law leaving the train station.

Themes and Meanings

According to March's biographer, Roy S. Simmonds, the genesis of "The Little Wife" was a simple observation that March made one day in a hotel lobby. He saw another guest open a telegram he had just been given. The man's facial expression changed; then he tore up the telegram, threw it away, and, seemingly unconcerned, returned to his conversation. Although March would never know the real story of the stranger and the actual content of the telegram, he developed the incident into a short story illustrating one of the author's primary themes: that for one reason or another, human beings choose to live in a world of appearances rather than in the more difficult world of realities.

At the end of the story, Joe tells Mrs. Thompkins that he did not open the second telegram because if he did not know the truth, he could keep Bessie alive, at least for a few more hours. However, though he does not realize it, Joe's choice is also motivated by a need for self-preservation. He had no warning that Bessie might die. The shock was a terrible one. Instinctively, Joe senses that only by retreating for a time from the full realization of his loss can he prepare himself to face it. When he receives the second telegram, Joe is not ready to read the words he knows it contains. He wants to run away. Because he cannot jump off the train and run into the woods, as he briefly considers doing, and because he cannot face the reactions of the other passengers if they see the grief on his face, he decides to escape the reality and to avoid their comments by acting a role, by putting on what is essentially a theatrical performance for the benefit of his fellow passengers.

Ironically, Joe never realizes that the passengers who make up his audience are just as involved in the world of appearances as he is. Although at first they are sympathetic to the new father, who is so excited about the birth of his son, they soon grow tired of his talk. Thereafter, they merely pretend to be interested, just as he pretends to be blissfully happy. In Joe's case, it is a matter of survival; in their case, it is simply a social code. Their training in good manners has included instruction in how one should behave when confronted with a bore.

Though in his fiction March often harshly ridicules what he sees as the falsities of his society—for example, snobbery, patriotic fervor, and even religious faith—he also understands that without their illusions, human beings may find life unbearable. One can only imagine how difficult the trip would have been, both for the passengers and for Joe, if he had told them the truth, only to see them embarrassed by his sorrow and helpless to provide him with consolation. They would have chosen not to hear Joe's real story, just as Joe chooses not to hear the woman with the goiter announce that she has a death sentence. Sometimes, March seems to conclude, people have to linger for a time in the world of appearances. For Joe, as for the woman with the goiter, reality would come soon enough.

Style and Technique

It has been pointed out that although "The Little Wife" was one of March's earliest works, in it he already displays the technical skill of a far more experienced writer. For example, the story is constructed as two parallel narratives. One of them is the actual journey, a train trip that takes almost exactly five hours. The other is Joe's account of his involvement with Bessie, which is told during the train trip, but goes back to their meeting and ends with their planning for the new baby. When the journey ends, Joe's narrative stops. However, as long as he is still on the train, he does not bring his story up to the present. Only when he is off the train, his journey concluded, does he admit that his love story, too, has ended.

March's handling of point of view is also highly effective. At first, it seems that the story will be told totally from Joe's perspective. Interspersed with Joe's thoughts are his observations about his surroundings, for example, the overwhelming heat and the ineffectual fan, as well as his impressions of the nearby passengers. Not until Joe returns from the back of the train and begins his story does the narrative voice change. At this point, the author begins to present Joe's account as a third-person summary, a tactic that enables March periodically to insert objective comments, noting, for example, how excited Joe appears to his audience and how bored the other passengers are becoming. When the girls get off the train, March reports their uneasiness about Joe, and later, after another long summary, he also mentions the elderly gentleman's unstated suspicions. These variations in point of view and even in style provide March's readers with a number of different perspectives. Although they can empathize with Joe, they can also sympathize with his captive audience, and every now and then, they can view events from the author's more objective viewpoint.

Much of March's fiction is an indictment of human nature and of the society that the human race has constructed. However, in the very different tone of stories such as "The Little Wife," in which all of the characters are well-meaning and only life is cruel, the reader can see another side of March, his respect for decent human beings and his compassion for those, like Joe, who should not have to suffer.

Rosemary M. Canfield Reisman

LITTLE WOMAN

Author: Sally Benson (1900-1972)
Type of plot: Domestic realism
Time of plot: The 1930's
Locale: An unidentified American city
First published: 1938

> *Principal characters:*
> PENNY LOOMIS, a short woman
> RALPH LOOMIS, her tall husband
> MR. and MRS. MERRICK, Ralph's client and his wife

The Story

From their first meeting, tall Ralph Loomis is attracted to Penny because of her tiny stature. They both enjoy the attention they receive because of the contrast between their heights. In the few months following their marriage, they entertain friends and seem to experience a satisfying relationship. Ralph enjoys being the protector of such a tiny dependent person; Penny relishes his attentive wonder over her ability to function as an ordinary wife.

Gradually their circle of activity diminishes. Even in the early days of their entertaining, the guests are mostly men. They have no children, and Penny makes few friends. Ralph encourages Penny to leave the apartment and meet with women friends, perhaps to play bridge, but Penny refuses on the grounds that renewing a friendship with the tall Louise Matson would make her look ridiculous.

Even their vacations are affected by Penny's size and helplessness. When they go on fishing trips to Canada, Ralph must carry Penny over rough terrain and protect her from such unpleasant sights and experiences as hooking a fish. Ralph eventually accommodates himself to Penny's size by choosing a lodge close to the fishing area.

This kind of accommodation pervades many aspects of Ralph's life, for example, choosing first-row seats in theaters, putting objects on low shelves, and walking slowly. The slightest suspicion of criticism, however, even if expressed as sympathy about the limitations imposed by her small stature, arouses Penny's resentment.

Penny protests that she stays busy, and this suggestion of constant physical movement supports Ralph's observation that her life is limited to physical activity. When he suggests she make friends with women, have interests outside the home, or read, she insists, even as she flits restlessly around the apartment, that she has all she needs to make her happy and satisfied. After ten years of married life, Ralph goes on a business trip to Chicago and makes a discovery: He not only does not miss Penny, he actually prefers the companionship of his client, Mr. Merrick, and his wife, Nellie. He writes Penny enthusiastically about his pleasurable experiences with the couple and tells her that they will take the Merricks to dinner when they visit.

At the ensuing dinner, Ralph observes the contrasts between Mrs. Merrick and his wife. Mrs. Merrick is slightly overweight, but she is unconcerned about her physical appearance. In contrast, Penny is carefully dressed in a ruffled pink taffeta dress and matching shoes that make her look extremely young. Even Ralph realizes that this young look is not appropriate for a thirty-five-year-old woman. In conversation, Mrs. Merrick expresses herself with dignity but not vanity. Penny speaks brightly and animatedly but apparently with little thought, because Mr. Merrick listens with a frozen smile. The two couples part, relieved, at the end of the evening. As Ralph and Penny return to their apartment in the rain, Ralph realizes that the raindrops reflect harshly on Penny's face. When he automatically picks her up so that she will not get wet, he realizes with surprise that his little woman has become a burden to carry.

Themes and Meanings

A good satire frequently employs a stereotype literally in order to undermine it. In "Little Woman," Sally Benson dramatizes a stereotyped version of the perfect wife. The protagonist, Penny Loomis, is small and helpless in the world outside her home, but a meticulous housekeeper, excellent cook, and devoted companion to her husband. This apparent recipe for a successful relationship backfires—both for the husband who chose his wife for these very characteristics, and for the wife who continues to pursue all the activities her husband originally admired, even though she realizes that he is losing interest in her company.

The main theme challenges the validity of the standards of attraction that society highlights. "Little Woman" is about two people who base life choices on the importance of appearances but find their happiness diminishing with each year of their relationship. Both Penny and Ralph accept the sexual stereotypes that the male should be physically bigger to be more protective, and the female should be tiny, vulnerable, and subordinate to her husband, and they now find themselves imprisoned behind this facade.

This story is not about a person who is unable to control the way people treat her because of her size. Two characters—Louise Matson and Nellie Merrick—point out that Penny could easily appear taller than her natural height of five feet by wearing high-heeled shoes instead of the flats that she wears. Penny's resentment of this helpful advice indicates that she is choosing to be regarded as small; she is deliberately making herself conform to the sexual stereotype imposed by society. Although Benson stresses that Penny and Ralph, representing society, are responsible for the unhappiness they have incurred by the use of superficial criteria, she also maintains a balance between satire and sympathy for the protagonist and her consenting spouse.

Style and Technique

The title of this story immediately introduces its theme and literal content. The phrase "the little woman," usually employed by a husband to refer to his wife, does not necessarily indicate the height of the woman. From one point of view, the term is affectionate; from another, the stress on the diminutive refers to the wife's subordinate position. Benson seems to stress the latter, negative interpretation.

The story maintains this stress on semantics. For example, Ralph takes Penny's side in her disagreement with Louise Matson by commenting, "You may be little, but you aren't small." Ralph, however, eventually decides that Penny's problem is that her worldview is small when he fails to talk her into extending her friendships and leaving the small world of their home. By the conclusion of the story, Ralph observes that Penny "seemed to grow smaller and smaller until there was nothing much left of her but a pink taffeta dress and a pink ribbon." The use of the name Penny—the smallest denomination of U.S. currency—is surely no accident.

Benson uses metaphors and similes extensively to support the theme. Penny pretends to denigrate her small feet with the phrase, "disgraceful little Chinese feet," when she is actually quite proud of them. The reference reminds the reader of a culture that once physically crippled its women because it supported the stereotype that small is better for a female. Another equivocal comparison appears early in the story when Ralph first describes Penny, dressed in short skirts and sitting in a large chair, as "just like a doll." His delight in an artificial toy dissipates when he looks for adult companionship in the ensuing years of their marriage.

From the positive image of being a doll, Ralph begins to see his wife as a bird. "She was as busy, he thought, as a canary in a cage, fluttering, picking, keeping up an incessant chirping." When she is wandering around the room one evening, he is ashamed of his outburst: "For the love of Pete, *light*, can't you?" The author's italics stresses that a bird lights, not a person. His changing feeling about his wife's size becomes explicit by the conclusion of the story, when he repeats the bird image and underscores its artificiality. He notes, "Her head was bent slightly to one side in the birdlike way she affected." The negative connotation is explicit.

The element of contrast is frequently used in this story. The author contrasts Ralph and Penny's marriage with that of Mr. and Mrs. Merrick as relationships based on different value systems. Ralph notes, Mrs. Merrick has "the appearance of a woman who had contemplatively set aside all personal vanity and turned to other things." The word "contemplatively" underscores Nellie Merrick's decision to disregard the emptiness of physical appearance, just as using the word "affected" to describe Penny's efforts to remain young in appearance emphasizes her choice to create a false illusion. Penny is quick to point out what she sees as negatives about Mrs. Merrick—not a stylish dresser, plain looking, and, above all, overweight. Ralph sees Mrs. Merrick as having dignity, while he notes his wife's face is unhappy, and she looks absurd in her ruffled pink taffeta dress. The Merricks' ability to enjoy themselves when they dine with Ralph in Chicago contrasts with their uneasiness when Penny joins the group. Although Penny is her usual bright, perky self, Mr. Merrick is "smiling a frozen sort of smile, but he didn't look very happy."

"Frozen" might describe the state of Ralph and Penny's marriage. Having accepted the standards of society as to what makes happiness, both seem unable to change. By the end of the story, their surname, Loomis, seems to foreshadow their unhappiness.

Agnes A. Shields

A LIVING RELIC

Author: Ivan Turgenev (1818-1883)
Type of plot: Social realism
Time of plot: The 1850's
Locale: The village of Alekseyevka, in Belyov province, Russia
First published: "Zhivye Moshchi," 1874 (English translation, 1895)

> *Principal characters:*
> PYOTR PETROVICH, the narrator, a landowner and hunter
> ERMOLAY, a serf, Pyotr's companion and guide
> LUKERYA, the protagonist, a paralyzed twenty-nine-year-old serf
> girl
> VASILY POLYAKOV, a freed serf and bailiff
> AGRAFENA, Vasily's wife
> FATHER ALEKSEY, a priest

The Story

The title, "A Living Relic," refers to a paralyzed serf girl, Lukerya, whom the narrator, Pyotr Petrovich, unexpectedly encounters lying alone and abandoned in a small shed on one of his mother's farms. Pyotr is stunned by the sight of the immobile, mummylike body that lies before him and cannot believe that the half-dead creature is the same lively, beautiful, robust young girl who loved to sing and dance a mere six years ago, when she lived in his mother's manor house as one of her household serfs.

Pyotr's compassion for the girl grows as he questions her about her misfortunes and learns that she fell, injured herself internally, and gradually lost the use of her legs. Because the doctors were unable to diagnose her illness and the gentry considered it inconvenient to keep invalids in the manor house, she was sent to the village of Alekseyevka. Her affliction caused her great grief because it separated her from the young peasant lad, Vasily Polyakov, whom she loved and to whom she had been betrothed. Vasily also grieved but eventually married another girl, named Agrafena. As Lukerya relates her misfortune, the narrator is astonished to learn that she harbors no resentment. She is grateful knowing that Vasily has found a good wife who has provided him with children. She weeps only after Vasily's visits, when she recalls the happy times that they shared together. For the most part she endures her suffering quietly and patiently, without dwelling on her affliction. She explains that as long as she still breathes, she is alive and she values that life. She takes delight in the beauty of the natural world around her: the aroma of wild flowers; the sounds of insects; the activities of birds, fowl, and other small woodland creatures that creep into her shed. Although it is with great effort, she continues to sing and even teaches the songs she remembers to an orphan girl. Pyotr is overwhelmed by the scarcely audible but pure sound that she emits from her trembling lips.

Deeply moved by the condition of the unfortunate Lukerya, he offers to transfer her to a hospital, but she declines, remembering the painful medical treatment she received. She asks only that he try to obtain for her more opium to help relieve her sleeplessness. Then, in a supreme expression of compassion and concern for others, she asks Pyotr to persuade his mother to reduce the quit-rent for the peasants because they are poor and do not have enough land. Pyotr agrees and departs. As he leaves, the foreman on the farm tells him that the local peasants call Lukerya "Living Relic," because she never complains and is grateful for everything. A few weeks later, Pyotr learns that Lukerya has died as she had foreseen in one of her dreams.

Themes and Meanings

Ivan Turgenev's story may be viewed as an allegory on the spiritual beauty of the Russian people symbolized by Lukerya, who personifies their longtime suffering and endurance. The story was written for a literary symposium that was published in 1874 to aid the victims of a famine. It was also included in the 1874 edition of Turgenev's *Zapiski okhotnika* (A Sportsman's Sketches, 1932), originally published by Turgenev in 1852 as an exposé on the evils of serfdom.

Thematically, "A Living Relic" stresses the dignity and moral worth of the peasantry and reflects Turgenev's humanitarian concern and compassion for suffering. He calls the reader's attention to the theme of suffering by introducing his story with a two-line epigraph from a poem by the Russian poet Fyodor Tyutchev (1803-1873): "Native land of long endurance, Thou land of the Russian people!" Lukerya becomes the major symbol of that endurance in the story. She accepts her suffering with patience and dignity approaching sainthood; she does not complain, and she makes no demands on others. Her needs are modest. She eats nothing and subsists only on the water contained in a jug at her side, which she can still reach herself with her one unparalyzed arm. She accepts her affliction, pointing out that others are more unfortunate than she, for they have no shelter or are blind or deaf. Furthermore, she considers her physical affliction a spiritual advantage, because it relieves her of the temptation to sin that burdens healthy people. She has even managed to overcome the sin of thought by training herself not to think. She interprets her suffering as a sign that God has sent her a cross to bear, which means that He loves her. She regards her solitude as an opportunity to become more spiritually aware, maintaining that this spiritual awareness would not be as highly developed if she were surrounded by people. She accepts her own misfortunes without malice and selflessly shows concern for the suffering of others when she pleads with Pyotr to request his mother to lower the quit-rent of the peasants to alleviate their plight.

Although Lukerya emerges as noble and compassionate, Turgenev depicts the members of the upper classes in a less positive manner, emphasizing their insensitivity. Unable to cure Lukerya, the doctors who treat her abandon her. Pyotr's mother, finding it inconvenient to keep the paralyzed Lukerya in the manor house, sends her to another village so she will not be in the way. Another doctor comes to examine Lukerya, not for the sake of helping a suffering human being but merely to satisfy his scientific curiosity. The doctor disdainfully refers to her and the other peasants he treats as fools.

Through his sympathetic portrayal of Lukerya, Turgenev suggests her moral superiority to those surrounding her. She emerges as a powerful symbol of the masses of the Russian peasantry, paralyzed, unable to help themselves, enduring misfortune and mistreatment, and regarded with disdain or indifference by the upper classes. Despite their suffering, however, the peasants, like Lukerya, persevere through patience, quiet humility, and resignation.

Style and Technique

Turgenev emphasizes the spiritual significance of Lukerya's suffering through a series of Christian symbols. Symbolically, Lukerya is given the name "Living Relic" by the peasants, who recognize her patience, meekness, and gentleness. The term "relic" has obvious religious overtones, associating her with sainthood or martyrdom. This religious symbolism is reinforced when Pyotr first encounters Lukerya and describes her face as "all of one color, bronze, for all the world like an icon painted in the old style; the nose narrow like the blade of a knife." The religious symbolism of her suffering is repeated in three of Lukerya's dreams. In the first dream, her parents appear to her and thank her for making it easier for them in the other world by suffering for their sins, asserting that she has already atoned for her own sins by her prolonged suffering and that she has now started to atone for the sins of others.

In the second dream, Lukerya sees herself standing in a field of golden rye and placing a moon on her head like a festive headdress. The circular shape of the moon suggests a halo. She begins to shine and light up the field around her as a beardless, tall, young man in white, whom she identifies as Christ, approaches her and soars with her to Heaven, leaving behind a vicious dog that keeps biting at her legs and that symbolizes her illness. The dream reveals to Lukerya that her suffering will cease only at her death, for the dog that is her illness will have no place in the Kingdom of Heaven. Her third and final dream both foreshadows her death and suggests her sainthood by associating her death with a religious holy day. Lukerya encounters a tall woman with large, yellow, falconlike eyes who announces to her that she represents death, which will come for Lukerya after the fast for Saint Peter's day. Lukerya dies as predicted, after Saint Peter's day, and on the day of her death, she reports hearing the sound of church bells "from above"—which the narrator, Pyotr, interprets as "from Heaven," thus acknowledging her saintliness and affirming her spiritual beauty, which is the major theme of the story.

Jerome J. Rinkus

LIVINGSTONE'S COMPANIONS

Author: Nadine Gordimer (1923-   )
Type of plot: Social realism
Time of plot: About 1970
Locale: Africa
First published: 1971

> *Principal characters:*
> CARL CHURCH, the protagonist, a British newspaper
>   correspondent
> MRS. PALMER, the owner of a hotel where Church takes a break
>   from an assignment
> DICK PALMER, her son, manager of the hotel, who wants to be a
>   pop musician
> ZELIDE, the secretary-receptionist at the hotel, with whom Dick is
>   having an affair

The Story

"Livingstone's Companions" is a somewhat indeterminate story, for it combines two tangential but still related plot interests: Carl Church and his fascination with the lake near the hotel where he is staying, and Dick Palmer's attempt to break the bonds of his domineering mother. Both these stories are undergirded by Church's reading the journals of the famous Scottish missionary/explorer of Africa, David Livingstone. Moreover, providing a social background (typical of Nadine Gordimer's fiction) is the story of the complex relationship between white colonials and indigenous Africans.

The story begins with Church's bored response to the petty political posturing of the minister of foreign affairs in an anonymous African country, a country, like most in modern Africa, which is newly independent. Church's story begins with an assignment from his British editor to do a piece on the one hundredth anniversary of the Royal Geographic Society's sending of a party to search for Livingstone during the 1870's. Church is told to retrace the steps of Livingstone's last journey. With this assignment, the central metaphor of the story is established, for although Church—less than delighted with what he considers to be the triviality of such a task—does not retrace Livingstone's steps literally, he does so psychologically and symbolically.

Church's journey begins in the airport with a chance meeting with a blond woman who runs a hotel in a neighboring country near the graves of Livingstone's companions, graves that the woman proprietorially calls "my graves." The central theme of the story, and that which connects the story of Church with the story of Mrs. Palmer (the hotel proprietor) and her son, is indicated when Church reads from Livingstone's journal about how a community of interests and perils makes everyone friends. Church says, as though referring to "Livingstone's Companions," that such an idea could be the lead for his own story. Indeed, it is the community of interests and perils that connects Church with Dick Palmer and thus with the story of Africa itself.

Church's involvement with the Palmers begins when he gets lost looking for Livingstone's trail, stumbles on Mrs. Palmer's hotel, and meets Dick and Zelide—he wearing diving fins and she dressed in a bikini, as if they were the inhabitants of an ocean world right in the middle of the African bush. Although it is getting lost that leads Church to the hotel, it is the lake that keeps him, for it is the lake that serves as Gordimer's central metaphor of irresistible allure, as the Livingstone journals (particularly Livingstone's account of the death of one of his companions) serve as a reccuring motif of interest. Church, in this hiatus in his journalistic tours, responds to the journals in place of the usual Gideon Bible he might find in a hotel. Although he plans to seek out the graves of Livingstone's companions, he has difficulty finding them, and thus discovers them more significantly in the journals themselves.

Dick's story is one of being dominated by his mother; even as she urges him to grow up, she tries to keep him from making decisions of his own. Dick tells Church about having his own band, about playing the guitar, about composing his own material, but when he cannot agree with his mother, he, like Church, heads for the lake and skin-dives. Church sees in him the image of a homosexual boy in the Berlin of the 1920's, the master-race face of a George Grosz drawing. It is this decadent sense that takes hold of Church, for he feels that such a pause or break as this is difficult for him: If he is not focused on what he will do next he knows not what to do. His mind turns to death, and he goes back to the lake.

In fishing with a spear under the lake surface, Church discovers the miracle of an unselfconscious technique of the hunt: the miracle of hitting the fish without thinking of it, a kind of magic typical of primitive intuitiveness. When the miracle occurs and he does spear a large fish, however, it twirls about so vigorously on the spear that it unscrews itself from the shaft and disappears with the harpoon point sticking out of its belly and its entrails floating out. At this point in the story, Church no longer remembers the error that brought him to this place; he simply accepts himself as "here"—an experience not common to him, for he is not accustomed to being present in the places and situations in which he now finds himself, and he identifies with the first travelers in Africa, who must have experienced each day as detached from the last and next.

The conflict between blacks and whites in Africa with which Gordimer is often concerned is embodied in Mrs. Palmer, who says that blacks simply do not know how to look after anything—a comment that Church ironically sees as the enlightenment the white man has brought to the Africans. She treats her son the same way. When Dick tells Church that he has just received a phone call from his fiancé in another city and that someone has told her that he is having an affair with the secretary-receptionist, the reader knows that the mother is the guilty party. When Dick disappears, the mother worries that he will "do away with himself" as his father did.

Such confessions prompt in Church a desire to go to the lake, to feel the cool mouth of waters close over him. However, he does not go back to the lake. As Church is leaving he finds the path to the graves of Livingstone's companions, the graves he was originally seeking. Among the five graves is that of Dick's father—a sixth companion to Livingstone. All of them look toward the lake, a lake that stretches as far as one can see.

Themes and Meanings

This is one of those stories that is so slight in plot that the reader is left with a feeling that it is not a story at all. It manifests a technique of inconclusiveness that Gordimer learned from the great modern, Anton Chekhov, for the story does not present its theme by means of plot or character dialogue but rather by implication and understatement. Carl Church is the central character, but he is less a character than a convention: the convention of the bored and jaded newspaperman who remains objective, aloof, and uninvolved with the lives of others, one who is usually not really "there," but who, because of the influence of the lake, now seems actually "here," who seems most alive when he is under the influence of the lake itself. Although he does not have any interest in Dick's dilemma, nor any sympathy for Dick's mother, he still somehow sees a relationship (though he never explicitly mentions it) between the experience of Livingstone and his own experience.

Thus, ironically, he does not write his newspaper story about following in the footsteps of Livingstone, and yet in a strange way he does, for this very story entitled "Livingstone's Companions" is an artistic version of that story he was assigned. Church somehow believes that he is following in the footsteps of Livingstone, exploring the mysteries of Africa; here, the mysteries of Africa are those of the proprietorial and paternalistic attitude of the white toward the black, reflected by the fact that Dick is an employee of his mother, who believes that neither her son nor the blacks can take care of anything. Thus, the story is really about the fact that all whites in Africa are Livingstone's companions, following in his footsteps, leaving graves in their wake. However, none of this is made explicit; all is suggested indirectly.

Style and Technique

The technique that Gordimer uses here is typical of her stories. The style is fairly straightforward and realistic, focusing on trivial events and only gradually revealing that there is a story at all, that there is indeed a conflict. Juxtaposition is the technique Gordimer uses to reveal the theme: juxtaposition of the story of Church with that of Dick, and juxtaposition of both of their stories with the journals of Livingstone. Moreover, Gordimer makes use of a central metaphor, the lake, to indicate the cool and mysterious submerged nature of Africa, where true reality is to be found, in contrast to the hot and complicated world of surface human interaction. Gordimer is a realist, but only if that term is understood as referring to the symbolic realism of Chekhov, Katherine Mansfield, James Joyce, and Sherwood Anderson. Her stories seem realistic in the sense of being detailed small slices of life, but they always carry more meaning beneath the surface than may at first appear.

Charles E. May

A LODGING FOR THE NIGHT

Author: Robert Louis Stevenson (1850-1894)
Type of plot: Historical
Time of plot: 1456
Locale: Paris
First published: 1877

Principal characters:
FRANCIS VILLON, a poet and thief
DOM NICOLAS, a Picardy monk, one of the band of thieves
GUY TABARY, another thief
REGNIER DE MONTIGNY, a thief and murderer
THEVENIN PENSETE, another thief, who is murdered by Montigny
ENGUERRAND DE LA FEUILLEE, a lord and veteran of the wars,
    who gives Villon shelter and hospitality

The Story

On a bitterly cold winter's night in 1456, Francis Villon, the greatest poet of medieval France, is huddled in a small house by the cemetery of St. John, trying to write "The Ballade of Roast Fish" while Guy Tabary slobbers over his shoulder, Regnier de Montigny and Thevenin Pensete play a game of chance, and the renegade monk Dom Nicolas watches. All of them are thieves, among whom there is no honor. Hearing the wind rattling the rafters, Villon reminds the others of hanged men dangling on the gibbet at nearby Montfaucon. Despite this memento mori, Montigny leaps up and stabs Thevenin to death after losing to him. The thieves divide the dead man's money, but then the others steal Villon's purse before they all flee into the night.

The snow has ceased, and Villon fears that his footprints will lead the authorities to him. Trying to elude a patrol, he takes refuge on the porch of a ruined house, where he finds the body of a woman frozen to death and steals two small coins from her stocking. Then, discovering his purse to be missing, he wanders in search of it, to no avail. Fearing that he, too, will freeze before morning, he seeks shelter from his adopted father, the chaplain of St. Benoit, but is turned away. Wandering once more, he recalls that wolves devoured a woman and child nearby. When he begs shelter from former friends whom he has lampooned, they drench him with a slop bucket, and his legs begin to freeze.

In desperation, he knocks at the door of a strange house in which he sees a light. The door opens, and an elderly gentleman invites him in. While his host goes for food and drink, Villon surveys the riches of the apartment and considers stealing the golden plate but thinks better of it. When his host returns, they strike up a conversation, and Villon learns that the master of the house is Enguerrand de la Feuillee, a great lord and a veteran of the king's wars. Villon confesses himself a poet and thief. They engage in a dialogue over the nature of honor, Villon claiming that the soldier is a greater thief than himself and that their different status is merely a matter of birth, the lord maintaining the traditional view of honor. When the host condemns Villon's rascality, the poet defends himself by claiming that he, too, has honor, which has kept him from stabbing Enguerrand and robbing him. By then, morning has broken, and the enraged host orders his unwanted guest to leave.

Themes and Meanings

"A Lodging for the Night," Robert Louis Stevenson's first published fiction, was also the first fictional treatment in English of Francois Villon (1431-1463?), the greatest poet of medieval France. Born as Francois de Montcorbier, Villon, author of *Le Petit Testament* (1456) and *Le Grand Testament* (1461), was neglected in subsequent centuries but rediscovered in the nineteenth century, when his bohemianism struck a kindred chord and his writing contributed to the romanticizing of the Middle Ages. In the 1860's, Dante Gabriel Rossetti (1828-1882) did three notable translations of Villon, and soon several other poets, including Algernon Charles Swinburne (1837-1909), did some translations and imitations of the French poet. The first complete translation into English did not appear until 1878, the year after Stevenson's story, and it may well be that "A Lodging for the Night" was the catalyst for the project. Just before writing the story, Stevenson wrote in 1877 an article entitled "Francois Villon, Student, Poet, and Housebreaker."

In it, Stevenson, an advocate of the heroic, stoic, and active life, condemned Villon as a whining, cowardly knave and used this portrait to attack the aesthetes and bohemians of his own day. Stevenson was both drawn to and contemptuous of Villon; he preferred the vigor and sometimes brutal realism of Villon to the work of more effete and languid poets of his own day, but he also disliked the extreme realism of the rising naturalist writers, of whom he saw Villon as an ancestor. "Not only his style, but his callous pertinent way of looking on the sordid and ugly aspects of life, becomes every day a more specific feature in the literature of France," Stevenson complained. Nevertheless, Stevenson was fascinated by the vitality of evil, a subject that he explored in *The Strange Case of Dr. Jekyll and Mr. Hyde* (1886), *The Master of Ballantrae* (1888), and elsewhere, and he was drawn to Villon's vivid picture of the Parisian underworld. He envied Villon an artistic freedom denied the Victorians: "No thought that occurred to him would need to be dismissed without expression; and he could draw at full length the portrait of his own bedevilled soul, and of the bleak and blackguardly world which was the theater of his exploits and sufferings."

Later authors were to transform Villon into a romantic hero. In *If I Were King* (1901), Justin Huntly McCarthy (1860-1936) makes Villon not merely a thief but also a king of vagabonds, whom Louis XI then makes Grand Constable of France for a week, during which Villon saves Paris from the Burgundians and wins the love of a highborn lady. This version of Villon, and variations on it, flourished in the operetta *The Vagabond King* (1925) and in several films, in which Villon is portrayed by Dustin Farnum, John Barrymore, and Ronald Colman. Stevenson's biographer J. C.

Furnas observed that "Louis would probably have been genuinely shocked by the distortions of *If I Were King*." According to Stevenson, the poor should bear their burdens with stoic fortitude and "smile with the fox burrowing in their vitals. But Villon, who had not the courage to be poor with honesty, now whiningly implores our sympathy, now shows his teeth on the dungheap with an ugly snarl."

"A Lodging for the Night" shows Villon doing both. He is so ineffective even in crime that his colleagues pick his pocket and call him a crybaby while he stands limp and trembling after the murder. During his dialogue with Enguerrand de la Feuillee, he is alternately swaggering and servile, justifying his unsavory life by blaming it on the poverty into which he was born. The snarl comes when he challenges the lord's claim to honor; Villon observes with bitter truth that the honor of a conquering army is that of plunder and rapine, that his own petty crimes are trivial compared to those committed by royalty and their troops. Villon says that his own honor consists in not cutting his host's throat and stealing his golden goblets; that is his thanks for the night's hospitality. He leaves with his neck still unstretched and his impudence intact.

Style and Technique

Like all of Stevenson's writing, "A Lodging for the Night" is notable for a clear, well-crafted style. There is nothing complicated about the construction of the story; it moves in a linear manner from beginning to end. Stevenson made his moralizing dramatic by couching it in the form of a dialogue between Villon and his host, and the argument between them is fairly well balanced, with Villon getting the last word. The genesis of the story can be found in Stevenson's earlier article about Villon, where he briefly recounted the murder of Thevenin and commented, "If time had only spared us some particulars, might not this last have furnished us with the matter of a grisly winter's tale?" On further reflection, he fashioned just such a tale out of the incident. The story contains a marvelous evocation of medieval Paris on a wintry night, when people were frozen to death on the streets and wolves were prowling over the snow. Furnas writes, "'A Lodging for the Night' has a high and valuable flavor of Balzac— the harsh little literary curiosity is still shapelessly cunning, and, for all its didactic dialogue, strangely alive."

As a novelist, Stevenson was to make his mark with vigorous historical romances, and "A Lodging for the Night" was his first work in that genre.

Robert E. Morsberger

THE LONELINESS OF THE LONG-DISTANCE RUNNER

Author: Alan Sillitoe (1928-   )
Type of plot: Social realism
Time of plot: The 1950's
Locale: Essex, England
First published: 1959

Principal characters:
SMITH, the narrator and protagonist, a rebellious teenager
THE GOVERNOR OF BORSTAL (an English reform school), who
    encourages Smith's long-distance running

The Story

In a reform school for delinquent youths, Smith, the streetwise son of working-class parents from Nottingham, is chosen to train and compete for a coveted long-distance running award. He is selected, he states, because of his build (he is long and skinny) and because his constant running from the police has made him an appropriate candidate.

Arising before dawn for a five-mile practice run through the countryside, Smith experiences a freedom of thought that allows him to confirm his philosophy of life and his perceptions of society.

Through self-revelation, Smith learns about himself: He evaluates his life on the street and in Borstal, weighs his options, and decides on the meaning of an "honest life." Running affords him this opportunity: "It makes me think so good that I learn even better than when I'm on my bed at night." His conclusions are strong: He is, and will always be, an "Out-law," pursued by society's "In-laws," who are forever looking to inform the authorities about his unlawful actions.

Smith draws definitive lines in this societal war. He is dedicated to the life of an "Out-law"; for Smith, life according to the laws and values of society is not a worthwhile existence. Along with this confirmation is Smith's decision that, despite his abilities, he will lose the race. As winner of the Borstal Blue Ribbon Prize Cup for Long-Distance Cross Country Running (All England), he would merely be the vehicle through which the Borstal governor would achieve glory and recognition.

Smith considers the attention to his well-being an act of hypocrisy by the governor, whose only intent is to mark the progress of the one he has chosen to win the much-desired award. In fact, Smith feels that he is spoken to as though he were the governor's prize racehorse, which only strengthens his resolve: "I'll lose that race, because I'm not a race horse at all. . . . I'm a human being and I've got . . . bloody life inside me."

It is this sense of aliveness that Smith appreciates and vows to uphold, rather than become what he considers "dead from the toe nails up," like any "In-law." Moreover, his idea of a valuable, honest life simply does not conform to that of society. Honesty is not, Smith relates, "a cosy six pounds a week job." Rather, it is being true to oneself and one's principles. It is dishonest, Smith has learned, to live life comfortably, without concern. It is dishonest to win a race that symbolizes the type of honesty Smith rejects.

As he ends his morning course, Smith recounts the events that led him to Borstal. Out on a winter night with a friend, he espies a bakery with its window opened barely enough to allow them entry. They steal a money box, the contents of which they decide to hide outside Smith's house in a drainage pipe and spend leisurely. Within a few days, a police officer arrives to inquire about the stolen money but is deterred by lack of proof of Smith's guilt. After many days of accusation, Smith is certain that the police officer is about to abandon his investigation. One rainy day, however, during yet another interrogation, money starts to fall out of the drainpipe. Smith is arrested and sent to Borstal in Essex.

As the day of the race arrives, Smith remains committed to his plan to sabotage the win, despite the governor's hint that on his release from Borstal Smith might receive assistance in making his living as a runner. The race begins, and Smith easily takes the lead. As his thoughts overtake him, he is motivated by the memory of his father's death (from a painful cancer, at home, without medical intervention) to stand firm in his principles. Despite an annoyance in his left arm that causes some discomfort, Smith nears the finish line favored to win.

At this point, he slows his pace down almost to a halt, enabling the runner behind him to overtake his lead. As the crowd cries for him to run the last hundred yards to win, Smith completes the course in second place.

In the aftermath of the race, his privileges removed, Smith is relegated to perform chores of the most menial nature, a response that he predicted would follow his act of defiance. In this manner, Smith endures his final six months in Borstal, all the while planning his next lawless act. The story ends on a note of further resistance: Smith entrusts the account of his Borstal experience to a neighborhood friend, who will seek its publication on Smith's next arrest.

Themes and Meanings

Themes of rebellion and isolation dominate this story. As Smith grapples with his life's meaning and direction, he comes to understand and defend his defiance of authority.

Smith rebels to retain control over his life and to ensure that conformity will not suppress his individuality. The result of his actions is isolation—in the form of removal to Borstal. Once at Borstal, his isolation is enforced: He runs a five-mile morning course alone, while the rest of Borstal is still asleep. The physical isolation of running encourages Smith to think, which, in turn, leads to an emotional isolation that is intense and resolute.

For Smith, the concept of individuality is understood only in terms of black and white; there are no shades of gray. Ultimately, the issue is whether one can retain individuality—the key to feeling alive—while belonging to a society that imposes laws and restrictions.

Smith views society according to definitions of social class, simply the haves and the have-nots. Only if one lives by the limitations of his class is one living honestly. Smith recognizes that his meaning of the word "honest" differs from the Borstal governor's, but he resents the authority's efforts to deny him his own perceptions.

Perhaps Smith's most significant discovery is this interpretation of an "honest life." It is running the race, not winning it, that is important, because running causes him to think, to feel; it is the ultimate expression of individuality, of being real. One perceives that Smith has always been running: first from the police and acceptance into society, now toward introspection and honesty.

To Smith, winning is not crossing the finish line. Instead, he sees beyond this aspect of winning to an underlying implication: A winner is one who chooses his life and lives according to his principles.

The reader senses that before Smith is sent to Borstal, he has lived his life with no thought to his actions. As a have-not, reared to get whatever he can by whatever means from those who have more, Smith acts naturally, impulsively. The experience of running long distance at Borstal, however, causes him to pause and consider where he has been and where he is going.

This process of thought paves an internal road toward self-discovery that Smith runs without hesitation. As he discovers a talent for running, which can be turned to economic advantage and a place in society, Smith is offered an opportunity for change. However, it is change according to someone else's intent, a condition that Smith cannot accept. The possibility of reform is thus replaced with the reconfirmation of rebellion and defiance. The only change that occurs is the nature of the rebellion itself: No longer instinctive, intuitive, Smith's noncompliance becomes deliberate, cognitive.

An antihero who wins his own race, Smith is able to achieve a measure of inner growth that, while rejecting assimilation and community, provides a model of determination strength and everyone can admire.

Style and Technique

Like its main character, the language of the story is aggressive, determined, defiant. Colloquialisms and profanities reflect the bold and contemptuous disdain that the poor have for the more advantaged. Speaking of the governor, Smith declares: "It's dead blokes like him as have the whip-hand over blokes like me, and I'm almost dead sure it'll always be like that, but even so, by Christ, I'd rather be like I am."

The author employs two types of storytelling that keep the reader and protagonist linked until the story's end. In a manner similar to stream of consciousness, Alan Sillitoe makes the reader privy to the unfolding of Smith's deepest thoughts, ensuring compassion and sympathy with his motives. In addition, he uses straight narrative to fill in the pieces of Smith's past and information about his family and his life in Nottingham.

The race is symbolic of internal and external life forces. Apart from representing the obvious conflict between the governor and Smith (for the governor the race will bring acclaim and recognition, although for Smith it is the means by which to strike back at authority), this contest contrasts Smith's physical and mental energies. As he races toward the finish line, where he will prevent his own progress, his mind races toward continued self-analysis and esteem.

As he achieves self-definition, Smith embraces the loneliness of the long-distance runner with enough courage to allow another runner to

> go right slap-up against that bit of clothes-line stretched across the winning post. As for me, the only time I'll hit that clothes-line will be when I'm dead and a comfortable coffin's been got ready on the other side. Until then I'm a long-distance runner, crossing country all on my own no matter how bad it feels.

Shelly Usen

A LONG DAY IN NOVEMBER

Author: Ernest J. Gaines (1933-   )
Type of plot: Psychological
Time of plot: The mid-twentieth century
Locale: A sugarcane plantation in rural Louisiana
First published: 1968

>*Principal characters:*
>SONNY HOWARD, the six-year-old narrator
>MAMA (AMY), his mother
>DADDY (EDDIE), his father
>GRANDMA, Amy's mother
>MADAME TOUSSAINT, a seer and adviser

The Story

Sonny wakens, shivering, from dream-filled sleep to the sound of his parents quarreling. Such tension between Mama and Daddy is new to Sonny; it turns him into a keen observer and his story into a series of dialogue-driven episodes. Although he cannot always interpret it, he knows well what people say around him. Daddy works hard and long cutting cane on a sugar plantation. Lately he has been neglecting his wife and son, devoting his free time instead to repairing an old car. When Daddy repeats that he needs love, Mama responds, "Get love from what you give love. . . . You love your car. Go let it love you back." When Daddy goes off to work, Mama and Sonny gather a bundle of clothes and leave for Grandma's, a short distance away in the workers' quarters. Sonny is sleepy and confused, not pleased to stay with Grandma, because he tires of Grandma's constant fussing. Besides, she is trying to get Mama to leave Daddy and go live with the despised Freddie Jackson. It is a relief to run off to his one-room school.

The second section, more dreamlike than the first, is set in the quarters' tiny school, which is always cold in November. Sonny shivers even more today because he does not know his lesson. Normally, Mama teaches it to him at night and Daddy goes over it again in the morning. With all the fussing today, however, no one has helped him. As Daddy has violated one of the adult rituals, so Sonny has done with his. Miss Hebert, his teacher, would understand if he explained, but the other children, especially those his age, would only laugh. So, when called on to recite, he simply cries and wets his pants. As the other children tease him and mop up the puddle, Sonny can only get colder.

Sonny takes home a note asking his parents to come to the school the next day. Grandma's place is hardly a refuge: she is still yelling, Freddie Jackson is still chasing Mama, and Daddy is still standing at the gate, begging Mama to come home. When Grandma drives Daddy away with her shotgun, Sonny follows him onto the road.

News of Freddie Jackson spurs Daddy to a desperate decision: "Madame Toussaint . . . I hate it, but I got to." Sonny hates it too, for he is afraid of the wizened old voodoo woman of the quarters. However, she is the last hope of men in trouble with their women. She knows everything that happens and seems to know Daddy's problem, but he does not have her three dollar fee. From a fellow cane worker named Charlie, Daddy gets both the money and the reassurance he needs. Charlie lends him five dollars, all he has, and tells him of the troubles he has been having with his own wife. "I'm following her advice, Brother Howard, and I wouldn't be a bit surprise if there ain't a little Charlie next summer sometime." Charlie is happy to do what he can to bring the family back together, believing that family love is the most important thing in the world.

Once Daddy pays Madame Toussaint, she gives him the very advice that he does not want, to set fire to his car. Dumbfounded, he pretends he has not heard. She repeats that he must burn it—another necessary ritual, this one of expiation. At most, he will sell it, he says. So he runs to Mama, seeking a reprieve. "Burn it," she commands.

With the whole community gathering to watch, Daddy parades the car, towing it a few miles to an unused field. There, with everyone agape—for the other men love cars as much as he—he pours gasoline and sets it on fire. Grandma is the most incredulous: "I never would've believed it . . . I just do declare. . . . He's a man after all." Like a Greek chorus, the people of the quarters agree.

Daddy believes all the rituals are over, but Mama knows better. She brings in a big switch and insists that he whip her before they can eat dinner. Only then will he save face in this tightly knit community; only then will the affair be concluded. Lulled to sleep by the familiar sounds of his parents' bedsprings, Sonny, feeling warm and happy, begins his best dreams in a long while.

Themes and Meanings

Best known for his novels, *The Autobiography of Miss Jane Pittman* (1971) and *A Gathering of Old Men* (1983), Ernest J. Gaines locates most of his fiction in Louisiana, focusing on black southerners, Cajuns, and Creoles. A century earlier, the locale of this story would have been the slave quarters. In varying degrees, all the stories recount the trials of being a man, woman, or child in a hostile environment. Here he underscores the rituals that protect a person and a family from despair and disintegration.

Decades have taught the need for codes and rituals if the African American family is to survive. The bleaker, the more difficult life is, the greater the need for rules of behavior. Although Eddie is a good worker and a good man, when he neglects his family—however briefly and unintentionally—he threatens the entire community. The women are preservers and transmitters of tradition and set in motion the series of gestures and countermeasures that make up this folk narrative. Amy's leaving precipitates all subsequent action, to the extent that she foresees her own ritualized whipping that resolves the tale. Grandma is willing to spur her on, because in her eyes, Eddie violates decorum. Miss Hebert teaches the Creole sense of learning and manners. Madame Toussaint is the community guide to the invisible mysteries of love and value.

Sonny's embarrassment at school is central to the meaning of the story. He does not know his lesson because no one has taught it to him. His father does not know the dangers of a car, because none of the women has yet taught him the lesson of where legitimately to place his love. Each initially appears woefully inept. Each quickly learns his lesson, for the whole community is watching. Each comes of age.

Style and Technique

This, Gaines's most widely reprinted story, is told through a notable blend of soft-focus narration and sharp-focus dialogue. Its frame is the mind of a cold, hungry, confused half-asleep six-year-old. This long day has been the most bewildering of his short life. At the same time it has made him unusually alert—to the point of precise transcriptions of the adult conversation flowing around him. Drawn from African American oral folk tradition, this dialogue ranges from Eddie's garrulous confusion, mirroring Sonny's, to Madame Toussaint's gnomic certainties. The differences between men's and women's language provide one of the leitmotifs of the tale.

There are few resources in the quarters, hence the struggle to preserve the ones there are. On one level, it is an account of how much can be achieved with so little. Although much is at stake in the story, it is told in a relaxed, humorous vein that pulls the reader into its orbit. Because Gaines remains so close to his characters, his readers cannot feel above them. Mama tells Daddy: "Go back to your car. . . . Go rub 'gainst it. You ought to be able to find a hole in it somewhere." Whenever he is bedeviled by something or someone, Sonny throws the only object he always has with him—his chamber pot. By the end, readers have joined the author in a total and sympathetic immersion in the characters—understanding of all, superior to none.

John Sekora

LONG DISTANCE

Author: Jane Smiley (1949-   )
Type of plot: Domestic realism
Time of plot: The 1980's
Locale: Iowa and Minnesota
First published: 1987

> *Principal characters:*
> KIRBY CHRISTIANSON, a teacher without commitments
> MIEKO, a Japanese woman with whom he has had an affair
> HAROLD, his favorite brother
> LEANNE, Harold's wife
> ERIC, Kirby's other brother

The Story

Kirby Christianson's Japanese lover, Mieko, calls from Japan to tell him that her visit to him, which was to take place in a few days, has been canceled. Her father has been diagnosed with lung cancer, and she must stay with the family. Kirby's first reaction is a feeling of relief, because he has been unsure of what to do about Mieko and does not think she will fit in with his American family and associates. Feeling guilty about his feelings of relief, he affects sympathy. She breaks down on the telephone and weeps. Wanting to be there for her in an American sense, he holds on to the receiver and listens to her weeping, reflecting that he has never felt that deeply about anything. After she gains control of herself again, she makes it clear that he should not have listened but should have hung up, as a Japanese man would. She has exposed herself to him by her display of grief, and she feels deeply embarrassed. The connection is broken.

Kirby travels from Iowa to his brother Harold's new home in Minnesota for their family Christmas reunion. While driving through a severe snowstorm, he fantasizes about being killed on the road and there being no one to tell Mieko about his death; it is evident that he has no intimate connections at all. Reflecting that no one would care more than Mieko about his death, and she probably would not even hear of it, he feels sorry for himself.

He arrives safely at his brother's house and slips back into an unsatisfying relationship with his family. He has only contempt for his older brother, Eric, who writes for a conservative think tank and specializes in family values. His brother Harold is affectionate but seems childish and ineffectual compared with Eric, who dominates the reunion. Kirby is repelled by the limitations of his brothers' lives and angered by Eric's domination and moralizing.

The holiday continues, with Kirby watching his family from the sidelines, drinking and becoming more and more unhappy with Eric. When Eric punishes his three-year-old daughter, Kristen, for not eating, his thirteen-year-old daughter, Anna, takes up for her sister, and Kirby joins the fray on Anna's side. He pushes Eric into a bald and blatant statement of his conservative values, but Leanne, Harold's wife, stops the argument before it goes further. As the day proceeds, each occurrence shows that the holiday tensions are still present. Eric's wife, Mary Beth, wants Leanne to unwrap the presents she has wrapped, fearing that the realization that Santa's presents were wrapped like other presents might tip off the children about Santa. To keep peace, Leanne agrees.

Kirby goes to bed but, at midnight, drunk and restless, comes downstairs and finds Leanne still working. She offers him cocoa, and he tells her about Mieko. Leanne is both sensitive to others and honest. Kirby hopes that Leanne will somehow absolve him of his selfish treatment of Mieko, and side with him against Eric, but she does not. She comments that Eric has his flaws but never tries to get something for nothing, which she admires. This comment makes Kirby take a look at himself, and he flinches from what he sees. As he leaves the room in the dark he stumbles; Leanne guides his hand back to the banister and kisses him on the cheek.

Themes and Meanings

Jane Smiley's plot brings to mind Henry James's story "The Beast in the Jungle." Both stories feature a character too self-centered to commit to another human being, a character who feels himself special or chosen; both conclude with the hero realizing that he has missed forever the chance to be fully human. Smiley's lighter touch and suburban setting allow a rueful identification on the part of the reader. Her close analysis of people's misreadings of one another provides insight into the isolation of much of contemporary life and the exploitation of others this isolation provokes.

Kirby both wants and does not want companionship. He is relieved when Mieko cannot come. He thinks that his family will not accept her and that he will fail her because he cannot provide for her the support that she needs. He is unwilling to ask her to marry him, to make the relationship permanent, yet he is driven to her by loneliness. She is the most beautiful woman he has ever seen, and she loves him, but he has a deep-seated horror of the conventions of married life and of the suburban lifestyle he sees as inseparable from marriage. His need for companionship is countered by the fear of intimacy. Kirby does not want to be alone but wants complete freedom.

In what could be described as a long-distance society, communication is difficult. The telephone is no vehicle for intimacy, and misunderstandings abound. Kirby violates Mieko in Japan by turning to her in his loneliness, allowing her to fall in love with him, and making her unfit for a normal Japanese life; he makes the situation worse by listening to her weeping over the telephone, sharing over the wire grief that he never would witness in person. He is also at a distance from his brothers, psychologically as well as literally. He has not seen them often since they reached adulthood, and he understands only the surface levels of their lives. As the story progresses, Kirby becomes more aware of the superficiality in his relationships with others and of the role his own nature has played in establishing distance between himself and others.

At the end of the story, Kirby becomes aware of his shallowness. He realizes that the relationship with Mieko is a missed opportunity that cannot be recaptured, for either himself or her. The precious freedom that he has so defended is illusory. He understands that his brothers' lives, however much they seem filled with cliché to him, have a substance that is missing from his own. Leanne's kiss on his cheek may be seen as a token that she forgives him for what he is and for what he perhaps cannot help being.

Style and Technique

Smiley's domestic realism may recall the stories of John Updike and other writers concerned with subtleties of relationships. Smiley, however, specializes in the portrayal of connections not made, communications not completed, because her protagonist lacks the depth of character and courage needed to complete them. These protagonists have an intellectual sophistication that makes them feel superior, but they are emotionally underdeveloped.

Smiley also has a characteristic structure in many of her short stories: a character who cannot feel or react honestly to life, who is in some sense an outsider unable to be intimate with another, is shown his or her limitation by exposure to someone who can. Sometimes the outsider is unmasked by his or her attempt to intervene in the life of another without knowing what that life is and means.

Smiley's dialogue carries much of the weight of her themes. In "Long Distance," it is direct and realistic, yet multilayered and subtle. Each speech sounds perfectly natural, yet communicates a wealth of information about the relationships and advances the action as well. Rather than placing her characters in the usual situations of their ordinary lives, saying their usual things, Smiley manages to imply the typical content of a life through contrast with a present, unusually strained situation in which characters step out of their usual roles and speak differently but fully in character.

The description is subtle and functional. Smiley's suburban home is presented as a wonderfully ambiguous place. It is a tidy little domestic hell, with all the standardized attitudes, activities, and equipment that her outsider character can mock, yet it may be the only real testing ground for character and values.

Janet McCann

THE LONG-DISTANCE RUNNER

Author: Grace Paley (1922-   )
Type of plot: Fantasy
Time of plot: The early 1970's
Locale: New York City
First published: 1974

> *Principal characters:*
> FAITH, the narrator, a middle-aged woman who takes up long-
> distance running
> JACK, her boyfriend
> RICHARD and
> ANTHONY, her sons
> CYNTHIA, an African American Girl Scout
> MRS. LUDDY, an African American woman

The Story

Faith explains that one day in her early forties, she became a long-distance runner, because she wanted to travel around the county, including the old neighborhood streets. One day Faith kisses her sons goodbye and travels to her childhood neighborhood, now populated primarily by African Americans. As she jogs through the area, she is suddenly surrounded by a few hundred African Americans, and there occurs a surreal, at times humorous, discussion of a number of unrelated subjects between Faith and the large crowd. A Girl Scout named Cynthia volunteers to take Faith to Mrs. Luddy, who lives in the apartment where Faith spent her childhood.

As they approach Mrs. Luddy's residence, Faith becomes apprehensive and states that she no longer wants to see her old home. She lies to Cynthia, telling her that she does not want to see her mother's house right now because her mother has died. The idea of her own mother dying terrifies Cynthia. She becomes lachrymose and reveals that her mother is her protector, who will not let the pushers and other dangerous people get her. Trying to reassure her, Faith tells Cynthia that the girl can come live with her and her two nearly grown-up boys if her mother dies. Apparently Cynthia has been warned by her mother that white boys have sinister sexual intentions, and she assumes that this "honky lady" has some perverse scheme in mind. She begins screaming for help, fearing that Faith plans to kidnap her. Hearing the voices of large boys coming to rescue Cynthia, Faith runs in fear to Mrs. Luddy's door. Mrs. Luddy allows the unknown white woman to enter her home. She orders her son, Donald, to hide the white lady under his bed; when someone knocks on the door, the boy sends him away.

Faith lives with Mrs. Luddy and her family for three weeks and helps her take care of three little girls and befriends Donald. She develops some rapport with Mrs. Luddy, and they discuss a number of matters, including the problematical relationship between the sexes. One morning Mrs. Luddy wakes up Faith and informs her that it is time for her to return home, to which Faith agrees. Near home, Faith jogs through a playground and sees a dozen young mothers handling their children carefully and says to them, "In fifteen years, you girls will be like me, wrong in everything." She does not say it maliciously but to prepare them.

Faith's boyfriend, Jack, and her sons, Richard and Anthony, do not seem particularly concerned about her three-week absence. Anthony leaves to visit his friends in various institutions, a task that often occupies him into the evening. When Faith explains to Richard that she has spent a few weeks in her childhood apartment, he responds by asking her what she is talking about. When she tries to explain her experience to Anthony and Jack, they cannot understand what she is talking about either.

Having failed to communicate her experience to her boyfriend and her sons, Faith ends the story by appealing to the reader for understanding: "Have you known it to happen much nowadays? A woman inside the steamy energy of middle age runs and runs. She finds the houses and streets where her childhood happened. She lives in them. She learns as though she was still a child what in the world is coming next."

Themes and Meanings

Grace Paley is known as one of the most politically committed writers in the United States, and this story was written to promote social change. The story avoids didacticism and does not exhort the reader to adhere to a specific political ideology, but it reveals Paley's ardent feminism and her fervent concern for racial justice.

Paley's narrator, Faith, is experiencing a midlife crisis. Her journey to her childhood neighborhood can be seen as an imaginative quest for her roots and a new sense of direction, now that she finds herself adrift in the uncharted seas of middle age. Long-distance running is a metaphor for her sense of inadequacy and her need to take action and search for a creative outlet for her vast energy and untapped talents. She has spent much of her life "lying down or standing and staring" and now feels the need to run. Divorced, with two grown sons who feel little need for a mother, Faith believes that she has reached the age in which society has little use for a woman.

By returning to her old neighborhood and living with a socially underclass African American family, Faith is tacitly expressing her solidarity with fellow victims. She hopes to transcend the barriers of race and class and affirm her liberalism, but she is only partially successful. Despite the differences in class and race, Faith and Mrs. Luddy do achieve a limited friendship for the several weeks they live together, based largely on their common experiences as women and their tacit repudiation of a patriarchal society. They share a skepticism of men, who, they believe, are too often guilty of infidelity, inebriation, and violence. Mrs. Luddy's demand that Faith return home to her spoiled boys suggests that they cannot completely overcome the barriers of race and class. In fact, Mrs. Luddy's demand that Faith leave comes as no surprise to the reader, for Faith's experience in her old neighborhood reveals that despite her good intentions and her desire to become part of the community, she does not completely understand the culture of the African American neighborhood. When Faith expresses surprise that Mrs. Goreditsky, a white woman from Faith's childhood days, continued to live in the neighborhood until just two years earlier, she asks Cynthia if Mrs. Goreditsky was not frightened, "So we all," the girl replies. "White ain't everything." On another occasion, appalled at the deterioration of the underclass neighborhood, Faith remarks to Mrs. Luddy that "someone" should clean up the area. "Who you got in mind? Mrs. Kennedy?" Mrs. Luddy sarcastically replies.

The lack of understanding and failure of communication among people of different classes, races, and sexes are key themes in the story. Significantly, when Faith returns to her home and tries to convey her experience in the African American neighborhood to her boyfriend and sons, they have no idea what she is talking about.

The story is not entirely pessimistic, however. Full of humor and playfulness, it ends affirmatively with the implication that Faith's spiritual return to her childhood roots will enable her, in contrast to the jaded, cynical people around her, to recapture the child within her. She will attain the child's uncorrupted vision and ebullient capacity to respond to everyday existence with joyful spontaneity and a sense of pristine wonder to see "what in the world is coming next."

Style and Technique

Reminiscent of another writer who also challenged the status quo with radical politics, Bertolt Brecht, Paley employs innovative techniques that undermine narrative conventions. In "The Long-Distance Runner," she may have deliberately employed Brecht's idea of the "alienation effect." By calling attention to the artistic nature of the play (its artifices), Brecht deliberately destroys the illusion of verisimilitude and the "you-are-there" emotional absorption in the story that writers traditionally have sought. By confounding an audience's expectations and making them keenly aware of the difference between reality and fantasy, he wants to emotionally distance his audience from the dramatic action in the hope that the audience will ponder the social problems that the work presented.

In "The Long-Distance Runner," Paley produces the alienation effect by including details that destroy the illusion of verisimilitude and remind the reader that this is a story deliberately crafted by the writer for a purpose. For example, the narrator deliberately undermines the story's verisimilitude by admitting her inability to decide on an age for Mrs. Luddy, "a slim woman whose age I couldn't invent." Like Brecht, Paley does not want the reader to become totally immersed in the story. She calls attention to the artificial nature of storytelling, reminding the reader that this is a made-up story, not reality, so that the reader can be detached and critically consider the complex social problems that are at the core of the work.

Laura Chavkin
Allan Chavkin

LOOKING FOR A RAIN GOD

Author: Bessie Head (Bessie Amelia Emery, 1937-1986)
Type of plot: Social realism
Time of plot: 1958-1964
Locale: A village in British Bechuanaland (now Botswana, Africa)
First published: 1977

> *Principal characters:*
> MOKGOBJA, the head of the family
> RAMADI, the father and supporter of the family
> TIRO, the mother of the family
> NESTA, an unmarried sister
> NEO and
> BOSEYONG, the children of Ramadi and Tiro

The Story

"Looking for a Rain God" is part of a larger collection of stories, *The Collector of Treasures, and Other Botswana Village Tales* (1977), an account of the history and people of Serowe, a large village in southern Africa. It is told in the third person by a member of the village. The main action takes place on the lands surrounding the village, where a family resorts to ritual murder to ensure rainfall for their crops.

The story begins in the lonely yet tranquil lands outside the village of Serowe, where people journey to grow crops each year. The edenic setting suggests mythic lushness and abundance. In 1958, however, a seven-year drought begins, and the once-idyllic land grows dry and barren. Initially, the people respond with humor, but during the seventh year, after two years of starvation, many succumb to despair. Some of the men hang themselves. The only people who prosper are those "charlatans, incanters, and witch-doctors" who make their fortunes off of others' misery and desperation.

The seventh year brings an early meager rain that promises an end to the drought, and the season for plowing and preparing the land to grow crops is officially announced at the *kglota*, or village center. In earnest anticipation, the family of the old man, Mokgobja, which includes a father, mother, unmarried sister, and two small girls, journey to the lands outside the village and clear the field of thornbush, create hedges around it, dig their well, and plow the field with oxen.

The earth comes alive and sings with insects. Without warning, the rain clouds depart, leaving the sun to soak up the last bits of moisture in the air. The earth dries, and the only remaining goat stops giving milk; the family waits in despair, unable to plant the seeds that will nourish them. Only the two small girls, Neo and Boseyong, are content as they play together with dolls, imitating their mother's chastisements and hitting their dolls as she might them.

Mindful only of their plight, the adults take no notice of the girls' activities. At their breaking point, Tiro, the girls' mother, and Nesta, the unmarried sister, commence a nightly wailing that begins as a "low, mournful note" and ends as a "frenzy," while stamping their feet and shouting. As a result, the men find it impossible to maintain their own equilibrium. The old man, Mokgobja, remembers an ancient tribal ritual, buried beneath years of Christian training, of sacrificing children to a rain god to ensure that crops will grow, and he consults Ramadi, the father of the girls, about it. Gradually, Mokgobja becomes more and more convinced of the authenticity of his recollection, and the idea is communicated to the women, then executed by the men.

Soon the bodies of the two small girls are spread on the fields. The act, however, is ineffective in bringing about rain, instead bringing terror to the remaining family members, who flee back to the village. The villagers notice the two girls are gone and ask the family questions, which they fail to answer satisfactorily. The police are brought in, and when asked to show the girls' graves, the mother confesses and tells what has happened. Mokgobja and Ramadi are sentenced to death for ritual murder, even though their actions are well understood by the villagers, who might have done the same in their place.

Themes and Meanings

"Looking for a Rain God" deals with survival and desperation. The act of ritual murder must be understood in the context of the harsh conditions that the villagers of Serowe live under, in terms of both the landscape, which is arbitrary in the suffering it assigns, and the government laws that punish ritual murder with the death penalty without regard to the circumstances that produced it.

The title points to how rain is crucial to the villagers' survival and to the ongoing, futile effort to bring rain to the dry lands. Although the land is edenic, it is also lonely. The drought brings about an unexpected fall from grace. The flight of the rain clouds and the oppressive presence of the sun suggest that nature and life themselves are faithless and arbitrarily cruel, even to the hardworking, patient villagers who have given up many customs and already survived many years of starvation.

Desperation is the product of a cycle of anticipation and frustration. The village is tantalized by the promise of rain, and Mokgobja's family works hard to ensure the crops' success but to no avail; the only people who thrive are those who lack virtue. The desperation of the people is pronounced in the suicides that precede the first rain, forecasting the ensuing tragedy.

It is desperation that awakens the buried memory in Mokgobja, but only after the two women break down completely. Blame for the men's act of ritual murder is assigned to the two women, suggesting that in this society, they are culpable, if not guilty. Likewise, the two small girls, whose talk foreshadows their demise, are the victims of the family's despair; they are a subset of the villagers, suffering under the family as the villagers suffer under the oppressive landscape.

The conclusion, that the villagers understand the act of ritual murder in this circumstance because they might do the same in the family's place, implies that outsiders would be unable to judge the act fairly as they have not lived through the harsh drought conditions that exist in this region and therefore are unable to understand the family's desperation.

Style and Technique

"Looking for a Rain God" resembles a fable in that the plot is rather brief, the characters less than fully drawn, and there is a clear moral. However, the story, inspired by a newspaper report that Bessie Head read in Africa, also belongs to a particular time and place, Serowe in 1958. Likewise, the focus is not on human behavior in general but on the worst human behavior, and the tale's moral is not one that invites consensus because it is a justification of ritual murder and does not make common sense as much as cultural sense.

In keeping with Head's background as a journalist and her goals as a writer, the story is written in compact reporting style, displaying taut prose, detailed description, and little dialogue. In the opening paragraph, Head presents a favorable picture of the physical and cultural landscape then quickly disrupts it, creating suspense and causing the reader to experience some of the shock that the villagers must feel. Embedded in the initial description of the edenic lands that the villagers go to cultivate are mere hints of the tragedy to come, such as "lonely," the second word of the story. Grafted onto the mythic present-tense description of the land is the historic event of the drought. Likewise, in the same paragraph is contained the villagers' initial humorous response in close proximity to men hanging themselves.

Similarly, in the fourth paragraph, Head presents the land as being ready to produce, then suddenly barren again, and tags the play of children to the end of the paragraph, foreshadowing yet another tragedy. Here, the only dialogue occurs, the girls' talk among themselves, characterized as "funny chatter," but which indicates their meager value in the society. The adults pay no attention to the girls' play, but the plot functions as though they were responding to it rather than succumbing to pressures brought on by the drought. This example of culture complicating where to place motivation and blame is characteristic of Head's work.

Head's writing is typically concerned with the encroachment of European culture on Africans and the resulting suffering. Although the questions Head presents are not clearly answered for the reader, she works to bridge cultural divides and create empathy, even in the worst circumstance.

Jennifer Vinsky

MASTERPLOTS II

SHORT STORY SERIES
REVISED EDITION

TITLE INDEX

A & P (Updike), I-1

Abenteuer der Sylvester-Nacht, Die
(Hoffmann). *See* New Year's Eve
Adventure, A

Able, Baker, Charlie, Dog (Vaughn), I-4

Abogado más hermoso del mundo, El
(García Márquez). *See* Handsomest
Drowned Man in the World, The

Absolution (Fitzgerald), I-7

Acceptance of Their Ways (Gallant), I-10

Ace in the Hole (Updike), I-13

Across the Bridge (Böll), I-16

Across the Bridge (Gallant), I-19

Across the Bridge (Greene), I-22

Act of Faith (Shaw), I-25

Adam and Eve and Pinch Me (Coppard),
I-28

Admiral and the Nuns, The (Tuohy), I-31

Admirer, The (Singer), I-34

Adulterous Woman, The (Camus), I-37

Adventure of the Dancing Men, The
(Doyle), I-40

Adventure of the German Student (Irving),
I-44

Adventure of the Speckled Band, The
(Doyle), I-47

Aeroplanes at Brescia, The (Davenport),
I-50

Africa Kills Her Sun (Saro-Wiwa), I-54

After Saturday Nite Comes Sunday
(Sanchez), I-57

After the Fair (Thomas), I-61

After the Storm (Hemingway), I-64

Aghwee the Sky Monster (Ōe), I-67

Albatross, The (Hill), I-70

Aleph, The (Borges), I-73

Alien Corn, The (Maugham), I-77

Alienista, O (Machado de Assis). *See*
Psychiatrist, The

All Shall Love Me and Despair
(Thompson), I-81

All Sorts of Impossible Things
(McGahern), I-84

All the Years of Her Life (Callaghan), I-87

"All You Zombies—" (Heinlein), I-90

Alpine Idyll, An (Hemingway), I-93

Altar of the Dead, The (James), I-96

Alyosha Gorshok (Tolstoy). *See* Alyosha
the Pot

Alyosha the Pot (Tolstoy), I-99

Amanda (Fernández), I-103

Amateur's Guide to the Night, An
(Robison), I-106

Ambitious Guest, The (Hawthorne), I-109

America! America! (Schwartz), I-112

American History (Ortiz Cofer), I-115

Amish Farmer, The (Bourjaily), I-118

Among the Dangs (Elliott), I-121

Amour, trois pages du livre d'un chasseur
(Maupassant). *See* Love

Amy Foster (Conrad), I-124

Anatomy of Desire, The (L'Heureux),
I-128

. . . and the earth did not part (Rivera),
I-131

Angel Levine (Malamud), I-134

Angel of the Bridge, The (Cheever), I-137

Angels at the Ritz (Trevor), I-140

Another Part of the Sky (Gordimer), I-143

Another Time (O'Brien), I-146

Apocalipsis de Solentiname (Cortázar). *See*
Apocalypse at Solentiname

Apocalypse at Solentiname (Cortázar),
I-149

Approximations (Simpson), I-152

April Witch, The (Bradbury), I-155

Aptekarsha (Chekhov). *See* Chemist's Wife,
The

Arabesque—The Mouse (Coppard), I-158

Araby (Joyce), I-161

Argentine Ant, The (Calvino), I-164

Ark of Bones (Dumas), I-167

Arkhierey (Chekhov). *See* Bishop, The

Art of Living, The (Gardner), I-170

Artificial Family, The (Tyler), I-173

Artificial Nigger, The (O'Connor), I-176

Artist of the Beautiful, The (Hawthorne),
I-179

C

TITLE INDEX